AF231095

America in Bible Prophecy

Our True Identity by Ancient Names

Jesse R. Cox

WORKBOOK PRESS LLC
187 E Warm Springs Rd,
Suite B285 Las Vegas NV 89119 USA

Website: https://workbookpress.com/
Hotline: 1-888-818-4856
Email: admin@workbookpress.com

Ordering Information:
Quantity sales. Special discounts are available on quantity purchases by corporations, associations, and others. For details, contact the publisher at the address above.

ISBN-13:   978-1-963718-33-1 Paperback Version
                978-1-963718-34-8 Digital Version

REV. DATE: 03/08/2024

TABLE OF CONTENTS

An intriguing study in Secular and Biblical History

America in Bible Prophecy is a must read for all concerned Americans. The purpose of this book is to prove our true identity as a part of the house of Israel and that we are now at the end of the age of time. It explains in detail our role in the soon coming cataclysmic events prognosticated to occur as we approach the Apocalypse spoken of in the Prophetic Scriptures. Yes, America is a prime player in all the future Prophetic events as recorded in the Holy Bible. America should be warned of the coming changes to our Christian way of life and we need to wake up to the reality of truth.

This book is based on ancient and Biblical history and the foundation for understanding Gods Prophecies. It proves the existence of Great Britain and the United States in prophecy by ancient historical and Biblical names as the house of Israel, Gods Battle Ax and protector of the Church. The King of England declared his throne to be "the protector of the faith" (the Apostolic Church) in 156AD. The thoughts theories or personal principles within this book are based upon actual fact of recorded history and Canonized Scripture. The Security of our soul lies within Gods omnipotent power to preserve the purity of his ancient Scriptures with undeniable truth and clarity. If we as humans deny God and his truths, the Holy Bible, then our lives mean nothing in the scheme of life.

"In the beginning was the Word, and the Word was with God, and the Word was God" John 1:1

If we elect as a nation to believe the lies of the liberal left that the truth of the Scriptures is not absolute and reject the fact that God established his Word for the guide lines of our daily lives and society itself, then we are truly an unwise people. This nation is slowly renouncing four hundred years of Gods inspired traditions and way of life in the guise of Political Correctness. If we continue our arrogance and denial of God, then, he has no choice but to judge this nation just as he did his Chosen People of Israel. They were judged and found guilty with a sentence of captivity and total destruction. Let's not be foolish enough to believe that he will not Judge our sins as a Christian nation for those same warnings pertain to our present time period. On February 29, 1892 by a vote of nine to zero, the Supreme Court of the United States declared America to be a Christian nation on which our Declaration of Independence, Preamble and Constitution is based. It is undeniable that our forefathers establish the birth of this nation on Biblical truth and this can be proven by the one-dollar bill and pledge of allegiance of our nation, "in God we trust" and "one nation under God".

Introduction

This book intends to show the reader that the early American founders of our country can be traced to the ancestors of Great Britain through the ancient descendants of the Hebrew tribes (Ephraim and Manasseh) of the house of Israel. The United States and Great Britain is mentioned in all the Old Testament prophecy books and can be identified whenever the Biblical writer speaks of the house of Israel, house of Jacob, Joseph, Ephraim, Manasseh, Lebanon, Bashan, Carmel, Gilead and Sharon. The ancient Biblical names of Gods patriarchs, the birthright tribes of Ephraim and Manasseh, can be associated with Lebanon, Sharon, Bashan, Gilead and Carmel. These nations are the only fruitful nations listed in the Bible that means they are Christian and this time frame places them within the last days. By studying the words tree, mountain, vineyard, fruit, plant, forest, wilderness, bough, branch, Zion and other key words, it is clear that Lebanon and Sharon are the modern-day Commonwealth of Great Britain and Carmel, Gilead and Bashan, the United States. Keep in mind that the Arab Lebanon of the Middle East is not the ancient Lebanon in God's Word.

There is another aspect that Christians must understand if we are to comprehend Gods Prophecies. We are being lied to as a people and nation. Satan and his human agents do not want us to know the truth whether it be our true national identity or world events that occur on a daily-bases. This is very important for them, for if they can keep the masses dummied-down they can accomplish their political agenda of forming their world Socialist system. They have full control of the world media rewriting history for the past one hundred years or more to include distorting our Christian and national heritage. Satan realizes that if the American people ever woke up to the fact of our true identity, we could and most likely repent of our national immoralities and return to our God in repentance. I pray that we as a nation have not gone beyond the point of no return, for if we have, God has marked us for destruction by having a full cup of iniquity. The American people must learn to read and study for themselves, to seek the truth that is happening around us and learn to recognize the lies that are being perpetrated upon this nation.

This introduction is just a few mind-grabbing events listed in this book that is recorded in the Scriptures but not being taught in our schools, Universities, and Churches. The truth is in God's Word and if we study with faith, he will reveal the truth to us, James 1:5, **"If any of you lack wisdom let him ask of God, that giveth to all men liberally, and upbraided not; and it shall be**

given him". The purpose of this book is to try to open the readers mind to the fact of how to study the Word in the proper prospective.

The historical and religious establishment of this nation has failed to connect the Hebrew Phoenician migrations that took place over thousands of years. This migration started as early as the Egyptian captivity around 1800BC and continued till the fall of Jerusalem in 70AD. With each war and invasion over hundreds of years, a portion of Israel migrated to escape captivity or death and a perfect example is Dan that disappeared during the time of the Judges, they leapt from Bashan (Duet 33:22) and not mentioned in the genealogies (I Chronicles chapters 4-8 and Rev 7:5-8). The reason people do not understand the true identity of Israel is because they do not realize that Israel exist as two separate houses divided into nations, the house of Israel and the house of Judah. This book will explain how the Prophet Ahijah in I Kings 11:30 divided Israel into two houses or nations and they are divided to this day. They will remain divided till the last days and brought back together as a whole nation under King David's throne. It will explain the true birthright role of Joseph's two sons to be kings of kingdoms and to be one single great nation and a company of nations as told in many verses. In other words, the house of Israel through Ephraim and Manasseh, were to receive the great blessing to be given to Abraham, Isaac, Jacob and Joseph to receive Christ's Church as the lost sheep of the house of Israel in Matt 10:6, 15:24, Acts 10:36, Eze 3:1-5 and Rev 10:2&8-11 as the "roll" and "little book" called the Gospel.

It will be presented in detail of how Britain's Commonwealth and the United States are the Christian nations of the house of Israel fulfilling all the blessing of greatness to God's Chosen People and fulfilled the promise to King David that his throne would survive all generations and a man would always occupy his throne. The 37th chapter of Ezekiel clearly divides the house of Israel and the house of Judah into two separate groups of nations during the end times, which is our present time.

The three gatherings of Gods people as recorded in the Scriptures will also be covered in detail and is a very important aspect in understanding Biblical Prophecy. The Lord has two main purposes for his Hebrew chosen people and will be explained why God divided Israel into the house of Judah and the house of Israel. Judah was to be the taproot of his vineyard, to always be located in Jerusalem to maintain the prophecies of Palestine. Israel was to be his Kingdom as branches to branch out into the earth to be fruitful and preach his end time Gospel for the salvation of the world as his Church. When we understand the division and the purpose of each house, many questionable

Scriptures become clear.

This book will explain the misnomer of the Jews of how they claim to be God's chosen people and their true identity. His chosen people were to be the Hebrew as a whole and not just the Jew, Deuteronomy 7:6 and 14:2, to be over all nations as these verses indicate. In no way can this historically pertain to the Jewish people for they have not fulfilled these, Scriptures. The Christian nations of the house of Israel, Great Britain and the United States are the only nations to fulfill these verses as indicated by history. The promises of being his chosen people was given to the new nation of Israel, all twelve tribes, before they entered into the promised land of Canaan while they were still in the wilderness in approx. 1451BC. The Tribes of Judah/Benjamin (the Jews) was only a small portion (two twelfth) of the Chosen people. Today, where is the house of Israel, the other 10 tribes of God's Chosen People?

We will explain in great detail the true meaning of Hebrew and the plan that God has for his people. The truth that will be brought forth in this book will shake the foundations of your belief system just as it has mine. By learning the truth of God's Word and the Secret that Daniel was told to lock up within the Scriptures till the time of the end, is now being released by Gods Spirit. The Hebrew language is the key to understanding for each word may have many different meanings and that is where his secrets lie. When we dissect key words within his Scripture and apply the word in correct context to whom, what, when and where, the Secrets pop out as demonstrated within this book. Study closely each Scripture and word as outlined and you will be astounded by the truth of God's Word.

We need to understand the difference between God's Chosen People and the Promised Blessings of greatness to Abraham, Isaac and Jacob. Only Jacob's son Joseph inherited the family birthright to receive the name Israel (Gen 48:16) and pasted directly to his sons Ephraim and Manasseh. They have two completely different purposes in Gods end time prophecies. This purpose is the heart of why God separated Israel into two divided houses or families. God's chosen people were the Hebrews of all twelve tribes. The Jews were chosen to provide the bloodline of King David (Gen 49:10) and his throne for the Messiah that is the house of Judah (the Jews of Judah and Benjamin). The Hebrew's of the Ten Northern tribes were to receive the blessings to be nations and kingdoms from the birthright of Ephraim to spread the Gospel worldwide in the last days (Gen 49:1, Matt 10:6, 15:24 and 21:43). Deuteronomy 33:17, **"with them he shall push the people together to the ends of the earth; and they are the ten thousands of Ephraim and they are the thousands**

of Manasseh." Today, Ephraim is the unicorn of the United Kingdom of Great Britain and Manasseh the bull of the United States of America. Both are brothers bound by a common language in ancient days just as they are today. Deuteronomy 33:17 refers to, **"His glory is like the firstling of his bullock, and his horns are like the horns of unicorns",** which refers to two Brothers. Today, England is the only nation that has a Unicorn as a national symbol and the Bull is a symbol of America's economic greatness of Wall Street stock market in New York City.

This book will cover the history of the ancestors of Calcol and Dara from the Judah/Zara bloodline. They were the Hebrew people from Judah and the ten northern tribes that migrated to Greece, Spain, Troy, Europe, Ireland and England to receive the blessings promised to Abraham, Isaac and Jacob as stated in Genesis 48:19; 49:22-24 and Deuteronomy 33:13-17. Ephraim and Manasseh were to be the tribal leaders and receive the lion's share of all blessings given to the 12 Tribes of Israel. They were planted in a land, England, I Chronicles 17:9-14, to receive the birthright blessings, **"and his seed shall become a multitude of nations"** (Gen. 48:19).

Where are the blessings that the Scriptures promised in Genesis 28:14; 22:17-18, and to Jacob in Genesis 35:11, where God states, **"And God said unto him, I am God Almighty; be fruitful and multiply; a nation and a company of nations shall be of thee, and kings shall come out of thy loins".** Read and study these verses for they cannot apply to the modern state of Israel, the Jews. They are only one nation and God promised a company of nations. There are only two nations today that fall into the category of these blessings, the 46 nations of the Common Wealth of Great Britain (Ephraim), which is a company of nations and the United States (Manasseh) that became the single most powerful Godfearing nation ever in history as given in the account of Genesis 48:16-22 and again in 49:22-26.

This book will describe the Hebrew meaning of British which is very interesting and means; "Brit" in the Strongs Concordance (1285), Briyth (Hebrew) a *"covenant"* and "ish" (eesh) (Hebrew) means *"man"*, Covenant Man or British the Covenant of Man. Britannia is a Roman name for the largest Island of the British Isles, England to include Scotland and Ireland. Isaiah 41 and 42 speaks to the Isles that is the Islands of Britannia of ancient Briton and carries the Hebrew name Hibernia in ancient times as listed on Biblical maps.

Jeremiah was commissioned by God to build and to plant Kingdoms, Jeremiah

1:10, **"See, I have this day set thee over the nations and over the kingdoms, to root out, and to pull down, and to destroy, and to throw down, to build, and to plant,"** It will be explained how Jeremiah overturned the throne of Israel to a far land in the wilderness of peace.

The many subjects listed above will be covered in detail along with the four major areas of Scriptures not being taught in our schools, Churches or Seminaries.

Area one: The division of Israel into two houses that still exist in modern times. Who is the house of Israel in conjunction to the house of Judah and where are they today?

Area two: Gods promise to King David that a man of all generations would sit on his throne forever. Where is his throne during modern times after it was overturned in Ezekiel chapter 17 and 21 by being taken from the high branch and given to the low branch?

Area three: Who received the Birthright inheritance blessing to be kings of kingdoms and many nations as promised to Abraham, Isaac, Jacob and Joseph? Where are these nations of Israel that were to bless the families of the earth promised to take place in the last days (Gen 49:1)?

Area four: Who are the lost sheep of the house of Israel where Jesus sent his Disciples (Matt 10:6 and 15:24) and gave his kingdom that he took from the Jews in Matthew 21:43 to a fruitful nation in the wilderness?

These are questions that must be answered if we are to understand end time prophecies and to know the true characteristics of the house of Israel. This book will explain in detail Gods lost sheep in the wilderness and their true identity.

The many hours of study and materials compiled to complete this book is totally predicated upon the truth set forth in the Holy Scriptures with the guidance of the Holy Spirit conducted in prayer. A note should be made that many Bible verses and subject matter will be quoted and emphasized more than once throughout this book. Many of the subjects overlap so it will be necessary to re-quote Scriptures and certain key phrases to cover each thought pattern from different angles in the course of completing the materiel within this book. Repetition fortifies memory and understanding of the perplexities of Bible Prophecy. The Greek and Hebrew definitions within this book is based upon the New Strong's Exhaustive Concordance of the Bible (KJV), Copy Right 1995.

Chapter 1

The Mystery

od says that his Word is a mystery and set forth, in parables. In Ephesians 1:9, he says, **"Having made known unto us the mystery of his will"**, and again in Mark 4:11 referring to the sowing of the seed of the Gospel, **"And he said unto them, Unto you it is given to know the mystery of the kingdom of God: but unto them that are without, all these things are done in parables"**. Rom 2:7, says **"But we speak the wisdom of God in a mystery, even the hidden wisdom, which God ordained before the world unto our glory:"** According to the Scriptures, God wants his Word to be a mystery. His mystery of the puzzle is based on linear time and comes in two parts. To understand the mystery, it takes evaluating the Bible for one part and analyzing accurate ancient and secular history for the other part. We must understand the history of man to fill in where the Bible leaves off.

The Hebrew Israelite people, God's chosen people, are the main players in the puzzle so we must know WHO, WHAT, WHEN and WHERE in studying the Scriptures. We all know that a mystery, a novel, an unsolved crime, or just a mysterious event, is often shrouded in symbols, code words, parables, or just unexplainable events. The Bible was written as a mystery for a purpose and God expects us as Christians to solve the mystery. Too solve any mystery takes time, diligent research, and a tremendous amount of study. II Timothy 2:15 states, **"Study to show thyself approved unto God, a workman that needeth not to be ashamed, rightly dividing the word of truth."** The Bible is a tool that God has given us as the truth and expects us to reverently study and search for the correct answers to solve the mystery. His design of the Scriptures through symbols and parables humbles the reader. It takes inspiration and guidance from the Holy Spirit for understanding and he does not give total insight to any one person. If a study was conducted using ten Christians, learned and educated in the same denomination and give them one doctrinal subject to perceive, they would most likely come up with at least five different points of view or aspects of the subject. This is why God calls his Word a mystery for he gives no man the complete picture of the puzzle and the Holy Spirit works differently with each individual. There would be no need for faith if he did. I Corinthians 13:8-9 states, **"Charity never faileth;**

but whether there be prophecies, they shall fail; whether there be tongues, they shall cease; whether there be knowledge, it shall vanish away. For we know in part, and we prophesy in part". This tells us that God reveals to each Christian or prophet only a portion of the overall puzzle or prophecy of his Word and gives no person a full understanding of his prophetic picture. The essence of God's Word and Gospel of salvation is through faith. The human mind cannot fathom the ultimate glory God receives when a Soul accepts his Word of salvation by faith and then lives a Christian life by that same faith.

The Strong's concordance gives the Greek definition of mystery as: to shut the mouth; a secret or mystery through the idea of silence imposed by initiation into religious rites. The Hebrew meaning and primitive root; to be slack or languid to imply sleep figurative to die, also to grow old, stale or inveterate, old (store), remain long, and make to sleep. In accordance to these definitions, God intended for his Gospel and Kingdom of Heaven to be a mystery, for otherwise, we would have no need to seek Gods Kingdom. The Mystery is related to death by not knowing the future of our souls, therefore, he expects us to seek him for the security in the afterlife of our spirits and souls.

In the Old Testament, God revealed prophecy and visions to his Prophets through Angels or by his Spirit in dreams. His Prophets had no written Word to find the truth, so God had to be more personal and direct. Today we have Gods written Word that gives the truth of man's existence in creation and the Holy Spirit to guide us through the Scriptures. Man wants to deny that truth by explaining it away through science and intellectual enlightenment separating himself from God and creating a void in their heart where he needs spiritual warmth. In Mark 4:11, Christ says, **"but unto them that are without, all these things are done in parables"**. If a man is not a Christian he cannot explain or understand the mystery even with all his science and intellectual knowledge. He will always be searching to fill the cold void within himself. Truth in this world today and forever is God's Word, the Bible, the Holy inspired Scriptures and Jesus Christ our Lord. John 1:1, tells us, **"In the beginning was the Word, and the Word was with God, and the Word was God"**. This is a comfort by telling us the Scriptures are inspired by God himself for the Word is God and to be trusted in total faith. John 1:14 says, **"And the Word was made flesh, and dwelt among us"** and **"full of grace and Truth"**, meaning Christ that was in the flesh is God's Word and the truth of man's existence. Throughout the ages of time, man has denied this fact.

II Timothy 1:20&21 tells us, **"Knowing this first, that no prophecy of the scripture is of any private interpretation. For the prophecy came not in old**

time by the will of man: but holy men of God speaks as they were moved by the Holy Ghost." II Tim 3:16 **"All scripture is given by inspiration of God, and is profitable for doctrine, for reproof, for correction, for instruction in righteousness"**. According to these verses, you have to believe the Bible is true in totality, not just portions or the part meeting your spiritual needs. In Revelation 22:18-19 states that if any man either adds or takes away from the words of the prophecy of this book God shall take away his part out of the book of life. Christians need to make a stand for God's Word and draw a line in the sand. Defending the Word is like defending a tiger, you really cannot because of its power, all we as Christians can do is let it out of its cage and brandish with a stand. The Word has supernatural spiritual properties to defend itself just as a tiger defends itself. II Thessalonians 2:15 makes the statement, **"Therefore, brethren, stand fast, and hold the traditions which ye have been taught, whether by word, or our epistle"**. Modern day thinking would have you believe that old traditions need to be changed and obsolete. Our salvation is based on faith of the shed blood of our Lord Jesus Christ that God's Word teaches. If the Scriptures are obsolete and outdated, our soul is at risk. We as Christians need to be a true Biblicist.

It is very important to understand that God's Word is true and the Scriptures have proven itself throughout history by the fulfillment of hundreds of prophecies. Just a little study can prove this fact. Are we willing to jeopardize our souls being separated from God by disregarding his Word and trusting in our own intellectual belief system? Read the Bible and look at world events each day and you can see the truth taking place in the daily media. If we humble ourselves in prayer with a pure heart and sincere desire to seek knowledge and wisdom with the guidance of the Holy Spirit, God will give the knowledge of what we seek (James 1:5-8; Heb 11:3; Proverbs 1:5).

We are living in times of delusion and cannot depend on the modern establishment of either our secular educational system or the overall Religion of our Churches to teach the truth. We are witnessing a rebellion against the Word of God where personal opinion replaces the truth, that there are no absolutes. It is called moral relativism when we explain away human sin as evil is good and good is evil (Isaiah 5:20). Humanist has maintained this excuse of wickedness for thousands of years and uses it as a tool in our modern society. Satan with his new age thinking teaches religion without Christ by diluting his absolute Word of Truth. God established his true Church, which he will never abandon, for there will always be a few congregations that maintain his candlestick till the end. Except for a very few, the true Church is dying, the candlestick is being taken away. The days of purity and innocence are over and a furious assault from all directions on anything that is good, moral or ethical is destroying our Society by Satan and his human followers. II Thessalonians 2:10 states, **"And with all deceivableness of unrighteousness in them that perish; because they received not the love of the truth, that they might be saved. And for this cause God shall send them strong delusion, that they should believe a lie; That they all might be damned who believed not the truth, but had pleasure in unrighteousness."** This verse is pretty much an accurate statement of our Hollywood Society of today called liberalism.

The Liberal Socialist agenda is out to destroy this nation and anything that stands for Christ. Isaiah explains the evils of a liberal very well, **"The vile person shall be no more called liberal, nor the churl said to be bountiful. For the vile person will speak villainy, and his heart will work iniquity, to practice hypocrisy, and to utter error against the Lord, to make empty the soul of the hungry, and he will cause the drink of the thirsty to fail. The instruments also of the churl are evil: he deviseth wicked devices to destroy the poor with lying words, even when the needy speaketh right. But the liberal deviseth liberal things; and by liberal things shall he stand"** (Isaiah 32:5-8). The Hebrew meaning of Churl; (3596) in the sense of withholding; niggardly, (3557) primitive root; hence to measure; figuratively to maintain in various senses; feed, forbearing, guide, make provision, receive, sustain, provide sustenance (victuals).

As you can see from the above Hebrew definition, the word churl is referring to the Liberal leaders that provide to the poor whether in ancient days as a King or our modern Liberal Social governmental Programs. The Liberal or Churl, by the Scriptures, is called vile, evil and wicked (Isaiah 32:7). This author believes that Isaiah is giving a futuristic picture of the masses of the world being enslaved into a Socialized Liberal System that is occurring today and will culminate into Satan's One World Order. Communism means that the people live in a Commune or community controlled by the government (Churl) under social programming and this system is being taught to our children in the government run school systems by the NEA (National Education Association). This system will be the platform for the Antichrist, the end time world leader, to enslave the masses of the world as the Red Horse of Communism (Rev 6:4). God's truth is based upon a strong family unit that produces wealth where Liberalism is based on social programming to destroy wealth my taking from the wealthy and giving to the poor. Who would have thought that Robin Hood was a Socialist? We can see this occurring in our present-day welfare system in this nation and throughout the world. The Liberals have destroyed the family unit worldwide through governmental social programs just as Isaiah prognosticated. Many Christians today still stand up for the liberal Democrats for they just cannot see the evil in Liberalism. They have been blinded!

The Church is in crises, for the few pastors that understand, fail to teach the truth due to retribution by not being politically correct. For a modern Church to teach the truth, they would have to be anti-government that would cause an immediate attack by certain organizations such as the IRS, state and federal government by being incorporated under a 501C3 tax program. They would lose their Tax-Exempt status or be sued for not being politically correct therefore, they refuse to teach the truth. The Bible is our salvation and our road map to the future but we are willfully taking the wrong road. Why are we so easily swayed in believing a lie and allowing our government to control our personal and religious lives in a supposedly free country? The reason is that the people of this nation has refused to base their lives and government on God's Word established by our forefathers. God has given the Bible to the world for man's benefit and in turn gave him absolute free choice to accept or deny his truth. The liberal world has taken individual responsibility and placed it on "Society" or the Government where they no longer need to make his or her own decisions. Man, with his humanistic wisdom, has been given the right to deny or accept the truth of God's Word. Man fails to realize that he or she will be found accountable for denial with the verdict of eternal separation from God.

In the Garden of Eden Satan planted the first seed of the lie and deceit to separate man from God by telling Eve that she would become as God if she ate of the forbidden fruit. Genesis 3:5, **"For God doth know that in the day ye eat thereof, then your eyes shall be opened, and ye shall be as gods, knowing good and evil."** Today, that same lie to separate man from God is alive and well but Satan has changed his tactics. Now he claims that there are no absolutes of truth, political correctness is in order, spiritual enlightenment of self-indulgence and you also can be as god and a lie is only what an individual perceives it to be. The idea of zero tolerance and three strikes your-out with no justice or mercy factored into the individual case. Satan knows human nature and uses it to his advantage. Basic psychology tells us that the average person of either gender has a learning curve that extends from the day they are born till approximately the time their formal education is complete. At this time their belief system is basically in tact to allow them to serve society in whatever capacity they elect. During the learning curve of early years, the persons social, educational, religious, political, moral and ethical values are formed for life. After the learning curve and mindset is complete a person basically becomes closed-minded. It takes an extreme event to change a person's mind concerning their belief system mainly due to pride and self-esteem. Satan and his agents know this aspect and is why he uses the media to program society targeting the young.

Let's look at the reason why the values of our Social System have changed so drastically in just the past fifty years. All great nations are based on solid moral and ethical values that are a must for good Government and a successful economic system. The truth is, our country was based on Christian values even though new age educators deny that fact. This goes back to Satan's lie in the Garden of Eden and if we fail to understand or see that fact then we will never be able to overcome the moral down fall of our country. The system that teaches our children is Satan's point of attack. Hitler knew this in Germany during the 1930's by forming the "Hitler Youth" to change the ideology of his country to meet his needs. Satan's Global Atheistic Socialist Liberal movement today realize the same thing so during the 1930's and 1940's, new age thinkers infiltrated our government, education, political and religious systems of this country. From the core of our belief systems, God has been meticulously removed.

We are now seeing the results of that infiltration and the changing of the mind set of our social and political system. Our children are being raised in a Godless society where we have become a dummied down, desensitized, sheep to the slaughter, mindless, apathetic and euphoric generation. The world media through television, WWW Net/computers/I-phones and Hollywood is indoctrinating our society by bombarding the world with satanic nefarious programming intended to control our minds. The intent is to change or destroy all old traditions and principled values to humanistic ideals, which is the basis in destroying a world-class moral society. It is only a matter of time before our system will fail and Satan's nefarious One World Order will be in place unless we as a nation wake up to the fact. Our political, religious and educational system along with every aspect of our society is being meticulously dismantled from within for one reason, to enslave us into a one world economic and political system.

Our nation became the single greatest nation in history for three reasons. The first is because we are the birthright tribe of Ephraim and Manasseh (the unicorn and bull) and it is our inheritance of greatness (Gen 48:19 and Duet 33:17). Secondly, this nation is an isolated land mass and the expanse of our land with natural resources to build a great nation and 3000 miles from shore to shore. Third reason, we as God fearing people produced a government and a free enterprise economic system that was based on Christian principles. Our nation has forgotten their ancestor Christian roots and the truth of God's Word. For Satan to establish his end time world government, he knows that the United States as a Christian nation has to be destroyed. You destroy a world dominating power through its education system. The Satanic liberal agenda has turned our nations school system, on every level, into a camp of immoral, socialistic, liberal, humanistic cesspool controlled by Satan's human agents of Progressive Professors and Doctors. This ideology became a force in our government and schools back in the 1920's and 30's and we are now reaping its corruptive fruits. The ENRON and WORLDCOM scandals are only the beginning of our economic malfeasants and the end of our power as a great economic nation.

Our children have been destroyed through the education system for they no longer know ethical values of right from wrong. They are not being taught our true history or traditions so how can they defend and love their own nation. These liberal university students are now the CEOs of government and big corporations and have totally eroded the ethical and moral base of our social system. We shall now fall as a great power just as Greece, Rome and all the other great civilizations. The same force that established the Luciferian Secret Societies and Communism, engineered the liberal ideologies aimed at destroying our nation. Until we as a people see the danger of liberalism and have the strength to eradicate it form our society, we will fail as a nation. The liberal agenda has only one thing in mind, to destroy the United States and its Constitution and anything pertaining to Christianity. It is Satan's tool. The American Constitution and its Christian patriotic citizens are the main retardant to Satan's world system. We must open our eyes to this fact and stop believing their lies. The only way you can eradicate evil liberalism is to eliminate it and its roots. We as a Christian based nation must realize, either we destroy the liberal socialist new age ideology or it will destroy us.

The one world idealist is dedicated in destroying our Constitution and what the people of this nation have built in the past three centuries. The idea of One World Government has been around for thousands of years and has been tried many times. The Illuminated leaders in pinnacle positions are now able and planning to implement this world system because of the computer and technological advancements in the past one hundred years. Illuminated or Illuminati means light or illumination. The Hebrew definition for Lucifer means light barrier or the Eastern Star and is why they call the illuminated secret organizations the Illuminati or Luciferian Occults. The human ideologies of Socialism, Communism, Liberalism, Humanism, Political Correctness and World Government along with many more subversive organizations is orchestrated by Satan and his human agents. If we cannot recognize the power source of these organizations, we cannot win the war against Satan and will lose our nation to a world system. Their power comes from Lucifer himself.

Their sole purpose is to enslave man into a Luciferian World System. They are named after Lucifer or Satan the Devil and believe him to be the true god.

This is Lucifer's modern perpetuated lie. The biggest obstacle in keeping these leaders at bay is Christ's Church protected by the Constitution of the United States that was established to be Gods Battle Ax and protector of the faith, Jerm 51:19-20. The one item in this document that scares them the most is the second amendment, the right to own and bare arms. Once we lose the right to defend ourselves, our country will fall to the Socialist Liberals (Communist). We are the only country left to defend the free world and when we fall, they all fall to the World System. The rights and liberties set forth in our Constitution protect the wicked as well as the innocent. The Liberal Agenda uses the Constitution as a protection while destroying it from with-in and only a matter of time before it will fail. They operate like a worm in a beautiful red apple, it's beautiful on the outside but rotten and hollow within.

The world has become very dangerous with terrorism and third world countries running around with unclear and biological weapons. The plan of the Socialist One World leaders is working very well. By creating a facade of illusion that Communism is dead, using the terrorist threat to take away our security and freedoms and flooding the world with weapons of mass destruction, the Illuminated ones are forcing the world into accepting the United Nations as a peace maker and world government. They are chipping away at a relentless rate with their goal of a One World Order. George Bush Sr. stated these words 210 times during his term in office as President, "The New World Order". The Globalist liberal mode of operation and method is to be very patient with the understanding that by taking one-step backwards and then two steps forward, they will win. Satan's human advocates lose battles but are still tirelessly fighting for victory and they expect to win in the end as indicated in the prophetic Scriptures. The human's that are working Satan's agenda for a Christ-less Society will be held accountable before God whether they believe the truth or not. We as Christians and patriotic citizens should be even more dedicated in upholding our Constitution of God given rights and Christian way of life. Surely the Constitution of this country was inspired by our Lord for only he could have inspired the forefathers of our nation to write the Preamble, Bill of Rights, Deceleration of Independence, and Constitution to be so profound and iron clad as to fight the Satanic forces trying so desperately to destroy our Christian way of life for the past 200 plus years. After one civil war, two world wars and multiple major wars, our stars and stripes still fly high and bright in the darkness of the world.

History of the Biblical Test

The intellectual Theologians tell us that there are thousands of errors in the

King James Bible. If God is omnipotent to create the universe and the heavens with man in his own image, don't you think he is powerful enough to preserve his Holy Scriptures to his specifications for man's salvation? As small as man is in the scheme of the universe, it is awfully presumptive of him to take God and his Bible so lightly.

King James I in 1611 authorized 47 scholars to translate the Bishop's Bible that was the basis of the new version, but the ancient Hebrew and Greek texts were studied and other English translations consulted with the view of obtaining the best results. This Authorized Version is now generally used by the English-speaking people around the world and later translated into hundreds of other languages that became the most renowned Bible worldwide. This author realizes that the King James version is not perfect when it comes to translation and verbal error but truly believe that God selected this Bible to spread his end time Gospel to evangelize common man. History proves the fact that only the KJV was authorized by God to translate ancient text into a modern language. We cannot refute this fact. God expects us as students to seek the truth in the original text, to teach the true meaning to layman and has used the KJV in common text for this purpose.

To ascertain the inspiration of the Scriptures, it is important to understand how the Biblical Text of the oldest manuscripts were compiled and organized into the present-day Canon of the Holy Bible. The very oldest written translation only date back to the fourth century AD ("Bible Encyclopedia Britannic, vol. III, pg. 859"). That means from the time Moses wrote the first five books, there were many copies transposed from script to script to the last copy in the fourth century. Many scholars make the statement that the Bible is full of inaccuracies so let's look at some statistics. The following statement is taken from Chronology of the Old Testament by Floyd N. Jones: *"As to the accuracy of the Hebrew Old Testament in our day, Bishop Benjamin Kennicott did a study of 581 manuscripts of the Old Testament which involved 280,000,000 letters. Out of that 280,000,000, there were 900,000 variants. Although seemingly large to the reader, it is only one variant in 316 letters which is only 1/3 of 1%. But there is more. Of those 900,000 variants, 750,000 pertain to spelling - whether the letter should be an "i" or "u". This has to do with vowel points for the purpose of pronunciation that were supposedly added c. 600AD by a group of Jewish scribes known as the Masoretes. Thus, we are left with only 150,000 variants in 280,000,000 letters or only one variant in 1580 letters, a degree of accuracy of .0006 (six ten thousandths). Most of those variants are found in only a few manuscripts; in fact, most are from just <u>one</u> corrupted copy."* This makes a clear statement that our God preserved his Word very well.

After Christ's Crucifixion, the Word of the Gospel was spread by mouth from the Apostles and their Disciples. As followers grew and Churches established there became a great need for the written Word.

According to "The Lost Books of the Bible" by Crown Publishers makes the flowing statement, "two major councils in North Africa, in Hippo (Augustine's Bishoprie) in 393 and in Carthage in 397AD, established the canons of the Old and New Testaments and Apocrypha. Since then, there have been changes in the Old Testament, and the Apocrypha dropped from the Protestant Bible at the Council to Trent (1545-63), but the New Testament has remained unchanged for almost 1600 years (Page 9)". Again stated, *"The compilation of the Bible was not an act of any definite occurrence. It was a matter complicated and abstruse. It was an evolution at the hands of Churchmen of various beliefs and purpose. In the formulation of early church doctrines there was dissension, personal jealousy, intolerance, persecution and bigotry. That out of this welter should have arisen the Bible, with its fine inspiration, would seem to present a plausible basis for belief in its Divine origin"*. (Page 11)."

Under the circumstances of how the early Bible was compiled at these conferences reminds me of our own Constitution. After months or years of heated debate there were dissension, personal jealousy, intolerance, persecution, bigotry and the most wonderful document man has ever produced was born, the US Constitution. There should be no doubt that God's inspiration was with each of the signers of our Constitution so his Gospel could be preserved till the end. Gods Battle Axe, Jeremiah 51:20.

Ancient Versions of the Bible

We must face two views presented to us in our uncertain world of today. The first is whether we accept Gods promise to preserve his Word with blind faith as a true Biblicist. The second view is in vogue today among scholastic seminary circles that the Scriptures have been corrupted over time and are currently in the process of being restored to their original form. All the new revised versions of the Bible that has been published in the last few years fall under this second view. They were not authorized by God! Should we trust modern Theological Professors over the time tested KJV Bible that God chose to evangelize the world during the past 392 years? It is this writer's belief that these new translations are a part of the great falling away as spoken of by Paul in Thessalonians 2:3.

The following information is taken from the Thompson's Chain-Reference Bible 4th Edition and "Chronology of the Old Testament" by Floyd Nolen Jones.

Masoretic Text- Translated in 600AD by a group of Jewish scribes known as the Masoretes. The earliest Masoretic Text that we have is dated 400AD. The Masoretic Text is the true text, not the Dead Sea Scrolls, even though the Scrolls are more than a thousand years older. The Dead Sea Scrolls were not written by Jews of the tribe of Levi but rather by the Essenes, a Jewish cult of ascetics whose teachings were rife with heresies. In Old Testament times, the Levitical priest (Scribes) copied and preserved the Living Words of God (Mal 2:7; Duet 31:25; Duet 17:18). *"The irrefutable fact is that the divine oracles of the Old Testament were given to the Jews and the Jews only to both write and preserve (Rom 3:1-3), never to the Greeks. It is therefore the Hebrew writings that is the true infallible Word of the Living God."* There were three portions of the Tripartite Hebrew Cannon that comprise the **Law, Prophets** and **Psalms** or the **Writings** (Matt 7:12; 11:13: 22:40; Luke 24:27-44). The Lord Jesus Christ showed great respect for the Old Testament Word and upheld it completely when-ever he addressed the Scribes and Pharisees. In Luke 4:16-21, Jesus stood up in the synagogue to read and being that the language used by the Jews in their synagogues was Hebrew, we can be assured that the scroll which was delivered to him was written in Hebrew. Matthew 5:17-18 **"Think not that I am come to destroy the law, or the prophets: I am not come to destroy, but to fulfill. For verily I say unto you, till heaven and earth pass, one jot or one title shall in no wise pass from the law, till all be fulfilled"**. According to these words Christ promised that not one letter of his Word would be lost and he was directly referring to the Masoretic Hebrew Text. This material was taken from the book, "Chronology of the Old Testament" by F.N. Jones.

The Septuagint version- The translation of the Old Testament Hebrew Scriptures into Hellenistic Greek was believed to be transcribed in Alexandria about 285-250BC by 72 Jewish scholars at the request of Ptolemy II Philadelphus or possibly his father, Ptolemy Soter. Little is known of the actual facts of the creation of the Septuagint and embellished with diverse fables of its origin that is still under debate. It has been determined that due to many of the Alexandrian expressions displayed in the text that the origin was from the Egypt Hebrew tongue and not administered by Hebrews from Israel. There are significant variations between the Septuagint and the Masoretic Text that is evident that the Septuagint was contrived by design indicated by the systematic way in which the alterations were made. Josephus did not consider the Septuagint to be reliable or it did not exist in his day for he did not use it in his writings.

The Samaritan Pentateuch- First published in 1632AD and quoted by Jerome, Eusebius and Church Fathers in the third and fourth centuries AD. This text is not actually a version but Hebrew Text perpetuated (preserved or maintained) in Samaritan characters or old pointed Hebrew script. The Samaritan text is believed to go back as far as the 9th century BC, Moabite Stone, or to possibly the time of Hezekiah in the 8th century BC but the actual age of the partial scrolls date to only the tenth century AD. There are discrepancies between the Samaritan Pentateuch and the Hebrew Text concerning the antediluvian Patriarchs fathering sons 150 years after the flood and differs in varying Scriptures in about 6,000 places. "In 1815, the text came under the careful scrutiny of the great Hebrew scholar Gesenius. He concluded that it was a vulgar text with corruption's, hence far inferior to the Masoretic Text with little critical value. In 1867AD, McClintock and Strong succinctly summed the Samaritan Pentateuch's status as the following: *This last (the Samaritan Pentateuch), however, need not come into consideration, since it is well understood that the Samaritan text, here (Genesis 5 and 10) as well as elsewhere, is merely fabricated from the Greek; and those who treat it as an independent authority only show themselves ignorant of the results of criticism on the subject"*. This makes it pretty clear of the reliability of this Samaritan Pentateuch text. This Material is taken from: "Chronology of the Old Testament" by F.N. Jones.

Peshito or Syriac- The whole Bible, date uncertain (first or second century?) apparently a translation into the common language of certain portions of Syria.

The Vulgate- The entire Bible was translated into the Latin language by Jeremy at Bethlehem and completed about the end of the 4th century AD. The Vulgate Bible was the first book ever printed in about 1455AD and for a thousand years was the standard Bible in the Catholic Church. The Gutenberg Bible edition was printed as the Latin Vulgate version of the Hebrew Old Testament and the Greek New Testament, only 49 copies survived.

English Versions of the Bible

During the dark ages, very little Bible translation was attempted with a few minor translations made on a portion of the Bible. The Word of God was locked up in the Latin tongue that was unknown to the common people. The truth of the Scriptures revealed to God's Chosen People that they were to bring righteousness and mercy to the world (Isaiah 41:2-5) and be a fruitful Christian bough or nation (Gen 49:22) as a commission and were to; **"shall push the**

people together to the ends of the earth" (Duet 33:17). This blessing was only given to Ephraim the unicorn and Manasseh the bull through the birthright blessing received by Joseph in Genesis 48:16-22. They became the English-speaking people that gave God's Word to the common man world-wide through the English translations of ancient Scripture giving blessing to the nations and families of the earth fulfilling Genesis 22:18, 26:4 and 28:14. Jesus himself in Matt 10:6 and 15:24 gave his lost sheep of the house of Israel the authority of the Church ruled by Ephraim and Manasseh given the birthright blessing by Jacob called Israel.

Wycliffe- (1320-1384) A great English scholar and Bible Student conceived the plan of translating the whole Bible into the common language of English. He first translated the New Testament about 1380 and exactly how much more he did before his death is uncertain. Wycliffe's friends completed the work after he died which rested upon the Latin Vulgate.

William Tyndale- (1525) He was the next great English Translator and an early courageous reformer determined to give the English common people the Bible in their own tongue. Persecution made it impossible for him to do his work in England, so he crossed over to the Continent of Europe where his New Testament translation was issued in 1525 and the Pentateuch in 1530. His Version does not rest entirely upon the Latin Vulgate, as did Wycliffe. Tyndale was a Greek scholar and had access to the Greek text of Erasmus and other helps which Wycliffe did not possess. He had a fine command of accurate English that left its impress upon all later versions. Tyndale was martyred before he completed the Old Testament but is generally thought that he left the material which appeared later in the Matthew's Version.

Miles Coverdale- (1535) a friend of Tyndale where he prepared and published a Bible dedicated to Henry the VIII in 1535. Coverdale's New Testament is largely based on Tyndale's and explicitly disclaimed originality but used the Latin, and other versions as helps, as well as Tyndale's Version.

Matthew's Bible- (1537) About the same time as the second edition of the Coverdale Bible another translation appeared. Its authorship is somewhat uncertain, but although it bears the name of Matthew's it is generally credited to John Rogers, a companion of Tyndale. The scholar, it is thought, had come into the possession of Tyndal's unpublished translation of the historical books of the Bible. It contains Tyndale's translations in their latest forms but also gives evidence of Coverdale's work.

The Great Bible- (1539) This translation is based upon the Matthew's, Coverdale and Tyndale Bibles. The first edition was prepared by Miles Coverdale and was ordered to be setup in every Church Parish. It was a large-sized volume chained to the reading desk in the Churches, where the people flocked to hear the reading of the Word of God.

The Geneva Bible - (1560) This translation was written in Geneva by Scholars who fled from England during the persecution by Queen Mary. It was a revision of the Great Bible collated with other English Translations. The Geneva Bible was a Scholarly version, handy in size and for many years a popular Bible in England.

The Bishop's Bible - (1568) Prepared under the direction of the Archbishop of Canterbury during the reign of Elizabeth and mainly a revision of the Great Bible although somewhat dependent upon the Geneva Version, used chiefly by the clergy, not popular with the common people.

The Douay Bible- (1582) A Roman Catholic Version made from the Latin Vulgate. The New Testament published at Rheims, 1582, the Old Testament at Douay, 1609-10. It contains controversial notes and generally accepted English version of the Roman Church.

The King James or Authorized Version - (1611AD) the English-speaking people of the world now generally use this translation. It was translated by forty-seven scholars under the authorization of King James I of England. The Bishop's Bible was the basis of the new version, but the Hebrew and Greek texts were studied and other English translations consulted with the view of obtaining the best results. It has held first place throughout the English-speaking world for almost five centuries: *FACT- The King James Version is the only Bible in history that was chosen and inspired by God to be printed into one single language. Since the 1611 King James Version, there has been hundreds of other bibles translated into modern thought, in many different languages, where words and whole sentience's has been changed by Religious University Professors and Theologians for the supposedly purpose of better understanding in modern thought. There is a belief that the old English is too hard to read so, with the help of Satan, uninspired men changed the wording and meaning of the Scriptures. The only Bible inspired by God with the guidance of his hand is the King James Version in 1611AD and this is an absolute fact weather Christians believe it or not. All modern versions of the Bible, except the original KJV, is not inspired by*

God but printed by unholy University Professors and organizations, follow the money. We must recognize that Satan is trying to destroy God's Word through modern translations for Many Christians follow after these modern bibles thinking it is Gods true Scripture when it is not inspired by God. The term "Authorized Version" means, authorized by God himself where no other Bible received this title.

The Apocrypha- Fourteen books translated along with the King James Bible that was an appendix to the Septuagint and Vulgate Bibles of the Old Testament. This makes the Apocrypha equal to the KJV Bible in Biblical correctness and translation as being God's Holy Word in the Last Days as a part of the KJV. Today, the Apocrypha is not considered Canonical by certain Scholars due to unknown reasons, man removed it from the Bible, not God. The following definition of the Apocrypha is given in accordance with the American College Dictionary: *1. Fourteen books, not considered canonical, included in the Septuagint and the Vulgate as an appendix to the Old Testament, but usually omitted from Protestant editions of the Bible. 2. Various religious writings of uncertain origin regarded by some as inspired, but rejected by most authorities. 3. Works of doubtful authorship or authenticity.* The Apocrypha was originally a part of the King James translation but later rejected by the established religious system. It is up to the individual reader to interpolate the reason why our Religious System rejected the Apocrypha. We need to determine for ourselves whether God inspires the Apocrypha for the inspiration of his Children.

The Revised Version - (1881-1884) Printed by a company in England and by American Scholars. Revision of the Authorized Version has one distinct advantage over all its predecessors for it reaches down and touches the most ancient copies of the original Scriptures. Some of these ancient copies were not available at the time of the translation of the KJV Authorized Version. <u>Question</u>: is the Revised Version Bible an authorized version by God. **No,** only the KJV was authorized by God, the Holy Spirit and the King of Israel for King James was in the inherited linage of King David through the house of Israel as Christ's lost sheep of the house of Israel as proven in Matt 10:6 and 15:24.

The American Standard Version- (1900-1901) This version incorporates into the text, the readings preferred by the American members of the Revision Committee of 1881-85.

A brief history of how the Bible was structured and by whom is necessary to make a major point. What is the Bible? John 1:1&14 tells us, **"In the beginning was the Word, and the Word was with God, and the Word was God" "And the Word was made flesh, and dwelt among us"**. According to these verses, the Bible or Scriptures is God in the flesh making his Spirit to be with us through his Word. With out the Bible, we have no salvation or guidelines to live by. This shows the importance of the Scriptures themselves and with this in mind, let's review several verses. Genesis 48:16, explains to us that the two sons or lads of Joseph, Ephraim and Manasseh, were directly given the birthright and the family name of Israel. They were to be a multitude in the midst of the earth. Only they received the name Israel through the family firstborn birthright. They were given the authority by Christ himself to evangelize the world by translating all Hebrew ancient texts into the English KJV Bible for the salvation of common man.

Genesis 49:22-24 says that the two Lads were to produce fruit (Christian) branches that ran over the wall and Deuteronomy 33:17 states that they shall push people together to the ends of the earth. Deuteronomy 7:6, 14:2 and 26:19 says that God's Chosen People (Birthright) would be above all nations. Isaiah 42:1 also states that Gods people shall Judge the Gentiles and Isaiah 42:6, 54:3 and 62:2 makes the statement that his Chosen People shall be a light to the Gentiles, shall inherit the Gentiles and the Gentiles shall see their righteousness. These verses can in no way be speaking of the modern-day nation of Israel for they are still in darkness by rejecting Christ our Messiah and do not believe the New Testament of the KJV Bible to be true. The light, judgment and righteousness these verses speak of can only be God's Word, the Bible, proclaiming Christ's end time Gospel, the light to the world. The people that translated, published, distributed and evangelized the world with Gods ancient Scriptures has to be his Chosen People according to these Scriptures. This is how we can trace and identify Gods Birthright blessed People in the end days.

In the light of the above Scriptures, history can prove the identity of God's fruitful nation spoken of in Matthew 21:43 which is the house of Israel, his lost sheep. This also proves the division of the house of Israel and the house of Judah during the end days of our present time period. The race of people that translated and evangelized the world with God's Word has to be his chosen people by establishing and publishing the Scriptures into a common language. They have evangelized the world with this truth and produced great universities open to the common people designed to teach and spread his Gospel. This race of people is the English-speaking people of the world, Gods fruitful nation in the wilderness.

Who is this race of people? They are the English people of the Anglo Saxons (Isaac's sons) of the British Empire authorized and protected by the English Crown. English scholars such as Wycliffe, Tyndale, Coverdale, Rodgers, Bishop and many more saw the need with great desire and clarity to translate and publish God's Word as his chosen people. They translated Gods ancient Word for the common people just as Prophesied in Isaiah 41:1-8, **"who raised up the righteous man from the east" "gave the nations before him and made him rule over kings"**. These men dedicated their lives under great persecution from the Roman Church to complete this task guided by Gods supervision. There is no doubt that the ensign spoken of in Isaiah 11:10 and 12 is the symbol of the Cross of Christianity and represents Christ's Church. This cross is flown on the flag of the King of England to this day. God's Word could not have been translated into a common language and the truth of his Word distributed to the common people without the power behind the throne of England that allowed this to occur. It took all the power and might behind the throne of England to fight the Roman Catholic Church and Satan's Principalities to unlock the truth of God's Word that was sealed within the Latin and Greek translations. This was a part of Daniel's secret, for the Scriptures that held Gods end time prophecies were literally sealed till the English translations were provided to the common people, fulfilling Daniel 12:4&9. The truth of the Scriptures was forbidden and sheltered in these languages simply to keep the Gospel of salvation from the people controlling the masses. If the truth of the Scriptures were ever revealed, the people would know the lies and distortion of the Gospel that the Roman Church perpetrates, even to this day. Due to the release of the truth, the war between the Catholics and Protestants still rages in Ireland. This was Satan's attempt to destroy Christ's true Apostolic Church and demonstrates the power of Gods battle ax, the servants of his fruitful nations and dust of his sword and stubble to his bow (Jerm 51:20 and Isaiah 41:2-8). The power of the Church is found in Matt 21:44, **"And whosoever shall fall on this stone shall be broken; but on whomsoever it shall fall, it will grind him to powder"** and in Dan 2:44, **"the God of Heaven set up a kingdom, which shall never be destroyed: and the kingdom shall not be left to other people, but it shall break in pieces and consume all these kingdoms, and it shall stand for ever"**. Gods' kingdom is the house of Israel as Christ's Church.

The official shield of the King of England has a cross with the Lion of Judah where the King swore in 156AD to uphold the faith of the Cross of Christ and his Gospel. This cross is the ensign to the people of England and to the nations of the world just as Isaiah predicted in chapter 11 and represents Gods Battle Ax. In 1611, King James authorized 47 scholars to translate the Hebrew, Greek and Latin ancient manuscripts into the King James version Bible based on the Bishop's Bible that has been used ever since to evangelize the world under Gods New Covenant, Christ's Church and Gospel. Gods end time Chosen

People, in light of all the above Scriptures, can only be the English-speaking British Common Wealth of Great Britain along with their brother, the United States (Ephraim and Manasseh).

This generation is extremely blessed in the fact that we have the full written Word at our disposal. Only within the past four hundred years the average person has had access to the Bible. Prior to the printing of the King James Bible, only the very wealthy and learned Priest or Monks had admission to the Scriptures and were only available in the original Greek, Hebrew or Latin. A person had to be educated eliminating common man for they learned the Word by mouth. In the last days, God needed a nation that was free from tyrannical Kingships and intolerant organized Religion so the Gospel could be spread freely and openly to all peoples of the world with-out interference. The United States of America was born out of Gods will as a nation on a continent protected by two oceans for this purpose which was founded and based on freedom of religion. He had to establish a Nation with an inspired Constitutional Government that provided education to its common people through schools and universities so his Gospel could be read and understood as the spreading of his Gospel. This nation had to be free of an intolerant King or Tyrant. The system of government had to be able to withstand the threat of tyranny and the direct onslaught from the evils of Satan himself, till the end time prophecies are fulfilled. To this day, people come from all over the world to attend our Schools and Universities.

Let's keep in mind that the Prophecies and Warnings given in the Old Testament prophetic books were given to the house of Israel and the house of Judah as two separate houses. They were separated in ancient days just as they are today and documented by Scripture. The duality of prophecies pertaining to ancient times were preached by word of mouth from Gods Prophets and personally given to the two houses. This was the first part of the dual prophecy for they did not have the written Word, as we know it today. The second part of the dual prophecy is the New Covenant presented in Gods Holy Scriptures to the house of Israel, house of Judah and to the world (Gods Church) spreading the plan of salvation in the last days. The Warnings of coming destruction is just as viable today as they were 2700 years ago. The prophecies and warnings to ancient Israel are identical and can be applied to our modern-day prophetic scenario. As we read the prophetic warnings of approaching captivity to the house of Israel prior to 740BC and the house of Judah in 586BC, it is astounding how we can apply every aspect of their idolatry and immorality to our present time period. It's as if God created a prophetic overlay through his Scriptures and all we have to do is change the date.

The English-speaking nations, generally Great Britain and the United States, became the most powerful force in spreading the Gospel during the end days by using the King James Version Bible. In viewing the success of this Bible in the past 413 years, don't you think that God's inspiration had to be with those 47 scholars and their translation? With this fact alone, you can see how God has used Jame's Bible to spread his end time Gospel. Therefore, it has to be acceptable by God. This writer understands that men translated the KJ Bible, therefore, making it imperfect. Anything man does is flawed for he is not perfect and God understands this for he created us. Translation errors and miss quotes within the King James Bible should not hinder or lead us away from the purpose of Gods salvation to the world for history proves, with no doubt, that he used this Bible to evangelize his world. In light of all the so-called errors and faults as identified by modern intellectuals, God has used and indorsed the inspired KJV to spread his end time Gospel. University Intellectuals cannot refute this fact so why use other Non-authorized Secular Translations.

Today, people say that the old English is hard to understand and follow so they buy the new revised versions written by University Professors that has been trained in New Age thinking. The Canons of Scripture were first compiled in 397AD and Satan himself has been trying to destroy it ever since. The Devil has realized the power of the Scriptures and Hebrews 4:12 tells us: **"For the word of God is quick and powerful and sharper than any two-edged sword piercing even to the dividing asunder of soul and spirit and of the joints and marrow and is a discerned of the thoughts and intents of the heart".** This is exactly why the New Age thinkers hate the Scriptures and try to denounce and destroy for the truth stings as sun light to a vampire. Satan has a new tactic for he understands that he cannot destroy the Word. Therefore, he has changed the Word in the guise of Political Correctness and New Age thinking as new revised versions by saying that the Old English is hard to understand and is obsolete. Be aware.

Christ said that in the last days there would be deceit and a falling away from the truth of his Word. II Thessalonians 2:3 **"Let no man deceive you by any means: for that day shall not come, except there come a falling away first, and that man of sin be revealed, the son of perdition:".** I believe that we now see the falling away that Christ spoke of in Thessalonians. Christians need to be careful and not fall into the trap of the New Age revised versions and stay with what we know to be time tested old fashion King James inspired Word. By understanding the history behind God's Word and how it was compiled, it will give us faith in Gods inspiration of prophecies and meanings within the Scriptures. God expects us as students to research and teach the correct translations not available at the time of the translating of the KJV.

Today, people say that the old English is hard to understand and to follow so they buy the new revised versions written by University Professors that has been trained in New Age thinking. The Canons of Scripture were first compiled in 397 AD and Satan himself has been trying to destroy it ever since. The Devil has realized the power of the Scriptures and Hebrews 4:12 tells us: **"For the word of God is quick and powerful and sharper than any two-edged sword piercing even to the dividing asunder of soul and spirit and of the joints and marrow and is a discerned of the thoughts and intents of the heart".** This is exactly why the New Age thinkers hate the Scriptures and try to denounce and destroy for the truth stings as sun light to a vampire. Satan has a new tactic for he understands that he cannot destroy the Word. Therefore, he has changed the Word in the guise of Political Correctness and New Age thinking as new revised versions by saying that the Old English is hard to understand and is obsolete. Be aware.

The Truth verses The Lie

There is a very profound statement spoken of by Paul in pertaining to the last days that we are presently in. We are in the time period of falling away mentioned in II Thessalonians 2:3. The period of falling away from the truth happens prior to and during the Tribulation before the Antichrist (Apotheosis) can take power in the middle of the Trib. This falling away from the Truth has been happening for the past four hundred years or more and has accelerated in the last fifty years to almost the point of completing Satan's One World System. The Church has been so diluted and brainwashed by Satan and his demons, it is almost to the point of being all but spiritually dead to the truth. Isaiah 5:20 makes the statement, **"Woe unto them that call evil good, and good evil; that put darkness for light, and light for darkness; that put bitter for sweet, and sweet for bitter."** This takes place through Moral Relativism, Political Correctness and the Liberal agenda that sounds like the order of our day with the current social ideologies and political system.

The American people base their belief system on emotional feelings and not fact. The problem with the world is that Satan can control emotion and play on them but hates the truth of factual information. The truth would divulge his intentions of enslaving the world into a One World system so he has to control the media in every aspect. Therefore, he produces news based on slanted opinion, a spin on the truth, fabrications and semi truth. Due to this process, Satan can alter our minds though disinformation within the media. The American people or the people of the world do no study for themselves but rely on the lies of the conglomerated world satanic controlled syndicated news agencies. Syndication means being controlled by a central source. This allows Satan's human agents to influence every aspect of our lives. We will eventually be over powered and lose our God given rights based on the Constitution before truth can be realized of their hidden agenda (conspiracy). The manipulation and destruction of our Constitution is already in progress and only a matter of time before they eliminate its power, strength and protection of the people by using Liberal Judges through the court system. I believe that time has already come. Yes, it is a conspiracy and we need to understand that fact.

A perfect example of this occurred in Alabama where the Liberal Judges of the Supreme Court forced Alabama to take a Monument of the Ten Commandments out of their State Justice building claiming the separation of Church and State. Acknowledging God as our Al-Mighty Creator is mentioned all through our Federal Documents to include State Constitutions. Nowhere in these Documents do our forefathers claim to have implemented a distinct separation between the Government and the Church. It basically states that the Government is not to interfere with freedom of Religion, the Church, not vice versa. Satan's Agents are using this falsehood to remove God from every aspect of our lives to include Government, Corporate and private segments. This lie is designed for two purposes. First, destroy States Rights of the people for this is where the strength of the people lay, not in a central Government. Secondly, it will eliminate God and his plan of Salvation of Christ's Gospel from every aspect of Society that has to occur before Lucifer (Satan) can establish his New World Order. When the Luciferian Liberals have full control of their Governmental agenda, our Christian way of life and four hundred years of traditions will end.

The old analogy of the frog in the pot of water is very true. If you take a frog and put him in a pot of cold water on the stove and turn the burner on high, he will jump out. He is warned of the danger. If you take the same frog and put him in a pot of cold water on the stove and very slowly turn up the heat, he will cook to death without realization. This is what is happening to the Church and our nation today. Satin is turning up the burner of lies and deceit extremely slow and we are dying from the heat of lies due to the lack of understanding. His tactics has been so slow and methodical that the Church and our nation are all but spiritually dead. The world has been so bombarded with false hoods and lies that the truth has been over shadowed. The truth is in Christ dying on the cross and his Word the Gospel, John 17:17, **"Sanctify them through thy truth: thy word is truth"**. Satan has declared all out war on the Word which is the Truth.

If we as Christians do not understand this spiritual war that is being waged around us, we will lose our personal battle with Satan. God has won the war for us through the blood of our Lord Jesus Christ, but the battle for our spiritual life's rages on. Our intellectual minds do not have the capability to comprehend Satan's lie without the help of the Holy Spirit for he calls his Spirit the Comforter that teaches and gives understanding. The reason I wrote this book is to wake America up to the truth and try to present an understanding of what is happening around us in the Religious and Political arena. We as Christians and the Church are failing to seek and search out the Holy Spirit through prayer as James tells in 1:5, **"If any of you lack wisdom, let him ask of God, that giveth to all men liberally, and upbraideth not; and it shall be given him"**. The Church is dying from the lack of knowledge, Hosea 4:6 **"My people are destroyed for lack of knowledge: because thou hast rejected knowledge, I will also reject thee"**. This verse makes it clear on why our nation has become so evil and corrupt. We have abandoned the knowledge of his Scriptures allowing Satan to enter. Therefore, he is rejecting us as a nation and will bring judgment upon us. We have allowed our nation to slip away and be taken over by Satan's human agents advancing their Liberal Agenda.

This writer has come to the realization that the severity of our spiritual degeneration as a nation is in great peril and gives this reading audience a dire WARNING. If we as a Nation and the Church do not seek Gods wisdom through prayer and ask for forgiveness of our National and individual sins, we will see Judgment come upon this country very soon.

State of the American People

We as Christians and patriotic citizens of this nation should be very aware that Satan's influence and diabolical plan to destroy God's creation and Chosen People has never changed. Satan failed in heaven when he rebelled against God and in revenge destroyed the earth. God recreated the earth and set dimensional barriers to prevent Satan from physically destroying man. From that point forward, Satan only has the power to destroy through man's spiritual world and his Spirit of mind. Satan's plan to destroy man has never changed, only his tactics. After Satan rebelled in Heaven and failed, he tried again in the Garden by tempting Eve that took man from the grace of God. Satan tried again at the tower of Babel with Nimrod to form a world system and failed. His new modern angle of attack is through spiritualism of false religions by trying to establish the One Word Religion and Government to enslave man by worshiping Lucifer Satan the Devil. This is why Christ is being taken out of our Society by destroying his Church which is a deterrent in proclaiming himself to be god. The Church and Spirit has to be removed first.

The Scriptures of Revelation states that this will occur during the Tribulation Period of Wrath and this government is culminating at this very moment through the United Nations world government, world economic system and the World Church. The World Church has the philosophy that all Gods are the same such as Buda, Jesus, Allah, etc. Evaluating the world situation, this system is almost in place and time is very short before it will soon be complete. This is called the falling away as mentioned in II Thessalonians 2:3 and occurring at this very moment through the guise of Liberalism, Relativism, Communism, Socialism, Spiritualism and all the other ideologies of Humanism. These are Satan's tools to demoralize mans spiritual mind through Moral Relativism of no absolutes which leaves out God and mans Salvation through his son Jesus Christ. We as a nation are in grave danger with no aptitude of its passive presence within our social and political systems.

The American people are passive and refuse to change anything. After each election and all the promises of change by the politicians, either Republican or Democrat, it is always business as usual after their election. Why, because they are all a part of the Satanic one world system. We as the people refuse to see this aspect and demand corrective change thinking that there is nothing we can do. The main reason we are ignorant of what is going on is due to the media dummying down the population by not giving facts of current events. The American people truly believe that our system of prosperity will last forever and never change. The American Christian believe that Trump is going to be re-elected and save the day but it is only a dream for he is a part of that system. We do not study history and due to the wickedness of man, it always repeats itself. This is why we desperately need to know the truth of the Scriptures about the soon coming prophesied destruction of our wealthy decadent system. If we as citizens are not willing to seek the truth with our intellect, then we will forever be swayed by outside forces called the media, whether good or evil. This author believes it would bring unspeakable enlightenment and give us a will to seek the truth if we knew who we are as a nation. Knowing that we as Americans of English descent is a part of Manasseh the bull, God's Chosen birthright people, should give each of us an overwhelming internal blessing. The knowledge that we are an intricate part of Gods end time Prophecy is the only way we will ever change our evil ways as a nation, simply by knowing our Heavenly purpose.

With this in mind, we should be able to realize why things are happening around us that is unexplainable and that our society is so easily swayed in believing all the seemingly harmless liberal ideologies that is taking our liberties and freedoms from us. It is simply a Satanic Spiritual influence that seems good to our feeble human minds. We should recognize how Satan is trying to take not only our minds but also our children from us through these satanic influences. Christians often think that we do not have the capability to understand Gods

Prophecies due to our low self-esteem. That is just not true. All through the Scriptures God has taken simple and unimportant people and made them great because they truly believed in him and had faith to seek his truth. Any person can be great in Gods eyes simply by reading and understanding James 1:5.

This nation is in a battle for our minds and we are in a state of duress without realization. If we do not wake up and realize the devastation that is occurring to the Christian moral fiber this nation was based upon, we will be judged and lose our nation as we know it.

Chapter 2

Hebrew Ancestry

Gods chosen race of people was the Hebrew, not the Jew, that became a broad spectrum of nations from King David down through the end of time. These nations, the House of Israel, are controlled by his covenant people governed by David's throne just as the Bible predicted. The house of Israel as a stone is designed to give mercy, righteousness and justice to the entire world, as his servant and battle axe which are the Christian western nations of today (Isa 41:1-8 and Jerm 51:20). This is Gods earthly kingdom called Israel which means in Hebrew, "he will rule as God" or to rule for God as a Prince till he comes in power to claim his throne. Zion (Gods spirit with man) and the throne of Israel go hand and hand and are not complete without each other. Israel as the Church will be Gods Heavenly Kingdom as his Bride, **"O virgin Israel".** Zion is no longer the Tabernacle in the desert or the Temple in Jerusalem where Gods Spirit dwelt with his people, but is now his Church of Christian people worldwide representing his Kingdom as the four Brigades of Israel as the four Beasts found in Num 2:3-34, Eze 1:10 and Rev 4:7. God reside within each of our hearts (Jerm 31:33 and Heb 8:10) and represents the New Covenant of the Church that is Christ's Gospel.

The term Hebrew "Ibriy" means the descendant of Eber "Eberite" (Hebrew) the "Great, Great, Great" Grand Father of Abram or Abraham, the first man called Hebrew (Gen 14:13). Do not fall for the falsehood that Abraham was a Jew for that term did not exist for almost 1200 years. Abraham was first called Hebrew in approx 1913BC and the Judeans of Judah were first called Jews in 742BC in II Kings 16:6.

Gods old and new covenants with man is a wonderful and fascinating interface between man and God. He used Israel as a nation and peoples of nations to set up and implement his end time Gospel, the New Covenant for his plan of Salvation and the coming of Jesus. As you study the Scriptures you can see how the United States played a big part in spreading his Gospel as indicated all through the prophecy Scriptures as Bashan, Carmel, Gilead, Lebanon and Sharon as his fruitful nations of Hebrew descent.

It all started with Gods promise to Abraham, Isaac and Jacob of great blessings and the coming of the Messiah through King David's Throne. Gods plan of Salvation was to go through the nation of Israel and the bloodline of his throne to provide the Savior, our Lord Jesus. He did not want his people to be under a King so he set up a system of Judges when they came out of Egypt and ruled the people for 350 years till the people demanding a king. There is a close resemblance to Gods system of Judges and the Republic of the United States. God wanted to rule his people directly through the Judges for he knew that a king would be wicked and his commandments would not be bestowed to the people properly. The Republic of the United States is basically the same system but rather than a ruling Judge, it is broken down into three elements, the Executive Branch, the Legislative Branch and the Judicial Branch, governed by a constitution based on the will of the people as a Republic. America was not created as a Democracy. God's original design was for government, religion and family to be a local independent entity, not controlled by parties, denominations or equal heads of the family unit. Whenever these changes occur, Satan can take over, control and destroy. This is what has happened to our government, Churches and society. We have allowed the power elite to take over our government, political parties, and religious denominations that would control every aspect of our personal lives. God's system was designed on absolute freedom not governmental control.

God knows the wickedness of a Kings heart (a man) and the cruel obstruction it would bring to the people. He wanted to rule his nation directly through his judges and prophets, not a King. The Israelites rebelled and wanted a King to rule over them as all the surrounding nations so God gave them King Saul as their first King. The Lord knew that the kingship would be wicked and unacceptable but he gave the people what they wanted. Israel's second king, King David, found great favor in Gods heart due to his righteousness and love for his Lord. David loved God so greatly that he promised to build a Temple for his Spirit to dwell with man, therefore, out of his love, he made a promise to David that he would always have a throne, Jeremiah 33:17, **"For thus saith the Lord; David shall never want a man to sit upon the throne of the house of Israel."** God knew David's heart but would not allow him to build the Temple because he was a man of blood, a warrior, so he allowed his son Solomon to build the Temple. This promise is given again in I Kings 9:5, **"Then I will establish the throne of they kingdom upon Israel for ever, as I promised to David they father, saying, There shall not fail thee a man upon the throne of Israel."** Note that God said the throne was given to Israel or the house of Israel as a whole and not just to Judah or the house of Judah for the birthright heritage of the name Israel went to Ephraim and Manasseh, Joseph's two sons, the unicorn and bull (Gen 48:16).

Judah was given the responsibility as caretaker to the throne and provides a man from David's linage to all generations. The throne was to be a symbol of God ruling over man through his earthly kingdom by righteousness, mercy and justice, governed by Israel to all the nations of the world. This same earthly Kingdom would later be open to all man under the New Covenant and become Gods heavenly Kingdom promised to Abraham, Isaac, Jacob, Joseph and to all that accept Christ as their Messiah (Matt 8:11). From the time David was crowned as King in 1056 BC, God has ruled his earthly kingdom through a man of David's linage of every generation till Christ claims his Throne and power Rev 4:1-2 where he will rule for eternity. The Judah/Phares Crown was overturned where Jeremiah gave the high Cedar Branch of Judah/Paraz to the low Cedar Branch of Judah/Zarah in approx. 584BC. Jeremiah took Zedekiah's daughters to Ireland and married the leader of the Judah/Zarah bloodline of the scarlet thread (Gen 38:28-30) established many years prior preserving the throne. At this point, David's Throne was overturned from the Pharez line of Kings of the house of Judah and given to the Zarah line of kings to the house of Israel. This event fulfilled the first overturn of David's throne as recorded in Ezekiel 21:27 and planted in the wilderness by a covenant of Christ's Gospel as the New Covenant. Hosea 2:14-23 states, **"Therefore, behold, I will allure her, and bring her into the wilderness, and speak comfortably unto her."** Verse 23 goes on to say, **"And I will sow her unto me in the earth; and I will have mercy upon her that had not obtained mercy; and I will say to them which were not my people, Thou art my people; and they shall say, Thou art my God."** Study these verses carefully for this nation in the wilderness received Christ's New Covenant as spoken of in Jeremiah 31:31 and Hebrew 8:8 placing them in the last days or the Church age of the lost sheep of the house of Israel in Matt 10:6 and 15:24. These verses also match Ezekiel 37 where Gods Kingdom is made whole in the wilderness now under the Zarah line of Judah's Kings. This event fulfilled prophecy of the overturned throne as a breach of the scarlet thread in Gen 38:27-30 making Pharez and Zarah eligible to be kings under the linage of King David.

This was the betrothal or engagement to be married (verse 19) of the house of Israel after being divorced in Jeremiah 3:8 due to their national sins. Judah was never divorced so it can only be the house of Israel God is speaking of in the wilderness. Verse 23 speaks of the fact that these people (house of Israel) did not believe their identity as being Gods people, **"and I will say to them which were not my people, Thou are my people:"** This is also mentioned in Hosea 1:10. These people did not believe they were Gods people (Hebrew) but God said that they were his people. This is what has happened today, for the house of Israel in the wilderness are the English-speaking Christian nations of Hebrew descent and do not recognize that fact. The English People know that we are Gods people through being Christian and the Church but still do not realize that we as a nation are of Hebrew descent, God's chosen covenant people a firstborn birthright tribe of the house of Israel.

The throne and Gods kingdom on earth was created for Christ to claim (Luke 1:32), **"He shall be great, and shall be called the Son of the highest: and the Lord God shall give unto him the throne of his father David."** God has plans for Christ to sit on the throne to rule over man forever so he has to maintain the pure bloodline for that purpose and to fulfill the prophecies. Even Satan understands the importance of King David's throne that it is promised to Christ, so he (Lucifer), takes claim of the throne during the Tribulation Period by claiming himself to be god of the universe.

At the time God split Israel into two nations or houses in I Kings chapter eleven, he had plans for each of his tribes as a nation to play a role in end time prophecies. II Kings 19:17, makes the statement that when the Assyrians took the ten northern tribes, they were called nations not tribes. This is significant for in the latter days each tribe was to be a nation within the world. The house of Judah was to provide the taproot of the vineyard that would produce the Messiah. Isaiah 5:7 states, **"for the vineyard of the Lord of hosts is the house of Israel and the men of Judah his pleasant plant"**. We need to understand that after the Babylonian captivity the house of Judah was divided where the majority of the Judah Hebrews migrated into Europe to amalgamate with the house of Israel. Only a remnant of Jews returned to Jerusalem to rebuild the Temple that produced the linage of Christ almost 600 years later. They are still divided to this day. The house of Israel as the lost sheep to include the Judah Hebrews were to be sifted through the nations and go into the wilderness to a new land and prepare to receive the Gospel when the Gospel came. They were to evangelize the world as Christ's Church. Matthew 10:5-6 tells us, **"These twelve Jesus sent forth and commanded them saying, go not into the way of the Gentiles, and into any city of the Samaritans enter ye not: But to rather to the lost sheep of the house of Israel"**. Again, in Matthew 15:24 Christ said to the Canaanite woman that he was sent only to the lost sheep of the house of Israel. The lost sheep are the planted nations in the wilderness (Hosea 2:14-23, Ezek 17:5, Hosea 1:10). At the time of Christ, supposedly, only the house of Judah as the Jews existed as a nation and it had lost the throne of David to Babylon in 586BC, then to the Media Persian Empire and later to the Roman Empire. The house of Israel had not existed since the Assyrian captivity, approx. 750 years before Christ made the statement for his Disciples to go to the lost sheep of the house of Israel. Christ knew where they were, for they were in Europe waiting for Christ's Gospel just as Jeremiah's Scribe Baruch knew their location when he sent an epistle to them on the neck of an eagle, Chapter LXXVII of "the Apocalypse of Baruch", page 122.

When the ten northern tribes went into captivity by Assyria, each of the tribes later departed internment and went their own way. Manasseh was the first tribe to be taken captive in approx. 740BC, about twenty years before the main invasion by the Assyrians. A small portion of each tribe migrated East and North to avoid captivity. The tribes of Dan, Ephraim, and Manasseh were located on the Mediterranean Sea allowing them seaports to be sailors. Keep in mind that during their captivity in Egypt they were merchant mariners for the Egyptians. When the invasion came, a small portion of each tribe escaped by sea to avoid capture and migrated to Greece, Spain and up the coast of Europe to France, Denmark and Brantania.

Their ancestors of Calcol and Dara prior to arrival already settled many of these areas. They had migrated during and after the Egyptian captivity to Greece (Javan or Ionia), Troy, Spain and Phoenicia (the Phoenicians) on the north upper coastal area of ancient Israel settled by Semitic migrations during the second millennium B.C. This Phoenician migration was the family of Noah, Shem and Eber or Semites that moved north and settled the coast of Phoenicia in upper Canaan. The ancient Phoenicians were great mariners and known for their sea trade throughout the Mediterranean and even up the Atlantic coast to Europe. Tarshish, a son of Javan (Greece) and a great-grandson of Noah (Gen 10:4), identified with Tartessus (Jonah 1:3), an ancient city located on the Atlantic coast of Spain. The ships of Tarshish supplied great wealth to King Solomon, I Kings 10:22.

The Phoenician Semites had an enormous influence on the Israelite people to the point that the Hebrew letters came from the Phoenician alphabet. God said that his Hebrew people would rule over all nations, Genesis 28:14, **"And thy seed shall be as the dust of the earth, and thou shalt spread abroad to the west, and to the east, and to the north, and to the south: and in thee and in thy seed shall all the families of the earth be blessed."** Through the migrations of his people, you can begin to see and understand how and why this domination occurred. They were never called Jews and never will be. The term Jew was created just prior to the captivity of the house of Israel by the Assyrians and only given to the Judeans and the Jews of Jerusalem. The ten northern tribes were never called Jews that included the mass of Judah that migrated into the wilderness and never returned to Judea. Only a remnant of the Jews, approx. 40,000 in Ezra chapter 6 returned to Jerusalem from the Babylonian captivity. They had a tremendous hatred for non-Jewish people due to the torment of their captivity and separated themselves by name from their brothers of the ten northern tribes. This was the beginning of the division between the Judah/Hebrew and the Judah/Jew of Jerusalem in Judia. The Jew, claimed for their own purpose, the sole name of God's chosen people to be the Orthodox Jew of Judaism. This deception has lingered to this very day and blinded the world to the true identity of the house of Israel and the Judah Hebrew that migrated into Europe.

This lie has permeated the world to the point that even the modern-day house of Israel, the English Christian speaking nations of the world do not believe their own heritage just as Hose 2:14-23 states. The name ISRAEL was given to the ten northern tribes in I Kings chapter 11 at the division of Israel to include the mass of the Judah Hebrew to be Gods whole Kingdom. The family name by birthright law of the firstborn is given in Genesis 48:16-20. Judah, the Jews, have no Biblical right to claim the name Israel for it was given to the ten northern tribes of the house of Israel given directly to Ephraim and Manasseh. Only they were to be leaders of Israel and from this time forward include the Judah Hebrew. The Jew only received the right to be called Israel through the chosen birthright tribes of Ephraim and Manasseh as clearly recorded in Gen 48:13-22 and confirmed in I Chron 5:1-2.

The ten northern tribes settled the world and applied Hebrew names to rivers, valleys and mountains where ever they went as proof of their migration. This was a commandment given by God for them to leave their trail during their migrations as stated in Jeremiah 31:21, **"Set thee up waymarks, make thee high heaps: set thine heart toward the highway, even the way which thou wentest: turn again, O virgin of Israel, turn again to these they cities."** Their waymarks of Hebrew names and high heaps of stone circles and mounds are found all through Europe and other continents throughout the world. The term "O virgin of Israel" is very interesting for the Hebrew meaning of virgin is "a bride". This term means "O bride of Israel" and a symbol of the house of Israel being the Bride of Christ as outlined in Isaiah 62:1-5. The house of Israel and the Church being the Bride of Christ is one and the same and explains why Joseph is called a fruitful bough (Christian nation) by a well, a fountain of living water that is Christ, Genesis 49:22.

We as Christians only have to do a little study to see and understand this fact but we refuse. The modern country of Denmark is no other than the Land of Dan or (Jutland) the cloth of Dan, a Hebrew name to this day. Jutland means the land of the Jews that were the mass of the house of Judah that migrated after the Babylonian captivity. Only approx. 40,000 Jews returned to Judea to rebuild the Temple in Jerusalem. After the Assyrian captivity, the remaining ten tribes began to migrate north across the Caucasus Mountains that divide modern Georgia and the lower part of Russia. The names of the ten northern tribes of Israel when taken into captivity were, Beth Omri (House of King

Omri), Bit Kumri, Kimmerian, Cimmerians or Gimmiri (Scythian), Danaoi (tribe of Dan), Sakai, Sacae or Sakasuna (House of Isaac) and later called Scythians. After hundreds of years wandering through Europe, they were called Gaels, Angles, Celts, Danes, Saxons and Anglo-Saxon (Isaac Sons).

There is a massive number of books and material on this subject that explains in great detail for the reader that would like to research and study the ancient migrating tribes of Israel. The object of this writer is to give just enough information to provide a good idea on the migration of the house of Israel.

It is very interesting to note that Paul in Romans 9:4 & 7 asked, **"Who are Israelites; to whom pertained the adoption and the glory and the covenants, and the giving of the law, and the service of God and the promises:"** The adoption, the glory, the covenants (both old and new Christian), the law, the service of God and the promises went from Abraham to Isaac's seed or descendants of Isaac's sons, the virgin of Israel called the house or children of Israel which is Christ's Bride, the Church. The seed of Abraham, Isaac, Jacob, Joseph, Ephraim and Manasseh clearly in Gen 21:12, Rom 9:4 and Heb 11:18 were to be named after Isaac as Isaac' sons or Saxon related to the Gales, Angles, Celts, Danes and Anglo-Saxon of the European tribes of Israelites. Keep in mind that the house of Israel, Isaac's seed or Saxon, were to establish and maintain the Church that was opened to all mankind under the New Covenant. The promises of greatness went to Ephraim and Manasseh the two sons of the birthright tribe of Joseph that received the firstborn birthright blessings of Israel. Rom 9:7 states, **"Neither, because they are the seed of Abraham, are they all children: but, In Isaac shall thy seed be called."** Genesis 21:12 also states that, **"in all that Sarah hath said unto thee, hearken unto her voice; for in Isaac shall thy seed be called."** It did not say for in Judah should thy seed be called (the Jews). From these verses it is clear that the great blessings of the Covenants and to be servants to God were to be of Isaac's seed, Isaac's sons and later to be called Saxons from migrating tribes into Europe. Romans 9:4 give the responsibility to the Israelites of spreading his new covenant, Christ Gospel, into the entire world. Even Paul had a question of just who the Israelites were for he was condemning the Chief Priest and Pharisees and the non-believing Jews that killed Christ and persecuting the Christian Church.

After the captivity to Assyria, all of these tribes settled in the steppe country of the Ukraine and were called the Scythians and later Goth. The twelve tribes of Israel took the name Gauthei, which means the people of God, and later changed to Goth (Abraham Ortels 1527-1632 German cartographer and geographer). They became great in number and began to invade neighboring countries such as the Roman Empire where they were called Goths, Ostrogoths and Visigoths. After years of wandering and fighting as Goths which were the descendant of the Scythians, Sakai and Danaoi, they entered Europe and Britain as Saxons, Jutes and Danes. These tribes of people were later called the Caucasian white skinned tribes that settled into Europe and became our ancestors along with the Hebrew tribes that migrated by ship into other parts of the world. Hosea 12:1 tells us that Ephraim feedeth on the East wind and in Genesis 48:19 said that his seed shall become a multitude of nations. As the east wind blows to the west so their direction of departure was to the east across the Jordan River and as the wayfaring Hebrew traveler, Eberite, he was blown to the west.

Ephraim was Joseph's younger son and destined to receive the lion's share of all the heritage blessings over the other eleven tribes of Israel (Gen 48 & 49). If you study these Scriptures, these blessings cannot be talking about modern day Israel for nations shall come out of Ephraim, **"his seed shall become a multitude of nations."** and Manasseh shall be one great nation (United States of America) (Gen 48:19). Of all the historical records, the Jewish population never increased above twenty million while dispersed among the nations. Where is the blessing that they would be, **"as the stars of heaven and as the sands of the sea shore and thy seed shall possess the gate of his enemies"** (Gen 22:17-18). Only Great Britain and the United States (Ephraim and Manasseh) ever fulfilled this verse for between the two they have controlled and colonized all shipping passages, trade routes and all major seaports throughout the world in the past five hundred years. The English once said that the sun never set on her British Empire that was a true statement.

As a whole, the people of the Middle Eastern nations never migrated to other parts of the world. They always maintained their land and ventured out to capture other nations in warfare but by history went back to their homeland. The Egyptians, Greeks, Babylonians, Medes, Persians, Romans and all the other great nations of the past did not migrate to other parts of the world so who are these tribes that settled Europe? All the colonizing nations over the past five hundred years such as the French, Spanish, Germany, Dutch, Portuguese, British and Americans are all of Hebrew descent. The English-Speaking people (Angle-Saxon) are the descendants of the ten northern tribes of the house of Israel fulfilling Gen 28:14 by colonizing the North, South, East and West. We are Gods lost sheep, the Hebrew travelers and wayfaring men that left waymarks (Jerm 31:21) after Abraham, the colonizer in a plantation style (Eze 17:7).

The migration of the Hebrew tribes began to take place during the Egyptian captivity and continued till 70AD when Rome destroyed Jerusalem. In every country the Hebrew migrated, they found other peoples of their ancestry already settled. Enoch's ancestors, the house of Enoch (Phoenician) and the Phoenicians of Abraham's descendants migrated years before. Both Shem and Abraham are from the line of Enoch (Phoenician), Shem, Aram, Salah, and Eber. The definition of the word Hebrew comes from the line of Eber making the Eberites the first Hebrews which would also make them Phoenician but God did not call them by their Biblical name of Hebrew till Abraham. According to the Strong's Concordance #5680, the term Hebrew means, Ibriy - an Eberite or descendant of Eber and is first mentioned in the Bible in Genesis 14:13 calling Abram the first Hebrew as descendants of Enoch and Shem which were a Phoenician/Semitic people.

There is an aspect that we need to consider for God's chosen people came from the birthright of Noah's three sons which were Shem, Ham and Japheth (Gen 10:1). Shem was the oldest and received the birthright to be Gods people which is very easy to trace through the Scriptures. Genesis 10:2 gives the genealogy of the third born son of Japheth as Gomer, Magog and Madal and others which are the European Communist bloc nations of today. Genesis 10:6 gives the genealogy of the second born son of Noah as Ham and he conceived Cush, Nimrod, Mizraim, Phut and more which are the Arab and African nations of today. No great Prophets, Patriarchs or men of God came from the linage of these two sons of Noah proving that God's Chosen People came from the line of Shem, the firstborn of Noah. If we closely look at today's world situation, we can easily see that the nations of Japheth, the Communist Bloc nations, and Ham of the Arab and African nations are diametrically aligned against the Christian industrialized nations of the world that is the house of Israel (Christian nations) and Judah as the Jews from the descendants of Shem.

The three sons of Noah were to be the building block of Civilization to fulfill the prophetic purpose of Gods plans for the Salvation of man. The structure of world politics today is based upon these three sons and each of their ideologies. Simply look at world events and this is extremely obvious so how can we deny the truth of the Scriptures. The Bloodline of Shem is dominated by the birthright sons of Jacob and represents the Christian nations of the house of Israel, God's Chosen People. The modern-day descendants of Ham have been subdued by the Islamic religion of Ishmael and represents the Islamic and black nations of the world. The descendants of Japheth, during modern times, is being dominated by the sons of Esau the red baby (Gen 25:25) and represents the Communist bloc nations as the Red Horse of Communism (Rev 6:4). This fulfills the hatred between Ishmael, Esau and Jacob in reference to who received the birthright that was taken from the eldest sons of Ishmael and

Esau and given to Jacob. This hatred exists today and has produced a world terrorist situation.

The jealousy and hatred begin when Genesis 17:6, 22:17-18, 28:14, 35:11 and 48:16-19 all emphatically state that Israel was to be many nations of world power, to be kings, to possess the gate of his enemies and bless all the families of the earth through them. They were to be a great nation and a company of nations. In other words, they were to be a blessing to the whole world as a World Class Power creating the hatred between descendants or nations of Ishmael (Arab) and Esau (Communist). This hatred can be seen through the centuries such as the Crusades led by England that took place from the 11th to the 13th centuries by the Christians of Europe to recover the Holy Land form the Muslims of the Islamic faith. This hatred has come full circle producing world terrorism created by the Arab and Communist block nations of the world simply due to who received the birthright that went to Jacob and not the eldest brother.

All these great nations were to fulfill the blessings given to Abraham, Isaac, Jacob and Joseph that was passed directly to Ephraim and Manasseh. They all came from the birthright of Shem, Noah's firstborn son to be God's Chosen Semitic people. This can be proven by the study of ancient languages. The oldest known language is Sumerian that would have been Noah's language at the time of the Tower of Babel.

Immediately after the story of the tower of Babel, Genesis 11:1-9, the genealogy of Shem is given which emphasis the Birthright and are the great names of Gods Patriarchs such as Noah, Eber, Pleg, Abraham which were the linage of David, and then to Christ. Gods Holy Scriptures was written in Hebrew, which is similar to Akkadian, Moabite, Phoenician, Greek, Latin and English and all derived from the northern Semitic ancestral language of Shem.

Ancestors from Noah's other two sons, Ham and Japheth, migrated to parts of Europe and Africa that never inherited the name Semitic or Hebrew. It is stated in Genesis 10:5 and 10:20 that they had their own language and nations. This clearly establishes a difference between the nations of Ham and Japheth verses the bloodline of Shem that produced God's Chosen People and birthright blessing to be fruitful as Christian nations. Spain in ancient times were indicated on maps as Ibernia and Ireland Hibernia that is a derivative of Hebrew from the line of Shem as Semitic. The names Ibrey and Heber is where the term Hebrew is derived which makes the ancient land of Ibernia (Spain) and Hibernia (Ireland), a Hebrew name indicating the earliest settlers of these lands were of Hebrew descent. Over thousands of years with many different Hebrew migrations from all directions and at different periods of time, God finally united all twelve tribes into Ireland, Scotland and later the throne of England which became the British Empire, in 1703. They became the 46 Christian nations of the Common Wealth of Great Britain and better known as the United Kingdom. This fulfilled the blessings to Abraham, Isaac, Jacob and Joseph (Ephraim and Manasseh) to be nations and kings of Kingdoms as recorded in Genesis 17:6, 35:11 and 48:16. This fulfillment brings ancient days and modern times of Gods prophetic purpose full circle in accordance to his timetable.

Who are the Jews?

The Scriptures are clear on the fact that God's chosen people are the Hebrew and not the Jews as a whole for they are only 1/12 of his people. Abraham was called a Hebrew in Gen 14:13 and never a Jew as our established system would have you to believe. The first time the term Jew is mentioned in the Bible is in II Kings 16:6, after the division of the house of Israel and Judah in approx. 742BC, two years prior to the starting of the captivity of the house of Israel. The house of Israel and Assyria was at war with Judah or the Jews and the Assyrians coined the term Jew for the Judeans that were Judah and Benjamin. Theologians and historical leaders of our time have misconstrued the difference of the two peoples of Gods divided kingdom, the houses of Israel (Hebrew) and Judah (Jewish Hebrew). Today there are a distinct division within the house of Judah called Jews and the house of Israel are Hebrew never called Jew. Only the house of Israel along with a portion of Jews departed into the wilderness and accepted Christ's Gospel at Christ's coming. Both houses are Hebrew. The Jewish Hebrews are the modern orthodox Jew that never accepted Christ as the Messiah. Their blindness is somewhat disturbing to this writer for the Church cannot correctly discern between the simple dictionary definition of the word Jew and Hebrew. Ephesians 4:18 tells us, **"Having the understanding darkened, being alienated from the life of God through the ignorance that is in them, because of the blindness of their heart"**. Our present-day religious system has been succumbed to the Gentile way of thinking as stated in Ephesians. Today, this blindness has infiltrated the Church to the point that we are no longer searching the Scriptures for the truth. The famous writer Josephus Ben Matthias was a Jewish historian and Pharisee that lived during the destruction of Jerusalem in 70AD and termed the name Jew as Yehudim or "the remnant of Judah" (the tribe of Judah). Josephus never called anyone Jew other than the house of Judah and Benjamin that lived around Judea in Jerusalem.

The Strong's Concordance list the term Jew as meaning, #3046 Yhuwdiy, a Judaite or Jew, of Jududah, Jew. #3063, Yhuwdah-also of the tribe descended from the first and of its territory-Judah. The term Jew can only apply to the Hebrew people that stayed in the area of Jerusalem of Judea after the Assyrian and Babylonian captivity and not the millions of Hebrews that migrated to other parts of the world. Romans 11:2 tells us, **"God hath not cast away his people which he foreknew"**. Amos 9:9 explains very well how God preserves his people, **"For, lo, I will command, and I will sift the house of Israel among all nations, like as corn is sifted in a sieve, yet shall not the least grain fall upon the earth"**. Of the millions of Hebrew people from all twelve tribes that migrated to Europe, God knows where each and every one of their blood descendants are located. When Christ was talking about the lost sheep and James and Peter the scattered strangers, they knew where they were. The word foreknew that the Apostle Paul is talking about in Romans are the migrated Hebrews which departed to other parts of the world after the two captivities. The present-day system has failed to understand and blind to the fact of how God divided Israel into two nations for his purpose of end time prophecy.

"The word "Jew" according to many sources, did not appear in the English language until 1620. The word used before this time was "Iewe" (pronounced hew'ee). The reason is that the word "Jew" is not to be found in the original Hebrew or Greek Scriptures. According to the esteemed Colonel Curtis B. Dall (Franklin D. Roosevelt's son-in-law), in his <u>Israel's Five Trillion Dollar Secret</u> (1977), the word "Jew" did not exist until 1775. The word itself was a corruption from the Latin Indaeus, which meant "Judean." It underwent numerous forms, from "Giwis, Gyues, Geus, Iuys, Iows, Iews," and finally "Jews." It appeared for the first time in an English Bible, when a mass printing was made of a new 18th-century edition that "updated" the 14th-century translation. This special edition was then distributed throughout the English-speaking world to people who had never before owned a Bible. Dall also asserts that the word "Iewe," or "Jew," when first translated in the Scriptures, referred only to the ancient Judeans of the Bible and not the modern "Jew (pp28-31)." ("Uncovering the Mysteries of your Hidden Inheritance" by Robert A. Balaicius)

This quote should shed some light as to just who the Jews really are. Whether this was a common mistake on the translator's part or a planned deception is for the reader to determine for it has created a delusion as to the true identity of the house of Israel. As we proceed through this book, it will be clear as to the separation of the house of Israel and the house of Judah that exist today. Note that the house of Judah is divided into two parts, the Judah Hebrew (approx. two million) and the Judah Jews (40,000), the only Hebrew to return to Judea after the Babylonian captivity (Jerm 44:28). Where is the modern house of Israel?

The Planted Nations of Israel

The breach or rift between the tribes of Israel began to divide the nation prior to King David's reign (Judges 21:15). David had problems in I Chronicles 21:5 when Satan stood up against Israel and tempted David to number the nation. The nation of Israel was very young during the time of the Judges and already started internal power struggles. Satan has always tried to destroy Israel, Gods people, even from the beginning.

Let's look at why our system is in a shadow of blindness to Israel's division and how God has divided time. The Prophet Daniel asked God to reveal the secrets of his visions but was told to close up his book, Daniel 12:9 **"And he said, go thy way, Daniel: for the words are closed up and sealed till the time of the end"**. This tells me that God does not want the mystery of his prophetic Word known till the last days fulfilling his timetable. God tells us that the number of man is six or (666), Revelation 13:18. Man was made on the sixth day of creation and allotted 6000 years to complete Gods purposes of his existence. God rested on the seventh day and the seventh millennium is his time of rest ruling his people. The earth could have been around for millions of years before Adam but the Bible says that Adam or man is only approx. 6000 years old. If we go back and divide the time man has been on Earth according to the Bible, we will find that there was approx. 1656 years from Adam and Eve to the Flood and 2344 years from the flood to the birth of Christ. The first two time periods equal 4000 years. We are now in the year 2024AD (AD Latin for Anno Domini, in the year of our Lord) and at the end of 6000 years of man's lease on earth. The Old Testament prophets speak of the end of time, the last days, at the end of the age, and they all refer to the present day which is at the end of man's 6000 years of self-rule. Man has lost calendar time so we are not sure of the exact date of Christ's death. We are quickly approaching the fulfillment of all end time Bible prophecy and at the end of God's timeline for man.

Daniel's secret and the blindness Paul spoke of in the book of Romans explain why God has purposefully blinded his people, the Church. The secular historians or theologians do not see the connection of the Hebrew Israelite-Phoenician migrations into Europe fulfilling the great blessings promised to Abraham, Isaac and Jacob. God had to change their name (Isaiah 62:2) and identity to preserve the secret of Daniel 12:9, till the time of the end of the age. God divorced Israel in Jerm 3:8, therefore, losing their name among the nations till the punishment of X7 of 2520 years were complete. After their punishment, God betrothed Israel in Hosea 2:19-20 regaining not only their birthright name of Israel but also their birthright heritage of greatness to be kings and kingdoms (Gen 35:11 and the 3rd covenant of Gen 17:2-11). The term "virgin Israel" is mentioned four times and "virgin daughter" referring to Israel mentioned twice in the Old Testament where Israel is called a Bride. The house of Israel was betrothed in Hose chapter two and the marriage will take place after the Church (Israel) is taken and the Marriage supper of the Lamb occurs in Heaven in Rev 19:9. The Spiritual Israel (the Church) will be taken (I Thes 4:14-17) but the physical kingdom of non-believers will be left behind which are the gathering of the 144,000 during the Tribulation Period (Rev 7:5-8 and Eze 37). This 144,000 are a special chosen people to represent his earthly kingdom to go into the seventh millennium to complete the prophecies of Jerusalem for Christ's coming in power to fulfill all prophecy.

God said that he would change their name and had to occur to complete the mystery. Isaiah 45:4 states, **"For Jacob my servant's sake, and Israel mine elect, I have even called thee by thy name: I have surnamed thee, through thou hast not known me"**. Here God makes a distinction between Jacob which is all twelve tribes. Jacob gave his name Israel to Joseph passed directly to his two sons Ephraim and Manasseh in Gen 48:16-22 to be "elect" by receiving the firstborn family birthright name to be leaders of the house of Israel being two separate kingdoms of nations. Jacob represents 11 tribes of the Children of Israel to include both houses but do not include the birthright tribe of Joseph (Ephraim and Manasseh). Israel is the ten northern tribes as divided in I Kings 11:11-13 called his elect; the leader as his birthright tribes of Ephraim and Manasseh (I Chron 5:1-2). Keep in mine, this verse was written in approx. 712BC eight to ten years after the house of Israel (ten northern tribes) went into captivity to Assyria. God changed their name and gave them a surname (Christian) under the new Covenant. Isaiah 65:15 also make the statement, **"And ye shall leave your name for a curse unto my chosen; for the Lord God shall slay thee, and call his servants by another name"**. God is speaking to the house of Judah in the first part of this verse referring to their curse for the chosen servants that is called by another name is the house of Israel that was planted in the wilderness waiting for the Gospel. A servant is Gods people that teach his Gospel. The Jews cannot be his servants (fruitful Christian) for they have not accepted Christ. The name of Judah as the Jews has never been changed, for they have always been identified and persecuted down through the ages.

This curse did not apply to the house of Israel but only to the inhabitants of Jerusalem, the house of Judah, for the Scribes and Pharisees rejected God by worshiping idols in ancient days and rejected Christ in modern days. Their blindness will be lifted and salvation held back till the time of the Tribulation period, Daniel's 70th week, then they shall see the light of Jesus Christ and be saved. Israel's blessings (Ephraim and Manasseh) were to be **"whose branches run over the wall"**, Genesis 49:22 and, **"his seed shall become a multitude of nations"**, Genesis 48:19. In Deuteronomy 33:17, **"His glory is like the firstling of his bullock, and his horns are like the horns of unicorns with them he shall push the people together to the ends of the earth: and they are the ten thousands of Ephraim and they are the thousands of Manasseh."** As you can see in these verses, the blessings of Jacob gave the birthright to Joseph that went to his two sons, Ephraim and Manasseh, to maintain the family name of Israel.

The children of Israel called the house of Israel became the fruitful Christian nations or righteous nations that preached God's Word, the Gospel. The house of Israel escaped the curse by accepting Christ and becoming his servants, the Kingdom of Daniel 2:32-45, Gods 5th Stone Kingdom in verse 44, **"And in the days of these kings shall the God of heaven set up a kingdom, which shall never be destroyed: and the kingdom shall not be left to other people, but it shall break in pieces and consume all these kingdoms, and it shall stand for ever"**. This kingdom has to be the Hebrew and Christian nations that has preserved the world from evil for the last three thousand years for it was to be in place during the end days and the only Kingdom on earth that will last forever is Gods people, the Kingdom of his Church. Dan 2:44 is almost identical to **"a nation bringing forth the fruits"** spoken of in Matt 21:43-44. In our present time period, this Kingdom can only be the 46 Christians nations of the Common Wealth of Great Britain and the United Stated or any other Christian nation that exist as the lost sheep of the house of Israel given by Christ in Matt 10:6 and 15:24. These nations are preserving Gods Kingdom on earth through the throne of England fulfilling the promise to King David that a man would always sit upon his throne (Jerm 33:14-17, I Kings 9:5, Ps 145:13, Ps 89:4 and II Chron 7:18). God's Word clearly states that his earthly kingdom and dominion will endure throughout all generations with a man sitting on David's throne and it is located on this earth today through the throne of England.

Great Britain is the only nation with a Unicorn as a national symbol and their great navy has pushed the people together throughout the world colonizing as stated in Deuteronomy 33:17. In true reality of history, they are the only nation that can fulfill Gods prophecy of these verses. Ephraim and Manasseh became the Hebrew Phoenician, Milesian, Celtic-Anglo-Saxons and later the English-speaking peoples of the world. A portion of all twelve tribes migrated and was planted in the wilderness or bush but the tribe of Joseph (Ephraim and Manasseh) was to receive a crown and lion's share of the blessing to be kings of nations and multitudes of peoples. The blessings were given only to the birthright tribe given in Genesis 48:13-22. These verses and blessings cannot be talking about the modern nation of Israel for they did not exist as a nation from 586BC till 1948. Israel did not control Jerusalem till 1967and still do not have a King to fulfill Scripture. David's throne was overturned three times in Eze 21:26-27 by Jeremiah in Jerm 1:10 where he pulled down David's throne from Jerusalem in 586BC during the Babylonian invasion. Jeremiah and Baruch his Scribe planted David's (diadem meaning Tiara, Crown or Turban of the King) into Ireland through the bloodline of King Zedekiah's two daughters in Jerm 41:10, and 43:6. He transplanted by ship the two daughters into Ireland where they married into the Zarah bloodline of kings that migrated hundreds of years before fulfilling the breach of "the scarlet threat" in Gen 38:29-30. David's crown was overturned 1st from Ireland, 2nd to Scotland and 3rd after the unification of all of Britain into London as the Throne of England where the Cross of Christ and the three crouched lions are displayed on the Kings flags and banners.

New Testament Facts in reference to the house of Israel

There are twenty-seven books in the New Testament and Paul is believed to have written ten of them. There is a big question that needs to be asked! If the twelve Apostles were chosen by Jesus to teach and spread the Gospel, why did God select Paul to do most of the writings of the New Testament? Paul did most of the teaching in Jerusalem and the surrounding area and not the Apostles. Christians fail to realize that Paul was sent to teach and spread the Gospel to the Jews and Gentiles in Judea, Asia, Greece and Rome to the population around the Mediterranean Sea. Romans 11:13, **"For I speak to you Gentiles, inasmuch as I am the apostle of the Gentiles, I magnify mine office"**. Again, Paul's mission was to the Jews first and then the Gentiles, Rom 1:16, **"For I am not ashamed of the gospel of Christ; for it is the power of God unto salvation to every one that believeth; to the Jew first, and also to the Greek"**. If Paul were sent to the Jews and Gentiles then to who were the Apostles supposed to teach? Matthew 10:5 and 15:24 tells the Apostles to not go to the Gentiles but to the lost sheep of the house of Israel. They were neither Gentile nor Jew but of Hebrew decent, Gods people.

After the 21st Chapter of Acts, the Apostles are not mentioned and only John,

James and Philip are referred to after chapter 15, where did they go? They did what they were told and went to the lost sheep of the house of Israel which were scattered all over Europe and England, the scattered people abroad, strangers scattered, and Barbarians which Paul were indebted to, Romans 1:14, **"I am debtor both to the Greeks, and to the Barbarians; both to the wise, and to the unwise".** Why would Paul be indebted to Barbarians if there was not a close connection to him? The Apostles remained in Jerusalem long enough to get the Church started on the right track and for Paul to be established. After the Church was developed and growing, the twelve Apostles departed to find the lost sheep of the house of Israel as commissioned by Jesus.

The Romans attacked Britain in 42AD and the word Barbarians became a common term for the British people spoken by the Roman population. Paul's first trip to Rome took place in 56AD and the Romans had been fighting the British for 14 years. Rome attacked Britain because of enter tribal warfare where one of the tribe leaders asked Rome to help fight for their cause. Joseph of Arimathea had started a Church in Avalon England in 36AD prior to the Roman invasion where a few of the British Royal family members had become Christian. During the war a portion of the Royal Family had been taken captive and imprisoned to Rome for trial prior to Paul's first visit. Caradoc (Caractacus a Celtic) as the Barbarian's leader, his daughter Claudia (Gladys British name), and his son Linus and was taken captive by the Romans. Linus, Claudia and Pudens her husband the senator is mentioned as Christians in II Tim 4:21. She had already started a Church in Rome before Paul arrived and his acquaintance with the Barbarians was these British Christians within the Roman Christian Church. The term Barbarian and Scythian as British is mentioned in Colossians 3:11.

Here is a brief history of Rome's attack on Briton by Geoffrey of Monmouth written in 1136AD of the legendary Arvirargus. In 52AD, King Caradoc known as Caractacus and King Arvirargus is believed to be the same person and legend as a Celtic leader. Rome first invaded Briton in 55-54BC by Juluis Caesar with two separate military campaigns to learn Ibernia's weakness, strength and resources and then withdrew. Emperor Claudius invaded in 43-44AD with 40,000 troops to stay in Briton till approx. 410AD when Rome cut off all aid and removed most troops except a few garrisons. They were sent to Europe to fight against the invasion of Rome. In 51AD Caradoc/Caratacus or Arvirargus and a portion of his Royal family was captured and taken to Rome as POW and put on trial in front of the Roman Senate. Because of Caradoc's/ Arvirargus great battle strategies, Rome could not take Britain and he was admired throughout Rome as a mighty warrior. Caradoc in Welch is the name of a baby that is delightfully beloved and Caratacus radiated this trait to the

Roman people. He was the only foreign leader to ever speak to the Roman Senate where he had a standing ovation. His sentence was a supernatural event for he was the only foreign leader captured that was not killed or imprisoned. The Emperor, Claudius became his friend and allotted him property in central Rome for his living abode and offered his daughter for marriage. Due to his greatness as a leader and diplomacy, Caradoc received a slight punishment of seven years on house arrest in Rome and with a promise to never take up arms against the Empire. It is uncertain if he died or later returned to Britain after his seven-year probation. During his seven years in Rome, enter marriage between the Royal families began. Caradoc's daughter Gladys (Claudia) married the Roman Senator Aulus Rufus Pudens and started the first Church in Rome somewhere between 51-56AD prior to Paul's first visit. Other inter marriages within the Christians and Roman families began. This was the beginning of Rome turning Christian for the British Royal family is referenced in II Tim 4:21. In 56AD was Paul's first visit to Rome invited by Claudia to minister the Gospel. The first Christian Church at Rome already existed at Paul's arrival in Palladium Britannicum where the British Royal Family lived also called Titulus or Hospitium Apastelorum then Pudentians to this day. The British Royal family of Claudia, a Roman name and Gladys her British name, was the first hostess to Apostle Peter and Paul during their visits to Rome. Gladys was the British wife of the Roman Senator Aulus Rufus Pudens, a Christian and Paul's half-brother also referred to in Rom 16:13. Romans 11:2 **"God hath not cast away his people which he foreknew, Wot ye not what the scripture saith of Elisa"**. This verse is talking about his castaways that God foreknew, the 10 lost tribes or the lost sheep of the house of Israel where the throne had been overturned to Ireland by Jeremiah. The book *"St. Paul in Britain"* by R.W. Morgan and *"The Origin and Early History of Christianity in Britain"* by Andrew Gray, D.D. are excellent reference books on the account of the Apostle Paul going to Britain. A few of the books of the New Testament were written to Gentiles or scattered strangers. Matthew, Mark, Luke, and John were mostly written to the Gentiles telling the story of Jesus. The book of James was written to all twelve tribes, Peter to the scattered strangers, Acts written to Theophilus and the Gentiles. John, Jude, and Revelation were written to Christians as the Church.

Study the word abroad in James 1:1 for it is very interesting, **"James, a servant of God and of the Lord Jesus Christ, to the twelve tribes which are scattered abroad, greeting."** The Greek word for abroad means #1290, dispersion of Israelite residents in Gentile countries scattered abroad. This verse is clear that James knew where the other ten tribes of the lost sheep of the house of Israel were located, for they had disappeared almost 800 years earlier. He was preparing for his trip as Christ commanded in Matthew 10:6. When James wrote this book, Jerusalem only consisted of the remnant of the house of Judah, Jeremiah 44:28, **"Yet a small number that escaped the sword shall return out of the land of Egypt into the land of Judah, and all the remnant of Judah, that are gone into the land of Egypt to sojourn there, shall know whose words shall stand, mine, or theirs."** We must note that the name Egypt in Hebrew Strong's ref# 4714, 4693 and 4692 means, *besieged places, fortified, siege, hemming in,* for this verse is speaking of the besieging of Jerusalem by Babylon. The word remnant indicates only a very small portion of the two million Jewish people that went into Babylonian captivity return to Jerusalem of Judea after their seventy-year captivity remained till the time of Christ. The term "land of Egypt" is a symbolic name for being besieged or being in foreign countries. By definition, this small remnant of Hebrew people is the only populace that have the right to be called Jews. Where is the rest of the 13 million Hebrews/Jews as the twelve tribes, the bulk of God's Chosen People? The above verse speaks to the people that migrated out of Palestine, for Egypt represent other parts of the world and that his Word is more powerful than theirs for their punishment of disobedience were to be taken into captivity. This brings up a big question? Where did the Hebrew's of the house of Israel (11 million) and the house of Judah (2 million Jews) depart and where are they now? There is no record in the Bible or secular history returning them to the promised land of Israel except for the remnant of approx. 40,000 Jews (Jerm 44:28 and Ezra Ch 6).

After the Babylonian captivity, the Bible only speaks of a vestige of Jews returning to Jerusalem out of an estimated 2 million (Ezra 6:14). Jesus knew where they were and also James for, he wrote to them, all twelve tribes. The twelve tribes scattered abroad in James 1:1 was scattered all over Europe and the word abroad explains their situation. Christ commissioned the Apostles in Matthew 10:5-8, 15:24, Acts 10:36 and Eze 3:1-5, to go to the Lost Sheep of the ten northern tribes of the house of Israel that became Gods fruitful nation in Matthew 21:43-44 and Dan 2:34-35&44 to spread his Gospel as the stone kingdom that grinds to powder. God knew that the house of Israel, Judah Hebrew, would accept his Gospel, where the Jew of the house of Judah would not, due to wealth, pride and entrenched religious traditions of hundreds of years. Keep in mind that even though the lost sheep of the house of Israel, Gods people of Hebrew descent, were still considered to be Gentiles for the term Gentile to a Jew means, an Edomite, a foreign nation, heathen or non-Jew. The ten northern tribes to include the mass of Judah had been separated from the tribe of Judah for so long and such a distance, they were considered to be Gentiles or Greek and not of there-own kind.

The Dividing of a Nation "Branches verses Root"

There is a verse in Deuteronomy that most Christians completely overlook when it comes to God dividing his creation. When God created the earth and divided it into continents, he did not intend for his beautiful earth to be settled and dominated by heathen people to worship idol gods. This is exactly why God established the North American Continent, Austria, New Zealand and others islands to be under English-speaking Christianity. God took the continents from the idol worshiping savages and gave it to his people called the house of Israel. This is clearly stated in Deuteronomy 32:8-9 and states, **"When the Most High divided to the nations their inheritance, when he separated the sons of Adam, he set the bounds of the people according to the number of the children of Israel. For the Lord's portion is his people; Jacob is the lot of his inheritance."** In this verse, God is not speaking of just a small portion of land in Palestine called Canaan but the bounds of the sons of Adam and the people that is the whole world. The world was to be divided in accordance to the number of the children of Israel and the inheritance and seed of Jacob were to settle to the North, East, South and West in the four corners of the world as God's earthly Kingdom. They were to represent the four Brigades as the four Beast of Israel as outlined in Numbers 2:3-34, Eze 1:10, 10:14 and Rev 4:7 as the Lion, Calf/Ox/Churbim, Man and Eagle. Jacob clearly gave his inheritance through Joseph and directly to Ephraim and Manasseh to receive the name Israel (Gen 48:16) and to no other tribe. In other words, the birthright inheritance that Jacob gave to Joseph's two sons were to control the boundaries of the people of the world just as Genesis 22:18, 26:4 and 28:14 states **"in thy seed shall all the nations of the earth be blessed" "will give unto thy seed all these countries" "and in thee and in thy seed shall all the families of the earth be blessed.".** All nations and families of the world were to be blessed by his inherited tribe of Ephraim and Manasseh. Only Great Britain and the United States fulfill these verses as Christian nations as brothers.

Deuteronomy 32:8 calls Israel nations just as they are called nations in II Kings 19:17 after their division and captivity to Assyria. The house of Israel never returned to Canaan due to their inheritance for they were to be nations and to be kings of kingdoms according to Genesis 17:6, 35:11 and 48:16. If the house of Israel had returned to the Promised Land after their captivity, they could not have fulfilled their commission to be many nations and Kings. These blessings only went to Ephraim and Manasseh through the birthright of Joseph (Gen 48:16-22).

Isaiah 7:17 speaks of the day that Ephraim (the house of Israel, ten northern tribes) departed from Judah due to the Assyrian captivity, **"from the day Ephraim departed from Judah: even the king of Assyria"**. This verse clearly divides Ephraim of the northern kingdom and Judah the southern kingdom. In other words, according to this verse, whenever the Bible speaks of Ephraim in a singular form, it is referring to the house of Israel as the 10 northern tribes with Ephraim as their leader. Ephraim and Manasseh were given the Birthright by Jacob to be over all nations on earth.

From the dividing of Israel into two separate nations in 1 Kings 11:30, the ten northern tribes from that time forward, the Old Testament Scriptures referred to them as the house of Israel (the branch or vineyard) and the two southern tribes as the house of Judah (the root). Judah was to be further divided after the Babylonian captivity as the Judah Hebrew and Judah Jew where only a remnant returned to Jerusalem. After the division of Israel, God always addressed each of them separately. This is a view that is not being realized by our religious leaders and by not understanding this point, they have lost the overall purpose and blinded to true end time prophecy. If you step back and look at Israel as two separate nations and realize that God has two deferent plans for each of his Hebrew nations, then you can better understand end time prophecies. Please do not take my word on this subject but research the Scriptures for yourselves as I have done. My authority on this point of view is the Scriptures and as pointed out in chapter one, the reader must go to the Holy Spirit in prayer for understanding.

The following is just a few verses taken from the prophetic book of Isaiah indicating the division of the two houses as two separate and distinct nations. Isaiah 5:7, divides the house of Israel as the vineyard representing the branches or vines that travel worldwide and Judah the pleasant plant as the root that is permanently planted in Jerusalem. This is an important verse for it indicates that Israel was to be Gods vineyard whose branches ran over the wall into the world. Judah was to be his pleasant plant or the root of the vineyard that stayed in the Promised Land to preserve prophecy for the last days and fulfill the linage of Christ and maintain Jerusalem as Jews of Judah. The house of Israel Hebrews and the majority of the Judah/Jew Hebrew migrated into the wilderness to help maintain David's Throne. Only a remnant returned to Judea.

The different names of Israel can be very confusing unless you understand the firstborn family birthright blessing. Many verses in the Scriptures describe Jacob as being the eleven tribes not including Joseph or Ephraim and Manasseh due to the fact that only they received the birthright. In some cases, the name Jacob refers to all twelve tribes. The house of Joseph refers to Ephraim and

Manasseh for only they received the family firstborn birthright blessing to be called Israel. When speaking in context, the house of Israel represents the ten northern tribes to be led by Ephraim and Manasseh and the house of Judah the two southern tribes. The Jews for prophetic purposes were to be a divided house as Judah Hebrew and the Judah Jew because of the Jewish non-belief in the Messiah.

We must realize that whenever the word Israel is used singularly, it is speaking of Ephraim and Manasseh as leaders of the ten northern tribes of the house of Israel. Only they were given the birthright name of Israel in Genesis 48:16, to be the inherent sons that received the blessings God gave to Abraham, Isaac and Jacob passed directly to Joseph's two sons, Ephraim and Manasseh. This blessing was not given to any of the other sons of Jacob but exclusively to Ephraim and Manasseh. The Jews of Judah were not included and did not receive the family birthright name of Israel as recorded in I Chronicles 5:1-2. What divides Judah (Jews) from the house of Israel is the fact that they still reject Christ as the true Messiah to this day where many of the Judah Hebrews accepted Christ in the wilderness.

We need to understand that Judah is the root of the vineyard representing all twelve tribes for prophetic purposes. A good example of this is seen in Isaiah 43:22 and 27 and can be proven by studying the word curse in verse 27. The curse pertains to Judah rejecting Christ at his coming and not to the house of Israel. They were to be blessed by the birthright. The house of Israel was to be many nations and kings where Judah were to maintain the promised Land to fulfill the end time gathering of all twelve tribes back into Jerusalem in the last days as stated in Gen 49:1. This process began in 1948 as a recognized nation within the world.

This can also be seen in Jeremiah 2:4, **"Here ye the Word of the Lord, O house of Jacob and all the families of the house of Israel"**. Here, Jacob is a completely different entity of the families of Israel. Jacob is referred to as the 11 sons of Jacob the Hebrew nations of Europe and the family of Israel is Ephraim and Manasseh, the sons of Joseph (46 Common Wealth nations of Great Britain and the United States) as the birthright tribes by blessings given in Genesis 48 and 49. All are indicated as separate nations to take place in the last days and the families of Israel means different nations within Israel. Jeremiah 12:14 states, **"that touch the inheritance which I have cause my people Israel to inherit; Behold, I will pluck them out of their land, and pluck out the house of Judah from among them."** These two verses clearly divide Judah, Jacob and Israel (the inherit birthright tribe) and goes as far as to say that Judah will be plucked out from among Israel indicating two separate peoples or nations. Study Jeremiah chapter twelve on how God planted Israel in the wilderness and for it to take root signifying their inheritance in a land of peace, the continents of the world.

Jeremiah 13:11 tells us, **"so have I caused to cleave unto me the whole house of Israel and the whole house of Judah,"** The term "whole house of" clearly means that they are individual families or nations. Jeremiah 30:3 further states, **"For, lo, the days come saith the Lord, that I will bring again the captivity of my people Israel and Judah,"** Verse 24 of this chapter places this verse in the last days giving them a distinct division. Jeremiah 31:27 also divides the two houses by saying, **"Behold, the days come, saith the Lord, that I will sow the house of Israel and the house of Judah with the seed of man, and with the seed of beast."** This verse indicates that Israel and Judah are two separate peoples when they are scattered into the world among the seed of man and the seed of beast means within the wilderness or continents of the world. This verse explains our current migration problems in how Satan is destroying the Christian nations through illegal migration in the last days. The Hebrew meaning of beast in this verse means, *dumb beast, large four-legged animal, beast or cattle.* This is calling the people of the world dumb cattle being ignorant of Gods laws by being used to destroy our Christian societies through migration.

The book of Hosea is basically written to the tribe of Ephraim, the birthright tribe for events that take place in the last days. Hosea was an end time Prophet. Chapter one explains the difference between the house of Israel and house of Judah very well and Hosea 1:10 matches the new covenant that takes place in Hebrew 8:8 and Jeremiah 31:31, verse 10, **"Ye are the sons of the living God"** (Christian). Hosea 1:11, **"Then shall the children of Judah and the children of Israel be gathered together, and appoint themselves one head, and they shall come up out of the land: for great shall be the day of Jezreal."** This gathering is again mentioned in Ezekiel chapter 37 as the gathering of the dried bones that take place during the last days of the Church age as indicated by the day of Jezreal and represent the nation of Israel as a whole Kingdom under the Throne of David (the Throne of England). According to this verse, Judah and Israel is divided prior to the day of Jezreal called the Tribulation Period of wrath.

Hosea 5:5 goes as far as to divide the nations even father by stating, **"And the pride of Israel doth testify to his face; therefore shall Israel and Ephraim fall in their iniquity; Judah also shall fall with them."** This verse divides the house of Israel as Israel and Ephraim (Great Britain and US verses the rest of the European Israelite nations). Hosea divides the Children of Israel into three different nations of Israel, Ephraim and Judah for events that take place in the last days. This division is again mentioned in Hosea 6:10-11 as three different countries. Study the whole book of Hosea in how it compares Ephraim to Israel and Judah. Lebanon is the name for the house of Israel in the last days and further broken down into Sharon, Gilead, Carmel and Bashan with Lebanon and Sharon being Ephraim (GB) and Gilead, Carmel and Bashan being Manasseh (USA). Study each of these ancient names in context as fruitful nations and you will understand that they are Christian in the last days. Refer to table two for the Modern Hebrew nations by name according to the twelve tribes.

Amos 7:9, is a very interesting verse for it calls the house of Israel Isaac (Saxon) for events that take place in the last days. **"And the high places of Isaac shall be desolate, and the sanctuaries of Israel shall be laid waste; and I will rise against the house of Jeroboam with the sword".** Refer to I Kings chapter 11 for the division of the kingdom to Jeroboam the Ephrathite (Ephraim) of the ten northern tribes of the house of Israel. This is a dual prophecy for this event is going to also take place in the last days. They were to be called Isaac's sons (Saxons) (Gen 21:12, Rom 9:7 and Heb 11:18) and speak of the soon coming end time World War.

Zechariah 10:6-7 also makes a distinction between the houses of Judah, Joseph (Ephraim and Manasseh) and Ephraim by being in far countries (verse 9). Ephraim was to be Christian for, **"their heart shall rejoice in the Lord".** Zechariah was a Prophet of end time events. The word saved in verse 6 can be related to all Israel being saved in the last days (Jerm 23:6 and Rom 11:26). Study Zechariah chapter ten through 11 and it also refers to these nations mentioned above as being Lebanon, a cedar tree, symbolic to King David's throne (England as Ephraim). Zechariah 10:7 says, **"And they of Ephraim shall be like a mighty man, and their heart shall rejoice as through wine: yea, their children shall see it, and be glad; their heart shall rejoice in the Lord."** According to this verse, Ephraim (unicorn) was to be a separate nation from Judah and Joseph and to be a great powerful nation as Christian, "rejoice in the Lord". The ancient house of Israel as the ten northern tribes during the time of Jeroboam worshiped Baal and did not follow the ways of the Lord. This verse has to be speaking in future tense after the coming of Christ's Gospel.

We can absolutely place the division of Israel and Judah in the last days by studying Hebrews chapter 8, Jeremiah chapter 31 and Romans chapter 9 through 11. These chapters refer to the New Covenant of the Church in the last days. Romans 11:26 refer to all Israel being saved (Jerm 23:6, Zech 10:6) indicating a division of the houses. Hebrew 8:8 makes a new covenant with the house of Israel and the house of Judah placing them in the Church age of the end time, our present time period. This new Covenant is mentioned in Jeremiah 31:31 almost word for word also placing them in the last days of the new covenant. The term virgin of Israel and virgin daughters of Israel indicate they are a Bride or the Bride to be which God betrothed in Hosea 2:19, Christ's Church. Israel is the Bride of Christ or the virgin Israel of the house of Israel given the birthright and family name Israel (Ephraim and Manasseh).

These are just a few important verses indicating the division of the house of Israel and the divided house of Judah as Hebrew/Jew that takes place in the last days. There are many Scriptures throughout the Bible signifying this division and placing the cedar tree of Lebanon (Ephraim), King David's throne, ruling and executing judgment in the world today (Jerm 23:1-6, Isa 41:1-8).

We all know the story of Moses, the Exodus, and how Israel became a nation in the Promised Land. Let's now look at how God filtered his chosen people from the other side of the Exodus that settled Greece, Spain, Troy, Hibernia (ancient Ireland), Iberian trade routes (Spain) and on into Europe. Historians fail to realize that each time Israel went into captivity, a large portion of the Tribes population migrated to escape slavery and persecution. Where did they go? We can trace these migrating Hebrews through writers of ancient history. "Tracing Our Ancestors" by Frederick Haberman, "Missing Links Discovered in Assyrian Tablets" by E. Raymond and "Tracing the Ancestors of Great Britain and America" by Gospel of the Kingdom Ministry is all good reference books along with reference material listed in table four. There are hundreds of books on this subject written by great ancient and modern English/European history scholars if we are willing to open our minds and research the truth of history.

It is time to take off the blinders and open the seal of the Word as stated in Daniel 12:9, **"for the words are closed up and sealed till the time of the end."** The purpose of this book is to tell the American people of our true identity as a nation and that we are now at the end of the age of time.

God's Chosen People or Covenant People

In Genesis 1:28, God blessed man and said **"Be fruitful and multiply, and replenish the earth, and subdue it; and have dominion."** God created the heavens and earth for man and this writer believes, by God's Word, that he selected his chosen people (the Hebrew) to be the building block or the established dominating race of civilization through the four Brigades of Israel as laid our in the encampment in Numbers chapter two to have dominion over all nations. The four Brigades of the Man, Lion, Ox and Eagle represent God's Kingdom of the four Beast in Eze 1:10, Rev 4:7 and 19:4. They were to be his Covenant People (Gen 17:2-9, Duet 7:6; 14:2; 26:15-19; 32:8 & 13; I Sam 12:22; Ps 4:3, Isaiah 43:1, Eph 1:4 and I Peter 2:10).

Deuteronomy 7:6, 14:2 and 26:19 are almost identical verses and states Israel as a Chosen People and to be above all nations, **"For thou art an holy people unto the Lord thy God: the Lord thy God hath chosen thee to be special people unto himself, above all people that are upon the face of the earth."** Deuteronomy 32:8-13 clearly states that Jacob (Israel) is the lot of his inheritance and was to make him to ride on the high places of the earth. In other words, Jacob of all twelve tribes under the leadership of the house of Israel, the birthright of Ephraim and Manasseh, were to dominate the world and control it. I Samuel 12:22 and Psalms 4:3 goes on to say that God will never forsake his people of these great blessings and always answer our prayer of need. Isaiah 43:1 divides Jacob, his chosen people, into other nations by calling them Jacob and now Israel separating them into different entities. To understand this verse, we need to be aware of the birthright and to whom it went. The family name Israel is the firstborn birthright of Joseph that directly went to Ephraim and Manasseh (Gen 48:16) and to them only in I Chron 5:1-2.

We can further trace who God's chosen people are by looking at the birthright blessing of Joseph (Ephraim and Manasseh). Genesis 49:22-24 states that Joseph was to be a fruitful (Christian) bough (nation) whose branches ran over the wall from thence are the shepherd, the stone of Israel. In other words, Joseph was to be the Shepherd (spread the Gospel) and stone (Christ Church) of Israel and responsible under the birthright to spread Christ's end time Gospel. This can be further verified in Deuteronomy 33:17 when Moses said that Ephraim and Manasseh were to be blessed worldwide and can be identified by the symbol of the bull and unicorn. This clearly states that Ephraim and Manasseh are to dominate the world by pushing the people together and dividing them as two separate nations. This process is to be identified by the Bull (US) and Unicorn (GB). The ten thousands of Ephraim represent many nations and the thousands of Manasseh represents one single strong nation. This can be proven in Genesis 35:11, **"And God said unto him, I am God Almighty: be fruitful and multiply; a nation and a company of nations shall be of thee, and kings shall come out of thy loins"**. "A nation" and "a company of nations" refer to two separate entities, one being singular and one multiple, matching together the two sons of Joseph. This verse is the blessing God gave to Jacob which was passed directly to Joseph, then to Ephraim and Manasseh in Genesis 48:16 as the birthright that went only to the two lads along with the family name. The other eleven did not receive this blessing for they in their right were to be their own single nations. This verifies Deuteronomy 33:17 by stating "a nation" matches Manasseh's thousands where "a company of nations" matches Ephraim's ten thousands.

After reviewing all the above verses on God's Chosen People, it is clear that they were to be many nations worldwide to dominate the people of the world under Gods Righteous Laws. These Covenant Laws ultimately were culminated to be Christ's Church and the Gospel of Christianity (fruitfulness) led by his fruitful nation of the house of Israel (Ephraim and Manasseh). Ephraim means in Hebrew double fruit as the Christian Birthright leader. After reviewing history, the only two Christian nations in the past two thousand years that can match these verses is the unicorn of the Common Wealth of Great Britain and the bull of the United States.

We can further trace the identity of God's Chosen people through the word ruddy for it is mentioned several times in the Bible and a key word to understand to whom God is speaking. The term Ruddy in accordance to the Strong's Concordance reference number 119 means Adam, to show blood in the face or be flush or turn rosy. Reference number 120 means human being, an individual or the species, mankind. This is very interesting for according to definition only the Caucasian people of Adam are described as ruddy. We know that the Caucasian people are from the linage of Abraham for I Samuel 16:12 makes a clear statement on the physical appearance of King David which produced the linage of Christ, **"And he sent, and brought him in. Now he was ruddy, and withal of a beautiful countenance, and goodly to look to. And the Lord said, Arise, anoint him: for this is he."** I Samuel 17:42, **"And when the Philistine looked about, and saw David, he disdained him: for he was but a youth, and ruddy, and of a fair countenance."** All the Hebrews of the nation of Israel fell under this same physical appearance of being tall, blond hair, blue eyes and strong since of person.

We also know that Christ was of this same stature. The following letter first appeared in the writings of Saint Anselm of Canterbury in the 11th century A.D. that was written to the Monarch of Rome by Publius Lentrelus (a resident of Judea in the days of Tiberius Caesar).

"There lives at this time in Judea a man of singular virtue...Jesus Christ...his followers love and adore him as the offspring of the Immortal God".

"He calls back the dead from the graves and heals all sorts of diseases with a word or a touch. He is a tall man, well-shaped, and of an amiable and reverend aspect; his hair of a color that can barely be matched, falling into graceful curls, waving about and very agreeable... His forehead high, large, and imposing; his cheeks without spot or wrinkle, beautiful with a lovely red; his nose and mouth formed with exquisite symmetry; his beard and of a color suitable to his hair... his eyes bright and blue, clear and serene. {His} Look innocent, dignified, manly, and mature; his arms and hands delectable to behold." (from pg. 75, Appendix B of the "Resurrection Tomb" by E. Raymond Capt).

This letter was taken from the book "Uncovering the Mysteries of Your Hidden Inheritance" by Robert Alan Balaicius. The same people of stature mentioned in this letter above can be traced through the ancient tribes of circumcised Caucasians that migrated into Europe as the Anglo-Saxons but called by many other names throughout time. The term Caucasian comes from the tall, blond haired, blue eyed and light skinned peoples that migrated across the Caucasus Mountains into Georgia and settled Europe, later to be called Caucasian people. The Caucasus Mountains are located in southern Georgia, south of Russia and north of Turkey between the Black and Caspian Seas.

Gods Covenant said that you could identify his people through his law of circumcision (Gen 17:11) and his perpetual covenant of keeping his Sabbath (Exo 31:16-17). These same ancient tribes that maintained circumcision and kept the Sabbath, became the English-speaking Celts, Goths, Angles and Saxons that became the Christian nations of Europe. They are God's chosen people of the lost sheep of the house of Israel that can be identified by observance of circumcision and keeping the Sabbath on the seventh day of the week. The Sabbath was later changed to Sunday, the first day of the week by the Roman Church, distorting Gods commandment to observe his Sabbath on the last day of the week.

There is a false teaching within the Black community that Christ was a Black man and that the Caucasian people were of the descendants of Cain, vagabonds that migrated across the Caucasus Mountains. We need to remind ourselves of the power of Satan and not let him use cultural or ethnic divisions to divide and destroy our Christian nation for that is exactly what Satan the Devil is trying to do. No matter what race, creed or color, we should not disregard the truth of the Scriptures and ancient history of who our Savior truly is, for he died for all mankind. Let's not let Satan's tactics of duplicity and lies destroy our nation from within.

The book of Solomon's Song is even more specific on the stature of God's chosen people. This book is said to have been written to Christ's Church and the kingdom of the Church was given first to the lost sheep of the house of Israel in Matthew 10:6; 15:24 and 21:43. Solomon's Song 5:10-16 states, **"My beloved is white and ruddy, the chiefest among ten thousand", "His eyes are as the eyes of doves by the rivers of water,"** Lamentations 4:7, makes a statement on the appearance of a Nazarite that Christ was a Nazarene (Mat 2:23). **"Her Nazarites were purer than snow, they were whiter than milk, they were more ruddy in body than rubies, their polishing was of sapphire".** From all of these verses that refer to the linage of Abraham through David to Christ and now to God's chosen people that are of Caucasian persuasion, they were to be white, tall, blond hair, blue eyes and of a stout physical appearance. The term **"Chiefest among ten thousand"** can also be found in Deuteronomy 33:17 when Ephraim of the house of Israel is called "the ten thousands of Ephraim". The word chiefest in Hebrew means *to flaunt or raise a flag* and corresponds with the word ensign as the nation's spoken of in Isaiah 11:10-12 under the flag or ensign of Christianity, the New Covenant of Christ's Church. This appearance of being ruddy (red faced) applies to the English-speaking Christian nations and the Germanic countries of Western Europe of the Anglo Saxons (Isaac Sons or Saxons Gen 21:12, Heb 11:18).

God's chosen people, the Children of Israel, are to be the shining light unto the world and his heavenly plan is for his people to carry the plan of Salvation to the continents of this planet. The way God divided the landmasses separated by oceans was for a reason and he always has a wonderful plan. The Continents were first settled by heathen idol worshiping people of Noah's sons that were descendants of Ham and Japheth. They also were given shipbuilding technology from Noah. Isaiah 41:3 says, **"that he had not gone with his feet,"** explains how Gods people populated the continents of the world for they went without using their feet, they went by ship. God divided Israel for the reason of planting to establish a commonwealth of nations. Again, the following verses need to be re-emphasized. Genesis 35:11 is very clear that Israel was to be Kings of many nations. It is necessary to re-quote Deuteronomy 33:17 for it clarifies,

"His glory is like the firstling of his bullock, and his horns are like the horns of unicorns with them he shall push the people together to the ends of the earth: and they are the ten thousands of Ephraim and thousands of Manasseh". The term "firstling of his bullock" represents Ephraim and Manasseh's birthright of double blessing given the family name of Israel, to be God's chosen people (the house of Israel), to go forth and spread his end time Gospel. They were to go to each continent on the face of the earth, and teach the plan of Salvation of our Lord Jesus Christ. His chosen people were to be God-fearing teachers of his Word and to receive the blessings promised to Abraham, Isaac and Jacob.

The term "thousands" and "ten thousands" in the above verses is very important to under and has two different Hebrew meanings. Ephraim is the only people mentioned as being ten thousands in number indicating his birthright as being first and was to be millions in population as multiple nations. The Hebrew meaning of ten thousand is as follows; abundance in number, many (*nations*), multiply, be many and a rain of accumulated drops. Ephraim was to be many nations as millions of people and indicated by its definition. Manasseh is mentioned as being thousands or one single nation with the symbol of an ox, café, cow or bull. The Hebrew definition of thousands means; the Ox's head being the first letter of the Hebrew alphabet, a family, the sense of yoking or training of an ox or cow with the primitive root meaning to associate with, learn and teach, and to utter. This definition associates Manasseh with the United States as our symbol as the bull and we have trained under the yoke of Christ's Church to teach the Gospel to the world, to utter his Word. When researching the Bible, only Ephraim is mentioned as being ten thousands or multiple nations where Manasseh, Israel and Judah is referred to as thousands or one single nation. This clarifies Genesis 35:11 and 48:19 as to who will be many nations that can only apply to Ephraim. This fulfills the blessing to Abraham, Isaac, Jacob and Joseph down to Ephraim and Manasseh as the chosen Birthright to be many nations as brothers.

The only commonwealth of nations that fit the parameters given in God's Word in reference to these blessings are the Christian nations and colonies of Great Britain (Ephraim) and the United States (Manasseh). After a close study of history and Scripture, it uncovers undeniable facts of how God's chosen people, the Hebrew, were selected and slowly traveled (traveler, meaning of a wayfaring Hebrew man, Eberite) over time into Great Britain and Europe. They slowly migrated over thousands of years where all twelve tribes are represented as the western Christian culture, a company of nations throughout the world. The Common Wealth of England and their brother, the United States, is the nation Jesus spoke of in Matthew 21:43, to spread his fruitful

Christian end time Gospel. Christ himself authorized this mission in Matt 10:6, 15:24, Acts 10:36 and Eze 5:1-5 to the lost sheep of the house of Israel.

The story of Tamar

Now let's take off the blinders and study facts that will show who the English-speaking people truly are. The story of Tamar and Judah is directly linked as to the reason God divided his Kingdom into two houses. It is absolutely critical in understanding the events that occurred between Judah and Tamar and their twin sons, Zarah and Pharez. This twin birth created a breach within Gods throne promised to King David and helps to explain critical verses on how God healed the breach by overturning his throne from the high branch Pharez to the low branch Zarah, the scarlet thread in Amos 9:11. The story begins in Genesis 38 with Jacob's son Judah and a Hebrew woman by the name of Tamar, the mother of the bloodline of King David's throne (Matt 1:3).

The promise of the coming Messiah was to be through Judah's bloodline that is linked to the throne of Israel and Christ is to sit on that throne over all of Jacob promised by God in Gen 49:10 and Luke 1:32-33. Tamar had twin sons by Judah, Pharez and Zarah. Pharez was the firstborn and heir to the throne by a controversial breach. In Hebrew, Pharez means breach or a break. Zarah's hand came out of Tamar's womb first where a scarlet thread was tied around his finger by the midwife indicating the firstborn. In Hebrew, Zarah means to rise or a rising of light. He drew back his hand with the scarlet thread tied to his finger but Pharez, his twin brother, was born first giving him the birthright. God works in wonderful ways for this incident also gave Zarah a right to the Throne as we will see later when the throne of David is overturned in Ezekiel 21:26-27. The Pharez bloodline occupied the throne up to the fall of the house of Judah, Jerusalem, in 586BC when Jerusalem fell to Babylon. To this day, the last King to sit on Israel's throne in Jerusalem was Zedekiah. Nebuchadrezzar of Babylon or Satan tried to destroy King David's bloodline by having all of King Zedekiah's sons killed. His two daughters escaped and were hidden by the Prophet Jeremiah (Jerm 43:6). In an earlier segment we showed how the throne was preserved through his two daughters by the first overturn.

The Pharisees came from the Pharez bloodline of the first Kings of Israel. Jesus took the kingdom from them because of their sins and disbelief in Matthew 21:43 and gave it to the low branch of Zarah which had been planted in Ireland hundreds of years prior healing the breach of King David's tabernacle or throne as recorded in Gen 38:29, Judges 21:15, Ps 60:2 and Amos 9:11.

The overturn of the throne can be traced through Zarah and his five sons, Zimri, Ethan, Heman, Calcol and Dara as recorded in I Chronicles 2:6. Calcol and Dara are the only brothers mentioned in other Scriptures or secular history and were to eventually inherit King David's throne when overturned by Jeremiah (Jerm 1:10). To indicate that Zarah has a right to the throne is stated in Matthew 1:3 where Tamar begot Pharez and Zarah which authorized both to be in the Royal Blood line and plays a very significant role in establishing the throne in Ireland fulfilling Ezekiel 17:22, **"Thus saith the Lord God; I will also take of the highest branch of the high cedar, and will set it: I will crop off from the top of his young twigs a tender one and will plant it upon an high mountain and eminent"**. Ezekiel 21:26-27 further states, **"Thus saith the Lord God: Remove the diadem, and take off the crown: this shall not be the same: exalt him that is low, and abase him that is high. I will overturn, overturn, overturn, it: and it shall be no more, until he come whose right it is: and I will give it him"**. This is the first overturn and it will stay in England. Note that the throne of Israel has not existed in Israel for the past 26 hundred years and according to Ezekiel 21:27, the throne will stay in England till Christ sets on it in Rev 4:1-2 when the Church is taken, "whose right it is", Christ's.

The second overturn occurred when the throne was moved to Scotland and later the last overturn to England where it is located today in Westminster Abbey in London. Jeremiah 33:17, **"For thus saith the Lord: David shall never want a man to sit upon the throne of the house of Israel:"** Again in I Kings 9:5 makes the statement, **"Then I will establish the throne of thy kingdom upon Israel for ever, as I promised to David thy father, saying, There shall not fail thee a man upon the throne of Israel"**. We know God's Word is infallible so where is King David's throne today, it is located within the throne of England transplanted by Jeremiah (Jerm 1:10). These verses make it very clear that a man will always sit on King David's throne and has been fulfilled through the throne of Ireland, Scotland, and now England, God's chosen people to be called Israel.

Migrations of Semitic Hebrews

The book "Missing Links Discovered in Assyrian Tablets" by E. Raymond Capt on page 61 states, states *Long before Moses led the Children of Israel out of Egypt (Exodus in 1453 B.C.) There had been continuous migrations of Semitic Hebrews to Greece and other parts of Asia Minor and Europe", "Egyptian" origin of the Greeks. Hecataeus of Abdere (sixth century B.C.) quoted by Diodorus Siculus (50 B.C.) tells us that the Egyptians "Expelled all the aliens gathered together in Egypt. The most distinguished of the expelled foreigners followed Danaus and Cadmus into Greece: but the greater number were led by Moses into Judea"* (British History Traced from Egypt and Palestine, Rev. G.A. Robert, p.122)". Danaus and Cadmus are Zarah's two sons Dara and Calcol spoken of in I Chronicles 2:5-6 and in ancient history. When the house of Israel went into captivity and later migrated, they lost their language and identity as God said they would. Deuteronomy 32:26, **"I said, I would scatter them into corners, I would make the remembrance of them to cease from among men."** They were forced by the Assyrians to use other languages and religions during their period of captivity causing them over time to lose Judaism. Therefore, the nations of the world no longer recognized them as Hebrew Israelites. They never returned to the promised land of Israel so they totally lost their language and national identity of being Hebrew.

Isaiah 62:2 said that his forsaken people would lose their name, **"And the Gentiles shall see thy righteousness, and all kings thy glory: and thou shalt be called by a new name, which the mouth of the Lord shall name."** This name was to be Christian after Christ himself who was righteous and they were to be a World Class nation and leader. Again, in Isaiah 56:5, **"Even unto them will I give in mine house and within my walls a place and a name better than of sons and of daughter: I will give them an everlasting name, that shall not be cut off"**. This name had to be Christian for it will never be cut off just as Christ's Church and Kingdom cannot be destroyed. Isaiah 42:16, **"And I will bring the blind by a way that they knew not; I will lead them in paths that they have not known; I will make darkness light before them, and crooked things straight. These things will I do unto them, and not forsake them"**. This verse says that God is going to give his people a new place or nation and an everlasting name giving them light (the Gospel) by not forsaking them. This verse is speaking of the Gospel of Christ's Church. The term "the blind by a way they knew not" and "I will lead them in paths that they have not known;" simply means that God guided their migrations on the wings of eagles, a way they had never traveled before (Eze 17:3&7). They traveled by ship into the wilderness to inherit their own land under Christ's Gospel as a New Spirit and Heart that man has never experienced before (Eze 34:13, 37:14 and 39:28).

Isaiah 28:11, **"For with stammering lips and another tongue will he speak to his people."** Isaiah 65:15, **"And ye shall leave your name for a curse unto my chosen: for the Lord God shall slay thee, and call his servants by another name"**. His servant's new name is Christian and the Christian nations that have preached his Gospel (Acts 11:26). Jeremiah 50:6 identifies the house of Israel, **"My people hath been lost sheep: their shepherds have caused them to go astray, they have turned them away on the mountains:**

they have gone from mountain to hill, they have forgotten their resting place". This verse explains how Israel lost their mountain that means nation and become a hill during the two houses captivity. They became a remnant of a people scattered into the world as lost sheep of the house of Israel and Judah where James 1:1 calls then twelve tribes scattered abroad and called lost sheep in Matt 10:6 and 15:24. Jesus knew where they were after almost 750 years of being dispersed worldwide and they were still individual Hebrew Israelite nations scattered throughout Europe.

Jeremiah 50:17, **" Israel is a scattered sheep; the lions have driven him away; first the king of Assyria hath devoured him; and last this Nebuchadrezzar king of Babylon hath broken his bones".** This verse speaks of both houses of Israel. First, the house of Israel being taken away by Assyria where the ten northern tribes were to never return to Palestine and then the house of Judah taken captive by Babylon 130 years later. They were both lost sheep but their bones were finally broken by Babylon and remained broken until the last days where the gathering in the wilderness took place under Christ's Gospel to become a whole house again (Eze 37:22). The taproot of the vineyard in Palestine, the house of Judah (Jews), never moved but sprouted re-growth and became a nation again in 1948 to fulfill Daniel's 70th week Prophecy. In Isaiah 65:5 God gave the house of Israel a new place or nation and a new name that would not be cut off (Christian) and Judah was to return and reestablish Jerusalem in the last days to fulfill the prophecy of Daniel.

These verses are speaking of the 10 northern tribes of the lost sheep of the house of Israel as in Jeremiah 50:6&17, along with all the migrated Hebrews over thousands of years. God scattered and planted his chosen people (Isaiah 65:15) into a new land of wilderness to wait for his Gospel. This new name was to be called Christian, Act 11:26, **"And the disciples were called Christians first in Antioch".** Jesus in Matthew 10:5-6, commanded his Disciples to go to the lost sheep of the house of Israel, to this new planted nation, Matthew 21:43, **"Therefore say I unto you, The kingdom of God shall be taken from you, and given to a nation bringing forth the fruits thereof".** Great Britain (Ephraim) and the United States (Manasseh), a branch of the vineyard, are the greatest and most fruitful nations that have spread Christ's Gospel around the world in the past five hundred years. Our nation meets the standards given in the Scriptures, certainly not the modern-day nation of Israel. They do not believe in the Lord Jesus as Savior so the Jews can never be fruitful and remain cursed till they accept Christ as the Messiah (Jerm 25:18).

Gods Fruitful Nations

The name Ephraim has a special Hebrew meaning and match the double blessing given as his primogeniture birthright in Genesis 48:20-22 but study verses 13-22. In Hebrew, Ephraim means, Ref. #669, "double fruit, fruitfulness". He was to be a fruitful nation, Genesis 49:22; Isaiah 29:17-18, **"fruitful field as an esteemed forest"** (wilderness) and the, **"deaf shall hear the words of his book"** (the Bible his Gospel). This is the nation Christ referred to in Matthew 21:43 when he told the Chief Priests and Pharisees that the kingdom of God shall be taken from them and given to a fruitful nation. Isaiah 32:15-18 speaks of the wilderness as a fruitful field after the Holy Spirit has been poured upon us and it shall be a peaceful habitation and a **"quit resting place"**. This certainly cannot be speaking of modern-day Israel with their history of war and continuous threat of war with the Arabs during the past 2000 years. Israel and the Middle East are not Christian so it cannot be fruitful as a "quite resting place". The Middle East has never been peaceful or restful and does not match these verses. Isaiah 33:13-21 refers to a nation afar off and verse 20-21 speaks of looking upon Zion, the city of solemnities (place of assembly). The term Zion, Solemnites and Jerusalem in this verse is referred to as a nation in the wilderness of broad rivers and not in the Middle East. The word Solemnities in Hebrew means appointment, a fixed time or season, a yearly festival, assembly, congregation, synagogue or in general terms a place of assembly. It also means engage for marriage or betroth which would make this verse refer to "O virgin of Israel" or the house of Israel as the bride of Christ, the end time Church (Hose 2:19-20). Study Jeremiah chapter 31 of how the house of Israel will be established in the wilderness as Christ's bride, calling them Ephraim that left waymarks and created a new thing in the earth, which is the New Covenant of the Church, his betrothed bride of the house of Israel. Study the word Solomites in table one.

Jeremiah 23:1-6 speak of God gathering his flock and bringing them to their folds, **"And I will gather the remnant of my flock out of all countries whither I have driven them, and will bring them again to their folds; and they shall be fruitful and increase"**. Note that God is speaking in a plural form, more than one-fold. Verse 5 speaks of a righteous branch which is Jesus Christ that executes judgment and justice in the earth, **"Behold, the days come, saith the Lord, that I will raise unto David a righteous Branch, and a King shall reign and prosper and shall execute judgment and justice in the earth"**, his Gospel (Battle Axe, Jerm 51:20). This is not speaking of Christ ruling on earth but a Christian righteous king under Christianity. The Jews have never fulfilled this verse, for they still to this day reject Christ as the Messiah. The fold of the house of Judah was planted back into Jerusalem in 1948 where the root has always remained, waiting to re-sprout as a nation. Jeremiah 23:8 says that the seed of the house of Israel shall dwell safely in their own land, **"But, The Lord liveth, which brought up and which led the seed of the house of Israel out of the north country, and from all countries whither I had driven them; and they shall dwell in their own land."** The land of Canaan has never been safe for the Jews and cannot fulfill this verse for this gathering is speaking of Christ gathering his Church (Gen 49:10) under his New Covenant of the Church. Jeremiah 23:6, **"In his days Judah shall be saved, and Israel shall dwell safely"**. This verse is referring to our present time period where the Christian nations of the house of Israel is safe and has protected or saved the modern nation of Israel under our umbrella of world power as Gods Battle Ax. Refer to Fruit; Fruits and Fruitful in table one.

Note the words **"his days"** to Judah indicates a difference between Judah, and Israel for they have different days of appointment. The term "his days" represent Daniel's 70th week where the Jews of Judah is allotted 3½ years during the first half of the Tribulation to repent and accept Christ as their true Messiah. The Gospel is finished in the middle of the seven-years of Trib as stated in Rev 10:7, 11:7 and Dan 12:7 where II Thess 2:6-7 is fulfilled when the Holy Spirit is removed. Today, Israel and Judah/Jew are two different nations or flocks dwelling in separate nations under two separate ideologies of religion. The Church age is allotted by appointment to the house of Israel as a whole nation to teach Christ's Gospel where Daniel's 70th week is allotted to Judah or the Jews. Where is the house of Israel dwelling today? They are the fruitful nations in the wilderness, the Christian English-speaking people of the world spreading Christ's Gospel as the house of Israel, Christ's Bride, as the Church. The Judah Jew was denounced by Christ and their Kingdom taken from them (Matt 21:43) due to rejecting his Gospel at his death and was given a chance to be a part of his Bride (Church) in Hebrews 8:8 and Jeremiah 31:31 and again they rejected his Gospel. The 17th chapter of Ezekiel explains how Israel was planted in the wilderness and where the Kingdom was to be overturned, the betrothed bride to be. Ezekiel 17:1 speaks in a riddle or a parable directly to the house of Israel, the ten northern tribes joined by the Judah/Hebrew to make a whole house. In Eze 17:3-4 a great eagle came into Israel and **"took the highest branch of the cedar: He copped off the top of his young twigs, and carried it into a land of traffic; he set it in a city of merchants"**. This verse represents how God moved his throne of David from Jerusalem to another nation, the highest branch is the throne and the young twigs is King David's blood line through Zedekiah's two daughters. The term "a land of traffic" is speaking of England in how they have controlled the world trade for the past 300 years, a land of sea traffic as the unicorn.

Eze 17:5 states, **"He took also of the seed of the land and planted it in a fruitful field; he placed it by great waters, and set it as a willow tree"**. Jeremiah overturned the Throne to Ireland after Babylon took Jerusalem where he was given authority by God in Jeremiah 1:10 and Ezekiel 17:22-24; 21:25-27. The highest branch was the throne of King Zedekiah and his Pharez bloodline where it was overturned to the Zarah low branch bloodline. They were chopped off when Babylon took Judah into captivity. Too preserve the throne, Jeremiah took King Zedekiah's two daughters, **"He cropped off the top of his young twigs,"** and fled into Ireland, the land of traffic and city of merchants (Eze 17:4). England has always been known for their merchant shipping and a very fruitful and Christian nation. Too better understand this chapter you need to study Jeremiah's commission and how God promised to overturn the throne in Ezekiel chapter 17 through 23.

King Zedekiah's daughter married into the Kingship of Ireland that were under the Zarah bloodline or the low branch of the throne of King David. This made the house of Israel whole under Israel and Judah as outlined in Ezekiel 37:22. The Zarah descendants settled Ireland after fleeing the captivity of Egypt by ship. Zarah is mentioned in Genesis 38:30 and 46:12 along with his sons Dara and Chalcol. Their names are mentioned in ancient chronicles to include Danaan or Tuatha de Danaan meaning the Tribe of Dara and Cadmus. Danaan and Cadmus are mentioned in the ancient Chronicles of Ireland, Scotland, England, and Greek history of how they came from Egypt and settled Greece, Spain, Troy, Italy and later into Ireland. When King Zedekiah's daughters married into the Zarah blood line established in Ireland by Danaan and Cadmus, this completed the first overturn of Ezekiel 17:22-24. The word fruitful is associated with the word plant and they both represent the planting of the lost sheep of the house of Israel, Ephraim and Manasseh as leaders and birthright tribes (Great Britain and the United States). Their fruitfulness represents Gods Christian Nations of today and the great blessings of their birthright to become the two greatest nations in history fulfilling Genesis 35:11.

Chapter 3

Israel, God's Divided House

Gods wonderful plan for his covenant people Israel is a fascinating mystery and warrants great study to understand. As we read through the Scriptures of the Old Testament starting with Genesis, the mysterious picture slowly unfolds. The nation of Israel begins with Jacob and his twelve sons with Judah, Joseph, and Levi as the key players. As progression takes place, we will see God's prophetic time table unfold in how it pertains to the house of Israel and the house of Judah as two separate nations with different identities. It is absolutely imperative that we grasp the understanding of the division of the two houses of God's people called Israel if we are to identify with end time Prophecy.

The three elements of God's Children of Israel are; the house of Judah (tribes of Judah, Benjamin); the house of Israel (the ten northern tribes) lead by Ephraim due to the birthright blessings; and the tribe of Levi which was dispersed between the two houses to provide spiritual and judicial wellbeing. The account of Israel being divided is recorded in I Kings chapter 11 and 12:21 when the Prophet Ahijah rent Jeroboam's garment into twelve pieces. This represents the dividing of the twelve tribes into separate nations but to be ruled by two houses. The house of Judah and the house of Israel are separate nations to this day and reunited as a whole Kingdom during the Church age as recorded in Ezekiel chapter 37. Throughout the Old Testament, the Children of Israel is mentioned by many names in different contexts. We as Christians, must dispose the idea that the Jews are Gods only chosen people in the last days. The name Jacob called Israel was only given to Joseph given directly to Ephraim and Manasseh as the two lads clearly stated in Gen 48:16.

The eleventh chapter of I Kings is the key in understanding why God divided his children of Israel and one thing that he will not tolerate, idol worship. The Lord warned King Solomon twice about having strange wives for he had seven hundred wives, princesses, and three hundred concubines. God told him that foreign wives would turn his heart to worship idols and I Kings 11:4 states, **"For it came to pass, when Solomon was old, that his wives turned away his heart after other gods; and his heart was not perfect with the Lord his**

God, as was the heart of David his father." These verses show how God is merciful for he gave King Solomon two warnings by coming to him personally. Any normal person would have been scared to death by the appearance of God but Solomon did not listen. Verse 11 gives us the consequences of Solomon's sin, **"Wherefore the Lord said unto Solomon, forasmuch as this is done of thee, and thou hast not kept my covenant and my statutes, which I commanded thee, I will surely rend the kingdom from thee, and will give it to thy servant."** This is a very important verse to understand for God is taking his Kingdom from Solomon and giving it to his servant, the house of Israel in I Kings 12:20. This occurs due to his idol worship and disobedience which is the beginning of the overturned throne mentioned in Ezekiel 21:25-27 where the throne and kingdom is taken from the Phares (Jews) line of Kings and given to the Zara line of Kings.

Gods Kingdom of Israel was taken from Solomon and given to the birthright tribe of Jeroboam (Ephraim) that has not been reunited to this day according to Scripture. Another thing that needs to be understood is that the physical kingdom of Israel belongs to God and not to the King that rule. I Kings 11:13 goes on to say, **"Howbeit I will not rend away all the kingdom; but will give one tribe to thy son for David my servant's sake, and for Jerusalem's sake which I have chosen."** These two verses make a clear statement that divides the nation and is an absolute distinction between the Kingdom and the Throne.

The kingdom was to be given to Solomon's servant Jeroboam and the throne was to stay with David's tribe of Judah. In this verse, notice the parallel between the branch (the Kingdom, Israel, Ephraim the Birthright tribe) and the root (Judah "Jews" Jerusalem and the throne). It is important to note that eleven tribes went to the house of Israel that is the majority of the kingdom and Judah or the Jews only received one tribe to be later joined by Benjamin. Our present-day teachings indicate that the Jews are all of God's Chosen People and this line of thought is absolutely wrong according to Scripture. The mass of Gods kingdom falls under the Hebrew people of the house of Israel (Christian nations of the world) and not the Jews of the house of Judah (modern Israel). Understand that the house of Judah is divided between the mass of the Judah Hebrews that migrated into the wilderness and accepted Christ's Gospel along with the house of Israel verses the non-believing Jews of Jerusalem in Judea as outlined in Jeremiah 44:28.

The verses concerning King Solomon's wives can directly apply to the United States today for we have allowed foreign peoples into our nation permitting them through liberal ethnic equalities to turn our heads and hearts from the one and true God that we based our nation upon. We shall see the same fate as King

Solomon and our nation will be divided and destroyed just as ancient Israel.

The inheritance blessing to each son as given by Jacob in Gen 49 was to be their future destinies. Genesis 49:10 explains Judah's role in more detail, **"The scepter shall not depart from Judah nor a lawgiver from between his feet, until Shiloh come; and unto him shall the gathering of the people be."** The throne and lawgiver were to be given to Judah or till Christ comes to establish his Church and gather his people under the Gospel. For understanding, study the word gather in table one. Because of Judah's sin, God took the throne from them when King Zedekiah fell to Babylon and will not return to Jerusalem till Christ returns in power. This may be confusing at this point of time for the throne and Kingdom are the same. Later we will see how Jeremiah was commissioned to unite the throne and Kingdom when it is taken from the high branch of Pharez and given to the low branch of Zarah, healing the breach between the two twins. Genesis 49:22 explain Joseph's inheritance or the house of Israel, David's Kingdom that was given to Jeroboam of the tribe of Ephraim, the house of Joseph and the birthright tribe.

Genesis 49:22 states, **Joseph is a fruitful bough, even a fruitful bough by a well; whose branches run over the wall"**. Refer to the word bough in table one. Bough means builder of the family name of Israel and went to the birthright tribe of Ephraim and Manasseh. This verse explains that Joseph as the house of Israel were to be fruitful which means righteous and wealthy. They were to run over the wall to spread or be scattered over the world to multiply in righteousness. Genesis 49:10 and 49:22 is tied together by this phrase, **"and unto him shall the gathering of the people be."** The inheritance of both houses will not be competed, till the gathering of the house of Israel under Christ's Gospel and then the last gathering as the Jews of Judah gathers back into Jerusalem which began in 1948 as the modern state of Israel. We must understand there are three gatherings that take place. The first in ancient times when the 40,000 Jews gathered or returned back into Jerusalem during Ezra's time to rebuild the Temple after the Babylonian captivity. The last two takes place in the last days. Verse 10 is clear that Judah will maintain the scepter or throne and be a lawgiver till Christ comes and establishes his Church. The gathering of the people is the house of Israel brought together as a nation in the wilderness where both houses became Gods kingdom excluding the remnant of the non-believing Jews where Christ himself took the Kingdom from them in Matthew 21:43 (I Chron 17:9-14, Zech 10:6-12: Eze 20:37, 34:13-18; Jerm 13:2-25; Hos 2:14-23; Micah 5:7-11).

After Christ came and his Gospel presented to the Jews, God gave them 40 years to repent and accept Christ as the Messiah but they refused. Jerusalem was totally destroyed in 70AD by General Titus of the Roman Army and remained unoccupied as a nation by the Jews till 1967, a total of 1897 years. Israel to this day has no King so where is Gods promise to David in I Kings 9:5 and Jeremiah 33:17 that a man would always be on his throne? Genesis 49:10 was to take place during the last days (Gen 49:1) and is not the gathering at his coming in power. This is the gathering of his sheep called the Church established in Ireland by Joseph of Arimathea where Gods Kingdom is given to the house of Israel by Christ in Matthew 21:43, his fruitful nation. The throne was taken from Judah, the Pharez line, and given to the house of Israel in Ireland, the Zarah line (Matt 1:3). This is the second gathering as Christ whole Kingdom.

We must understand who Jeroboam was and I Kings 11:28 explains, "**And the man Jeroboam was a mighty man of velour: and Solomon seeing the young man that he was industrious, he made him ruler over all the charge of the house of Joseph.**" Keep in mind that the house of Joseph is Ephraim and Manasseh, Joseph's two sons that received the birthright blessing in Gen 48:16-23. Verse 26 tells us that Jeroboam was of the tribe of Ephraim, **"And Jeroboam the son of Nebat, an Ephrathite of Zereda, Solomon's servant,"** This is very significant for it fulfills two verses, Genesis 48:16 making Ephraim and Manasseh the birthright tribe and 49:8-12 giving the scepter (the throne) and lawgiver to the coming Messiah in the linage of Judah.

This is a separation that we must comprehend if we are to understand the division of the houses of Israel. After studying these verses, you can see how God divides the ten northern tribes of the house of Israel (I Kings 11:35) to be his kingdom and the two southern tribes of the house of Judah to be his throne and lawgiver, the government (I Kings 11:36), the root of the Children of Israel. This division created a severe problem and power struggle between the two houses. The house of Israel, the ten northern tribes lead by Ephraim was the birthright tribe and given a double portion of blessing to be Kings of Kingdoms (Gen 35:11). The house of Judah (Gen 49:10) was given the throne of Judah/Phares bloodline to be the Kings of Israel. The house of Judah is a divided house within their people that departed into the wilderness along with the house of Israel. They also lost their Hebrew language and identity as did the house of Israel. The remnant of the house of Judah that returned to Jerusalem in Ezra chapter six remain divided to this day where the Kingdom was taken from them in Matt 21:43 due to non-belief in Christ.

According to the Scripture, both houses were to be Kings so God had to separate the two and when he did, he gave his kingdom to his birthright tribe of Ephraim which fulfilled the primogeniture of Mosaic Law as the firstborn.

By understanding the division, we can now trace both houses of Israel through the Old and New Testament when looking for key words. The house of Judah or the Jews never had a name change but when the house of Israel and the house of Judah Hebrews went into captivity, God changed their name (Isaiah 45:4 and 65:15). Their name was changed due to sin so Christ divorced Israel (Jerm 3:8). Note, Judah of the Jews was never divorced so they did not lose their name or language. Taking Israel's name from them was a way of totally separating the two houses by language and identity.

You can trace the house of Israel through the Old Testament by the names of Ephraim, Manasseh, house of Joseph, Lebanon, Unicorns, the Bull, Sharon, Bashan, Carmel and Gilead. The house of Israel is called Mystery Babylon all through the book of Revelation which is the USA and GB that control the world financial system. In the New Testament, their names are more obscure such as: Lost Sheep of the house of Israel (Matt 10:6 & 15:24); cast away his people (Rom 11:1); dispersed among the Gentiles (John 7:35); the children of Israel (Act 9:15); to the Barbarians (Rom 1:14); Barbarian and Scythian (Colossians 3:11); new covenant with the house of Israel and with the house of Judah (Heb 8:8); but in Isaac shall thy seed be called or *"modern day Saxon"* (Rom 9:7); remnant (Rom 11:7); Gentiles (Rom 11:13); to the twelve tribes which are scattered abroad (James 1:1); and to the strangers scattered throughout (Peter 1:1).

If we study each of these phrases carefully, it indicates a connection to the scattered strangers of the lost sheep of the house of Israel, Gods given kingdom and birthright tribe of great blessings to be Great Britain and the United States. The English-speaking countries are Gods fruitful, righteous, Christian nations spoken of in Matthew 21:43 as Christ spoke to the chief priests and Pharisees, **"Therefore say I unto you, The kingdom of God shall be taken from you, and given to a nation bringing forth the fruits thereof"**. Bear in mind that when God speaks of fruits or fruitful, it means God fearing, righteous and Christian bearing fruits of righteousness.

We have established that the house of Israel was to inherit Gods earthly kingdom but Judah, the house of Judah, was to provide the Royal Blood line of the Scepter and lawgiver **"till Shilo come"**. Christ was to establish his Church and new covenant (Zion) Hebrew 8:8, Jeremiah 31:31 along with his overturn of David's throne to the house of Israel (Eze 21:25-27) to take place in the wilderness. The Jews rejected Christ (Mat 21:43) so the kingdom was taken from them and given to the house of Israel in the wilderness that also included the mass of the house of Judah Hebrew (the lost sheep of the house of Israel Matthew 10:6, 15:24). Judah (Jews) was to be the root of the vineyard **"the**

pleasant plant" that never leaves the land (Isaiah 5:7). The house of Judah is the stock of the nation through being the root of the vineyard and produced the bloodline for the Messiah. They were to preserve Gods homeland till all prophecy is fulfilled and Christ sits on his Throne with power and glory in Jerusalem. Modern day Israel is the house of Judah of the Jews responsible in maintaining the root of the vineyard in the beloved city of Jerusalem in Judea.

We all know that the Bull is the symbol of Wall Street, the center of world trade, controlled by the United States in New York City. This paints a clear picture of the true identity of the United States (Manasseh) and Great Britain (Ephraim). The house of Israel (the ten northern tribes) were the branch or vine of the vineyard that ran over the wall and departed the vineyard or Promised Land of Canaan (Isaiah 5:7 and Gen 49:22) to be Kings of Kingdoms as stated in Genesis 35:11. Levi were to be the priestly tribe that provided spiritual guidance for both houses and by the authority of being the lawgiver they coronated the European Kings separated but controlled by David's throne of England (Duet 17:18 and Isaiah 9:6).

Gods Kingdom on Earth

Now that we have established the division of the kingdom of Israel into two separate houses, we need to understand just what a kingdom is and how it relates to Gods People. Let's take a look at the Hebrew meaning of the word kingdom as stated in I Kings 11:11 when the kingdom was taken from Solomon and given to his servant Jeroboam of the tribe of Ephraim. The Hebrew meaning as by the Strong's Concordance in reference #4467 means; dominion, the estate (rule) or the country (realm); kingdom, Kings reign, royal. Primitive root is to reign, to ascend the throne; to induct into royalty; hence to take counsel. The Greek meaning of Kingdom in reference #932 means royalty, rule or a realm, kingdom and reign.

God's kingdom has certain elements that we need to understand for it is actually two kingdoms. It consists of his earthly physical kingdom of Israel represented by the number four identifying the four Brigades or Beast of Israel. They were to settle into the four corners of the world (Numbers chapters 2:1-30, Zech 6:1, Eze 1:1&10 and Rev 4:7) bringing judgment as his earthly Kingdom and Church. His second Kingdom is Spiritual and identified by the number seven representing his heavenly kingdom of the Temple and Church and is Spiritually open to all man. They are the seven Spirits of his Church in Heaven as the four Beasts standing before the Throne in Rev 4:7, 5:6, 14:3, 15:7 and 19:4. These four Beasts give power to the seven Angles or Spirits that bring

Wrath upon the earth (Rev 5:5 and 15:7) making the Beast and Seven Spirits the Church. The four Beast that is like a lion, calf/Cherub/bull, man and eagle (Rev 4:7, Eze 1:10) represent the encampment of the four Brigades of Israel as outlined in Numbers 2:1-30 being his earthly Chosen People and Church. The four Beasts represent the Spirit of the Church and are found to be in Heaven during the Tribulation Period. The four Beasts are mentioned at least ten times throughout the book of Revelation.

Christ's earthly kingdom that deals with man has basically four elements; his Chosen People (12 tribes of Israel), the throne of King David, the Tabernacle or Temple (Christ's Church) and his Spirit (Zion). These four elements encompass dealing with his people. At some point in the future his two kingdoms will be combined when Christ takes his earthly throne in power and rules forever. By understanding Gods kingdom and its rudiments, we can see why it appears God has abandoned his Jewish people for his Glory was taken from them and overturned into the wilderness to the lost sheep of the house of Israel. They became the Christian nations of today. When we combine all the elements of Gods kingdom it becomes Zion, the capital or guiding pillar of his people as the Church called New Jerusalem in Rev 21:9-14. The Church is called Israel and New Jerusalem is its Capital City as these verses state.

As we study the Scriptures, we can see the four stages of Gods earthly Kingdom of Israel. The first stage of Glory and greatness began under the throne of King David and Solomon where God establish Zion in Jerusalem. The second stage of turmoil and sin began when the kingdom was divided in I Kings chapter eleven and continued till God took his Spirit and Glory from Jerusalem when it travailed and was plowed (moved or overturned). His Glory departed when the throne was overturned with the last king, King Zedekiah, in 586BC when it fell to Babylon. Gods Spirit continued in Jerusalem till the coming of the Messiah was complete when Christ died on the cross and the vail rent in the Temple (Matt 27:51). The renting of the veil in the Temple at Christ's death represented Gods Spirit departing Jerusalem to the already planted fruitful nation in the wilderness. The third stage of his Kingdom was the planting in the wilderness where Jesus gave the kingdom to a fruitful (Matt 21:43) nation under his New Covenant combining the house of Israel and Judah as his whole Kingdom. The non-believing Jew is an entity of their own making due to the rejection of the Messiah. The four Beasts are the Church and Gospel as the four Brigades of Israel outlined in Numbers chapter two. They were to spread into the four corners of the world (Eze 1:10-15, Rev 4:7 and Isaiah 11:12-16) under his New Covenant (Heb 8:8 and Jerm 31:31) to be righteous men (Isaiah 43 1-10 as the Savior). They were as the spokes of a "wheel" traveling throughout the world. The fourth stage of Gods kingdom will be the combination of his earthly kingdom and heavenly kingdom when Christ comes in power to establish his throne in Jerusalem to rule the earth during the millennial reign.

We need to consider a special time that has been set aside for the house of Judah, the Jews. This is the prophecy of Daniel's 70th week as told in Daniel 9:24-27 and is for two purposes. One is for the salvation of the Jews to realize the true Messiah and the other is to finish sin, prophecy and begin righteousness to anoint Christ at his return to earth. It also allowed for the twelve tribes to be sealed as the 144,000 or 12,000 from each tribe to advance Gods people into the Millenium or all would be killed as Rev 13:15 states.

God's ancient kingdom of the house of Israel that was divided into two houses is the same kingdom of the Church as recorded in Matthew 8:11. All men were accepted into Gods kingdom if they worshiped the God of Israel and kept his commandments in either ancient time under the Temple or modern times as the Church. Faith in maintaining Gods commandments in the Messiah before his coming and after he came is the same belief system to inherit the Heavenly Kingdom. The earthly inheritor was Abraham, Isaac, Jacob and Joseph (Ephraim and Manasseh) as the birthright tribe of Gods earthly sovereignty to maintain the family heritage as Gods Battle Ax, protector and responsible to teach God's Word in ancient and modern times. This same kingdom was opened to all man before and after Christ died on the cross. God's physical kingdom exist today as the house of Israel preserved through the throne of England which fulfills the promise to David that his throne will be for all generations and forever. The kingdom was divided in I Kings chapter eleven where it was given to Ephraim of the house of Israel but a small portion of Gods people remained with Judah as the throne was overturned into the wilderness.

Judah fulfilled their prophetic mission by providing the Messiah through King David's bloodline as prophesied and were to accept his Gospel in which they rejected. They refused Christ's Gospel; therefore, their part of the kingdom was taken from them in Matthew 21:43 by Christ himself. Due to this fact, Zion (Gods Spirit with Jerusalem) travailed in Isaiah 66:7-8 and plowed in Jeremiah 26:16, Micah 3:12 meaning that Gods Glory (Eze 10:18-19) and Spirit departed Jerusalem. When Gods Spirit departed Jerusalem, the name Jerusalem went with it and was placed on his new nations in the wilderness that became Zion (Isaiah 33:20, 52:9, 64:10 and 66:19-20). These verses indicate Jerusalem being many cities or mountains (nations Isaiah 66:20) for in Hebrew, Jerusalem means duel or dual meaning as a peaceful place in the wilderness, to teach or as a capital city of Israel. When the throne and Zion was overturned into a peaceful place in the wilderness and the kingdom taken from the Jews in Jerusalem, the name Jerusalem was attached as a part of its Hebrew definition. This indicates that one element of Gods kingdom cannot exist without the other. The throne, the people of Israel as the twelve tribes and the Temple are all one and if one is overturned, then, all are overturned to another land along with the name Jerusalem just as Revelation chapter 21 indicate.

Because of their rejection, his kingdom was given to the fruitful nations of the lost sheep of the house of Israel (Matt 10:6, 15:24 and 21;42-44 the Church) planted in the wilderness within their own land making them ruler over the whole kingdom under both houses. This is the location where Jeremiah overturned the throne in Jeremiah 1:10 and Ezekiel 21:25-27, 17:22-24 and 20:34-41. They were given a new name as Christian to spread Christ's end time Gospel representing the cedar tree of the throne. We need to understand that the Throne established in the wilderness consist of the mass of the house of Israel and Judah after the Assyrian and Babylonian captivities making his Kingdom whole. Only the Jews of the house of Judah rejected Christ. God's earthly kingdom of the house of Israel will be his Heavenly Spiritual Kingdom to any man that accepts Christ as their personal Savior under the New Covenant (Jerm 31:31 and Heb 8:8). This is the same kingdom of the Church mentioned all through the New Testament as Gods kingdom of the house of Israel opened to all of man through the new Covenant of Christ's Gospel, his vineyard. The New Covenant under the Gospel is the new thing, spirit and heart in the earth (Jerm 31:22, Eze 11:19 and 36:26) open to man through all generations.

There are several other words that are critical in understanding the division and separation of Gods Children of Israel. These words are house, nation and mountain. The Hebrew meaning of house in accordance to Strong's Concordance #1004, court, daughter, door, palace, steward, temple, a dwelling place, family or race wherever dwelling, "household" or "family". (#1008), "Beyth El", House of God. Basically, the word house means a family unit in light of Gods Children. Whenever the house of Israel and the house of Judah are mentioned separately, they are referred to as two separate family units. A house is sacred to God for he calls it "Beyth El", his dwelling place, the house of Israel, where Israel means "he will rule as God", and with this came the responsibility of spreading his Gospel.

The Hebrew meaning of nation or nations, (#1471), a foreign nation, hence a Gentile, figurative for troop of animals or flight of locusts, Gentile, heathen, nation, people, (#1484) Whelp. By Hebrew terms, a nation can be a Gentile foreign nation or referred to as a nation of Israel (Gen 12:2). The house or nation of Judah is referred to as a whelp (Gen 49:9) and in other aspects of

Scripture is referred to as mountains (Isaiah 65:9-10) that represent nations. Isaiah refers to Jacob (all of Israel), Judah (modern Israel) and Sharon (Great Britain and the United States) being Christian as mountains or nations). These verses confirm that mountains represent nations. Isaiah 65:10 states, "inheritor" (Christ) "of my mountains" (nations) "and my servants shall dwell there" is speaking of the modern Christian nations of today's world. They were planted in the wilderness and her boughs were sent out into the sea and river to spread Christ's Gospel, Psalms 80:8-12, Isaiah 41:1-8 and Hosea 2:14-23. The house of Israel became Christ's Church or the Kingdom of Heaven through the spreading of his Gospel.

The Hebrew meaning of mountain, (#2022) a mountain or range of hills sometimes used figurative, hill (country) mountain, promotion and to loom up a mountain or hill. When reading all the Scriptures referring to a mountain, many refer to them as a country or nation as depicted by the above definition. The word "hill" refers to a small nation. Ezekiel 17:22-23 explains how God is going to overturn his throne from Jerusalem and plant it on a **"high mountain and eminent" "In the mountain of the height of Israel"**. This planting was Jeremiah's commission to overturn David's throne from Jerusalem to Ireland that became the throne of England. In other words, the British Empire became **"the mountain of the height of Israel"**. The planting in the mountain or nation was Christ's Gospel for in verse 23 it speaks of boughs and bear fruit that indicates Christianity or Christ's Church. Therefore, whenever the Scriptures speak of the mountains of Israel it is referring to the house of Israel and the Christian nations of Ephraim the unicorn, Britain and the United States. Study the word mountain; bough and fruit in table one for better understanding.

The term kingdom is directly related to nations as the tribes of the Children of Israel. Let's prove this fact by reviewing II Kings 19:17 and Zechariah 2:11. We know that the Prophet Ahijah in I Kings chapter 11 rent Jeroboam's garment into twelve pieces representing the twelve tribes being divided into separate nations to take place in the future. From that time own the nation of Israel were called the house of Israel and the house of Judah. A short time later, the 10 northern tribes were taken into captivity by Assyria to never return to the Promised Land but were sent into the wilderness to fulfill Gods promise to Abraham, Isaac and Jacob and Joseph. II Kings 19:17 tells us that when Assyria took the ten northern tribes into captivity, they were called nations and not tribes, **"Of a truth, Lord, the kings of Assyria have destroyed the nations and their lands."** When Assyria took the ten northern tribes of Israel into captivity and destroyed their land, they were called nations to take place in the last days and very important if we are to understand our current times. Therefore, when they migrated into Europe after the Assyrian captivity, they were considered nations and not tribes which were Gods kingdom given to the house of Israel in I Kings chapter eleven.

We also know that Israel was to be nations in the last days (Gen 49:1) and also indicated in Zechariah 2:11, **"And many nations shall be joined to the Lord in that day and shall be my people: and I will dwell in the midst of thee and thou shalt know that the Lord of host hath sent me unto thee. And the Lord shall inherit Judah his portion in the holy land, and shall choose Jerusalem again. Be silent, O all flesh, before the Lord: for he is raised up out of his holy habitation."** This verse is speaking of the last days, Christ's Church, and the fruitful nations God gave his Kingdom that was taken from Judah the Jews (Matt 21:43). Verse 11 speaks of his fruitful nations in the wilderness that is the house of Israel but verse 12 speaks of Judah, the house of Judah and Jerusalem in the holy Land of Israel, **"and shall choose Jerusalem again"** to fulfill end time prophecy. The word again indicates Gods Glory left Jerusalem to return again for his Glory first departed in Ezekiel 10:18-19 and returned to the Holy Land in 1948 fulfilling Matt 24:32-36 as a parable "Now learn a parable of the fig tree".

In accordance to the Scriptures, it is clear that God is speaking of a physical nation of people being governed by a throne as a kingship ruled by a man. A Kingdom is synonymous to being ruled by a royal throne responsible for keeping Gods laws as given to the nation by his Prophets and Priests. This is emphasized in Deuteronomy 17:18-19, **"And it shall be, when he sitteth upon the throne of his kingdom, that he shall write him a copy of this law in a book out of that which is before the priest the Levites: And it shall be with him, and he shall read therein all the days of his life: that he may learn to fear the Lord his God, to keep all the words of this law and these statutes, to do them."** This verse could very well be speaking of how King James of King David's linage authorized the translation of the Holy Scriptures of the Bible into a common language for not only the Kings to follow but for the people called the Authorized King James Version Bible. Verse 15 of this chapter states that God is to choose the king over his people, **"Thou shalt in any wise set him king over thee, whom the Lord thy God shall choose: one from among thy brethren shalt thou set king over thee:"** According to these two verses, King James was chosen by God. Israel is Gods kingdom so he will select the King and expects his chosen King to write down and obey his commandments or punishment will occur. King Solomon did not keep Gods commandments so he took the kingdom from him as stated in I Kings chapter 11 and divided the nation for his future prophetic purposes. Many verses state emphatically that Gods kingdom and throne will be forever and a man will always sit on his Throne, I Kings 9:5; Gen 49:10; I Chron 17:14;

II Chron 13:5; Jerm 33:14-17; II Sam 7:12-17; Ps 89:4 & 27-37; 145:13; Eze 17:22; 21:25-27; 29:21 and Luke 1:32. King David's throne will be covered in a following segment.

After a study of all these Scriptures, there is a big discrepancy between God's Word and modern theological teaching. If we go by what we have been taught, then, King David's throne does not exist today. According to the Scriptures, from the time God appointed David as King over Israel in approx. 1056BC, his kingdom would last forever and ever more till Christ sits on the earthly throne (Luke 1:32-33). Where is his throne today? We know that King Josiah was the last sovereign King and Zedekiah the last puppet King under Babylon's rule to sit on David's throne in 586BC. If one generation of the Phares and Zarah blood line is lost in the genealogy of the Royal Throne of King David, Christ's heir to the throne would be null and void for the blood line of King David has to be maintained.

Another aspect that we must understand is that God or Christ himself is the overall King of the world (Ps 47:2 & 7) **"For the Lord most high is terrible; he is a great King over all the earth"**. Man is only in temporary charge till his time of judgment is complete or his cup of iniquity is full. This will be proof in Gods judgment that man cannot be just or righteous without God at his center and then God will be the King of his kingdom or the world at the beginning of his millennial. For this reason alone, there can be no break in a king sitting on David's throne for it has to always exist to complete Gods plan.

God's kingdom and the Tabernacle or Temple (symbol of the end time Church, Zion) is one and cannot function without the other. This is indicated when Solomon built the Temple in II Chronicles 2:1&12, **"And Solomon determined to build an house for the name of the Lord, and an house for his kingdom."** verse 12, **"that might build an house for the Lord, and an house for his kingdom."** The scepter or throne and lawgiver (Levite tribe representing the Temple) are together in Genesis 49:10 making them inseparable. God created his earthly kingdom consisting of the throne and lawgiver (Temple/Church is Zion) to be forever but when Jerusalem and the throne fell in 586 BC and the Temple destroyed in 70AD, where did they go for God did not destroy his kingdom?

We need to establish the fact that Gods kingdom begins here on earth with King David's throne and the importance of maintaining a pure bloodline for Christ's return. King David's throne is Gods throne to be King of the world. Psalms 22:28 makes a clear statement, **"For the kingdom is the Lord's: and**

he is the governor among the nations." God is the governor of all nations on earth as Christ's Church whether wicked or righteous and Daniel 4:17 explains in even more detail, **"to the intent that the living may know that the most High ruleth in the kingdom of men, and giveth it to whomsoever he will, and setteth up over it the basest of men."** God sets up the rulers over men but in most cases, he will let the people make their own choice whether good or bad. The term basest means, humble, low, debase and subdue establishing God above man.

In other words, God makes us live with our mistakes. Psalms 145:13, **"Thy kingdom is an everlasting kingdom, and thy dominion endureth throughout all generations."** According to this verse, there will be a king sitting on David's throne in every generation from the establishment of his throne in 1056BC till Christ comes to inherit his throne fulfilling Luke 1:31-33 where Jesus sits upon his promised throne in Rev 4:1-2. Isaiah 9:6-7 is an excellent verse that explains Gods rule on earth, **"For unto us a child is born unto us a son is given: and the government shall be upon his shoulder; and his name shall be called Wonderful Counselor, The mighty God the everlasting Father, The Prince of Peace. Of the increase of his government and peace there shall be no end, upon the throne of David, and upon his kingdom, to order it, and to establish it with judgment and with justice from henceforth even for ever, The zeal of the Lord of hosts will perform this."** God states in these verses that his government, kingdom and throne will be no end from its beginning till eternity and he will establish peace judgment and justice forever upon the earth. If there is to be no end of Gods government, throne and kingdom, where is it in modern times? It is preserved through the throne of England and the Hebrew name of Israel, "he will rule as God". The house of Israel of Ephraim and Manasseh will bring righteousness and judgment to the world as Gods Birthright tribe and Battle Ax sitting on David's throne.

We have established that the nation in I Kings chapter eleven divided by God is his physical kingdom on earth. He gave the Kingdom to Jeroboam, the tribe of Ephraim of the house of Joseph, the birthright tribe to receive the double blessings of wealth and greatness to be nations and kingdoms (Gen 35:9-12). He gave Judah of the house of Judah, Jerusalem, the throne and the lawgiver (government). When Judah (the Jews) rejected Christ and had him crucified, God took the kingdom from them (Matt 21:43) and gave it to a righteous nation that is the house of Israel, Gods lost sheep in the wilderness (Eze 20:34-47 & Amos 9:8-15). This repaired the breach between the Judah Phares/Zara bloodlines making his kingdom whole again as the Kingdom that was given to Jeroboam. God overturned the throne from Judah and healed the breach between Phares and Zara (Amos 9:11; Matt 1:3) by giving the throne to the Zara blood line in Ezekiel 17:22-24 & 21:25-27 as commissioned by Jeremiah, (Jerm 1:10).

Christ's death on the cross was the final authority and overturn (Eze 21:27) of David's throne from Judah in Jerusalem (Matt 21:43) to his fruitful nation (Ireland, house of Israel) at the renting of the veil (Matt 27:51) and represented the travailing of Zion (Isaiah 66:8 Gods Spirit). This was the planting and gathering of Gods new fruitful nation in the wilderness of a peaceful new land (Isaiah 14:1, Jerm 23:8, Eze 34:13, 36:17&24, 37:14). The receiving of Gods Spirit and New Covenant (Eze 37:14) were the branches that ran over the wall and over the seas to a new land (Gen 49:22, Isaiah 16:8). The house of Israel as the mass of Gods kingdom led by Ephraim and Manasseh were the birthright tribes and planted in the wilderness, in their own peaceful land (peace meaning Jerusalem #3389 Strong's Concordance).

They were to wait for his Spirit and New Covenant, Christ's Gospel the Church. Ephraim was to be the birthright son to lead Gods Kingdom, the house of Israel, that was given the family name Israel and responsible in establishing the end time Church. The planting occurred under Christ's New Covenant (Heb 8:8-10 and Jerm 31:31-33) and represents the valley of Achor, the Church (Isaiah 65:10, Hos 2:15). This is a subject that takes extensive study and a great desire to understand by seeking wisdom and truth through the Holy Spirit, (James 1:5-6).

After studying the Scriptures of Gods earthly Kingdom, we can see how it is symbolic to Christ's Church. The three elements of his Kingdom are the Throne (promised to King David), the Tabernacle, Temple and Church (Levite tribe as the lawgivers) and Gods Children of Israel (12 tribes of Israel and any true believer of his Covenant the Church). Gods overall plan of creating man was to save the world so he used his chosen Covenant People for that purpose. The final stage of his plan was to create the Church so his Spirit (Zion/Sion) could be with all man throughout the world in peace that means Jerusalem (Ps 48:2). Christ's Gospel and Church opened his Kingdom to all mankind using the nations of the house of Israel to spread and protect ("Battle Ax" Jerm 51:20) his dominion within the world in a peaceful land called Jerusalem. A close study on the Hebrew meaning of Jerusalem indicates a dual meaning for not only is it the city of Jerusalem, the Capital of Zion (Temple), for when it travailed and was plowed, Jerusalem became the Capital of Sion (Church) planted in the wilderness and the fruitful nations of the house of Israel. See the next segment on Jerusalem.

As we study Gods Scripture, we can see how the nations of Israel has been a shining light unto the world and a symbol ("ensign" Isaiah 11:12) of his end time Church. This makes it even more important to understand why God divided his Kingdom into two houses and how each has a certain role to play in his Prophetic plan. Gods Spirit in the Holy of Holies within the Tabernacle and Temple as Zion was the fore runner and symbol of the Holy Spirit given to the Church as Sion in Acts 2:1-2 at Pentecost.

During Old Testament times, a lamp was always burning within the family house and the Temple. It was a symbol of prosperity and righteousness and the lamp was never extinguished. A continuous burning lamp or lamp stand (candlestick) within the home or Temple was a symbol of Gods acceptance and if the oil lamp was snuffed out, it signified sin and the coming of judgment (Job 29:3; Ps 18:28; Proverbs 24:20; Jerm 25:10; Rev 2:5). Within the Temple there were 10 lamp stands and each stand held seven continuous burning lamps of oil representing the seven Churches (Rev 1:20). The Bible is clear, punishment or judgment (Rev 2:5) will come on a nation (the Church) if they refuse to repent of their sins and their lamp or candlestick will be extinguished. Our modern-day Church is in the state of falling away (II Thess 2:3) and our candlesticks are slowly burning out for the Holy Spirit is the oil or fuel and when the Spirit leaves the Church the light will go out. Rev 2:5 gives a dire WARNING, **"Remember therefore from whence thou art fallen, and repent, and do the first works; or else I will come unto thee quickly, and will remove thy candlestick out of his place except thou repent"**. It appears that our current Church candlestick has been removed from the Church due to our falling away into sin. Another WARNING is given in Rev 3:5, **"He that overcometh, the same shall be clothed in white raiment; and I will not blot out his name out of the book of life, but I will confess his name before my Father, and before his angels"**. This verse is clear, if we fail to repent "often" (Heb 9:25-26) our salvation will be taken from us just as the candlestick of the Church. The best Scriptures indicating the Tabernacle and Temple symbolizing the Church with Christ as our High Priest is in Hebrews 9:8&25-26 where Paul refers to the Holy of Holies as the Holy Spirit and the Church. Study all of Hebrew chapter nine.

Jerusalem "a peaceful land"

We know that Jerusalem is the center of the creation of man and Gods Kingdom for he truly loves this wonderful City. Jerusalem on this earth is where God establishes his throne of power during the millennial reign and New Jerusalem in Heaven (Rev Ch 9) where he judges and rules his people forever. As we study this segment, we need to open our minds to the facts of the Scripture for what is being presented is riveting and hard to believe. If we are to understand Prophecy, we need to have absolute belief in the Scriptures for that is our only truth. Christians need to put aside what we have been taught and go to prayer for understanding. With an open mind, thinking logically, lets dissect the true meaning of the word Jerusalem in Hebrew to get its full meaning.

Let's review the Hebrew meaning of Jerusalem as given by the Strong's Concordance reference number (3389) Jerusalem means; a <u>dual in allusion</u> to its two main hills, <u>founded peaceful</u>, the capital city of Palestine. (3384) Primitive root; to flow as water, to rain, to lay or throw especially <u>an arrow to shoot</u>, to point out as by aiming the finger, <u>archer</u>, cast, direct, <u>to teach</u>, <u>inform</u> and <u>instruct</u>. (7999) Primitive root; <u>to be safe</u> in mind, body or estate, figurative; to be friendly, to reciprocate, make amends, make an end, <u>finish</u>, restore and reward. We need to go into each root meaning to get a full comprehension and relate the underlined word definitions to the house of Israel being in a peaceful land of their own scattered into the wilderness where they are called Sion in Isa 18:1-7 as Jerusalem being a dual allusion.

Certain key words ring out from the definition above that refer to Gods Kingdom. According to this meaning, Jerusalem were to be a very peaceful city, strong with an army as an archer shooting arrows, to be very wealthy and prosperous, and to be a teacher of the world, informing the world of Gods Laws and finally restore Gods Kingdom as a reward of our works in his earthly Kingdom.

Let's realistically look at the actual history of Jerusalem and see if it fulfills the literal definition of its true meaning. Something seems to be incorrect for the City of Jerusalem as the capital of Palestine has never been peaceful and lay in rubble just as the Bible predicted for almost two thousand years. Look at the violence of the European Christian Crusades during the Dark Ages. Could there possibly be a meaning of Jerusalem that we are overlooking and this writer believes that there is another meaning not being understood.

The first definition in the concordance is the word duel of allusion referring to the two mountains that Jerusalem was built upon. This has an extreme significance for Jerusalem has a dual purpose to fulfill and is an allusion that we all have overlooked. The two mountains or nations that Jerusalem was built upon represent its division into two houses of the Children of Israel. The house of Judah that was promised the throne and the linage of the Messiah and the house of Israel, the birthright tribe to fulfill the great blessings of Abraham, Isaac, Jacob and Joseph to be nations and kings of kingdoms. The dual meaning also represents the name Jerusalem as one being physical, the taproot of the Children of Israel in the Promised Land to never move and fulfill end time prophecy. The other is a Spiritual name that departed Jerusalem when God overturned, travailed and plowed his Throne, Zion and the Spiritual name Jerusalem into a peaceful land or resting place in the wilderness to spread his end time Gospel, the land of Ephraim. Isaiah chapter 18 clearly identifies this new land. The definition of Jerusalem fulfills the Spiritual name, not the physical name.

The kingdom that Jesus took from the Chief Priests and Pharisees in Matthew 21:43 is the nation mentioned in Isa 18 where he gave the whole kingdom to his lost sheep of the house of Israel in the wilderness included the Throne, Zion and now the name Jerusalem as its dual Spiritual meaning. Study closely the words overturn, travailed (birth of Christ), plowed (be silent), plucked (moved), wilderness and all the words listed in chapter eight and table one to get a full understanding. The true meaning is hidden within the Hebrew root words.

Now we need to go to the Scripture to prove our synopsis of the dual meaning of Jerusalem. Let's start with Isaiah 33:20 and to understand this verse, we need to read the context of the whole chapter for it is speaking of the end days. Verse 9 is speaking of Lebanon, Sharon, Bashan and Carmel in the wilderness losing their fruits referring to his Christian nations (GB and USA) in the last days and the great falling away from his truth, the Church. Verse 13 speaks to the people afar off, the sinners of Zion, and verse 15 says that he has walked righteously, and speaks uprightly which is referring to the Church age of his Gospel. Verse 19 speaks of a people with a stammering tongue that is the house of Israel where God took their language and national identity from them as their punishment of idolatry and changer it slowly from Hebrew, Phoenician, Galic to English the speech of Isaac's sons, Saxon in Gen 21:12, Rom 9:7 and Heb 11:18.

Verse 20 states, **"Look upon Zion, the city of our solomnites: thine eyes shall see Jerusalem a quiet habitation, a tabernacle that shall not be taken down; not one of the stakes thereof shall ever be removed, neither shall any of the cords thereof be broken,"** If we read this verse literally as being the city of Jerusalem and not factoring it being a symbol, this verse is incorrect. Jerusalem and the Temple or Tabernacle was totally destroyed by Titus of the Roman army in 70AD and still has not been rebuilt. This verse is referring to Jerusalem and the Tabernacle as being his Church, his Heavenly Kingdom that will never be destroyed. This is the same Kingdom that Jesus took from the Jews in Matthew 21:43 and gave to his lost sheep to spread his end time Gospel of Christ. Lebanon, Sharon, Bashan and Carmel as listed in verse 9 is the fruitful nations God gave his Kingdom and they became the Anglo-Saxon of the sons of Isaac or Isaac's sons as the birthright tribes of Ephraim and

Manasseh, the bull and unicorn of Great Britain and the United States. We are the only nations in history as a whole to spread his end time Gospel. Study the word solomnites in table one.

Isaiah 66:20 calls Jerusalem Gods Holy Mountain or nation. Again, to see the complete meaning of this verse, we need to study the whole chapter in context. Isaiah 66:1 begin by calling Heaven his throne and the earth his footstool. God is asking a question, **"Where is the house that ye build unto me? And where is the place of my rest?"** The Lord is asking where is his Kingdom that is his earthly throne and his Temple, Zion, the place where his Spirit rest with man. This is a symbol in the future for the whole earth to be Zion/Sion, his Church, open to all men. This question is being asked because his throne and Temple, his people were performing idolatry in Jerusalem and the Kingdom of the house of Israel was in captivity to Assyria. Isaiah wrote this verse in approx. 698BC, 20 years after the house of Israel went into captivity and 112 years before Judah went into captivity to Babylon. Isa 66:7-9 refers to Zion laboring where the Messiah is born into the world. Verse 7 and 8 says, **"Before she travailed, she brought forth; before her pain came, she was delivered of a man child." "Shall the earth be made to bring forth in one day? Or shall a nation be born at once? For as soon as Zion travailed, she brought forth here children."**

When Zion travailed by bringing forth the Messiah, the man-child, this fulfilled Genesis 49:10 where Christ gathered his people into the Church which was the second gathering, "until Shiloh (Christ) come". This second gathering into nations is referred to when Isaiah mentions, **"Shall the earth be made to bring forth in one day? Or shall a nation be born at once"**. This phrase is speaking of the Kingdom taken from the Jews in Matt 21:43 and given to a fruitful nation in the wilderness. This is speaking of his Christian Nations under the New Covenant and the new spirit, heart and thing in the earth in Eze 36:24-27 and Isa 43:1-20. These verses describe God gathering his people the Church in the wilderness of a new land washed with water meaning baptized. The term, **"for as soon as Zion travailed, she brought forth her children (Church)",** for they were planted into the wilderness as the lost sheep of the house of Israel (Ephraim and Manasseh).

Isa 66:10-11 states, **"Rejoice ye with Jerusalem, and be glad with her, all ye that love her: rejoice for joy with her, all ye that mourn for her: That ye may suck, and be satisfied with the breasts of her consolations; that ye may milk out, and be delighted with the abundance of her glory."** This verse is referring to the birth of Christ the Messiah and Jerusalem as his mother by the sucking for the breasts of her consolations. Jerusalem has to be the

Church or Gods Children suckling on their mother, Christ the Savior. Verse 12, **"I will extend peace to her** (Jerusalem) **like a river, and the glory of the Gentiles like a flowing stream: then shall ye suck, ye shall be borne upon her sides, and be dandled upon her knees."** This verse gives the living water of Christ to Jerusalem and can only be the Christian nations of the world that has been the light to the Gentiles as Gods Battle Ax and any one that accepts Christ as their Messiah. They are the Christian nations of the west dwelling in safety and peace like a flowing stream, giving Glory (the Gospel) to the Gentiles. They are like a child on a mother's knee, suckling and bouncing (Jerm 23:5-6, 33:14-17, Eze 28:24-26 and 34:22-25). These verses are speaking of the Church being nourished by Christ, the stone and Savior called Jerusalem. These Scriptures are referring to Jerusalem being plucked, plowed and travailed into the wilderness.

According to Isaiah chapter 66, Jerusalem is the Church that is the capital of Zion, Gods Spirit with man and the Christian nations of Ephraim and Manasseh planted in the wilderness, Christ's fruitful nation (Matt 21:43). There are key words that match the definition of Jerusalem within these verses such as peace, a river of running water and a flowing stream further indicating a referral to Jerusalem where all nations are comforted.

Isaiah 66:13 sums it up, **"As one whom his mother comforteth, so will I comfort you: and ye shall be comforted in Jerusalem."** This verse is clearly speaking of the comforter that is the Holy Spirit of the Church open to all mankind and calling Jerusalem his Church of the world as a "dual allusion". Isaiah 64:10 refers to Zion and Jerusalem as a wilderness and when we study the word wilderness in table one, it indicates where God drove his lost sheep of Israel into a peaceful place to wait for his Gospel. After reviewing all the above Scriptures and many more throughout the Bible, Jerusalem is mentioned in a dual role as his Christian nations scattered into the wilderness that has spread his end time Gospel. By historical fact, only the English people has translated God's Word into a common language and taken the Authorized King James Version of the Bible into every corner of the world evangelizing, "ye shall be comforted in Jerusalem". Jerusalem's Spiritual name is the birthright tribes of Ephraim and Manasseh called Israel that has spread Christ's end time Gospel into the World being the light to the Gentiles. Gods Kingdom can only be complete with all the elements that is, the Throne of David, his Children of Israel (12 tribes or the Church), Zion/Sion. Jerusalem as the capital of his Kingdom is preserved through the Crown of England and his brother, the United States of America. Reference the following verses, Psalms 47 and 48, Isaiah 33:20, 52:9, 64:10 and 66:1-20.

King David's Throne

We have established that the Kingdom of Israel is Gods Kingdom and his throne is his rule over man. This seat of rule has been entrusted to Israel (Ephraim and Manasseh Gen 48:16) to be maintained by man, God's chosen people, till Christ comes in power and sets on his throne and Kingdom in Jerusalem. God set up his earthly throne with the man of his choosing as shown in a prior segment to represent him on earth. To be eligible to sit on King David's throne, Christ had to be in the flesh as a man. Let's keep in mind the overall purpose of David's throne and that was to establish Gods Kingdom on earth. This kingdom was to be called Israel, "he will rule as God" and given the authority through the birthright tribe of Ephraim and Manasseh to maintain the throne till the fulfillment of his prophetic Time Table. Christ is to claim his THRONE in Rev 4:1-2 when the Church is taken or raptured into Heaven. Christ rules from his throne in Heaven during the Tribulation of Wrath and brings his Throne back to Jerusalem at the beginning of the millennial reign to rule over Israel for ever, Luke 1:32-33.

We have lost the connection with God and our nation no longer abides by his established commandments due to being politically correct. It will only be a matter of time before our cup of iniquity is full and God will bring judgment, unless, we repent as individuals and as a nation.

Understanding Gods kingdom and his forever ruling throne is the key to comprehending the division of Israel and to why. The Scriptures are clear that his throne and kingdom would be forever and for all generations of man, **"and in thy seed shall all the families of the earth be blessed"**, through his kingdom and birthright blessing to the world (Gen 28:13-14). The land spoken of in this verse is the exact spot that the Temple in Jerusalem was built, the most Holy ground on earth. The facts within the Scriptures are an issue that the modern-day Church fails or refuse to understand and is a part of the blindness mentioned by Paul in the book of Romans. When we finish with this segment, by the Scriptures, there should be no doubt in the reader's mind that the Throne of Israel exists within the world today.

There is an important aspect as to why God loved David so much and a subject that we need to understand to comprehend Gods purpose for David's everlasting Kingdom. I Samuel 16:12 says that David, as a boy when chosen by God, that his skin, **"was ruddy, and withal of a beautiful countenance"**. This indicates that David's blood was from a pure descendant of Abraham and very important for the Messiah was to come from this same bloodline. Christ was also recorded as being tall, fair skinned, blue eyed and blond hair. There is an ancient letter found written by Publius Lentrelus (a resident of Judea in the days of Tiberius Caesar) that describes the physical appearance of Christ. This letter is quoted for your reference in chapter two in the segment on God's Chosen People.

The word ruddy is the key for it also proves that God's chosen people were to be of this nature. The description of human stature matches the tribes of the Anglo Saxons that migrated through the Caucasus Mountains into Europe were tall, blue eyed, blond hair and circumcised, Caucasian people (God's chosen people). Keep in mind that this is not the Writers opinion but as recorded history.

God also knew that David had a pure heart for II Samuel 7:1-6 tells us how David loved God so much that he chose to build God a beautiful temple so he would no longer have to dwell in the Tabernacle Tent. Because of this selflessness, God blessed David that his Kingdom would be forever. Israel would be divided and planted in a place of their own away from the children of wickedness (middle eastern countries), a place of peace over-seas as recorded in Eze 34:13-14; II Sam 7:10; Isaiah 16:8; Ps 89:25-37. Keep in mind that Jerusalem has a dual meaning for Isaiah 66:6-20 calls Jerusalem a city, Zion and a mountain that means nations indicating it was planted in the wilderness to be called Jerusalem. David's house (the Jews) was to remain in the Promised Land to provide the Messiah. This planting has to be speaking in a future context for Israel had received the inheritance of the land when this verse was written. The city of Jerusalem has never been apart from the children of wickedness. Palestine has been at war from the moment Israel became a nation in the Promised Land in approx. 1445 BC and the same hatred exist to this very day. They have never been at peace. Study the word plant and see table one. The moment David became King of Israel in 1056 BC, God promised that his throne would endure forever and never be destroyed (Isaiah 9:6-7).

I Samuel 16:1-13 gives the account where God physically chose David to be king of Israel fulfilling his Word. God chose King David himself, not Samuel his Prophet. The ultimate heir to the throne is Christ but King David's seed is to set on Israel's throne till Luke 1:32-33 is fulfilled, **"He shall be, and shall be called the Son of the Highest: and the Lord God shall give unto him the throne of his father David: And he shall reign over the house of Jacob for ever: and of his kingdom there shall be no end."** This verse clearly states that from the time of King David till Christ sits on the throne in power, there shall be no end of his throne, so where is it today and who is sitting upon it?

Let's start with Gen 49:10 and for better understanding, we need to re-quote this verse, **"The sceptre shall not depart from Judah nor a lawgiver from between his feet, until Shiloh come: and unto him shall the gathering of the people be."** According to this verse from the time God established his throne with first Saul and then King David his chosen, his scepter or throne would not depart or be destroyed till Shiloh (Christ) comes to create his Church and gather his people under his Gospel. Shiloh's coming is not in power but to establish his Church by sending his disciples to the lost sheep of the fruitful nation in the wilderness (Mat 10:5-6, 15:24 and 21:43). The term Shiloh and why God called his son by this name will be covered in another segment. According to man's history, David's throne was conquered by King Nebuchadrezzar in 586BC to never exist again in Jerusalem to this very day. Our history is not compatible with the Scriptures. II Chronicles 13:5 makes the statement, **"Ought ye not to know that the Lord God of Israel gave the kingdom over Israel to David for ever, even to him and to his sons by a covenant of salt?"** This verse is clear that his sons would rule King David's Throne forever by a covenant of salt. Salt was used years ago to preserve meat or food and as long as the salt existed the food would be protected. David's throne is the same, it was meant by this verse that David's throne would always exist as protector and Battle Ax till Christ comes and exalt himself on the throne. The salt is also a symbol of Gods Holy Spirit within the Church that is Gods Kingdom as long as the Church exist as salt of the Earth as King David's Throne. Daniel also makes a statement about Gods kingdom, Daniel 4:3, **"How great are his signs! And how mighty are his wonders! His kingdom is an everlasting kingdom, and his dominion is from generation to generation."** Daniel's prophecies were to take place in the last days which indicate that Gods kingdom and throne were to be perpetuated into the end times and for all generations to include our present, so where is God's promised throne today?

We need to establish by Scripture that King David's throne exist in the last days or the Church age of our present time period. The first example in Scripture is located in Genesis 49:1 when Jacob said that all the blessings given to his twelve sons of Israel would take place in the last days, **"And Jacob called unto his sons, and said, Gather yourselves together, that I may tell you that which shall befall you in the last days."** Verse ten of this chapter gives Judah his blessing in preserving the throne of David that would take place in our present time period. This verse was quoted above and is a literal verse that takes place in the later days so the scepter or throne of David has to exist today some-where in the world. The term, **"until Shiloh come;"** is when Christ came to establish his Church and, **"and unto him shall the gathering of the people be"**, represent the house of Israel and all the people of the world that would accept his Gospel to be gathered into the Church planted in the wilderness. This is not speaking of his coming in power at the end of the age but of establishing his Gospel during his ministry. Study the word gather from beginning to end in the Scriptures and you will see the picture.

Ezekiel chapter 34 is very interesting for it places Gods scattered sheep where he gathers them to their own land (verse 13) to be feed by David or his throne and David would be their shepherd as stated in Eze 34: 13 & 23, **"And I will set up one shepard over them, and he shall feed them, even my servant David; he shall feed them, and he shall be their shepherd"**. This indicates that King David's Throne exists during this time period and **"one shepherd over them"** indicates Christ and his Gospel. Verse 25 states, **"And I will make with them a covenant of peace, and will cause the evil beasts to cease out of the land: and they shall dwell safely in the wilderness and sleep in the woods."** This covenant is the same new covenant mentioned in Hebrew 8:8 and Jeremiah 31:31 (a new heart and spirit, the Gospel, Ezekiel 36:24-34) of peace and prosperity of the Church age. The nations cut out of the wilderness and woods were the Christian Commonwealth nations of Great Britain and the United States under the new covenant. The evil beast is speaking of dumb cattle or the evil heathen Indian indigenous tribes of the world that is ignorant of God's Word.

Jeremiah chapter 30 falls under the same time frame of being in the last days of Jacob's trouble, as did Ezekiel chapter 43. Study Jeremiah chapters 29 through 31 for a better understanding. Jeremiah chapter 30 is speaking to both the house of Israel and the house of Judah (Jerm 30:4) of a time frame of great tribulation during Jacob's trouble. Any Bible student knows that Jacob's trouble (verse 7) takes place just prior too and during the Tribulation period. Verse 9 falls within the period of Jacob's trouble placing it in the last days, **"But they shall serve the Lord their God, and David their king, whom I will raise up unto them."** This verse directly places King David's throne in the period of Jacob's Trouble which is the last days of our present time where we are serving the Lord in the Church under David's throne, the throne of England. The Anti-Christ will move the throne from England to Jerusalem during the Tribulation when he sits on the throne in power claiming to be god the Apotheosis.

Another aspect of Israel in the last days is recorded in Acts 2:17, **"And it shall come to pass in the last days, saith God, I will pour out of my Spirit upon all flesh: and your sons and your daughters shall prophesy, and your young men shall see visions, and your old men shall dream dreams"**. Compare this verse to Joel 2:27-28, **"And ye shall know that I am in the midst of Israel, and that I am the Lord your God, and none else: and my people shall never be ashamed. And it shall come to pass afterward** [last days same as verse above]**, that I will pour out my spirit upon all flesh** [Holy

Spirit in Acts 2:1-4]: **and your sons and your daughters shall prophesy, your old men shall dream dreams, your young men shall see visions"**. This verse clearly calls the Church Israel. Paul in Acts and the Prophet Joel was speaking of the same new covenant (Spirit) given to the house of Israel, the Church, in the last days and the pouring out of his Holy Spirit. These verses do not mention Judah Jews for they rejected Christ but it was given to all flesh, even to Judah that rejected the Gospel (Heb 8:10 and Jerm 31:33).

We have established that the throne will exist during the last days so now let's prove that a man will always set on David's throne. Several verses make the statement that there would always be a man wearing David's Crown. Again, we need to quote I Kings 9:5, **"Then I will establish the throne of thy kingdom upon Israel for ever, as I promised to David thy father, saying, There shall not fail thee a man upon the throne of Israel."** Jeremiah 33:17, **"For thus saith the Lord; David shall never want a man to sit upon the throne of the house of Israel"**. II Chron 7:18, **"Then will I establish the throne of thy kingdom, according as I have covenanted with David thy father, saying, There shall not fail thee a man to be ruler in Israel."** According to these three verses, there has to be a man somewhere in this world sitting on David's throne at this very moment for Christ has not returned to claim his crown. The throne is called the house of Israel making the Crown of England Israel or the house of Israel. II Chronicles 7:18 states that where the throne is located, that nation is called Israel, **"There shall not fail thee a man to be ruler in Israel."** Ephraim and Manasseh represent the birthright tribe of the family name to be called Israel that is England and the throne preserved through the Judah Zarah bloodline of their Royal family. The Royal Family of England has a proven family tree through ancient documents tracing their bloodline back to King David.

Where are Gods promise to King David today that his throne would be forever and to his seed for all his generations? This promise leaves no break in time till Christ comes to claim the throne. Psalms 145:13 go on to say, **"The kingdom is an everlasting kingdom, and thy dominion endureth throughout all generations."** The word endureth indicates a struggle and this writer believes that Satan has tried all through history to destroy Gods earthly throne but it shall endure through all generations till Christ comes to claim his right, it has to still exist. Psalms 89:4 and 89:25-37 makes an exact statement, **"Thy seed will I establish for ever, and build up thy throne to all generations"; "his seed also will I make to endure for ever, and his throne as the days of heaven." "His seed shall endure for ever, and his throne as the sun before me."** Again, the throne is for all generations as the days of heaven and the sun is forever before God. The sun is the most powerful natural force in the universe and cannot be destroyed just as it is impossible to destroy Gods throne. To destroy Gods throne would be like destroying the days in heaven and we know that cannot happen. Three infallible forces are mentioned in the last three verses, throne to all generations, as the days of heaven and as the sun before God. These verses clearly make it identifiable that Gods throne is infallible and cannot be destroyed, not even by Satan himself. The Scriptures are unmistakable in that when Babylon subjugated the throne in Jerusalem, it was only planted to another location and not destroyed. Ezekiel chapter 17 thru 21 explains Jeremiah's commission to relocate the throne to be placed overseas in Jerm 1:10, **"nations and kingdoms, to root out, and to pull down, and to destroy, and to throw down, to build, and to plant"**. Jeremiah was commissioned to overturn the throne to another location in a far-away land, the wilderness over the sea in Isaiah 16:8 "they are gone over the sea" and Ps 89:25 "set his hand also in the sea" (speaking to David's seed) that was given to the seed of the house of Israel not to Judah, for they are cursed (Jerm 24:9).

Isaiah 9:7 also speaks of David's Throne and makes the statement, **"Of the increase of his government and peace there shall be no end, upon the throne of David, and upon his kingdom, to order it, and to establish it with judgment and with justice from henceforth even for ever."** The word "henceforth" is the key for it means that from the moment David's throne was created by God, it would last forever till the Wonderful Counselor (Christ) claims the throne in power. This verse says that his throne will bring justice to the heathen world fulfilling Deuteronomy 7:6 and 14:2 and to be kings of kingdoms in Genesis 17:6 and 48:16 to be given to the birthright tribes of Ephraim and Manasseh.

To understand present world events and how King David's throne plays a roll through the Throne of England, we must study the Scriptures that explain the overturn. Ezekiel 21:25-26 says that David's throne would be overturned, **"Thus saith the Lord God; Remove the diadem, and take off the crown; exalt him that is low, and abase him that is high. I will overturn, overturn, overturn, it: and it shall be no more, until he come whose right it is** [Christ]; **and I will give it him."** If you read these verses out of text and not compare it to other Scriptures, it makes no sense. Alone, this Scripture seems to say that the throne will be overturned and be no more till Christ returns. That is not what this verse says. In light of the above Scriptures that David's throne will be forever as the sun of the days of heaven and that Christ sent his disciples to his lost sheep in Matthew 10:6; 15:24 and how Christ took the Kingdom from the chief Priests and Pharisees in Matthew 21:43 to overturn it to a fruitful nation, we can begin to understand Gods division of his nation of Israel.

This explains the other Scriptures that speak of cropping off from the high branch and giving it to the low clearly indicating that God moved his throne to a high mountain or nation, Ezekiel 17:22-24, **"Thus saith the Lord God: I will also take of the highest branch of the high cedar, and will set it: I will crop off from the top of his young twigs a tender one, and will plant it upon an high mountain and eminent: In the mountain of the height of Israel will I plant it: and it shall bring forth boughs, and bear fruit, and be a goodly cedar: and under it shall dwell all fowl of every wing; in the shadow of the branches thereof shall they dwell and all the trees of the field shall know that I the Lord have brought down the high tree, have exalted the low tree, have dried up the green tree, and have made the dry tree to flourish; I the Lord have spoken and done it."** What mountain did God move his throne to; he moved it to the mountains or nations of the height of the house of Israel where it was planted in the wilderness (Unicorn, Duet 33:17, symbol of England).

The words bough, plant, fruit and branches all refer to the firstborn and birthright blessing to Joseph (Ephraim and Manasseh) in Genesis 49:22 which were the branches that ran over the wall and over the sea. John 15:1-5, Jesus is called the <u>vine,</u> God/Christ/Church the <u>husbandman</u> and in verse five the Church members are called <u>branches</u>. Isa 5:1-7 describes Gods Vinyard where the house of Israel is called his vineyard (branches) and Judah his pleasant plant the root of the vineyard. Christ's parable in Matt 21:33-44 describes this same <u>Vinyard</u> and how the vineyard husbandman was the house of Judah of David. They sinned by rejected the Messiah so the husbandman authority was replaced with a fruitful nation of the house of Israel in the wilderness as the overturn. Matt 21:42 calls this vineyard "the kingdom of God", therefore, all these verses explain how God overturned his throne of David by fulfilling the breach of the throne from the husbandman of Judah and gave it to the new husbandman of the house of Israel.

Study the Hebrew definitions of vineyard, bough, plant, fruit and branches for understanding. These words refer to a fruitful bough (BRANCH or Christ Jerm 23:5, 33:15) planted in the wilderness, a symbol of Christ's Church. Isaiah 16:8 speak of a people wandering in the wilderness and branches that are stretched out over the sea. Isaiah 16:1 sent the lamb (Christ's Church) to the ruler in the wilderness that sat upon the mountain (nation) of the daughter of Zion/Sion. Verse five states that in this nation within the wilderness David's throne would be established and judging and seeking judgment and hasting righteousness. The Jews could never fulfill this verse for they have never ruled a nation of power in the wilderness. Isaiah 16:5 clearly states that David's throne was established after Christ's death for the lamb was sent which is this ruler and he was righteous (Christian). Christ commissioned his disciples to go to his lost sheep (Matt 10:6) in the wilderness where the house of Israel accepted Christ's" Gospel. This ruler over the sea can only be the throne of England. England's parliament declared their nation to be Christian in 156AD to be defenders of the faith (the Apostolic Church) and only the United States has made this same statement in 1892 by the Supreme Court of a vote nine to zero.

This nation was to be a fruitful bough and by tracing the word fruitful in the last days it takes us to Lebanon, Sharon, Gilead, Carmel and Bashan (Isaiah 33:9). These ancient names correlate with Ephraim and Manasseh that settled in the upper portion of Bashan in northern Israel and they were the birthright tribes to inherit the family name of Israel. The dried-up green tree and making the dry tree to flourish is the moving or traveling of Zion (Isaiah 66:8) from Jerusalem to Gods planted nation in the wilderness under his new Covenant. He knew that Judaism with its wealth and old entrenched religious traditions would never accept Christ's Gospel.

To prove this, go to Gen 49:22 where Jacob gave his blessing to Joseph calling him, **"fruitful bough by a well; whose branches run over the wall."** Study the word bough; plant, wilderness and mountain in table one. The branches that ran over the wall simply mean they departed the promised land of Israel for another land. His young twigs, tender ones, were the two daughters of King Zedekiah, the last king of Israel, where Jeremiah took them into protective custody. They departed by ship to Ireland where the oldest daughter married their leader or King that was of the Zarah bloodline preserving the purity of the throne. This event overturned the scepter, giving it to the low branch of Zarah and taking it from the Pharez blood line healing the breach of Gods throne (Amos 9:11). Ireland was settled hundreds of years earlier by the dissidents of Zara that were his sons, Calcol and Dara. They were also a portion of the tribes of Dan that amalgamated with the Zarah blood line along with portions of the other eleven tribes of Israel. They were called Danaan, Danai, Danites and Tuatha de Danaan along with the Milesians and other Hebrew tribes of the Zarah bloodline of Judah healing the breach of the throne as recorded in the story of Tamar in Genesis chapter 38:27-30. A Cedar tree is the symbol of David's throne (II Sam 7:2).

One last important verse that pertain to King David's throne in reference to the national blessing promised to Abraham, Isaac and Jacob is Genesis 35:11. This verse promised that Israel's kingdom would be, **"a nation and a company of nations shall be of thee, and kings shall come out of thy loins:"** This blessing and promise was given to only Ephraim and Manasseh and no other sons. At the beginning of World War One, all the major Royal families of Europe were related by marriage with a direct link to the Royal Family of England. The historical events of European Royalty having family ties to the English Throne and Royal family is a distinct fulfillment of Genesis 35:11; 48:19 and 17:6. The Monarchs of England, Russia, France, Germany and all the other European Royal families were related by blood or marriage.

The tribe of Levi was given the authority through the law to anoint these kingdoms when Moses gave his inheritance blessing in Deuteronomy 33:8-12. They were divided into all twelve tribes (Gen 49:7) as the lawgiver, priests and servants to teach Gods laws given by Moses. This verse again clearly indicates the division of Jacob (representing all 12 tribes through Judah, modern Israel) and Israel (the family birthright of the 10 northern tribes) to take place in the last days. The law giving authority is also mentioned in Genesis 49:10 allowing the individual tribes to have their own line of Royal Kings but attached and connected to the head throne of David controlled by Judah/Hebrew (Jerm 33:21). The Royal bloodline of England is of Judah but overturned from the Phares line (Jew) to Zarah/Judah Hebrew. An example of this is seen in Genesis 49:20 when Asher (modern Germany and Belgium) was given their national destiny and inheritance, **"and he shall yield royal dainties."** If the tribes are not separate nations, how can Judah and Asher have a King? Gad in Deuteronomy 33:20-21 also is indicated as having a crown, **"Blessed be he that enlargeth Gad: he dwelleth as a lion, and teareth the arm with the crown of the head."** The term crown of the head indicates that Gad has power through a Royal Crown making battle. Study these verses for they match the Royal Dynasties that were established in Europe by the Anglo-Saxon Caucasians (Isaac' sons) and were basically controlled by the English Throne through family and inter marital relations for hundreds of years. This is why the nations and Monarch symbols of the different nations of Europe all resemble each other. Moses gave the twelve tribes their inheritance in Deuteronomy chapter 33 that correlates with Jacob's inheritance blessings given in Genesis chapter 49 to take place in the last days. The Royal Crowns of Judah, Gad, Asher and others as recorded in Genesis and Deuteronomy are the Royal Dynasties of Europe fulfilling Genesis 17:6, 35:11 and 48:19.

There is another aspect that many Christians over look and explain away of how Gods Hebrew Battle Ax (the 5th Stone Kingdom) has been around since the Babylonian Empire. When you closely study Daniel's interpretation of King Nebuchadnezzar's dream in Daniel 2:31-45, he speaks of four world powers and where God sets up his 5th Kingdom made of uncut stone (Christ Kingdom of an uncut stone) that destroy the first four world kingdoms made of Gold, Silver, Brass and Iron and clay. Christians want to believe that this is

Christ coming in power and glory at his millennial reign. If we closely study theses Scriptures, it speaks of a 5th Kingdom that destroys the first four ancient world powerful Empires. We have a tendency to read into these verses for most readers do not understand the division of Israel into two houses or families. It clearly states in Daniel 2:44-45, **"And in the days of these kings shall the God of heaven set up a kingdom** [his Chosen Hebrew People of the Temple/Church], **which shall never be destroyed: and the kingdom shall not be left to other people, but it shall break in pieces and consume all these kingdoms, and it shall stand for ever."** This verse simply proves the existence of Gods earthly Kingdom given to Jeroboam of the ten lost tribes after they disappeared into the wilderness and became great nations.

When it says "In the days of these kings" God set up a kingdom that shall never be destroyed and not left to other people is speaking of the establishment of King David's throne consisting of the twelve tribes and Gods Temple/ Church, Gods earthly kingdom. When it says that "this kingdom shall not be left to other people" simply means that Gods Hebrew (peculiar people) were responsible for being his Battle Ax given to Jeroboam of Ephraim of the house of Israel in I Kings 12:20. They are the birthright tribe and cannot be reckoned with in I Chron 5:1-2. Jerm 51:19-20 called the house of Israel his battle ax that "with thee will I destroy kingdoms" just as Dan 2:35 states, **"the stone that smote the image"** verse 45 **"brake in pieces the iron, the brass, the clay, the silver, and the gold;"** and Matt 21;44 **"grind him to powder"**. These Scriptures clearly says that this Kingdom made of uncut stone (Christ's Hebrew Temple) is God's battle ax which is his Earthly Kingdom and future Church that destroyed not only the <u>Babylonian Empire</u> of Gold but also the <u>Medo-Persian Empire</u> of silver, the <u>Greek Empire</u> of brass and the <u>Roman Empire</u> of iron and clay just as stated in Dan 2:35&44. God destroyed the first three empires through the power of his Temple in Jerusalem but the fourth empire was destroyed by Christ's Church as his battle ax and weapon of war.

It has been proven through historical findings and ancient writings that Greece was settled by the Hebrews of Calcol and Dara (I Chron 2:5-6) where many people of the ten lost tribes migrated after the Assyrian captivity allowing them to become great. It is also recorded where Cyrus, King of Media Persia (Ezra 1:1), had great compassion for the Jews and allowed them to return to Jerusalem to rebuild the Temple. Why would a heathen king do this? It is very simple for he was a descendant of the Hebrew ten northern tribes taken into captivity by Assyria. The captured northern tribes amalgamated with the Assyrians where they populated and became a great people within the Assyrian Empire. After the 70-year captivity was complete, the main body of the Hebrews departed to the north country into the wilderness. A remnant of the Hebrews stayed behind and were called Median as the Guti, Catti or Gadil of the tribe of Gad and a portion of Judah that became a crucial part of the Media/Persian Empire. They helped destroyed the Babylonians. See "Tracing our Ancestors" by Frederick Haberman page 124. The Hebrew King Cyrus helped to destroy Babylon.

We all know how Rome fell to the Christian movement by Emperor Constantine who was the great-grandson of Arviragus or King Caratacus, Pendragon and leader of the Silurian Army (the British Barbarian). Arviragus was the most powerful leader of the royal house of the Silures and the most famous Christian warrior in history while fighting the Roman invasion of England starting in 43AD. Briton had become Christian due to the establishment of the first above ground Church in Ireland in 38AD by Joseph of Arimathea, Christ's Uncle. Arviragus is believed to have had a daughter Claudia and a son Linus that started the first Apostolic Church in Rome where Linus became it first Bishop. Constantine was the son of the famous Empress Helen, a British princess and an heir to the British throne which brought Christianity to Rome during the 2nd century AD. The Apostolic Church grew and fulfilling Daniel 2:44-45 and Matt 21:43-44. This is how Paul knew Claudia and Linus in II Tim 4:21 as members of the British Royal Family and her husband Rufus Pudens, a Roman Senator. After Claudia established the Church in Rome, Paul and Peter was invited to came for the Church had been established prior to Paul's visit. Paul was also related to the Puden family by marriage of his mother and was his half-brother as indicated in (Rom 16:13). See "The Drama of the Lost Disciples" by George F. Jowett, page 86 and 94. Also, read the note warning in the bottom of the Table of Contents in the beginning of this book.

When we apply documented history to the Scriptures, the full picture unfolds just as Gods Battle Ax of the ten lost tribes (Gods 5th Stone Kingdom) can be seen and understood. There is no doubt in this writer's mind that God preserved history of fables, myths, legends and true history hidden through ancient writers and story tellers for this purpose. He expects Christians to study and research the facts of history to show ourselves approved so we can understand his Word.

From the moment God established his earthly Kingdom through King David's throne, it was to be forever and always a man sitting on his throne for all generations and of the days of heaven. This is a clear promise to David from God, so why does it appear that he destroyed his kingdom? According to secular and Christian history there has been no king of the Kingdom of Israel since King Zedekiah in 586BC, where is the promise? This theory is absolutely contrary to the Word of God as proven in this segment. God's Kingdom has existed through the house of Israel from David till the end of the age that is the preserving salt and Battle Ax of the earth, Gods Christian people. The Church is Gods Kingdom, the New Covenant, led by his birthright tribe of Ephraim and Manasseh given the name of Israel according to Genesis 48:16 (Great Britain and the United States) the unicorn and Bull. Our mission as the Church was given by Christ in Matt 10:5-8 as a fruitful nation (21:43) to preach the end time Gospel world-wide in which we have completed as a fruitful nation and people.

Gods Covenant with Man

The word covenant is simply the way God spiritually deals with his Children of Israel (true believers) and the people of the world. The Hebrew meaning of Covenant "briyth" means a compact, confederacy, and league. The prime root means to create, qualified to cut down a tree, select, feed, and dispatch. From the time God dwelt with man and Israel till today, he has made eight recorded covenants with his people and the human race. When studying these covenants, we need to take into consideration the Who, What, When and Where scenario.

The first covenant recorded in (Gen 9:9) was to Noah and all his seed or man promising that the earth would never be destroyed by water again binding with the sign of the Rain Bow. This is a covenant to all of mankind.

The 2nd covenant (Gen 15:18) was to Abraham and all his seed giving the promised land of Canaan to his Hebrew people, Abraham the first Hebrew (Gen 15:18). This is a covenant given to all of Abraham's seed, the Hebrew people, not just to the Jews. The Jew is simply the caretaker, the root set in Jerusalem of Judea but the house of Israel branched out as vines over the wall into the world.

The 3rd covenant (Genesis 17:2-9) makes a covenant with Abraham and all his seed choosing the Hebrew as his chosen people for them to multiply and be many nations. This is a key in understanding today's political situation between the house of Israel and the house of Judah for his Hebrew people were to be many nations, verse 4. Realizing that Gods people were to be many nations helps us to understand the division of Israel in Romans chapter 11. Under this covenant, Abram's name was changed to Abraham that means father, to be many peoples or nations as a colonizer. Verse 6 explains that he was to be the father of his chosen people that under the birthright tribe of the house of Israel were to multiply into many nations and kings of kingdoms (Gen 35:11) to take place in the last days in Gen 49:1. Abraham's seed were to become exceedingly fruitful (Christian), which only applied to the house of Israel, as we will see in the following Scriptures. We are so blind to believe that God only wanted one little country in Canaan (Israel) to be his nation. It is clear in these verses and many more throughout the Bible that God wanted his Hebrew people to be many nations and dominate all families and tongues of the earth. Circumcision, verse 11, is the way we can trace Gods Hebrew people through the centuries and binds the Covenant. Verse 21 passes the covenant on to Isaac, Isaac's sons (Saxons as English) (Gen 17:21; 21:12, Rom 9:7, Heb 11:18) and not to Ishmael. This is an everlasting Covenant exiting today that there were to be many nations of Hebrew multiplying as the stars of heaven.

The fourth covenant took place (Exodus 24:7-8) as the blood covenant given to all twelve tribes of Israel. This was the covenant to the Children of Israel and the beginning of God's plan to save man through animal sacrifice and ultimately the blood of Jesus Christ our Messiah. The verbal acknowledgement of obedience from the people accepted by God and that they would obey his Book of the Covenant by the righteousness of his laws. The everlasting Covenant was bound by blood, first by animal and then by Christ himself. This blood Covenant represents the Messiah and his future New Covenant of his Church open to all man. The Old Covenant was given to only the 12 tribes of the Children of Israel as caretaker or husbandman of his vineyard but open to anyone or nation that accepted and obeyed his laws under the rule of his chosen people. This is explained in Matt 21:33-44, John 15:1-5 and Isa 5:1-7. This explains why his chosen people were to be over all nations for they received the responsibility to enforce Gods Laws. They were to rule and judge all nations as the Beast of the four Brigades of Israel (Ezek 1:10 and Rev 4:7); "he will rule as God" till Christ comes in power and Glory.

The fifth covenant (Exodus 31:16) was the Perpetual Covenant that all generations of the Children of Israel would keep and obey the Sabbath. This covenant is forever, **"It is a sign between me and the children of Israel for ever:"** and another way we can trace Gods people through time by tracing the people that maintain the Sabbath and Circumcision.

The sixth covenant (Exodus 34:27) gives Moses the Ten Commandments on Mount Sinai after forty days and forty nights on the mountain. The commandments and covenant were given to Moses and the Children of Israel by God to be obeyed through-out all their generations.

The seventh covenant (Exodus 34:10) given to the Children of Israel to enter the Promised Land of Canaan and destroy all peoples and nations, to obliterate all false Gods and alters. This was to be a covenant proving the power of God to the entire world and for his children to have no other Gods before them.

The eighth covenant is Gods new Covenant (the Church and found in Jeremiah 31:31 and Hebrews 8:8). Hebrew 12:24 clearly states that this new Covenant is Christ's Gospel and Church. Study closely the 31st chapter of Jeremiah and Hebrew chapter 8 from beginning to end. Jeremiah chapter 31 explains how God sent Israel into the wilderness and caused him to rest, Jerm 31:2, **"Thus saith the Lord, The people which were left of the sword found grace in the wilderness; even Israel, when I went to cause him to rest."** This is God gathering his people from the nations of captivities through-out the world and bringing them into a nation in the wilderness of peace, the continents of England, North America, Austria, New Zealand etc. First to Briton in the British Isles and then to America that corresponds to Ezekiel chapter 17 and Isaiah 18. Jerm 31:9 calls Ephraim Israel for Ephraim was the birthright tribe to receive the double portion of great blessings and to carry on the family name of Israel, which became one great nation and a company of nations (Gen 35:11).

Their symbol is the bull and unicorn that represents Great Britain (unicorn) and the United States (the bull), Ephraim and Manasseh. Jerm31:12 calls the fruitful nations the height of Zion (Christ's Church as Sion) as a watered garden and shall not sorrow any more. These verses cannot be speaking of the Jews for they have been persecuted in every nation for the past two thousand years. Jerm 31:31 explains, **"Behold, the days come, saith the Lord, that I will make a new covenant with the house of Israel, and with the house of Judah".** This whole chapter is speaking of the last days and the new covenant is to the house of Israel and the house of Judah as two separate nations. The new covenant is the righteousness of Christ's Gospel for verse 32 states that it is not the same covenant that was made with their fathers coming out of Egypt.

Jeremiah 31:33 sums it up by saying, **"But this shall be the covenant that I will make with the house of Israel: After those days, saith the Lord, I will put my law in their inward parts, and write it in their hearts; and will be their God, and they shall be my people."** The Covenant was given to both Israel and Judah (Zara/Phares) in verse 31 but in this verse only the house of Israel and Judah/Zara received and obeyed the covenant. Why? The house of Judah (the Jews of ancient and modern Israel) rejects Christ as their Messiah to this very day. The law and lawgiver were given to Israel through the Levites in Deuteronomy 33:10 which enabled the ten northern tribes to establish King David's throne in England and a line of Kings through-out Europe. This verse goes on to say that Judah/Phares could receive this covenant but they refused by not believing in Christ as the true Messiah. Therefore, God took Judah's

(Jews) portion of the kingdom from them and gave it to a fruitful nation as the lost sheep of the house of Israel (Matt 21:43).

Keep in mind that this is Jeremiah speaking and was written in the Old Testament around 606BC, 2600 years ago. This took place almost 120 years after the house of Israel went into captivity and ceased to exist or that is what we have been told. According to Jeremiah, the house of Israel was to be a great nation of people in the last days and separated from Judah. To prove that this new covenant is speaking of the end days, let's go to Hebrews 8:8 and read of the same new covenant, verse 8 states almost the same as Jeremiah 31:31, **"For finding fault with them, he saith, Behold, the days come, saith the Lord, when I will make a new covenant with the house of Israel and with the house of Judah".** Hebrew 8:10 states almost exactly as Jeremiah 31:33 by stating, **"For this is the covenant that I will make with the house of Israel after those days, saith the Lord: I will put my laws into their mind, and write them in their hearts: and I will be to them a God, and they shall be to me a people".** Compare these verses.

Again, the laws of righteousness are planted in their hearts by the authority of Levi and the Holy Spirit (Duet 33:10). There is no doubt that the verses in Jeremiah chapter 31 and Paul's writing in Hebrew chapter 8 is speaking of the same new covenant of Christ's Gospel. According to these verses, the house of Israel and the Church is the same for the new covenant was to the house of Israel, Judah and all Christians born into the Church. They all fell under the new covenant to Israel for the Church is called Israel, we inherit Jacob's name when we are born into Christ's family. This is the heart of why God separated and divided his Kingdom into the house of Israel and the house of Judah Phares/Zara for he knew that the established Hebrew religion of the old laws of his covenant would reject his coming Messiah. Therefore, he divided his kingdom and sent the ten northern tribes (his lost sheep) called the house of Israel into the wilderness to wait for his Gospel.

The house of Israel and Judah/Zara in the wilderness was to be the base, the spring board and protector of Christ's new thing in the earth, the Church (Jerm 31:32) and commissioned to spread it worldwide. Christ sent his twelve Apostles to his lost sheep in Matthew 10:5 and 15:24 that was the house of Israel waiting for his Gospel planted in the wilderness. The planted nation in the wilderness can also be found in I Chronicles 17:9-14; Ezekiel 20:34-37, 34:13-18; Hosea 2:14-23; Micah 5:7-11; Zechariah 10:6-12 and Jeremiah 13:2-15. All this was to take place in the last days just as Acts 2:17 states, **"And it shall come to pass in the last days, saith God, I will pour out of my Spirit upon all flesh: and your sons and your daughter shall prophesy, and**

your young men shall see visions, and your old men shall dream dreams:" This is the same pouring out of the spirit that gave the laws in the minds and hearts of Gods Christian people that is mentioned in Hebrews 8:10 and Jeremiah 31:33 under the New Covenant to take place in the Church age, our present time.

We need to keep in mind that these Scriptures are not speaking to the Jews but to Gods kingdom in the wilderness, his fruitful nation. They are his Christian nations or the mountains of Israel. The word Jew or Judaism was not coined till II Kings 16:6 by the Assyrians after the division of Gods Kingdom just prior to the ten northern tribes going into captivity to Assyria in 740 to 720 BC. The ten northern tribes of the house of Israel lead by the birthright tribes of Ephraim and Manasseh were never called Jews to this vary day.

Gods eighth covenant actually falls under the fourth covenant of blood, making only seven total covenants, the number of perfection. Gods new covenant of his Gospel under the shed blood of Jesus Christ fulfilled the old covenant of the law as stated in Romans 10:4, **"For Christ is the end of the law for righteousness to every one that believeth."** The old covenant was fulfilled with the renting of the veal in the Holy of Holies when Christ died on the cross, Matthew 27:51, completing the way for our salvation and planting the Holy Spirit within our heart as stated in Jeremiah 31:33 and Hebrews 8:10. Gods new covenant with man, covenant "<u>Brit</u>" man "<u>ish</u>", British, planted in the wilderness to wait for his new covenant, the Gospel.

To sum up the covenant, let's give its components. The covenant was given to Gods Children of Israel that consisted of the Kingdom of all twelve tribes, the throne controlled by Judah and the lawgiver (the Levite priest) that controlled the Temple/Church or Zion/Sion (Gods Spirit with man). The elements within the Kingdom are the throne given to King David's linage as the scepter, the lawgiver or the ruling government to fulfill prophecy (Gen 49:10). Zion/Sion represents the Temple or the Church (Gods spirit with man in the Holy of Holies and Church) and the Birthright tribe that was given to Joseph's two sons Ephraim and Manasseh. They were to be fruitful branches that run over the wall and nations and kings of nations to spread Christ's end time Gospel (Gen 48:22 & 35:11). The other tribes fell under the leadership of Ephraim and Manasseh. Therefore, we have the Kingdom consisting of the Throne of David, the law-giving government, the Birthright tribe representing all of Israel and Zion (Gods spirit with man). Zion is the Tabernacle or Temple of the Holy of Holies where God dwells with man on earth that culminated into the Church and his Holy Spirit. Jerusalem was its capital till Christ died on the cross and then it became Sion (New Testament Greek) where God dwells in each individual heart, Jerusalem, a peaceful place (Jerm 31:33, I Peter 2:6 and Heb 8:10).

When God gave Jacob the blessings to each tribe in Genesis chapter 49, he knew that by giving the throne and the birthright to different tribes would create a rift within Israel. Most Christians believe that the Birthright went to Judah but according to Scripture, it went to Joseph and his two sons. The initial throne went to Judah/Phares as the overturned throne went to Judah/Zara to fulfill the breach of the scarlet thread. Both of the breached kingships were under the Judah bloodline of King David. Moses established the Tabernacle (Tent) to be mobile at Mt. Sinai in approx. 1491BC so the twelve tribes could travel. Numbers 10:14-27 listed the tribes by name and Ephraim and Manasseh replaced Levi and Joseph indicating the importance of the birthright tribes. Due to this replacement, Levi and Joseph never had inherited landmass in the Promised Land. This created a power struggle beginning as early as King David's reign and finally divided the kingdom after the death of King Solomon in I Kings chapter 11. God used this to fulfill his prophecies for he promised Abraham that he would be many nations and kings of nations but he still had to maintain his throne in Jerusalem to provide the Messiah. To complete this scenario, God had to divide his kingdom and I Kings chapter eleven gives the account.

Total separation and loss of contact occurred between the houses of Israel and Judah when the Assyrians took the ten northern tribes lead by Ephraim into captivity. This allowed the house of Israel to be the fruitful branches that ran over the wall into the wilderness fulfilling Genesis 49:22. From this point, they never associated with the Jews or Judah again. The house of Israel and Judah/Zara of Colcal and Dara that departed Egypt by ship lost their national identification, language, Religion and planted in their own faraway land (Isaiah 14:1-2 & Jerm 23:8). (Reference *"Missing Links Discovered in Assyrian Tablets" by E. Raymond Capt. page 85*) On the other hand, the tribe of Judah was later taken into captivity by the Babylonians further dividing the two and only a remnant returned to Jerusalem to preserve the prophecy of Jerusalem for the coming of the Messiah. The mass of Judah departed into the wilderness where they joined the house of Israel under David's throne of the Judah/Zara bloodline established in Tara Ireland. The Jews almost lost their language as did the house of Israel due to captivity and Nehemiah had to reteach the people their own Hebrew language (Nehemiah 13:24). Out of an estimated thirteen million people, 11 million Hebrews from the house of Israel and two million Jews from the house of Judah, only 40,000 Jews returned to Jerusalem to rebuild the city and Temple (Nehemiah Ch 2 & Ezra Ch 6). Keep in mind that according to secular history, King David's throne has not existed since King Zedekiah fell to Babylon in 586BC. Up till this point, all of Israel fell under the covenant of animal sacrifice and circumcision but the moment Christ died on the cross and the veil was rent in the Holy of Holies, we all fell under the New Covenant of Christ's blood under the Gospel.

God dwelt with man through his covenant in a Spiritual form differently during each dispensation of time. As we research the Scriptures, we find that there are three periods of dispensation where God strives with man through his Patriarchs, Prophets, Kings, Angles, visions, personal appearances and finally his Holy Spirit. There is an evolution of how God has dwelt with his elect Children. The first period range, from the Creation of Adam and Eve to the flood, approx. 4004BC to 2348BC, 1656 total years. During this period, Gods Spirit did not directly dwell with man on earth but spiritually communicated through angles and his human patriarchs. The second period begin at the flood or deluge to the birth of Christ, 2349BC to approx. 3BC, or 2344 total years. During this period of time God physically sent his spirit to dwell with man through his chosen people of Israel in the Tabernacle (Arch of the Covenant) and then the Holy of Holies in his earthly Temple within Jerusalem, Zion. There is almost exactly 4000 years between the first two periods. The third period starts at the birth of Christ to the end of the Church age and takes place at the close of 6000 years that is the number of man (6 or 666). This period of time is considered the last days for it is the last period of dispensation. We are presently at the very end of this time period. During this period, God dwells with man in each believer's heart and became Gods Temple on earth during the Messianic Age, Sion (I Peter 2:4-6). Gods return is so secret that the angles in Heaven or Christ himself do not know the date or time which closes man's rule on earth. His Children were told to watch for the seasons for there is no doubt we are in the last days.

The first period of time from Adam to the deluge is very silent in the Bible with very little information given. By studying the Holy Scriptures, the Books of Enoch, the Apocrypha, the book of Jasher and the Apocrypha of Baruch, more information is exposed. This writer would like to make the note that these books are not a part of the inspired Word of God but of history that God gave his patriarchs and prophets to write for Christians to better understand his Scriptures and especially in the last days.

The period of time from Adam to the deluge was very evil. When the angels tasked to watch over the earth saw that the human women were beautiful, they began to mate and teach the human race very evil ways along with the secrets of God's creation. Gods Spirit did not dwell with man directly during this period of time but his knowledge and spiritual contact was conducted through angles and his patriarchs. These angels were called Watchers and their interference with man took place in the days of Jared, Enoch's father. The Books of Enoch and Jasher explains how the mating between the Watchers and human women created giants and polluted man's genealogy. According to the first few chapters of the Book of Jasher, God dealt with man through Enoch, his Patriarch and gave Enoch knowledge and wisdom. Enoch was directed to teach man "the ways of God" so the men of earth gladly made Enoch their leader. God communicated with man through his Patriarchs starting with Adam and ending with Noah. By the time Noah was born and became a man, the earth had become so evil that the Lord decided to destroy the earth and all inhabitance due to Satan's corrupting the human gene pool through DNA.

There is evidence that the Watchers began to breed with human women and taught man to gene splice or cross breed humans with animals. In the book of Jasher chapter IV verse 18 states, *"And their judges and rulers went to the daughters of men and took their wives by force from their husbands according to their choice, and the sons of men in those days took from the cattle of the earth, the beasts of the field and the fowls of the air, and taught the mixture of animals of one species with the other, in order therewith to provoke the Lord; and God saw the whole earth and it was corrupt, for all flesh had corrupted its ways upon earth, all men and all animals."*

This writer has no opinion on the Greek period of mythology but when you study this material and the Greek period of half humans and half animals, it brings up a huge question if these myths were possibly true. Jasher goes on to state in Chapter V verses 5 and 21, *"And all who followed the Lord died in those days, before they saw the evil which God declared to do upon earth." "And all the sons of men who knew the Lord, died in that year before the Lord brought evil upon them; for the Lord willed them to die, so as not to behold the evil that God would bring upon their brothers and relatives, as he had so declared to do."* By these writings, Noah's family was not the only pure humans alive before the flood but there were thousands maybe millions of uncorrupted God-believing people that he took through death to not see wrath. Before God executes judgment on man, he always gives a warning and this is documented through-out the Scriptures. These verses are very important for it establishes the fact that God does not bring wrath on his beloved people. God took all his people by death before the flood representing the rapture of the Church prior to Gods Wrath of Tribulation Period. There are certain Christians that do not believe in the pre-trib. Rapture for they have not studied Gods Word and ancient history.

There is a teaching today that Gods Church is going to go through the Tribulation period of wrath, but if you study Jasher and the Scriptures, it proves that God does not punish his people that love him and keep his commandments for the sins of the earth. The Church will not see Gods wrath that comes during the Tribulation Period for his Church is warning the world at this very moment. They will be taken away just as Gods beloved people were taken prior to the flood and the destruction of Sodom and Gomorrah. Jasher V:8-9, gives this warning, **"For thus saith the Lord, Behold I give you a period of one hundred and twenty years; if you will turn to me and forsake your evil ways, then will I also turn away from the evil which I told you, and it shall not exist, saith the Lord. And Noah and Methuselah spoke all the words of the Lord to the sons of men, day after day, constantly speaking to them."** This same warning that Noah and Methuselah gave to the people of the earth is being warned today of Gods soon coming destruction, Matthew 24:37, **"But as the days of Noah were, so shall also the coming of the Son of man be."** We as Christians today, are beginning to see the same abundant evil on earth just as the days of Noah. The technology of DNA cloning (genetic copying) is an absolute sign that we are in evil days as in the days of Noah. The American people need to wake up to Gods truths and stop the moral backslide of this nation. If we fail to return to his commandments, we will see the destruction prophesied in his Holy Scriptures.

To sum up the word Covenant, as stated above, let's explain its Hebrew meaning. Covenant man or the word British is derived from two Hebrew words, "Beriyth" (ref#1285) meaning covenant and "ish" (376) meaning man. British means covenant man. The word English (Angles) is also derived from two Hebrew words, "AY-ghel" and "ish". AY-ghel (5695) means, a male calf, bullock, steer or a female calf, heifer. The symbol of Manasseh as one of the firstborn birthright tribes of Joseph. The word English means "people of the bull" descends of Manasseh, (Jerm 31:18; Hosea 10:11). Ephraim was the unicorn and both are described in Duet 33:17 and Isaiah 34:7. These verses refer to Ephraim and Manasseh as a bullock and unicorn and can be traced through ancient tribes of Europe as their symbols. It is believed that the word America comes from two Gothic words Amel and Rich meaning Kingdom of Heaven and we also carry the bull as a symbol of our economic strength as the tribe of Manasseh. There is also a belief that the name America came from the Aztec's meaning the "plumed serpent". Research these facts for yourself. We, America as the Christian house of Israel, took the responsibility of establishing Gods Kingdom on earth by setting up his Church world wide, the local independent New Testament Church, not the Universal Catholic Church. Ephraim and Manasseh (Common Wealth of Great Britain and the United States) have established and evangelized Christ's New Covenant (the Church) worldwide.

Understanding the Law of the Birthright

Gods Birthright for all the families of the world to be blessed was to go through Enoch (Phoenician), Noah, Shem (Semitic), Eber (Hebrew), Abraham to Isaac Jacob and finally to Joseph of the 12 tribes of Israel. For end time purposes (Gen 49:1), this Birthright was passed directly to Ephraim and Manasseh (Gen 48:16-22) and to no other Israelite. Only they were to be called Israel, "he will rule as God" as a Prince to prepare and be a forerunner to Christ's Gospel and Church. The other eleven tribes were to be called Israelite through the Birthright tribes. The book of Jasher mentioned in Joshua 10:13 and II Samuel 1:18 is an extremely interesting book and in Hebrew means, "the upright or correct record". Jasher goes into more detailed events and help to explain where the Bible leaves off. A good example is the record of Enoch through Jacob as recorded in "The book of Enoch or 1 Enoch" by R.H. Charles and the book "Josephus the Complete Works" by William Whiston with the original manuscripts written my men of God. These seven generations are the building block for God's Chosen People from Abraham through the Church age of our present time. The Bible states that Enoch and Noah "walked with God" and Jasher says that Noah, Shem and Eber taught instruction of the Lord and "his ways".

This is very important for what was the name of Gods "ways" for it had no name at that time. God has many names that relate to his people such as, "The Lord our Righteousness", (Jerm 23:6), "house of Israel" (Jerm 7:14) and "City of Jerusalem" (Jerm 25:29). All these names and many more match the Hebrew meaning of Israel, "He will rule as God" to be a Prince of the world ruling. According to these names and definitions, Israel were to rule the nations of the world bringing righteousness and justice to man, Duet 7:6, 14:2, and Isaiah 16:5. The house of Israel were to be over all nations of the world with justice as his battle ax, Jerm 51:19-20 in the absence of Christ's rule till the Messiah claims his Throne in power, Luke 1:32. The principles taught "in the ways of God" resemble the Druid religion scattered through-out Europe.

Noah lived 950 years and Shem his son lived 600 years. Eber lived to be 464 years of age. They were the last of the Long-Lived Patriarchs of God. According to Jasher 9:5, Noah and Shem taught Abraham the "ways of the Lord", Isaac was sent to the house of Shem and Eber to learn the "ways of the Lord" (Jasher 24:17), and Jacob was sent to the house of Shem and Eber to learn the "ways of the Lord" (Jasher 28:18). God allowed these last three Patriarchs to live long lives for one reason, to teach "his ways" to the birthright tribes that were to be called Israel. Abraham, Isaac and Jacob were given Covenant blessings to be passed to Gods Birthright Tribe of Joseph given directly to his two sons Ephraim and Manasseh. God's "ways" were taught from generation to generation down to Jacob and finally to Joseph inherited by Ephraim and Manasseh by Jacob himself. The teaching of Gods "ways" were the forerunner of Christ and his Gospel to be passed by Birthright to the selected sons of Ephraim and Manasseh to be called Israel, "he will rule as God". They were to be responsible in spreading Christ's end time Gospel as the lost sheep of the house of Israel recorded in Matthew 10:6, 15:24 and 21:43, the fruitful bough or nation to be kings of kingdoms.

There is an aspect of the birthright that must be understood if we are to trace the lost tribes down through the ages of time and more importantly the last days. God called Jacob Israel to be a Prince making his 12 sons the Children of Israel (God's chosen covenant people). They were to be led by Ephraim and Manasseh.

The chosen birthright tribe is to rule the families of the world as Israel and again "he will rule as God", to bring righteousness and judgment to the nations. The birthright was given directly to the unicorn of Ephraim (GB) and the bull of Manasseh (USA).

When Jacob gave his heritage blessings to his sons in Genesis 48 & 49, he did a very strange thing. By tradition, the first blessing went to the birthright Child that by inheritance law was presented to the oldest son. In Jacob's case, he gave the birthright to Joseph, the eleventh born son as recorded in Genesis 48:15 and not to Rueben the eldest son. The key to this mystery is that Jacob gave the birthright blessing not to Joseph but directly to Joseph's two sons, Jacob's grandsons, Ephraim and Manasseh (Gen 48:16). God did this for a reason and it was to emphasize the double portion birthright to not be reckoned with (1 Chron 5:1-2). After the special birthright blessing was given in Genesis chapter 48 to Joseph and his two sons, Jacob then gave his normal inheritance blessings directly to all twelve sons to include Joseph. Joseph was blessed twice, first for the family firstborn birthright to receive the name Israel and secondly the normal family blessing by order of birth along with all his brothers in accordance to Mosaic Law. This proves that the first blessing to Joseph and his two sons were the family birthright blessing to be leaders of all Israel. During the inheritance blessings to all the sons, no other grandsons were involved again proving the importance of the double portion birthright to Ephraim and Manasseh. From this point on in the Scriptures, Ephraim and Manasseh were listed as inheriting a double portion of land when Israel settled into Canaan (Joshua 17:17).

Another key element in being able to trace the Children of Israel, namely the ten lost tribes of Israel, through time is by the traits and or symbols given to each son within his respective inheritance. These blessings were to take place in the last days as recorded in Genesis 49:1. For example, Judah and Gad is the Lion, Ephraim the unicorn, Dan the lion and adder, Manasseh the bull, Benjamin a wolf, Naphtali the hind or deer and Issachar the strong ass of burden. See table two for details on the Tribes symbols and traits.

Genesis chapter 48, 49 and I Kings chapter 11 are the key chapters in understanding the birthright blessings and why God divided Israel. Israel's division and the birthright go hand and hand and give us comprehension of one of the reasons why God divided his people. God applies the rule of authority in any event that occurs to his Kingdom, the throne or nation of Israel. He gave Ahijah the authority to divide his kingdom in I Kings chapter 11 and gave Jeremiah the authority over all nations to root out, pull down, to destroy and to throw down Israel under the Old Covenant. Jeremiah was to build and plant his new nation of Israel to be under the New Covenant in the wilderness (Jerm 1:10). This same authority was then passed on through Ahijah to Jeroboam to rule the mass of Gods kingdom (I Kings 11:30) of the house of Israel the ten northern tribes. Note that God took Solomon's Kingdom and gave it to Jeroboam of Ephraim consisting of ten tribes. Rehoboam, Solomon's son, was given the authority through the house of Judah, the two southern tribes, to maintain King David's throne fulfilling Genesis 49:10, preserving the throne till Christ establishes his Church when Shiloh comes in Gen 49:10. Levi, the priestly tribe and lawgiver, was divided between the two houses completing all three elements of Gods Kingdom, making available the lawgiver and judgment to the people. The authority of Levi is given in Genesis 48:5-7 and Deuteronomy 33:8-11 to provide laws and judgment to sustain the kingdom of the two separate houses till prophecy is fulfilled at the end of the age. It is absolutely imperative to understand the authority of the birthright of Ephraim and Manasseh and how it is manifested in the inheritance role in Gods divided kingdom. Let's trace Gods authority.

God gave Jacob the authority to transfer all the Birthright blessings of Abraham, Isaac to Jacob and now transferred to Joseph, directly given to Ephraim and Manasseh, the birthright in Gen 48:16-22 (the double portion). This same authority was given to Jeroboam, a decedent of Ephraim the birthright tribe, by Ahijah in I Kings chapter 11 as leader of the northern Kingdom that exist to this day. Rehoboam was given charge over the house of Judah and the throne. There is a distinct separation between Gods kingdom of the house of Israel and the throne of the house of Judah as indicated in Genesis 48, 49 and I Kings chapter 11. This authority stayed with Israel in Jerusalem till the throne was overturned in Ezekiel 21:27 and the coming of Christ (Shiloh) in Genesis 49:10 where the Messiah gathered his Church, "and unto him shall the gathering of the people be". Judah's portion of the kingdom to include the throne (Judah/ Phares "Pharisees") was taken away by Christ himself in Matthew 21:43 due to sin and rejection of the Messiah and his Gospel. The complete Kingdom was then given to the lost sheep of the house of Israel (Matt 10:6 and 15:25) the fruitful nation planted in the wilderness (Matt 21:43, Hos 2:14-23, Eze 17:5 fruitful field "Christian"). From this point forward, the children of Israel are under the Judah Zarah bloodline of the scarlet thread as the story of Tamar is told in Gen 38. This planting and overturn of the throne (Eze 21:27) into the fruitful field by the authority of Jeremiah healed the breach between Zarah of the red hand due to the scarlet thread and Phares birthright to (Gen 38:29-30) the bloodline of the Israelite Kings.

The overturn or planting in the wilderness healed the breach of the throne as recorded in Amos 9:11 and Jerm 33:15, **"and I will cause the Branch of righteousness** (Christ) **to grow up unto David"** (the throne) that occurs in the last days. Jeremiah was commissioned (Jerm 1:10) to tear down, to destroy and to rebuild Gods Kingdom in the wilderness. His commission allowed him to overturn the throne form Jerusalem when it fell to Babylon in 586 BC where it was replanted in the wilderness to keep Gods Promise to David that there would always be a man reigning on his throne for all generations. God allowed his judges and kings of Judah to rule his earthly kingdom of the land of Israel from Jerusalem till he divided his kingdom in I Kings chapter 11. This is where he gave the leadership to Jeroboam the Ephrathite, descendent of the tribe of Ephraim. See table two for the leaders of Israel from Moses to present.

It is plain by Scripture that Ephraim was to lead Gods Kingdom after the division due to the birthright responsibility and also carrying on the family name Israel. Ahijah made Rehoboam (Solom's son) King over two tribes in Jerusalem called the house of Judah, I Kings 11:37, **"And I will take thee, and thou shalt reign according to all that thy soul desireth, and shalt be king over Israel."** Remember that the name Israel was to stay with Jerusalem's kingship till Christ called Shilo come in Gen 49:10. Ahijah calls the ten northern tribes the house of Israel and not Jerusalem for I Kings 12:20 gives Jeroboam of the house of Israel leader of the ten northern tribes the throne over all Israel, **"and made him king over all Israel".** From this point on in the Scriptures, Jerusalem is called the house of Judah and the birthright name of Israel went to the house of Israel, the ten northern tribes fulfilling the Mosaic birthright law.

Zion travailed (Isaiah 66:8 Christ's birth) and was taken from Jerusalem when Christ died on the cross and the veil in the Temple (Gods house) was rent, representing its planting and plowing into the wilderness. When Jesus died on the cross and the vail in the Temple rent, the authority of David's throne departed Jerusalem and overturned to the house of Israel in the wilderness (Tara Ireland) where Joseph of Arimathea had established the first Church in Ireland. Gods Spirit (Zion) moved into the wilderness under his new covenant that was given to the house of Israel (the Church, Heb 8:8 and Jerm 31:31 the new thing in the land). David's throne was planted and established under the British throne first in Ireland then Scotland and England becoming Gods Covenant People. They were led by Ephraim the unicorn where the descendants of Ephraim and Manasseh under the Zarah blood line (Matt 1:3) reigns to this day.

Jeremiah 10:16 make the statement of who received his inheritance, **"The portion of Jacob is not like them; for he is the former of all things; and Israel is the rod of his inheritance".** We need to understand that Jacob consisted of the other eleven tribes to include the house of Judah. This **"portion of Jacob is not like them"** is speaking to the house of Israel, Gods birthright tribe of Ephraim and Manasseh as the family firstborn birthright protectors of the Church, under the New Covenant. They were to be different than any of the others, just as the US and GB are today. The house of Judah has always rejected Christ and his Gospel but will be given their chance during Daniel's 70th week during the Tribulation period. A proving factor is recorded in Genesis 49:7 when Jacob gave the inheritance to Simeon and Levi. They were rebuked by Jacob due to their cruelty and were to be divided between Jacob and Israel, **"Cursed be their anger, for it was fierce; and their wrath, for it was cruel; I will divide them in Jacob, and scatter them in Israel."** This verse explains why Simon and Levi as Priests of the house of Israel were scattered throughout the word into almost every nation for the past 2500 years. The name Jacob (reefers to all eleven tribes not including the Birthright tribe of Joseph) and Israel is the other ten tribes as divided in I Kings chapter 11. This verse refers to Judah, Jacob and Israel as three groups of different nations during the last days (Gen 49:1). The birthright tribes of Ephraim and Manasseh, leaders of the ten northern tribes, were given the name Israel in (Gen 48:16) and to be the rod of Gods inheritance to be kings and kingdoms of a company of nations (Gen 17:6, 35:11 and Duet 33:17).

God knew that when he established his laws among the people, the law of blood sacrificing, the temple, his priest, and all the other Moses laws would present a problem when the time came for them to change and except Christ as their Messiah. This is why he sent John the Baptist as a forerunner of Christ to prepare the people. The poor people listened but the Chief Priest and Pharisees along with the wealthy rejected the Messiah as a whole. They could not or would not give up old traditions and their wealthy way of life for hundreds of years. Christ's death on the cross fulfilling the old Laws and traditions was no longer needed (Romans 10:4 and 13:10). Mans salvation now fell under his new covenant of grace (Matt 5:17, Heb 8:8 and Jerm 31:31) to include the world along with Israel and Judah as two separate nations in the last days. The old laws were given to Gods Hebrew people not just to the Jews. When you view this reason as to why the Jews did not accept Christ at his coming, it gives a better understanding and most likely the reason God divided his people. He needed to maintain his system of Old Covenant Laws of sacrifice till Christ came to fulfill his destiny as the Messiah. God knew that if he did not divide his people and remove the mass of his people from the old laws and traditions, none would believe at his coming. He sent the house of Israel, the rod of his inheritance, into the wilderness almost 800 years prior to wait for Christ's Gospel and the Church. The majority of the Jews also settled in Europe Denmark (Jutland) after their captivity losing the Hebrew language and identity just as the house of Israel. Christ sent his disciples to the ten northern tribes of his lost sheep to include the migrated house of Judah/Hebrew so they would be the fruitful nation and platform of his Church to spread worldwide. This fulfills Matthew 10:6, 15:24 and 21:43.

We must go to the Old Testament Scriptures and fine Gods laws on the first fruits and firstborn blessings if we are to understand the correlation with Israel, his Children. Let's start with Exodus 22:29, **"Thou shalt not delay to offer the first of thy ripe fruits, and of thy liquors: the firstborn of thy sons shalt thou give unto me".** The first fruits of the field and the first son were to be given to God. Exodus 13:2 further clarifies the blessing of the firstborn, **"Sanctify unto me all the firstborn, whatsoever openeth the womb among the children of Israel, both of man and of beast: it is mine."** Leviticus 27:26, **"Only the firstling of the beast, which should be the Lord's firstling, no man shall sanctify it; whether it be ox, or sheep: it is the Lord's."** Numbers 3:13, **"Because all the firstborn are mine: for on the day that I smote all the firstborn in the land of Egypt I hallowed unto me all the firstborn in Israel, both man and beast: mine shall they be: I am the Lord."** Genesis 43:33, **"And they sat before him the firstborn according to his birthright, and the youngest according to his youth: and the men marveled one at another."** II Chronicles 21:3, **"but the kingdom gave he to Jehoram; because he was the firstborn."** According to these verses, the firstborn is Holy to God and belongs to him.

God also knew that if he took the firstborn son, it would cause instability within the family unit so he established the tribe of Levi to be his Holy Priest (Num 3:12). This allowed the firstborn son to inherit the responsibility of the family name and fortune with the blessing of the father. The stability of the family unit is the strength of any nation or peoples. Satan knows this and is why he is destroying the family unit of our nation today. With all these verses referring to the Holiness of the firstborn as honored by God, we can better understand why he changed Jacob's name to Israel for it was to be applied to his chosen firstborn son. Whom-ever Jacob chose as the birthright of Israel were to be the pinnacle of all great blessings passed from God to Abraham, Isaac, Jacob and then to Joseph directly to Ephraim and Manasseh. Only they were to be the birthright nation to fulfill the definition of Israel, "he will rule as God" bringing justice and righteousness through Levi to the nations of the world.

The double blessing of the firstborn is mentioned in Deuteronomy 21:17, **"But he shall acknowledge the son of the hated for the firstborn, by giving him a double portion of all that he hath: for he is the beginning of his strength; the right of the firstborn is his."** This verse gives the right of the inheritance of double portion to the firstborn son and with that, the responsibility of maintaining the family unit along with the family name. Even the secular world goes along with this rule. After studding all these verses, it produces a question? If you ask any Christian today which of the twelve sons of the tribes of Israel received the birthright firstborn blessing, most of them would say that Judah (the Jews) received the right. This is incorrect for Gen 48:16 clearly gave the family name to the firstborn birthright blessing to Joseph's two son Ephraim and Manasseh. The main reason is that Christians refuse to study God's Word. Secondly, there is a satanic influence of false teaching creating a Spiritual blindness and a falling away from the truth. These false teachings divert the truth form Gods Covenant People, the house of Israel, generating a blindness of our true identity as a nation.

It is important to understand who received the birthright if we are to comprehend just who the houses of Israel and Judah is today and their division 2700 years ago. This division still exists according to Scripture. The anointed blessing of the firstborn fruit went to Ephraim (Great Britain) and Manasseh (United States of America) in a double role (Gen 48:16&22) along with the responsibility of carrying on the family name, Israel. Refer to fruitful in table one.

Israel's Inheritance the Birthright Blessing

Now that we have covered the birthright law of Moses, let's look into the Scriptures and see who actually received the firstborn birthright double portion inheritance. Genesis chapter 48 and 49 covers the blessings that Jacob (called Israel Gen 32:28) gave his sons and was to take place during the last days or our present time period. Genesis 49:1 makes it very clear when this time period was to take place, **"And Jacob called unto his sons, and said, Gather yourselves together, that I may tell you that which shall befall you in the last days."** Chapter 49 gives the family blessings to all twelve sons as the twelve tribes of Israel to include Joseph.

We need to note that Abraham and Jacob were two of the greatest men in the Bible and chosen by God to play a very important role in his Prophetic plan as families of nations. The unique character about these two men is that God personally changed their names that is a rare occurrence within the Bible and shows their importance. Abram was chosen to be Abraham or the high father of the seed of Gods Chosen people where Jacob's name was to be changed to Israel meaning he will be a Prince to rule, "He will rule as God" controlling Gods earthly Kingdom during the last days.

Let's back up just a little. Joseph, the eleventh son born to Jacob, was actually blessed twice for in Genesis 48:16-22 Jacob called Joseph and his two sons Manasseh and Ephraim into him to be blessed. These blessings were separate from the ones given in chapter 49 to all twelve tribes. This was a special birthright blessing to Ephraim (the second born) and Manasseh (the first born) to receive Jacob's name "Israel", for his name Israel were to be named upon both of the lads, Gen 48:16, **"The angle which redeemed me from all evil, bless the lads; and let my name be named on them, and the name of my fathers Abraham and Isaac; and let them grow into a multitude in the midst of the earth."** It is important to note that all the blessings of greatness and promises of kings and kingdoms to Abraham and Isaac went to the sons of Joseph, Ephraim and Manasseh, as the birthright blessing in Genesis 48. We need to understand that the end time language was to come from the seed of Isaac for Gen 21:12, Rom 9:7 and Heb 11:18 clearly state almost word for word, **"for in Isaac shall thy seed be called"**. Their language was to be after Isaac's sons for in Welch means Saxon as Celtic which is Phoenician of the house of Enoch. The Hebrew language is the basic langue for the Phoenicians, Welch and later English. (Tracing Our Ancestors by Frederic Haberman page 73-76)

There must be no doubt that Ephraim and Manasseh were of Joseph and consisted of two different tribes to perform different prophetic functions. This is indicated in Joshua 14:4, **"For the children of Joseph were two tribes, Manasseh and Ephraim",** and note that Manasseh is mentioned first due to being the firstborn and both brothers play a dual role in the birthright blessings (Gen 48:16). Refer to table two for their prophetic functions and blessing to be a nation (Manasseh) and a company of nations (Ephraim).

When Jacob gave the inheritance blessing to all of his sons in Genesis 49, the blessing to Abraham and Isaac is not mentioned. This indicates that only Ephraim and Manasseh were to multiply as a people to be as the dust of the earth and stars of the sky, to be kings of kingdoms and the other 11 tribes were to be single nations. The blessings that God gave Abrahan, Isaac and Jacob passed through Joseph directly to the two lads of Ephraim and Manasseh and to no other tribe. This blessing did not apply to Judah or the Jews. There is a distinction between the Birthright blessing and the inheritance blessing. The birthright blessing went to Joseph directly to Ephraim and Manasseh in Genesis chapter 48 and the inheritance blessings went to all twelve sons to include Joseph in Genesis chapter 49 by Jacob and Duet 33 by Moses and these blessings indicate they were to be nations in the last days.

When Moses gave Levi their inheritance in Deuteronomy 33:10, it breaks down and groups the nations of Israel in the last days by stating, **"They** (Levi) **shall teach Jacob thy judgments, and Israel thy law,"**. Jacob represents all eleven tribes to include the Hebrew nations of Europe and modern Israel to be taught judgments. Israel was to be separate from the other eleven as the birthright tribes, to teach the law representing Great Britain and the United States (Ephraim and Manasseh). Only they received the name Israel under the birthright to be leader of all the tribes. To be a leader, you have to know the law and this is why God gave them the Gospel, to teach the world. Study the inheritance to Levi for they were given the power of the Lawgiver that authorized them to produce kings within each tribe or nation in the last days.

Genesis 35:9-12 is the key verse. Jacob's name was changed to Israel, therefore, when you apply the Hebrew Primogeniture law, the family name Israel would be passed to the son Jacob selected as the birthright son. Jacob selected Joseph that was directly given to Ephraim and Manasseh by Jacob himself (Gen 48:15-16) and this birthright was not to be changed or reckoned with (I Chorn 5:1-2). This blessing to Ephraim and Manasseh as leader of Israel was to be a company of nations and kings of kingdoms. This is an irrefutable fact by Scripture but our religious system refuses to understand or blinded to the truth. Also refer to table two on the birthright leadership of Ephraim and Manasseh from Moses to King David.

Genesis 35:9-12 and 48:16 transfers the family name to Ephraim and Manasseh and allows us to understand all the other verses that mentions the house of Israel being planted into the wilderness in I Chronicles 17:9-14; Zech 10:6-12; Ezekiel 17:1-24; 20:34-37; 34:13-18, Jeremiah 13:2-15; Hosea 2:14-23 and Micah 5:7-11. The seed of Jacob (Israel) were to be a nation and a company of nations. Jacob's birthright blessing only went to Ephraim and Manasseh. All Scriptures pertaining to planting in the wilderness is tied to Genesis 17:6;

35:9-12 and 48:16, **"And I will make thee exceeding fruitful, and I will make nations of thee, and kings shall come out of thee." "a nation and a company of nations shall be of thee, and kings shall come out of they loins"; "And let them grow into a multitude in the midst of the earth".** These verses clearly state that Israel was to be fruitful (Christian) and divided into one single nation of power and a people that became a multitude of nations throughout the world.

Ephraim and Manasseh as Israel, the inheritance tribes, were to fulfill Jeremiah 51:19-20, **"The portion of Jacob is not like them; for he is the former of all things: and Israel is the rod of his inheritance" "Thou art my battle ax and weapons of war: for with thee will I break in pieces the nations, and with thee will I destroy kingdoms".** According to these verses, Ephraim (UK multiple) and Manasseh (USA single) as the inheritance nations fulfilled Daniel 2:35&44-45 and Matt 21:43-44 as the Stone Kingdom, protecting the faith. These verses describe the same Kingdom being Gods Kingdom taken from the Jewish Chief Priest and Pharisees and given to a fruitful nation (the lost sheep of the house of Israel the birthright tribe). The **"multitude in the midst of the earth"** (wilderness) is the double fruit birthright to Ephraim and Manasseh only. The other eleven tribes were to be single nations within the world and separate to receive the family name of Israel through Ephraim and Manasseh. When God took the Kingdom from Judah, only they were to be without a nation plucked out from Israel (Jerm 12:14-15) due to their curse. The Jewish nation or portion of the Kingdom is withheld till Daniel's 70th week begins as the whole house where Jerusalem lay in rubble for almost 2000 years. The modern nation of Israel is still not of Christ's Kingdom for they still reject Christ as the true Messiah. From the time Jesus rebuked the Chief Priest and Pharisees in Matthew 21:43-45, the Jews of Judah were the only tribe to be without a nation since Christ's death. This was their curse for rejecting Christ as the Messiah and illustrates how the house of Judah is divided to this very day. You can only be a part of Christ's Kingdom if you believe in Christ as the Messiah but the Jew is still a very big part of Gods prophetic plan to be completed in Daniel's 70th week, the seven-year Tribulation Period.

The nations and boundaries of the earth were pre-selected by God himself and ordained to Jacob, the twelve Tribes of Israel. Deuteronomy 32:8-9 states, **"When the Most High divided to the nations their inheritance, when he separated the sons of Adam, he set the bounds of the people according to the number of the children of Israel. For the Lord's portion is his people; Jacob is the lot of his inheritance."** Deuteronomy 32:13 goes on to say, **"He made him ride on the high places of the earth, that he might eat the increase of the field; and he made him to suck honey out of the rock, and oil**

out of the flinty rock;" Compare these verses of the earth's natural recourses to the blessings given to Joseph (Ephraim and Manasseh) in Deuteronomy 33:13-17. Only they received the blessing of the earth's natural recourses. This inheritance did not go to the other sons or tribes of the Children of Israel. Refer to table two for the blessing given to all tribes. Until recent years, Great Britain and the United States dominated most of the earth's natural resources and commerce fulfilling these, Scriptures.

This verse clearly states that God selected the boundaries of the earth for his children of Israel and not just restricted to the Promised Land of Canaan or Jerusalem of Judea of the house of Judah. Judah were to be the root or pleasant plant of his Children. Israel (the ten northern tribes) was to be his vineyard within the world (Isaiah 5:7). These boundaries are reserved for Gods birthright tribe to fulfill the promise to Abraham, Isaac and Jacob, to be a nation and a company of nations, to be kings of kingdoms. God did not want the boundaries of his world to be settled by idol worshiping people but to be set aside for his chosen, to spread his end time Gospel for the salvation of the world. The Jews cannot fit into this scenario for they have rejected Christ.

Through-out the Bible there are instances where the father has the right to give the birthright to the most fitting if the firstborn sins against the family. Here is just a few cases listed in the Scriptures; Cain firstborn of Able ejected from the family due to murder (Gen 4:14); Japheth firstborn to Shem but Shem received the birthright (Gen 9:27); Esau firstborn to Jacob but Esau sold his birthright to Jacob (Gen 25:31); Reuben the first born of Jacob but Joseph received the birthright (I Chron 5:1) and Joseph's two sons to receive the family name and firstborn birthright; Manasseh first born but given to Ephraim due to sin (Gen 48:17-19).

Jacob loved Joseph more than the other brothers and due to this jealously, his brothers threw him into a pit to be later sold into captivity. Because of this sin, the birthright was taken from his brothers and given to Joseph that went directly to Ephraim and Manasseh Genesis 48:16-22. This is to be further confirmed in I Chronicles 5:1-2, **"Now the sons of Reuben the firstborn of Israel, (for he was the firstborn; but, forasmuch as he defiled his father's bed, his birthright was given unto the sons of Joseph the son of Israel: and the genealogy is not to be reckoned after the birthright. For Judah prevailed above his brethren, and of him came the chief ruler; but the birthright was Joseph's,".**

There is another aspect of Jacob blessing Joseph's two sons that we need to understand for Genesis 48:16-22 and I Chronicles 5:1-2 are land mark verses. This is the only event in the Scriptures where the family blessings went to the grandsons and not the elder son. Jacob did not tell the other eleven sons to bring in their sons or Jacob's grandsons to be blessed but only Joseph's two sons. Why? They were the only sons to receive the family birthright name Israel and to receive the great double portion of greatness that God bestowed upon Abraham, Isaac and Jacob. I Chronicles 5:1 sealed the birthright. This is why there is no land in Canaan given to Joseph but to Ephraim and Manasseh that is a direct indication of the birthright to Joseph's two sons. The house of Joseph is mentioned several times in the Scriptures and refers to the birthright of Ephraim and Manasseh as leaders of Israel.

The above verses make an absolute statement by saying that Joseph's two sons were to receive the family name Israel by Hebrew Law and that the genealogy is not to be reckoned after the blessing was given. In other words, this was a message to the other eleven sons that the birthright was sealed and final and there were to be no other reckoning or fighting over the birthright given to Joseph (Ephraim and Manasseh). They clearly received the right. The name Israel was bestowed upon Ephraim and Manasseh and all the other eleven tribes or sons received their right to be called Israel through Ephraim and Manasseh, their leader. This caused a paradox within the nation of Israel and later the division.

We have established that Ephraim and Manasseh of the ten northern tribes received the birthright blessings. Now let's see what the Scriptures say of the blessings to be inherited by Abraham, Isaac and Jacob. Abraham's blessing (Gen 15:18-21, 16:10 and 17:6) were to father a multitude of people and be many nations producing kings. This same blessing was passed to Isaac (Gen 22:17-18) where his seed were to be called Isaac's sons or (Saxon English), and then to Jacob (Gen 28:13-14) to be called Israel (Genesis 32:28). God changed Jacob's name to Israel and Genesis 48:16 passes the name Israel to Joseph's two sons Ephraim and Manasseh, **"and let my name be named on them, and the name of my fathers Abraham and Isaac,"**. The Scriptures are clear that the name Israel went to Ephraim and Manasseh to be called "Isaac's son", Genesis 21:12, **"for in Isaac shall thy seed be called."** Hebrews 11:18, **"That in Isaac shall thy seed be called:"** It should be made clear that Israel were to be their Biblical name where Isaac's Sons or Saxon were to be their earthly name. During their migrating travels they were to leave waymarks to be identified as Hebrew that means traveler.

The term Saxon (Phoenician the house of Enoc) comes from the migrating Hebrew tribes of the Sakai, Sacae, and Sakasuna of the sons of Isaac for

"Saxon" means "Isaac's sons". The Saxons of Europe and England are portions of the ten northern tribes of Ephraim that received the inheritance blessings and their migrations can be traced through ancient and secular history of archeology. Ephriam in Duet 33:17 was given the symbol of the unicorn displayed throughout England today. We can follow the Isaac's sons or the Saxons through the blessing given to Jacob in Genesis 35:11, **"And God said unto him, I am God Almighty: be fruitful and multiply; a nation and a company of nations shall be of thee, and kings shall come out of they loins"**. You cannot apply this verse to the Jews for it does not fit. According to this verse, the Saxons or Isaac's sons will be Kings of a nation and a company of nations. This sure fit the description of the United States as a single nation and the 46 nations under the Kingship of the Common Wealth of Great Britain (the Lion and Unicorn). Genesis 28:14 states that the seed of Jacob would be as the dust of the earth and spread abroad to the west, east, south and north and in thy seed shall all the families of the earth be blessed. You cannot say that this verse pertains to the Jews for it would not be correct. This is a direct correlation to the British Empire where the sun never sets.

Now let's go to the direct blessings to Joseph and his two sons. It starts with the blessings that Jacob gave his two grandsons in Genesis 48:19 which occurred prior to the blessing of all twelve sons. This was the birthright blessing to Ephraim and Manasseh, **"he also shall become a people, and he also shall be great: but truly his younger brother shall be greater than he, and his seed shall become a multitude of nations."** Again, it speaks of Manasseh being one great nation and Ephraim being a multitude of nations. There are no other nations in the history of the world that meets this description other than the United States as a single great power and the British Empire or United Kingdom of Great Britain as the multitude of nations spoken of in this verse as brothers. The next blessing is given when Jacob blessed all twelve sons in order by birth given in Genesis chapter 49. Genesis 49:22 give the blessing to Joseph and it states, **"Joseph is a fruitful bough, even a fruitful bough by a well; whose branches run over the wall."** Verse 26 further states, **"The blessing of thy father have prevailed above the blessings of my progenitors unto the utmost bound of the everlasting hills: they shall be on the head of Joseph, and on the crown of the head of him that was separated from his brethren."**

Verse 22 states that Joseph is a fruitful bough that means they were of Gods covenant of being righteous or God fearing. The Hebrews of the house of Israel departed the land because their branches run over the wall due to captivity and refused to return to Jerusalem as recorded in II Esdras 40-45. Verse 41 states, *"But they took this counsel among themselves, that they would leave the multitude of the heathen, and go forth into a further country, where never mankind dwelt"*. It goes on to say that their inheritance blessing was above their brothers or progenitors to be unto the utmost bound of the hills of the earth or scattered and to be crowned on their heads to be kings as Genesis 35:11 states. They were to be above their brothers unto the utmost bounds of the everlasting hills or earth that means, they were to be masters of the world and corresponds with the British Empire.

Deuteronomy 33:13-17 is even more explicit on Joseph's blessing. Verse 17 states, **"His glory is like the firstling of his bullock, and his horns are like the horns of unicorns with them he shall push the people together to the ends of the earth: and they are the ten thousands of Ephraim, and they are the thousands of Manasseh."** The firstling of his bullock designates the birthright blessing and the horns of the unicorn pushing people together through-out the world indicate their economic and military might worldwide. Again, Ephraim is shown to be multiple and Manasseh to be singular. The Bull and the Unicorn is their national symbols; therefore, the Bull represents the United States and Wall Street's world economic system. Scotland is the only nation in the world that has a Unicorn as one of their national symbols and indicated on most of the 46 national commonwealth seals, flags or ensigns.

After reviewing all of these Scriptures, it is absolutely clear that it cannot be speaking of the Jewish state of Israel. As stated in the segment of King David's throne and Gods promise to always have a man sitting on his throne, only England can fit the description and inheritance of preserving Gods overturned throne (Ezekiel 17:22-24 and 21:25-27). The Isaac sons or Saxons of the English-speaking Christian fruitful nations as described by the above Scriptures can only be the house of Israel (the ten northern tribes of the lost sheep) Ephraim (England) and Manasseh (the United States of America). They were to be leaders of the other eleven tribes or nations of Europe just as the European NATO nation of today. Israel were leaders in ancient days just as they are leaders of the free world today for their birthright gave them the responsibility and authority from God himself. The United States and Great Britain has always been leaders of the free world and cannot be denied. Only they fulfill the birthright promise of leadership of the family and the Scriptures that say his chosen people will be over all nations just as factual history records. It is clear by scripture that the Anglo-Saxon (sons of Isaac) was to rule the world and to be above all people on earth **"above all the nations that are upon the earth"**. (Duet 7:6, 14:2 and 33:17).

Judah's Inheritance

We have covered how the birthright was given to Joseph and his two sons and that Judah was not given the birthright. Of all the twelve sons, Joseph, Levi and Judah were the most righteous and because of this factor they received the greatest of the blessings. Judah, because of the goodness of his heart, received the blessing to rule and maintain the throne as recorded in Genesis 49:8-12. He was the fourth son born to Jacob and his descendants, the Jews, were to make up only 1/12th of the mass of the Hebrew people, God's chosen people. They were not called Jews till II Kings 16:6, approx. two years before the ten northern tribes went into captivity to Assyria. Their purpose was to play a special role in Gods Prophetic plan for his Children of Israel. After studying the Scriptures for the past thirty years and asking the Lord to show me wisdom, God has given me a clear picture of why he divided his people.

When God gave the throne to Judah, he knew the corruptive power it had and the pride and evil that it would produce. He still had to maintain David's throne for Christ to claim at his return. This was Judah's responsibility but God new the forces of power and greed and how it would destroy his people. The Israelite people wanted a king against Gods will but because of his love, he gave them one. Between the power of the throne, the rigged rules of the Old Covenant Laws, the great wealth accumulated over time, the ingrained religious ceremonies and hundreds of years of building powerful intrigues within the nations, God knew that the Jew of Judah would not accept Christ (the Messiah) at his coming. This non-belief created a division within the house of Judah. The whole purpose of Gods plan of salvation was to the world and not just to the small nation of Israel in the Middle East (Ps 48:2). This is why God promised Abraham, Isaac and Jacob great blessings to be kings and kingdoms of many nations, to go into the world and prepare for Christ coming with his Gospel. The key phrase, **"whose branches run over the wall"**, in Gen 49:22, Isaiah 16:8, Eze 36:8-9, Hos 14:6 demonstrate Gods house of Israel branching out into the world after the Assyrian captivity and became his lost sheep in the wilderness Matt 10:5-6 and 15:24 where Jesus personally gave them the responsibility of his Church. Isaiah chapter five explains the role of the house of Judah and the house of Israel. Verse 7 states, **"For the vineyard of the Lord of hosts is the house of Israel, and the men of Judah his pleasant plant"**. In other words, the vineyard is the house of Israel as the Church the birthright tribes, to branch out into the world to spread Christ's Gospel. Judah is his pleasant plant or the tap root in Jerusalem to maintain the promised land in Jerusalem for prophetic fulfillment. This is why God divided his nation of Israel into two separate houses for different prophetic purposes.

God allotted the non-believing Jews 490 years or 70 weeks to fulfill their prophetic Time Table under the Old Covenant. This is why the last week or the 70th week of the Old Covenant is to be fulfilled during the Tribulation Period. The time of Christ or Church age fell between the 69th and 70th week of the Old Covenant. The Messianic Age of the New Covenant and the Old Covenant of Daniel's 70th week cannot overlap so the Church has to be taken prior to the beginning of the 70th week Prophecy. Daniel's 70-week prophecy started when Ezra and Nehemiah (445 BC) rebuilt Solomon's Temple after their captivity to Babylon, as recorded in Daniel 9:24-27. This was the division of the house of Judah. The 40,000 Jews that returned to Jerusalem never accepted Christ as the Messiah where the mass of the Jews that departed into the wilderness with the house of Israel accepted the Gospel. Prophetic time abruptly stopped after 69 weeks or 483 years when Christ entered Jerusalem on the donkey (Matt 21:5) in 30 AD. Christ knew that the Jews would reject him as their Messiah therefore, he stopping the prophetic countdown when entering Jerusalem just prior to his trial and crucifixion. It is this writer's belief that if the Jews would have accepted Christ as their Messiah the prophetic time table would not have stopped and only God knows what the future would have been. At the same time, only God knew that the house of Israel planted in the wilderness waiting for the Messiah would accept him as his lost sheep and would later become his whole Kingdom at the coming of Shiloh (Matt 10:6; 15:24; 21:43). History records how his lost sheep of the house of Israel, Common Wealth of Great Britain and the United States, has preached and spread his Gospel world-wide in the past two thousand years under the New Covenant.

Daniel's 490 year or seventy-week prophecy never pertained to the house of Israel but only to the divided house of Judah (the Jews) due to their disbelief. This is why God has preserved the 70th week or the seven years Tribulation Period for the house of Judah, the orthodox Jew or modern State of Israel in Jerusalem. The Church will be taken away prior to the Tribulation Period and possibly the starting event of this period of wrath for the Anti-Christ cannot come on the scene till the Holy Spirit or Church is taken away (II Thess 2:7). The sealing of the 12,000 from each tribe (Rev 7:5-8), 144,000 total, represents God taking his physical Kingdom into the 7th millennial where each tribe except Dan is represented. The house of Israel during this period of time is Gods selected Holy Hebrew people (the Physical Kingdom) that have been left behind for they accepted Christ during the first part of the Tribulation. This seven-year period are for the Jews to accept their true Messiah and the house of Israel to be punished for breaking Gods covenant and realize their true identity as Hebrew. This period is also allotted for God to bring wrath on the wicked fulfilling prophetic prophecy, therefore, the 70th week Prophecy of the Old Covenant and the New Covenant of the Church cannot overlap. The Church has to be taken prior to the starting of the seven-year Tribulation.

This is one reason the Church is taken away (Raptured) so the Old Covenant Prophecy can be fulfilled for each represent a completely different time period between the Old and New Covenants.

Judah's Curse "The Jews"

This writer would like to be clear on the fact of not being an anti-Semitic. The Jewish people play an important role in Gods prophetic plan as part of his chosen people and should be loved and respected but we also should not be blind to the facts of the Scriptures. Their prophetic role was to produce the Messiah and preserve the throne of David till Christ came to establish his Church (Gen 49:10). They were not included in the birthright but were to maintain the Promised Land till all Prophecy can be fulfilled in the end days.

We must study closely the facts of the Scriptures when regarding Judah "The Jews" as a divided people. God chose Abraham's seed to be his chosen race of people by Covenant, Genesis 17:2-11, which was then passed to Isaac, Gen 17:19-21 and 26:3-4. From these verses, it is very clear that all the earth were to be blessed through Isaac, Isaac Sons or Saxon as English-speaking people. The Jews of Judah are not mentioned at this point and the first time the term Jew is recorded is in II Kings 16:6 (742 BC), approx. 700 years after Israel became a nation when entering Canaan in 1445 BC. Deuteronomy 14:2 narrows God's chosen people down to the twelve tribes of Israel making them a Holy and peculiar people above all the nations on earth. The Tribe of Judah "the Jews" only represent $1/12^{th}$ of God's chosen people of the Hebrews and further divided where only 40,000 out of two million returned to Jerusalem. These 40,000 are the orthodox Jew of today represented by the modern state of Israel where the other two million departed into Europe and the world losing their Hebrew language and identity. Only the 40,000 Jews that returned to Jerusalem after the Babylonian captivity maintained the Hebrew language and then, they had to relearn their own language taught by the Prophet Nehemiah.

Review all the Scriptures presented in the Bible referring to the great blessings of Gods chosen people pertaining to Abraham, Isaac and Jacob. Look at the historical facts pertaining to the non-believing Jewish people from the fall of Jerusalem in 70AD to our present time. Something is very wrong for the Jews were only cursed and rejected by every nation they migrated and certainly not a blessing for they were persecuted and killed. According to recorded history, the Jews never had an army or government of themselves till 1948, but Abraham's blessings were to be a company of nations and to be kings of kingdoms. There is an absolute difference between what we have been taught and what the Scriptures have to say about the Jews.

God's chosen people were to be nations and kings of kingdoms (Gen 17:6 & 35:11); all the families of the earth were to be blessed by his people (Gen 28:14); they were to be Gods battle ax and weapon of war (Jerm 51:20); they were to poses the gates of their enemies (sea ports and trade routes Gen 22:18); they were to be a fruitful bough or nation meaning Christian (Gen 49:22 & Matt 21:43); they were to push the people together to the ends of the earth colonizing (Duet 33:17); they were to be as the dust of the earth and stars of heaven (Gen 22:17). After truthfully and carefully studying these verses, there is no way they can pertain to the Jews of Judah according to accurate recorded history during the past two thousand years.

To further prove this point, let's review a few Scriptures indicating the curse God applied to Judah "the non-believing Jews" of the divided house of Judah, a remnant of the two southern tribes of Judea. This curse was applied due to idol worship, rejecting their Messiah and having him crucified. The proving factor is that they, to this day, reject Christ as the Messiah. We need to make it clear that the house of Israel and divided Judah are two separate peoples when referring to the curse. Zechariah 11:14 makes it simple, **"Then I cut asunder mine other staff, even Bands, that I might break the brotherhood between Judah and Israel."** This clearly breaks the brotherhood between the two houses and when the curse speaks of Jerusalem, it almost always refers to the house of Judah (the Jews). There are no Scriptures rejoining this brotherhood till Ezekiel 37:11&15 is fulfilled. Jeremiah 25:18 makes the statement, **"To whit, Jerusalem, and the cities of Judah, and the kings thereof, and the princes thereof, to make them a desolation, an astonishment, and hissing, and a curse; as it is this day;"**. This curse clearly went directly to the Jews of Jerusalem.

Jeremiah 44:8, **"In that you provoke me unto wrath with the works of your hands, burning incense unto other gods in the land of Egypt, whither ye be gone to dwell, that ye might cut yourselves off, and that ye might be a curse and a reproach among all the nations of the earth?"** This curse is in direct relation to all the non-believing Jews that live in other nations for the term Egypt is a symbol of foreign nations and how the Jew will be cursed and reproached by all nations where they live. Jeremiah 44:12 further states, **"and they shall be an execration, and an astonishment, and a curse, and a reproach."** Jeremiah 44:22, **"and because of the abominations which ye have committed; therefore is your land a desolation, and an astonishment, and a curse, without an inhabitant, as at this day."** The term "without an inhabitant, as at this day" clearly states that they will not have a home or nation in any country, "at this day" means till the end of the age. This is exactly what recorded history tells us about the Jew, for they had no national home till 1948 when Palestine became the modern State of Israel. We also need to note Scriptures that pertain to the house of Israel referring to living in their own peaceful land (Jerm 23:3-8, Eze 34:13, 36:24-26, 37:14) all refer to a new spirit and heart meaning Christian.

Isaiah 65:15, **"And ye shall leave your name for a curse unto my chosen: for the Lord God shall slay thee, and call his servants by another name;".** Isaiah is speaking to the people of Jerusalem which makes this a very interesting verse. If you carefully study this verse it speaks of two different people. He is speaking to the Jews "your name" and will leave there name the Jews as a curse to "my chosen" the house of Israel and will call his servants (the house of Israel) by another name. The Jews have never lost their name in any country they have traveled. The "servants by another name" can only be the house of Israel for the Jews still reject Christ and cannot be his servant.

Isaiah 43:28, **"Therefore I have profaned the princes of the sanctuary, and have given Jacob to the curse, and Israel to reproaches.** In this verse both houses have sinned against God and both are rebuked but Jacob (house of Judah and Benjamin) received a curse and Israel or the house of Israel (birthright tribes to include the 10 northern tribes) was reproached. This verse plainly divides the two houses. Ezekiel also makes it clear on how the Jews of the bloody city (Jerusalem) will be cursed and mocked by all countries, Ezekiel 22:4, **"Thou art become guilty in thy blood that thou hast shed; and hast defiled thyself in thine idols which thou hast made; to draw near, and art come even unto thy years; therefore have I made thee a reproach unto the heathen, and a mocking to all countries."** You can take this verse and apply to modern Israel today in how they are killing thousands of Palestinians in Gaza today. All the above verses plainly states that the Jew was to be cursed, mocked, killed and hissed at by all the nations of the world. When you study the word curse in the Strong's concordance, you will find in most cases, when referring to a nation of people, it is speaking to the Jews of Jerusalem. If we closely study the house of Israel and the house of Judah (the Jews), it is plain to see that the great blessings of wealth to be nations and kingdoms cannot be relevant to the verses pertaining to the curse for the curse only applies to the divided house of Judah (Jews).

Due to the Jews rejecting Christ and having him crucified on the cross, they paid a very dear price. After Christ died on the cross at the hands of the Jews, God still had mercy and gave them 40 years or one generation to repent. They still refused due to pride and blindness. Because of their rejection, God cursed them, destroyed Jerusalem in 70 AD (exactly one generation after his death) and scattered the Jews into the face of the earth to fulfill prophecy. This 40-year generational period corresponds with the 40 years of wandering in the wilderness where God would not allow that generation to enter into the Promised Land of Israel due to the same sin, rejection and idol worship. The Jews became a modern nation in 1948 after 1878 years of destruction and homelessness to fulfill Daniel's 70th week Prophecy (Dan 9:24-37). This will complete the prophecy of the Old Covenant.

Where are Gods promise to David that a man would always sit on his throne for all generations and the Scriptures that pertain to the blessing of greatness to Abraham, Isaac and Jacob to be nations and kingdoms? If you fail to rightly divide the house of Israel (the birthright tribe of Ephraim and Manasseh) and the house of Judah (modern day Israel "the Jews"), then it is impossible to understand the Scriptures of blessing and end time Prophecy!

Both houses of Israel were very sinful and dealt in idol worship. God punished and judged each house in a different manner, for each had a separate role to plan in his prophetic plan. The mass of Gods people was the house of Israel, approx. 13 million Hebrews that included most of the house of Judah for only approx. 40,000 from the house of Judah returned to Jerusalem of Judea. The rest were sifted through the nations of the world and become the whole house of Israel as they accepted Christ's Gospel and his Church, Eze 38:22. Even though God calls his ten northern lost tribes the house of Israel, Judah were included through migration. The house of Israel was given the authority of the throne of David in I Kings 12:19-20 and overturned into the wilderness to Ireland, Scotland and finally to England. Today it bringing righteousness and judgment to the free world just as prophesied as Christ's whole Kingdom under his New Covenant (Isaiah 41:2-3 and 43:1-20).

Thirteen million Hebrews and Jews disappeared into the wilderness to never exist again as a nation according to religious and secular historians. The Scriptures teach differently. God punished the house of Israel first by captivity to Assyria and sifted them into the nations of the world (Amos 9:9). None of the house of Israel returned to Jerusalem or Canaan. God punished them by divorcement in Jerm 3:8, dispersion and name change in Eze 36:19 and Isaiah 45:4. After their period of judgment was complete, he betrothed (bride to be "O virgin of Israel" Jeremiah 31:4&21, Amos 5:2) the house of Israel for they were to be Christ's Bride as a virgin in Hosea 2:19-20 when they received Christ's Gospel in the wilderness, for he knew that they would receive his teachings. They became Gods 5th Kingdom as stated in Daniel 2:35&44-45 and inherited Battle Ax in Jerm 51:20. The house of Israel lost all ties to

Jerusalem and the house of Judah.

On the other hand, God knew that Judah would not accept Christ's Gospel till the time of the end so he cursed them and dispersed Judah into the nations of the world to be mocked and hissed at as recorded in history. The blessings of wealth and to be great nations given to Abraham, Isaac, Jacob and Joseph (Ephraim and Manasseh) did not pertain to the Jews as they were not the birthright tribe and they rejected Christ. Notice that he did not divorce Judah, for that would have nullified the inheritance of King David's throne and the coming of the Messiah. The root of Judah and Jerusalem were revived as a nation in Canaan in 1948 as modern Israel. This was to fulfill their role in Gods prophetic plan preparing for Daniel's 70th week. The house of Judah never lost ties to the land of Jerusalem of Judea, their language or religion indicating a significant difference between the two houses. Understanding the punishment of Judah's curse and Israel's divorcement (betrothal "O virgin of Israel) as two separate nations during the end time is absolutely essential if we are to identify with end time Prophecy and the occurrence of future prophetic catastrophic events.

Chapter 4

Gods Spirit with Man
(Zion "Hebrew", Sion "Greek")

God is a spirit of great power and blinding to the sight of man and cannot be looked upon for he is pure energy. It is extremely hard for man's earthly mind to understand the trinity of how he can be one God of three spiritual entities of the Father, Son and Holy Spirit (the Comforter). He is a power of immeasurable energy that would destroy man simply by being in our presence. For God to associate himself with his creation of man, he had to reduce a part of himself to physically adapt to man's environment, therefore, creating his son as a Savior on the same level as man, making himself man. To further break down and make this process complete, God had to create a Spirit that could interact with man's spirit, to bring him to God and guide him through life. God created humans as a Spiritual being so man could communicate on his level and physically be able to enter Heaven as his creation or child.

When studying the following Scriptures, Matthew 28:19, John 14:26, 15:26, II Corinthians 13:14, and I Peter 1:2, they give the roles of each God Head. God represents the Father that is love where the Son (Christ) establishes obedience, sprinkling of blood for Salvation and grace. The Holy Spirit or Comforter provides sanctification, communication, teaching, learning, remembrance and spirit of truth. When combining these elements, we can see Gods brilliance, power and glory that place man on his level through our spirit when combined with the Comforter. The Holy Spirit or comforter through his son (Christ) brings us to Gods level in a spirit form and we will claim his Kingdom as Christians (believers) when given our heavenly bodies.

He appeared on mount Sinai as a cloud (Exodus 19:16) and while guiding the Israelites through the desert, his spirit appeared as a cloud by day and a pillar of fire by night. God did not directly dwell with man till he chose his people, the children of Israel, and dwelt with them in the Tabernacle behind the veal of the Holy of Holies. When the Tabernacle was being moved, his Spirit went with his people in the Arc of the Covenant. During the colonial years of war when establishing the territory of the land under the leadership of the Judges, the Tabernacle was temporarily placed in Shiloh just north of Jerusalem in the land of Ephraim. Note that Ephraim controlled the Tabernacle in ancient days just as they were given authority to control the Church in modern times, Matt 10:6 and 15:24 as the house of Israel. The Tabernacle and Temple represents Christ's Church and is why Christ is referred to as Shiloh in Genesis 49:10. Hebrews chapter nine refers to the Tabernacle as the Church after establishing his new Covenant of his Gospel in Hebrews chapter eight and Jeremiah chapter 33. David moved the Ark of the Covenant to Jerusalem in approx. 1042 BC from the house of Abinadab (II Sam 6:1-6) and from this time forward, Jerusalem is called Zion. When Solomon built the Great Temple in Jerusalem, God declared this city the capital for his throne and Spirit to reside with his people in Zion (I Kings 8:1). Gods Spirit with man is called Zion, (Ps 9:11) and the whole earth is called Mount Zion in Ps 48:2. According to these Scriptures, Jerusalem is the capital of Zion making the earth habitation of Zion and Jerusalem. This clarifies a lot of Scriptures and shows how the Church and Gods Christians in the end days are Sion in Greek, I Peter 2:2-6. Refer to Zion in table one. When God overturned his throne and Zion traveled and plowed (moved) from the City of Jerusalem, the name Jerusalem went with the throne for it was the Capital of Zion. It would only be fitting that if the throne and Zion was planted in another land, the name Jerusalem would also go with the other elements of his Kingdom as indicated by its dual definition. Isaiah 66:18-20 refers to Jerusalem as a mountain or nation where the people are drawn to her bringing offerings indicating it being the Church of his Christian nations. Isa 66:20 is an excellent example of how people from all over the world came to our harbors seeking freedom of faith and prosperity. This verse is not speaking of the millennial reign.

We know that God created man and his environment from the history of the Scriptures and after a deep study, there is still no complete explanation of the purpose of his creation. God has demonstrated his love for man and his magnificent creation of the universe simply for one reason, the glory of Adam to be in his own image. The God of the universe has not given a complete documented explanation for his creation of the human race, therefore, creating a great mystery. He understands human nature and created it for a reason, simply so man has to believe by faith. Through-out all of his Scriptures and writings of historians, poets, Philosophers, Patriarchs and Prophets, he has not shown man a complete understandable mission statement for his creation. This has created a tremendous question within the minds of man. *Who are we and why are we here?* The Scriptures is our guide as Gods Children but even the Bible does not give a complete understanding of why God created man.

The relationship God has with man is in direct correlation with the association of God and Lucifer (Satan), his most beautiful Arch Angel. It is very important to understand the link between God and Lucifer or Satan, and the evil events that occurred in Heaven that separated them through rebellion. Man plays a large role in the outcome of this confrontation between good and evil and a direct connection of why God allowed Satan to separate man from his creator.

Mans Spirit

Before we can understand Gods prophecies, we must first understand the spiritual connection between God and Spiritual Man. The purpose of this segment is to establish a connection between the two. Just as God is a spirit, he had to create man with that same spirit for us to inherit his kingdom. God created man from the dust of the earth but gave him an eternal spirit that fuels our fleshly shell. Once our corrupt flesh dies the spirit departs our four-dimensional world and enters Gods multi-dimensional spirit kingdom.

It is not clear which came first, Satan's rebellion in heaven or the creation of man for there is a direct connection between the two. It would appear that Satan fell first for God created man with two sides to his nature. One side patterned after Gods good traits of nature and the other after Satan's evilness and rebellion. God created all the creatures in heaven to include the beautiful Arc Angels to serve and obey him. They were not made of flesh or had free will. This did not satisfy God for his creation had no choice but to obey him. He wanted and needed a spiritual creation that would love him by free determination. This is why God created man in his own image. He fashioned man to have a choice, to choose between right and wrong and this is where the forbidden tree with beautiful fruit in the Garden of Eden comes into play. God had to create a dimension of quantum theory that was solid and organic so that man could live in.

The amount of time Adam and Eve spent in the garden before partaking of the forbidden fruit is unknown. This is where Satan played his part in deceiving man and has continued the lie and deceive from the moment, he tempting Adam and Eve in the Garden. God created man to be his sons making him the heir to the throne of David (Rom 8:17 & James 2:5). This is why he created man to have a free spirit to be able to choose between good and evil, God his creator or Satan the deceiver. If man is wise and chooses God and his Righteousness, he will stand beside God and the throne in ruling power for eternity. If man elects to reject God and his Messiah, Jesus Christ, then he will eternally be separated from God in Hell (Matt 10:28 and Rev 19:20, 20:14). Yes, there is a lake of fire and brimstone waiting for those that rejects Christ, whether man believes or not and it was created not for man but for Satan and his demons. If you chose to follow Satan the Devil, then, you also accept Satan's fate to be cast into the lake of fire and brimstone.

There is a Spiritual war raging around us for the souls of mankind and it seems that Satan is winning but we know the Scriptures say differently. I realize this is simple common knowledge but say this to make a point. If we as a nation fail to realize the significance of the Spiritual war occurring around us, the consequences of not fighting the evil forces, we will lose the war. If we fail to fight and defeat the Liberal Socialistic evil forces attacking our nation and Christian way of life, we will be defeated to Satan and his human agents to the One World System. This means individual enslavement into evil where we will also receive the damnation of Satan at his end.

We know there is two Spirits working within the world. The Spirit of God that is the Holy Spirit and the Angelic dominion. The other is Satan with his demonic Spiritual principalities. The porthole or the median into either spirit realm of good or evil is through man's mind, spirit and soul that operate on quantum mechanics or quantum reality. There is a battle to the death raging within the quanta level of dominions around us pitting Gods truth of righteousness against Satan's evil destructive force. It is vital for Christians to understand why God warns us against mind control whether it be drugs, alcohol or mind hypnotic techniques. Satan can only have access to us through our mind so it is critical to not alter our mind with drugs or control techniques, allowing him to enter. This is why Satan has flooded our streets with crack houses, drug dealers, drug stores (Pharmacy) and beer or liquor stores on every corner. The media advertising Physic Networks, Channeling techniques, remote viewing, hypnotics, fortune telling, children's games such as dungeons and dragons and many more mind control methods are medians for Satan to enter and control our minds. Man fails to understand this aspect because he refuses to believe in God and the Scriptures. Many people refuse to believe that Satan exist! Our world is full of mind control and we are not aware of this danger. The battle for our minds rages every day through our TV sets, on line computers, smart phones and all kinds of electronic technologies that effect our daily lives. We must be perceptive of these brain washing methods that has produced a spiritual blindness within our society. This is Satan's plan before he moves in for the kill. If we are in full control of our mind with God given abilities, then we can somewhat control Satan's influence. A person without Christ's Salvation does not have the Holy Spirit to protect them and only has the God given traits of natural man such as honesty, integrity, basic goodness etc. Without the presence of the Holy Spirit within a person soul, they are basically at the mercy of Satan for the earth is his domain or spiritual dominion.

Wake up America to Satan's battle for our minds before it is too late and accept

Christ as your personal savior! He is our only protection against the soon coming apocalyptic prophetic events that will destroy this world and bring Gods WRATH on Godless man.

The natural Spirit of man with-out God

From the creation of the human race there has been forces that man has never been able to understand. Through education, intellectual sophistication, mind probing techniques, drugs, massing huge fortunes with great power and hundreds of other ways, man has still not found his inner self to fill the void that exist within him. There is no doubt that forces and powers exist in this world that cannot be touched or explained. The spirit world reaches out and touches man but in return he cannot touch it directly. Hebrews 11:3 states, **"Through faith we understand that the worlds were framed by the word of God, so that things which are seen were not made of things which do appear."** Our dimensional world was made by the Word of God and does not appear, as they seem. In the writings of Baruch of "The Apocalypse of Baruch", he makes a statement in LI. 8, page 84, **"For they will behold the world which is now invisible to them, and they will behold the time which is now hidden from them."** From these verses, there is a world around us that we as humans cannot see or touch but is waiting for our spirit after physical death.

For man, this is confusing, fascinating and very mysterious. This is the mystery that man has been trying to solve from the beginning of his creation. WHY? What is this force or power? Man has the insatiable nature of wanting to know the unknown. Nature seems to be the most basic idea of man's creation and the key to understanding the universe and its secret is to understand nature itself. The question of man's existence is in the natural order of the universe making nature the unsolved question. What is nature and where did it come from? What is the NATURE of man and why are we here? This is the preverbal question. Without seeking the answer through God, man can only go within himself to find the answer. Physical man only has the power to look for the answers in his environment that surrounds him that is the natural planet, the heavens and the spiritual soul within. The natural spirit of man reaching out for his void within him to be filled with security and happiness but what is the final answer and where does he go to fulfill the answer? The physical man can only go to nature for the answer and the most fascinating source that nature produces is LIGHT.

Man is always looking for answers, but because of his nature, he looks in the wrong place. From the most advanced societies to the deepest darkest continents, man believes in a god but due to his nature and the influence of Satan, he turns to the dark side of Satan's dominion and not to his creator. Man refuses to realize who his creator is, therefore, failing to understand how God placed a space within each man's soul or spirit just for him and gave each individual a choice to accept or reject his spirit. This void can only be filled if we as humans accept Christ as our Savior and God as our almighty creator. If man rejects, he will live a lifetime trying to fill this void with tangible wealth or untenable ideologies and still feel empty. This empty void was created when man was separated from God in the Garden of Eden due to Adam's sin. Because of man's sin, we have to have a mediator even as Christians and that is Christ where only the Messiah can feel the void within us.

To understand the Spirit of man, let's make an analogy. If we enter into a court of law and stand before the judge under the presumption of ignorance or stupidity, the judge will say, "Ignorance of the law is no excuse" and will execute judgment under the letter of the law. The same applies to man in accordance to Gods truth (the Bible). If we go through life accepting the philosophies of man or our own belief in self and reject Christ and the truth of his Word, then God will be just in giving us the sentence of death and separation from him because of our ignorance of his Law. Ignorance of the law by man's standards or Gods righteousness does not provide justification or justice. Mercy cannot apply to ignorance or stupidity just as in a court of Law. God gave Lucifer the choice to love and follow him or to not. Lucifer chose poorly and rebelled against God. When Lucifer the Devil (Satan) becomes ruler of the earth (apotheoses) as recorded in the book of Revelation, he will also give man the choice to accept him (the mark 666) or die. What choice will man make? This will be basically the same choice God gave Lucifer (the Devil) before he rebelled in heaven.

The Spirit world consist of the Spirit of God the Father (Jesus Christ) and Lucifer, the Devil, Satan (the Angle of Light). God's Word explains the war in heaven when Satan rebelled against him and for his sin; the realm of earth was given to him. Lucifer was the most powerful angel and called the angel of light for he was the most beautiful brilliant angel in Heaven, the head Arch Angel. Why would Satan willfully rebel against God knowing that he will die at the end? Simply due to pride just as man's pride divided him form God. Satan believed his own lie that the told Eve in the Garden, "you can also be as God". This is why God hates pride over all sins because it's a powerful destructive force. During the time of Wrath, Satan will not have access to heaven as he does now. He was put in charge of the earth and his rebellion in Heaven happened possibly before God created man.

Why did God create man? This writer believes that God's creation was simply to prove to Lucifer that his love, kindness, mercies, righteousness and purity would prevail over Satan's wickedness, destruction, death, and rebellion. God wanted to create a being that was equal to his righteousness so he created man in his own image and gave him self-choice to be good after God or be evil after Satan. He then gave him a lifetime of being tempted of the pleasures of this world and at the end he has the choice to accept God or Satan. The Creation of man is the proving factor and earth is the battleground. This is why God had to provide a plan of salvation to man by sending a part of himself as their Savior. The final proving factor to Satan is that God's Love will prevail over Satan's evil lies.

There are two spiritual forces that exist in our world today and man cannot see or understand their realm of influence (angelic and demonic). Man feels their presence but these dominions are elusive to him. Understand that God created the heavens and the earth in natural order and set laws of nature in place that all creation observes, even himself. Satan has no power over the laws of Gods dimensions and if he did, he would immediately destroy the earth, Gods creation. Satan is bound by Gods laws of nature just as man. With these laws in place to protect us from Satan, God created his plan of salvation to overcome him and prove that in the end, Satan's plan of rebellion, destruction and death will not prevail.

If we are to understand why there is death and destruction in the world then we must study Satan's kingdom on earth. God did not create death or destruction for it was Satan's creation. The most asked question of God is, "Why does God allow death and destruction if he is so loving and just?" The answer is simple, he gave man free will to choose Satan's evil order of death and destruction or to accept life through Christ. Man chooses to live in darkness that represents death and not the light of his creator that produce life, therefore, death and destruction on earth prevails. We are judged on how we encounter and adapt to Satan's evil world by the way we live our lives.

Mans environment consist of Gods spiritual angelic kingdom of love and justice and Satan's evil demonic dominion of death and destruction that separates man form God. Man is willing to accept the good side but due to his nature, out of ignorance and lack of knowledge refuses to recognize the evil side. Mans nature works to Satan's advantage for it is easy to fall for the lusts and temptations of sinful pleasures of this world believing Lucifer's lie that Satan and sin don't exist verses the stringent law of maintaining God's commandments. If a person doesn't believe that Heven and Hell exist, then why not partake in the pleasures of the world. Christian's today fail to realize the forces of evil in the world due to the lack of knowledge (Hos 4:6). Without the knowledge of God's Word, Satan will attack and destroy. God tells us that his Word is sharper than any two-edged sword and to put on his armor of knowledge, for without them we are defenseless against Satan. This writer has a great desire and burden to WARN this nation of the soon coming destruction and Christian persecution, which will occur if we fail to repent of our sins. We desperately need to arm ourselves with the knowledge of God's Word.

For God to receive the love and adoration that he deserves, he had to give Lucifer his Arch Angle of light and the Angels in Heaven the same choice he gave man, a free will to choose their own destiny. Lucifer and one third of the Angels in Heaven choose to reject God. God's nature is love and righteousness so Satan's nature can only be rebellion, death and destruction opposite to God. DEATH was and is the punishment for rejecting God. If man rejects Christ and God the Father due to Satan's influence, then he will receive the same sentence of Satan's rebellion, DEATH and separation from God (Rev 19:20). This is why God gave man the knowledge and truth of his Word, the Scriptures of his Holy Bible, so we can reject Satan's lies and overcome the ignorance of refusing God and escape the punishment of death. His Law Book, the Word, justifies the punishment of death. If we reject Christ and the Father, our judgment will be by this same Law Book as we stand in Heaven before God.

Reference: (Helmet of Salvation Isaiah 59:17 and Eph 6:17, Spiritual War Eph 6:12 & 6:11, God's Word as Armor Eph 6:17 Rom 13:12, Heb 4:12, II Cor 6:7 I Tim 5:8)

Satan's Kingdom

When God created the universe, he established absolute laws to hold it together. One of these major rules are the three laws of motion, "For every action there is an equal and opposite reaction." When we view the two major forces of good and evil in this world, this law also comes into effect. We have the forces of good and evil working against us just as we have the forces of motion against our bodies. We must understand that for every good thing that happens in this world of God, Satan counter acts with evil in one way or the other.

We know that God has his earthly Kingdom established on this earth through the house of Israel and King David's throne that will never be destroyed. If God has a kingdom, Satan will also try to have a kingdom. At this point of time Satan cannot have his kingdom on earth for the presence of the Holy Spirit through the Church prevents him. II Thessalonians 2:7 states, **"only he who**

now letteth will let, until he be taken out of the way." This verse is speaking of the presence of the Holy Spirit as the preserving salt of the earth and will stay that way till removed. Therefore, Satan cannot establish his kingdom till Gods Spirit is taken away. This is why the Rapture or taking away of Christ's Church has to take place prior to the Anti-Christ taking power in the middle of the Tribulation.

A good example of how Satan imitates God is found in Revelation chapter thirteen. We know the account of how Christ died for our sins and rose from the grave to be in heaven with God till his prophetic plan is complete and then returns to claim his throne in power. Satan tries the same thing for Revelation 13:3 gives the account of how one head of the Anti-Christ is wounded to death and he also resurrects from the dead. This event makes the people of the world wonder after him as being god just as Christ rose from the dead and claims to be God. This is symbolic of how Satan is going to imitate God by resurrecting himself from the dead to establish his Satanic Kingdom on earth.

Satan has not established his kingdom as of this time but according to Scripture, he has power over the kingdoms through his spiritual influence where Satan is called the god of this world (II Cor 4:4). This power is also demonstrated in Matthew 4:8-9 and Luke 4:6 where Satan tempted Christ by trying to give him the kingdoms of the earth if Christ would bow down to him. He is restricted from physically entering our three-dimensional world till Christ's Church is removed (the spiritual house of Israel) and the third gathering is complete with uniting the whole house of Israel (the ones left behind). This is why God divided his kingdom for the house of Judah (the Jews) and the Hebrew's of the house of Israel that is left behind are to fulfill the last part of Gods prophetic plan during the Tribulation Period. They are to fulfill Daniel's 70th week prophecy under the Old Covenant bringing Judah to believe in the true Messiah and the house of Israel to realize that they are Hebrew of Gods lost ten tribes.

Christians represent the Church and must understand the power of Satan along with his earthly influence for we are in great danger. The following is just a few verses that state the power of Satan on our physical earth. John 12:31, 14:30 and 16:11 calls Satan the Prince of the world. He is called a Prince because of his great power but only Christ is King. The Apostle Peter typifies the danger to Christians and to all man, I Peter 5:8, **"Be sober, be vigilant; because your adversary the devil, as a roaring lion, walketh about, seeking whom he may devour:"**. Christians can be destroyed just as well as any man if we allow the Devil to enter by falling away from his Word. This is a very powerful and awakening verse that should bring us reality to Satan's supremacy on this earth. Let's not fool ourselves and believe that because we are Christians, we cannot be influenced by Satan for Matthew 4:3 and II Corinthians 2:11, 11:3, 3:5 says differently.

To close this segment on the power of Satan's dominion of principalities, Rom 8:38, Eph 6:12, Col 1:16 and Titus 3:1 explain how the Devil can be defeated. Satan controls principalities of great power within this world. God calls his Word the sword and his salvation a helmet, **"And take the helmet of salvations, and the sword of the Spirit, which is the word of God"**, Hebrew 4:12, **"For the word of God is quick and powerful and sharper than any two edged sword, piercing even to the dividing asunder of soul and spirit and of the joints and marrow, and is a discerner of the thoughts and intents of the heart."**

If we allow the Satanic Liberal agenda to take away God and his Word (sword) out of our Society, we are defenseless against Satan and his principalities. Satan's goal is to eliminate God's Word (the Holy Bible) and all that deals with his Kingdom, the Church. For him to establish his earthly kingdom he has to destroy the power of God and we can clearly see this taking place in our nation today. Let's not be ignorant God's Word and use it as a sword of power to defend our nation against evil before its too late.

The Dark Ages Satan's time period

(Period of X 7 punishment of the house of Israel and Judah)

We have been taught in school about the history of the Dark Ages or Mid-Evil times. Let us stop and ask our-selves a question as to why God allowed this horrible period of death and destruction to occur upon the human race. The arts and sciences, education, religion and politics were subdued by ignorance and superstition. It was as though Satan had a stronghold on the human race during this period of time. Why would God allow this to happen for such a long period in the light of his promises of greatness to Jacob and the Children of Israel? Israel did not exist as a nation during this period, or did they? It has taken this writer 40 years of study to realize why God allowed the misery, death and destruction by war, disease, and plagues of Black Death to occur during the Dark Ages. This is proof that the house of Israel and the house of Judah did exist during this time for they were both in a period of punishment in accordance to Leviticus 26:18&24 and Deuteronomy 26:19. During the period of this punishment, the burning and destruction of Gods Scripture and literature dealing with his truth occurred worldwide and his true Church persecuted and killed. It would seem that his salt or preserving force had been taken away during this time period. God told both houses of his people that if they would obey his commands, they would be greatly blessed but if they refused to obey his commands they would be doubly punished.

The American College Dictionary places the Dark Ages as time in history from about 476AD to 1000AD. The same dictionary gives the term for the middle-Ages as follows, "The time in European history between classical antiquity and the Italian Renaissance (from the late 5th century to about 1350AD); sometimes restricted to the later part of the period (after 1100); sometimes extended to 1450 or 1500AD". Keep in mind that this is man's definition and not Gods.

The normal period of punishment was 360 years or one Hebrew year for each day of the year. In this case it was seven times punishment due to the sin God hated more than any-thing in this world, IDOL WORSHOP. As the Bible tells us, they refused to heed his warning so God sent both houses into captivity, the house of Israel starting with the captivity of Manasseh and the northern part in approx. 740BC and ending with Ephraim in 720BC to the Assyrians. The house of Judah went into captivity in 586 BC to the Babylonians. Due to their idol worship, God multiplied their punishment by seven, 360 years times 7 equals 2520 years of punishment for each house.

God's children, the Hebrews of the house of Israel and the house of Judah, are the center of his world. To prove this point lets look at Genesis 12:3, **"And I will bless them that bless thee, and curse him that curseth thee: and in thee shall all families of the earth be blessed."** Genesis 28:14, **"And thy seed shall be as the dust of the earth, and thou shalt spread abroad to the west, and to the east, and to the north, and to the south: and in thee and in thy seed shall all the families of the earth be blessed."** Deuteronomy 33:17, **"His glory is like the firstling of his bullock, and his horns are like the horns of unicorns, with them he shall push the people together to the ends of the earth: and they are the ten thousands of Ephraim and they are the thousands of Manasseh."** From studying these verses, it is clear that the nations of the world will be blessed only through the nations of Israel. According to Genesis 28:14, Israel was to spread to all corners of the world, west, east, north and to the south for their multitude was to be as the dust of the earth. Deuteronomy 33:17, is even more clear on the identity of these nations. It was to be his birthright tribes of Ephraim and Manasseh that the world was to receive their blessing as the symbol of the Bull and Unicorn. The Bull is the symbol of Wall Street of New York City that feeds the world economically and technologically, the United States of America. The Unicorn is one of the national symbols of almost all the 46 nations of the Common Wealth of Great Britain mainly Scotland. These verses are saying that the world will be blessed through the United States (Manasseh) and the Common Wealth of Great Britain (Ephraim), the Bull and Unicorn. Study these two words in the Scriptures to get a clear picture of their meaning.

Let's get to the point of why God did not bless the nations of the world during the Dark Ages. From the verses above, it is clear, if God did not exalt his nations of Israel the world will not be blessed either. The last nation of Israel to go into captivity was Judah in 586BC and only a remnant of 40,000 out of two million returned to Jerusalem after the captivity to Babylon that means they were still under the 2520 years of punishment. The majority of Jews were sifted through the nations of the world. Only a remnant returned to Jerusalem for they were to fulfill the prophecy of Christ coming as the Messiah. Judah went into captivity in 586BC so add 2520 years and you will get approx. when their punishment was complete and that was 1934. This is the period of time that the Jews went through the Holocaust in Germany and due to this horrific event; the Jewish nation was formed in 1948 fulfilling the Christ's parable in Matt 24:32. Their blessing began after their punishment was complete by becoming a nation and to fulfill prophecy.

The house of Israel starting with Manasseh (USA) in the northern section of Israel went into captivity in approx. 740 and completed in 720 BC with Ephraim (UK) as the southern tribes. Add 2520 years to 720 BC and you get 1800 AD. This is about the time Great Britain (Ephraim) exploded with their colonies worldwide forming the 46 nations of the Common Wealth of Great Britain. Add 2520 years to the time Manasseh was taken captive, 740 BC, and you have 1780, approx. the time the United States became a nation. The Dark ages occurred approx. from the time Jerusalem fell in 70AD till the time of the printing press with the first book to be printed, the Holy Bible, in 1455 AD. Keep in mind that the Americas were discovered in 1492. During the period of the dark ages, both the house of Israel and the house of Judah were under their period of punishment and God's blessing had been taken from them, therefore, the world was not being blessed. This allowed Satan to create death and destruction through-out the world with very little opposition from God. This is also the time period of the Roman Empire that was Godless, ruthless and destructive to any God-fearing nation or people. It is almost as if the Roman Empire was Satan's tool during this time and it took the righteousness of Gods nation, England, to break away from the stranglehold of the Roman Catholic Church. The same blessing will be taken away from the world when God takes his Church and his wrath begins during the seven-year Tribulation of the end days.

Isaiah 8:22 explain darkness over the earth that matches the period of the

Dark Ages almost exactly, **"And they shall look unto the earth; and behold trouble and darkness, dimness of anguish; and they shall be driven to darkness."** This verse is not speaking of the Tribulation Period for if you study the chapter before and after this verse, it refers to the wickedness of the 10 northern tribes and their punishment. Jeremiah also speaks of a time period that was dreadful for Gods people in the wilderness and could very well be speaking of the Dark Ages when the Roman Catholic Church killed millions of Christians in the name of Rome, **"Oh that my head were waters, and mine eyes a fountain of tears, that I might weep day and night for the slain of the daughter of my people! Oh that I had in the wilderness a lodging place of wayfaring men; that I might leave my people, and go from them! For they are all adulterers, an assembly of treacherous men."** The words "wayfaring men" is the key for in Hebrew it means a Hebrew traveler, Gods people. See the word wayfaring in table one. During this period, Satan had very little opposition from God and tried to destroy not only the Druid and Christian faith but also the Christian nations of Europe at the same time performing his punishment of their rebellion. Satan thought he had destroyed Jerusalem during the German holocaust and the Hebrew faith through Judaism but that also failed for its rebirth took place in 1948. Rome tried their best to destroy England by invading in 55-54 BC and again in 43-410AD but failed. Its as if God used this period of time to prove to Satan that he could not destroy his Kingdom on earth. Christ made the statement in Matthew 16:18, **"That thou art Peter, and upon this rock I will build my church; and the gates of hell shall not prevail against it."** The rock is Christ that is the Church, Zion/Sion, God's earthly spiritual kingdom of Israel as his Spirit with man. This verse is clear that Satan or man cannot destroy Christ's Church.

Satan realized that he could not destroy Christ's Church so he joined it through the Roman Catholics Religion. It is not this writer's intent to upset the Catholic Religion but simply stating historical facts. The Roman Church dominated the religions of the world during ancient times by blocking access to the Bible in Latin keeping it from the common people. Wycliffe, an English Scholar, began translating the first Bible into English in 1380 and completed by William Tyndale, "The Pentateuch" in 1530. Ancient and present-day historians would have us believe that the Roman Catholic Church was God's chosen Church and they were then and now the worlds dominating religious force. The pagan Romans tried their best to destroy the Apostolic Church from the time Christ died in 30AD till Constantine became the first Christian Emperor of Rome in 306AD. The first Catholic Pope of Rome was established in 610AD. Even after Rome became Christian, they persecuted the Protestants of England and Ireland and any one that did not conform to the Roman Catholic Religion. This hatred and war still linger in Ireland to this day. Christ did not establish a denomination by name but local Churches independent of each other. The

Roman Catholic Church became a great denomination controlled by a Pope and began to kill and destroy any people or religion that did not conform to their belief system. This included Gods original local independent New Testament Apostolic Church. The Roman Church killed millions of Christians in the name of God and has been documented very well by John Foxe in his book, "Foxe's Christian Martyrs of the World". During this dark age of the Roman dominance of Europe and the subjugation of the fundamental Apostolic Church, thousands of true Christians were persecuted and killed in the name of Rome by their self-proclaimed authority to be the head of Gods Church. This is the darkest and most destructive period in the history of man, the absence of Gods blessings to his house of Israel. One of the ancient names of the Saxons was Cimmerians/Cymri that means "those in darkness" in Latin indicating a period of punishment without Gods direction. The name Cimmerians relates to the Hebrew word "kimriyr" #3650 meaning eclipse or blackness.

The Roman Catholic Church during the dark ages destroyed literary works, Bibles, and records of history that did not meet their desired state of conquest. Therefore, the Romans dominated the world along with their historical view of literary history. Mr. Frederick Haberman makes a statement in his book "Tracing Our Ancestors",

"Once our 'broad-minded" critics admit the existence of British civilization before the Romans and British descent from the Hebrew-Phoenicians and other eastern Aryan tribes, the whole artificial structure of our evolution from primates collapses like a cardboard house and some of our theology also. Every evidence is on our side, and only a rigidly enforced program of keeping the reading public in ignorance uphold, this pre-Roman British (Savage Story)". (p. 107)

"There is a voluminous literature in existence which indicates that up to the end of the Eighteenth Century the scholars of Britain knew that their people descended from the seagoing Hebrew-Phoenicians and from the Anglo-Saxons, who came from the shores of the Summerland on the Black Sea. But since the beginning of the Nineteenth Century the trend of thought of British and Continental scholars has been permeated by an attitude of critical skepticism towards their descent and toward Scripture." (p. 110)

We as Christians need to understand that there are Satanic forces that do not want the truth to be told and even God told Daniel in 12:9, **"for the words are closed up and sealed till the time of the end."** His command was repeated in Daniel 12:4, **"O Daniel, shut up the words, and seal the book, even to**

the time of the end". The sealing of Daniel's secret was emphasized twice. God inspired his writing of the books of Prophecies to be written in mystery, symbols, parables and the truth, to not be revealed till the time of the end that is our present day. A part of the sealing of God's Word was the fact that the Roman Church sealed it in Latin and away from the common people till Gods Birthright tribe (Ephraim) translated his Word into a common language of English and released to the world that created reformation.

This author believes that the United States and Great Britain is Gods lost sheep house of Israel (the blessing of the world) and the truth of Daniel's secret that God said would be revealed at the time of the end. As Mr. Haberman mentions above, the English-speaking people of the world is in a state of skepticism and denial of our true history of heritage to fulfill Gods prophetic plan for his Children. Even Hosea 2:23 states that God knew where his people were but they did not realize their heritage of Hebrew descent of the house of Israel. Hosea pertains to end time Prophecy of our present time period.

The significance of the Dark Ages indicates the duality of the prophetic warning of ancient times verses the end times of today. The Dark Ages or Mid-evil times separated the ancient period of blessings to Israel and Judah and the last day blessing due to their national disobedience and completion of their 2520 years punishment. This indicates that the great birthright blessing to Ephraim and Manasseh (the house of Israel, GB and USA) would occur after the Dark Ages and during the Church age of the end time. The world has truly been blessed through the greatness of the British and American influence through-out the world during the past five hundred years fulfilling the birthright blessings promised in the Bible verses listed above.

The Scripture that says, **"And ye shall know the truth, and the truth shall make you free",** is very true (John 8:32). God's Word (the Bible) is truth and when we use its power through prayer, we can be free physically, mentally and spiritually. There is historical proof of this fact if we simply review history in the proper perspective.

We have covered the 2520-year punishment of both the house of Israel and Judah which extended through the period of the dark ages where there were no blessings given. During this period of time, Satan knew that as long as he could keep God's Word locked within the Hebrew, Latin and Greek language and under the total control of the Roman Church, the mass of the people would not know the truth of his Word. This allowed for only the Church Clergy and leaders of the Roman Catholic Church to control the ancient Scriptures for even the wealthy and influential were refused full access. They either killed or burned any person or writings, whether poetry or literature pertaining to Gods truth. Satan had full control and thought he could destroy God's Word under a false religion of humanistic rituals.

The power of Gods truth lies within the printing press invented in 1455 in which the Roman Church tried to band. They knew the destructive power in regard to their purposes of dominating and controlling the Scriptures. God's Word is Truth and sharper than any two-edged sword and Satan knows God's Holy Bible is like body armor to a Christian. Keep in mind that around 1455 time was approaching the end of the 2520-year punishment of Gods people and he began to prepare for the great blessing that were promised to Abraham, Isaac, Jacob and Joseph (Ephraim and Manasseh). They were to be great nations (Genesis 35:11). Let's keep in mind that the Hebrew meaning of Abraham means colonizer to be father of multitudes and was the branch that ran over the wall to push people together to the ends of the world and to dominate the worlds leadership as promised in Genesis 49:22, Deuteronomy 7:6 and 33:17. Abraham's seed were to be a multitude of nations as promised which is a key in understanding end time Prophecy.

The proof of the power of God's Word is demonstrated in the Reformation that took place around the 16th century establishing the Protestant Church within England. The Reformation was nothing more than the struggle for religious rights which opened man's eyes to their God given rights. The Reformation actually began when Wycliffe translated the Holy Scriptures into English in 1384AD and King Edward III began to break away from the power of the Roman Church due to the enlightenment of the newly translated Scriptures. At this point, we need to keep in mind of Jeremiah 51:20 and Daniel 2:35&44-45 of how God has used his Chosen People to be his Battle Ax and the 5th Kingdom that has destroyed evil nations as the salt of his earth, the house of Israel, his fruitful nation. This demonstrates how God needed a strong nation to protect his Chosen People and the Church. It took the authority of the Throne of England (King David's throne) to defy the power and domination that the Roman Church had on Britain and Europe. The truth and power of Gods Scriptures gave physical, spiritual and mental freedom to England and the world when presented and open to the common people. This is proof that England and the United States is the house of Israel for God's Word says that the Kingdom would be given to a fruitful (Christian) nation in Matthew 21:43. The only nation that translated God's Word under the authority of the government and King gave it to the common people for salvation and evangelized the world is England through the Authorized King James Version of the Holy Scriptures. Later, the United States as England brother evangelized the Word with this

English Translation. There were other Christian nations of Europe that also established Christian colonies but basically, they fall under the authority of the Crown of England which is King David's throne planted by Jeremiah.

The struggle for the Reformation has led to our present day Democratic and Republican system of governance, "under God we trust", guided by his laws of Christian moral and ethical values as stated on our currency and coinage. These Christian nations are the British Empire and the United States of America. As long as Gods truth was locked-up under the control of the Roman Church, the world was in ignorance and non-prosperous. The truth of God's Word has produced two of the greatest nations ever in history of the world, the United Kingdom of Great Britain (Ephraim the Unicorn) and the United States of America (Manasseh the Bull) fulfilling Gods promise to Abraham, Isaac, Jacob and Joseph (Ephraim and Manasseh) to be kings of kingdoms.

How can anyone refute the history and facts of the dominance of our present Republic representing the free world based on religious freedom of Gods principles founded on the English translation of the King James 1611 Bible produced by Wycliffe and his followers. The English-speaking people of the birthright of Ephraim, the Anglo-Saxon (Isaac's sons), were to dominate the world just as prophesied by translating God's Word into a common language, the Hebrew/Phoenician/Welch and English translation of ancient Scripture.

Chapter 5

The House of Judah verses The House of Israel

his writer has studied Bible prophecy for the past five decades and read hundreds of books on the subject but it has always been a mystery. There has never been a true understanding in my studies till realizing the division of the house of Israel and the house of Judah that exist in end time prophecy. Fundamental Churches all teach that modern day Israel is the Old Testament house of Israel and that the house of Israel and the house of Judah are the same. This segment is going to try to prove by the Scriptures, the truth of who Israel really is and what the Church should be teaching Christians concerning end time prophecy.

Pastors teach that modern day Israel represents all twelve tribes of Israel of the Old Testament and the lost 10 tribes were absorbed into the surrounding nations and have no national ID in modern day but is presently part of Israel. Woe to the pastors that are leading their flocks astray and not teaching the truth. Jeremiah chapter twenty-three not only pertains to ancient times but also to our present end time falling away of the Church. We fall under the same warnings Jeremiah predicted. The Scriptures indicate differently than what we are being taught and there are a few questions that need to be answered to understand Prophecy.

To comprehend the Bible, you have to begin by knowing the following: who wrote the book you are reading, to whom the book was written, and when and where the book was written (WHO, WHAT, WHEN AND WHERE). If you understand these basics then you can begin to understand prophecy. We must believe in the absolute truth of the Bible. The next thing you have to understand is, who is Israel? Israel was divided into two houses in I Kings chapter eleven and twelve by the Prophet Ahijah, so the time frame is very important to understand. The brotherhood between Israel and Judah was broken in Zechariah 11:14, **"Then I cut asunder mine other staff, even Bands, that I might break the brotherhood between Judah and Israel."** This brotherhood between the house of Judah and the house of Israel is not restored till the gathering of the bones in Ezekiel chapter 37. To further complicate things, each tribe was divided into separate nations in I Kings 11 when Ahijah split Jeroboam's garment into twelve pieces representing nations, for II Kings 19:17 calls the ten northern tribes nations when they went into captivity to Assyria. Deuteronomy 32:8-9 also calls Israel nations when he divided their inheritance. Isaiah 7:17 calls Ephraim the house of Israel when they were divided from Judah, so when the Bible speaks of the house of Israel it is referring to Ephraim and Manasseh as the Birthright tribes and leaders.

Through-out the Scriptures, the Bible speaks of Israel in many different names which represents different time frames. We must study each name of Israel in proper context if we are to understand prophecy. Names such as: Israel, the house of Israel, the Children of Israel, Judah, the house of Judah, house of Jacob, house of Joseph, Ephraim, and Manasseh and many more. The Scriptures even speak of the mountain of Esau and Edom. In the Old Testament prophetic books, you have to understand to whom the Prophets are talking about, **When, Where** and to **Whom**.

Names of the Children of Israel

<u>Israel</u>: Hebrew meaning an inherited name of God to all Christians "he will rule as God". Remember, the Scriptures state that Christians will be Priests, Kings and Queens ruling with God in Rev 1:6. Genesis 35:9-12 changed Jacob's name to Israel which was the beginning of Gods earthly kingdom and his Chosen People. Who ever received the name Israel were to receive the great blessing given to Abraham, Isaac and Jacob, to be many great nations dominating the earth and were to rule the earth as King, Queens and Priest (Gen 17:6, 22:17-18, 26:4, 28:14, 32:28, 35:11, 48:19, Rev 1:6). Jacob passed his God given name Israel "he will rule as God" to Joseph in Genesis 48:15-16 and then directly to Ephraim and Manasseh. The other eleven sons of Jacob received the name Israel only through Joseph or Ephraim and Manasseh for they were to be leader of the family name (Gen 48:16 and I Cron 5:1-2). Each tribe is considered a separate nation after the division in I Kings chapter eleven (II Kings 19:17) to be different nations during the end days (Gen 49:1). The tribes of Israel were to be individual nations but the birthright tribe of Joseph (Ephraim and Manasseh), were to be one single great nation (Manasseh) and a company of nations (Ephraim), fulfilling the promise to Abraham, Isaac, Jacob, Joseph and then to his birthright sons to be called Israel. They were to separate from the other eleven tribes, and in certain context, they are called the house of Ephraim, the house of Israel, Lebanon, Sharon, Gilead, Carmel and Bashan.

God promised that a multitude of people, nations, and kings would come out of Jacob, Gen 35:11, **be fruitful and multiply; a nation** (Manasseh USA) **and a company of nations** (Ephriam GB) **shall come out of thee, and kings shall come out of they loins** (European Monarch)". The birthright and the family name of Israel went to Ephraim and Manasseh and not to the other tribes but they were also to be kings. The covenant and Birthright went with the house of Israel (Gen 17:2). The covenant spoken of in Gen 17:7 was the Old Covenant of the Law to be changed to the New Covenant of the Church as recorded in Jerm 31:31 and Heb 8:8. The house of Israel or Ephraim as the birthright tribes was in charge of keeping and protecting the Covenant (Gods Battle Ax Jerm 51:20). Whenever you see the name Israel, you must look at what context the writer is speaking to understand to whom he is talking. It is taught that Israel is only one little country in the Middle East and it did not exist as a Jewish nation for almost 2500 years. If this was true, who and where are the multitude of nations and kings as promised?

Children of Israel: When speaking of the Children of Israel the Bible refers to all twelve tribes as the complete nation or Kingdom (Num. 34:2 Act 9:15). This encompasses all Christians (the Church) under the New Covenant of his divided house (Jerm 31:31 and Heb 8:8).

House of Israel: Inherited the definition of "he will rule as God" through the birthright sons of Joseph. The house of Israel was to be the rulers of the free world as Gods battle ax and Church during the last days as outlined in the blessings to Abraham, Isaac, Jacob and then to Joseph and his two sons Ephraim and Manasseh. All twelve tribes in Exodus 19:3-6 was established at Mt. Sinai as Gods People as a whole nation till I Kings when the Prophet Ahijah divided King Solomon's kingdom. At this time the house of Israel became the ten northern tribes of Ephraim and Manasseh, Reuben, Simeon, Zebulun, Issachar, Dan, Gad, part of Levi, Asher and Naphtali. They were given the mass of the Kingdom in I Kings and were destined to receive the complete Kingdom when Jesus took the portion form Judah in Matthew 21:43. This completed the overturn (Eze 21:25-27), the travailing of Zion (Isa 66:8), the plowing of Jerusalem (Jerm 26:18) and the plucking of Judah (Jerm 12:14) that represent the Kingdom being moved from Jerusalem to a peaceful resting place in the wilderness as a nation spoken of in Isa 18. Because of their sins, the house of Israel went into captivity to Assyria and lost their ID as a nation and language (Isaiah 65:15, 56:5, 28:1-11) to fulfill their punishment and to receive their great blessing to be kings of kingdoms and multitude of nations in the last days as recorded by Scripture.

The Hebrew meaning of Israel is very fascinating and an important key to understanding end time Prophecy. Its definition explains the mission of the house of Israel as the birthright tribe given the responsibility to rule as God till Christ comes to claim his throne in power. It represents the Master (Jesus) that departed into a far country where the husbandman (Temple/Church) waits for his return. The definition of Israel in Hebrew means, "he will rule as God" is a very important commission and explains a lot of misunderstood verses. The word "he" is referring to the birthright tribe called Israel given to Ephraim and Manasseh, giving them the responsibility to fulfill the verses that state that the families and nations of the world would be blessed through them. They were to be political and economic world leaders just as the Hebrew Phoenicians, the Hebrew ancestors of the Common Wealth nations of Great Britain and the United States. This also explains why he divided his kingdom into the branches that ran over the wall as the house of Israel which became the Christian fruitful nations to spread his end time Gospel as being a fruitful vineyard (Gen 40:10). The Jews of Judah were to be the root of his vineyard to maintain the homeland of Jerusalem to fulfill Prophecy. The house of Israel is his Battle Ax (Jerm 51:20) under the overturned throne taken from the non-believing Jew (Matt 21:43) to be the salt of the earth bringing judgment and righteousness to the world (Jerm 33:14-17) under the New Covenant of the Church.

The house of Israel is an essential part of the Church for their mission is to be its caretaker as the political and military arm, the battle-ax just as the whole kingdom of Israel in King David and Solomon's day. A great army was needed to protect Gods People and Temple in ancient times. If God did not have a strong military (Battle Ax) within his Kingdom, Satan would have destroyed it thousands of years ago. This same principal of needing a Battle Ax or protector of the Church exist today. The British and American Army, Gods Battle Ax has been the world police force for the past two hundred years, protecting Gods Church or his Kingdom. The Church is the people of the world that accepts Christ and his Gospel and could never have survived the tyrannical assault and destructive power from the Roman army and Catholic Church. Napoleon, Hitler and Communism tried, and so far, failed. Without the political and military power of the English Throne and Christian America, Satan would have destroyed the Church during the Dark Ages. We are the Christian nations fulfilling the prophecy of Jeremiah 51:20 as being Gods battle ax and the 5th kingdom mentioned in Dan 2:35&44-45 and Matt 21:43-44.

The only nations in recorded history to claim to be the protector of the Christian faith is the throne of England declared by decree in 156AD by the English Crown and the United States Supreme Court with a ruling of nine to zero on

29 February 1892, claiming our nation to be Christian.

The following verses refer to the lost sheep of the house of Israel being scattered into the wilderness to become fruitful and Gods Christian nations promised to his inheritance tribe of Ephraim and Manasseh, in Jeremiah 50:6&17; Ezekiel 34:5-31 (planted in their own land, not the promised land of Canaan). This nation is referred to in Matt 21:43; 10:6; 15:24; John 7:35; and Romans 1:14. The term barbarian, were referred to by the Romans as foreigners from Britain where the sun sets in the West. John 7:35 refers to, (unto the dispersed); Romans 11:5 (Remnant & election); James 1:1 (twelve tribes which are scattered abroad); Peter 1:1-2 (to the strangers scattered). Colossians 3:11 speak of the Greek, Jews, circumcised, Barbarians, Scythians and the free or bond to all be in Christ. Paul knew that the Greeks, Barbarians (Britons) and the Scythians were of the Hebrew stock.

God had two different plans for his people. Israel was to be divided into the house of Israel planted in the wilderness, which is the main body of his people. The house of Judah was to maintain the throne and Jerusalem for the coming of the Messiah. God removed the name of Hebrew and religion as Israelites from the house of Israel and scattered them into the wilderness to populate the earth. They were to prepare for the Gospel, his lost sheep waiting for the shepherd and the teachings (see the meaning of Jerusalem) of Christ to spread it through-out the world. Their mission was to receive the Kingdom, the overturned throne of David by Jeremiah when Zion (Jerusalem) was plucked, plowed and traveled. God moved his Kingdom from Jerusalem. The terms travailed (moved or traveled) and plowed means that all the elements of Gods Kingdom was moved. This includes the name Jerusalem/Israel/Throne/Temple that went with his Kingdom as the duel meaning listed in chapter three. Jerusalem was to be a teacher and instructor of his Gospel as his Christian English-speaking people of today using the translated version of the King James Bible, Gods authorized Word.

The house of Judah was to be the two southern tribes, Judah, Benjamin and part of Levi with the capital in Jerusalem. God used them to maintain the Law and Judaism for the lineage of Jesus to fulfill the prophecy. Israel will be united as a whole nation in Daniel's 70th week, Daniel 9:24-27, and Ezekiel 37. It is important to understand that in the prophecy books when speaking to only one or the other, it is not speaking as a whole nation but only to tribes or as a single nation. The tribes or nations were divided and significant to understand the time frame and context of the Biblical writer speaking. If we fail to apply the who, what, when and where scenario when reading the Scriptures, we will not understand the prophetic picture. Scripture can switch from present time in one verse and the next verse can switch to future time or vice versa. We must always keep this in mind while studying the Scriptures.

The Brotherhood between Judah and Israel was broken (Zech 11:14) and will remain broken as Hebrew/Jew till the end of the Church age (New Covenant) and the beginning of Daniel's 70th week (completions of the Old Covenant) during the Tribulation Period. The Bible speaks of Samaria being the capital of the ten northern tribes and list their names in the last days as Lebanon, Gilead, Carmel, Sharon and Bashan. The birthright went to Ephraim and Manasseh, leaders of the 10 northern tribes of the house of Israel in I Chronicles 5:1-2. The 70th week period of wrath is exclusively for the Jews and the unbelievers of Gods physical kingdom that were left behind. God will use the Tribulation Period to unite his whole earthly kingdom to prepare for his coming in power evangelizing the world by using the two Prophet Witnesses and the sealed 144,000 Hebrews in the absents of the Church.

House of Judah: (Judah in Hebrew meaning **"celebrated"**) Only the two southern tribes. The divided house of Judah the Jews never through history lost their language or ID. They always attempted to keep the Sabbath and the Law, I Kings 11:28-43, 12:21. The Jew is a person of the faith Judaism, the Tribe of Judah or Jew. If the name Jew is so important to God, why is it that the term Jew is not mentioned in the Bible till II Kings 16:6 (into the first one third of the Old Testament) and even then, the Jews of Jerusalem are fighting Assyria and the King of Israel, the ten northern tribes. This is an absolute indication that the house of Judah (the Jews) and the house of Israel (the ten northern tribes) are two separate nations even to this day. Judah was not blessed but cursed due to their non-belief in Christ (Jerm 25:18; 44:8-12&22; 49:13&15; 42:18; Isa 65:15). If you study these verses, it is clear that the Jew could not have received the birthright blessings due to Gods curse and matches the actual history of the Jewish people down through historical times of their persecution and deportation from almost every nation. Even a few of the early American Colonies outlawed Judaism at their beginning.

Joseph or the house of Joseph: (Joseph Hebrew meaning **"future of"**) Joseph was the 11th born son of Jacob, one of the twelve tribes of Israel. His two sons were Manasseh (1st born) and Ephraim by an Egyptian wife (Gen 48:16-22). The term "future of" means the house of Joseph (Ephraim and Manasseh) were to be the future of Israel through the birthright blessing from Jacob. In Gen 48:22, God gave Joseph and his sons the lion's share of all the birthright blessings over the twelve tribes of Israel to become Kings and great nations, to be the **Stone of Israel** (the leader Gen 49:24, Duet 33:16-17; I Chron 5:3). His sons were to become the future of the world planted in the wilderness and inherit the Hebrew name of Israel (future of the world to rule as God) and to spread Gods end time Gospel as the house of Israel.

Manasseh: (Hebrew meaning **"causing to forget"**) first son of Joseph. He sinned against the family so he lost his birthright inheritance to his brother Ephraim blessed in a dual role (Gen 48:16-22). Genesis 48:19, **"he also shall become a people, and he also shall be great: but truly his younger brother shall be greater than he, and his seed shall become a multitude of nations."** Manasseh was the first tribe to go into captivity commanded by Tiglath-Pileser III to Assyrians in 740BC. He is spoken of in a singular form and to be one single great nation of people to be identified through Bashan, Gilead, Carmel and the symbol of the Bull (the United States).

Ephraim: (Hebrew meaning **"double fruit"**) second son of Joseph received the lion share of blessings in Gen 48:19, **"but truly his younger brother shall be greater than he (Ephraim), and his seed shall become a multitude of nations."** Ephraim and Manasseh were to be separate individual tribes and to be leaders of the ten lost tribes. They went into captivity to the Assyrians in 721-719 BC which ended their kingship in Israel. Ephraim is spoken of in plural form, to be great nations and kingdoms due to his birthright double blessing and to be a commonwealth of nations. Ephraim received the double portion of birthright blessing to be many nations and can be identified through the term Lebanon, Sharon and the symbol of the unicorn (Common Wealth of Great Britain, 46 nations).

Jacob or the house of Jacob: (in Hebrew means **Supplanter**) Identifies all twelve tribes prior to Jacob's name change to Israel (Gen 32:28). In some cases, the name Jacob includes Judah as the subject in accordance to context. It can be a mystery of how God speaks of his Children for in some cases when he speaks of Jacob, it refers to Judah and in other cases to all twelve tribes. When either the house of Jacob is mentioned or just Jacob and the term house of Israel is spoken in the same sentence or paragraph as two different peoples, then Jacob is being referred to as the house of Judah which is Judah and Benjamin. Otherwise, the house of Jacob is all twelve tribes prior to Jacob being called Israel or only the other eleven tribes that did not receive the birthright. We must realize that the name Israel went only to Ephraim and Manasseh in Genesis 48:16, therefore, when the Old Testament speaks of the house of Jacob, it is referring to the other eleven tribes to not include Joseph for his two sons were called Israel the birthright tribes.

When Jacob's name was changed to Israel, from that moment all twelve tribes were called the whole house of Israel till the division in I Kings chapter 11. After the division, God spoke of each house differently. He called the ten northern tribes given to Jeroboam the Ephrathite of Joseph, his kingdom of the house of Israel. This is the first stage of the complete Kingdom being taken from the Jews due to disbelief in the coming of the Messiah (Matt 21:43). From that point of time, he called Judah and Benjamin the house of Judah. Israel is now referred to as two different houses (families) through-out the rest of the Old and New Testaments. They are spoken of as two separate nations and peoples till the whole house of Israel is brought back together in Ezekiel chapter 37. The gathering takes place during the Church age prior to the period of wrath marking the completion of the Church at the beginning of the Tribulation Period. This begins Daniel's 70th week to fulfill the prophecy of the Jew due to disbelief in the true Messiah that is the divided house of Judah (Dan 9:24-27). Daniel's 70th week prophecy does not apply to the house of Israel, the ten northern tribes which became the Christian fruitful nations of the world for they did not reject Christ's Gospel but became his Battle-ax to spread his end time Gospel. Only the portion of the house of Israel that are none believers (again rejecting Christ) will fulfill Ezekiel's Prophecy of the gathering of the dried bones of the whole house of Israel in Ezekiel chapter 37. We must correctly separate the two houses of Israel in the above context or we cannot understand Bible Prophecy. The different names of Israel play separate prophetic roles in fulfillment of the Scriptures.

Zion or Mount Zion: (Zion Hebrew or Sion in Greek mean **"as a permanent capital, a mountain of Jerusalem"**) The city of Jerusalem (King David's Throne) II Samuel 5:7, Psalms 87:2. The word Zion or Sion is a very difficult word to understand for it is referred to in so many different ways. After reviewing Gods Word from the beginning to the end, this writer comes to the conclusion that Zion is no more than Gods Spirit with man and its original Capital was Jerusalem (I Kings 8:1). Zion is not mentioned in the Bible till I Samuel 5:7 where Zion reefers to Jerusalem. Zion is always connected to the Tabernacle and Temple of the Holy of Holies during ancient days that were in Jerusalem and Gods Spirit dwelling within man during the last days. Isaiah 66:1 says that heaven is his throne and the earth his footstool and he is asking where is his place of rest with man (Zion the Temple and Sion the Church). Christians fail to realize that God came to save the world and the Tabernacle and Temple was his resting place for the world, not just to the Hebrew and Jewish people.

The Jews in Jerusalem were Gods caretakers of his Temple by being his chosen people just as God chose the house of Israel to carry on and protect his

Church in the last days. Psalms 48:2 states, **"the joy of the whole earth, is mount Zion,"**. We know that by studying the word mountain means nation or nations and this verse clearly indicated that Zion is Gods joy of the nations of the whole earth. Isaiah 66:7-8 makes the statement that Zion travailed which means pain by birth and says that it produced a man child which was the Messiah (Christ), **"Before she travailed, she brought forth; before her pain came, she was delivered of a man child", "for as soon as Zion travailed, she brought forth her children."** The word travailed in this verse can mean child birth or to travel by walking, horse or ship. There is no doubt by this verse that Christ and his established Church is Zion/Sion for it states that as soon as Zion travailed, she brought forth her children of the Church through the salvation of birth of Christ's Gospel. To prove this fact we need to go to I Peter 2:4-8 where he calls Christians, the Church, Sion, **"To whom coming, as unto a living stone," "He also, as lively stones, are built up a spiritual house," "Wherefore also it is contained in the scripture, Behold, I lay in Sion a chief corner stone, elect, precious: and he that believeth on him shall not be confounded."** Jesus Christ all through the Bible is referred to as a STONE and these verses clearly declare Christ as being Zion or Sion, the living stone making his spiritual house his Church. Zion, Gods Spirit, resides with the world through his Chosen People in Jerusalem during ancient days. Sion is Greek and represents Christ's Spirit through his Church overseen and protected by his earthly kingdom, the house of Israel during end times.

Isaiah stated that Zion travailed and Jeremiah mentions in Jerm 26:18 that Zion would be plowed, **"Thus saith the Lord of host: Zion shall be plowed like a field, and Jerusalem shall become heaps, and the mountain of the house as the high places of a forest."** The Hebrew word plowed in this verse means, a singer, harp, player as being festive by playing music. This verse indicates that Zion and Jerusalem were to be plowed and Jerusalem to become heaps or destroyed. In other words, Zion was to be moved when Jerusalem fell to Babylon so where did it go? Zion and Jerusalem are Gods capital, so if one moved, both had to move along with their name. Study Jerm 1:10 for his commission was to protect King Zedekiah's two daughters and through their bloodline was to overturn King David's throne to another land (Eze 17:22-24 & 20:34-47 and 21:25-27) to be plowed as a happy musical singing nation. The throne was overturned to the house of Israel in the wilderness, a safe resting place moving all three elements of Gods Kingdom.

God's kingdom on earth consisted of the throne, the lawgiver, his divided Hebrew people and Zion or Sion as the Temple representing the Church in the last days. The throne was taken away to be preserved for the end times and given to the house of Israel to fulfill Jeremiah 33:17, II Samuel 7:12-17 and

Ezekiel 17:22-24. Where did the capital of Israel go for Jerusalem did not exit as a capital of the Israelite people from 70 to 1948AD. God had to preserve the promise of King David's throne and to be pure during all generations for Christ to accept the inheritance of the throne in Luke 1:32-33. Each generation has to be pure in genealogy for Christ to set upon David's Throne in Rev 4:1-2. The Bible speaks of Zion (Isa 40:9, Joel 2:1&17) as his Holy People, the mountains or nations of Israel, his Battle Ax of the house of Israel.

History of Israel's Captivity

In approx. 960BC (II Sam 2:1-10), King David's house became the house of Judah and at that time were all 12 tribes. King Solomon sin caused the Prophet Ahijah to divided the nation and set Jeroboam over the northern 10 tribes. Keep in mind that Jeroboam was not of King David's royal bloodline but from the tribe of Ephraim (I Kings 11:28-43; 12:19-24). When God split Israel into two houses, I Kings 11:30-37, the house of Judah became the two southern tribes of <u>Judah</u>, <u>Benjamin</u> and part of the Tribe of <u>Levi</u>. The house of Israel became the 10 northern tribes. The house of Joseph in I Kings 11:26&28 is <u>Ephraim and Manasseh</u> the blessed leaders of Israel in the last days (Gen 49:1).

The term Jew comes from the name of the tribe of Judah and Israel were never called Jews. II Kings 16:6 is the first time the word Jew is referred to in the Bible and the reason Jeroboam changed the laws and Sabbath, to keep the ten northern tribes from reverting back to Judaism. He was afraid he would lose his throne back to Jerusalem and is why all the Kings of the house of Israel maintained the Baal worship for they were afraid the people would return to Judaism and reunite under the throne of Judah in Jerusalem. Due to the changes Jeroboam made in traditional religious laws, the northern tribes never returned to the Jewish orthodox Religion but turned to idol worship that brought Gods wrath and captivity. When God divided his Kingdom, he gave the northern Kingdom to Jeroboam for the house of Joseph (Ephraim and Manasseh) to rule. Ephraim was to always maintain the throne just as Judah in the south. Due to their sin and Baal worship, there were a continuous power struggle for the throne between the other tribes causing disruption, death and destruction. This greatly displeased God and eventually sent them into captivity as a max punishment for 2520 years. Refer to table two for details on the line of kings. Israel had a total of 19 Kings that ruled from Samaria, Capital of Israel, separate from Jerusalem and all their leaders were evil. They did not keep Gods commandments and paid the price for disobedience by being taken captive to Assyria.

The house of Israel, 10 northern tribes, because of their wickedness, Assyria took them into captivity in approx. 745 to 717BC and they never became a nation again according to present day teaching. II Kings 10:32-33 records the beginning of Israel's fall in the north along with the small country of Phoenicia located along the northern coastal border of Israel. Beth-Sak was the Phoenician name for "The house of Isaac which was the old house of Enoch" (Amos 7:16-17). In 745 the Assyria General Tiglath-Pileser took the tribes of Asher, Zebulun, Issachar, and Gad into captivity according to II King 15:29. Gilead and Manasseh (Bashon) were taken due to being the most northern tribes that bordered on Assyria. In 720 BC, King Shalmaneser of Assyria placed a siege on Samaria, the capital, and it fell in 717 to Sargon II, King Shalmaneser successor (II King 17:5-6 and 18:11). To this day the house of Israel (the 10 northern tribes) and the house of Judah are two separate nations of peoples. These Scripture describe the house of Israel being the Phoenician, Bashan, Gilead, Sharon, Lebanon and Carmel being the northern territory of Ephraim and Manasseh as the lost sheep of the house of Israel. On the title cover of this book, these names identify these ancient names to be Great Britain and America as brothers. They were scattered into the wilderness becoming the English-speaking people of Ireland, Scotland and England waiting for Christ's Gospel in Matt 10:6, 15:24, Acts 10:36 and Eze 5:1-5 to become Christ's Church.

Keep in mind that according to Genesis 48:16-22, 49:22-24 and Deuteronomy 32:8-9, Joseph and his two sons Ephraim and Manasseh, as the ancient names listed above, were to receive the birthright blessings to always be the leader of Israel to include the end times. Their blessings were to become wealthy Kings of all these countries and to be great nations because they received the lion share of the blessings from Jacob that was called Israel. Jeroboam, the first King of Israel, came from the tribe of Ephraim and dominated Israel's leadership. Ephraim received the overall Birthright blessing to be kingdoms and nations and Manasseh the firstborn blessing, therefore, Manasseh received more landmass than any of the other tribes. The birthright blessing from Jacob is the only blessing recorded in the Bible where it was given in a dual role to two grandsons at the same time.

To understand Bible prophecy, you have to realize time frames of events. For example, the book of Ezekiel was written in approx. 595BC and according to Ezekiel 2:3 it was written to the Children of Israel, a rebellious nation that disappeared 122 years after the capitol of Samaria fell as the capitol of ten northern tribes. They still exist as a whole people or nation according to the prophetic Prophets for they wrote their books to not only Judah but to the house of Israel after their captivities. Understand, they went into captivity starting as early as 745 in the north and ended in approx. 717BC in the south. Ezekiel wrote his prophetic book in approx. 595, 122 years after the captivity and Jeremiah was written in 626BC approx. 88 years after captivity and both called the house of Israel a nation. They knew that the house of Israel still existed as a people after they disappeared into captivity. Through all the Old Testament books of prophecy, Israel, Judah and Ephraim are mentioned as three different nations or houses as in Hosea 5:5. Zechariah was also written in approx. 520 BC and in chapter 9:10-13, Ephraim's dominion was to be, **"and his dominion shall be from sea even to sea, and from the river even to the ends of the earth"**. The date of when these books were written is taken from the Thompson chain reference Bible and is approximate.

This dominion from "sea even to sea" and "from the river even to the ends of the earth" is the British Empire and America during the last days. How can present day pastors of Churches not see and understand that present day Israel is the Old Testament Judah which is the Jews and were not called the house of Israel. Matthew 21:43 states that the kingdom (duty of the husbandman Temple/Church) will be taken from Judah and given to a nation that will bring forth fruits which is the Church and modern-day countries that is serving Christ as the Church. This can only be the Christian nations of the United States and Great Britain or the English-speaking nations, the only nations as a whole that identify as Christian nations. Present day Israel cannot be whole, all twelve tribes, till the Church age is over as the Rapture takes place and the 144,000 sealed (Rev 7:5-8). That means, present day Israel is the house of Judah, rejected the Messiah, where the Kingdom was taken from them in Matthew 21:43 and given to the lost sheep of the house of Israel (Mat 10:6) representing the nations bringing forth the fruits thereof (Christian). According to Scripture, the third gathering is not complete at this point and will not be till the joining of the sticks in Ezekiel 37:17. If present day Israel is the Old Testament house of Judah, then who is the present-day house of Israel? It has got to be the United States as the Bull and the Common Wealth of Great Britain (46 Nations) as the Unicorn in Duet 33:17. These are the only two world-class nations on earth to ever claim themselves to be Christian by government decree.

This writer has listened to famous television prophetic commentators that do not see the division of Israel and call the Jews, God's Chosen People. The Jew is a part of his Chosen People but only represent 1/12, so where are the rest of his people? They cannot see the division of Israel as being separated into the Hebrew Israelites of the house of Israel and the Jews, the house of Judah. We must separate the two and without understanding this aspect, we will never realize who we are as a nation. The Jewish Religion is very nefarious and riddled with occult beliefs. God/Christ is not happy with this and that is why he curses the Jews to include the rejection of Christ as their Messiah. To be a part of Christ's Kingdom, you have to believe in him as the Messiah. How about the Islam God Allah for its definition is stunning for it means CURSE. The Hebrew word "curse" in Isa 24:6 saying **"There hath the <u>curse</u> devoured the earth"** and Jerm 29:18, **"to be a <u>curse</u> and astonishment"**. According to the Strong's Concordance in ref#423 means, "alah", an imprecation, cure, cursing, execration, oath, swearing, 422, "alah" prime root; to adjure usually in a bad sense, imprecate, curse or swearing. We know that the Muslim name for there one and only god is "Allah" and the Arabic name is Al-Iah. According to the Hebrew definition and the verses listed above, "alah" or Allah is a Muslim curse to the world. This writer is simply quoting definitions and it is up to the reader to research and determine for yourself the truth of this subject.

This is the reason God divided his kingdom, to separate his elect, the birthright tribes from Judaism and sent them into the wilderness to wait for the Gospel. God knew that if they remained under Judaism or the old Hebrew religion that fell under the law, they would never accept Christ as the Messiah and his new Gospel. God gave forty years or one generation of warning to the Jews, from his death to the date Jerusalem was burned in 70AD by the Romans. This again demonstrates Gods mercy for he gave them approx. forty years to repent and accept Christ as their Messiah before he implemented his curse upon the Jewish people.

The English Language

The oldest and greatest Monarch left today is the Throne of England, the old Common Wealth of Great Britain that has played the greatest role of any nation in spreading Christ's Gospel in a common language. Over the years, may countries have tried to over throw the small Island nation of England with the intent of destroying the last great European Monarch. Rome tried in 55 and 54BC and again in 43AD and failure. France with Napoleon and Germanys Hitler attempted, and all failed. Communism has tried during modern times and also has failed thus far, but they have their foot in the door in both England and America and on the verge of total control. God has preserved his throne and earthly kingdom of his Church through England till Christ claims his seat on the throne and no principality or nation shall destroy his Church or Kingdom till his taking away occurs. It is this Authors belief that the Church will be taken prior to the total takeover by Communism as the NWO, world Government. The rise of evil empires such as Fascism, Nazism and Communism has destroyed all the European Monarchs in preparation for the New World Order except for England, the Throne of King David.

There are several ways we can prove who Gods end time Chosen People are with simple logic and deduction with Scripture simply by identifying their language. We must first realize that these verses are not speaking to the Jews of the house of Judah for they never lost their name or language of Hebrew and represent the modern state of Israel. The following Scriptures only refer to the house of Israel and identifies who they are in the last days of our present time period. Genesis 17:6, 22:17-18, 28:14, 35:11 and 48:19 clearly says that the seed of Abraham, Isaac, Jacob and Joseph, which were past directly to Ephraim and Manasseh, were to be many nations and kingdoms. We are now at the end of the age so we need to identify Ephraim and Manasseh, the birthright tribes as modern nations.

It would only be logical that God would give his nations and company of nations under a king, one common language. Genesis 22:17-18 says that his people will multiply as the stars of heaven and sands of the seashore and possess the gate of his enemies as one people being many nations. The phrase "possess the gate of his enemies" is very important for it means that his people will control all major sea ports and trade routes of the world making him a world power over other nations. Note, the English language has controlled both ancient and modern world commerce and aviation (FAA). Every commercial airline pilot in the world has to speak English to all control towers through the world. This can be further proven in Genesis 28:14 when God said his people will spread abroad to the west, east, north and the south and in his seed shall all the families of the earth be blessed. He was to spread throughout the earth. This verse can be verified in Deuteronomy 33:17 where the bull and unicorn (US and GB) of Ephraim and Manasseh push the people together to the ends of the earth. God's Chosen People were to be world travelers by ship, air and control international trade by possessing the gates of his enemies, world seaports and airports. Today, the bull represents world trade through Wall Street in New York City that controls most of the wealth of the world. The unicorn is on the seals and emblems on most of the 46 nations of the Common Wealth of Great Britain. The British and Americans are brothers (Ephraim and Manasseh) bound together by a common language of English derived from the Semitic Hebrew/Phoenician/Welch dialect that controls the world.

Before we identify Modern English, we need to cover a little history of where our language came from. The oldest language written by man is the Sumerian dialect of Mesopotamia in the first period of Archaic around 3100 BC. Very little is known about this language. It is important to note that the first Phoenician dynasty of King Barat also appeared around 3100 BC making Sumerian and Phoenician almost the same age. The descendants of King Barat, were the settlers of ancient Britain and is where the term Briton is derived which means covenant man in Hebrew. The first King of the Western Isles of Briton was Brutus of Troy about 1100 BC where he gave the name of his own race, Barat, B'r't, Brit, Prat, Prut or Prydi, the B and P being interchangeable in the Phoenician, as well as the unwritten vowels. ("Tracing our Ancestors" by Haberman, p. 35-36).

We can further trace the descendants of King Barat to Hebrew by the meaning of British derived from Barat. The Hebrew meaning of "British" means Covenant man and can be traced from Brutus to Troy and from Troy to Greece where Zarah's descendants of Calcol and Dara settled prior to the exodus from Egypt. The descendants of Calcol and Dara amalgamated with the Phoenicians for they are related by Tribal blood.

At this point, I would like to make an important note. If the oldest known language was Sumerian, then that must have been the language at the time of Babel that was the one world language of Noah. The event of the Tower of Babel took place just after the deluge or flood that would make the world language from Noah and his family. We know that God confounded the languages of the people to speak different dialects to divide them so they all went into the world (Gen 11:7-8). To identify God's Chosen People, we must look to the language that he gave his people and to write his Holy Word. Noah had three sons, Shem, Ham and Japheth and by Mosaic Law, Shem received the Birthright, therefore Shem's language was to be God's chosen language and people. It is this writer's belief that the birthright son of Noah, Shem, was to carry on the birthright family name under God's chosen language and people to be Semite and later Israel under the language of Hebrew/English of the sons of Isaac or Saxon. It would also be logical that the language of Noah and Shim was not changed or confounded by God, therefore, his Semitic language were the original speech of Noah. This can be seen by comparing other languages that are similar to the North Semitic Alphabet and is of the Phoenician (Canaanites) and Hebrew languages. The language of Abraham was Hebrew in which the Old Testament was written.

This brings up an important point that we need to consider. From my study of history, there is no direct link between the origin of the Phoenicians and Hebrew people but their language and religion of Druidism is very similar. Why? My idea is that they separated to the north and settled the upper coastal region called Phoenicia to escape the very evil times of Nimrod prior to and during the time of the Tower of Babylon. According to the book of Jasher, the houses of Noah, Shem, Aphaxad and Eber (Hebrew) followed the "ways" of God and a portion of their people departed the land settling Phoenicia. This would explain several factors such as the Phoenicians being ship builders and sea going people for it came from the technology given by Noah. It would also explain why the Phoenician and Hebrew Israelite languages and religions are so similar, Judaism and Druidism. The Phoenicians heaped up stones and monuments (Waymarks Jerm 31:21) and were wayfaring men just as their brothers the Hebrew in which God Commanded during their travels.

The early Phoenicians were of the house of Enoch through Noah and Shem, to settle in the northern coast of Canaan. It is important to know that Noah lived to be 950 years, Shim 600 years and Eber 464 years making them the last generations to live extremely old. The Book of Jasher explains why and how the house of Noah, Shem and Eber taught the "ways" of God to Abraham, Isaac and Jacob for the purpose of preparing the way for the coming of the Messiah and establishing Christ's Church in the wilderness. The selected birthright tribe were to be many nations with power given the responsibility in spreading the end time Gospel to the world. We can see how God passed his knowledge and righteousness as salvation to the world first through Noah, Shem and Eber as the "ways of God" that became "Druid" taught to Abraham, Isaac and Jacob to teach the birthright tribes that were to become Israel. We know that "Druidism" was subverted by Satan just as Judaism and Christianity has been subdued by Satan. The house of Israel lead by Ephraim and Manasseh was to inherit the birthright and be great nations of Kingdoms settling the world preaching Christ's Gospel. They were to spread Christ's end time Gospel taught by the house of Noah, Shem and Eber and later by Christ himself, "The Ways of God" as the Gospel.

We can see how the Word of God was passed from generation to generation first called "the ways of the Lord" taught by Noah, Shem and Eber to Abraham, Isaac and Jacob. God's Word then evolved into the Old Covenant of blood sacrifice from Moses to Jacob and the Children of Israel for Salvation to prepare the way for the Messiah and his Church through the established nations of Israel by the power of the throne of David. Christ then gave the authority to spread his Gospel to the lost sheep of the house of Israel Matt 10:6 and 15:24 to settle into the world teaching. The last and final stage of the "ways of the Lord" was established in 1455 AD with the creation of the printing press and the printing of Gods ancient Word "his ways" into what we now call the Hold Scriptures, the Bible. God then gave his Word in written form to the single nation of his firstborn birthright tribe of Manasseh (United States) to complete spreading his end time Gospel creating schools and Universities to teach the common man his Word, "his ways". People from all over the world come to American and British Universities for technical education to run the world. We can now see how the Phoenicians amalgamated with Judaism and Christianity to pave the way for God's Word, "his ways" to be taught to the world through his birthright tribes of the house of Israel.

The New Encyclopedia Britannica volume 9 gives the Phoenician definition as "Kenaani (Akkadian; Kinahna) or "Canaanites". The Hebrew secondary meaning of Phoenicia is merchant to arrive around 3000 BC and thought to have come from the Persian Gulf region. They settled in the upper costal portion of Canaan. This would explain several important aspects. The Semitic family that settled to the north in the coastal region of Tyre and Sidon that became the Phoenician race of people, took with them the ship building technology passed down from Noah. This would also explain why the Phoenician and Hebrew language is very similar and both races of people became great ship builders and mariners of the world throughout time. The Hebrew and Phoenician language were to be his chosen language of Gallic (Stammering) to become English where the King James Bible was written and controlled by his Chosen People for one reason, to spread Christ's end time Gospel. The Hebrew word stammering is found in Isa 28:11 and 33:19 with the meaning, #3934 "laeg", a buffoon, *a foreigner*, mocker, *stammering*. The word "laeg" means Danish in Old English in ancient Greek means "of the people". These two verses are speaking to Zion/Sion in Isa 33:14 as the house of Israel and Isa 33:9 called them Lebanon, Sharon, Bashan and Carmel being in the wilderness where they have a stammering (foreigner) language that became Gallic English of the French Gaul's. The old Covenant were taught by the house of Noah, Shem and Eber to Abraham, Isaac and Jacob but Christ's New Covenant was to be taught by the house of Israel as his birthright tribe to all the world with stammering lips as a foreigner. They became the fruitful nation that Jesus took from the Jews and became the Kingdom of the house of Israel under the birthright of Ephraim and Manasseh in Matt 21:43 as a stammering people of the Gallic language just as the above Scripture state. Gallic means French Gaul's. The Saxon's invaded Britain in approx. 410AD and called Anglo (Angle) Saxon after they converted to Christian. They migrated from North Germany and South Scandinavia and settled into Wales as Welsh Britain's speaking Brittonic a Celtic language that developed into Welsh, Cornish, Briton and came from the Phoenician language.

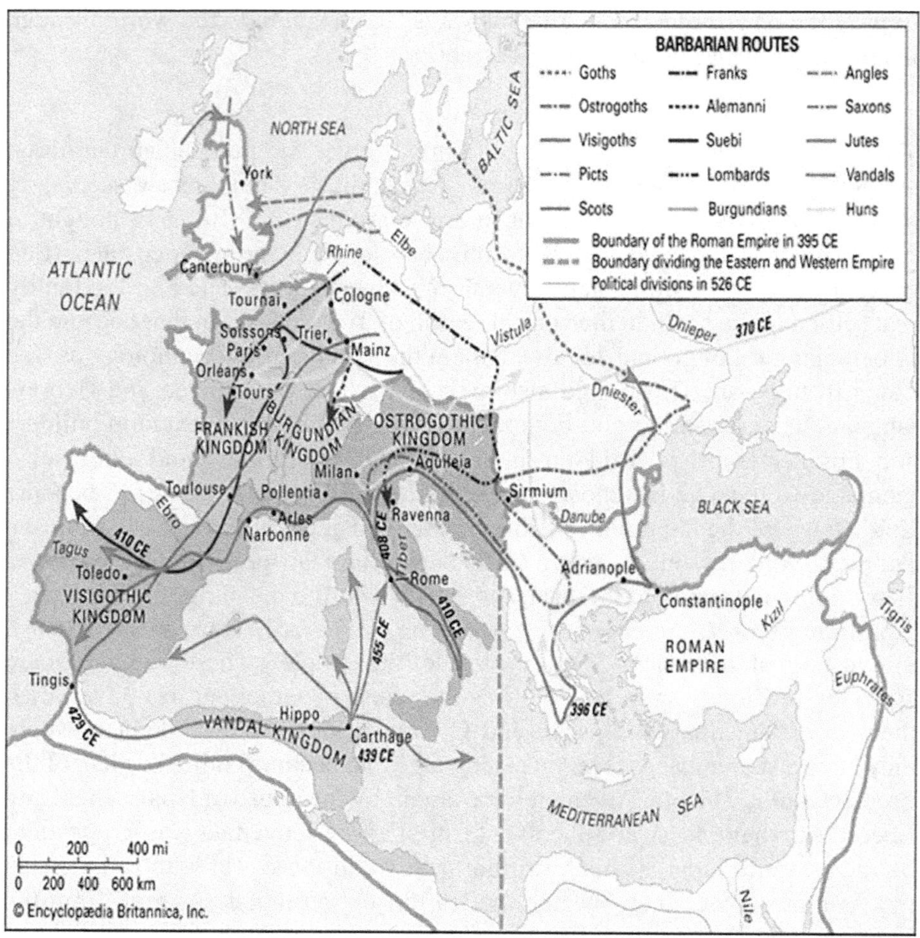

This in itself proves that we are God's Chosen People of the house of Israel where God took away the old Hebrew language and national identity as Israelite, Isaiah 28:11, 45:4, 56:5, 62:2, 65:15 and Deuteronomy 32:26 and gave us a new language of English (Stammering lips means Gallic). The Hebrew term for stammering means, stammering lips, another tongue, an everlasting name and a new name by the mouth of the Lord. This indicates that his new identity and language would be Christian (Acts 11:26) where his people would be called by this name. With a simple and common deduction of who spread Christianity over the past five hundred years, fulfills Matthew 21:43 as being Gods fruitful nations where Jesus sent his lost sheep to preach his Gospel. Matthew 10:6 (lost sheep of the house of Israel) can only be the English brothers of the United States and England bound under a common language as Christians, Gods new name.

To further prove this fact, lets study the word Covenant. In Hebrew, the word covenant spells "Brit" and man spells "ish" spelling Man or <u>Covenant of Man</u> which is the tribe of Ephraim (birthright tribe) that became the greatest commonwealth of nations in the history of the world settled by the ancient Phoenician Hebrew tribes of King Barat and Brutus. Ephraim is listed as, "and a company of nations", in Genesis 35:11. They received the greater blessing from Jacob and to this day Great Britain has a Lion and Unicorn as their national symbols. His brother Manasseh, the United States is called, "a nation", also in Genesis 35:11 which has become the single greatest nation on the face of the earth with the symbols of the Eagle, olive branch (peace) and bundle of arrows (power) on our national seals. The bull is a symbol of our nation's financial wealth based on Wall Street in New York City. The symbols of the olive branch and bundle of arrows represent peace and weapons of war as the Christian nation of the United States, Gods Battle Ax (Jerm 51:20). The olive branch also represents a peaceful resting place which is found in the definition of Jerusalem, Shiloh and the Hebrew word for peace, Shalam". Again, refer to Genesis 49:22-24 and Deuteronomy 33:13-17. Ephraim and Manasseh were brothers in ancient days just as the United States (the bull) and England (the unicorn) are brothers today.

Over 75 percent of the English language comes directly from Hebrew words or their roots. You can take any sentence in Hebrew and change it into Gaelic, word for word, without altering the order of a single word or particle and you will have the correct Gaelic idiom in every case. You cannot do that with any other language in Europe. God changed the language or tongue (stammering) of his people in Isaiah 28:11 and it states, **"For with stammering lips and another tongue will he speak to his people."** The Young's Concordance list stammering as "laeg", where the Strong's (3934) spells it as "gael". An old name for stammering in Irish is Leagael and in Hebrew "leagael" means stammering people. You can spell leagael from right to left or left to right, just as Hebrew is read from right to left and English from left to right. ("Tracing our Ancestors" by Haberman P.120)

Welsh scholars and writers of early days also noticed a remarkably close resemblance and connection between the ancient British (Welsh) and the Hebrew language. It is evident that the Hebrew formed a very important part of the language of Britain. Let's take a look at where the English language was actually derived. By reviewing the structure of the Phoenician/Hebrew language, there is a good argument that would make the Phoenician/Hebrew from the North Semitic Alphabet the monogenesis of world languages. The Phoenicians were international mariners controlling the world trade routes and ports, therefore, if you conducted trade with these sea going people, you would need to speak their language. The fact of being mariners and great ship builders, dates back to Gods technology to Noah that was passed to the Hebrew people as a part of their inheritance. The Hebrew language came from or is the same as the early Phoenician language.

Original Hebrew was believed to be derived from the Phoenician language just as Gaelic English was a resultant from the Hebrew language as the ancient migrating tribes arrived in Europe by ship which were the lost sheep of the house of Israel (the ten northern tribes of the house of Israel). The following paragraph is taken from "Tracing our Ancestors" by Frederick Haberman, page 120 and will give you an idea of where our English language came from.

"Irish chronology places the coming of these Gadelos about 700 to 650 B.C. Their landing in Uladh were fiercely contested by the Danaans in the land; but the Gadelos held their ground and became the aristocracy of Erin. As they were of the same race of Israel, but of the house of Judah, they of course amalgamated with the Danaan; and out of the various forms Gadil, Gadelos, Gadels, Gaidheil, the term Gael and Scot emerged and Gaclic, the name of the language of Ireland, and the related Gaelic of Scotland, both of them branches of the Phoenician, as is also the Welsh and the Manx. In Isaiah 28:11 we read, "For with stammering lips and another tongue will the Lord speak to his people". Strong's Concordance gives the Hebrew word for stammering as "gael." while Young's Analytical Concordance gives stammering as "leag". It is most striking, therefore, that one of the old names for the Irish should be "Leagael." or, in Hebrew, a stammering people, the double word representing the left to right Phoenician and the right to left Hebrew."

The Lost Sheep of the House of Israel (Ten northern Tribes)

Early English, French, Greek and Roman historians have amassed a great amount of documentation indicating that Hebrews settled in Cornwall, Wales, Ireland, Isle of Manx and the south-west coasts of Scotland, beginning about the days of King Solomon. Egyptian writers wrote about the migration of Semitic Hebrews to Greece and other parts of Asia Minor and Europe long before Moses led Israel out of Egypt in 1453BC. This could be one reason the New Testament was written in Greek due to their Hebrew influence. "Hecataeus of Abdere (sixth century BC) quoted by Diodorus Siculus (50 BC) tells us that the Egyptians "Expelled all the aliens gathered together in Egypt. The most distinguished of the expelled foreigners followed Danaus and Cadmus (Hebrews) into Greece: but the greater number were led by Moses into Judea."

Danaus and Cadmus were descendants of Calcol and Dara in I Chronicles 2:5-6. (British History Traced from Egypt and Palestine, Rev. GA Robbers, P.122).

From my research, there is a vast amount of information on the history of the lost ten tribes of Israel migrating into Europe and the British Islands. Hosea 12:1 gives an idea of how we traveled and matches Isaiah 41:3 by ship, **"Ephraim feedeth on wind, and followeth after the east wind: he daily increaseth lies and desolation and they do make a covenant with the Assyrians, and oil is carried into Egypt"**. Following after the east wind means, Ephraim was blown by the east wind to the west. His increase of lies and desolation and the covenant with the Assyrians along with oil carried into Egypt represents evil dealings and merchandizing with nations of the world. This certainly indicates the worlds free trade system of today.

The Sea and the Isles are mentioned all through the Old Testament (Isaiah 49:1-6) *"to raise up the tribes of Jacob, and to restore the preserved of Israel: I will also give thee for a light to the Gentiles, that thou mayest be my salvation unto the end of the earth. "* He is talking of two separate peoples. The tribes of Jacob are the 11 tribes not of the birthright blessing of Joseph. Israel is the Birthright name that went only to Joseph to be passed directly to Ephraim and Manasseh. Only Joseph (Ephraim and Manasseh) received the Birthright blessing to be a great nation and a company of nations of kingdoms (Common Wealth). The term, **"that thou mayest be my salvation unto the end of the earth** ", represent the responsibility given to the Birthright tribe to take the Gospel to the world evangelizing (Joseph the Stone of Israel Gen 49:24). The tribes of Israel are the Christian nations or Mountains, Amos 6:1, **"Woe to them that are at ease in Zion and trust in the mountain of Samaria, which are named chief of the nations** [12 tribes], **to whom the house of Israel came."** The Hebrew meaning for mountain, "range of hills" figuratively as countries. Samaria was the capital of the house of Israel in ancient times with Ephraim and Manasseh their leader. These verses indicate that Ephraim will be a nation in the later days teaching the Gospel as a world leader, **"give thee for a light to the Gentiles,"**. Manasseh and Ephraim represent the Christian nations of the United States and Great Britain evangelizing the world in the end times and indicated as being chief of the nations. Samaria was the capital of the ten northern tribes of the house of Israel lead by Ephraim and indicated as a World Leading nation. The United States and Great Britain surely fit's this description. Modern day Israel has never been a light to the gentiles (Christian).

The Brotherhood between Judah and Israel is broken and Judah is the outcast, **"the idol shepherd, clean dried up, right eye utterly darkened."** Zech

12:2 makes, **"Jerusalem a cup of trembling and burdensome stone."** Judah or Jerusalem rejected Christ and had him killed so God blinded Judah till Daniel's 70th week Prophecy is complete. Jerusalem as a cup of trembling and burdensome stone can also be applied to the Christian nations of the western world as the peaceful resting place representing the dual definition of Jerusalem. The US has truly been a burdensome stone to Islam and Communist nations that are anti-Christian to include the modern nation of Israel. We can see this in our terrorist activity of today.

The whole book of Hosea is to the inherited blessed nation of Ephraim or Britain and the United States, the world's Christian Nations. Hos 2:14-17, **"Therefore, behold, I will allure her, and bring her into the wilderness, and speak comfortable unto her. And I will give her vineyards from thence, and the valley of Achor for a door of hope", "For I will take away the names of Baalim out of her mouth, and they shall no more be remembered by their name".** These verses are clear on how God will allure the house of Israel into the wilderness to wait for her name and language change. Her old name will be removed and her new name will be Christian also called Gods holy mountain of Jerusalem Isa 66:20 where people migrate from all over the world. The valley of Achor is where Joshua set up a monument to God in honor of the captured land of Canaan or the Promised Land of Israel representing justice and righteousness under the Law. The valley of Achor for a door of hope is a symbol of their new promised land in the wilderness in ancient days and mentioned several times in the capacity of being Gods fruitful planted nations in the wilderness. The symbol of this same valley brings justice and righteousness as his Church under the New Covenant in the end days (Joshua 7:24, Isa 65:9-15, Hos 2:14-23).

Isaiah 65:10 refers to Sharon as one of the Christian nations that accepts the inheritor (Christ) in the last days which is directly associated with the fruitful Christian nations of Ephraim (Bashon, Gilead, Carmel, Sharon and Lebanon Isa 33:9, 35:2). Remember that in Zech 11:14 the brotherhood of Israel and Judah were broken so they are not the same people for this verse is speaking to the house of Israel. A staff is a stick and this staff will be broken till the sticks are rejoined as the whole house of Israel in Ezekiel 37:16-19 which takes place during the Tribulations Period.

For the reader to get a broader picture of the facts presented on this subject, we must go to Gods Patriarchs that wrote books that were not included in his inspired Word but of history for us to understand. The writings of Baruch, Jeremiah's Scribe, in "The Apocalypse of Baruch" gives a clear picture of the separation of Israel and Judah. In LXII 4, on page 104, states, **"And the time of their captivity which came upon the nine tribes and a half, because they were in many sins."** Baruch is speaking of the ten northern tribes of Israel that was taken into captivity by Assyria in 721BC. The ½ tribe he is speaking of is the tribe of Levi that was split between the ten northern tribes of the house of Israel and the two southern tribes of the house of Judah. LXIII. 3, on page 105, states, **"When, moreover, Hezekiah the king heard those things which the king of Assyria was devising, to come and seize him and destroy his people, the two and a half tribes which remained:"** Baruch is clear on the separation of the two houses, Israel and Judah.

The writings of Baruch took place approx. 581 BC, five years after the captivity to Babylon, and the ten northern tribes of the house of Israel had already departed and migrated beyond the Euphrates River into Europe. LXXVII. 17-25 page 122 explains by stating, **"And now go and tarry not in (any) place, nor enter a nest, nor settle upon any tree, till thou hast passed over the breadth of the many waters of the river Euphrates, and hast gone to the people that dwell there, and cast down to them this epistle."** Baruch wrote two epistles, one to the people left in Jerusalem and one to the lost sheep of the ten northern tribes of the house of Israel that migrated beyond the river Euphrates into Europe. He attached the epistle to the neck of an Eagle and sent him to fly beyond the water of the Euphrates. This was the last known contact between the house of Judah and the house of Israel.

Esdras was another Prophet that spoke of the lost tribes of the house of Israel. In the Apocrypha of II Esdras 13:40-45, he states, **"Those are the ten tribes, which were carried away prisoners out of their own land in the time of Osea the king, whom Salmanasar the king of Assyria led away captive, and he carried them over the water, and so came they into another land. But they took this counsel among themselves, that they would leave the multitude of the heathen, and go forth into a further country, where never mankind dwelt, That they might there keep their statutes, which they never kept in their own land. And they entered into Euphrates by the narrow passages of the river. For the most High then shewed signs for them, and held still the flood, till they were passed over. For through that country there was a great way to go, namely, of a year and a half: and the same region is called Arsareth. Then dwelt they there until the latter time; and now when they shall begin to come."** Esdras is very clear on how they departed by the valley of the Euphrates River and migrated into Europe where they were to remain till the last days which is our present time. This is basically the same account Baruch gave in LXXVII. 18-25.

How can we disregard all the archeological stone tablets and writings of the great ancient writers describing the lost Hebrew tribes of Israel that migrated and settled into Europe? After reviewing all the historical data, modern historians and Theologians do not believe that the two houses have been separated as the English-speaking nations of the house of Israel and the Jewish state of Israel as the house of Judah.

Christ unmistakably commissioned his Apostles to go to the lost sheep (house of Israel) in Matthew 10:5-8 and do not mention the Jews. He restates his authority in Matthew 15:24. This verse is absolutely fascinating for it clearly says that Christ was only sent to the lost sheep of the house of Israel and again, do not mention the Jews. God knew that the house of Judah, the Jew, would reject him so he sent his twelve Apostles to the lost sheep of the house of Israel. He reserved Paul to teach the Jews and the Gentiles in the area of Palestine and the surrounding area but sent his Apostles into Europe, Africa and deep into eastern Asia to reach the migrated tribes of the house of Israel, his lost and forgotten sheep of the birthright tribe of Ephraim and Manasseh.

Christ's Commission to the Lost Sheep (house of Israel)

Isaiah 62:2, 56:5 & 65:15 changed the name of the house of Israel so God divorced them because they would not repent of their sins after going into national captivity to Assyria. Jeremiah 3:8 declared a divorcement, **"And I saw, when for all the causes whereby backsliding Israel committed adultery, I had put her away, and given her a bill of divorce; yet her treacherous sister Judah feared not, but went and played the harlot also"**. Note that the divorcement did not pertain to Judah but to only the house of Israel. After God divorced the house of Israel, he sent them into the wilderness to inherit their own land (Eze 34:13-18, 36:24-26 "a new heart" Gods Spirit of the Church) and wait for his Gospel. He knew they would accept Christ's Gospel and Judah would not. This is the reason for their division for he had to separate the 10 northern tribes from the stubborn religion of Judaism or none of his people would have accepted Christ as the Messiah. When Genesis 49:10 was fulfilled and his people gathered into Christ's Church (Shiloh), God betrothed (in Hebrew means to engage) the house of Israel (Hos 2:19-20). The marriage of the betrothal is to take place at the marriage supper of the Lamb in Rev 19:9. This betrothal took place in the wilderness of the earth and vineyard of the valley of Achor under Christ's new Covenant to be sown unto all the earth (Hos 2:14-23) for the branches of his vineyard to run over the wall (Gen 49:22), the birthright tribe of Joseph (Ephraim and Manasseh).

Hosea 2:23 also indicates their name being changed to Christian, **"And I will sow here unto me in the earth; and I will have mercy upon her that had not obtained mercy; and I will say to them which were not my people, Thou art my people; and they shall say, Thou art my God."** His People are the house of Israel as his Church sown into all the earth and by saying "Thou art my God" indicated that they accepted Christ's Gospel under another name, not Hebrew Israelite. In Isaiah 28:1-11, God changed Ephraim's language, verse 11 says, **"For with stammering lips and another tongue will he speak to this people"**. This name was changed to Christian in Act 11:26&27 and sent the twelve disciples to teach the lost sheep, **"And the disciples were called Christians first in Antioch"**.

Christ made two commandments to go and teach. The first is in Matthew 10:5-8, **"These twelve Jesus sent forth and commanded them saying, Go not into the way of the Gentiles, and into any city of the Samaritans enter ye not: But go rather to the lost sheep of the house of Israel. And as ye go, preach, saying"**. The disciples were not trained so they could not be called Apostles at this time but Christ commanded them to go only to the lost sheep of the house of Israel. We need to realize that God knew the Jews would reject Christ and they would kill him. Paul was commissioned to go to the Jews of Judea and the Gentiles not the Apostles. This command was only to the Disciples because the Church did not did not have the authority till the Holy Spirit was given in Acts chapter two.

Matthew 15:24 clearly states that Jesus was only sent to his lost sheep of the house of Israel, the ten northern tribes or Ephraim, leader of the birthright tribe, his elect, **"But he answered and said, I am not sent but unto the lost sheep of the house of Israel."** This verse is clear that Jesus was sent to teach only the house of Israel and not the Jews. It also verifies Luke 1:80 when Jesus was a child, **"and was in the deserts till the day of his showing unto Israel."** This verse is speaking directly to the house of Israel. We need to remind ourselves that Israel is the family name of Jacob given only to the birthright tribes of Ephraim and Manasseh in Genesis 48:16 which means "he will rule as God", his elect, the birthright of the house of Israel (Ephraim and Manasseh). Jesus was only to show himself to his lost sheep, Israel, of Ephraim and Manasseh. Paul was to go to the Jews, not his Disciples, for they were given a bigger commission. They were to go to the world through the lost sheep of the house of Israel, Ephraim and Manasseh planted in the wilderness waiting for his Gospel to evangelize the world.

The second command was the Great Commission in Matthew 28:19-20 which was to the Church, all Christian Members not just to the Apostles. Notice the difference between the two commands, **"Go ye therefore, and teach all nations, baptizing them in the name of the Father, and of the Son, and of the Holy Ghost: Teaching them to observe all things what so ever I have commanded you: and, lo, I am with you always, even unto the end of the world"**. This command was given to the twelve Apostles that were the heads of Christ's Church, therefore, the commandment to go and teach unto the end of the world was given to the Church, not to the individual Apostles as in Matthew 10:5. In other words, Matt 10:6 and 15:24 was given to the twelve Apostles but Matt 28:19-20 was given to the overall Church.

God chose Paul to go to the Gentiles. Keep in mind that we have been taught that the lost 10 tribes have been filtered back into the remnant of Israel and don't exist as a nation. Christ knew where they were, scattered through Asia, Europe and Great Britain. In Matthew 15:22-24, Christ was talking to the woman from Canaan and most likely a Gentile, asked Christ to heal her daughter but Christ said, **"I am not sent but unto the lost sheep of the house of Israel"**. Only because of her great faith he healed her daughter but he was not to cast the bread of his Gospel before dogs of the non-believing Canaanites. This is why the Jew is not included in Matthew 10:5-8, 15:11-24 and 22:24 for Christ knew they would reject him as their Messiah for this verse clearly states that Christ were only to go to his Hebrew lost sheep of the 10 northern tribes to teach and instruct (Jerusalem in the wilderness).

Christ was teaching his disciples to be missionaries to foreign countries and go to the lost house of Israel that was not in the area of Judea but far off. Again, when Christ was talking to the Chief Priests in Matthew 21:43, he knew they were going to reject him so he said, **"Therefore say I unto you, The kingdom of God shall be taken from you, and given to a nation bringing forth the fruits thereof"**. He was speaking to the Pharisees for they were of the Royal bloodline of his throne representing his kingdom. Who is this nation? It's not the Jews, they killed Christ and no other nation accepted Christ in that area. It can only be the lost sheep of the house of Israel that was already scattered and migrated into Britain years before where Tea Tephi and Scotia, King Zedekiah's daughters, establish the royal bloodline into the British Throne (Eze 17:22-24 and 21:25-27).

According to the book, "Missing Links Discovered in Assyrian Tablets" by E. Raymond, quotes from page 150, concerning the daughters of Zedekiah, the last king of Judah. Scota departed Jeremiah's protection while in Egypt before he departed.

"The name "Scotia" is, by ancient historians, applied to Ireland more often than any other name. Orosius, a third century geographer, used the term "Hibernia, the nation of the Scoti." The ancient poets and seanachies (historians) of Ireland claim the name "Scotia" was derived from "Scota," queen mother of the Milesians (Story of the Irish race by, MacManus page 192). *Undoubtedly, this was Scota, the daughter of Zedekiah, the last king of Judah. Scota married a Milesian prince in Egypt and their son Eochaidh (Heremon or Eremon) married Tea Tephi and founded a dynasty in Ireland"* (Missing Links Discovered in Assyrian Tablets: by E. Raymon page 150). Many of these people migrated to Scotland and took this name with them.

The story of Tamar and Judah and their two sons Pharez and Zarah (Gen chapter 38) explains Zarah being of the royal blood line through Tamar and the diadem taken from Pharez line and given to Zarah's line (Eze 21:25-27). Matthew 1:3 place both Zarah and Pharez in the lineage to be eligible for King David's throne and fulfilled the overturned throne from the high to the low branch as stated in Jeremiah's commission (Jerm 1:10; Eze 17:22-24 and 21:25-27).

The name Tamar is scattered all through England to this day and is traced through secular history. This would trace King David's bloodline through Zarah of the Milesians, to Ireland and later to the Throne of England. After Christ descended into Heaven, the Church was not official till the Holy Spirit came into the upper room. Act 1:2 & 8 **"unto the uttermost parts of the earth."** Most of the twelve Apostles departed shortly after to never be heard of again, to preach the Gospel to the lost sheep of the house of Israel (Mat 10:6). This is why Paul was chosen to teach all that would listen in Jerusalem, Judea, Samaria and all surrounding areas of the known world and why he dominated the writings of the New Testament Scriptures and not the Apostles. He was chosen by God to be the Apostle to the Gentiles (Rom 11:13), **"I am the apostle of the Gentiles,".** The 12 Apostles were chosen to go to the lost sheep of the house of Israel (Mat 10:6) afar off and Paul was chosen to preach to the Gentiles.

British Historians, Publis Discipulus, Usher, Fuller and Sir. Henry Spelman all state in their history books that Joseph of Arimathea (a Disciple of Jesus) Matthew 27:57, Mark 15:43, Luke 23:51 and John 19:38, the younger brother of the father of Virgin Mary was a wealthy tin miner. He mined out of Britain and contracted tin to the Roman Empire creating powerful political standings that allowed Arimathea to be able to take Christ's Body at his death. British folklore indicates that Joseph possibly took Jesus as a young boy to Britain on his business trips. This would explain Luke 1:80 as Christ being in the desert as a child **"and was in the deserts till the day of his shewing unto Israel"**. A word deserts means the wilderness of the world. This verse indicated that Jesus as a child were to be in deserts (plural) symbolizing the world explaining his travels with his uncle prior to his ministry. According to English historians, Joseph of Arimathea established the first Church in Britain in approx. 38AD in Glastonbury.

There are twenty books of the New Testament not including the repeated Epistles and 11 were written by Paul, 10 for sure, and possibly the book of Hebrew. They were all written to Gentile Churches that he established, except, the Book of Hebrew and that was to the Jewish Christians, the only book to Jews. Matthew wrote to the lost sheep of the house of Israel in Matthew 10:6 and 15:24. Mark, Luke and John indicate the telling of the story of Christ to the scattered Gentiles that is the lost sheep of the house of Israel. The Book of Acts in verse 1:2 refers to the command to the Apostles in Matthew 10:6 to go to the lost sheep of Israel. James 1:1 is to all 12 tribes and includes the lost sheep. Peter 1:1 is to the strangers scattered throughout which indicate the lost sheep. The book of John is written to all Christians. The books that the Apostles wrote seem to indicate they were written to a people or a group of people. The books written by Paul were to an established Church of Christians indicating a different group of people written in reference to Paul and the Apostles.

This writer believes that Great Britain and the United States (Ephraim and Manasseh Gen 48:17-19 & 49:22-26) was the nation that Christ spoke of in Matthew 21:43 when he told the Chief Priests and Pharisees that the kingdom would be taken from them. When Jesus spoke of this, both the house of Judah and Israel had been utterly separated by two captivities and only till 1948 did the house of Judah became a nation as the modern Jewish state of Israel. Where is the house of Israel? The Jew's were the ones that killed Jesus in unbelief so the kingdom was taken from them and given to a fruitful (Christian) nation.

The only two nations since Christ's death to claim themselves, by their government to be a Christian nation, is the throne of England and the United States. The Constitution of the United States was inspired by God through our leaders to ensure freedom so that the Gospel could be spread worldwide without demonic intervention as indicated in Matthew 21:43, Gods fifth kingdom (Dan 2:44-45). The United States is the only country ever in history to have a national motto, "In God we trust".

The **Nations**, as in multiple (Gen 35:11, 48:19), that Christ mentioned can only be Great Britain and later the United States for it has been the dominating nations in the last three hundred years that has truly spread the Gospel. The Gospel came from England, Ephraim, the common wealth of nations, Genesis 48:19 & 49:22-24, **" the branches run over the wall",** and spread the Gospel throughout the world. God sent his lost sheep to the Island of Great Britain (Ephraim and Manasseh) so they could be safe from invasion surrounded by water. He established the United States by Manasseh through Great Britain again surrounded by water to be safe from invasion to spread the Gospel in the last days, **"In God We Trust".** The nation of Ephraim (GB) and Manasseh (USA) is a symbol where the two great eagles of diverse colors (Eze 17) planted these nations in the wilderness to be many colors or diverse people throughout the world spreading Christ's Gospel to all man.

Chapter Six

Gods given Technology of Ship Building

There is an aspect that we need to consider when we review the fact that God plainly scattered and dispersed his people worldwide to spread his end time Gospel. Isaiah 16:8 state that Gods branches of the house of Israel went over the seas and Genesis 49:22 tells us that these branches were Joseph or Ephraim and Manasseh of the birthright tribe. Many Jews departed with Ephraim and Manasseh and fell under their control but according to Ezra, a remnant remained in Judea to maintain Jerusalem for the coming of the Messiah. Isaiah 41:1-3 explains how God gave his righteous people from the east (house of Israel) the nations of the world to rule and said that they would get there without using their feet (Isa 41:1-8). They went by ship for the Hebrew people-maintained Noah's technology of shipbuilding.

There are certain key words in the Bible that refer to Gods People being travelers and they are; wayfaring, east, waymarks, ensign, scattered, sifted, dispersed, abroad, without feet, Zion, ships and many more. Study these words for it produces a clear picture of how God dispersed his fruitful nation (Matt 21:43 house of Israel, lost sheep) into the wilderness to the east over the Caucasus Mountains (Eze 43:2) (to be blown by an east wind to the west, Isa 43:5). The migrating Hebrews can be traced through time because they left ensigns, high heaps and waymarks (Isa 11:10 and Jerm 31:21) along their way for the purpose of future identification. They left mounds, circles and monuments to trace their path of migration. Isaiah 66:7-12 says that Zion was to travail (travel) after she brought forth a Man Child (Christ the Messiah) and produce a nation that will be the glory of the Gentiles. The Hebrew definition of Zion is the same as; wilderness, desert and waymark which is a Capital or mountain (nation). A close study of all these words clearly establishes how the house of Israel of Ephraim and Manasseh were planted in the wilderness to institute a new thing or a new heart and Spirit in the earth, Christ's Gospel (Isa 36:26 Jerm 31:22 Eze 11:19 & 18:31).

Let's start from the beginning in how the Hebrew people first became ship builders in Egypt. Joseph was in grace with the Pharaoh of Egypt when Jacob,

Joseph's father, who was called Israel, arrived in Egypt along with his sons in approx. 1706BC. They became prosperous and multiplied as a family. During Joseph's reign of power, the Hebrew people helped Egypt to become a great nation with their technology of Noah's shipbuilding. This was the zenith of the strength of the Egyptian people. During the Hyksos Dynasties from 1730-1580 BC, the Hebrew Semitic Shepherd Kings ruled the western portion of the fertile crescent of Egypt with great power. These Hebrew Shepherd Kings were of Abraham's sojourn starting in 1921 BC. They became ship builders and produced trade routes throughout the Mediterranean area and up the Nile River basin. The first Hebrew migration took place during the time of freedom before Joseph and his Pharaoh died. These migrating Hebrews became part of the Phoenicians that settled Phoenicia in the northern part of Canaan in ancient times. The new Pharaoh saw the danger of how the Hebrew people multiplied and became afraid, he began to enslave the Hebrews.

The Tribe of Dan was an adventurous people along with Calcol and Dara of the tribe of Judah. They departed Egypt by ship and settled into Greece, Spain and Troy due to their shipbuilding and navigating ability which allowed them to migrate. Some Pastors teach that the Israelites were not of ships but by Scripture, is not true. The Scriptures indicate, the tribes of Dan and Zebulan were always great ship builders for they maintained the technology that God gave Noah to build the Ark prior to the flood. The tribes of Dan, Asher, Zebulun, Ephraim and Manasseh lived by the sea and were seaman after they settled the Promised Land. Genesis 49:13 **"Zebulun shall dwell at the haven of the sea; and he shall be for an haven of ships; and his border shall be unto Zidon"**, and again in Deuteronomy 33:19, **"for they shall suck of the abundance of the seas, and of treasures hid in the sand."**. These verses indicate that they were sailing the world for treasure. The tribe of Dan and Asher were also of the sea for Judges 5:17 states, **"and why did Dan remain in ships? Asher continued on the sea shore, and abode in his breaches."**.

Throughout the ages, the tribe of Dan and the other tribes used this technology. They became great ship builders and mariners where ever they migrated. The nations they combined with all had a great navy such as Spain, England, Norway (Vikings) and Denmark (the cloth of Dan). The writer of these verses was placing each tribe location in Israel but Dan had no landmass, they all abode in ships. This is why Dan disappeared from the Scriptures and dealings with his brothers of the other tribes as indicated in I Chronicles chapter 4-6. The tribe of Dan was shippers and mariners and disappeared from the Scriptures. They opted to depart and go into the world giving up their brethren of the other tribes. Due to this fact, they are not mentioned in the sealing of the 144,000 of the twelve tribes listed in Revelation 7:5-8. They elected to not fight and be a part of the establishing of the nation of Israel in Canaan, therefore, God took their part away in the sealing of the tribes during the tribulation period, giving it to Manasseh, the firstborn birthright tribe (Rev 7:6).

The tribe of Levi was divided between all twelve tribes to be Priest and had no landmass (Num 3:12). This is why Levi is never listed as being a tribe for they were divided among the other eleven tribes. Because of the Priestly authority given to Levi by God, as the lawgiver, each tribe could then in the eyes of God produce their own nation and line of Kings which occurred after they migrated into Europe. This authority was given to Levi in their inheritance blessing recorded in Deuteronomy 33:8-11, **"They shall teach Jacob the judgments and Israel thy law"**. Only through the authority of Levi could each tribe become an individual country with Kings that became the nations of Europe with their own line of Royalty. Joseph was not actually a tribe but divided between his two sons Ephraim and Manasseh which received blessings of the firstborn, Genesis 48:20. Joseph received their blessing (Primogeniture) because of the sins of his brothers that sold him into Egypt (I Chron 5:1-2). He later saved his family when they went into Egypt due of the grace that the Pharaoh showed to Joseph, therefore, receiving the Lion's share of the family blessings.

God wanted his people to populate the worlds continents (Gen 26:4) that were divided by great oceans. It would only be fitting for him to give them shipbuilding technology so they could circumnavigate the earth to be Gods earthly Battle Ax through a navy (Jerm 51:20) and fulfilled the blessing promised to Abraham, Isaac, Jacob and Joseph then passed to Ephraim and Manasseh as the Bull and Unicorn.

Celt Druidism verses Judaism and Christianity

We have already established that God's Word is a mystery and Daniel says his prophetic puzzle is a Secret. An important piece of the mysterious puzzle is the connection of Druidism, Judaism, and Christianity. To figure out this connection, we need to ask ourselves a question. What religion did Gods Patriarchs practice prior to Moses receiving the Law and establishing the Tabernacle in the wilderness under the Covenant? The Covenant with Moses was Gods first formal religion of doctrinal faith given to his Chosen People through the seed of Abraham.

From Adam to Moses, what religion was practiced? This author believes, through documented evidence, it was Druidism, a monotheistic practice. God's number one law with man from the beginning of time is to have no other Gods before him, no idol worship. This would answer many puzzling questions and fill in blanks such as who created the Pyramids and Stonehenge. The creation of these mysterious objects is a part of Gods Secret for he wants us to believe by faith, therefore, not knowing the whole truth of his nature.

A close study of Druidism will show an uncanny parallel between the practice of Druidism and Judaism that is very compatible with Christianity. R.W. Morgan in his book, "St. Paul in Britain" page 12 states, *"At its beginning Druidism was in its original form as created by man or possibly by God, but, like all religions, Satan finds a way to corrupt and turn it into evil. Just as Judaism and Christianity, Druidism was absorbed into the Satan's Ancient Baal religion".*

As R.W. Morgan states, *"Druidism commenced, i.e. 3903 years before the Christian era, 181 years after the creation of man, and 50 years after the birth of Seth."* He goes on to say, *"Druidism became the religion of Mithras in Persia, Baal in Assyria, Braham in India, Artarte or the Dea Syria in Syria, Apis in Egypt and later transferred from Egypt, of the two "Apis" or calves as they are rendered in our version of the Scriptures of the Kingdom of Israel."*

Of all these religions, the Bull or Taurus was their sacred animal given to the house of Israel in Duet 33:17. This could very well be why the birthright tribes of Ephraim and Manasseh to this day is dominated by the Bull, the Bull of Wall St. in New York City that dominates world economics. They are called his bullocks in Duet 33:17 and an ox in Eze 1:10, cherub in Eze 10:14 and a calf in Rev 4:7.

Before we get into Druidism, we need to understand where it came from and what nations produced it. God preserved and planted his fruitful nation (Matt 21:43), his British people (Covenant Man) on an Island called Hibernia and Britannia, and protected them from invading armies. Their old faith was called Druid that resembles the faith of Abraham and later Christianity. God protected his special people and would not allow the power of the Roman army to conquer during two different envisions. Rome had taken most of Europe except for Hibernia (Hebrew Britannic Isles) for Druidism had crept into the Roman Society and became an ideological threat. They invaded Britannia on August 5, 55BC with total failure and returned in 54BC that also failed. Their third invasion took place during Paul's ministry in 43AD. The third invasion was not a coincidence but occurred due to the influence of the Druids accepting Christianity and that God had planted them in the wilderness to wait for Christ's Gospel. The migrating Hebrew tribes of Calcol and Dara (I Cron 2:5) departed Egypt by ship prior to the exodus and over hundreds of years settled into Ireland (Hibernia), Scotland (Caledonia) and

England (Britannia). The house of Israel after the Assyrian and Babylonian captivities also slowly migrated into Europe and settled the Britannic Islands where they amalgamated with their other Druid Hebrew descendants fulfilling the preparation for the coming of Christ's Gospel.

We know that there are several verses that refer to Gods Hebrew travelers as departing on great eagle wings of diverse colors in Eze 17:3&7 and calling them a speckled bird in Jerm 12:9 indicating their travels as migrating flocks. The settling of Gods Hebrew people into Ireland, Scotland and England was not a coincidence but a heavenly calling just as migrating birds return to their home nest each year. Their way of travel is mentioned in Isaiah 41:3, by ship on the wings of an Eagle as Phoenician ships. The planted nations in the wilderness were to be the home nest of the house of Israel as the speckled bird planted in their own land, separate from the house of Judah rooted in Jerusalem (Jerm 23:8, Eze 34:13-14, 38:14&21 and 39:28). They were given the Gospel and accepted the responsibility as the fruitful nation, the Birthright tribes of Ephraim the unicorn and Manasseh the bull to spread Christ's end time Gospel. They are identified as the lost sheep of the house of Israel in the wilderness where God overturned his throne and later his complete Kingdom taken from the Jews in Matt 21:43.

The Druid religion is based on the worship of the God of Creation called Du-w or Duw (the one without darkness). The Druids did not commit their religious traditions to writing but only by memory that has caused a great misunderstanding down through time. Falsehoods have been created that they were barbarous, uncivilized, uneducated people that practices human sacrifice. The falsehood of human sacrifice was created by the Romans to demoralize the Druid people and to deter their influence within Rome and Europe. Just a little study will show that their civilization and culture ranked with the Greek and Romans in Literature, Arts, Architecture and Universities. We also need to understand that if this is Gods faith prior to establishing his Gospel, then Satan would try to destroy it just as he has Judaism and Christianity.

We also need to understand that Druidism over hundreds of years became distorted and departed from Gods true ways just as Judaism fell into idol worship and the falling away of Christianity from Gods truth today. The Church is presently seeing the great falling away that Paul spoke of in II Thessalonians 2:3 where Satan in attacking the Church just as he tried to destroy Druidism and Judaism in the same manner.

"Duw had a trinity which represented the past, present and future or Beli, Taran, and Esu or Yesu. In Hebrew the term Jesus means, life (having

Salvation), to live or living which is basically the same meaning as Yesu in Druid. According to the Druid faith, the essence of the soul was the will and the essence of religion the willing hood. Therefore, without freedom there is no humanity, for freedom of conscience is the birth and breath of manhood". (R.W. Morgan, "St. Paul in Britain").

The Scriptures teach freedom and equality for all men and a blessing of the Christian faith. God founded our Christian nation on liberty that created the atmosphere for freedom of Religion to spread Christ's end time Gospel without the influence of a tyrannical government.

The parallel between Druidism, Judaism and Christianity are based on the same basic principles and is why the Druids merged with Christianity in Britain so easily during the first century after Christ's death. The Druids had a strict belief in hospitality of strangers in their land and based on Scriptures such as II Samuel 12:4, Exodus 12:48-49 and Leviticus 19:33. The tradition of hospitality to stranger's date back to the old faith before the Law was given by Moses and is based on God's love and mercy to all people. According to the old faith, a stranger in the land could very well be an Angle of God so all strangers were treated with great respect.

There is no recorded persecution of any foreign people in ancient Britain due to their political or religious faith and is based on the same principles of Christ's Gospel. Historians claim that the Druids worshiped nature and that is not true. They worshiped the one true God that created nature but did not worship nature itself (I Corinthians 15:44-45). The Great Pyramids and Stonehenge built by the Druids were created as a monument to the God of creation and was not worshiped as Gods themselves (Isaiah 19:18-20 and Exodus 20:24). The ancient Irish stone circles were called Bothals by their people and meant, "The house of God." The Hebrew meaning for the "House of God" is Bethel and indicates a connection between the ancient Irish and the original Hebrew faith of Jacob (Gen 28:19).

We can trace why the Hebrew descended Druids of Calcol and Dara built stone circles and mounds where ever they went. There are certain key words in the Scriptures that explain why Gods people left this trail to follow. The term Wayfaring man and Highway has a direct correlation as recorded in Isaiah 33:8, **"The highways lie waste, the wayfaring man ceaseth: he hath broken the covenant, he hath despised the cities, he regarded no man"**. In context, this verse is speaking of the falling away in the last days for it mentions Bashan and Carmel shaking off their fruits. They were the fruitful nation that Christ took from the Chief Priest and Pharisees in Matthew 21:43.

By Hebrew definition, wayfaring man is a Hebrew traveler that departed to the East on Gods highway of righteousness as indicated in Isaiah 35:8, **"And an highway shall be there, and a way, and it shall be called the way of holiness; the unclean shall not pass over it; but it shall be for those the wayfaring men, through fools, shall not err therein."** The highway of holiness is nothing more than Gods Hebrew tribes as the lost sheep of the house of Israel that spread Christ's Gospel worldwide as they traveled. Ezekiel chapter 10 calls the four brigades of Israel the "four living creatures" as the Man, Lion, Ox and Eagle and refers to them as a "wheel" ten times in Ezekiel chapter ten. This same listing of living creatures are found in Rev 4:7. A wheel is a way of travel. They were commanded to leave waymarks or high heaps of stone during their travels in Jeremiah 31:21, **"Set thee up waymarks, make thee high heaps: set thine heart toward the highway,"** as to mark their track of migration. This is why Dan is called **"the adder in the path,"** (Gen 49:17) for it leaves an identifying trail fulfilling this commandment. In context, this verse reverts back to the Church age and the period of migration for a highway is Gods Salvation that can only be Christ's Gospel. This writer believes that it was also a Spiritual calling to all the wayfaring men of Gods twelve tribes of Israel guiding their migrate trail to a central location in the wilderness (England). Gods overall prophetic plan was to establish Gods highway of Salvation (end time Gospel) to all men. As we study the definition of the word highway, a couple of interesting aspects appear, for it means to mound up, raise up and to exalt oneself. This could very well explain why mounds were erected all over Europe dating back thousands of years and also why the early Celts and Goths exalted themselves by saying they were "the people of God".

To sum up this idea, a wayfaring man is a Hebrew man by definition and highway means to mound or raise up, so when God dispersed and scattered his people, they built stone circles and mounds where ever they went. This was an honor and monument to the one true God of creation in Druidism. Ezekiel 22:15-16 makes the words scattered, dispersed, wilderness and inheritance synonymous with each other. The Hebrew word dispersed means cast abroad so when we associate these words with wayfaring and highway, we can see a beautiful picture of how God took his inheritance tribes of Ephraim and Manasseh and dispersed them. We must understand that when Druidism was the British religion, Christianity had not arrived but when it, they accepted it. The Druid Hebrew branches that ran over the wall (Gen 49:22 and Isa 16:8) into their own land in the wilderness (Eze 34:13-14) and became the mountains (nations) of Israel, Gods Christian nations in the end days.

Isabel Hill Elder has an excellent book on the history of the Celt Druids called "Celt Druid and Culdee". She states on page 87 that the three foundations of

Druidism are Peace, Love, and Justice. The three primeval unities are, one God, one Truth, and one Liberty. *"The Druid duties of every man: worship God; be just to all men; die for your country."* The motto of the Druidic Order of Wales states, *"The truth against the world"*. Now we can see why the Romans had to destroy this influence by invasion in 55 to 54 BC and again in 43AD with the merging of Christianity. The wealthy families of Rome were sending their children to Britain for a Druidic education and the influence began to affect the Roman Empire. By 43AD the Druids began to merge with Christianity and became even a bigger threat that promoted the second invasion of Britain. In 43AD, the Emperor of Rome declared a decree to destroy Druidism and Christianity in Briton, for every man, woman, child, and its institutions of learning were to be totally eradicated. This included a capital offence for any person declaring to be Druid, Christian, a descendant of King David (aimed at the British Royal Family) and Jews claiming to be of the Orthodox Jewish faith. Historians fail to mention that the Druids were included in the Christian and Jewish persecution by Rome. The influence could very well be why approx. 500 years later Rome fell to the Christian faith.

Other information that comes from Mr. Morgan's book, "St. Paul in Britain" on page 24 and 25 tells us, *"The Druids required 20 years to master the circle of knowledge which consisted of nature, philosophy, astronomy, arithmetic, geometry, jurisprudence, medicines, poetry and oratory with severe exactitude on philosophy and astronomy"*. The Greeks called the Druids "Saronidoe" which means astronomers". Even our modern-day Doctorate Degree do not require this amount of study. This also clarifies why Stonehenge is based on the movement of the sun and moon for precise growing seasons and religious festivals.

Britain consisted of 40 Druidic tribes and each produced a university that was the capital of each clan and used a form of writing in all areas of learning except Religion. This is why they are so misunderstood and created a mystery due to little written knowledge of their beliefs ("Celt Druid and Culdee" by Elder. P56). Ancient historians and writers such as Cicero, Caesar, Pliny, Tacitus, Diodorus Siculus and Strabo all speak highly of the Druid abilities in astronomy and their education system (Celt page 25). Britain is filled with megalithic remains of unhewn stones that were placed in circles and piles. These piles were called "si'uns or cairns" and were usually placed on the summit of hills and mounds. It is striking that these Celtic si'uns were placed on mounds or mounts for the word Zion in Celtic means the Mount of Stones. In other words, the Celt word si'un and the Hebrew word Zion means basically the same thing, Mount Zion (fortress), Gods Spirit with man. This also matches Christianity where Christ and his Christians are called living stones (I Peter 2:4-5). These mounds were simply a place of worship just as the Temple in Jerusalem for no identifiable idol or image of any god has ever been found in Britain prior to the pre-Roman period (Celt page 84).

It would be fitting to make a couple of quotes from Mrs. Elders book "Celt Druid and Culdee" at this time. *"The educational system adopted by the Druids is traced to about 1800 B.C. when Hu Gadarn Hysicion (Isaacson or Saxon), or Hu the Mighty, led the first colony of Cymri into Britain from Defrobane, where Constantinople (Istanbul in Turkey) now stands. In the justly celebrated Welch Triads, Huy Gadarn is said to have mnemonically systematized the wisdom of the ancients of these people whom he led west from the Summerland. He was regarded as the personifications of intellectual culture and is commemorated in Welsh archaeology for having made poetry the vehicle of memory, and was the inventor of the Triads. To him is attributed the founding of Stonehenge, and the introduction of several arts including glass-making and writing in Ogham characters."* (page 53)

"The primitive religion of Britain associate in so many minds with the heavenly bodies. In reality, they worshiped the 'Lord of hosts', the Creator of the Great Lights, the sun, moon and stars, not the worship of the heavenly bodies themselves. The Universe was the Bible of the ancients, the only revelation of the Deity vouchsafed them. The wonders of nature were to them as the voice of the All-Father, and by the movement of the heavenly bodies they ordered their lives, fixed religious festivals and all agricultural proceedings." (page 61)

Study the word solemnite for Isaiah 33:20-21 makes a clear statement, **"Look upon Zion, the city of our solemnites: thine eyes shall see Jerusalem a quiet habitation, a tabernacle that shall not be taken down; not one of the stakes thereof shall ever be removed, either shall any of the cords thereof be broken. But thee the glorious Lord will be unto us a place of broad rivers and streams; wherein shall go no galley with oars, neither shall gallant ship pass thereby"**. By this verse the Church is called Jerusalem is a place of broad rivers and streams representing a foreign land. We know by fact that in 70AD the Roman General Titus totally destroyed the Temple in Jerusalem but according to the verses above says that "a tabernacle that shall not be taken down; not one of the stakes". This verse seems to contradict history unless you understand the key word solemnite. When we study other verses such as Zion shall travel "travail" (Isa 66:8), Zion shall be plowed like a field and Jerusalem shall become heaps (Jerm 26:18), destruction of the Temple (Matt 24:2), we can better understand why God planted his fruitful nation in the wilderness to be his Church. He moved his throne, Zion and the name Jerusalem to a fruitful peaceful land. All these are the elements of his Kingdom given to the fruitful nation in the wilderness (Matt 21:43).

Solemnite means, *an appointment or a fixed time or season, an annual festival, an assembly or place of meeting and synagogue.* The house of Israel and the world, were to become Gods Zion solemnite temples and synagogues under the new Covenant of the Church making Isaiah 33:20-21 a true statement and it was called Jerusalem (Isa 33:20, 66:19-20). Gods Temple, Throne and Church will never be destroyed as Isaiah states. The Druid's developed solemnite stone circles based upon seasonal movements of the sun and moon simply to mark precise religious festivals for assembly and agriculture planting.

"Stonehenge, the Greenwich Observatory" is the great solar clock of ancient times and pre-eminently an astronomical circle. Heliograph and beacon were both used by the ancient British astronomer in signaling the time and the seasons, the result of observations, for the daily direction of the agriculturist and the trader." (page 59)

"While the Druids used writing for all other subjects taught in their colleges, they never used this medium in connection with the subject of religion. To the spread of Christianity, we owe most of the information possessed of the Druidic religion; their secret laws gradually relaxed as they became Christian, and some of their theology was then committed to writing. Dr. Henry, in his "History of England", has observed that collegiate or monastic institutions existed among the Druids." (page 56)

After only a quick study of the massive amount of material on the civilization of the Celtic Druids, it is clear that their history and beliefs have been misjudged, misconstrued and blatantly distorted by the Romans, ancient and modern historians along with our Theologians. There are two reasons for the lies and distortions. The belief system of truth and justice under one God of creation threatened the Romans and other civilizations that believed in multiple Gods. Druidism, Judaism and Christianity was a direct threat to their belief systems. Secondly, it threaded Satan himself for the original Druid belief was the religion of Gods Patriarchs prior to Moses and the Covenant. We know that Judaism and Christianity is of God, therefore, Satan has tried to destroy all three systems of Gods worship throughout time. Due to the similarities and belief in the same God, Druidism merged with Christianity during the Christian area of Britain and Europe. We need to understand that Christ's Gospel was a new thing in the earth (Isa 43:19) to include a new heart and Spirit, the coming of the Holy Spirit in the upper room (Eze 36:26). Judaism could not merge for they still do not believe in the true Messiah. The Jews will not accept Christianity till their allotted 70th week of Daniel's prophecy (Dan 9:24-27) begins which will occur during the Tribulation Period of wrath.

This writer believes, with study and logic, that the Druid faith was the religion of the Phoenicians and migrating Hebrews of Calcol and Dara (I Chron 2:6) that maintained the faith of Abraham. The descendants of Noah and Shem knew the ways of God and departed the land of Shinar of Nimrod to escape his evils. They settled Phoenicia and became the Phoenicians of the Druid faith, "the ways of God" where they migrated prior to the Exodus along with portions of the tribes of Israel during the reign of David and Solomon. These ancient Hebrew tribes settled into Ireland and England as early as 1800 BC. The Bible indicates that the tribe of Dan departed the Promised Land and did not return. Deuteronomy 33:22 says that Dan shall leap from Bashan and I Chronicles chapters four, five and six indicate they were not in the land for Dan is not listed in the genealogies. Dan is an example of how the Hebrew Israelites slowly migrated through time. Asher also migrated for they blended in with the sea going Phoenicians by being their neighbors. Zebulun departed by ship according to Genesis 48:13 for he abodes in ships.

All these migrations along with Jeremiah's commission (Jerm 1:10) completed the overturn of the throne of David (Eze 21:25-27) and travailing of Zion (moving of Gods Glory form Jerusalem, Ezekiel 10:18-19). They were to wait for Christ's Gospel. This was a part of Gods overall prophetic plan to replant his overturned throne and Kingdom in the wilderness as the migrating speckled bird (diverse races or nations of people Jerm 12:9).

Several good references on the Pyramids can be found in the books, "A study in Pyramidology" by E. Raymond Capt. and on Stonehenge by Bonnie Gaunt, "Stonehenge…a closer look".

Bible Prophecies in Ancient and Modern times

Gods Prophets and Patriarchs were simply a medium for his spiritual communications to the King and his Children of Israel. His voice was open not only to Israel but to all nations and people that would hearken to his Word just as his Spirit is today. Israel was his chosen people but his Salvation was open to all the world and the Prophets were his form of communication till the fulfillment of Christ's Church and coming of the Holy Spirit. Don't confuse the duty of the High Priest and the Temple for they only atoned for the sins of the people and not for the purpose of communication. The Temple was Gods dwelling place on earth, Zion. Christ's death on the cross as our Savior fulfilled the need for the Prophets, Priest and Temple. Christ became our high Priest, our bodies became Gods Temple, and the Holy Spirit became a direct communication link from individual Spirit to Christ our mediator, and then to the Father on High. John the Baptist and Agabus were the last Prophets ordained by God directly. Paul was the last Apostle ordained by Christ himself on the road to Damascus in Act 9:5.

To have a better understanding of Prophecy, we must pay particular attention to when the Prophets wrote the Scripture in direct correlation to whom it was written and to when and where the Prophecy is to take place. A good example of this is the Prophetic book of Ezekiel. This book was written to the Children of Israel but predominately to the house of Israel, the ten northern tribes. Ezekiel mentions the house of Israel 78 times, house of Judah five times, house of Jacob one time, and the house of Togarmah twice. The house of Israel is considered to be destroyed and never to return but is mentioned 78 times, many times more than any other house. All the different houses in Ezekiel are referred to as divergent peoples and nations. This brings up a very interesting point for Ezekiel speaks of being on the river Chibar during the Babylonian captivity. This had to be written after 586 BC or approx. 135 years after the house of Israel disappeared into captivity to Assyria and never returned or heard of again as a nation or people. Why would Ezekiel write to the house of Israel with a Prophetic warning after their captivity if they did not exist as a nation? The reason is simple, Ezekiel knew where the house of Israel was located and that they were to be many nations in the last days for his prophecies were to the house of Israel to take place in the end days of our present time period. This fulfilled Gods promise to Abraham, Isaac and Jacob that under the birthright blessings they would be one great nation, a company of nations and kings of kingdoms (Gen 17:6; 35:11; 48:16-19).

These promises are clear and absolute within the Scripture and irrefutable, but the modern Church refuses to see the truth. Many of the Prophetic books of the Old Testament were written to the house of Israel and Judah after their division and subsequently had been taken into captivity. The house of Israel (Ephraim) is mentioned more than any of the other houses but they were first to go into captivity and never returned. This tells us that the warnings and Prophetic books of the Old Testament of destruction due to wickedness and idol worship applies to not only the ancient times but also the end days or the end of the age. Why would the Prophets write after the fact? God knew that the evil ways of his rebellious house never change and would come full circle to the end of the age for history always repeats itself. In other words, all the Old Testament Prophetic books were written to Christ's Church of the last days which is Gods Children of Israel under the New Covenant (Zion) (Heb 8:8 and Jerm 31:31).

Chapter 7

The Phoenician and Milesian connection

There are three groups of people that must be considered when evaluating the migrating tribes of Hebrew. The first group is known very well as the Hebrew tribes that came out of the Egyptian captivity by the leadership of Moses into the wilderness where the nation of Israel was established. These were God's Chosen People under his Covenant in the desert. They were dominated by the Judah/Phares line of Kings and produced the linage of David and Christ. The second group came from the descendants of Calcol and Dara of the tribe of Judah and Dan along with possibly portions of other tribes that migrated from Egypt by ship to escape slavery by the Egyptians. They can only be traced through ancient writers and archeological findings and were the sons of Zarah, the Judah/Zarah bloodline of the Milesian and Danites that settled Greece, Spain, Troy and Italy where they later migrated into Europe and England. This group of people fell under the blessings that Abraham, Isaac, Jacob and Joseph were to receive but were not a part of the Chosen People. When all the ancient tribes of Zarah amalgamated with the house of Israel in the wilderness, they also fell under Gods' chosen people. The second group sojourned into Egypt with Jacob but did not depart the Exodus with Moses for some escaped by ship. When the new Pharaoh saw the danger of the Hebrew population, he began to enslave them. To avoid this persecution, some fled by ship and land into other regions. The Hebrews of the different tribes that elected to depart by ship gave up their right to be an Israelite. These Hebrews of Judah and parts of the other tribes elected to depart on their own but later merged with the house of Israel as God's Chosen People and accepted Jesus at his coming. The blood lines of both Phares and Zarah are eligible to be king of Israel through their mother Thamar as the genealogy of Christ is recorded in Matthew 1:3 which is very important to understand for it plays a great role in the history of King David's throne. This group is very unique due to their birth breach from Tamar as recorded in Genesis chapter 38. It is important to understand the breach and where they come into play as being eligible to the throne if we are to comprehend Gods end time Prophecies. The people of the scarlet threat (Zara blood line of Judah) were not a part of God's chosen Israelite people but were to play a very important role in the overturn of King David's throne into the wilderness. This completed their role as Gods people and their prophetic function when they accepted Christ's Gospel.

The third group is another important migrating segment of Hebrew people that need to be recognized and identified. They are the Phoenician ancestors of Enoch, the house of Enoch, which Noah was a part of and very little is known of their origin and history. They were the beginning of the Hebrew bloodline or birthright from Enoch to Abraham and the first in the line of Hebrews. This writer believes that God gave the Phoenicians the small region of coastline called Phoenicia in northern Israel because they were brothers. All through history, the Phoenicians and Israelites worked and traded together just as if they were family. The Phoenicians came from the ancestors of Enoch, Noah, Shem, Eber (Hebrew), Nahor, Terah and Abraham. Most likely, they had already settled Phoenicia in northern Canaan when Abraham was told by God to sojourn into Egypt. This would explain why the Phoenician and Hebrew languages are so similar for they were related by blood. All three elements of Gods people as Semitic, Phoenician and Hebrew meet the definition of Hebrew as being a traveler and wayfaring people. God knew that all three migrating elements of Hebrew people would join in unison and accept Christ's Gospel at its coming. They left behind high heaps and waymarks as identifying features throughout history within the continents of the world where ever they migrated as the speckled bird of diverse colors representing different races of people.

The small nation of Phenice in northern Palestine was only the beginning point for the Phoenician people. Their ancient sea going merchant dynasty of capitalism influenced every major seaport throughout the globe just as Great Britain and the United States today. The Phoenicians became a broad spectrum of different races of people due to world trade just as the English-speaking nations of the British Empire. You could say that with the amalgamations of all three elements of the Druid Phoenician people with the Hebrew Israelite tribes of Britannia, under the birthright blessing of the British Empire to include the United States, has become the Phoenician dynasty during modern time. We have become the speckled bird (Jerm 12:9) and the eagle with diverse colors dominating the world fulfilling the great blessings to Abraham, Isaac and Jacob, as being a blessing to all the families and nations of the world. The symbol of Manasseh as the united State of America in Duet 33:17 is the bull but in real life we carry an eagle for Dan the eagle is replaced by Manasseh in Rev 4:7 where Manasseh inherited Dan's eagle. The Greek word for eagle and Phoenicia means "Phoenix" or eagle in reference 5403 and 5404 of the Strong's Concordance. In Hebrew, it means "nesher", an eagle as a bird of prey or a region of northern Palestine. When you understand the Hebrew and Greek definitions of eagle and then read the prophecy of Ezekiel 17:1-7, we can see how the symbol of the eagle with great wings of diverse color is nothing more than the Phoenician ships migrating the Hebrew tribes into the wilderness.

The Israelites were a very pretentious people and often did not want to cooperate with their leader. In several cases throughout the Bible, when God told their leader to comply with his commands, the people rebelled and refuse to conform. This is what happened in Moses, Abraham and Solomon's case, for a portion of their people broke off and went their own way. God allowed this to happen, for he had special plans for each division. When the Hebrew people splintered into the world, you better believe Gods knows where they are and protects each and every one of his People. God is a master historian and if he knows each hair of our heads then he can certainly trace each of his Hebrew people down through the ages of time and know their whereabouts. Even though the Druid Phoenicians, Milesians and Danites of Calcol and Dara, were not of God's Chosen People of Israel, they were given a Heavenly mission and fell under the great blessing to be given to Abraham, Isaac and Jacob when blended with the house of Israel. They were to amalgamate among the birthright tribes as a calling into Europe where the house of Israel migrated to complete end time Prophecy as the diverse bird (different races of people). This is why God separated them as the Phoenicians, Milesians and Danites verses the Celts, Goths and all the other splintered tribal names of the house of Israel for they were to be a diverse people. God sent them into the world to settle as a preparation for the Gospel.

If you look in the back of your Bible that has ancient maps of Israel, Phoenicia is a small strip of land about twenty-five miles wide that runs along the coast of the Mediterranean Sea from Mount Carmel north into Syria. It was a costal nation bordering Asher and renowned for being sea going merchants. We have already covered in Chapter five how the Hebrew alphabet derived from the Phoenician language for they had great influence on the Israelite tribes because of their merchandizing. Their language was international just as English is today due to world trade and diplomatic influence.

Asher was known to be Phoenician after the conquest of their territory and established trade with Britain before the Trojan War of 1190BC. Britain was considered to be the trading center of the world prior to 900BC. This is an example of how the migrating Israelite tribes blended in whenever they settled in areas under Phoenician influence, therefore, losing their language and national identity. (Celt Druid and Culdee" by Elder)

The following historical information were taken from "Tracing Our Ancestors" by Frederick Haberman, page 22. The Phoenicians were colonizers and mariners after the name of Eber and Abraham, the first Hebrews, which means colonizer or High Father. The Greeks were the first to call the sea going mariners and merchants Phoenician for the small nation of Phoenicia existed at least 1000 years prior to the Hebrew Greek Empire of Calcol and Dara. The Phoenician language was Punic, being the commercial language of antiquity, as English is today. They derived their name from the forests of date Phoenix palms which grew in great abundance. The historian Horapollon says, "A palm branch was the symbol of the Phoenix" and Sanchoniathon, the Phoenician writer, states that "Phoenix was the first Phoenician" making Phoenix a man. The word Phoenix is the Greek form of the Egyptian term "Pa-Hanok," the house of Enoch. In Hebrew, Enoch is also Hanok, Strong's #2585 "Chanowk". This could very well mean that the first Phoenicians came from the house of Enoch.

According to Chambers Encyclopedia page 136, volume 8, gives the origin of the Phoenicians. Ancient historians such as Herodotus, Strabo, Pliny and others wrote that they dwelt anciently on the shores of the Persian Gulf where they migrated by land to Syria and settled on the coast of the Mediterranean. They were run out of their land by a great earthquake and settled the north west coast of Palestine called Phenicia. (Haberman p. 22)

There is very little recorded history on the Phoenicians that make them a mystery just as God's Word is a mystery. God wrote his Scriptures based upon symbols, analogies and parables hinged together on his Spiritual Truths. This is why God calls his Word a MYSTERY for he expects us to believe in faith and to study his history to puzzle his mystery together. We are to be Jerusalem, to teach and instruct his Word in a peaceful land. Studying ancient history has fortified my absolute belief in Gods Holy Scripture, to believe in total faith. From my studies, it is obvious that the ancestors of Enoch through Abraham were the building blocks of civilization. They were to be God's Chosen People through the Semitic people of Shem to become the Phoenician, Hebrew and English peoples, to be the birthright of Israel and spread Christ's end time Gospel to the entire world. His inherited birthright tribes were to be the Isaac sons or Saxons of Great Britain and their brother, the United States of America. They were to be the Battle Ax and protector of Christ's New Covenant where the Church is called Jerusalem and inherited the name Israel under the leadership of the lost sheep of the house of Israel in Matt 10:6 and 15:24.

Tracing Ancient names of the house of Israel
(Great Britain and the United States)

At this point, the author believes the reader is most likely saying to themselves that there is no evidence in history or Scripture indicating a clear identity of England or the United States in Bible prophecy. The reader most likely things this writer has lost it. American Christians believe that we are not mentioned in Prophecy because it is not clearly stated in the Bible and in that we have not studied the Scriptures for ourselves. The fact that we are in the Scriptures is clear if we read and study in the proper perspective for our historians and Theologians are not teaching the truth in our Churches, schools or Seminaries. The more we read and study the Scriptures the further they prove themselves to be true and accurate in every aspect and comes full circle from ancient days to modern times. The ancient names of Great Britain and the United States are, Ephraim, Manasseh, house of Israel, Lebanon, Sharon, Carmel, Gilead and Bashan as given by the Scriptures. There is also abundant evidence within accurate ancient history of the migrating Hebrews of the lost sheep of the house of Israel into Europe and England. The regions of northern Israel where Ephraim and Manasseh received the portion of the Promised Land was in the land area of Lebanon, Sharon, Carmel, Gilead and Bashan. When the Bible speak of these names, it is them the house of Israel as the ten northern tribes.

The way of identifying Great Britain and the United States in Bible Prophecy is rather simple and will be laid out in an orderly and understandable fashion in this segment. Before we study the ancient names of Israel, we must first cover a little Biblical history. Prior to understanding Biblical facts, we must first have total belief in the Scriptures, for without them, we have nothing to base our belief upon. There are certain facts that we must address before getting into this segment.

Today's world situation is based upon two Biblical stories that is critical in understanding if we are to appreciate end time Prophecy. There are several people representing separate ideologies diametrically opposing the Christian nations of the house of Israel. This puts light on why we have a world terrorist situation during these end days. We can trace this history through the Old Testament Prophetic books to the last days that encompass a hatred that dates back thousands of years. This abomination has created a terrorist mentality among the Arab (Ishmael "Islamic") people and a Socialist ideology within the people of the Communist bloc nations, Esau of Edom. These Islamic nations are diametrically opposed to and determined in destroying the western Christian culture. See Tyrus in table one.

The story of Hagar and Ishmael is recorded in Genesis chapter sixteen and although Ishmael was the firstborn, God gave the birthright to Isaac (Gen 17:21) due to Abraham's disobedience. Genesis 16:10 states that the descendants of Ishmael would be multiplied exceedingly and would become nations which are the Arab nations within the middle east of today dominated by the Islamic Religion of Ishmael. Esau and Isaac were Hebrew of Abraham's descent and to be nations (Gen 25:23). Esau was born first, a red baby that represents the color of Communism (Isa 63:2, 65:1-3), the color ruddy (Gen 25:24), making him eligible to be the birthright son. He was very sinful and against God just as his descendants are atheistic in modern times. The color of red represents the Red Horse of Communism (Revelation 6:4) that is an Age-Old ideology of Anti-Christian and is beginning to dominate the world of today. It will be the platform of the soon coming world leader of the Anti-Christ. We must realize that the Liberal Socialist agenda is demanding change of our economic, Political and Social environment. It is determined to eliminate all moral values and Christ from our system and is nothing more than the Philosophy of Communism preparing the way for the Red Horse of Socialism.

The ancestors of Esau (Seir), 1ⁿᵈ son of Isaac, became the Communist bloc nations of Europe with red as the color of Communism based on his color at birth as stated in Gen 25:25, **"came out red, all over like an hairy garment"**. He was a red hairy baby at birth. Esau was evil in the sight of God causing his birthright to be given to the younger son Isaac. Both Ishmael (1ˢᵗ son of Abraham) and Esau were firstborns but chose to not follow Gods Covenant, therefore, forfeiting the right to receive any of the birthright blessings given to the Children of Israel. Because of sin and rejection of God, they lost their Hebrew descent along with their birthright. We can now see the Liberal Nefarious Social dogma of Ishmael (Islam "terrorism") and Esau (Communism) trying to reclaim their birthright and how Satan uses this ancient hatred to catapult himself to be god, the Apotheosis. As covered in an earlier segment, the Islamic god of the Muslims is called Alah and the Hebrew meaning of curse in Isa 24:6. In ref#422&423 the word Hebrew CURSE means "alah", a swear word that devoured the earth as an astonishment. This verse and definition describe the terrorist situation during the last days or Tribulation for it says that **"the earth are burned, and few men left"**.

These reciprocal stories have one thing in common in that their birthright was taken from them and given to the younger son due to sin against God. This created an unfathomable hatred for the Arabs and the people of Esau towards Isaac because he received the birthright that they believed were due them. This is why it is so important to understand the birthright blessings and to whom received the right. The son that received the birthright also received the family name Israel (he will rule as God) and was to be a great nation and a company of nations, to be wealthy or fruitful (righteous or Christian).

The Everlasting Covenant was given to Abraham in Genesis 17:2-11 for he was to be nations and kings to be identified by circumcision, **"And I will make thee exceeding fruitful, and I will make nations of thee, and kings shall come out of thee"**. This blessing was passed to Isaac in Genesis 26:1-4 for his seed was to be as the stars of heaven and given all nations in the known earth for all the nations of the earth will be blessed through Abraham. He was to be a powerful nation as leader that has culminated into the Christian nations of the United States and the Common Wealth of Great Britain.

There are no nations in recorded history that can fulfill this scenario with symbols of the Bull and Unicorn given during their blessing in Duet 33:17. Four facts stand out that we must understand and study if we are to comprehend Biblical Prophecy:

Fact one: The division of Israel into two houses (I Kings 11) that still exist during our end times or end of the age.

Fact two: King David's throne and Gods promise that a man of all generations shall sit on his throne. (I Kings 9:5, Jerm 33:17 and II Sam 7:12-17).

Fact three: Who received the Birthright to be called Israel, only Joseph and his two sons (Gen 48:16-22) Ephraim and Manasseh of the house of Israel, not the Jews of Judah.

Fact Four: The Jews of Judah are only a remnant of God's chosen people or $2/12^{th}$ percent of the Hebrew Israelites of all twelve tribes and not just the Jew of the tribe of Judah/Benjamin for they only represent the modern state of Israel (Duet 7:6, 14:2).

Ancient names listed in Ezekiel chapters 27, 28, and 38 give a present day aligned coalition with modern Russia and Communist bloc nations. See Tyrus in table one. The above Scriptures prove the accuracy of the Bible for it is identical to the modern-day alignment of nations in Europe and the Middle Eastern Communist coalition.

England	**US**	**Israel**	**Ishmael (Arab)**	**Esau (Communist)**
Lebanon	Gilead	Jebusite	Egypt	Gebal
Sharon	Carmel	Jews	Palestine	Idumaea
	Bashan		Syria	Hamon-Gog
			Saudi Arabia	Magog
			Libya	Gog
			Arvah (Palestine)	Gomer
			Zidon	Togarmah
			Persia	Russia
			Cush	Bozrah
			Phut	Edom
			Lud	Tyre or Tyrus
			Ethiopia	Seir
			Sheba & Dedan (Saudi Arabia)	
			Ashkelon (Palestinian)	
			Gaza (Palestinian)	
			Ekron (Palestinian)	
			Ashdod (Palestinian)	
			Philistines (Palestinian)	

The following European countries are believed to be the ten lost Hebrew tribes of the house of Israel to include the mass of Judah and Benjamin. Out of 13 million Hebrews that went into captivity only approx. 40,000 Jews returned to Jerusalem and Judea after the Babylonian captivity (Ezra 6:14). All eleven million of the houses of Israel had already disappeared 130 years prior and never returned to their home land of Canaan. After the Assyrian and Babylonian captivities, the tribes of Judah/Phares which include both the house of Israel and Judah migrated across the Caucasus Mountains as the Sakai, Kumri, Schythians, Danaoi, Cimmerian, Gimmiri, Omri (of the house of King Omri I Kings 16:16), Celtae, Gatae, Goths, Visigoths, Ostrogoths, Celts and many more. They settled into the southeastern portion of Europe and became what is the Caucasian people. The Gothic word "Gauthei" means "the people of God". This definition explains why the Anglo-Saxon people are so arrogant for they were to exalt themselves above other nations just as God commanded. The descendants of Judah/Zerah of Calcol and Dara (I Chron 2:5) entered into Britain as Milesians and Dan (Danes, Danaoi or Tuatha de Danaan). These are just a few of the many names of the migrating Hebrew tribes entering Europe over hundreds of years.

Beth-Sak is Phoenician for "the house of Isaac" (Gen 21:12, Amos 7:16, and Heb 11:18) making Hebrew Israelite their Biblical name. The heathen name for Isaac, as recorded on the Amarna Tablets were Habiru, Habiri or Abire. These were the men that conquered Palestine under Joshua and were called

Saga or Saka, men that later became Sakai or Saxon as the sons of Isaac as they migrated into Europe. Their Biblical names were Hebrew but their heathen neighbors and enemies spoke of them as Habiru or H'Abiri, and Saga or Sakai, sons of Sac or Isaac (Saxon). ("Tracing our Ancestors" by Haberman page 122)

The ancient names of Judah or the Jews were Gadelos and landed in Uladh England in 700 to 650 BC. They had several heathen names such as, Gadil, Gadelus, Gadels and Gaidheil where the term Gael and Scot merged as the language of Ireland and Scotland. They were both branches of the Phoenicians as well as Welsh and Manx. The Judah-Zara bloodline came from Gallam of Ireland and descended from Brutus of Calcol and Dara (I Chron 2:5).

The migrating Hebrew tribes of Israel that crossed the Caucasus Mountains (Akkadian, Semitic or Aryan, people from the mountains) represent the modern nations of Europe as follows: Reuben denotes (France); Simeon (Spain), Levi was scattered between the houses of Judah and Israel and had no land. The tribe of Judah (denotes modern Israel and also settled Spain and Germany); Zebulon (Holland or the Netherlands); Issachar (Finland); Dan (Denmark "Jutland", Spain, Scotland, Wales and Ireland); Gad (Switzerland, France and Italy); Asher (Belgium, Sweden and Germany); Naphtali (Sweden); Benjamin (Norway and Iceland), Joseph is Ephraim (Great Britain and Canada) and Manasseh (United States). Note the similarities and design of the flags of each tribe as depicted on the illustration. Many portray the cross of Christ, Gods ensign to the world (Isa 11:11-12 Christianity). Notice the colors of red, white and blue and three strips that represent the Holy Trinity. The similarities within the flag design of all these Hebrew European nations cannot be a coincidence.

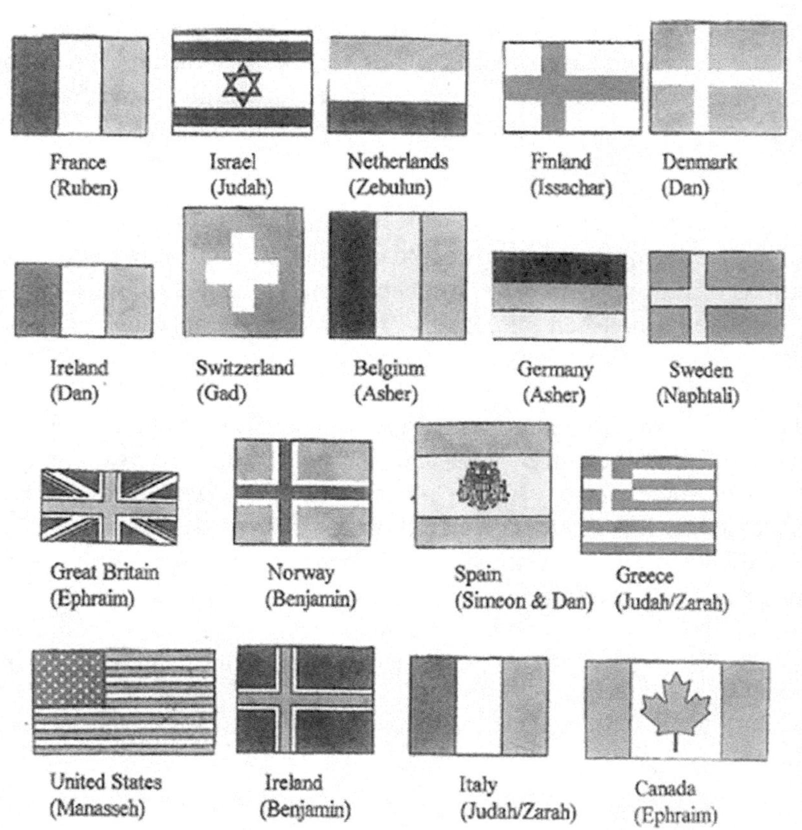

These tribes have been traced through bits of archeological findings found on the Behistun Rock inscription, the Topez of the Sachi, the Rosetta Stone, the Moabite Stone, Abiri of the Tel-el-Amarna Tablets and other archeological findings through-out Europe. Ancient writers such as Strabo, Josephus, Herodotus, the books of Maccabees and II Esdras, the four Masters, the Chronicles of Ireland, Scotland and England, Tacitus, Nennius, Lumisden, Welch Triads, Geoffrey of Monmouth, Diodorus Siculus (60 BC) and many others all speak of these ancient tribes. These tribes can also be traced through the symbols and traits of inheritance given by Jacob in Genesis chapter 49 and by Moses in Deuteronomy chapter 33 through symbols such as the lion, adder, bull, unicorn, deer, ass and the wolf. These symbols can be found in many of the modern European nations listed above. The massive amount of documented evidence tracing the ten northern tribes of the lost sheep of the house of Israel into Europe is overwhelming if you are willing to study and research with an open mind and a desire to learn the truth.

Ancient Lebanon (Ephraim or Great Britain)

As we study Lebanon in the Scriptures, it is referred to as a cedar tree (Isa 14:8) and the most renowned tree in God's Word for it typifies beauty. The Temple was made of cedar (I Kings 6:20) and represents the Throne of King David preserved through the throne of England, the unicorn (Eze 17:3 and 17:22-23). God's earthly creation was made of trees and his nations were named after them, Isaiah 60:13; Psalms 1:3 & 92:12. Lebanon and Asshur are one and the same for Genesis 10:11 states that Asshur, a son of Shem (Phoenician), built the city of Nineveh in Assyria (Lebanon). This could very well be why God sent Jonah to Nineveh to prophecy coming destruction due to their sins for they were a part of Gods Semitic people. They were descendants of his chosen people and played an important role as his Battle Ax of judgment.

The Hebrew definition associates Lebanon with the cedar tree and of righteous mountains that are symbolic as nations in the last days when referring to the house of Israel. Psalms 80:8-12 gives the account of the house of Israel being the bough that branched out over the sea and was a goodly cedar by being Christian or righteous. Lebanon is called the White Mountain covered with snow representing the purity and righteousness of Christianity (along with being fruitful). The glory of Lebanon is spoken of in Isaiah 35:2 and 60:13 as the glory of God and means it has to be righteous. Songs 5:15 speak of the great countenance of Lebanon and the excellence of its cedars. Lebanon is the cedar or leader over Sharon, Bashan, Gilead and Carmel just as Ephraim was leader over all the other tribes making Lebanon and Ephraim the same nation. They were to possess and preserve the cedar of David's Throne through the crown of England (the unicorn and bull).

Ancient Lebanon is not associated with modern day Lebanon in the Middle East but Gods Christian nations in the end times. There is a big question as to why the house of Israel was associated with Lebanon? It is fairly simple to understand for God used Assyria to punish Israel for their national sins. Ancient Assyria controlled the area called Lebanon in which Israel was forced to settle during their captivity. In essence, this was the house of Israel's first settlement after leaving their promised land. Assyria was settled by descendants of the tribe of Asshur (Gen 10:22) as a part of Gods Semitic people of Shem. The Hebrew meaning of Lebanon; the White Mountain is the heart as the most interior organ. God called them Lebanon so we could trace them through time for it was the last known existence of the ten lost tribes of the house of Israel before God sent them into the wilderness to the far reaches of the earth. They were also the heart of his Kingdom as portrayed in its definition. From this point, they were never whole again as all ten tribes but split into remnants of each tribe as nations (II Kings 17:6 and 19:17) and totally lost contact with the house of Judah. They lost their name as Hebrew Israelite, national identity and language (Isa 45:4 & 65:15).

Most of the ten northern tribes migrated into Europe and became the European Caucasians by crossing over the Caucus Mountains. The ones that remained show up in ancient writings where it is evident, they became part of the Media Empire and in 536BC along with the Persians, attacked and destroyed Babylon. This fulfills Jeremiah 51:19-29 for God used Jacob of Israel as his Battle Axe ("Tracing our Ancestors" by Frederick Haberman, page 124). This cannot apply to the Jews for when God dispersed them, they never became a nation with an Army to be his battle axe and Israel, the ten northern tribes received his inheritance of greatness through Ephraim and Manasseh (Gen 48:16).

Lebanon is always associated with the cedar tree and is the symbol of beauty in God's creation. Isaiah 29:17 states, **"Is it not yet a very little while, and Lebanon shall be turned into a fruitful field, and the fruitful field shall be esteemed as a forest?"**. Lebanon, Bashan, Carmel, Gilead and Sharon are all listed in the Bible as fruitful trees or forest and Lebanon is usually listed first. Being Fruitful is the key for it represents Christian trees or nations and Ephraim (England) the unicorn means double fruit in Hebrew. They became a fruitful field and esteemed forest (nations) under Christ's New Covenant of the Church (Jerm 31:31 and Heb 8:8) planted in the wilderness of the world. God's Christian nations are named after trees for they bear fruit (Ezekiel 17:24) (Refer to the word fruit and tree).

In other words, to fulfill Gods promise to King David that a man would always sit on his throne (I Kings 9:5), God had to move his throne to another location. The throne was to be taken from the Phares bloodline and given to the Zara bloodline (Matt 1:3, Gen 38). After studying Ezekiel chapters 17 and 21, it is clear that the cedar tree represents the throne and Lebanon is a cedar tree so the throne of Israel must be Lebanon. We can trace King David's throne to the throne of England; therefore, ancient Lebanon must be modern England or the Common Wealth of Great Britain. The throne was preserved to fulfill Gods promise to King David and the blessing to his inheritance tribes of Ephraim and Manasseh to be kings of Kingdoms and nations. The Cedar of Lebanon is the fruitful nation where Jesus took his Kingdom (throne) from the Jews and gave to a fruitful nation (Matt 21:43).

Ancient Sharon (Ephraim or the Isles of Great Britain)

The valley of Sharon is considered one of the most beautiful valleys in Israel and a coastal plain between Joppa and Mt. Carmel. The beautiful plant, rose of Sharon (Songs 2:1) is named after the valley due to its beauty and matches its definition. Sharon is used as a symbolic name for Ephraim or the house of Israel in ancient days as well as prophecies of the end times and can be found in Isaiah 33:9, 35:2 and 65:9-10.

Ancient names of Lebanon, Sharon, Bashan, Gilead and Carmel are listed as Christian (fruitful) nations in these verses and with Lebanon as their leader. This is referring to the falling away from righteousness (the Church I Thes 2:3) in the last days of our present time period. As we read and study these ancient names, we need to keep in mind that they are referring to Christian nations just prior to the Tribulation Period of Wrath. This can be proven in the following verses for Isaiah 33:9 states, **"Lebanon is ashamed and hewn down: Sharon is like a wilderness, and Bashan and Carmel shake off their fruits"**. Fruits is Christian and speaking of the nation Jesus spoke of in Matthew 21:43 as being fruitful. In this verse they are losing their righteousness during the period of falling away as prophesied in I Thessalonians 2:3, **"Let no man deceive you by any means: for that day shall not come, except there come a falling away first"**. We are presently in a period of apostasy of great falling away as recorded by Scripture.

Isaiah 35:2, identifies the Church, **"the glory of Lebanon shall be given unto it, the excellency of Carmel and Sharon, they shall see the glory of the Lord"**. This verse is referring to blossoming and rejoicing where Lebanon, Carmel and Sharon see the glory of the Lord and the Excellency of our God. This can only be speaking of the Church and these ancient names have to be his flock or Herd of sheep as the Church, the lost sheep of the house of Israel.

Isaiah 65:9-10 identifies the Church in more detail, **"And I will bring forth a seed out of Jacob, and out of Judah an inheritor of my mountains: and mine elect shall inherit it, and my servants shall dwell there. And Sharon shall be a fold of flocks, and the valley of Ahcor a place for the herds to lie down in, for my people that have sought me."** The seed out of Jacob and the inheritor of Judah is Christ the Messiah and the mountains his Christian nations. There are four different elements of people mentioned in this verse. The "seed out of Jacob" is Israel as a whole nation that produced Christ and his flock, the Church. "Out of Judah and inheritor" represent the linage of Christ as the Messiah, "my elect shall inherit" is any person that accepts Christ as the Messiah (the Church) and "his servants that dwell there" is the house of Israel, Gods Christian nations where he sent his Disciples to teach and to preach the Gospel in Matt 10:6 and 15:24. The phrase, "for the people that have sought me" is the Church of Christ's end time Gospel. The word mountain refers to nations where the valley of Achor is located within the world and where Sharon shall be a fold of flocks (the Church) of the people that seek Christ. These are the Christian nations of the world that have promoted Christ's Gospel fighting tyranny as Gods Battle Ax during the end days.

The valley of Achor is the continents in the wilderness (his vineyard) where he sent his lost sheep to spread the Gospel in peace that is England and the United States and all the other Christian nations of the British Common Wealth. Millions of people from all over the earth have come to the United States to seek religious freedom where they look for Christ in peace and prosperity. The United States and Great Britain, with our Christian coalition, is the only nations in history that can fulfill this verse that refer to the planting in the wilderness. Lebanon, Sharon, Bashan, Carmel and Gilead were located in the northern part of ancient Israel controlled by Samaria, the Capitol of the house of Israel. They were ruled by Ephraim and Manasseh, as the birthright tribes and this is why their ancient names are mentioned as being fruitful. The house of Israel was tasked by God to spread his end time Gospel as the Birthright tribes of Ephraim and Manasseh.

Ancient Bashan (Manasseh or the United States)

Bashan is an ancient region to the far north bordering Assyria and east of the Jordan River, the largest landmass of any tribe. This area belonged to Manasseh as one of the Birthright tribes being entitled to a double portion of land. We know that Manasseh is the Birthright tribe given double blessings and called the Bull for Deuteronomy 33:17 says "His glory is like the firstling of his bullock", indicating the firstborn birthright as being a single nation to be called a Bull. The horns of unicorns went to Ephraim his brother and indicated as being plural or many nations as "horns of unicorns" that match "his seed shall become a multitude of nations" (Gen 48:19). In Hebrew, the word unicorn means, #7214, a wild bull.

We know that Bashan and Carmel are a part of the house of Israel for Isaiah

33:9 states, **"and Bashan and Carmel shake off their fruits"**. We also know that the word fruit means a righteous nation in Gods eyes, a nation that bears fruit (Mat 21:43). The tribe of Dan was from Bashan and a part of the house of Israel for Deuteronomy 33:22 states, **"and of Dan he said, Dan is a lions whelp; he shall leap from Bashan"**. Bashan was a region of 13 cities consisting of the tribes of Issachar, Asher, Naphtali, and eastern and western Manasseh (I Chron 6:62 & 71). Being Manasseh was of the birthright tribe, it would only be fitting to say that they were the leader of the Bashan region.

Mt. Carmel was most likely a part of Bashan for it was located between eastern Manasseh and Asher on the north east coast of Israel. A portion of Dan leaped from Bashan by ship when Assyria took the house of Israel into captivity in 721 BC. Where did Dan go when he leapt from Bashan, they went west into the wilderness for Jeremiah 9:2 states, **"Oh that I had in the wilderness a lodging place of wayfaring men; that I might leave my people, and go from them! For they be all adulterers, and assembly of treacherous men."** Wayfaring in Hebrew means Heber or Hebrew men to cross over. In other words, the Hebrew men that crossed over into the wilderness across the sea that God prepared for them to complete their punishment of X7. When you multiply 7X360 years equaling 2520 total years and then add to their year of captivity of 740 BC. Their punishment would be complete in approx. 1780 AD (Leviticus 26:18). This is the approx. date when America became independent of England. Gods Spirit departed from them during their period of punishment which means he divorced them, Jeremiah 3:8.

Note that the divorce only pertained to the house of Israel and not to Judah. Judah's roots were then and always in Jerusalem where they are today. Jeremiah 50:19-20, again associates Carmel and Bashan with Israel, **"And I will bring Israel again to his habitation, and he shall feed on Carmel and Bashan, and his soul shall be satisfied upon mount Ephraim and Gilead. In those days, and in that time, saith the Lord, the iniquity of Israel shall be sought for, and there shall be none; and the sins of Judah, and they shall not be found; for I will pardon them whom I reserve."** Verse 20 refers to the last days that is happening now. It is clear that in these verses, Israel and Judah are two separate nations. This writer truly believes that verse 19 and 20 is modern day Israel where the gathering of the dried bones is presently taking place as the whole of Israel with all twelve tribes to be complete during the Tribulation Period, Ezekiel 37:11. Verse 19 is the key for modern day Israel is the house of Judah but is being drawn together back into the Promised Land to fulfill end time prophecy. In 1948, Israel became a nation with the help of Great Britain and the United States, (Carmel and Bashan). Israel is being protected by GB and the US, **"and he shall feed on Carmel and Bashan"**, and **"and**

his soul shall be satisfied upon mount Ephraim and Gilead". Carmel and Bashan represent the physical nation of the United States. The Christian Spirit of the Church represents the house of Israel that is broken down as Ephraim being Great Britain (the government of London) and Gilead of Manasseh as the United States (Washington DC). The Phrase, "whom I reserve", is the key for the Jews are being reserved till the last to complete the end time prophecy of the ancient city of Jerusalem.

Ephraim is the leader of the ten northern tribes of the house of Israel that became the Common Wealth of Great Britain. Amos 4:1 makes the statement, **"Hear this word, ye kine of Bashan, that are in the mountain of Samaria, which oppress the poor, which crush the needy, which say to their masters, Bring, and let us drink".** The word kine in "ye kine of Bashan" means in Hebrew #6510, a heifer, cow, kine. In Eze 1:10&10:14 and Rev 4:7 refer to the "the four living creatures" as the four brigades of Israel where the bull, calf or ox is referred to as Ephraim and Manasseh, the western tribes of their encampment during the Exodus and the western world in modern times. We know that Samaria was the capital city of the ten northern tribes with Ephraim and Manasseh as their leader (I Kings 21:18, II King 13:1). Samaria is synonymous with Ephraim and would make Samaria modern day Great Britain. See Samaria.

Again, in Micah 7:12-14 Carmel, Bashan and Gilead is associated together. Verse 14, **"Feed thy people with thy rod, the flock of thine heritage, which dwell solitarity in the wood, in the midst of Carmel: let them feed in Bashan and Gilead, as in the days of old."** The heritage of the birthright went to Ephraim, the modern-day Christian nation of GB and the US with symbols as the bull and unicorn (wild bull). They have fed the world with his Gospel of the rod of Christ as the fruitful nation taken from the Jews, Matthew 21:43. God planted them in the wilderness to dwell in solidarity within the woods, to live safely as a nation of un-walled cities (Eze 38:11). This verse would make Carmel, Bashan and Gilead to be Manasseh for these were the ancient regions of Manasseh. The phrase, "as in the days of old", means they were leader as the birthright tribe in the wilderness during modern time just as they were in ancient days.

Nahum 1:3-4 demonstrates how God will punish his Christian nations and will not acquit the wicked, Bashan, Carmel and Lebanon. Zech 11:2, **"howl, O ye oaks of Bashan; for the forest of the vintage is come down".** This verse refers to Bashan as an oak tree that is a wilderness of trees and the vintage representing a vineyard, the fruits of a vintage of Christ's Gospel the Church.

God's vineyard is the house of Israel and Judah in the wilderness that accepted the fruit of his Gospel. This verse refers to the great falling away from the truth of his Gospel that is happening now. Refer to Wilderness and Vineyard.

Ancient Gilead (Manasseh or United States)

Bashan is the leader of the coalition between Gilead and Carmel and it is this writer's belief that Bashan is the United States as a whole but broken down into two groups of people. Gilead is the northern states within the United States and its leader with the capital in Washington DC, Jeremiah 50:19, **"And I will bring Israel again to his habitation, and he shall feed on Carmel and Bashan, and his soul shall be satisfied upon mount Ephraim and Gilead."** The Excellency (Christian) of Carmel (Isa 35:2) is the Bible belt of the southern states. The Civil War between the north and south of the nation of Israel is recorded in Ezekiel 20:46 through 21:4. Remember that the Bible is written for the last days but there was also a war between the north and south of the nation of Israel in ancient days as recorded in II Kings 16:5. The Bible is a mirror of time and history repeats itself for everything that happened to Israel in ancient days also occurs in modern times. The Bible and its prophecies come full circle just as the Civil War between Judah and Israel in approx. 742 BC in ancient times verses the war between the north and south in 1860 in modern days.

We know that Gilead was from the tribe of Manasseh that received the double blessing of the birthright along with Ephraim, Genesis 48:16-22. Gilead was the son of Machir and Machir the son of Manasseh (Gen 50:23) which puts him in line to receive the birthright blessings of greatness. The one-half tribe of Manasseh was given the north half of Gilead, all of Bashan, and the region of Argob (Duet 3:13) which makes the people of Gilead and Bashan the same descendants as referred to in end time prophecy and national alignment. In Jeremiah 8:19 thru 9:2, refers to Gilead as the daughter of my People, verse 22, **"Is there no balm in Gilead; is there no physician there? Why then is not the health of the daughter of my people recovered?"** These verses indicate the unrighteousness of Gods people in ancient times and parallel in the last days that is our present time period of Liberalism. Gilead is referred to as the daughter of Gods people, the house of Israel as a part of Manasseh the bull therefore, Gilead has to be the United States.

To prove this fact, let's review Jeremiah 8:22 referring to Gilead. He is referred to as being the daughter of Gods people and is a key in understanding Gilead during the end times. The secrets lie within the root meaning of daughter for the

Hebrew meaning as given in the Strong's Concordance, (1323) as a daughter of relationship. The primitive root (1129) means to build by obtaining children and the secondary feminine (1319) means to announce (glad news), messenger, preach, publish, tell good tidings. At this time, if you go to the word bough given in Genesis 49:22 as Joseph's birthright blessing and reference (1121) gives its meaning as, a builder, nation, young bull or calf, firstborn and very fruitful. Reference (1121) gives a cross reference to (1129), bough, which is a root meaning of daughter in reference 1323. After reviewing the meaning and all the cross-reference meanings, daughter represents the definition of, a building by obtaining children, a preacher or messenger bringing, carrying or bearing good news or tidings, a nation, young bull or calf, firstborn and to be very fruitful. Through root word meanings, we can trace the definition of daughter as referred to Gilead, to bough in Genesis 48:22 where Joseph is called a bough as the birthright firstborn blessing given to his two sons Ephraim and Manasseh.

Gilead is the tribe of Manasseh as the young bull to be builder of the family name of Israel and was to preach and teach the new Covenant of God's Word, the Gospel. They were given this responsibility through the firstborn birthright blessing and were to be the Shepard, the stone of Israel, to preach the end time Gospel (Gen 49:24) to the world as a bough whose branches run over the wall. Gilead is a part of Bashan and Carmel as the United States fulfilling their great blessing as the Bull. Another interesting cross reference is the meaning of Jerusalem in (3389 and 3384) for it also means to teach and be an archer (Confederate 1167) in a founded peaceful place and Jerusalem has a dual meaning that also departed with the Throne and Kingdom.

We need to connect Gilead with the words bullock or bull, covenant, archer, confederate or confederacy. The secret identity of Bashan, Carmel and Gilead as part of the southern States of America lie hidden within the cross referencing of these words. The word confederate is found six times in the Scriptures (Isa 8:12,7:2, Gen 14:13, Ps 83:5 and Obadiah 7) and has a Hebrew meaning of; (1285) covenant, compact, league, join together, (1167) chief man, Lord, archer, captain, a husband as being married, master, (5115) to rest, etc. The unicorn is the symbol of Ephraim and has the Hebrew meaning of, to rise or be lifted up and a wild bull. You can clearly see that this definition matches the history and greatness of the British Empire as being raised up in power and strength. Keep in mind that "Brit" in Hebrew means covenant and "ish" means man, therefore, British (Angles or Angel) means covenant man which is Gods Covenant People of the lost sheep of the house of Israel as Anglo-Saxon.

The Hebrew definition of Bullock; (6499) a bullock as breaking forth in wild strength, (6565) utterly, to plow, (1241) bull, cow, heifer, ox or herd, (7794) a *bullock as a traveler, cow, bull or Ox,* (7788) travel about as a harlot or *merchant, go sing,* (7891) *to sing or singing man.*

The word bull has a slightly different meaning; (47) Angel, chief, mighty one, (46) spoken of God, (82) primitive root; to soar or fly, (5022) fruits, (5011) fruit (5108) produce fruit (as being Christian, 5107) to germinate, to make flourish, to utter, bring forth (fruit as Christian), make cheerful and increase. It can be seen how through the definition of bullock and bull, the American people as travelers (migration), through military strength, being merchants (world economics), singing praise by uttering God's Word worldwide and bearing fruits as Christian nations, has spread Christ's end time Gospel. America is the bull of Manasseh and was to be a very fruitful powerful people as a chief or mighty one. They are to be Gods spokesman as Christian and fulfill Deuteronomy 33:17, Gen 22:17-18, 35:9-12, 48:16-19 with the bull as their national symbol. This is the fulfillment of the great Birthright blessing given to Abraham, Isaac, Jacob, Joseph and then to Ephraim the Unicorn (GB) and Manasseh the Bull (USA). They were to be Gods powerful battle ax and protector of the Church during the past 2000 years.

The southern states of Manasseh, Carmel, can be identified through the word Confederate and the symbol of the Bull "**X**" (the flag of St. Andrew of Scotland) found on the British flag and the southern Confederate (Covenant) states of America. The Bull is a symbol of the strength of Gods Covenant People as indicated by being the first letter of the Hebrew alphabet where Manasseh is referred to as "thousands" in Deuteronomy 33:17 (Strong's Concordance ref. #505, 504 and 502). They are the bull of Gods people in ref. # 46 and 47 (spoken of God and mighty one, angel "Angles" Anglo-Saxon, Chief or mighty one).

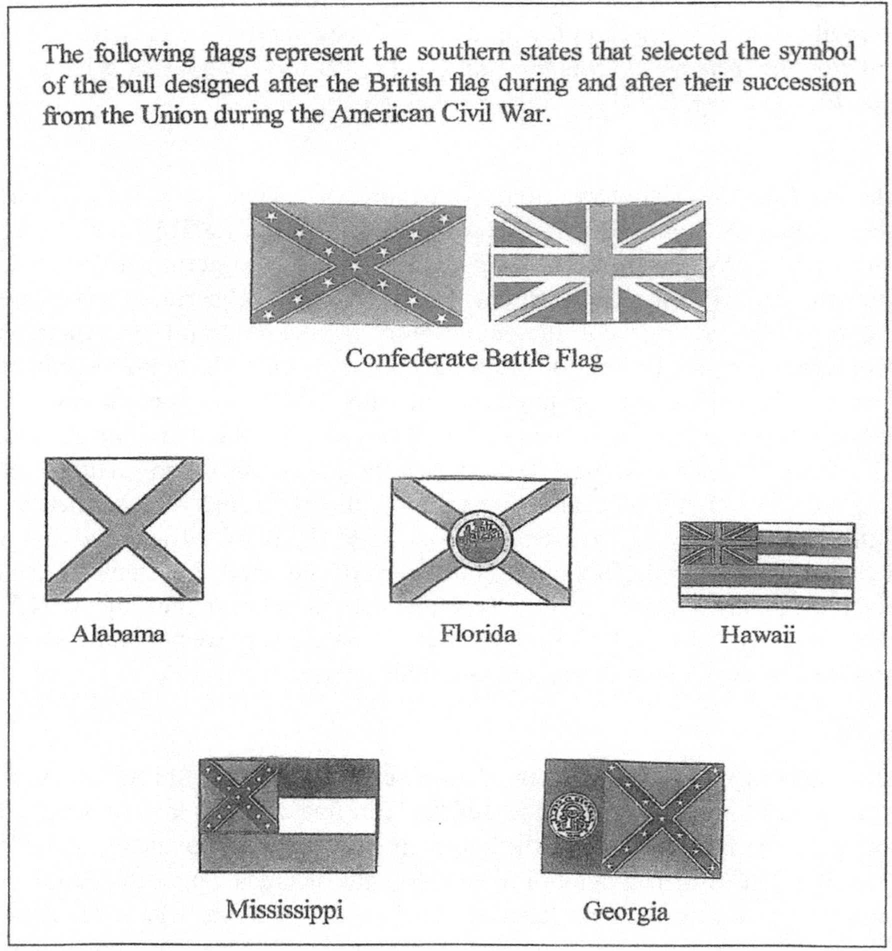

The following flags represent the southern states that selected the symbol of the bull designed after the British flag during and after their succession from the Union during the American Civil War.

If we study the Confederate flag and the **X** chosen as their symbol at the time of succession from the union in January of 1860 through June 1861, we can understand as to why Alabama, Florida, Georgia, Hawaii and Mississippi has an **X** on their state flags prior to being politically incorrect. We can now see the present falling away from Gods Covenant and this explains some of the hatred toward the Confederate flag and the planed destruction of every aspect of Gods covenant by Satan and his agents.

We need to understand the symbol of the **X** and why it was chosen to represent the Bible belt of the southern states (Carmel). It is common knowledge that the southern states have always been more prevalent in keeping God's Word, therefore, being called the "Bible belt" of the south. The south is also great cattle keepers fulfilling the definition of "Thousands", the name given to

Manasseh in Deuteronomy 33:17 as a family and "yoking or taming of cows" (504). The cowboy is <u>a singer</u>; to sing or <u>singing man and traveler as in the definition of bullock</u> (7788 and 7891). We can see how the Scriptures imply how the bull or cow was to be the economic wealth (merchant) of our founding forefathers, the settling of the old west and the wealth they provided. The expanse of the western wilderness in the western states is perfect for raising cattle and settling our west just as our brothers of Austria, New Zealand and other Christian (Saxon or Isaac Sons) nations. They have always been cattle keepers called the Bull.

The settling of this nation to include the old west represents plantation life as referred to in Ezekiel 17:7. This was a way of establishing the wilderness of our nation and creating great wealth. Reference (4302) of the Strong's Concordance gives the Hebrew meaning of Plantation (ing) as; something planted, the place as <u>a garden or vineyard</u> or a thing by the act of planting. Study the words planted, garden, vineyard and other related words in table one. The plantation is a nation planted in the wilderness by the great eagle (Eze 17:3&7) to be a fruitful field, garden or vineyard as Christ's Church (Christian) and planted by great waters (USA, Isa 18) to fulfill the end time Gospel (Matt 21:43). This is why the bull of strength is the symbol of our economic wealth of today. We know that our forefathers, overall, came from the English (Saxon), therefore, when the south succeeded from the union, they took the symbol of the Bull (**X**) from the British flag (the flag of St. Andrew).

The British flag is the symbol of the wild bull's (strength as a unicorn), an X, first letter of the Hebrew alphabet superimposed on a + (plus), the last letter of the Hebrew alphabet. The X also represent the crossing of Jacobs arms in Genesis 48:16 when giving the birthright blessings to the two lads or sons of Joseph, Ephraim the Unicorn and Manasseh the Bull (Duet 33:17). The colors of the British flag are red, white and blue just as their brother of American and the Confederate states of the south. When the South succeeded from the Union, they encompassed the colors and symbol of the bull (**X**) from the British flag. The thirteen stars on the Confederate flag represent the thirteen tribes of Israel as the thirteen colonies on the original American flag. It should be noted as to why the Confederate flag had thirteen stars but only eleven states succeeded. Manasseh represents the United States and were the thirteenth Tribe therefore, the number 13 was incorporated into our flag, standard or ensign. The American Continental flag had thirteen stars representing the original colonies but symbolize the thirteen tribes of Israel. Can this be a coincidence for it is up to the reader to make that determination?

If we closely study and complete a cross reference of confederate, bullock, covenant, branch, bough, Jerusalem, Carmel, Gilead, fruitful and nation, we can begin to understand the identity of the Hebrew travelers (the bull). They are the fruitful nation taken from the Jews by Christ (Matt 21:43) as the lost sheep of the house of Israel (Matt 10:6 and 15:24) that was scattered abroad into the wilderness and continents of the world to become fruitful Christian nations. Gilead is a portion of Bashan and Carmel and represents the bull of the United States as a whole.

Jeremiah 9:2 tell of the resting place in the wilderness for Gods planted people, the lost sheep of the house of Israel. Refer to the word wayfaring men, for they are Hebrew people that migrated to far countries as indicated by the Hebrew definition. It is believed that in approx. 1800 BC, Hu Gadarn Hysicon (Isaacson), or Hu the Mighty, established the first Cymri colony in Britain and credited as erecting Stonehenge after the faith of Abraham that was Druidism. The same Hebrew race of Calcol and Dara where their descendants erected the great Pyramids of Egypt prior to migrating from Egypt before and after the Exodus.

God left his people in the wilderness till his 2520-year punishment was complete (Lev 26:18). He then restored them as a great nation to receive the birthright blessings to be a nation and a company of nations (Gen 35:11) that is the United States and Great Britain of today. Jeremiah wrote these verses approx. 600 BC, 140 years after Manasseh had been taken into captivity to Assyria in 740 BC (II Chron 33:11). Manasseh or Gilead was the first tribe taken into captivity during the 20-year Assyrian war. This indicates that Jeremiah knew where they were and later overturned King David's throne into Ireland where the Hebrew people of Calcol and Dara had already combined with the Hebrew travelers of the house of Israel called Isaac's sons (Saxon). This was the joining or gathering of Gods people to include the Druidic people of the old faith of Abraham (I Chron 2:6) where they had migrated hundreds of years before and planted by God to wait for Christ's Gospel. This fulfills Jeremiah's commission as recorded in Jeremiah 1:10.

Ancient Carmel (Manasseh or United States)

The Hebrew definition of Carmel directly links the meaning to the house of Israel. We see the words mountain, hill, fruitful field, planted garden, orchard, vineyard, a son or builder of the family name, obtain children and to build. All these definitions can be applied to the nations that were planted in the wilderness in Ezekiel 17:23. Through-out the Old Testament, verses that refer to the word Carmel is associated with Lebanon, Sharon, Bashan, Tabor, Mt.

Ephraim, and Gilead. Carmel is generally referred to as Mt. Carmel and often used as an illustration of a beautiful and fruitful place. These ancient names represent end time nations as the Christian countries that are fruitful and bearing fruit of God's Word as a flowering nation. They migrated north as the house of Israel after their captivity to Assyria in 740 to 718 BC to never return but are mentioned in the Old Testament prophetic books during the last days as Lebanon, Sharon, Bashan, Gilead, and Carmel.

We need to re-quote Isaiah 33:9 that refers to Carmel, **"The earth mourneth and languisheth: Lebanon is ashamed and hewn down; Sharon is like a wilderness; and Bashan and Carmel shake off their fruits"**. These nations are a coalition and at one time righteous nations but have lost their righteousness as Christian by shaking off their fruits that is happening today in our liberal world. We are shaking off the fruits of Christianity by taking God out of our Society as a liberal movement and Socialist agenda of the Red Horse of Rev 6:4 (Political Correctness). This is speaking of the end time Christian nations that have lost the righteousness of God and his Word by allowing Satan's Liberal agents to come in and take over our nation. We are now seeing the corrupted state of falling away from the truths of his Gospel (II Thes 2:3) by not staying faithful to Gods Commandments. Again, we need to re-quote Jeremiah 50:19, **"And I will bring Israel again to his habitation, and he shall feed on Carmel and Bashan, and his soul shall be satisfied upon mount Ephraim and Gilead'.** This is when God brings the Children of Israel back into the Promised Land (modern Israel) during the end days and is helped by Carmel and Bashan (United States). This event takes place just prior to Israel becoming a whole nation with the gathering of the dried bones in Ezekiel chapter 37. **"Satisfied upon mount Ephraim** (England) **and Gilead** (Washington DC)" represents all the military and economic aid given to modern Israel (house of Judah) to maintain their nation in the midst of the Arab states. Without our aid, Israel could not exist as a modern state. We are presently in this time period.

Bashan and Carmel (United States) are the nations that helped Israel sprout again in 1948. Mt. Ephraim and Gilead were districts in the heartland of ancient Israel of the northern region of Bashan making them of the tribe of Manasseh. As we have studied, Manasseh is one of the birthright tribes and represents the Bull (United States) and encompasses the regions of ancient Carmel, Bashan and Gilead. When we read Scriptures pertaining to these three regions, it is speaking of the United States or Manasseh during end time events.

Micah 7:12-20 says, **"In that day",** referring to the last days, shall come from the river and from sea to sea or mountain to mountain (nations to nations) feeding their people with **"the rod, the flock of thine heritage"**, (the rod and flock is the Gospel and the Church). The heritage is the inheritance of the birthright tribe of Ephraim and Manasseh that is Lebanon, Sharon, Bashan, Carmel and Gilead mentioned in verse 14 to be called Israel through the birthright. They shall be a mighty people for the nations of the world shall see their strength, verse 16. They will be Christian for verse 17 says, **"they shall be afraid of the Lord our God, and shall fear because of thee."** Verse 20 states, **"Thou wilt perform the truth to Jacob,"** which indicate the Gospel or truth will be given to Jacob or all twelve tribes through the New Covenant just as Hebrew 8:8-10 and Jeremiah 31:31-33 states.

If we closely study these verses, we can see how God planted his fruitful nation in the wilderness to spread his end time Gospel and the responsibility that fell upon the birthright Christian nations of the house of Israel. History tells us that only the English-speaking nations (Protestant) and Hebrew European countries such as Germany has helped evangelize the world during the past five hundred years. The rod and flock mentioned in these verses cannot be speaking of the Roman Catholic Church for it tried to destroy the original Apostolic Church established in England and Europe during the past two thousand years. At one point in time, the Roman Church even ordered all Bibles to be burnt. How can that be of God and spreading his Gospel? The United States were originally settled by immigrants that fled Europe for religious freedom to escape the grip of the Roman Church and represented Christ's original Church established by the Apostles. This is exactly why God reserved the North American continent as a safe haven, a place for the people of the world to escape religious persecution and seek peace and prosperity during the last days. With the freedom of religion establish under a Republic ruled by the people, God was able to spread his Gospel worldwide into every nation within the globe under the protective arm of his Battle Ax, his 5th Stone Kingdom which is the Church (GB and USA).

When we combine the Scriptures that refer to Lebanon, Sharon, Bashan, Carmel and Gilead, we begin to get the overall picture of who they are. These five ancient nations fall under Lebanon of the Cedar (Ps 29:5-6) that represents King David's throne and the symbol of the calf or bull of Manasseh and the unicorn of Ephraim (Duet 33:17). Lebanon is almost always mentioned first as the leader and Isaiah 60:13 refers to it as a beautiful forest and states, **"The glory of Lebanon shall come unto thee, the fir tree, the pine tree, and the box together, to beautify the place of my sanctuary; and I will make the place of my feet glorious"**. According to this verse, Lebanon has to be his Temple or Church as the house of Israel, under the leadership of Ephraim as the birthright tribe for it is his sanctuary and the place or Glory for Gods feet, the earth where his Gospel is to be spread. The fir, pine and box trees represent Christian nations under the leadership of Lebanon which is the Common Wealth of Great Britain, controlled by David's throne, the cedar tree of the Crown of England which includes their brother, the United States.

Lebanon is Gods earthly Kingdom as the house of Israel according to this verse and will be his Heavenly Kingdom in the fruitful field of his Church. Ezekiel 17:3-5 explains how the Cedar of Lebanon of the house of Israel was chopped off and carried into the land of traffic by Jeremiah. The Commission of Jeremiah 1:10, planted Lebanon as the house of Israel in a fruitful field (Christian) and also means abundant and wealthy. Ezekiel chapter 17 through 23 explains how the high Cedar branch was chopped off which represents the throne of David (Eze 17:22-24) and was planted or overturned (Eze 21:25-27) into a fruitful field in a land of traffic which can only be the Islands of Britannia or England, Angle-land (England) of the Anglo Saxon, the seed of Isaac. Isaiah chapter 41 also explains these Islands for the Islands of Britannic has always been the center of world shipping of **merchants** (Bullock) even in ancient times accommodating the Phoenician ships of Tarshish (II Cron 9:21).

After reviewing all of these verses, the first bird with diverse colors (Eze 17:3&7) was the migrations of Lebanon or Ephraim where the throne of David is preserved through the Crown of England "a city of merchants", London England. This would fulfill the promise to David that his throne would be to all generations and that a man would always sit on his throne. Sharon is a part of Lebanon or Ephraim as the Common Wealth of Britain with the symbol of the unicorn and represents the bird of diverse colors of different nations of people, colonizing (Plantation) the world. Lebanon represents Gods Kingdom under his throne (England) that is all his Christian nations controlled by the original British Common Wealth to include the United States. Lebanon is further broken down into Sharon being England controlled by the government in London as the city of merchant where Bashan represents the whole of the United States. Bashan is divided into Gilead being the government of Bashan controlled by Washington DC and the northern states. The Excellency of Carmel represents the Southern States that has always been outstanding in preserving the Christian faith, therefore, given the name Bible belt of the south. This is the Excellency of Carmel (Isa 35:2) spoken of as keeping God's Word.

Bashan, Carmel and Gilead represent Manasseh the bull which was the second bird that gained independence from the first bird as their own country and became the Republic of the United States (Eze 17:7). Lebanon and Bashan were the land of freedom of religion and prosperity of great wealth promised to Abraham, Isaac, Jacob and Joseph given directly to Ephraim, to be **"a company**

of nations shall be of thee" and Manasseh to be **"a nation".** Between the two, they were to receive the inheritance blessings to be kings of kingdoms and a nation and a company of nations (Gen 17:6, 22:17-18, 28:14, 35:11 and 48:16-19).

Ezekiel 17:1-7 speaks of a great bird that took the house of Israel into the wilderness. Verse three says that this bird was of diverse colors which is important to understand for diverse in Hebrew means variegation of color, embroidery, needlework on both sides and to variegate color. This nation of the house of Israel was to be diverse races of people or colors. This can be verified in Jeremiah 12:9 where God said that his heritage, the birthright inherited tribe of Ephraim and Manasseh, were to be as a speckled bird. The Hebrew meaning for speckled, dyed in stripes as the hyena, to dip into coloring fluid of dye and diverse colors. This means that Israel was to be inter-racial as different colors of people just as the United States is represented as a melting pot of nations and corresponds with Christ's Gospel being open to all man, races, creeds or color.

Jeremiah 12:8-15 speaks of the inheritance of Israel as his vineyard and how his Pastors have destroyed it. Verses 11-13, explains the falling away from Gods truth that can be applied to ancient days as well as our present period of falling away. Verses 14-15 states the inheritance of Israel and how they will be plucked out of the Promised Land along with Judah and given their own inheritance. Judah is not mentioned as the inheritance tribe. Whenever the inheritance is spoken of, it is referring directly to Ephraim and Manasseh as the birthright tribe and not the Jew of Judah for they did not receive the birthright. Judah shall be plucked out from Israel and sent back to the Promised Land fulfilling the prophecy of Jerusalem by becoming a nation in 1948. Read and study these verses carefully.

Ezekiel chapter 17 is a fascinating chapter for it speaks to two different birds taking away Israel into the wilderness indicating two separate nations of diverse people. Verse 3 says that a great eagle came into Lebanon and took the highest branch of the cedar where God cropped off the top of his young twigs and carried it into a land of traffic and placed it in a city of merchants. This is London England.

This brings up another very interesting scenario for if you study the word eagle, in Hebrew, it means a large bird, eagle or vulture that is very tender, loving, compassionate and merciful towards its young. In Greek, eagle means Phoenix or palm tree which is a symbol of the Phoenician Sea going merchant empire that matches and fulfills Ezekiel 17:4, **"He chopped off the top of his young twigs, and carried it into a land of traffic, he set it in a city of merchants"**. The term "young twig" means branch, the two daughters of King Zedekiah and matches Genesis 49:22 where the throne was overturned (Eze 21:25-27) from Jerusalem and given to the birthright of Joseph of Ephraim as leader (Matt 21:43) to be the whole Kingdom. The throne was to be carried into a land of traffic into a city of merchants that matches Ephraim the unicorn or the city of London.

The tender twigs were the two daughters of King Zedekiah, Israel's last King in 586BC that preserved the bloodline of King David and the promise of his throne. This represents the traveling of Zion and how Jerusalem was plowed and David's throne being overturned into another land. This new land was given the name Lebanon for when the great eagle took the cedar, the name Lebanon went with it. This fruitful nation is the unicorn of Ephraim where Jeremiah was commissioned to overturn David's throne into Ireland. Today this land is called England and 46 nations of the British Common Wealth representing the diverseness of many nations, creeds and colors of people to include their brother Manasseh, the United States. They were carried by the wings of a great eagle that is a symbol of the Phoenician merchant ships into London, the center of world sea trade during ancient days as well as modern.

Verse seven speaks of another great eagle, **"There was also another great eagle with great wings and many feathers: and behold, this vine did bend her roots toward him, and shoot forth her branches toward him, that he might water it by the furrow of her plantation."** This verse says that another great eagle came from the first eagle as one of her vines and branched toward him and was watered by Lebanon. This vine or branch was Manasseh where the United States branched out from England and broke away by becoming independent in 1776. This nation was called a plantation just as our colonies were based on plantation life that allowed us to civilize and settle our great wilderness. Verse 8 speaks of this branched out nation, **"It was planted in a good soil by great waters, that it might bring forth branches, and that it might bear fruit, that it might be a goodly vine."** This vine was to be fruitful and righteous (Christian) planted in good soil by two great oceans on either side for protection. This verse is speaking of the continent of America as the regions of Manasseh, Bashan, Carmel and Gilead. The American continent is one of the most fertile and poses the greatest natural resources of any continent in the world. Isaiah chapter 18 also refers to this continent in more detail and calls it Mount Zion that means a Christian nation.

The first great bird or eagle mentioned in Ezekiel chapter 17 is Ephraim the unicorn of the house of Israel being taken or plucked out of the Promised Land of Canaan and given their inheritance in the wilderness. Ephraim represents ancient Lebanon and Sharon. The United States is the second great eagle of Manasseh, the bull, representing the regions of Bashan, Carmel and Gilead of ancient times. The diverse bird with great wings in Ezekiel 17:3 and the speckled bird in Jeremiah 12:9 represent migrating nations of the house of Israel as nations of diverse race, creed and color of people. When we study the history of how Britain colonized all the continents of the world to include America and represented all national creeds, races and colors of people, we can see the meaning of the diverse or speckled birds of color. An important aspect is that even though the house of Israel consisted of all creeds and colors of people, these colonies were controlled, educated and governed by the Caucasian ruddy people of the house of Israel under the Crown of England representing the throne of David. This fulfills Deuteronomy 33:17, Genesis 22:18, 28:14 and 35:11 that the inheritance tribe of Abraham, Isaac, Jacob, Joseph and then to Ephraim and Manasseh would control the gates of their enemy and bring righteousness and judgment to the world under Gods New Covenant of his Gospel. Study the words mountain, plant, vineyard, wayfaring, highway and all the other words that pertain to the house of Israel in table one for better understanding.

Chapter 8

Understanding the Hebrew meaning of the following words and applying them to the birthright tribes of Ephraim and Manasseh gives meaning to the identification of Zion and the Branch of Christ. This helps us to unfold Daniel's secret and to realize the responsibility that went to Ephraim and Manasseh. They were to carry on the family name and receive the firstborn blessing that went with this accountability. We must note that evangelizing the world went to the house of Israel in Matt 10:6, 15:24, Act 10:36 and Eze 3:1-5 where authority was given by Christ himself. The house of Israel is England as the bull and unicorn in Duet 33:17 given the family name as the firstborn birthright blessings of the tribes of Ephriam and Manasseh in Gen 48:16-22. Only they were to be called Israel. This places King James I of England into the lineage of King David and authorized him to translate all known ancient text into the King James Version Bible in 1611AD by 47 of the greatest Scholars in the world. This is the only bible in history to have Gods authorization by Scripture.

The words bough, plant, vineyard, branch, tree, wilderness and mountain are all in common by definition through-out the Old Testament and in direct reference to the house of Israel, the nations planted in the wilderness. They do not refer to the house of Judah that is the Jews. Judah was the root of the promised land of Israel and could not be replanted in the wilderness for they had the important role and destiny to return to the promised land in Judea to re-sprout which they did in 1948 as the modern nation of Israel fulfilling Matt 24:32, "Now learn a parable of the figtree". In reality, the modern nation of Israel should have been called, the nation of Judah not Israel, for the name Israel was reserved for the house of Israel in accordance to the birthright primogeniture Mosaic Law given to Ephraim and Manasseh. They became the English-speaking nations of Great Britain and the United States, the God given symbol of the unicorn and bull. These words over lap and interconnect so it will be necessary to re-quote certain verses and phrases to get a full understanding.

Bough

The word bough is a fascinating word and in direct correlation with the birthright blessings to Ephraim and Manasseh. The primogeniture of the birthright is indicated by the Hebrew definition of bough which means; a son (builder of the family name), anointed one, appointed to; nation, a branch, bright green foliage; firstborn bull or young calf (synonymous with the United States), a basis for building a foundation, a forest, fruitful and reward. These are the primary meanings and refer to bough as being a nation that received the birthright and to be fruitful as servants and Stewarts (Christian). Isaiah 16:1-8, 41:1-8 and Jeremiah 23:3-6 speak of a nation planted in the wilderness bringing judgment and righteousness under David's throne where their branches are stretched out over the sea. This nation bringing judgment is the kingdom Jesus took from the Jews in Matthew 21:43. Study these verses closely.

Whenever you see the word bough in the Scriptures, it is speaking of the birthright tribe of Ephraim or Manasseh with the symbols of the bull and unicorn. This is proven by the definition of being the firstborn and young calf or bull which is the builder of the family name as mentioned in the meaning of bough and found in Genesis 49:22. Joseph received his blessing in the capacity of being the Birthright son given to Ephraim and Manasseh. They were to be the leaders of God's chosen people, the house of Israel, and meet the elements set forth in the definition to be the birthright sons to carry on the family name of Israel as great nations within the world. These nations were to be fruitful (Christian) giving righteousness and judgment to the nations and having the symbol of the Bull and Unicorn. Their symbol of blessings was given in Genesis 49:22 (bough means bull) and Deuteronomy 33:17 (bullock and unicorn). Simply trace the symbol of the Bull and Unicorn through time and we see that the Bull represents the financial institutes of Wall Street in New York City (Manasseh) that controls world trade by the United States and the Unicorn is found within most of the governmental symbols of the 46 Common Wealth nations of the United Kingdom of Great Britain (Ephraim) and the financial institutions of London linked directly to Wall Street in New York City. No other nation in the world places a Unicorn on their national symbol and seals. These financial institutes of Gods Birthright tribes became the evil merchants of Mystery Babylon the Whore through corporate influence as recorded in Revelation chapter 18.

Note that the word bough means fruitful (Ephraim) as a part of its definition and stated in Matt 21:43. This links fruitful or Christian to the birthright tribes of Ephraim and Manasseh in Genesis 49:22 indicating them to be Christian nations of Bashan and Carmel (Manasseh Isa 33:9). Lebanon, Sharon, Bashan, Gilead and Carmel are end time fruitful Christian nations of Ephraim and Manasseh (Great Britain and the United States). The Hebrew definition of bough is a firstborn, bull or young calf which directly links Genesis 49:22 to Manasseh, the single great nation in Genesis 48:19 to the symbols of the United States, the Bull. The words plant, mountain (nations), bough and fruit are the key.

Whenever the Scriptures refer to the word fruit or fruitfulness it is speaking of righteousness or Christians of Christ's Gospel. The only fruitful nation that has fulfilled the birthright blessings are the English-speaking Christian nations of Ephraim and Manasseh in the past five hundred years. Germany and the other Christian European Anglo-Saxon Hebrew nations of the house of Jacob would also fall under Gods blessings but Jeremiah 10:16 says that a portion of Jacob is not like them referring to the other eleven tribes not including the birthright tribe, **"The portion of Jacob is not like them: for he is the former of all things; and Israel is the rod of his inheritance: The Lord of hosts is his name."** The rod of Gods inheritance was given to Ephraim and Manasseh and the birthright tribes were not to be like the other eleven tribes of Jacob but were to be named after God himself, "Israel, he will rule as God", the fruitful bough or nation to judge the world.

Genesis 49:22 is prophesied to take place in the last days (Gen 49:1) **"that I may tell you that which shall befall you in the last days"** and calls Joseph a fruitful bough or a righteous Christian bough (firstborn, bull or young calf). The blessing to Joseph mentioned in this verse, in reality, are the blessing that went to Ephraim and Manasseh, the recipients of the birthright lads (Gen 48:16). They received the name Israel and were to be a fruitful bough by definition and anointed as Gods people. Keep in mind that according to modern teaching, Ephraim and Manasseh has been non-existent since their captivity to Assyria in 721 BC, for approx. 2723 years. If this is true, why is the book of Hosea written to Ephraim as a warning to take place in the last days?

The Scriptures are clear in saying that Ephraim and Manasseh are to be a fruitful bough or nation of people in the last days (the Bull and Unicorn), so where are they? They are the English-speaking Christian nations of the world, Gods battle ax (Ps 80:8-16) **"Thou hast brought a vine out of Egypt: thou hast cast out the heathen, and planted it. Thou preparedst room before it, and didest cause it to take deep root, and it filled the land. The hills were covered with the shadow of it, and the boughs thereof were like the goodly cedar. She sent out her boughs unto the sea, and her branches unto the**

river. Why hast thou then broken down her hedges, so that all they which pass by the way do pluck her?" These verses are an overview of Israel's history from the time they departed Egypt and planted in the promised land and the period of great wealth and power during King David and Solomon when their influence covered the world.

When Israel's hedges were broken down by the heathen nations of their captivity and the division into two houses, the branches and boughs of the house of Israel were sent out unto the sea and rivers. The key is the Words Sea and rivers. By sea means, they departed by ship over the oceans and by river they went by boat up into Europe by land and river routes. This is how their branches and boughs migrated into the world on the wings of an eagle as a symbol of wind sales of the Phoenician ships. The term, "boughs thereof were like a goodly cedar", refers to the throne of Israel (the cedar tree) and its overturn into the wilderness in Ezekiel 21:25-27. The twelve tribes are referred to as boughs to the sea and her branches unto the river. Israel's hedges in the Promised Land were broken down and her boughs and branches (twelve tribes) went over the seas, "whose branches run over the wall" (Gen 49:22).

This is mentioned also in Isa 16:8, **"For the fields of Heshbon languish, and the vine of Sibmah: the lords of the heathen have broken down the principal plants thereof, they are come even unto Jazer, they wandered through the wilderness: her branches are stretched out, they are gone over the sea."** This verse also explains how the house of Israel, the lost sheep, wandered through the wilderness of Europe to become a fruitful nation waiting for Christ Gospel to fulfill Mat 21:43. Between these two Scriptures, it is clear that the boughs and branches of the house of Israel departed and went overseas to other lands.

Through-out the Old Testament, the word bough refers to a group or grove of trees and often to the cedar tree which is the symbol of the throne of Israel, Ezekiel 17:22-23, where it was overturned into the wilderness, England.

Plant

To help understand Bible prophecy you must study the word Plant for it is a key word. Plant or planted is mentioned at least eighty times in the Old Testament and explains how the Hebrew people, the Children of Israel, were planted in new nations to fulfill the blessings of Abraham, Isaac, and Jacob.

The first nation planted was the promised land of Palestine or Canaan, Zion, the nation of Israel to be rooted in Jerusalem of Judea. The promised land of Israel was to be the tap root of the vineyard to produce the Royal Blood Line of the Throne and our Savior, the Lord Jesus Christ. Isaiah 5:7 states, **"For the vineyard of the Lord of hosts is the house of Israel, and the men of Judah his pleasant plant"**. This makes it clear that Israel is divided and the house of Israel (10 northern tribes) is his vineyard (the world to be evangelized) and the house of Judah (two southern tribes of Judah and Benjamin) is the root of his promised land (Israel of Judea) that will never change or move. In verse 5 God says, **"I will tell you what I will do to my vineyard: I will take away the hedge thereof, and it shall be eaten up; and break down the wall thereof, and it shall be trodden down"**. The breaking down of the wall was the captivity of Assyria and Babylon causing the branches to run over the wall. This means they departed the vineyard and went into other countries. The root or the house of Judah always stayed in the vineyard of Gods Promised Land to represent the nation of Israel as a whole. God sent his vineyard, the house of Israel, into the world to spread his Gospel, Isaiah 5:7. Vineyards have to be planted with plants or by grafting and God replanted his Vineyard through-out the world by the branches that ran over the wall. People of the world that accepted Christ's Gospel were grafted into his Kingdom (Rom 11:17-26) but his original Chosen People were planted as his plant, not grafted. Refer to table one, the word PLANT.

The replanting of the Children of Israel as a nation or nations always pertain to the house of Israel in direct correlation to the birthright blessings which is not relevant to the house of Judah. This is why there were two separate captivities of the Children of Israel, the house of Israel (ten northern tribes) to Assyria in 721BC and the house of Judah (Jerusalem) to Babylon in 586BC. The two captivities created a separation that exist to this day and will exist till Ezekiel chapter 37 is fulfilled during the Tribulation Period.

The house of Israel lost their language and identity and after their captivity filtered into the world. God replanted the house of Israel in their own land (Eze 36:24-27) to fulfill Genesis 35:11. Ezekiel 36:24-27 states that they were given a new heart and new spirit and will walk in Gods statues which is the Gospel of Jesus and the Holy Spirit within them, **"For I will take you from among the heathen, and gather you out of all countries, and will bring you into your own land. Then will I sprinkle clean water upon you [baptize the Church], and ye shall be clean: from all your filthiness, and from all your idols, will I cleanse you. A new heart also will I give you, and a new spirit will I put within you: and I will take away the stony heart out of your flesh, and I will give you an heart of flesh. And I will put my spirit within you, and**

cause you to walk in my statutes, and ye shall keep my judgments, and do them". Do not mistake this verse **"you into your own land"** to mean the original promised land of Canaan for it is speaking of a whole new land as described in Isaiah chapter 18 in a far-away land. This planting has taken place in the last days during the Church age and can in no way pertain to the house of Judah for they still do not accept Christ as the Messiah. These verses are speaking of the New Covenant of the Church age (Heb 8:8 and Jerm 31:31) and Gods Christian nations. They were given a new land (Eze 34:13 and Isa 18) and were baptized or sprinkled with the Holy Spirit and given a new heart (the Church). God caused them to walk in his statutes and to keep his judgments by providing God's Word through the King James Bible and a nation (GB and USA) that produced schools and Universities to educate his people.

The house of Judah was filtered into the world and did not lose their language or identity by being called Jews and maintained Orthodox Judaism. According to the Scriptures, the ten northern tribes of the house of Israel were never called Jews but were divorced by God due to their national sins of idol worship (Jerm 3:8). Because of their divorcement, they were sent into the wilderness as their punishment (Jerm 31:2) and to fulfill Genesis 17:6-7, 35:11 and 48:19 to be a nation and a company of nations of kings and kingdoms under Christianity of the New Covenant. Their divorcement terminated the chances of ever returning to the promised land of Canaan. The world became their new promised land as a vineyard. These verses fulfill the blessings to Abraham, Isaac and Jacob through the birthright tribes of Joseph, Ephraim and Manasseh. This fruitful nation in the wilderness cannot be modern Israel. Study the whole chapter. The following is a few key verses pertaining to the house of Israel being sent into the wilderness: Eze 20:34-47; 34:13-31; Hos 2:14-23; and Isaiah 16:1-8. Refer to other segments in this book to understand the three different plantings of the Children of Israel over hundreds of years. The divorcement mentioned in Jeremiah 3:8, did not pertain to the house of Judah, for if it had, the Messiah and his throne would have been negated.

The Vineyard

Through-out the Old Testament, the nation of Israel is referred to as a Vineyard. The Hebrew meaning of vineyard is, garden, vines, increase, vintage, plant, brother and kindred. We can see how this relates to a growing garden or vineyard that produce fruit. God uses a brilliant analogy of the vineyard, vines and branches as a symbol of his growing Children that produced fruit of righteousness for the Salvation of the world as a builder of the family unit, the Church of Gods Children that inherited the name Israel.

We know that a grape vine or vineyard has a taproot that grows vines and needs nourishment and pruning to produce good fruit. The vineyard of God is the house of Israel and he gave one growing season to produce fruit. The vineyard plant provides two parts. The taproot plant that produces a root or stalk is the house of Judah and the vine or branches growing fruit is the house of Israel. This is why God chose the vineyard to symbolize his nation of the Children of Israel. The vineyard has walls to comfort and protect the plants, the tap root and stalk is stationary and never moves to provide nourishment. The branches and vines run out from the stalk which is pruned by the master to produce good fruit, and you have the master to oversee, to water, and prune the vineyard. If one element of the vineyard dies, the whole vineyard dies. When the master expands his vineyard, he plants a part of the root in a selected new soil with nourishment and care. The type of soil the root is planted in gives the quality of the vintage of the fruit. To change the quality of his vintage he can graft in other vines that represent Gentiles being accepted into his vintage or Kingdom (Rom 11) that is grafted into the vines (house of Israel the Church) nourished by the root (house of Judah).

Symbolic meanings are as followed when pertaining to Bible prophecy. The wall represents the protection and security as a nation when God planted Israel in the Promised Land. Isaiah 5:7 states, **"For the vineyard of the Lord of Hosts is the house of Israel, and the men of Judah his pleasant plant"**. A vineyard plant has two parts with two different functions. The tender plant or root is the house of Judah that produced the Royal Bloodline and lawgiver of the Messiah and never moves or changes. The root never moved from Judea or died after 2500 years and sprouted as a nation again in 1948. They are the tribe of Judah and Benjamin and a portion of all twelve tribes that migrated back of Israel since 1948. They represent the Jews that never lost their identity. They only lost their nation till the time of the end due to sin and rejecting Christ (Matt 21:43) to fulfill Daniel's 70th week. The Branches or vines are the house of Israel which is the ten northern tribes that went into captivity and lost their identify as a nation and people. They were to be replanted through-out the world to wait for Christ's coming as the Savior and for the Gospel (Gen 49:10). The house of Israel that were the lost sheep became God's pruned Christian nations to spread Christ's Gospel during the end times and were the fruitful and grafted branches that ran over the wall (Gen 49:22 and Matt 10:6). The branches of the Hebrew lost tribes became Gods wayfaring people that ran out and away from the promised land of Israel. They were to become God's tool to preach the Word and save the world at Christ's establishing the Gospel by grafting Gentiles or any man that believes in his Gospel to be a part of his Church (Heavenly Kingdom). The world became Gods vineyard after the establishing of the Gospel and the branches ran over the wall into the world to become his Christian nations but the Jews were to remain as the tap root stationary in Jerusalem. Jerusalem of Judah was to be his pleasant plant or the root of his Children of Israel to fulfill all Biblical prophecies.

The words plant, root, vine, wall and prune are synonymous to a vineyard and an analogy of the Children of Israel and ultimately the Church (Christ). John 15:1 state, **"I am the true vine, and my Father is the husbandman."** This is Christ calling himself the vine of the vineyard and gave the birthright tribe of Ephraim and Manasseh the responsibility to spread his end time Gospel as the branch of his vineyard (Gen 49:22 and Isa 36:8).

The term child or children of Israel represents a period of growth just as a child grows and learns. A Child has a growing cycle just as a vineyard. When Gods Children went into the wilderness after their Egyptian captivity, this represented the first stage of Gods vineyard. They established the Tabernacle in the wilderness where Moses personifies the Throne as the future Church and Lawgiver. The vine grew wild so God pruned the vine by killing that generation and would not allow them into the Holy Land. When the twelve tribes under Joshua's leadership established the Tabernacle in Shiloh (symbol of Christ and the Church) he planted it in a pleasant soil for it to grow. His vineyard grew and flourished but began to run wild and produce bad fruit through their idol worship. When God destroyed the wall around the vineyard through their national captivities, the wild branches were planted into a far-away land after they ran over the wall. This is when God pruned his vines and branches by sending Christ and his Gospel for his vines to run through-out the world to produce fruit of his Word. We are now at the end of the growing season and time for his vines to be pruned again due to present day sin and falling away from his Word. If you study each of the words, vine, vineyard, plant, prune, branch, fruitful, bough, tree, forest and mountain in perspective, the Old Testament prophecies will unfold before you and you can understand how God used the term vineyard, forest and mountain (nations) to spread his end time Gospel through-out the world. This fulfilled the promises of greatness to Abraham, Isaac and Jacob, to be fruitful nations and kingdoms.

Isaiah chapter 5 explains how Israel, the vineyard, sinned so he broke down the wall and did not prune the vine so it ran wild. Breaking down the wall and running wild represents his tribes departing the vineyard, to branch out and settle in other nations. Israel, the promised land, is the vineyard root which never moves but the branches leave the vineyard, Genesis 49:22 **"whose branches run over the wall;"** which means the house of Israel (ten northern tribes) departed Israel, the promised land, and was planted in other nations and prospered by receiving their blessings given to Jacob. The book of Hosea was written to Ephraim (Great Britain). Hosea 2:14-17 states, **"Therefore, behold, I will allure her, and bring her into the wilderness, and speak comfortable unto her. And I will give her vineyards from thence, and the valley of Achor for a door of hope: and she shall sing there, as in the days of her youth, and as in the day when she came up out of the land of Egypt. And it shall be at that day, saith the Lord, that thou shalt call me Ishi; and shalt call me no more Baali. For I will take away the names of Baalim out of her mouth, and they shall no more be remembered by their name."** This verse explains how Ephraim were allured into the wilderness, a new land (Eze 32:13), and given a vineyard, a nation, and worshiped God, the Gospel of Christ. Their name Hebrew was taken from them in verse 17 along with the Baal idle worship when they came out of Egypt. Problem, in the last days due to Satan's influence, the house of Israel as the Church fell back into Baalim worship and became Mystery Babylon spoken of throughout the book of Revelation. They became wild where in Rev 3:17 calls them wretched, miserable, poor, blind and naked. They departed God's vineyard and ran over the wall again bringing the wrath spoken of in Revelation.

The lost sheep of the house of Israel lost their identification as a people (Hebrew) along with their language and became a God-fearing people in their new land or vineyard. Ishi is a name for Israel and of the tribe of Manasseh, the birthright tribe that represents the end time Church by turning form Baal idol worship back to God under Christ's Gospel. "Achor for a door of hope" is a symbol of redemption through the Church as recorded in Joshua 7:20-26. Again, Isaiah 65:9-10, **"And I will bring forth a seed out of Jacob, and out of Judah an inheritor of my mountains: and mine elect shall inherit it, and my servants shall dwell there. And Sharon shall be a fold of flocks, and the valley of Achor a place for the herds to lie down in, for my people that have sought me."** These verses are speaking of Gods end time Church for Christ and his elect (Christians) are the inheritors of his mountains, Gods Christian nations of Israel. Sharon (Manasseh the US and Ephraim Great Britain) shall be a fold of flocks in the valley of Achor a place for the herds to lie down in as Christ's Church in the new land in the wilderness, Gods Christian nations during the end days (Eze 20:34-43, 43:13-18, Jerm 12:2-15, Micah 5:7-11 just a few verses). The valley of Achor is a symbol of Gods people turning from idol worship in Joshua's day and the Christian nations of the Church during the end of the age.

Just as Satan always do, he infiltrates and destroys just as he did the Druid religion, Judaism and now Christianity under the Church. There is always a remnant that does not fall of Satan's lie. He always takes the nations back to his old Baal religion for he wants to perform the tower of Bable all over again. Lucifer wants to be God in his New World Order, this time through AI or Advanced Intelligence (Alien or Demon Intelligence) for he knows his time is short.

Hosea 2:19-20 states **"And I will betroth thee unto me for ever; yea, I will betroth thee unto me in righteousness, and in judgment, and in loving kindness, and in mercies. I will even betroth thee unto me in faithfulness: and thou shalt know the Lord"**. These verses are the engagement of the virgin (Bride to be) of the house of Israel and the establishment of his Gospel for they shall know him through Christianity. Israel as the Birthright of Ephraim and Manasseh is mentioned as "O virgin of Israel" in Jeremiah 31:4 and 21 and Amos 5:2 as being the Bride of Christ. Prior to this verse, God divorced the house of Israel in Jeremiah 3:8, **"And I was, when for all the causes whereby backsliding Israel committed adultery, I had put her away, and given her a bill of divorce; yet her treacherous sister Judah feared not, but went and played the harlot also."** Note that God only divorced Israel and not Judah and sent the house of Israel into the wilderness after the divorcement to wait their punishment of X7 or 2520 years, Leviticus 26:18&24. If God had divorced Judah, then David's throne and the linage of Christ would not be been legitimate.

These verses cannot be talking about modern day Israel for the Jews do not believe in Jesus Christ, even today. Hosea explains the division of Israel. The house of Israel is the vine that ran over the wall and planted in the wilderness and the house of Judah is the pleasant plant or the root. God put his plan into motion when their branches began to run over the wall and the planting of the new nations started with the migration of the Hebrews during their Egyptian captivity.

Again, for this segment, we need to explain how Calcol and Dara of Judah's decent departed Egypt by ship and settled Greece years before Moses departed with his people into the wilderness. This was the second planting and the key in uniting the throne in England for the first overturn of the throne of David (Eze 21:27). God's plan for his nations (Mountains), are brilliant for he began to divide Israel before they ever became a nation. If you study the words plant and mountains in the Old Testament, you can see the picture of how God performed this miracle. The first planting of Gods nations was the Promised land of Israel to be one single nation represented by the Jews after the division and till the end of the age. The second planting was to be the starting of the first migration of the Hebrews led by Calcol and Dara during and after the Egyptian captivity to be later joined by the ten northern tribes of Israel after the Assyrian and Babylonian captivities.

These tribes of Hebrews were to wait in the wilderness till Jeremiah established the overturn of the throne, Ezekiel 21:26, **"Thus saith the Lord God: Remove the diadem, and take off the crown: exalt him that is low and abase him that is high".** The crown was taken from the house of Judah (the Pharez blood line) and given to the house of Israel, where the Zarah blood line amalgamated with the authority of the house of Israel through the birthright blessing of Ephraim and Manasseh, the establish Zarah blood line in Ireland. God's plan was for his people to be planted in the wilderness and to establish a new nation to become strong and to be ready when Christ delivered his Gospel to the twelve Apostles in Matt 10:5. This new fruitful nation is the nation mentioned in Matthew 21:43, that kingdom which was taken from the Chief Priests and Pharisees because of their disbelief, **"be taken from you, and given to a nation bringing forth the fruits thereof".** Be reminded that a fruitful nation is a Christian nation that is serving God by preaching his Gospel.

The Branch

The migrations of the Hebrew people during the early period of history were the branch running over the wall as mentioned in Gen 49:22, **"Joseph is a fruitful bough, even a fruitful bough by a well: whose branches run over the wall".** The well is our Lord Jesus Christ and his Salvation of living water. The Hebrew meaning of bough is a branch, forest, hedge up, sprig or house of the vineyard. In other words, the branches of the vineyard departed the promised land of Israel and ran over the wall into the world to produce fruit, righteousness and spread the Gospel, Isaiah 16:8, **"the lords of the heathen have broken down the principal plants thereof, they are come even unto Jazer, they wandered thought the wilderness; her branches are stretched out, they are gone over the sea.".** This verse is clear and states that the branches of the house of Israel ran over the wall and away from the Promised Land that the heathen destroyed (Jerusalem) and ran over the sea too far away countries.

From the Egyptian captivity, 1706-1491BC to the fall of Jerusalem in 70AD, almost 1800 years of migrating Hebrews had departed and settled in Greece, Spain, Troy, Ireland, Denmark, Norway by ship, and into Europe through the Caucasus Mountains. These people were the fair skinned, blond hair, blue eyed Caucasians as Celts, Goths and Anglo-Saxon along with many more tribal names. These tribes were related by traditions, language, clans and were the Hebrew Phoenicians that became the English-speaking nations. Historians have traced these clans or tribes through European history as Sakai, Sacae, Sakasuna (name of Isaac), Omri, Kumri, Kimmerians, Humri, Cimri, Gimmiri (established name for King Omri, King of Israel 930BC). The Persians called the ten northern tribes of Israel "Scythia or Saka", the Babylonians called them the "land of the Cimmerians or Gimiri", and the Romans called them "Goths".

The early Israelite names of the Saxons were, Sakasuni, Saki, Guti, Getai, Sak-Geloths, Skuthai, Skoloti and Scythians. Ptolemy mentions a Scythian race that sprung from the Sakai, called Saxones. The Ephraimite warrior names of Isaac slowly translated into Isaac-I-Saccasuns, I-Sad-suns, Sakasuna, Suksens and Saxons. ("The Drama of the Lost Disciples" by George F. Jowett page 130)

God planted his people, the lost sheep of the house of Israel, to become great nations for a reason and that was to spread his end time Gospel. Jesus gave the commandment for his twelve Apostles to go teach his lost sheep starting with the Jews first in which they rejected (Matt 10:5-8). This is a strange verse and hard to understand unless you match it with other verses speaking of the lost sheep of the house of Israel as listed below. In Matthew 15:22-26, a woman of Canaan, a gentile, came to Jesus for help but he told her, **"I am not sent but unto the lost sheep of the house of Israel"**. This is a very profound statement for Christ himself said that he was only sent to the lost sheep which is the ten northern lost tribes of the house of Israel. Christ was sent to save the world as the Messiah so why only to the lost sheep? The reason is that he was sent only to the lost sheep in that he was going to use them as a tool to spread his end time Gospel worldwide through the last day generation. The Jews of Judah rejected him so he used the lost sheep, his birthright tribes as his tool in spreading his Gospel.

Keep in mind that the ten northern tribes were taken into captivity by Assyria 750 years prior never to return but Jesus knew where they were. The ten northern tribes can only be the lost sheep that Jesus is talking about for it could not be the Jews, they are not lost and never were. In John 7:35, Jesus was talking to the Pharisees and told them that where he is going, they cannot go, this is what they said, **"Then said the Jews among themselves, Whither will he go that we shall not find him? will he go unto the dispersed among the Gentiles, and teach the Gentiles?"**. This verse indicates that the Pharisees also knew about the dispersed the lost sheep of Israel among the Gentile nations.

The best verse that refers to the planted nations of the lost sheep of the house of Israel is Matthew 21:43, when Jesus is talking to the Chief Priest and Pharisees telling them that they are going to reject him, **"Therefore say I unto you, The kingdom of God shall be taken from you, and given to a nation bringing forth the fruits thereof.".** What nation is Jesus talking about? The Jewish nation of Israel from that time till now has never believed in Jesus so they could not bring forth fruits. This nation Jesus is talking about is the nation of Ireland where Jeremiah was told by God to plant and establish, Jerm 1:10, **"See, I have this day set thee over the nations and over the kingdoms, to root out, and to pull down, and to destroy, and to throw down, to build, and to plant.".** The word plant or planted is mentioned seventeen times in the book of Jeremiah. The first Epistle of Peter was written to the strangers scattered, I Peter 1:1, **"Peter, an apostle of Jesus Christ, to the strangers scattered throughout Pontus, Galatia, Cappadocia, Asia, and Bithynia. Elect according to the foreknowledge of God the Father".** Who are these strangers? James 1:1 is written to all twelve tribes scattered, **"James, a servant of God and of the Lord Jesus Christ, to the twelve tribes which are scattered abroad, greeting".** The word abroad in Greek is the key for it means, the converted Israelite residents in Gentile countries which are scattered abroad and sown throughout and distributed in foreign lands. Again, the ten northern tribes have been gone for over 750 years, so James and Peter knew where they were for James's Epistle was written to all twelve tribes. As mentioned in a prior paragraph, the word fruitful or fruitful nation is a direct relation to a people or nation that is righteous, God fearing and spreading his Gospel. In other words, a fruitful nation is a Christian nation that is serving God by spreading his Word and cannot pertain to the Jews (Judaism) for they have never accepted Jesus Christ.

Tree

Isaiah 61:3 calls Zion the trees of righteousness planted in the wilderness of the old cities of desolations of many generations. This verse also indicates that Zion is the nations or people of the world. From the definitions listed above and the 291 times tree is listed in the Scriptures, it is clear that the trees is the center of the beauty of God's creation, Isa 60:13, **"The glory of Lebanon shall come unto thee, the fir tree, the pine tree, and the box together, to beautify the place of my sanctuary; and I will make the place of my feet glorious."** The place of Gods trees is in the earth and he has named his righteous nations after the trees such as Israel the fig tree, Lebanon the cedar, fir and box tree (David's Throne of England) and Bashan (Manasseh the United States) the oak tree.

His nations are called mountains and trees. The tree is a symbol of strength, height and in reference number (352) referred to as the mightiness of man.

The word bough in reference number (6288) and (2793) represents Israel as stated in Gen 48:22, and is referred to as bright green foliage and a forest. The definition of Israel in reference number (410) means, mighty as in God the mighty one. Again in (352) Israel means an oak or strong tree and the Hebrew word branch which is a high portion or summit of the tree as referred to in reference number (534), (of a tree or mountain) bough or branch. From all the definitions relating to tree and forest, it is clear that the fruitful trees are a symbol of Gods righteous nations. From the Scripture, trees in the forest bear fruit, some good fruit and some bad fruit. Whenever the word fruitful is used, it indicates a righteous tree or nation, Genesis 49:22, **"Joseph is a fruitful bough"**. Joseph was given the birthright blessings to carry on the family name of Israel and again bough means forest. We need to re-quote Matthew 21:43 to illustrate where Jesus was talking to the Chief priests and Pharisees and made the statement, **"Therefore say I unto you, The kingdom of God shall be taken from you, and given to a nation bringing forth the fruits thereof."** These two verses are only two of many examples in the Bible referring to the tree, forest, fruitful, vineyard and wilderness to his righteous Christian nations of the world.

We know that Satan is an imitator of God and this explains why Pagan tribes worshipped trees and believed in tree Gods. Some of Gods fruitful nations are named after trees. The ancient name of Lebanon and Bashan are named after the cedar, fir, box and oak tree, Isaiah 2:3, **"And upon all the cedars of Lebanon, that are high and lifted up, and upon all the oaks of Bashan."** We have already covered that Lebanon and Bashan is the great Christian nations of Great Britain and the United States. The cedar represents Gods beauty, for the Temple and throne house was made of cedar representing David's throne and the oak is the symbol of Gods strength. Psalms 1:3 says that man is like a tree, **"And he shall be like a tree planted by the rivers of water** [the Gospel of living water]**, that bringeth forth his fruit in his season"**. Again, fruit if mentioned as righteousness and the rivers of water represents Christ and his Gospel. Isaiah speaks of man springing up as trees and being feed by water and of his Holy Spirit, **"For I will pour water upon him that is thirsty, and floods upon the dry ground: I will pour my spirit upon thy seed, and my blessing upon thine offspring; And they shall spring up as among the grass, as willows by the water courses."** Men that are thirsty seek after God, Christians, or God will poor out his Holy Spirit upon his righteous nations of willow trees that flourish by the water given by Christ's Salvation.

The fig tree is a symbol of Israel as given in Matt 24:32, and Mark 13:28, as the parable of the fig tree. Christ was hanged on a tree or a wooden cross in Acts 5:30 and 10:39 and the speculation or folk lore is that it was a dogwood tree and cursed by God and is spindly to this day. Rev 2:7 states, **"To him that over cometh will I give to eat of the tree of life, which is in the midst of the paradise of God"**. So, what is the tree of life, it has to be Christ himself, Christ is a symbol of a tree. The Olive tree is a symbol of the Church that is the house of God, his Church. Psalms 52:8, **"But I am like a green olive tree in the house of God"**. The Palm and cedar tree is a symbol of righteousness, Psalms 92:12, **"The righteous shall flourish like the palm tree: he shall grow like a cedar in Lebanon."** The palm tree is a symbol of the Phoenician Empire (the descendants of Enoch), Gods ancient people prior to this Covenant and how he dispersed the house of Israel into the wilderness (Eze 17) on the wings of an eagle (Phoinix or Palm Tree). Lebanon is the modern-day Christian nations and not the Arab Lebanon in the middle east of today. Refer to Lebanon.

The Scriptures list green trees as nations of the world. Some are evil and some are righteous, Jeremiah 6:13, **"she is gone up upon every high mountain and under every green tree, and there hath played the harlot.",** and also in Ezekiel 6:13, **"Then shall ye know that I am the Lord, when their slain men shall be among their idols round about their alters, upon every high hill, in all the tips of the mountains, and under every green tree, and under every thick oak, the place where they did offer sweet savour to all their idols"**. Notice that in these verses, nations of the world are mentioned as high hills, tops of the mountains, every green tree and thick oak. This is very important to understand for as we read and study end time prophecies, it allows us to know who ancient and present-day names of nations are during modern times.

The righteous man is like a tree, Jeremiah 17:7-8, **"Blessed is the man that trusteth in the Lord, and whose hope the lord is. For he shall be as a tree planted by the waters, and that spreadeth out her roots by the river, and shall not see when heat cometh, but her leaf shall be green; and shall not be careful in the year of drought, neither shall cease from yielding fruit."** This sure sounds like the modern Christian nations of today with the great blessing that has been bestowed upon us. Notice that the heat cometh and the drought are evil forces against Gods fruitful and righteous people. Satan is slowly draining the water of life from the modern-day Church through liberalism, socialism and communism.

In Jeremiah 11:19, Satan tries to destroy the fruitfulness of the tree, **"Let us destroy the tree with the fruit thereof, and let us cut him off from the land of the living, that his name may be no more remembered."** This verse is the antichristian movement of today trying to destroy our Christian way of life.

Our nation is under assault through moral relativism of the liberal agenda and the influx of immigration into our country promoting socialism. It has created an ethnic equality that is slowly taking God and Christ out of our Society and Culture. When it gets to the point that the immigrants have more voting power than natural born citizens, this nation will no longer be the great nation we once were. We are also being assaulted by the growing Islamic religion within this country and Arab Islamic nations around the world determined in destroying our Christian way of life. Hundreds of Mosques have been built within this country to undermine and dilute our Christian Society. In the last few years, the Moslem or Islamic faith has been the fastest growing Religion within the United States. Again, the Hebrew word "curse" means in #423, "alah", the god of Islam, a curse that devoured the earth in Isa 24:6.

It has been established that during the end times, Israel is divided. The following verse was written to the planted house of Israel and to the house of Judah as two separate nations, Jeremiah 11:17, **"For the Lord of hosts, that planted thee, hath pronounced evil against thee, for the evil of the house of Israel and of the house of Judah, which they have done against themselves to provoke me to anger is offering incense unto Baal."** This destruction is happening today and in the very near future as the true Church is falling away and joining the one world religious system of Baal called Mystery Babylon found in the book of Revelation. Our punishment of wrath is due. We can see how God has weakened this nation through all the terrorist activity happening in our country today with our freedoms and rights being taken away in the guise of protecting the people. The rights of one are more important than the rights of many. When God finally gives up on his Christian nations, this means that our cup of iniquity is full and beyond the point of no return. At this point, we will fall to Satan's evil forces under his New World System.

There is a massive amount of Bible verses pertaining to trees but we need to cover one more tree that is critical in understanding the identity of the house of Israel during the last days. Ezekiel chapters 17 and 21, explains it very well and calls for a deep study into this subject. Ezekiel 17:5, **"He took also of the seed of the land** [twelve tribes of Israel]**, and planted it in a fruitful field: he placed it by great waters and set it as a willow tree."** This is a very interesting verse for it states that God took the seed of the land of Israel and planted it in a fruitful field far away from the promised land of Israel and placed it by great waters as a willow tree. Judah's roots never departed Israel for they were not divorced from God (Jerm 3:8) and returned as modern Israel. This verse can only be referring to the house of Israel, the ten northern tribes. Let's keep this verse in mind as we go to Ezekiel 17:22-24, **"Thus saith the Lord God; I will also take of the highest branch of the high cedar, and will set it;**

I will crop off from the top of his young twigs a tender one, and will plant it upon an high mountain and eminent: In the mountain of the height of Israel will I plant it; and it shall bring forth boughs, and bear fruit, and be a goodly cedar: and under it shall dwell all fowl of every wing; in the shadow of the branches thereof shall dwell. And all the trees of the field shall know that I the Lord have brought down the high tree to flourish: I the Lord have spoken and have done it." Jeremiah was commissioned by God to fulfill these verses in Jeremiah 1:10 with the authority to tear down, to destroy and to build and plant. The highest branch of the cedar tree spoken of in Ezekiel 17:22 is the King of Israel, King Zedekiah the last king of Israel in 586BC, under the Phares bloodline of King David, Matt 1:3. The Phares bloodline was of all the kings of Israel through King Zedekiah. King Josiah was the last sovereign king and the rest was puppet kings under Babylon as were Zedekiah.

Isaiah 16:8 states, **"the lords of the heathen have broken down the principal plants thereof, they wandered through the wilderness: her branches are stretched out, they are gone over the sea."** This verse explains how Israel migrated after their captivity and branched over the wall or over the seas into far away countries. This fulfills all the Scriptures promising King David that a man would always sit upon his throne forever, Jerm 33:14-17; I Kings 9:5; II Sam 7:12-17 and many more. We know that the King of Ireland was of Israel for verse 23 states, **"In the mountain of the hight of Israel will I plant it; and it shall bring forth boughs, and bear fruit."** This verse indicates that the King of Ireland had to be of the bloodline of Zara and of Hebrew descent. Zedekiah's daughters were of the Phares bloodline where the King of Ireland descended from of the Zara bloodline, therefore preserving the throne correctly through the tribe of Judah (Gen 49:10).

The word bough and fruit are mentioned as a forest and righteousness in fruit. This cannot be speaking of the Jews in Jerusalem for they have never been fruitful through our Lord Jesus Christ but their time will come during the Tribulation Period. Keep in mind it is referring to the last days, Gen 49:1. Ezekiel 17:24 state that all will know that God brought down the high tree and exalted the low tree.

He overturned and planted the old throne of King Zedekiah of Israel to the new throne of the New Covenant waiting in the wilderness to receive Christ's Gospel to be fruitful nations (cedar tree) in the new nation of Ireland, Scotland and later into England where it is today. Israel became a nation in 1948 and still does not have a King sitting on their throne. Why? The throne is still in

England and cannot be moved back to Jerusalem because of what is stated in Ezekiel 21:27, **"and it shall be no more, until he come whose right it is; and I will give it him"**. The Throne stayed in Jerusalem till Gen 49:10 was fulfilled at the coming of Christ for it states, **"The sceptre shall not depart from Judah, nor a lawgiver from between his feet, until Shiloh [Christ] come"**. These verses state that it shall be no more in Jerusalem till Christ claims his throne in Power and is why the throne remains in England. The Antichrist moves the throne to Jerusalem during his reign but not of Gods authority. The throne is moved to Heaven in Rev 4:1-2 when Christ sets upon it and he brings it back to Jerusalem when he returns in power at the end of the Tribulation.

It is clear in the Scriptures that the cedar tree is the ancient name of Lebanon and England, the United States and English-speaking Christian fruitful nations are of the ancient cedar of snow-covered Lebanon (purity of the Church) representing the Church and the throne of England.

Zion (Hebrew) or Sion (Greek)

The city of King David is Jerusalem and called Zion, I King 8:1. God dwells in Zion according to Ps 9:11. David in Psalms 48:2 called, **"the joy of the whole earth, is mount Zion"**. We have been taught and believe that Zion is only associated with the nation of Israel. If we closely study the word Zion and Sion, we will see that is not totally true. Jerusalem and Israel were Gods Capital and protector of Zion, Gods Spirit with all mankind, till Christ came and fulfilled his role as the Messiah of the world (Ps 48:21-2; 49:1-2; 50:1-2). After Christ's death, Jerusalem was no longer the Capital of Zion but in each believer's heart, the Church. This explains why Jerusalem laid waste for almost two thousand years and no king in Israel to this day. The Capital of Zion, the throne of King David and the name Jerusalem was overturned to a fruitful nation as a protector and commissioned to spread his Gospel. This commission was given to the twelve disciples by Jesus himself for them to go to the lost sheep of the house of Israel to teach his Word for they were to be that fruitful nation to be called Zion/Sion (Mat 10:6; 15:24; 21:43). Study the key words of mountain, forest, wilderness desert and waymark to get a better understanding.

According to Isaiah, a corner stone will be laid in Zion, **"Therefore thus saith the lord God, Behold, I lay in Zion for a foundation a stone, a tried stone, a precious corner stone, a sure foundation; he that believeth shall not make haste."** (Isaiah 28:16). Christ is the stone of Bethel that has always accompanied his nation and the corner stone of Israel. The house of Israel is the birthright tribe and their inheritance blessing by Jacob, Joseph, Ephraim and Manasseh, to be the stone of Israel (Gen 49:24). This same stone of Israel (Christ) is also the foundation stone of the Church. In other words, Ephraim and Manasseh were to be given the responsibility to be the stone of Israel by evangelizing the world with Christ's Gospel. Gods new covenant is with his children, the Church of the modern Christian nations of the house of Israel that is righteous and fruitful as stated in Psalms 48:2 as the joy of the whole earth. Zion is his creation of righteous people and nations with Christ the corner stone at their head. Zion is called by several different names such as, **mountains of Zion** (*nations*) (Ps 133:3); **children of Zion** (Ps 149:2, God's Chosen People); **daughters of Zion** (in the last days) or the house of Israel (Isa 1:8) and **sons of Zion** (*nations of people*) (Zec 9:13). In other words, Zion is Gods Spirit in the company of man on earth within the Tabernacle or Temple (Holy of Holies) his resting place, Gods House as the end time Church. God chose to place Zion in Jerusalem which consisted of three elements that is, the Throne of David, the Law Giver (the government of Israel from the authority of the Levite tribe Duet 33:10) and the Temple (Gods House and end time Church) Genesis 49:10. The Tabernacle and Temple with the Holy of Holies represented and is a symbol of the end time Church in ancient times.

This presents a huge problem for all three elements has disappeared and we need to find out where they went. God would not allow his Spirit with man to disappear from the earth no more than we can lose our Salvation. The last King that sat on King David's throne was Zedekiah and taken into captivity in 586BC by Babylon. After the invasion, King Nebuchadrezzar left a remnant of Jews behind in Jerusalem (Jerm 39:9-11). From 586BC, Jerusalem no longer maintained the throne of David or the lawgiver of the government and was occupied by Babylon, Persia and then the Romans till 70AD when the Temple was completely destroyed. Of the 11 million Hebrews as the house of Israel and 2 million Jews of the house of Judah, only a remnant of approx. 40,000 returned to Jerusalem, a total of .003 percent (Ezra 6:14). Where is Zion today? Israel became a reestablished nation in 1948 but still has no throne or temple. Zion cannot be in modern Jerusalem for they have rejected Christ as I Peter 2:6 states, **"I lay in Sion a chief corner stone, elect, precious: and he that believeth on him shall not be confounded."** This corner stone of Sion is Christ and his Church. The term Zion is directly associated with the throne of Israel so again it cannot be modern Israel of today.

Let's look at the facts by studying the word Zion and what God did when Jerusalem fell to Babylon in 586BC. God gave a warning to Judah, **"Shall I not, as I have done unto Samaria and her idols, so do to Jerusalem and her idols? Wherefore it shall come to pass, that when the Lord hath performed his whole work upon mount Zion and on Jerusalem, I will punish the**

fruit of the stout heart of the king of Assyria, and the glory of his high looks" (Isa 10:11-12). These verses are interesting for it warns Judah that captivity is coming to them just as it did to Samaria or the house of Israel, the ten northern tribes. This verse also indicates that when his whole work upon mount Zion and Jerusalem is finished, he shall bring captivity to Jerusalem the Jews. This is the wrath of the captivity to Babylon and where his work in Jerusalem is complete. At his point, Jerusalem was overturned (Eze 21:25-27), travailed (Isa 66:7-8), plowed (Jerm 26:8 and Mic 3:12) and plucked (Jerm 12:14) from the Promised Land (moved) and given to a fruitful peaceful nation in the wilderness (Jerm 9:2 and Eze 34:25).

Isaiah 16:1-8 and 18:1-7 explain Gods plan for Zion. Isaiah 16:1-2 sends the mount of the daughters of Zion (house of Israel) into the wilderness to become a wandering bird cast out of its nest (wayfaring men), the destruction of Jerusalem, to dwell with Moab or the Gentiles. The term daughter of Zion means, the descendants of old Zion that became the new Sion in the last days under the Church. Verse five is very interesting for it states, **"And in mercy shall the throne be established; and he shall sit upon it in truth in the tabernacle of David, judging, and seeking judgment, and hasting righteousness"**. This establishing of a throne cannot be speaking of Jerusalem for it is in past tense of its destruction and can only be established in another location for there is no history of the reestablishing the throne in Jerusalem. This establishing also fulfills the Scriptures in that there will always be a throne and law giver. Verse 8 explains where, **"For the fields of Heshbon languish, and the vine of Sibmah; the lords of the heathen have broken down the principal plants thereof, they are come even unto Jazer, they wandered through the wilderness; her branches are stretched out, they are gone over the sea."** Heshbon, Sibmah and Jazer are Levitical cites of the tribes of Reuben and Gad and represents the destruction of the principal plants of the Throne and Temple in Jerusalem and that housed the Levitical Priest Hood.

These were cities of the ten northern tribes of the house of Israel that had already been taken into captivity 135 years prior and this verse gives a connection between the two houses, the house of Israel and Judah. After the destruction of Jerusalem and the throne, her branches are stretched out and they branch out over the sea. This verse states that the branches of the house of Israel and Judah stretched out over the sea and can only mean that between verse 5 and 8, the throne was reestablished over-seas. This verse also correlates with Gen 49:22 and the birthright blessing to Joseph (Ephraim and Manasseh), **"whose branches run over the wall:"**, which means Ephraim and Manasseh were to stretch over the seas. Isaiah 18:1-7 confirms this account. Verse 3 states that God will plant a flag, a signal or a banner on the mountains or nations of the world, **"All ye inhabitants of the world, and dwellers on the earth, see ye, when he lifteth up an ensign on the mountains; and when he bloweth a trumpet, hear ye"**. The Hebrew meaning for ensign is, a flag, a sail, a signal, banner or pole. This is Gods reestablishment of his throne in a far country that represents his flag of righteousness, Christian, his Gospel being spread through-out the world. This ensign can be seen on the European Flags of the Hebrew nations, the twelve tribes, as the cross of Christ carried on the banner of the King of England.

The blowing of a trumpet means that God is going to identify himself through his Gospel preaching worldwide that all shall know him. Verse 7 states, **"In that time shall the present be brought unto the Lord of hosts of a people scattered and peeled, and from a people terrible from their beginning hitherto; a nation meted out and trodden under foot, whose land the rivers have spoiled, to the place of the name of the Lord of hosts, the mount Zion."** This new land over-seas are given to Gods people that is scattered and peeled and terrible form the beginning to be trodden under foot. These people are the scattered people of his nation of Israel of both the houses of Israel and Judah Hebrew not Jew. This is their resting place spoken of in other parts of the Bible. The land is also to be spoiled by large rivers, which divides the continent and to be a place named of the Lord of host, the mount Zion as the Church. This land can only be the Christian nations of Great Britain and the United States for they are the only two nations that fit the scenario of the Scriptures by being Christian, named after the Lord.

God will always protect Zion and will not let her go into total oblivion, **"For the Lord shall comfort Zion: he will comfort all her waste places; and he will make her wilderness like Eden, and her desert like the garden of the Lord; joy and gladness shall be found therein, thanksgiving, and the voice of melody,"** Isaiah 51:3. The United States is the only nation on earth having a national holiday of Thanks Giving to our Lord of Host and sing praises to his name. The phrase "whose land the rivers have spoiled" means this new land is spoiled or divided by great rivers such as the Mississippi, Tennessee, Ohio, Missouri, Rio Grande, Colorado, Snake, Columbia and other great rivers and water ways throughout this land. Five hundred years ago the United States was a total wilderness or wasteland but look at it today. We are like a Garden of Eden of great wealth and blessings as a Christian nation.

Now let's connect Zion to Ephraim the recipient of the name Israel and birthright tribe of the house of Israel to receive the blessings to be a nation and a company of nations. They were to be of great wealth spoken of in Genesis 12:2-3 (all families on earth be blessed); 22:17-18 (possess gates of enemies, seaports and trade routes); 21:12 (be called Isaac's sons, Saxons); 35:11 (be a nation and a company of nations); and Duet 33:17 (to push people together to the ends of the earth). Amos 6:1 clearly connects Zion to Samaria which was the ancient and modern capital city of the ten northern tribes of the house of Israel and Ephraim was its leader, **"Woe to them that are at ease in Zion, and trust in the mountain of Samaria, which are named chief of the nations, to whom the house of Israel came!"** In this verse Zion is at ease and trust in the mountain of Samaria the leader of all nations, the United States. You could say that this means modern Israel is trusting in the United States, but then, Israel is not at rest and has never been since their captivity and reestablishment in 1948. When you trust in something or someone you are a part to them. We know that Zion is Gods people or his Christian nations of power, so in this verse it has to be speaking of the nations of the world trusting in our government for protection just as the United States has been the Worlds police force for the past hundred years.

Jeremiah 26:18 states, **"Thus saith the Lord of host; Zion shall be plowed like a field, and Jerusalem shall become heaps, and the mountain of the house as the high places of a forest."** This writer does not believe that God will remain in a place of heaps where his Throne does not exist for over 2588 years, in a place of war and destruction as Jerusalem is today. He is with his Throne that Jeremiah overturned to England and became his righteous Christian nations of Great Britain and the United States where our Constitution, Preamble and Bill or Rights exalt God as the Almighty. Please do not take this writer in the wrong context for Jerusalem and the modern nation of Israel is Gods beloved chosen nation and people. We need to understand Gods over-all plan to correctly see the total picture. Jerusalem fell to Babylon hundreds of years prior to Christ dying on the cross, but his Tabernacle (Gods House) always remained in Jerusalem. Up to this point of time, Jerusalem was Zion, but the moment Christ died on the cross and the veil in the Temple was torn down, this symbolically ended Zion being in Jerusalem (Matt 27:51 and II Cor 3:13-16). We know that Jerusalem was still Zion as stated in Matthew 21:5, when Christ entered on the donkey. The house of Israel (Zion) was up rooted, I Kings 14:15, and officially planted in Ireland which become the Christian Hebrew people of England and later the Common Wealth of Great Britain (46 nations) to wait for the coming of Zion/Sion, Christ's Gospel. The renting of the veil was the last official act of moving Zion, David's preserved throne and the Lawgiver (government) to Ireland to wait for Christ's Gospel. This was the travailing of Zion spoken of in Isaiah 66:8 and, **"the glory of the Gentiles"** in verse 12 (Christ Gospel to the world).

Jeremiah had the Throne overturned (Eze 17:22-24; 20:34-47; 21:25-27) and became the Christian nation spoken of in Matthew 21:43. They became the fruitful nations that God took form the Chief Priest and Pharisees. This fulfilled Matthew 10:5-6 after the Church and Paul was established to preach the Gospel to the Gentiles. This made the Apostles free to go to the lost sheep of the house of Israel through-out Europe, Asia and England to preach Christ's Gospel. The New Testament spells Zion as Sion that means, *a hill of Jerusalem, the Church (militant or triumphant) Sion* in Greek (Ref #4622 Strong's Concordance). Sion became the Christian nations worldwide under Christ the corner stone of his Gospel, I Peter 2:4-6, **"To whom coming, as unto a living stone, disallowed indeed of men, but chosen of God, and precious, Ye also, as lively stones, are built up a spiritual house, an holy priesthood, to offer up spiritual sacrifices, acceptable to God by Jesus Christ. Wherefore also it is contained in the scripture, Behold, I lay in Sion a chief corner stone, elect, precious: and he that believeth on him shall not be confounded"**. We know that Christ called Sion is the corner stone of his Church but according to this verse, Christians is a living stone that completes Christ Church of stone. If the Chief corner stone (Christ) is laid in Sion, then all Christians (living stones) have to also be called Sion. In other words, we as Christians of living stones are actually a part of Christ being the corner stone which is the building material of the Church, Sion or Zion, **"Behold, I lay in Sion a chief corner stone,"**.

We complete this study of Zion with Hebrew 12:22-24, **"But ye are come unto mount Sion, and unto the city of the living God, the heavenly Jerusalem, and to an innumerable company of angels. To the general assembly and church of the firstborn, which are written in heaven, and to God the Judge of all, and to the spirits of just men made perfect. And to Jesus the mediator of the new covenant, and to the blood of sprinkling, that speaketh better things than that of Abel."** If Zion and the city of the living God are called the Heavenly Jerusalem in this verse, then the Church must also be called Jerusalem as indicated in (Isa 33:22, 66:10&20). The name Jerusalem also departed ancient Israel along with Zion, the Throne, and birthright tribes to the new nations or Kingdom in the wilderness.

When God moved Zion from Jerusalem at the moment of Christ's death, it was the beginning of the New Covenant. Up until this point, the Holy Spirit was with Zion in the Temple of the house of God in Jerusalem, the symbol of Gods nation of Israel and chosen people sprinkled by blood in the Sinai that represented their baptism. The New Covenant fell under the shed blood of the Lord Jesus Christ and the baptism of the Holy Spirit symbolic of water. Under the old covenant they used blood of sacrificed animals for Christ had not died on the cross at that time. The general assembly and Church of the firstborn falls under the new covenant. The Laws of Moses of the firstborn means that all firstborn or fruit of the field was given to God. This means that Ephraim and Manasseh were given to God as the Birthright tribe of Israel, "he will rule as God", to spread his end time Gospel. When a person under the New Covenant is born again unto God, he belongs to the Church of the firstborn and is a part of Mount Sion or Zion the city of the living God, the Heavenly Jerusalem. The Church is also called the earthly Jerusalem.

After a close study of all the verses on Zion/Sion, it is clear that Zion is the Spirit of God that presides with his ancient children of Israel within the Temple of the Holy of Holies in the city of Jerusalem. Zion remained in the Temple in Jerusalem till Christ died on the cross and the veal in the Temple was rent (Mat 27:51 and II Cor 3:14-16). At that moment Zion became Christ's Church called Sion and the Church became Israel, Gods Children of Jerusalem (a teacher or instructor in a founded peaceful place).

Wilderness

According to Hebrew definition, the term wilderness can be related to a place that cattle is driven, a desert, a wasteland or empty place. Wilderness is also associated with a sterile valley, an aridity dry desert, a barren dry solitary land of wild beast and nomads that inhabit the wilderness. In other words, a wilderness is where civilized man does not live. Another close analogy is the word Zion for the two definitions are almost the same in accordance to the Strong's Concordance. Zion and wilderness are one and the same and explains the plowing and travailing of Zion into the wilderness as recorded in Isaiah 66:8. Zion is Gods Spirit with his Chosen People and directly connected to David's throne and Gods Kingdom. Wilderness and Zion together helps explain how God overturned the throne from Jerusalem and gave his Kingdom to a fruitful nation in the wilderness.

We have already covered the word plant and how it relates to vineyard, branch, mountain and bough. The house of Israel is Gods vineyard that is a mountain of nations. They represent a branch (Christ's Church), a bough (firstborn birthright) that was planted in the wilderness to bring judgment to the world (Isa 42:4). Study Isaiah chapter 41 and 43 of how God is going to bring Righteousness, Law, and Judgment to the wilderness of the Isles. This is where his people, the lost sheep of the house of Israel has gone by ship, **"by the way that he had not gone by feet"** (Isa 41:3, 40:18, 42:11-12). They did not go by foot so their mode of transportation had to be by boot or ship that took them to the wilderness of the Islands in Ireland and Briton and later to the continents of the world colonizing.

God says that the wilderness would be a fruitful field and judgment shall dwell in the wilderness (Isa 32:15-16). God will plant his trees (nations) in the wildness and water them with Law, Judgment and Righteousness (Isa 42:18-19). Jeremiah 9:1-2 states that God has a lodging place in the wilderness for his wayfaring people, daughter of Zion (house of Israel) that he might depart from them during their time of judgment of X7 or 2520 years. This wilderness is in the Isles of Britannia as stated in Isaiah chapter 41 and 43. Ezekiel 19:13, states that Israel was planted in the wilderness in a dry and thirsty ground which indicated a desert or uncivilized place. Ezekiel 20:34 goes on to say how the house of Israel will be gathered out from all countries to a place in the wilderness where God pleads with them under the bond of the New Covenant (Eze 20:37). This bond of the Covenant corresponds with many verses (Jerm 31:31, 33:14-17, Heb 8:8, Rom 11:26-27).

We have established that God is going to gather the house of Israel and plant them in the wilderness under a new Covenant in a land over the seas (Isa 16:8), **"they wandered through the wilderness: her branches are stretched out, they are gone over the sea."** We know this verse is speaking of Joseph (Ephraim and Manasseh of the house of Israel) for it corresponds to Gen 49:22 where Jacob is calling Joseph a fruitful branch that ran over the wall and according to Isaiah it went over-seas when it departed over the wall. Now he says that they shall dwell safely in the wilderness under a New Covenant (the Church) and sleep safely. This cannot be speaking of modern Israel in Palestine for they have never been peace or safety from their beginning. Hosea gives even a better account of how the house of Israel (Ephraim and Manasseh) will be allured into the wilderness under a new Covenant and be betroth or engaged to be married as (the bride) (divorced in Jerm 3:8) as a servant knowing Christ (Hos 2:14-23). This chapter is not speaking of the Jews for they still reject Christ as the Messiah.

We know by definition that when God planted the house of Israel in the wilderness, it was desolate and uninhabited. Isaiah 16:8 states that this wilderness was a far-away land overseas and even speak of the isles or islands. After reviewing all the verses in the Bible that refer to Gods fruitful bough (Christian) whose branches ran over the wall and seas (Gen 49:22 and Isa 16:8), can only be speaking of Christian nations under Christ's New Covenant. When we match these verses with Genesis 17:6, 35:11 and 48:19 that states the house of Israel (Ephraim and Manasseh) are to be a single Great (fruitful Christian) nation and a company of nations to be kings of kingdoms, only the United States and Great Britain meets these standards through-out world history under the throne of England.

Mountain means Nation

Through-out the Bible, the word mountain or mount is referred to as a nation of Gods people. God reveres the term mountain for he named many things starting with Mount such as: Mount Ephraim; Mount Zion; Mount of Esau; Mount of Olives and many others. Exodus 15:17 is a good example, **"Thou shalt bring them in, and plant them in the mountain of thin inheritance, in the place, O Lord, which thou hast made for thee to dwell in, in the Sanctuary, O Lord, which thy hands have established."** This verse is where God plants his Children of Israel in the Promised Land to become a mountain of his inheritance that is Gods nation of Israel. This was the first planting (refer to plant) and refers to his nation as a mountain, a dwelling place. The inheritance went to Ephraim and Manasseh in accordance to Law of Moses referring to the firstborn. This was the inheritance to the house of Israel, the recipient of the promises to Abraham, Isaac, Jacob and Joseph to be nations and kings of Kingdoms and became the mountains or eminent nations of Israel.

Jeremiah 26:18 states, **"Zion shall be plowed like a field, and Jerusalem shall become heaps, and the mountain of the house as the high places of a forest."** This verse calls Zion the mountain of his house or simply calling the house of his people a mountain or forest. They were to be plowed and removed from power through destruction. Isaiah 13:4 calls his nations, **"The noise of a multitude in the mountains like as of a great people, a tumultuous noise of the kingdoms of nations gathered together: the Lord of hosts mustereth the host of the battle."** Again, mountains are referred to as great people or nations getting ready for battle. This verse clearly states that the noise of his gathered people is kingdoms of nations which is referred to in Genesis 49:10 as Christ's Christian nations gathered in the wilderness. This is the gathering for World War III that is presently taking place for we can hear the noise of sabers rattling of terrorist activity.

Ezekiel chapter 17 and 21 gives the account of how God overturned his throne of King David from the high cedar branch of the Phares bloodline and gave it to the low branch of the *Zara* bloodline. This healed the breach between the two twins (Amos 9:11) and God plants his throne on a high mountain or a powerful nation. Ezekiel 17:22-23, **"Thus saith the Lord God: I will also take of the highest branch of the high cedar, and will set it: I will crop off from the top of his young twigs a tender one and will plant it upon an high mountain and eminent: In the mountain of the height of Israel will I plant it: and it shall bring forth boughs, and bear fruit, and be a goodly cedar".**

There is no doubt in this verse that the mountain God is speaking of is a nation where he replanted his throne and call it a cedar tree. Through-out the Bible the cedar refers to Gods throne of Israel. From these verses and many more, whenever God speaks of a mountain in reference to Israel, he is calling them a mountain or a nation that became many nations.

Jeremiah 51:24-26 speaks of Babylon as being a destroying mountain and because of their evil; God will make them a burnt mountain. Jeremiah 50:6 calls his people Israel a mountain when they were great and believes in him but went from mountain to a hill (captivity) when they forgot their resting place in God through disbelief and disobedience. Ezekiel 20:40, call the house of Israel the mountain of the height of Israel again calling them a mountain. Daniel 2:35 calls the stone that smote the image a great mountain. This is the 5th Kingdom of the house of Israel, Gods Christian nations or his Battle Ax. Joel 3:17 calls Zion his holy mountain referring to them as a nation or nations. Amos 4:1 calls Bashan (United States) the mountain of Samaria and 6:1 speaks of trusting in the mountain of Samaria which is the house of Israel for Samaria was the capital of their northern territory under the leadership of Ephraim and Manasseh.

Ezekiel 34:6 makes it clear that Gods sheep were scattered upon all the mountains and hills of the world and in context can only mean the nations of the earth. Micah 4:1 state, **"But in the last days it shall come to pass, that the mountain of the house of the Lord shall be established in the top of the mountains, and it shall be exalted above the hills; and people shall flow unto it."** This verse is almost word for word with Isaiah 2:2. In context of logic and the Scriptures, the mountains and hills can only be established nations within the world and this verse even states that it will take place in the last days, which is our present time period. This exalted nation above the hills or other nations is the fruitful nation Christ spoke of in Matthew 21:43 that were to be righteous and fruitful and be a world leading nation. The phrase, **"people shall flow unto it"**, can only be speaking of England and the United States where Christians migrated from all over the world by millions for freedom of Religion. Great Britain and America are the only two Christian nations in history that fit's the scenario of these two verses.

The last verse we will cover pertaining to mountains as nations is covered in Habakkuk 3:6 and it states, **"He stood, and measured the earth: he beheld, and drove asunder the nations; and the everlasting mountains where scattered, the perpetual hills did bow: his ways are everlasting"**. The everlasting mountains mentioned in this verse is God's chosen people of the house of Israel spreading his end time Gospel as the Church, Gods everlasting Kingdom. His everlasting Kingdom is Christ and his Gospel under the New Covenant that subdues all nations.

After reviewing all the verses referring to mountain, it is clear that in some context, the word refers to a nation or nations whether evil like Babylon (Jerm 51:21) or fruitful (Christian) nations as the house of Israel (Eze 20:40).

Chapter 9

Daniels Secret and Mystery of Prophecy

Bible Prophecy is a fascinating subject that most people do not understand. The average Christian feels that prophecy is beyond his or her capability of understanding unless taught by someone else. This writer, in the past, believed in that same manner till realizing, God will give understanding if you truly study and seek knowledge. True knowledge comes from the Holy Spirit being one on one with deep study in the Scriptures and not from reading man's books. Having the desire to seek Gods knowledge is the key to understanding when it comes from the heart. James 1:5 tells us, **"If any of you lack wisdom, let him ask of God, that giveth to all men liberally, and upbraideth not; and it shall be given him"**. The responsibility of learning God's word is given to the individual Christian and not the Church. This is a very true verse when you have faith in prayer. Our nation and the Christians therein have lost their faith in God and prayer, therefore, losing our understanding of God. The Pastor has a duty to teach and guide his flock but the ultimate responsibility of learning the Scriptures falls upon each individual Church member and we have failed in this task.

There is an aspect of Gods mystery that the Church of the last days are over looking. Paul makes the statement in Romans 11:25-27 that Israel is partially blinded. Who was Paul telling this too, the Church or to Israel? Israel and the Church is one and the same according to Paul for in verses 26 and 27 he states, **"And so all Israel shall be saved: as it is written, There shall come out of Sion the Deliverer, and shall turn away ungodliness from Jacob: For this is my covenant unto them, when I shall take away their sins."** After closely looking at these verses, all of Israel will be saved by the Deliverer that is Christ and his Church. His New Covenant mentioned in Hebrews 8:8 and Jeremiah 31:31 is to the house of Israel, so Israel has to be his Church. The term "all of Israel" is plural and means both the house of Israel and the house of Judah that is Jacob, all of Gods Children. The time period of this saving takes place during the end days prior to the rapture for it falls within his covenant of the Church age.

The Hebrew meaning of Israel, "He will rule as God", which means, Israel will govern the families of the world through Gods New Covenant by judging with righteousness and justice till Christ claims his throne. At this very moment, there are Churches preaching the Gospel in the world and in the nation state of Israel that overall rejects Christ as their Messiah. This fulfills the Scriptures of Matthew 10:5-8 and 21:43 confirms Paul's statement in Romans that all Israel will be saved. This is where Jesus told his disciples to go to the lost sheep of the house of Israel to teach his Word. Because of rejection, Jesus informed the Chief Priest and Pharisees that he was going to take his Kingdom from them and give it to a fruitful nation. This fruitful nation was England that had already been established and where his throne and lost sheep of the house of Israel was plucked and overturned. This can be proven by the Roman invasion into Briton in 43AD where Gladys (Claudia) of the captured British Royal family had already been converted to Christian and been taken to Rome under Diplomatic immunity (II Tim 4:21). Claudia established the first Church in Rome before Paul arrived in 56AD for she was under immunity by being a part of the British Royal Family. The Roman Senate gave property to the Royal Family within Rome and was not subject to Roman law just as a foreign Embassy today.

We have already determined that God declares his word a mystery for he receives great glory from man believing in him by faith. Daniel presents another mystery that would appear God is keeping a secret from his people till the time of the end. Daniel 12:4 states, **"But thou, O Daniel, shut up the words, and seal the book, even to the time of the end: many shall run to and fro, and knowledge shall be increased."** Daniel reemphasizes the secrets being sealed again in 12:9, **"And be said, Go thy way Daniel: for the words are closed up and sealed till the time of the end"**. The subject Daniel was speaking of prior to both of these verses were of the tribulation wrath of God but I believe the Secret pertains to the last days which is now, **"many shall run to and fro, and knowledge shall be increased"**. This term is speaking of our present time period, the computer age of great knowledge increase. What is Daniel's secret that could be so important for God to keep from us till the time of the end?

Daniel 2:28 makes it clear that Christ's Church, Gods 5th Kingdom, is the corner stone, an uncut stone by hand. Daniel 2:34, says it was to be a secret in the last days. By Hebrew law, the Alter of blood Sacrificing could only be built with uncut stones without hands. The uncut stone Daniel speaks of represents Christ and his Church and the stone Kingdom or 5th Kingdom was to be a world power. Daniel chapter two refers to his interpretation to King Nebuchadnezzar's dream, the word secret is mentioned three times indicating its importance during the last days. The Secret is the identity of the 5th Kingdom that destroys the first four world kingdoms and establishes an ensign (flag or symbol) to the nations of the world (Isa 11:12). All of Daniel's interpretations of the visions within his book were to be a Secret and sealed till the end of the age. This would mean that all end time Prophecy was a Secret for every vision and interpretation within the book of Daniel compose the Old and New Testament Prophecies. Daniel's secret is the identity of the 5th kingdom that is his end time Battle Axe of Christian nations, Great Britain and the United States. The British and American flags have flown in more countries representing world power and justice than any other flags in history and fulfills Isaiah 11:10-16 as an ensign or flag to the world. This is simply a historical fact that cannot be denied and fulfills Scripture.

There is an aspect that we need to consider when we think of the availability of the Scriptures to mankind. From the time Christ established his Gospel and died on the cross, approximately 1973 years has expired. God's Word has only been available to common man since AD 1611 with the printing of the King James Bible, which is only 413 years out of 6,000 from Adam and Eve. This alone fulfills Dan 12:4 and 9 as being in the time of the end or the last days. Daniel's Secret could not be revealed till several things occurred. God's Word had to be available to the common man and then spread worldwide (Isa 11:11-12 and 41:2-3). Secondly, God needed a powerful nation (his battle ax Jerm 51:19-29) to complete this task. The printing and establishing of God's Word within the world allowed the fulfillment of Gods inheritance blessings given to Abraham, Isaac and then to Jacob passed directly to only Ephraim and Manasseh. They were to be many powerful wealthy nations and kingdoms. This time period also matches the completion of Gods times 7 punishment of the families or houses of Israel and Judah's 2520 years to be complete after the Dark Ages of no blessings. This occurs in the end days just as Daniel's Secret states. These nations fulfilled Scripture under a Republic and Democratic System that became our western Christian culture dominated by Gods Birthright inherited tribes of Joseph's two sons (Gen 48:16-19). This greatness could only have occurred through the establishment of God's Word under his New Covenant given to his Battle Ax, the house of Israel (Heb 8:8-10 and Jerm 31:31-33), Great Britain and the United States.

If we look back over time, there has been no change in Biblical doctrine or a major revelation in the Church. It is my personal belief that when God took the name and identification away from his people of the house of Israel, he did not want the world to know their identity till the time of the End. As the world grows more and more evil, it explains why the English Christian nations are hated due to their birthright inheritance of wealth and rule over kingdoms just as Deuteronomy 21:17 states that there would be family hatred for the firstborn. Certain prophetic teachers and writers are beginning to reveal the truth of our nations true identity and unlocking Daniel's secret of Gods end time prophecy. Refer to the 5th kingdom in chapter nine.

The Satanic world naturally hates Gods Children of Druid prior to Judaism, and Christianity as the house of Israel (the Christian nations) and the house of Judah (modern Judaism). He has tried desperately to destroy both from their beginning. The nations of the world, hates any nation that portrays righteousness or goodness and can be seen in the politics of today. Because of our fight against terrorism, the world (United Nations) is gathering against us and could very well cause World War III. The United States have been taken over from within through the Communistic Democrat Party. Our destruction will be predicated upon the advancement of the one world economic, religious and political system of the soon coming government controlled by the leaders of the New World Order. God's Prophetic destruction as indicated in the Old Testament Scriptures will occur if we do not repent of our national sin in which it may be too late. The Hand Writing could already be on our walls.

Blindness in Part

Paul speaks of the blindness that would occur to Israel during the last days in Romans 11:25-26, **"For I would not, brethern, that ye should be ignorant of this mystery, lest ye should be wise in your own conceits; that blindness in part is happened to Israel, until the fullness of the Gentiles be come in. And so all Israel shall be saved: as it is written, There shall come out of Sion the Deliverer, and shall turn away ungodliness from Jacob: For this is my covenant unto them"**.   These verses are very interesting for they also indicate a division of Israel between the house of Israel and the house of Judah till the fullness of the Gentiles be come in. **"As it is written"**, refers to Jeremiah 33:14-21 placing King David's throne, the Deliverer (Christ's Covenant the Gospel) and all Israel being saved (house of Israel along with house of Judah) in the last days. All three of these elements are mentioned in Jeremiah 33:14-21 placing a man on David's throne during our present time. This is Gods whole Kingdom under the Throne of England.

Paul speaks of the everlasting covenant in Genesis 17:6 where they were to be nations and kings of nations which is also mentioned in Genesis 35:11 of the blessing given to Abraham, Isaac and Jacob. The deliverer, Christ, was to turn away ungodliness from Jacob by establishing his Church that is his Hebrew Christian nations. This blindness that Paul is talking about speaks to Jacob and is both houses of all the Children of Israel. The house of Israel is blind to their true identity and Hebrew ancestry due to the fact of being planted in the wilderness as a fruitful nation commissioned to establish the Church and Gospel world-wide till Christ's coming in power. Liberalism, Socialism and Communism has blinded the Church. The house of Judah is blind to the fact that Christ was the true Messiah. Habakkuk 1:5 states that Gods people will not believe the truth even after being told by the Prophets, **"for I will work a work in your days, which ye will not believe, though it be told you."** The Prophet Habakkuk makes a statement concerning our end times. He prophesied to the nations of soon coming destruction by the Prophets, but they will not believe or listen. The term "in your days" refer to the last days of the end of the age.

The subject that Paul is speaking of in Romans chapter eleven is grafting in of the Gentiles that is the branches that represent the wild olive tree. During this period of time, it was extremely hard for the Hebrew Jews to accept Gentiles into the Church. This was a problem Paul had to correct for all people, nationalities and color or creed were open to the Church. The ten northern tribes of the house of Israel were considered to be Gentiles by the Jews along with the rest of the heathen world. The mystery is that God will graft anyone into his tree of life if they truly believe in our Lord. We need to understand that a person as a believer in Christ and an actual blood descent of Jacob is already a part of the physical plant but both Hebrew or Gentile believers has to be grafted into the Spiritual Kingdom to be called an Israelite.

It was impossible for the Chief Priests and Pharisees to accept Christ during that period of time and due to this fact, the kingdom was taken from them, Matthew 21:43, and given to a fruitful nation in the wilderness. Verse 26 states that all Israel shall be saved but that will not occur till the fullness of the Gentiles come in. The term "all Israel" indicates the separation of the house of Israel and the house of Judah that also explains the controversy of the bad branches of the olive tree. The term **"fullness of the Gentiles be come in"** means when the work of the Church is complete and the Gospel has been spread worldwide to all nations either Hebrew or Gentile.

The Jewish Hebrew Church of Paul's time had a hard time in accepting the Gentiles of the house of Israel into the Church. Remember that Christ sent the twelve Apostles to the lost sheep of the house of Israel, his fruitful nation, in Matthew 10:6 for they were the nation to inherit the Kingdom (Mat 21:43). Also keep in mind that the term Gentile simply means, a non-Jew. The 10 northern tribes of the house of Israel had been separated from the Jews for so long, they had become Gentile to the Jewish people. Paul goes on to say that "all Israel" which includes both the house of Israel and the house of Judah will be saved after the fullness of the Gentiles is complete. This fulfills Ezekiel 37:11, the gathering of the dried bones. Ezekiel 37:22 even states that Israel will not be divided into two kingdoms any more placing this time of gathering in the last days. During the Tribulation Period, the blindness will be lifted and the Jews of Judah will understand that they crucified the true Messiah two thousand years earlier and accept Christ as the Messiah. The house of Israel will finally realize their true identity and the roll of Gods inheritance of his birthright tribe. This will be the part of the house of Israel that was not Christian but of Hebrew descent after Spiritual Israel (the Church) is taken (Ruptured).

The fact that the Jews (Judaism) of the house of Judah rejected Christ as the Messiah is a distinct indication of the separation of the present-day house of Israel and the Jews of the divided house of Judah. The study of the word fruit and fruitful is the proof of the separation. The Old Testament speaks of Gods fruitful nations in the last days and even calls them by their ancient names of Lebanon, Sharon, Bashan, Carmel, and Gilead, **"The earth mourned and languisheth; Lebanon is ashamed and hewn down: Sharon is like a wilderness; and Bashan and Carmel shake off their fruits"**. Jeremiah 23:3 **"And I will gather the remnant of my flock out of all countries whither I have driven them, and will bring them again to their folds: and they shall be fruitful and increase."** Notice that folds are in a plural form meaning more than one. There are three gatherings of his people that we must not confuse. The first is the gathering of approx. 40,000 Jews back into Jerusalem after the Babylonian captivity to rebuild the Temple in Ezra's day. The second is the gathering of his flock in the wilderness country where they will be fruitful as Gods Christian nations of his Church as his whole Kingdom (Gen 49:10, Eze 37). The third is presently happening as the parable of the fig tree back into Israel in 1948 and during the Tribulation Period in the promised land of Israel to complete Daniel's 70th week Prophecy to the non-believing Jews of Jerusalem.

Paul in Romans 11:26 refers to Jeremiah 23:5-8 explaining the separation of Israel and Judah and the time frame is in the last days, **"Behold, the days come, saith the Lord, that I will raise unto David a righteous Branch, and a King shall reign and prosper, and shall execute judgment and justice in the earth. In his days Judah shall be saved, and Israel shall dwell safely: and this is his name whereby he shall be called, THE LORD OUR RIGHTEOUSNESS. Therefore, behold, the days come, saith the Lord, that they shall no more say, The Lord liveth, which brought up the children of Israel out of the land of Egypt; But, The lord liveth, which**

brought up and which led the seed of the house of Israel out of the north country, and from all countries whither I had driven them; and they shall dwell in their own land." This writer believes that these verses are speaking of our present time period and important to understand. Jeremiah 23:5, says that God will raise unto David a righteous Branch which is Christ and his Church, his earthly Kingdom. It goes on to say that a King shall reign and prosper and execute judgment and justice in the earth. This verifies Jeremiah 33:17, I Kings 9:5 and Psalms 89:4 that a physical man would always sit on David's throne during all generations and is not a Spiritual King **"There shall not fail thee a man upon the throne of Israel" "and build up thy throne to all generations"**. This King of Israel will dwell safely in a faraway land. Jeremiah 23:5-6 and 33:14-17 are almost identical verses that Paul in Romans 11:26 refer to. Jeremiah 23:6 states, **"Judah shall be saved, and Israel shall dwell safely"** as two separate nations. In other words, Jeremiah 33:16 is calling Israel Jerusalem, the nation dwelling safely in the wilderness (the Church) as already covered in chapter three as the Christian nations of the western culture.

When Jeremiah wrote his book, he was warning the house of Judah of coming destruction due to their sins of idolatry. These verses were written by Jeremiah around 599 BC, approx. 130 years after the house of Israel had been taken into captivity and no longer existed as a nation. They never reentered the Promised Land, but he was writing to them. Why? This is a warning during ancient times to the house of Judah of their eminent captivity to Babylon for the house of Israel had already been taken captive to Assyria. The dual warning is to the houses of Israel and Judah in the future that is our present time. This is a current warning of our eminent destruction due to our separation from God as indicated in the Scriptures above.

Jeremiah 23:6 states that in his days Judah the Jews shall be saved and Israel shall dwell safely which is exactly what is happening in the world today. The term "his days" is referring to the days of the righteous branch or the Church age of our present time period. Judah or the Jews are being brought back to their promised land and being saved for Gods future plans. Israel or the house of Israel which is the English-speaking Christian nations are dwelling safely throughout the world in their own lands and calling the Lord "THE LORD OUR RIGHTEOUSNESS" through the new Covenant of the Church as Gods whole Kingdom. The Jew do not believe in Christ so this does not pertain to them and that is why they are separated in these verses. Jeremiah 23:7 states that the days will come when they will no longer believe in the Lord. This is our present day of falling away and God being taken out of our Society. Verse eight explains how God in the last days will take the seed of the house of Israel in the north country and bring them back to their own land of the promised land of Jerusalem in Canaan. Note that Jeremiah uses the word seed of the house of Israel out of the North Country and from all countries. The word seed indicates that only a small portion of each tribe will return to Judea as a gathering. This is the re-gathering in Israel that is happening at this very moment of time. After reading these verses and many other verses throughout the Bible, it is clear that the house of Israel and the divided house of Judah the Jews are two separate nations during the last days just as our current situation exist between the USA, UK and modern Israel as brothers.

The word fruitful is the key in understanding the separation of Israel and Judah. The house of Israel was to be fruitful and multiply due to the birthright blessing and because they were given the Kingdom of the Gospel for, only they believed in Christ and not the Jews. Judah or the Jews of Jerusalem rejected Christ and the kingdom was taken from them due to disbelief (Matt 21:43) and received a curse (Jerm 25:18; 44:8, 42:18; Isa 65:15). Isaiah 32:15-18 explains the fruitful righteous nation in the wilderness, **"Until the spirit be poured upon us from on high, and the wilderness be a fruitful field, and the fruitful field be counted for a forest. Then judgment shall dwell in the wilderness, and righteousness remain in the fruitful field. And the work of righteousness shall be peace; and the effect of righteousness quietness and assurance for ever. And my people shall dwell in a peaceable habitation, and in sure dwellings, and in quiet resting places;"** Verse 15 speaks of the Spirit being poured upon us and the wilderness being a fruitful field which speaks of how God poured the Holy Spirit (the new covenant Jerm 31:31 & Heb 8:8) upon the Church and the Gospel was spread worldwide into the wilderness. The term **"Then judgment shall dwell in the wilderness"** is the inherited authority of the divided tribe of Levi as the lawgiver. They were to judge the other eleven tribes dispersed and scattered in the wilderness to teach judgment and law to all the other eleven tribes under the New Covenant and laws of Christ's Church (Duet 33:10). This is where King David's Throne was cut, chopped off and moved to a faraway land in the wilderness which is today's throne of England as Gods whole Kingdom. For better understanding study the words wilderness, fruitful and forest.

Being fruitful is simply being a Christian. Verse 16 and 17 states that judgment shall dwell in the wilderness which means that Gods Christian nations shall judge the world through righteousness which is exactly what has taken place during the past four hundred years with the domination of Great Britain's Commonwealth and the United State. Verse 18 states **"And my people shall dwell in a peaceable habitation, and in sure dwellings, and in quiet resting places:"** This verse cannot be speaking of Jerusalem of the promised land for there have never been peace during the last 2700 years due to the Arab

Islamic problem. The word **"places"** speaks in a plural since and indicates multiple countries so it cannot be speaking of the single nation of modern Israel. The United States and England has been placed on a secure continent or Island secure from conquering invaders and the freest peaceful loving nations in history.

We love peace as a nation and were considered to be a nation of isolation till WW II. America represents truth and justice when we become Gods Battle Axe to fight tyranny. Who is this verse speaking of that is in the wilderness, Isaiah 27:6, **"He shall cause them that come of Jacob to take root: Israel shall blossom and bud, and fill the face of the world with fruit."** This verse clearly states that the house of Israel, Ephraim and Manasseh, will evangelize the world with Christ's Gospel as Christian nations. (I Chron 17:9-14; Ezekiel 20:34-47; 34:13-18; Hosea 2:14-23; Micah 5:7-11: Zechariah 10:6-12). All these verses need to be studied vary carefully for they indicate the house of Israel being planted into the wilderness of faraway nations and mountains **"to fill the face of the world with fruit"**, spreading Christ's Gospel. The fruits of Christ's Gospel are a symbol of the house of Israel as a vineyard (Isa 5:7) and the "branches that ran over the wall" is the fruit bearing or Christian nations of Ephraim, the house of Israel, Gods first fruit or double fruit of the birthright tribe (Matt 21:43). Ezekiel chapter 37 explains in detail of how the dried bones and rejoining of the two sticks as Gods divided Kingdom will be re-gathered and joined during the Church age of the New Covenant governed by David's Throne of England (Eze 37:16-19)

One of the main reasons the Church has been blind to the true identity of the house of Israel in modern times is because of the world revival of Judaism that occurred around the turn of the nineteenth century. Till this time, Gods Kingdom was whole as his Christian nations under the Throne of England. This is when the Jews began to return to the area of Palestine in the region of Jerusalem under the control of the British Empire. The Christian people of Gods worldwide Church saw this and believed that this re-gathering represented all twelve tribes of Israel. It seems that the Church cannot get beyond this point of understanding. If you study the birthright and its proper recipient, you will see that modern Israel is the Jews of the divided house of Judah fulfilling prophecy pertaining to Jerusalem in the last days.

The house of Israel as Gods whole Kingdom still exist elsewhere within the world just as Ezekiel 37:11 states where God takes his Church under his New Covenant just prior to the beginning of the Tribulation Period (I Cor 15:51). The birthright tribes of the house of Israel were to be nations and kingdoms so it would not be fitting for them to return to Jerusalem and does not fit the scenario.

The Church is all twelve tribes representing the house of Israel during our present-day recognizing Israel as being whole as one under Christ's New Covenant, **"Then he said unto me, Son of man, these bones are the whole house of Israel: behold, they say, Our bones are dried, and our hope is lost: we are cut off for our parts"** (Eze 37:11). When the bones are gathered during the Church age under the Spirit of Christ's Gospel it becomes the whole house of Israel, all twelve tribes. Ezekiel 37:22 speaks in more detail of the end time division, **"And I will make them one nation in the land upon the mountains of Israel; and one king shall be king to them all: and they shall be no more two nations, neither shall they be divided into two kingdoms any more at all"**. These two verses occur during the last days and clearly make the distinction between the nations of Israel and Judah the Jews placing this time period in our present time. This places Christ's whole Kingdom under the Throne of England where it was planted in the wilderness making modern Israel a separate entity because they rejected the Messiah.

The Church today will not see or comprehend that the houses of Israel and Judah of the Jews are still separated until they understand the birthright blessing went to Ephraim and Manasseh (house of Israel) and not to the Jews or Judah (modern Israel). This separation still exists and makes all the Old Testament Prophetic warnings of destruction pertinent for today's end time Church.

Isaiah told us that the house of Israel would lose their name and language and would not know that they were Gods people, **"For Jacob my servant's sake, and Israel mine elect, I have even called thee by thy name: I have surnamed thee, through thou hast not known me"**, Isaiah 45:4. This verse groups all of Israel into two different peoples. The first is Jacob his servant that is all his Children of Israel and the second is Israel his elect, the ten northern tribes of the house of Israel controlled by the birthright tribes of Ephraim and Manasseh. The term elects' referrers to Christian as his elected birthright tribe to receive his double blessings. God states that he surnamed them by changing their name to another and that they do not know him. In other words, they don't know God as his Hebrew people because of their name and language change. That truly match in how the Church today cannot see that they are a part of the house of Israel, there are blind to Matt 10:6 and 15:24. When the house of Israel was taken into captivity by Assyria, they were forced to speak another language, worship other Gods and live under different customs so they slowly lost their identity as Hebrew Israelites.

Isaiah 65:15 also states, **"And ye shall leave your name for a curse unto my chosen: for the Lord God shall slay thee, and call his servants by another name"**. Again, it shows where God changed their name to fulfill his purpose. The name change did not only include the house of Israel but the millions of people from the tribe of Judah and Benjamin that also migrated into Europe. Keep in mind that only 40,000 out of 13 million Israelites gathered back into Jerusalem of Judea after the Babylonian captivity till Christ came and fulfilled prophecy when riding into Jerusalem on the donkey.

The reestablishment of Israel in 1948 was only the first step in Gods planning to prepare for Daniel's 70th week Prophecy to save the Jews. Modern day Israel is the house of Judah called the Jews and still separate as the Judea Hebrew from the lost sheep of the house of Israel as Gods whole Kingdom under Christianity. It is interesting to study the word whole for its mentioned only twice prior to Ezekiel 37:11 when referring to the whole nation of Israel. The first is in Leviticus 10:6 when Moses was talking to the whole house of Israel prior to entering the Promised Land and Jeremiah 13:11 when Jeremiah was talking about the division of the two houses and made a distinct difference between the two, **"I caused to cleave unto me the whole house of Israel and the whole house of Judah"**. After studying this verse, how can anyone not see the division of Israel as two individual houses or nations? The Church is blind to this fact and refuse to study the Scriptures for the truth which is the blindness spoken of by Paul in Romans 11:5-27 "God has given them the spirit of slumber" as quoted above. The blindness will remain till the fullness of the Gentile age is complete and the Church is taken by the rapture. Only then are the Jews saved and fall under the whole house of Israel spoken of in Ezekiel chapter 37. Daniel's 70th week Prophecy pertains only to the non-believing Jews of Jerusalem.

The partial blindness spoken of by Paul in the above verses is a fascinating and absolute phenomenon. You can truly see Gods Blindness within the Church as recorded in history and even more so within Society itself.

Since the revival of Judaism and the establishment of Israel in Palestine, we as Christians have been inundated to the so-called fact that the Jewish State of Israel is the whole house of Israel and that the houses of Judah and Israel are one and the same. This is just not true for many verses throughout the Scriptures indicate the division. This blindness can only be overcome by a true desire to learn the truth with total faith in the Scriptures through prayer asking the Holy Spirit to give us wisdom and understanding as mentioned in James 1:5. If you truly seek this understanding in prayer, God will give you the truth of his Scriptures.

Gathering of the People

The gathering of the people Moses spoke of in Genesis 48:10 is a very interesting scenario. When you take a good concordance and study the word gather from the beginning of the Bible to the end you come up with approx. three different gatherings of Gods people. The Hebrew meaning of gather; prime root to grasp, assemble bring selves together and heap. Acts 7:38, says that the gathering of the Israelites in the wilderness at Sinai was called a Church just as the gathering of his people planted in the wilderness. A gathering could not take place till the tribes had gone into captivity to Assyria and Babylon. All of Israel had to be regathered if they were to be a whole nation again. The first gathering was only for the Jews of Judea that took place when approx. 40,000 Jews returned to Jerusalem of Judea after the seventy years of Babylonian captivity (Ezra 6:14) to rebuild the Temple. This gathering preserved Jerusalem till The Messiah could come to fulfill prophecy and represents the division of the house of Judah. The rest of Israel dispersed separately into the wilderness of Europe.

The second gathering applies to the house of Israel/Judah gathered in the wilderness (Gen 48:10). This gathering is the fruitful nation that received the Kingdom taken from the Jews completing the whole house of Israel as mentioned in Ezekiel 37 (Matt 21:43, Isa 43:5, 54:1-7, 56:8, 60:1-16, Eze 34:13, 36:24-27, Hosea 8:10). They gathered together as the Monarchs of Europe for all of them were connected by family and the throne of England was their leader. The third gathering is recorded in Matthew 24 as the fig tree parable to complete Daniel's 70th week Prophecy.

To have a gathering you must first have a scattering or dispersal. When Israel first went into the Promised Land, it was called a planting not a gathering (Exodus 15:17). There was no need for a gathering of Gods people till the first captivity of the ten northern tribes of the house of Israel that took place between 740 to 720BC by the Assyrians and then the captivity of Judah to Babylon in 586BC. For God to complete his prophetic plans, he had to re-gather his people from the two captivities where he divided the two houses for his prophetic purposes. They were to be separated and remain separated as two distinct houses till his plans are completed in the last days and during the Tribulation Period. The house of Israel and the house of Judah is mentioned as two separate nations all through the Old Testament and even Paul speaks of "all Israel being saved" indicating two different houses in Rom 11:26. There is no record in the Bible reuniting the two houses till Ezekiel 17 and Jeremiah 3 takes place during the Church age. Hebrews 8:8 also speak of Israel and Judah being separate people or nations in the age of the Gospel or the last days.

To understand the gathering of Gods people we must first have a total acknowledgment of one key verse that is a critical piece of Gods prophetic puzzle (Gen 49:10). When we break down the different segments of this verse into proper perspective, we can see one of the reasons God divided his two houses. In this verse, Jacob gave Judah his portion of inheritance that has influenced the nation of Israel throughout time. In this segment, we need to re-quote for a full understanding that is as follows, **"The sceptre shall not depart form Judah, nor a lawgiver from between his feet, until Shiloh come; and unto him shall the gathering of the people be."** This writer always believed, as most Christians that verse 10 is speaking of Christ coming in power at the end of the age to receive his Children that is the remnant of his nation of Israel in Jerusalem. In reality, this verse is simply speaking of Christ coming to establish his Church and Disciples in the wilderness prior to his death. Christ is called Shiloh for he represents the Temple in the form of a man (Gods Spirit with man as a MAN). When closely studying the word Shiloh, lawgiver and gather, you begin to understanding this verse which is absolutely critical in appreciating prophetical occurrences during our present times. Genesis 49:10 is a pivotal spring board for the house of Israel and Judah in end time prophecy.

Let's dissect this verse word for word so we can have a complete understanding. The words, **"The sceptre shall not depart form Judah,"** is simple. The scepter or crown of the throne of David will not depart from Judah till Christ or Shiloh comes to gather his people. The authority of the throne remained with Judah in Jerusalem till Christ established his Church and the rejection by the Jews complete. When Christ died on the cross and his Spirit departed, the veil was rent within the Temple. The authority of the throne was then moved to the Zarah line of Kings established and planted in the wilderness by Jeremiah and King Zedekiah's daughters in Ireland approx. 615 years prior. Zion travailed by producing the birth of the Messiah and departed Jerusalem (Isa 66:8). Physical Jerusalem was then plowed (Jerm 26:18 in 70 AD) and the Spiritual name Jerusalem and Israel, the house of Israel, was planted into the world to produce the Gospel. The word plowed in Hebrew in this aspect means, to be silent, to let alone, to be deaf as of dumbness, leave off speaking and speak not a word. In other words, Gods Spirit departed Jerusalem and will not return till Christ set on his Throne during the millennial. When Christ died on the cross and the vail in the Temple rent, the authority of King David's Throne moved from Jerusalem to the wilderness and given to the Zarah bloodline in Britain, today, the Throne of England.

Travailed in Hebrew means, to twist, to dance, to writhe in pain or fear, <u>drive away</u>, wait carefully or patiently, make to calve and be wounded. It also means that Israel produced a Man Child, the Messiah, with pain. Being plowed and travailed applied to both the Jews of Jerusalem and the house of Israel scattered into the wilderness, to be driven away. According to the meanings of travailed and plowed, Jerusalem was silenced as Zion after Christ's death due to rejection and is why God moved Zion and planted it in the wilderness so it could grow and produce fruit. His Kingdom would be taken from the Jew and given to the care of the birthright tribe of Ephraim and Manasseh (double fruit blessing). They were responsible for the family name under the Old Law, therefore, Zion and the authority of King David's throne was overturned and traveled or moved to another nation that was fruitful. The Scripture also makes it clear in many verses that there will always be a man of every generation sitting on his throne, which means in essence, that it exists today somewhere in this world (England).

The phrase, **"nor a lawgiver from between his feet,"** is very important for we must learn who the lawgiver represents. We know that ultimately the lawgiver is God or Christ himself but for the purpose of this verse, it means someone different. The original lawgiver in correlation with Gods Children of Israel was Moses. The name Moses in Hebrew means to pull out, draw, rescued and Israel's lawgiver. He was a physical man that God first gave his Children the laws of righteousness on stone tablets and by verbal rule. In this verse, the lawgiver has to be in direct correlation with the throne that we already know is an earthly man. The lawgiver has to be the government or the authority of judgment of the Levite tribe (Deut 33:10) in relationship to the throne of power. Keep in mind that Gen 49:1 places this verse in the last days so we are speaking of our present time, for Christ has not returned to rule as of this date.

The next part of this verse is, **"until Shiloh come;".** The Hebrew meaning for Shiloh is, tranquil, an epithet of the Messiah, secure or successful, be happy, prosper and be in safety. According to these definitions, Shiloh is the Messiah or Christ. The term, "be in safety" relates to his planted nation that dwells safely in the wilderness under his New Covenant, his Christian nations as Jerusalem. Why would God call the Messiah Shiloh? We need to go further into the Bible to find the reason and it is so clear. If we look on an ancient map of Canaan as divided among the tribes, Shiloh is a small town approx. 18 miles north east of Jerusalem and about 12 miles north east of Bethel (Gods House). Shiloh is where Joshua established the Tabernacle of Congregation during the early years prior to all the territory being taken for Israel's inheritance. Keep in mind that Moses, the Lawgiver, is the person that first established the Tabernacle in the desert, the Church (Acts 7:38).

The event of Joshua establishing the Tabernacle in Shiloh is a sacred time to God, for this is the beginning of his Children being established as a nation and Shiloh is a symbol of that creation and his Spirit with his Children. Shiloh was established in the land of Ephraim to indicate the birthright and leader of the family name, Israel. The reason God called Christ Shiloh in Gen 49:10, is to be a symbol of the creation of Israel as a nation in Canaan just as the creation of Christ's Church at the gathering of his people during his ministry. Why did God choose Shiloh in Ephraim? The Tabernacle and Holy of Holies establish in Shiloh is a symbol of Gods Spirit (Zion) with his people and represents the end time worldwide Church "until Shiloh come" where he instituted his Church and Gospel 2000 years ago. Joshua was born from the tribe of Ephraim to be their leader for they were the birthright tribe and inheritor of the family. This is the key reason Christ was called Shiloh of Ephraim for he was to be a forerunner of great nations with wealth and power (Battle Ax) to protect his Church. The interesting part of this verse is that Moses was a Levite and Lawgiver that gave the Tabernacle and Ark of the Covenant to Joshua the Ephraimite for him to be leader of the family and Children of Israel that fulfills the birthright Mosaic Laws.

Shiloh was a special place to God for it was the original location of his Tabernacle establishing his people in the Promised Land as a nation. Shiloh and the Tabernacle, later to be the Temple, represents Zion (Christ Church), Gods Spirit with his people in the wilderness and as a nation, his end time Church.

The three different gatherings are very import to understand so let's break each one down as to why by Scripture? The first gathering is recorded in Ezra where Jerusalem and the Temple restoration take place and the beginning of Daniel's seventy weeks of prophecy. This prophecy only pertained to the Jews of Jerusalem and not to the house of Israel of the ten northern tribes. The rebuilding of Jerusalem and the Temple were to maintain the authority for Gods Kingdom and the coming of the Messiah. We need to remember that Jeremiah had overturned the throne to Ireland in 584BC as a preparation but the authority remained in Jerusalem till Christ fulfilled the prophecy of the coming of the Messiah. When Christ died on the cross as the Messiah, the veil in the Temple was rent indicating the travailing of Zion (Isa 66:8). The plowing took place 40 years later and one generation of Jews rejecting Christ's Gospel

(Jerm 26:18) and completing 69 weeks of Daniel's prophecy of the Jews and Jerusalem. The third gathering will complete Daniel's 70th week that only applied to the Jews of Jerusalem. Judea and Jerusalem were totally plowed (destroyed) in 70AD by the Roman General Titus. Just as God did not allow the incredulous Hebrews in the wilderness to enter the Promised Land, he took David's portion of the Kingdom from the unbelieving Jews (Matt 21:43). He then gave David's share of the kingdom (I Kings 11:35-37) to the house of Israel, his lost sheep. This make Gods kingdom complete and whole within the nation that had already been planted in the wilderness, England (Matt 10:5-8). As a writer, I cannot believe that God would allow his Kingdom and Spirit to lie in rubble within Jerusalem for almost 2000 years. Gods Kingdom is not only physical but also spiritual. The Scriptures indicate a continual existence of his Kingdom (Zion of David's throne) as multiplying and being fruitful.

When Jerusalem was destroyed in 70AD, this ended the first gathering and shifted to the second gathering that had already begun. In reality, the second gathering began with early migration of Hebrews into the British Isles after the exodus from Egypt to establish the nation that Christ said would be fruitful. They were to be the fruitful bough of Joseph (Ephraim and Manasseh) in Genesis 49:22 and Deuteronomy 33:13-17 (the unicorn and bull), the ten thousands of Ephraim (46 nations of Great Britain) and the thousands of Manasseh (United States territories). This corresponds with a nation and a company of nations as promised to Jacob (Isaac's sons "Saxon" Gen 21:12, Heb 11:18) in Genesis 35:11. Isaac's sons mean Saxon and this was to be their name according to the Scriptures above.

According to secular history of the Four Masters, the Chronicles of Ireland, Scotland and England, Jeremiah had established Zedekiah's bloodline through his daughters in Ireland in approx. 584 BC. This preserved David's throne and the beginning of the overturn mentioned in Ezekiel 21:25-27 where Zedekiah's daughters of the Phares bloodline married into the Zara blood line which was under Druid law (Religion of Gods ancient Patriarchs) fulfilling Matthew 1:3 and healing the breach mentioned in Genesis 38:29 and Judges 21:15. The healing of the breach was the overturn of David's throne to heal the promise of the firstborn to Zara when they were planted in the wilderness in Ireland. This completed the healing of the breach and rebuilding of David's throne (England) to judge the world during the last days under Christianity as mentioned in Amos 9:11. The ancient Druid religion was the faith of Gods ancient Patriarchs of one true God and the coming of a Messiah. The Druid religion blended perfectly with Christianity for both taught basically the same moral principles.

When Gods Spirit (Zion) departed the Temple at his death, the role of the first gathering of the Jews was complete. The authority of the overturned throne was now planted in a new land over the seas (Isaiah 16:8), Ireland, and complete with the travailing of Zion at the renting of the veil in the Temple. The moving and plowing of Zion was to culminate into the Common Wealth of Great Britain and later the single nation of the United States as their brother, fulfilling Genesis 17:6, 35:11 and 48:19. They were to be nations and the name of these nations were to be called Israel which was not inherited by the other tribes as recorded in Genesis 48:16. The name of Israel only went to the two lads of Ephraim and Manasseh and the other eleven tribes received the authority to be called Israel through the birthright blessings of Joseph or Ephraim and Manasseh.

The second gathering commenced when Christ established his Church Ministry and sent his disciples into the wilderness to gather his lost sheep of the house of Israel and begin his worldwide Gospel, "Good News" (Matt 10:6 & 25:15 and Gen 49:10). The role and responsibility under the birthright of the second gathering went to the house of Israel, Ephraim (Great Britain) and Manasseh (United States) as leaders of Israel. The Monarchs of Europe are the other eleven tribes. The authority to create the European Monarchs came from Levi in Deuteronomy 33:8-11 (as the lawgiver). Dan (Denmark and Iceland) was to judge his people under a throne (Gen 49:16), Gad (Switzerland) was to have a crown of the head in Duet 33:20 and Asher (Belgium and Germany) shall yield royal dainties in Gen 49:20. We have already established that Ephraim (England) was given the complete kingdom to be under David's throne to preserve Christ's throne through the Crown of England till his coming. This is why there have been so many Monarchs in Europe over the centuries and most of their flags or ensigns carry the cross of Christ's Church.

Isaiah chapter 43 is an excellent chapter describing God gathering his Christian people of the house of Israel in the wilderness to their own land. They had already been Christianized by the fulfillment of Matt 10:5-8 and 15:24, where Christ sent his Disciples to teach his Gospel to the lost sheep of the house of Israel. Isaiah 43:5-8 states, **"Fear not: for I am with thee: I will bring thy seed from the east, and gather thee from the west; I will say to the north, Give up; and to the south, keep not back: bring my sons from far, and my daughters from the ends of the earth; Even every one that is called by my name"**. Verses one and seven of this chapter states that God will, **"I have called the by thy name; thou art mine,"**, **"Even every one that is called by my name"**. What is God's name that he is speaking of in these verses, it is the term Christian under his new Covenant (Acts 11:26). The term "bring my sons from far" is referring to bringing his Christian people from the four corners of the earth to a new land in the wilderness that is not the Promised Land in Canaan. This verse cannot be speaking of modern Israel for they have never been Christian as this verse indicates.

Isaiah 43:1 is speaking to Jacob and Israel as two separate entities that is the Church in the last days. "O Jacob" is referring to all twelve tribes as a whole family of Israel where "O Israel" is directed at the family name of Israel which was the birthright tribe of Joseph (Ephraim, GB and Manasseh, US) Genesis 48:16. The whole family of Jacob, all twelve tribes received their right to be called Israel through the birthright tribe of Joseph and that is why the Scriptures separate the two in this chapter. Isaiah 43:8-10 speaks of gathering Christians, **"Every one that is called by my name,"** from all over the world and when carefully studying these verses, it could very well be speaking of the emigrants entering the Christian nation of the United States into our harbors of New York City, San Francisco and Seattle in the past four centuries.

God's punishment of seven (2520 years) to the house of Israel and the house of Judah took place during the dark ages. The signing of the Magna Charta in 1215 was the beginning of the coming out from under his retribution. The English laws and statutes establish under the Magna Charta was based on Gods principles from the Scriptures which exist today within our God given Constitution of the United States and British law that actually date back to old Druid laws. These laws are mentioned in Deuteronomy 33:10 when Levi was given the responsibility to, **"They (Levi) shall teach Jacob thy judgments, and Israel thy law"**. These laws and statutes of Gods commandments has played a vital role in the end time gathering. These laws culminated with God's Word, the commission of the King James Bible, creating the two most powerful political economic and military powers (Battle Ax) in the history of the world, Common Wealth of Great Britain (Ephraim) and the United States (Manasseh). This creation of nations fulfills Genesis 17:6, 35:11 and 48:19 that was the blessings to Abraham, Isaac (Saxons), Jacob and Joseph (Ephraim and Manasseh).

The following is a few verses that speak very clear on the second gathering of Gods people, Israel (ten northern tribes) and Judah (the Jews). This gathering directly related to the Assyrian captivity in the wilderness. Isaiah 11:11-16 makes a distinct difference between Ephraim and Judah and the establishing of an ensign for the nations by assembling the outcast of Israel under the flag (ensign) of Christianity. Jeremiah 23:3-8 also explains how Israel will be gathered and dwell in their own land under Christ's Church (fruitful Jerm 23:3) to be ruled by King David's throne and shall execute judgment and justice in the earth under Christ's New Covenant. Again, this kingdom is Gods 5th Kingdom, his "Battle Ax". These verses refer to what Paul spoke of in Romans 11:26 when all of Israel shall be saved during the last days under the protective hand of King David's throne. Compare Romans 11:25-27 to Jeremiah 23:5-6, for they have similar meanings.

Another excellent verse referring to the gathering is located in Ezekiel 34:13-18 where God brings Israel out from the countries to their own land. This land is not referring to the promised land of Canaan but where God feeds his flock under Christ's Church and new covenant of Christianity (Eze 34:14) in a good pasture and high mountain (nation). This certainly cannot be speaking of modern Israel for they still reject Christ as the Messiah but is the fruitful nation that God gave his Kingdom in Matthew 21:43. Again in Ezekiel 36:24-27 God speaks of giving the house of Israel their own land after gathering them from among the heathen and gave them a new heart and spirit (Christian). In this new land, the house of Israel was to receive Gods new spirit and walk in his statutes and keep his judgments. This speaks of a great Christian nation of today and can only be the God-fearing nations of Great Britain and the United States.

Hosea 2:14-23 refers to Israel being allured into the wilderness and given a new covenant to be betrothed (the bride of Christ's Church) in faithfulness to be sown into the earth. These verses can only be speaking of Christ's new covenant, his end time Church and Gospel given to his lost sheep of the house of Israel, "O virgin Israel" as the Bride of Christ. Micah 4:10-13 states that Israel, daughter of Zion, will travail, be plowed and plucked meaning it will depart Jerusalem to dwell in the field. God will make his hoofs of brass, the house of Israel and shall beat in pieces many people and will consecrate their gain unto the Lord. To beat many people into pieces could only occur through Gods Battle Ax as Christian nations. Their substance will be unto the Lord of the whole earth (Micah 4:13 and refers to Duet 33:17). This verse is clear that the house of Israel will be a great nation within the earth and fear God under Christianity.

When we go to the concordance and look up the word "gather" in Hebrew, it means, to grasp, assemble, gather together, selves together and heap. The Hebrew word for "Bethel" (House of God) in the Strong's Concordance #1004 and #1008 means, a house especially family, house of God, daughter, door, home born, palace, place or temple. The Greek word for "Church" in 1577 is "ekklesia" which means, a calling out, a religious congregation (Jewish synagogue) and assembly. "Daughter" means house of God or Bethel and when you cross reference daughter to 1323 and then to 1121 and 1129, daughter means a builder of the family, nation and young bull or calf. We know that the symbol of the young bull is the tribe of Manasseh which is the United States, therefore, after cross referencing all these words, the United States is the daughter of Zion which is the builder of the family unit, Christ's Church.

When reviewing these definitions, the words gather, Bethel, Church and daughter have basically the same meaning. The gathering of the house of Israel as listed in those Scriptures can only refer to the gathering of Christ's Church (assembly or congregation) into the wilderness (Gen 49:10). The word fruitful, branch, bough and mountain can also be related to gather the Church. These words are directly linked to the family blessings given to the firstborn birthright tribes of Ephraim and Manasseh (US and GB) to be many wealthy nations as stated in Gen 49:16-22 to take place **"which shall befall you in the last days"** in Gen 49:1.

The second gathering fulfills the birthright blessing of Greatness to Joseph or directly to Ephraim and Manasseh to be a nation and a company of nations fulfilling Genesis 35:11. This is the gathering of the Church in the wilderness and will continue till the world becomes evil as the days of Noah (the last days) almost to the brink of Satan destroying the Church. We must not forget that the first 6000 years of man's rule fall under Satan's influence. Gods people, Israel and the Church, is simply a salt to preserve (Gods Battle Ax, Jerm 51:19-20) till Satan's rule on earth is complete.

The third gathering will be the completion of Daniel's 70th week to the Jews when they finally realize the truth of Christ being their Messiah. The Church will have been taken away at this point. This gathering is the remnant of Hebrews and Jews from each tribe gathered back into Israel to complete end time prophecy pertaining to physical Jerusalem. It also includes all the orthodox Jews around the world that is currently waiting for the Messiah where they finally realize that Jesus Christ, that they had crucified, was the true Messiah. The house of Judah (modern Israel) and the house of Israel (Christian nations of US and Europe) are still separated at this time due to the Jews rejection of Christ.

The United States and England in Bible Prophecy

(Manasseh US and Ephraim GB)

The Americas are relatively a young continent in light of population by our civilized European ancestral linage. To understand our national identity and heritage we must first know who our founding fathers were and the linage of their ancestors. This would make it important to understand the modern and prehistoric history of England and Great Britain. Who are the Brits and where did they come from? This writer realizes that a large portion of our heritage is traced to Germany, France, Italy, Spain, Danish and other European and Asian countries but England was the dominating nation of our forefathers. This fact is due to the influence of the Anglo-Saxon races and the power of the Throne of England allowing their language to be chosen as our national language. England and France invested large amounts of money into <u>North</u> (French Canada) and <u>South</u> (Spain) <u>America</u> (England) for commerce and natural resources through their shipping trade routes. Trade produced colonization which allowed the masses to seek freedom of Religion. The Americas was born.

Today, the American historians have fallen into the same trap as our British brothers for we denied our own heritage. The British and Americans do not interest themselves in true antiquity of our own race but had rather search in the tombs of ancient Egypt while the creation of Stone Hinge is basically ignored. Why? Subversion of the truth began with the domination of the Roman Catholic Church hundreds of years ago and continues through the agenda of the Liberal New Age Secret Societies by trying to play down and destroy the heritage of the Caucasian race. We are presently being destroyed through Liberal Socialism based on the Red Horse of Communism as referred to in Revelation 6:4. Satan does not want us to know our true inheritance of greatness created by our forefathers and promised by God to the house of Israel through Abraham that were to be passed down to his descendants of today.

The United States and England is not directly mentioned in Bible Scripture by name but can easily be linked and identified through ancient names. The English (Christian "fruitful") speaking nations can be traced by a close study of the Birthright blessing and Israel's division. Isaiah 41:2 and Micah 7:12-20 links Christianity to the rod and flock of heritage of Carmel, Bashan and Gilead (Manasseh of the USA).

The regions of Sharon, Carmel, Bashan and Gilead were located in the northern portion of the house of Israel representing their tribes as nations and were called Lebanon. Lebanon was the leader or cedar of David's throne representing Sharon, Carmel, Bashan and Gilead. These are the ancient nations of Israel that the great eagles with diverse colors carried on his wings with many feathers as a symbol of their migration into the wilderness as recorded in Ezekiel 17:3&7. During their migration they left symbols, names, waymarks and heaped stones to ID their peoples. The first eagle or phoenix was a bird of diverse colors making Lebanon a nation of different colors of people or races. This eagle took the cedar of the highest branch and carried it into a land of traffic in a city of merchants. The cedar of the high branch is the Throne of Israel overturned into another land or the Isles of Britannia as recorded in Ezekiel chapter 17 and 21:25-27 representing both Ephraim and Manasseh. These Islands are mentioned all through Isaiah chapters 41-43 as being a righteous people (Christian). The following symbols came from the house of Israel during the migration through the wilderness of the world:

The Hebrew word Phoenicia has a secondary meaning as merchant which would indicate this city being a Phoenician city of merchant shipping, a city of traffic. In Hebrew merchant also means bullock. The Hebrew Phoenician cities of Ireland (tin mining) and Briton were famous for international trade in ancient days when Jeremiah was commissioned to overturn the throne (Jerm 1:10). When Zion travailed and was plowed (Isa 66:7-9 and Jerm 26:18) means that Gods Spirit departed Jerusalem to a faraway land and verifies the overturn of David's throne to Ireland by Jeremiah.

We have already covered the term plowed in Hebrew which means diverse, be silent, to let alone, to be deaf and to hold one's peace. The meaning of diverse identifies the bird of diverse color as being plowed (moved) or migrating just as the migration of birds. The meaning of travail has also been covered as, bring forth, travail with pain and trouble. When we apply these definitions to Isaiah 66:7-8 (Zion travailing) and Jeremiah 26:18 (Zion being plowed), we can better understand its meaning. Zion in Jerusalem were to travail by bringing forth a man child (Christ) and then was to be plowed by Gods Spirit indicating silence within the Jews by removal to a faraway land. This occurred in 70AD with the destruction of Jerusalem. In other words, Zion travailed and was plowed by being planted to another location when Jeremiah overturned David's throne to a fruitful nation (Matt 21:43). The Spiritual name of Jerusalem has a dual meaning and departed with Zion as indicated in certain verses.

This bird of diverse color was the unicorn of Ephraim as the British Common Wealth of 46 nations and Manasseh as the bull that colonized America. Both represent diverse colors of races of peoples and nations all over the world. This can be verified in Jeremiah 12:9 when the house of Israel as Ephraim and Manasseh is called Gods heritage of the speckled bird. The Hebrew word diverse and speckled means to be of different colors indicating these birds of Gods heritage as the promise to Abraham, Isaac, Jacob, Joseph and directly to Ephraim and Manasseh as the inheriting tribes to be nations and kings of kingdoms as recorded in Genesis 48:16-19. This can be further verified by Isaiah 16:1-2 where the lamb (the Gospel of the Church) was sent, **"to the wilderness unto the mount of the daughter of Zion. For it shall be, that as a wandering bird cast out of the nest"**. Isaiah chapter 18 describes the land that this bird traveled which describes the North and South American continent. Note that these verses use the analogy of a bird that carries the house of Israel into the wilderness on their wings of feathers representing their migration just as birds migrate using their wings.

There is one more bird migration that must be recognized for it indicates the separation of Ephraim and Manasseh to complete Gods end time Gospel dividing the birthright tribes of the Unicorn and Bull. Ezekiel 17:7, "**There was also another great eagle with great wings and many feathers: and behold, this vine did bend her roots toward him, and shot forth her branches toward him, that he might water it by the furrows of her plantation**". This is a very interesting verse for the second great eagle carries a vine that grew from the nation that the first eagle of diverse colors carried into the wilderness. This would also make the second eagle or vine multiracial nations of diverse colors. We should make the note that the Jews never accepted other people into their inner circle or did other nations accept the Jew for they were persecuted by every nation just as the curse stated. The second nation watered by the furrows of her plantation just as England nourished the colonies of America prior to our independence. The wilderness of this nation was colonized on the principles of a colonial plantation just as Ezekiel 17:7 indicates. This verse matches Genesis 49:22-24 and Isaiah 16:8 where the birthright tribe of Joseph (Ephraim and Manasseh) became a fruitful bough whose branches run over the wall and over the sea. Isaiah 16:2 speaks of a bird falling out of the nest which is the shepherd, the stone of the house of Israel as the birthright tribe of Manasseh, a growing vine where it branched out and became independent from England (Ephraim) as quarreling brothers.

The American colonies fell out of the nest from the Common Wealth of Great Britain when we became independent in 1776. This can be verified in Isaiah chapters 16 through 18 where it progresses through the Scriptures. Isaiah 16:5 speaks of David's throne bringing truth, judging and seeking judgment and hasting righteousness to the nations and verse 8 even says that his throne, "**wandered** (bird) **through the wilderness: her branches are stretched out, they are gone over the sea.**" Isaiah chapter 17 is basically speaking of events during the Tribulation period where Ephraim loses their strength in a falling away from the truth. Isaiah chapter 18 describes a continent identical to North America where the house of Israel branched out over the sea as a nation and was meted out and trodden under foot spoiled by great rivers and called Mount Zion. Remember that Zion travailed and was plowed indicating that it was moved to another location and Isaiah chapter 18 is that location. Isaiah skips through time periods and is very important to carefully study these chapters with this scenario in mind. We must realize that the Bible and the Prophecies within were written to the end time Church. One third of the Holy Scriptures is dedicated to Prophecy and two thirds to history and doctrine. This should give us an idea of the importance of end time Prophecy for these prophecies were to be fulfilled by the house of Israel or the seed of Isaac, the Saxon of the Caucasian race where God said they would be kings of kingdoms and many nations.

The word England is very interesting for it is related to the word Angle or possibly Angel. The Hebrew word angel means to dispatch as a messenger, a prophet, priest or teacher, ambassador or king's messenger. European history establishes the Angle people that departed Schleswig in Germany and southern Denmark in the first century and was called the people of the bull of Angle-land or England. When we match the Hebrew meaning of Angel which means messenger, dispatch, teacher and ambassador, to the fruitful nation that Jesus took from the Jews and gave to the lost sheep of the house of Israel in Matthew 21:43, it then correlates with the commission in Matthew 10:6 and 15:24. The Angles (Angels) or Anglo-Saxon's called England took the message of Christ's Gospel to the world as an ambassador. This nation was the migrating sons of Isaac (Saxon) where the Scriptures state **"fore in Isaac shall thy seed be called"** (Gen 21:12, Rom 9:7 and Heb 11:18). The term bull and unicorn can be directly linked to Ephraim and Manasseh for their symbols are given in Deuteronomy 33:17. The Hebrew definition of Angel has been fulfilled by the English Christian nations by being Gods messengers, teachers and Ambassador to the world spreading his Gospel into every nation fulfilling Matthew 21:43 as a fruitful nation, Christian.

The sons of Isaac were called the house of Isaac or Beth-Sak, Saki, Sacae, Sakasani, Saxones, Sachsen and Saxons that were the Scythian empire of Eastern Europe. The Romans called the Scythians (Colossians 3:11) Goths and Guthi an important branch of the Scythian nation as the Getae. This race of people is mentioned in II Esdras 13:45 as Arsareth (Gautheir) where the seed of Isaac decided to depart the Assyrian captivity to a faraway land across the Euphrates River which would take one and a half years to be guided by God through signs. Study II Esdras chapter thirteen for these facts. During the Assyrian invasion, the ten northern tribes were called Beth Kumri or the house of King Omri (930 BC I Kings 17:6). The Achoemenian Inscriptions call them the Saka (Aryan) where the Babylonian Transcripts of the Persian and Seythic Columns call them Gimiri. The ten northern tribes called themselves the Tsaki, Isaacites or Beth-Isaac (house of Isaac) Amos 7:9-14. The Cunciform Inscriptions (648 BC) calls the house of Israel Sacae (Sakai) where the term Scythian first appears. These ancient tribal names are the descendants of Lebanon, Sharon, Carmel, Bashan and Gilead, which were regions of the northern ten tribes of the house of Israel.

It is believed that the Galatians of Asia Minor were Benjamin who escaped from Babylon for Galutha means prisoners in Babylonian. The Galileans of Christ's time were Benjaminite's and must have been immigrates into Palestine. When Christ ascended into Heaven, he spoke to the "men of Galilee".

The forefathers of the above ancient tribes became our forefathers from England and Europe bringing their symbols and inheritance with them. The United States became the most God fearing and powerful nation ever in history because of our old time Christian beliefs. Why is it that we are not mentioned in Bible Prophecy or are we? The Prophecy is there if we open our eyes and minds to the truth and look beyond what we have been taught from youth. The Scriptures of the Old Testament tells us plainly if we just read and study through prayer and seek knowledge. America and Great Britain are Mystery Babylon due to falling away from God's Word.

It is important to understand that Manasseh (United States the Bull) was to be one single great nation, therefore, we have territories under one central government that corresponds to Genesis 35:11 and 48:19. On the other hand, Ephraim Common Wealth of Great Britain the "Unicorn "was to be a company of nations that consisted of 46 self-ruled colonies that fell under the authority of the English Crown that also corresponds to the verses listed above. Gods Kingdom was to be maintained under the unity of the United Kingdom (a company of nations) ruled by the English Crown as King David 's throne tasked to spread Christ's Gospel. On the other hand, the United States was to be a Republic ruled by the people also tasked to finish spreading the end time Gospel by a nation not under the influence of a tyrannical king. God patterned the United States Constitution after the rule of the Judges for he knew a King would be evil and destructive to people in spreading his Gospel. God did not want his Children of Israel to be ruled by a king for he told them in I Samuel 8:11-19 that a king would enslave their sons under his rule and tax them but the people wanted a king anyway.

Israel's being ruled by the Judges and our present system of government under a Republic is very similar for both were ruled by the people. Our forefathers saw the danger and tyranny of government and the end result was our Constitution of America inspired by God himself as a Republic not a Democracy as we are told. Again, we are being lied to as a nation for our forefathers established our Constitution as a Republic form of Government. The word Democratic is not found anywhere within our founding documents for a reason. A Democratic form of government is not a very good system and a close study will show that they last a very short period of time before being taken over by a tyrannical system. The masses can be controlled and manipulated just as the situation of today due to open borders, ethnical exploitation and media control. Eventually a certain party or leader will gain full power causing confusion and finally collapse. A Republic is a nation controlled by the letter of the law where the Law is enforced by highly qualified moral leaders voted into office by the people and not governed by mob rule or a whim of the people agitated by extreme events.

There is an uncanny resemblance to our Republic, Christ's Church and the governments of ancient Israel that we need to identify. Our forefathers not only patterned our government after the structure of the Church but of ancient Israel governed by the Judges. Compare the follow forms of government as listed below.

United States   Executive Branch President as leader

                    Judicial Branch (preserves the law)

                    Congress by the people (vote laws)

Ancient Israel   Judges as leader

                    Tabernacle Priest (Law makers inspired by God)

                    Elders of 12 tribes (the people vote laws)

The Church   Pastor as leader

                    Deacons (preserve Gods laws of Scripture)

                    Congregation (the people vote by-laws)

All three of the above elements represent Gods earthly kingdom to be his Heavenly Kingdom in the future. God meant for his people to rule themselves as a Republic established upon moral law (the Holy Bible) patterned after the Church and system of Judges in ancient Israel and not by a tyrannical King or Democratic form of government that could be controlled and manipulate as a Democracy. A Democracy will fail for they believe in individual rights that eventually causes corruption and disorder dominated by a corrupt few where a Republic is based upon moral laws of the people and not the individual. We can see today how a corrupt few can dominate and control a Democratic

System and a perfect example is the nefarious Gay Rights Movement forcing their belief on the people of this nation. Due to evil forces, we cannot seem to stop their unnatural evil agenda and is why a Democratic system will fail in the end.

God knows that a form of government based on individual rights would hinder the spreading of his Gospel as can be seen in our Democratic system for it has taken God out of our Society based upon infringement of individual rights. If one single person hates Christianity, then, due to their single right, Christianity must be eliminated. This is exactly why Satan wants our Federal Government to be a Democracy, so it can control every aspect of our lives individual rights. The changing to a Democracy has allowed the government to eliminate God from our schools, business and Society itself. The Liberal Democratic and Communistic Godless form of government is perfect for Satan's agenda. Due to the corruption of our Constitution, we are presently in an extreme period of falling away from Gods principles because of Democratic governmental control. Our system has been changed from a Republic to a Democracy. This is why certain organizations want our borders open to the world, to dilute and liberalize our system.

God's Christian nations that were to spread his end time Gospel is predicated upon the birthright name of Israel that went to Ephraim and Manasseh. They were chosen to fulfill the blessing to Abraham, Isaac and Jacob to be a single great nation and a company of nations as the house of Israel. The only fruitful Christian nations in history that can fit this description is the United States and the United Kingdom of Great Britain that has demonstrated the power to fulfill, "he will rule as God" as righteous judges to the world under the power of the Crown of England. Jacob, the house of Jacob, was to be the other eleven tribes of Israel for many Scriptures make a distinct difference between the two. It is important to understand that the term house of Jacob, Ephraim, Manasseh, house of Judah, house of Israel, Children of Israel are all a part of Israel but in certain cases emphasized as separate nations which play different roles in prophecy. The house of Judah is called Judah or Jews all through the Prophetic books for they never lost their name or language as the root of Jerusalem.

The northern territories of the house of Israel were named after Lebanon, Sharon, Carmel, Gilead and Bashan and called these names in future Prophecies as Gods vineyard that branched over the wall. They were divorced by God in Jeremiah 3:8 to complete their X7 punishment of 2520 years and betrothed again in Hosea 2:19-20 as the "O virgin of Israel", Christ's Bride to be because only they accepted Christ's Gospel. The house of Israel are the nations and kings of kingdoms promised to Abraham in Geneses 17:6 and to Jacob in Geneses 35:11 and 48:19. These different names are the Children of Israel for they received their name and authority to be called Israel through the birthright tribe of Joseph but given directly to Ephraim (GB) and Manasseh (US). This is clear if you closely study the blessings to each tribe in Genesis chapters 48 and 49 along with Deuteronomy 33.

With the above paragraph in mind, read and study Deuteronomy 7:6 and 14:2, for God clearly states that his chosen people were to be above all nations of the world. In no way can these verses be speaking of the Jews for they do not meet the requirements of these verses. They can only be speaking of the house of Israel under the birthright of Ephraim and Manasseh as the English-speaking nations that has dominated the world for the past five hundred years. They have dominated the world not only politically but through world trade and banking.

A close study of bough, mountain, vineyard, plant and other corresponding words covered in chapter eight only applies to the house of Israel that is Ephraim and Manasseh. These words do no relate to the house of Jacob, but to the house of Israel leader of the other eleven tribes. The fruitful BRANCH (Christ, Jerm 23:5 & 33:15, Ps 80:8-12) that ran over the wall into the sea of the world and became a bough by a well (water of life Christ); the stone of Israel (also Christ); the everlasting hills (Gen 49:22-26); firstlings of his bullock and his horns are like the horns of unicorns; push the people together to the ends of the earth and they are the ten thousands of Ephraim and the thousands of Manasseh (Duet 33:13-17). Clearly the other eleven tribes of Israel are not mentioned in these verses as the great Christian nations of the double fruit firstborn (bough) of Ephraim and Manasseh. Branch also means a twig, tender branch or young twig, which corresponds to the overturn of the throne from the high branch to the low branch of Ephraim and Manasseh as recorded in Ezekiel 17:22-23; 21:26-27. In other words, the throne was overturned from Jerusalem and given to the bough that bears fruit of Ephraim (the throne of England the unicorn).

The key words are the bull and unicorn for they are unique to the Scriptures and only Ephraim (the unicorn) and Manasseh (the bull) are called by these names. This fact cannot be refuted and certainly not a coincidence. To further prove this point, all these nations are Christian (fruitful, Matt 21:43, Eze 17:23).

To unlock the understanding of the firstborn inheritance begins in Genesis 48 and 49. The blessings were given to Joseph and his two sons, Ephraim and Manasseh, where only they received the birthright inheritance. The next key in understanding the kingdom of Israel and the importance of the birthright takes place when the kingdom was taken from King Solomon in I Kings chapter eleven and given to Jeroboam. His servant was of Ephraim, leader of the ten northern tribes of the house of Israel. They went into captivity beginning in approx. 740 to 719BC to Assyria when Manasseh was taken first. The invasion of captivity was completed in 721 to 719BC (II Kings 10:32-33) when Ephraim fell in the south. The house of Israel never returned to the Promised Land of Israel as a nation and according to secular and Christian history, was absorbed into the countries of the world as individual peoples. This theory is in conflict with the Bible in accordance to the promises of Abraham, Isaac and Jacob that the birthright tribe of Ephraim and Manasseh (the house of Israel) were to be a single great nation and kingdoms of nations.

The two southern tribes (house of Judah) continued till approx. 586BC and the last king was King Zedekiah of the Jews. The house of Judah was no longer a sovereign nation and became a Governor ship ruled by Babylon (603BC), the Mead and Persian's and then Rome till 70AD when Jerusalem was destroyed. It became a wasteland and plowed like a field (Jerm 26:18) and scattered till 1948 when Israel became the modern nation of Judah but did not take Jerusalem till 1967. This writer believes it is possible that the parable of the fig tree mentioned in Matthew 24:32-36 begins when Jerusalem was taken in the 1967 war with the Arabs. We need to remind ourselves that the parable was based on Jerusalem for that was the subject asked by the Disciples. This is the first time the Jews had full control over Jerusalem for over 2553 years. If you add 40 years for one generation to 1967 you will get 2007, for this generation shall see the Tribulation mentioned in Matthew 24.

Jerusalem was the house of Judah when it fell in 586 BC and only the Jews returned to occupy Judea till 70AD when it was destroyed. The house of Israel never returned to Judea, therefore, in 1948 when Israel became a nation by the returning Jews, it would only be fitting to call modern Israel, the land of Judah. Technically the name Israel cannot be attached to modern Israel till Ephraim and Manasseh returns and claims the land for only they were named Israel the Law of Moses. Therefore, the name Israel can only be given through the birthright authority of Ephraim and Manasseh. This will occur at the sealing of the 144,000 in Revelation 7:5-8. The authorized name of Israel can be reattached to Jerusalem when all twelve tribes unite during the Tribulation Period. The following is complicated! By Hebrew law, God's throne cannot return to Jerusalem because it was given to the house of Israel to be over all Israel in I Kings 12:20 when they departed into the wilderness. They were divorced in Jerm 3:8 making the Throne ineligible to return to Jerusalem till remarried. The house of Israel was betrothed to be remarried in Hosea 2:19 to take place at the Marriage Supper of the Lamb in Rev 19:7-9 in Heaven during the Tribulation Period. We must understand that David's throne under Sion of the Church do not fall under Hebrew law, therefore, Christ set on his Throne when the Church is taken in Rev 4:1-2 and it stays in Heaven till the end of the Tribulation. After the Marriage Supper of the Lamb takes place, David's Throne, by Hebrew Law, can now be moved back to Jerusalem after the Tribulation is over by Christ himself. Gods Glory will return to Jerusalem to fulfill Daniels 70th week of Prophecy but the throne will stay in Heaven not to return to Jerusalem till Christ's return in power and restores David's Throne in Jerusalem. This explains why there is no throne in Jerusalem today for the authority and name of Israel is not there due to Mose's Law of the firstborn birthright that was not given to the Jews. God will not allow the house of Israel to return the Throne back into Jerusalem till Christ comes back to rule himself.

According to the book of Genesis, the promise of greatness of multitudes of peoples, nations and kings went to the house of Israel and not the house of Judah. Ephraim and Manasseh received the double portion of blessings to be great, not Judah. There is a span of approx. 2667 years of nonexistence of the house of Israel but yet the Bible said they were to be great nations of peoples and Kings. Modern teaching and attitudes toward Israel are not correct and obvious if you study the Scriptures.

When Moses departed into the wilderness out of Egypt with the main body of the twelve tribes, a small portion from each tribe departed by ship into Greece led by the descendants of Danaus (Dara) settled the ancient Greek city of Argues and Calcol (Cadmus) departed into Pontus. A small portion from the other tribes also departed with them such as Dan and is told by an Historian by the name of Mueller "Fragmenta Historicum". Dara's decedent Darta migrated to western Turkey and settled the City of Troy. After Troy fell, Anus, Darta's decedent took his remaining peoples and migrated to Italy. There he married Latinus that became Latin and later built Rome. Brutes, Anus grandson, migrated to Malta and the local inhabitants advised him to go to the Great White Islands. The white Islands were England, the white cliffs of Dover. Brutes settled New Troy or Seir Troy that changed to Londenium due to Latin influence and later to the modern name of London. An old stone tablet was found that stated when Anus settled New Troy in England, Beli (Eli) the Priest ruled in Jerusalem that would indicate around 1103 BC.

The Harmsworth Encyclopedia states that Dara and Calcol founded Athens

Greece and Calcol later migrated along the coast of the Mediterranean Sea into Spain and settled the valley of Zarah Gosa setting up Ibernie, Hibernia and Erni became Hebrew trading posts. Their name Hebrew and language slowly changed over the years into the local languages. Calcol's descendants migrated across Spain and settled into Ireland (Britannic Hibernia Isles) in approx. 1700BC. These Islands are the British Isles and some are named after the migrating Hebrews of Calcol and Dara of the Zarah bloodline (Matt 1:3) and can be found on most ancient Biblical maps. According to The History of Ireland by Moore, states the Dans or Dani Tiwath DeDanan left Egypt at the Exodus of the Hebrews to Greece and then to Ireland and were called Tribes of Dani Tiwath DeDanan (The people of God). Many old writings and ancient history books tell of the Hebrew people settling in Ireland and England as early as 1800 BC. Calcol's descendants settled in Ireland around this same time and later Dara's descendants settled England in approx. 1103BC. Keep in mind that the Phoenicians of King Barat settled these Islands hundreds of years prior, giving the name Briton and later called Britannia by the Romans.

How can we disregard all the artifacts and writings of ancient history that God's People, the Hebrews, settled Britain long before David became King. To understand the early history of Britain helps us to understand how the Gospel was to be spread worldwide by Ephraim and Manasseh during the last days. God's plan for his people and the Gospel is brilliant. He sent a portion of his people into these lands to prepare the way for the Gospel when the time was right. The ten northern tribes were taken into captivity by the Assyrians and never heard of again and never returned to Palestine. They migrated into Europe over the Caucasus Mountains and became the Caucasians of Eastern and Western Europe. They fulfilled Isaiah 18 and 33:21-22 that became a great nation (United States and Great Britain) in the wilderness and cannot be speaking of the small nation of Israel in Canaan.

The ten northern tribes of Israel slowly lost their language and identity of being Hebrew as they associated with local tribes. Eventually they migrated to Ireland and England as if there were a Heavenly calling to these lands (II Esdras 13:44 by signs from God) just as a calling of a migrating bird with great wings (Eze 17). All across Europe there are mountains, rivers and valleys to this day that has Hebrew names as they migrated through Europe. If you review a European map, you can see these names even today. God reserved the North American Continent to be the last and the greatest of all nations, to be God fearing and a people terrible from their beginning trodden under foot and spoiled by rivers, the United States of America (Isa 18:7). North America was founded and settled on Gods principles and Commandments under his New Covenant as recorded in Hebrews 8:8 and Jeremiah 31:31.

The British Islands were a perfect safe haven for Gods people, for it was surrounded by water and reasonably safe from invasion. The United States was to be the last safe haven for Manasseh to migrate and set up the Greatest Nation ever to be on Earth. The purpose is for freedom of Religion and Ezekiel 17:1-10 explains how God set up two great nations and cannot be talking about the land of Israel. Verse 3-7 establishes Britain and verse 7-10 the United States. Read and study these verses. We know that the United States came from the roots of Britain as stated in Ezekiel 17:7-10 and 21-24 for the words vine, branches, bear fruit and bough, links these nations to Ephraim and Manasseh recorded in Genesis 49:22 as the firstborn birthright to Joseph.

Zarah's bloodline of Judah (Matt 1:3) through Dara and Calcol, two of his sons, migrated and settled Ireland and England. As we know through history, King Zedekiah (Pharez bloodline of the Pharisees) was the last King of Israel when taken captive by the Babylonians in approx. 586BC (Eze 17:22-24). This was the first overturn of the diadem or Crown. Remember that Pharez and Zarah were twin brothers of Judah, so King David is in both of their bloodlines making each eligible to be King. This is where Jeremiah comes into play. Jeremiah was the prophet during the fall of King Zedekiah and the Babylonian captivity. According to this pivotal time period, Israel fell as a nation and their throne came to an end as history records the event. Israel never regained their throne even to this day according to secular history and certainly not in Jerusalem. There are certain promises God gave to King David that has not been fulfilled in the past 2584 years if we believe modern history. Where are the promises of his throne: Ps 89:4&25-37, Jerm 33:14-17, II Sam 7:12-17 and Luke 1:30-33? God is great and man has not maintained his history and searched the Scriptures to teach us correctly. There are absolutely no mistakes in Gods Scripture and Jeremiah tells a beautiful story.

God gave Jeremiah a tremendous commission as recorded in Jeremiah 1:10 **"See, I have this day set thee over the nations and over the kingdoms, to root out, and to pull down, and to destroy, and to throw down, to build, and to plant.".** At this point in time, Jeremiah was to be the most powerful man ever in history, for God placed him over all nations. This is important to understand for he was given the power to remove and replant Gods throne of King David. He was to destroy the old and plant a new nation and there is no other Scripture where God gives a single man this type of power, not even King Nebuchadrezzar that was the most powerful man ever in history to this point of time. This is the first overturn but where was the throne to be planted? Remember that kingdoms by the Zarah bloodline through Dara and Calcol had been set up in Ireland and England some 1114 to 517 years earlier.

When Nebuchadrezzar of Babylon took King Zedekiah captive, all of his family and sons were killed except for two daughters (Jerm 41:10). The Captain of the Jewish forces, Johanan, was afraid and asked Jeremiah what to do (Jerm 42:2-16), either to flee or stay. Jeremiah was told by God to stay in Judea or be killed but Johanan elected to flee to Egypt taking Jeremiah and Zedekiah's two daughters, therefore, they were all killed except for the two daughters and Jeremiah's party (Jerm 43:6). Jeremiah 46:27-28 tells the servants of Jacob (Jeremiah and remnant of Judah) to not fear for his seed (King Zedekiah's daughters) shall be saved by a far off country, Ireland where Jeremiah took the two daughters, **"But fear not thou, O my servant Jacob, and be not dismayed, O Israel; for, behold, I will save thee from afar off, and thy seed from the land of their captivity; and Jacob shall return, and be in rest and at ease, and none shall make him afraid"**. These verses cannot be speaking of the land of Canaan for there has never been rest or peace for Jerusalem has always been a burdensome stone to the world (Zech 12:3). The Scriptures speak no more of the two daughters but we can trace them through ancient and secular history. Keep in mind, for David's throne to maintain the purity and the proper royal bloodline, at least one daughter has to marry into the Zarah bloodline which fulfills Matt 1:3. Read the account of Pharez and Zarah of Tamar in Genesis chapter 38.

Eugene O. Curry, an English historian tells of how the ships of Dan brought Jeremiah, his servant Baruck, King Zedekiah's two daughters, Tea Tephi and Scota, the Stone of Destiny and a chest of artifacts that landed in Ireland around 584BC. Jeremiah's party took approx. two years where they departed Joppa by ship to Tahpanhes Egypt and from there, by ship, to eastern Spain at the mouth of the Zaragoza Valley. Scota the younger daughter married Gallam Malesius of Zara-Gossa of Spain, a tribe of Mileaian Hebrews that migrated from Egypt at the Exodus. Gallam were the King of the Mileaian's. They departed from Zaragossa through the Pillars of Hercules up the coast of Europe to Ireland, the City of Tara. Early historical records, Plantation of Oldster history of Ireland, Milasian Record (warrior) Gallam records William the conqueror that belonged to the Scarlet or Zarah Branch of Judah. These ancient records date settlements as early as 700 BC and tells the story and landing of Jeremiah's party. Tea Tephi, one of King Zedekiah's daughters of the bloodline of Judah-Pharez, married Heremonn (Leader) Eochaidh of the line of Judah-Zarah setting on the thrown in Tara Ireland. The ceremonies were presided by Jeremiah with the Stone of Destiny at foot. This event took place in approx. 580BC and was the first overturn of the Throne mentioned in Ezekiel 21:27 to fulfill the promise from Judah to Tamar in Gen 38:11. The Throne of King David was now overturned from the Pharez line to the Zarah line and moved from Jerusalem to Tara Ireland. This fulfills Ezekiel 17:3-4, 17:22, 21:26-27, Jeremiah 1:10, I Chronicles 17:9-14, Ezekiel 28:25

and Palms 72:2-10.

This event also heals the breach of the throne caused by the scarlet thread as recorded in Genesis 38:28-30 and the healing of David's throne in Amos 9:11. The verses above cannot be talking about the old or new Israel in Judea but the new promised nations of Duet 32:8-9, 33:13-17, Gen 48:16-19, 49:22-26, Isaiah 11:12-15 and 18:1-7. These Scriptures are speaking of great nations, multitudes of peoples from sea to sea sending ambassadors by the oceans. The house of Israel (10 northern tribes) vanished into captivity in 721 BC. The house of Judah went into captivity to Babylon and the end of King David's Kingship in 586BC. Where did they go? The difference between the two captives is that the Jews never vanished but maintained their language and national identity. The captivity of the house of Israel lost the Hebrew language, national identity, religion and most of all their pride and sense of belonging. They were forced to establish their own nations.

Jerusalem experienced obscurity in 70AD when the Roman Army burned the city. A remnant of Jews remained till approx. 130AD when there was another Jewish uprising and the Romans finally totally vanquished the Jew from Jerusalem. A small portion of Jews began to return to Palestine around the middle of the 1800's when under British control and finally became the modern nation of Israel in 1948 due to political influence of Great Britain and the United States (Ephraim and Manasseh) after the Jewish Holocaust. We can see how God used his own house of Israel to re-unite the nation of Israel in the Promised Land of Palestine. The Israelites took total control of Jerusalem in the 1967 war fulfilling prophecy and starting the 40-year generation of the parable of the fig tree in Matthew chapter 24. Where are Gods promise to Ephraim and Manasseh of great blessings and the Throne of King David during our day? It does not exist in Jerusalem as God's promise to David that he would always have a throne, so where is it located? This is a question that we must ask ourselves as Christians and seek the answer, for if we believe secular and Christian history, the Scriptures are at odds with the facts.

First read all of Genesis chapters 48 and 49, then Hosea that is to the house of Ephraim and the house of Israel. The book of Jeremiah is to the house of Israel and Judah and speaks of two different nations of peoples. Ephraim, Manasseh and the houses of Israel and Judah are all spoken of as different nations of peoples all through the Old Testament as by the division into nations by Ahijah in I Kings chapter eleven. The twelve pieces of garments representing the twelve nations of Israel as told in II Kings 19:17 when their land was destroyed by the Assyrians, **"Of a truth, Lord, the kings of Assyria have destroyed**

the nations and their lands". As you can see by this verse each tribe was considered a nation. Christians believe that all of these names are just one little country of present-day Israel because they do not study the Word. Great Britain (Ephraim) and the United States (Manasseh) can be traced by ancient names of the house of Israel, Lebanon, Sharon as Ephraim and Bashan, Gilead and Carmel as Manasseh.

Now that we have painstakingly covered the ancient history of the overturn of David's throne, let's look at ancient Biblical names of Ephraim (GB) and Manasseh (US) that do not apply to the other eleven tribes. This is due to the birthright blessings that only they were to receive and no other tribe. The Great blessing to Abraham, Isaac, Jacob and Joseph as recorded in Genesis chapter 48 produce the ancient names of Hebrew of the house of Israel as Cumri, Celt, Goth, and Anglo-Saxon etc. These are secular historical names but the Scriptures called them by their actual ancient names of Bashan, Gilead, Lebanon, Carmel and Sharon. We know this by the actual location within the Promised Land of Israel inherited by each tribe and can be seen on a Biblical map as the boundaries divided by each tribe.

To close out this segment, we should consider an aspect that is very important. We know that God established the English language as stated in chapter five and gave us the King James Bible in that language for the world to receive his Gospel. God needed a nation that would educate the world and spread his Gospel through Christian schools and Universities. This responsibility went to Manasseh, the birthright tribe as recorded in Genesis 48:19 to produce the single most powerful nation in history as a Republic to take place in the last days, Genesis 49:1. The United States is the only nation that can fulfill this verse in the light of accurate history. As stated, many times throughout this book, Manasseh was the first tribe to be taken into captivity to Assyria in approx. 740BC. To fulfill the X7 punishment in accordance to Leviticus 26:18 which would be seven times 360 years or 2520 total years of punishment due to their idolatry. Manasseh's punishment would be complete in 1780AD that is about the time the United States broke away from England and became our own independent nation in 1776. Our nation was based upon Christian moral values as the settlers escaped Europe seeking religious freedom and our forefathers wrote the Constitution to reflect these principles.

God knew that his birthright tribe of England, Ephraim, under a King would subdue his Church and the reason he created a Republic ruled by the people. They were to complete the spreading of his end time Gospel under freedom of religion, the United States of America. People from all over the world have sought freedom of religion in this great nation (Isa 11:11-16, 41:2-8, 43:5-10 and Jerm 31:6-10). Study Jeremiah chapter 31 for it surely indicates the gathering of Christian people from all over the world (Jerm 31:9-10 his flock the Church) into the harbors of New York City and Golden Gate of San Francisco as immigrants seeking freedom of religion and prosperity. Jeremiah 31:9 say that this nation is Israel, and Ephraim his firstborn. We exalt God in our Constitution and all of our national documents and symbols but present-day liberals would have us believe differently. This nation has become corrupted and returned to the Baal religion where we are not Mystery Babylon.

The North American continent was preserved by God till the end days for one sole purpose. This country was to be a safe protected land separated by two oceans or seas (Isa 16:8, Ps 80:11, Eze 27:25 and II Esdras 13:40) to be planted in the wilderness and multiply in safety. This protected land was given great natural resources to produce a great powerful nation independent of all nations with a people determined to build a country based on freedom of religion dedicated to Christianity. Isaiah chapter 18 gives a detailed description of the American continent and our vast territory. Verse, one says, "Woe to the land shadowing with wings" and Ezekiel chapter 17 shows how they were taken into the wilderness on the wings of a great eagle of diverse colors representing different races of people. The wings of an eagle symbolize the sails of Phoenician ships. Our Constitution provided the right of the States to provide schools to educate the common people from elementary to the greatest Universities ever developed. Our national emblem is an Eagle with spread wings just as Ezekiel 17:7 states. The United States is the only country in history by Constitution to provide education to its people as a common right by state law. People from all over the world has come to the United States to be educated over the past three hundred years and has produced the greatest minds in history and is why each state has its own Universities.

The facts are clear of who we are as a great nation if we only open our minds to the truth of history. We are Manasseh the Bull, given the birthright blessing to be a single great nation, **"a nation and a company of nations shall be of thee"** (Gen 35:11), **"he also shall become a people, and he also shall be great:"** (Genesis 48:19), and **"His glory is like the firstling of his bullock, and his horns are like the horns of unicorns with them he shall push the people together to the ends of the earth; and they are the ten thousands of Ephraim, and they are the thousands of Manasseh."** (Duet 33:17). Match these verses with Genesis 22:17-18 and 28:14 for they clearly state that the families and nations of the world will be blessed by Ephraim and Manasseh as the birthright tribes. God's blessings of these verses have produced the two greatest nations ever to exist on earth, the 46 Common Wealth Christian nations of Great Britain and the Republic of the United States of America.

Gods Stone Kingdom "the 5ᵗʰ Kingdom"

Gods Stone Kingdom is his people scattered and peeled and terrible from their beginning (Isa 18:2 & 7 "Zion"). They were sifted into the wilderness and gathered into their own fruitful (Christian) land on wings of an eagle (Eze 17:3-8). We have already established that fruitful means Christian for they were to be powerful and great, the 5ᵗʰ Kingdom as Gods Battle Ax (Jerm 51:20) fighting for righteousness and justice in the world. Isaiah 41:15 say that God will make them a new sharp threshing instrument having teeth and shall beat his enemy small making the hills as chaff. Isaiah 33:9 even names this Kingdom by calling them Lebanon, Sharon, Bashan and Carmel. We know they were Christian because of their fruits and inheritance of Ephraim and Manasseh for Ephraim means double fruit in Hebrew.

This kingdom is one single nation (United States) and a company of nations as recorded in Genesis 35:9-12, the promise of greatness to Jacob called Israel. Genesis 48:19 passed this birthright blessing on to Ephraim and Manasseh not to the other eleven tribes. Their ensign can be seen in the cross symbolizing the Church placed on many European flags. The British flag has two super imposed crosses, representing the cross of Christ. It is also said that the two crosses on the British flag represents Jacob crossing his arms to bless Ephraim and Manasseh as recorded in Genesis 48:14. Jacob was to place his right hand on the oldest son in front of him. He crossed his right hand to lay it upon Ephraim and not Manasseh. The blessing of Ephraim and Manasseh as the birthright tribes was the beginning of a physical earthly kingdom and cannot be speaking of Christ's coming in power and glory to claim his throne at the millennial. Isaiah 28:16 calls his kingdom a stone Kingdom after Christ being the corner stone, the New Covenant and a light to the Gentiles unto the end of the earth (the stone Church built on Peter meaning stone) as stated in Isaiah 49:6-8.

Study the word stone and you will see how the uncut stone in Daniel's interpretation is Christ's Church, the stone of Israel (Gen 49:24 and I Peter 2:4-5), and how his Christians are his living stones or his battle ax, the 5ᵗʰ Kingdom. Daniel 2:35&44 and Matt 21:43 clearly states that all four kingdoms is destroyed by this stone Kingdom, the kingdom made of the uncut stone (Christ's Church), **"And in the days of these kings shall the God of heaven set up a kingdom, which shall never be destroyed: and the kingdom shall not be left to other people, but it shall break in pieces and consume all these kingdoms, and it shall stand for ever."** This kingdom is his people of the house of Israel and had to be on earth during each of the four world kingdoms spoken of by Daniel, therefore, this uncut stone cannot be speaking of Christ coming in power to rule.

Gods Battle Ax started with the 10 lost tribes of the house of Israel, his northern kingdom. Cyrus of the Meads and Persians were Hebrew (II Cron 36:22-23), remnant of the 10 lost tribes and is why he had sympathy with the Jews returning to Jerusalem to rebuild the Temple. Alexander the Great of Greece was also Hebrew and a remnant of the 10 lost tribes. Calcol and Dara of Judah were joined by other migrating groups of Hebrew over hundreds of years (Zara Matt 1:3 and I Chron 2:5-6) and settled Greece and later became a world power under Hebrew influence. Rome was settled by descendants of Dara after the destruction of Troy and became Latinos creating the Roman Empire. The Hebrew Goths, descendants of the lost sheep of the house of Israel sacked Rome in 408AD enabling their fall to Christianity. Christ's Church of the throne of England basically destroyed the old Roman Empire for Emperor Constantine was born of the British throne and the Christian faith. All the civilizations mentioned above were part of Gods Battle Axe that culminated into his Christian nations of today. It amazes this writer that with all the documented evidence, recorded history and archeological finding of the 10 lost tribes migrating into Europe, the modern Church refuses to accept these facts. The Scriptures clearly supports all the data and findings. We as a Christian nation and Church are truly blinded to the truth. This Author understands that many segments within this book is repetitious and maybe boring but necessary to quote Scripture from every angle. Please bear with me.

There is a piece of history most people do not know for it matches Gods Battle Ax of his Hebrew people. In the year 390BC, Belinus and Brennus, sons of the most famed British King Dunwall, assaulted and captured Rome with a British army. From 113 to 101BC, European observers affirm that the Cimbri-Keltoi of Britain was the terror of Rome and could have brought the Empire under their own subjection if they had so desired. ("The Drama of the Lost Disciples' by George F. Jowett) This could very well be why Rome was so intent on destroying Britain with their invasions in 55 and 54BC and again in 43AD for they knew their fierceness and military capabilities.

Gods stone Kingdom was to be an ensign to the people of the world and gather to this ensign with speed and not stumble. Study closely the following Scriptures and compare them to the Christian nations of today (house of Israel) and the modern nation of Israel (Judah).

The word ensign is a key in understanding the following Scriptures and the Hebrew meaning is as follows: a flag, a sail, a flagstaff, pole, a signal, a token, banner, sign, and standard. After a close study of the word ensign in the following verses, the word ensign is either a flag or symbol representing a nation of power protecting Christ's Church. This nation is called Zion in Isaiah 18:7.

Isaiah 5:26-27, **"And he will lift up an ensign to the nations from far, and will hiss unto them from the end of the earth: and, behold, they shall come with speed swiftly: None shall be weary nor stumble among them; none shall slumber nor sleep; neither shall the girdle of their loins be loosed, nor the latchet of their shoes be broken"**. This verse can very well be associated with the emigrants from all over the world gathering to the Christian flag (ensign) into the harbors of America under the shadow and symbol of the Statue of Liberty in New York City. Isaiah 11:10, **"And in that day there shall be a root of Jesse, which shall stand for an ensign of the people; to it shall the Gentiles seek: and his rest shall be glorious"**. This verse makes it clear that the ensign was Christian (fruitful) for the root of Jesse (Matt 1:6) is Christ's linage and his Gospel (the Church). The ensign and gathering cannot be of the modern nation of Israel for only Jews returned and not Gentiles as the above verse states. Gentiles as a whole never migrated to the modern state of Israel. From the moment Israel became a nation, they have been at war so the term **"and his rest shall be glorious"** in no way could be speaking of modern Israel. This gathering is the second gathering in the wilderness making Great Britain and the United States the most sought-after nations ever in history by Gentile emigrants. They came from every nation in the world under the shadow of Liberty and freedom as a gathering stated in Gen 49:10 when Christ gathered his people worldwide.

Isaiah 11:12, **"And he shall set up an ensign for the nations, and shall assemble the outcasts of Israel, and gather together the dispersed of Judah from the four corners of the earth."** This is also the second gathering in the wilderness and included the house of Israel, house of Judah and Gentiles drawn from all nations into their own land in the wilderness where they are betrothed to God under the New Covenant of the Church as Christ's Bride to be (Hos 2:14-23). There are millions of Jews that have migrated to the shores of the United States for religious freedom and many of them have accepted Christ's Gospel. Isaiah 42:4 states, **"He shall not fail nor be discouraged, till he have set judgment in the earth: and the isles shall wait for his law."** This law of judgment is set forth by his New Covenant of the Church established by Joseph of Arimathea in 36AD, the first above ground Church in Ireland. The law and judgment in the earth is an established system of government first established as the Magna Carta in England and as a Republic (USA), "the rule of law" enforcing Gods Covenant of righteous law and order (Jerm 23:5, Isa 16:5 and 32:15-16). According to the American College Dictionary, a Republic is, any body of persons viewed as a commonwealth, a state in which the supreme power rests in the body of citizens entitled to vote and is exercised by representatives chosen directly or indirectly by the people. A Republic is when the rule of law is enforced by elected officials of the people and not by mob rule as a democratic system.

The Hebrew tribes of Calcol and Dara were to be a part of this established nation in the wilderness. They settled England as early as 1800 BC and later joined by the lost sheep of the house of Israel which were the Celts, Kumri, Anglos, Engles (angles), Saxons and Goths to name many more. This is the gathering of Gods people under Shiloh (Gen 49:10) which is Christ's Church that later migrated to the shores of America.

Isaiah 18:3, "**All ye inhabitants of the world, and dwellers on the earth see ye, when he lifteth up an ensign on the mountains; and when he bloweth a trumpet hear ye**". The word, "he lifteth up an ensign" is speaking of Christ and his Gospel from his Christian nations to all the people of the earth and "a trumpet hear ye" is the calling of his Holy Spirit of his Church and the thousands of missionaries dispersed worldwide. This is a calling to the world to flow into Gods land of freedom, justice, righteousness and land of opportunity (United States of America). Study this whole chapter for verse 7 could very well be speaking of the American Continent for it is divided and spoiled by great rivers. This land was meted which in Hebrew means: the sense of a fastening, stalwart, a cord for measuring, a rule, also a rim, a musical string or accord, line. Prime root, to balance, measure out by weight or dimension. The American College Dictionary list mete as, to distribute or apportion by measure; allot; to measure, a limiting mark, a limit or turning post. It is important to understand the word "<u>mete</u>" for Isaiah 18:7 indicate, by definition, that the Hebrew and English meaning is basically the same. The Americas were the only known land that was meted or measured (surveyed land) by the early colonist and today use almost the same method from the founding of this nation. The United States was broken down into territorial measurements as we colonized the continent. You can see this if you look at an early map of the colonies and their boundaries. There is a measurement system of appraising land still used by realtors and surveyors called "metes and bounds" derived from the Hebrew word "mete" or meted connecting the United States to Isaiah 18:7. The meaning of Gods prophecies lie within the cross referencing of Hebrew root words.

The American people have always been terrible from their beginning for we started with revolution. **"A nation meted out and trodden under foot, whose land the rivers have spoiled, to the place of the name of the Lord of hosts, the mount Zion"**. You could certainly say that it was trodden down for we took it from the Indians and parts of this nation, has at one time or the other, belonged to at least five different invading countries culminating into our United States after many wars. Pensacola Florida is called, the City of Five Flags, meaning that they at one time or the other was controlled by five different nations, Spain, French, England, Confederate States of America and the United States of America. This great nation God speaks of is to be called Zion after his own name that was trodden under foot (Gods Spirit and Church).

Isaiah 30:17 states, **"till ye be lift as a beacon upon the top of a mountain, and as an ensign on an hill."** This verse indicates that the ensign is a shining light that represents Christ's Church and the mountain and hill is a nation protecting the beacon (the Church). Isaiah 31:9, **"And he shall pass over to his strong hold for fear, and his princes shall be afraid of the ensign, saith the Lord, whose fire is in Zion, and his furnace in Jerusalem."** According to this verse the world will be afraid of the ensign on the mountain or hill (the Church) for this Christian nation must be very powerful. The important aspect of this verse is that the "fire in Zion" is Gods Spirit (the Church) and "the furnace of Jerusalem" the house of Israel as its dwelling place in the wilderness, where the fire burns, indicating it as a protector. The house of Israel is called Jerusalem as a company of nations under Zion (the Church) and guardian as its Battle Ax.

This verse can be explained by the words fire and furnace. According to the Strongs Concordance, fire means a flame, East (the break of day), luminous, and fires. Furnace means, fire pot, oven, burning lamp, candle light, to till the soil, break up, to shine and fire. Therefore, the "fire in Zion" is Gods Holy Spirit as a fire and where does a fire burn, within a furnace, Christ's Church which is the house of Israel as Gods Kingdom, a burning candle stick, the light to the world and salt of the earth. This verse would make Jerusalem the furnace where the fire of his Spirit lives which can only be the "O virgin of Israel", a bride to be as the Bride of Christ representing the Holy of Holies in the Temple. It represents the Apostolic Church of Christ under the birthright of the house of Israel, the STONE of Israel (Gen 49:24). The tilling and breaking up of the soil matche Jeremiah 26:18 and Micah 3:12 where Jerusalem was laid in rubble and plowed which means it was moved to a fruitful location in the wilderness. Jerusalem has a dual meaning and its name went with Zion, the Throne and his people of the house of Israel when plowed and moved, just as this and other verses indicate.

The analogy of the **"fire in Zion"** and **"the furnace of Jerusalem"** coincides with God making the connection with the house of Israel being **"his vineyard of the Lord of hosts"** or branches that departed over the seas and Judah being his root of the vineyard **"his pleasant plant"** (Isa 5:7). A root is stationary and never moves and provides life for the vineyard. This clearly makes a distinction between the two houses of Israel during end time prophecy and indicates different roles for each house.

After a close look at all of these Scriptures, it is obvious that the great mountain (Christian nations) must be the 5th Kingdom spoken of in Daniel chapter two for it is called Zion the beacon or the trumpet that can only be the shining light of Christ's Church. This ensign was for all the nations, the outcast of Israel, dispersed of Judah and for Gentiles to seek this light. With an open mind, this ensign can only be speaking of the Christian nations of Great Britain and the United States of how we opened our shores to the emigrants of the world and have been a shinning Christian light to all the earth through the cross of Jesus Christ as indicated on our national flags. In reality and truth, these verses cannot be speaking of the gathering of the Jews back into the modern state of Israel for they still reject Christ. With no doubt, they refer to the building of the single greatest Christian nation in the history of the world, the North American Continent.

The American Christian has been the most powerful political force ever in the history of man under Gods rule of law and undoubtedly a portion of the fifth kingdom mentioned in Daniel 2:44-45. This force has created the greatest economic, political and military system under a single nation ever recorded in history. The American dream is no happenstance but a direct result of Gods guiding Spirit and fulfillment of his birthright promise of blessings to Abraham, Isaac, Jacob, Joseph and then to Ephraim and Manasseh (Gen 48:16&19). They were to bring mercy and judgment to the world (Isa 32:1&16, 41:1-3). These are Gods Christian nations of Great Britain and the United States that has been a preserving salt (Luke 14:34; II Chron 25:11) and the **inherited** Battle Axe (Jerm 5:19-20) against Satanic forces for the past 2000 years. Genesis 49:22-24 states that Joseph or Ephraim and Manasseh is the stone of Israel, the branch that ran over the wall and became the stone Shepard's, a mighty army which became the 5th Kingdom or the stone Kingdom mentioned in Daniel chapter two. Before Satan and his human agents can establish his one world system, he has to dilute or eliminate the preserving salt of the Christian faith of Gods fifth kingdom. The Republic of America was founded on Christian principles and declared a Christian nation in 1892 by the Supreme Court just as England in 156AD by the British Parliament and Crown. They are the only two governments in recorded history claiming their nation to be Christian. This is why Satan and his human agents have targeted us for destruction.

This book is written as a WARNING to our Christian way of life. If we continue to be blinded to the lies being perpetrated upon our Society and the satanic assault directed at destroying our religious and political system, we will be enslaved into this one world satanic government. This writer truly believes that America and Great Britain is Gods fifth kingdom established under his new Covenant (Heb 8:8 & Jerm 31:31) to evangelize the world and a part of the Children of the house of Israel. The information and Scriptures provided in this book proves this point. The warning of Gods judgment of destruction to Judah and the house of Israel prior to their captivity due to national sins apply today just as they did 2700 years ago. We must not fool ourselves in believing that we as a Christian nation will escape Gods judgment. The Hebrew people of ancient Israel did not listen to Gods warning from his Prophets and their cities were destroyed and people taken into captivity. God's law of judgment does not change as stated in Leviticus chapter 26 and Deuteronomy chapter 28. The same warning applies to the United States today.

The only way we will repent of our present immoral turpitude is to be shocked by the realization of our true identity as a Hebrew nation and the plan God has for us as his people. Most Americans do not know that the U.S. Congress, after our national independence, came very close to voting Hebrew as our national language. Many of the early Universities and Colonies spoke Hebrew and it was common throughout the nation. America and Great Britain has always had an unbreakable spiritual bond with the Hebrew Jewish people because we are of the same stock.

The terrorist attack of 09-11-2001 in New York City did not bring us to repentance, so what event will? Will it take a nuclear strike to make us repent of our national sins? The United state is a part of Gods Kingdom given to the house of Israel in I Kings chapter 11, preserved through the tribe of Manasseh. The Common Wealth of Great Britain is Ephraim and both received the birthright blessing of greatness that is the Christian English-speaking people of the world. The overwhelming proof is documented throughout this book repeated many times to fortify our memories. We need repetition to remember the Scriptures and secular history when we study the details. Due to the fact that the English-speaking nations are the Children of Israel and Gods Church is why Satan has to destroy our system of politics and faith before he can establish his world system. Gods Time Table is set in stone and our destruction will take place unless one thing happens, we as a nation must repent (Jerm 9:13-15) if time is to be extended. All through the Scriptures there are stories of how God would have forgiven his judgment if only the people repented. Can we as a nation repent or is it too late?

A Nation to protect Christianity "Gods Battle Ax"

The Bible indicates in several cases that Satan has tried to destroy God's creation after his rebellion in Heaven. The first attempt took place in Genesis 1:1-2 and states, **"In the beginning God created the Heaven and the Earth. And the earth was without form, and void,".** When God creates, he designs it perfectly. Verse, one states that God created the Heaven and the Earth and it was perfect but verse two says the earth was without form and void. A cataclysmic event occurred between verse one and two destroying the earth but not the Heavens. It is believed that when Satan rebelled in Heaven and failed, he then returned to earth and totally destroyed God's creation out of anger due to his failure to become god. God then created the earth anew to prove a point to Satan, through his Prophetic plan of man's Salvation through Christ that love and mercy will prevail over death and destruction.

The second attempt to destroy man took place with the story of how Satan tempted Adam and Eve in the Garden causing them to lose favor with God and being cast out of Eden. This was the beginning of Satan's death and destruction of man and the physical war between God and Lucifer (Satan the Devil) with man as the pawn.

The third attempt to destroy God's creation occurred prior to the flood or deluge by destroying the genealogy of man. Satan and his demons had diluted man's gene pool so drastically that Noah and his family were the only people left of pure blood (Gen 6:9). This was Satan's attempt to destroy the pure bloodlinage and to prevent the Messiah's birth as the Salvation of the World. The book of Jasher IV: 18, explains how Satan and his human followers mixed animals of one species with the other to include gene-splicing man. This created giants and monsters in the earth and can be verified in Genesis 6:1-9. Satan tried to totally destroy man's genealogy, therefore, destroying his spirit. The Book of Enoch or I Enoch gives this account in more detail by listing the names of the two hundred demons by name (VI 1-8 and VII 1-6). The giants became so strong they began to devour mankind. God had no choice but to destroy man for his genealogy had become so polluted that only Noah and his family had pure blood as a descendant of Adam.

The fourth attempt for Satan to destroy man and to take him from God will be his endeavor to become god during the Tribulation Period. This occurs just prior to being thrown into the bottomless pit (Rev 20:3) for a thousand years and proves Gods mercy. God gives Satan another chance to redeem himself and to show that love and mercy always prevails over death and destruction.

After reviewing the above Scriptures, we can see why God had to create a nation to protect his Prophetic plan for his Chosen People and the Salvation of man through the Messiah. The great Kings of Israel played the role of protector through the ages but they ceased to exist in 586BC with the last king, King Zedekiah. They had fallen from maintaining God's commandments just as the world today. God promised that Israel, the rod of his inheritance, would always be his Battle Ax (Jeremiah 51:19-20). This verse is very important for it identifies three elements of Gods people, Jacob, his inheritance tribe and his Battle Ax or protector. These two verses identify Jacob as being all 12 tribes but his inheritance tribe is the only one called Israel. Verse 20 calls his inheritance tribe his Battle Ax and weapons of war meaning they are to be a strong powerful nation. Genesis 48:16-19 clearly states that Joseph's two sons, Ephraim and Manasseh were to be called Israel for only they, of all twelve sons of Jacob, were selected as the birthright inheritance tribe. This made them powerful nations as Gods Battle Ax and protector of this end time Church.

God divided his kingdom in I Kings 11 for the purpose of being his Battle Ax that was taken from the Jews in Matthew 21:43. Where was it moved? The whole kingdom and throne went to the lost sheep of the house of Israel (Matt 10:5-8 and 15:24) that was planted in the wilderness and given their own land (Jerm 23:3-8 and Eze 34:13-18, 36:24-27, 39:28). The house of Israel was to be planted in a new land and not the promised land of Canaan as an unsettled land in Europe and the Americas promised to the birthright tribe of the rod of Gods inheritor, Ephraim and Manasseh (Gen 48:16). They were to be the caretakers for the ultimate inheritor, Christ and his Church.

The Kingdom was divided for a short period of time before he reunited it under the birthright of the house of Israel. Mark 3:24 states that a divided Kingdom cannot stand, therefore God had to maintain his whole Kingdom to prevent destruction. The Battle Ax culminated under the throne of England and became the English Christian nations of the world spreading Gods end time Gospel and became his fighting force against Satan's tyranny for the past two thousand years.

When we objectively view this theory in light of the birthright blessing to Ephraim the Unicorn (Great Britain) and Manasseh the Bull (United States), we can clearly see how they are the only fruitful (Matt 21:43) or Christian nations that can fit this scenario after the coming of Christ. It also fulfills the promise to Abraham, Isaac, Jacob and Joseph (Ephraim and Manasseh) to be a great nation (single) and a company of nations (multiple 46 of the UK) and Kings of Kingdoms (Gen 17:6, 35:11 and 48:19). These nations in the wilderness were to be Gods Battle Ax and protector of his Gospel, the 5th stone kingdom mentioned in Daniel 2:35&44-45 which Christ will inherit in accordance to Luke 1:32-33.

The Church and the Gospel was given to the house of Israel to evangelize the world. This was the purpose of the birthright blessing to Abraham, Isaac and Jacob to be many nations. They were to become great nations and kingdoms as a weapon of war or bow. The birthright son was to be Gods "Battle Ax" an army of God-fearing nations, a platform and protection for the Gospel to be spread worldwide and the fruitful nation Christ spoke of in Matt 21:43. Think about it, if Great Britain had not been a wealthy colonizing nation with a powerful navy to sail the oceans of the world and a great Army to support the security of their Christian colonies, how could the Gospel be spread? This fulfills Jeremiah 51:19-20, **"The portion of Jacob is not like them: for he is the former of all things: and Israel is the rod of his inheritance and Lord of host is his name. Thou art my battle ax and weapons of war: for with thee will I break in pieces the nations, and with thee will I destroy kingdoms"**. This verse clearly says that Gods Battle Ax is Israel, his rod of inheritance that is Ephraim and Manasseh, GB and the USA. Isaiah 41:2 and Micah 7:12-20 also speak of Gods righteous people being mighty with sword. The United States and Great Britain has fought many wars pitted against evil tyranny for the past four hundred years and they are the only nations in recorded history that can fulfill these verses as fruitful (Christian) nations.

We, as a Christian nation, need to keep in mind and be vigilant to Satan's tactics of his Liberal agenda. America have been targeted for destruction by Satan's human agents and represent the last Sebastian of Christianity, Gods Battle Ax. We are presently fighting for the survival of our nation and our way of life.

The Roman Connection

By understanding Satan's tactics, we can better understand how Rome has influenced Gods People for the past 2000 years. Again, this writer would like to make it clear that my intent is not to insult the Roman Catholic Religion but simply stating historical facts.

We have already established that God provided his Battle Ax, the early Hebrew descendants of Calcol and Dara and the lost sheep of the house of Israel, to protect his people. Therefore, Satan would have to counteract by developing his own nation of evil simply to destroy Gods people. Satan is the master of deceit and emulates all that God creates. Let's set back and review history just for a few minutes and ask ourselves a question!!! What single nation in history has given Gods people and his Church the most persecution and destruction? There is only one answer and that is Rome that became the Roman Catholic Church. We know that Satan is over all kingdoms of the earth for he tempted Christ in Matthew 4:9, that he would give Christ all the glory of the kingdoms if he only worshiped him as God. We know that Satan has this kind of power so let's not fool ourselves and be naive to the strength of Satan the Devil.

The Book of Revelation tells us that Satan is going to use the fourth beast or kingdom mentioned in Daniel's visions as the catalyst to form his New World Government. This government will be the platform to establish his leadership as the Antichrist, World Leader, to catapult himself into power as God, the Apotheosis. This fourth kingdom is the old Roman Empire revived through the Roman Catholic Church and the nationalization of the status of the Vatican's territory controlled by the United Nation under Socialism that is culminating at this very moment. The color red represents Communism where two thirds of the world's population is presently enslaved. World War III will be the catalyst to enslave the West under this Socialist system. The American people fail to realize that the Liberal Agenda is nothing more than a Socialist movement to disarm American so the war of Ezekiel chapter 38 can be fulfilled. We will then be absorbed into the Socialist system of the Apocalypse as Revelation chapter 6 states.

Vatican City, through its creation of the first Pope in 610AD, has always been honored by all nations as a sovereign monarch or territory and exist within the city of Rome. This fulfills Daniel's vision of the fourth beast and Revelation 17:5-6, **"of the Mother of Harlots drunken with the blood of the saints"**. Over the years, the Roman Church has killed more Christians in the name of God than Communism during the past century. This Harlot is the false religion or the Beast of the Antichrist system and believed to be the Roman Church. We do know that Rome is at the center of this Satanic Political Religion just as they have been the worlds dominating religious force from the first Pope in 610AD.

Let's review past history pertaining to Rome and the influence on Gods people. We have already established how God allowed his Hebrew people to migrate into Ireland, Scotland and England as early as 2000 to 1800 BC where they establish the old Patriarchal faith of Druidism. Satan knew this and he also knew their mission so he had to create a nation powerful enough to destroy them. He created the Roman Empire with tremendous power infused with greed and the pretentious idea of world domination with the intent to destroy all nations of God. This is the reason Caesar was to be worshiped as a god of many gods.

Gods People are the salt and preservation (Lev 2:13 and Matt 5:13) of the earth even before the establishment of the Church and Christ's Gospel. Satan, from the beginning of time, even in the Garden, has tried to destroy God's creation of man. Lucifer the Devil could not destroy Christ's Church even with the great power of the Roman army so he joined religion through the Roman Catholic religion.

It has been documented that Joseph of Arimathea brought Christianity to Briton in approx. 38AD where he established the first Church. The old Patriarch faith of Druidism had been created hundreds of years earlier within the Isles of Britannia and had a tremendous influence on Rome. Let's review history. Due to this influence, Rome first invaded Briton in 55BC and failed. They regrouped and attacked again in 54 BC that also ended in failure. The Silurian British warriors were fierce and called barbarians by the Roman soldiers. The Romans did not pressure Briton again till 43AD when Christianity/Druidism began to grow becoming a threat to Rome through its influence. An all-out attack with the intentions of destroying all aspects of Druidism, Christianity, the British Royal Family and any one claiming to be of the Jewish faith along with their educational institutions. The Romans could not conquer all of the main Island of England and only advanced to the upper one third where they built the Plautian Wall. They never entered Ireland or Scotland and remained in Britain till approx. 410AD. The influence of the Roman Army became weak and began to fade away from Europe when Constantine, the great-grandson of the British warrior Arviragus and son of the famous Empress Helen, a British princess, converting Rome to their form of Christianity in approx. 312AD. The great power of the Roman Army was slowly converted to the tremendous influence and authority of the Roman Catholic Church where its religion was physically forced upon the European countries.

Just a little study will show that the original Apostolic Church arrived in England and Europe long before the Papal jurisdiction of the Church of Rome where they tried to subjugate the Churches of Europe. The Scriptures were locked up in Latin under the authority of the Roman Church where history was written on a slant to benefit the agenda of the Roman Church. The Scriptures were kept from the common people to maintain their ignorance so they would forever be suppressed as subjects to the Crown and Church. Truth of the Holy Scriptures if given to the masses was a threat to the Roman Church, therefore, they sealed the Scriptures in Latan and Greek hidden from the people.

There is a tremendous amount of documentation of how the Roman Church subverted, controlled, and dominated the Scriptures for hundreds of years simply for power over the people. The tyrannical feudal system of the Dark Ages was maintained till the Reformation took place where Wycliffe and other English Scholars translated the Scriptures into English. This event was able to occur due to the invention of the printing press in which the Roman Church tried to subdue. They knew that if the Bible were readily available to the common people, the Church would lose control of the masses. The truth of the Scriptures was finally taken from the control of the Catholic Church and published to the common people in the form of the King James authorized version of the Bible in 1611.

This created the single most important aspect of the human race, knowledge of the truth of God's Word and freedom from tyrannical governments and religion. In reality, it created the free democratic nations of the western world. John 8:32 portray a very true statement, **"And ye shall know the truth, and the truth shall make you free."** The great western Christian nations is based on the Holy Bible and this single verse rings true bringing freedom of religion under a Republic of a Democratic system. The knowledge of God's Word allowed true freedom to abound worldwide, which has created the greatest governmental system of the human race, the Republic/Democratic System of the Western Christian Culture, based on freedom of Religion. The Arab nations can never be Democratic for they will not allow freedom of Religion or government for their regimes is based on a tyrannical system.

Chapter 10

Communism Satan's Tool

Volumes of books could be written on Communism but this segment is only to give a brief description of why Satan developed this system for his evil purposes. We know that Christ has established his Church and Battle Axe of nations to bring Righteousness and Judgment to the world and we also know that Satan is to establish a New World System during the Tribulation Period. Let's ascertain the fact of how Satan can overcome Christ's Church and construct his government and ultimately become the Apotheosis. This would take a lot of time and effort on Satan's behalf to accomplish this feat. He would have to come up with an ideology that could counter act and powerful enough to destroy Christ's Church. We know that Christ's Church or Kingdom cannot be destroyed so this fact brings up a very interesting scenario. The most powerful force on the face of God's creation is the salt of the earth (Matt 5:13) that is nothing more than Gods Spirit within the Christians of Christ's Church. Salt preserves and fights Satan's evil ways so he knows Christ's Church has to be destroyed if his nefarious agenda is to be accomplished.

These destructive forces can be seen within the United States through the Islamic Religion with the Liberal Agenda and the Socialist nations that has sympathy to each other. The Socialist, Communist and Muslims are working together. This evil ideology (curse) of Islam and Liberalism is spreading to nations throughout the world such as France, Germany, Belgium and other so called Democratic nations. Muslims are migrating to every nation in the world building their Temples to infiltrate and destroy the western way of life. They are not here to assimilate but to infiltrate and subvert. God cursed the world through the god of Islamic for the word *curse* in Isa 24:6, **"Therefore hath the curse devoured the earth"**. In Hebrew curse means in ref#422&423, "alah", a swear word that devoured the earth as an astonishment. According to this verse, the Muslim god Allah is a curse to the world. This is why the world is filled with terrorism. Since the Berlin Wall fell and the so-called illusion that Communism is dead, it has allowed Communist/Muslim agents to act freely within the Western nations and Europe and Americaq. The world is slowly falling into the Socialist trap just as West Germany, Belgium and Mexico. The illusion that Communism is dead is the final stage to establish Lucifer's World

System and has created blindness in the Western nations as to their Liberal Socialist Agenda. The Socialist White Horse of Revelation 6:2 is on the loose. The politically correct liberal view is allowing the Islamic religion to spread worldwide unchecked. It takes a blind person or nation to not see how Islam teaches death and destruction supported and paid for by Socialist Liberalism just as the terrorist portray.

This nation and the world are presently going through a Cultural, Religious, Social and political transformation due to liberalism. They are presently in the process of destroying all Christianity. We are currently shaking off 400 years of Christian morals, honor and ethical values that has created the greatest political and economic system, as a Republic, in the history of man. The American people need to ask ourselves, why do we want to change our Constitutional System from wealth and freedom to a World Order that will enslave everyone under socialism? This system has been forced upon us by Corporate and Political forces and we are falling for their liberal lies shrouded as individual rights which sounds good to human nature but destroys our Constitutional system. Bible Prophecy clearly foretells how the world will be enslaved into the New World Order and we are being driven into this system like cattle.

There is an aspect of Communism that we need to consider that dates back to ancient Reuben (Modern France) and Edom of Moab that is located east and south of the Dead Sea aligned with Gog (the Communist bloc nations of Russia, Dumaea). In I Chronicles 5:4 Gog is listed as the son of Joel. It is not clearly stated but Joel is believed to be a part of the house of Reuben for he is not listed as being one of his sons. It is this writer's belief that Joel was not a son but a part of the house of Reuben possibly from Edom of Moab being their land was adjacent to each other. This is unique for it explains why Reuben (Modern France) produced early writings of the Communist Manifesto that Adam Weishaup wrote (leader of the Masonic Illuminati) and masked as Carl Marks being its original author. The ideology and early writings of Communism came from the Secret Societies of the Illuminati and the Masonic Lodges based in France (Reuben) during the early 1700 hundreds. Joel (Edom of Esau) of the house of Reuben is a part of Gog, a place east of the Dead Sea. They became the northern nations believed to be Russia, a Communist country with the ideology of Communism derived from Reuben. In the last days, Reuben (modern France) and Joel (Gog of Russia), as listed in I Chronicles 5:4, has united under the same ideology of Socialism. This explains why France portrays Socialism in their modern-day Politics.

The connection of Socialism can be traced to Ishmael through the coalition of the Arab and Communist states. From the time Ishmael lost his birthright to Isaac, his descendants self-proclaimed the right to the land that was clearly given to the seed of Isaac. For justification of their claim, they had to produce an ideology and religion contrary to God's Word. Satan has used this 4000-year family feud to destabilize the world not only in ancient days but also in our modern times. It has culminated into the Islamic terrorist activity of our present end days with the establishment of Islam and Socialism (Liberalism). The American people must wake up to the fact that Liberalism is used to subvert as the first stage of Communism. All these problems stem from the fight over the birthright of Ishmael given to Isaac and the next generation of Esau's birthright given to Jacob. The feud and war of these brothers claiming the birthright has now come full circle culminating into the terrorist activity of our present time.

We are quickly approaching the war that begins the time of Wrath ending the Church age of the house of Israel. The Church being taken away is two-fold for it prevents Christ's Church from seeing Wrath and begins a new time period. There are many Christians that do not think the Church is going to be taken away by the Rapture but the Scriptures state that it will happen for several reasons. The first reason is that the Church is the salt of the earth and if not taken out of the earth, the Anti-Christ could never come to fulfill Gods Prophecy of Wrath to the wicked. II Thessalonians 2:7 clearly states, **"For the mystery of iniquity doth already work: only he who now letteth will let, until he be taken out of the way."** This verse states that the mystery of iniquity, Satan's influence, already works but he cannot physically come as the Anti-Christ till the Spirit of the Church is taken away. He will not be able to appear on the world scene till the Church and Holy Spirit is removed. Gods Spirit or Kingdom (Church) and Satan's spirit kingdom (New World Order) cannot co-exist at the same time (II Thess 2:7). The second reason is that Daniel's 70th week has to be fulfilled and the unique thing about this is that the two time periods cannot overlap. These two time periods represent the New Covenant of the Church and the last week of Daniel's Prophecy (Dan 9:24-27) to complete the 70th week under the Old Covenant. The time periods of the Old and New Covenants cannot overlap due to the presents of the Holy Spirit and divided by the seven-year Tribulation Period. This is why the Spirit of the Church has to be taken or raptured and explains II Thess 2:7, "until he be taken out of the way". The man of sin (Satan) cannot come in power till the Spirit of the Church is taken. The two specific time periods are the Church age pertaining to the Spiritual house of Israel and the seven-year period of Daniel's 70th week involves only the Jews and the 144,000 sealed Hebrews. This also includes the non-believers of the physical house of Israel (Christian nations) that has been left behind.

The Church age is for the Spiritual house of Israel to fulfill the mission of the Gospel and completes the time period for "O virgin Israel", as Christ's betrothed Bride. Daniel's 70th week occurs when the Church is taken and the last week prophesies of the Jews of Jerusalem prior to the sealing of the 144,000. This is the physical Israel that has been left behind. If the Church and Holy Spirit were present during the time of Wrath, the 12,000 from each tribe would not have to be sealed. The Holy Spirit is their seal for they would be a part of the Church as Christians.

The reason Christ selected Paul (Saul) as an Apostle on the Damascus Road (Acts 9:3) was for several reasons. First, Paul was a man of God with a pure heart but he was totally blinded to the truth of Christ's Gospel and still entrenched in Judaism just as the Jews are today. Secondly, he was selected to perform a special mission as a replacement to the Apostles for they were to go only to the Lost Sheep of the house of Israel (Matt 10:6 and 15:24). The third reason is a symbol of blindness. The same loss of sight or blindness Saul experienced on the Damascus Road exists today within modern Judaism. This is why he came to Paul personally and is a symbol and example of the Sealing of the 144,000 in Revelation 7:5-8. This represents the same type of blindness Paul spoke of in Romans 9-11 when the sealing in Revelation chapter 7 takes place, for if Christ does not personally seal each of the 144,000, no one would believe. The Church and Holy Spirit has already been taken; therefore, the Holy Spirit has to come to each of the 144,000 just as he did to Paul or no one would believe due to Satanic blindness.

Another proof that the Church will not be on earth during the seven-year period is found in Revelations 18:23-24. The war that destroys Babylon in Rev 18:2 is the same war that occurs at the beginning of the Tribulation Period in Ezekiel 38 and 39. Revelations 18:23 clearly state that the voice of the Spirit and Bride that is the Church is not present when Babylon is destroyed. According to verses 23-24, Babylon is the house of Israel that has been subdued by Satan through deceit, therefore, they have deceived the nations of the world with Satan's new age agenda of sorceries and Social Liberalism through great wealth. The Church and Holy Spirit are no longer on the earth and have been taken (Ruptured). Daniel's 70th week is a full seven-year period that matches the time of the Tribulation under the Old Covenant and is a period for the Jews to redeem themselves for rejecting Christ. They will finally see the truth of the Messiah when the two witnesses provide the Gospel to them. The 144,000 are sealed in the middle of this seven-year period and given the commission and responsibility to physically take Gods earthly Kingdom into the seventh millennium for Christ to claim at his coming. The seal is to protect the 144,000, Gods physical Kingdom, from being killed by the Anti-Christ. We must understand that the Church is taken at the beginning of the Tribulation but the Holy Spirit is not taken till the Gospel is finished in the middle of the Trib. in Rev 10:7, 11:7 and Dan:12:7. The Holy Spirit cannot be taken with the Church for many people during the first half of the Trib. has to be saved under Christ's Gospel mistered by the two Witnessed due to the absence of the Church.

Millions of people will be saved due to the two prophets sent by God preaching and teaching Christ's Gospel during the first half of the Tribulation Period. The Holy Spirit appeared on earth in the upper room at the day of Pentecost (Act 2:1-2) when the Church was established and will remain on earth till the Gospel is "finished" in the verses listed above. There will be millions of people saved under Christ's Gospel only during the first half of the Tribulation prior to the mark of the Beast. During the second half the Holy Spirit is not present so no one is left to be saved for all will be killed in Rev 13:15 except the sealed 144,00.

Let's not fool ourselves and fall for Satan's humanistic lie that there are no God or Christ through the teaching of humanism, atheism, polytheism, moral relativism, political correctness, Socialism and Communism. This is just a few of Satan's nefarious tools of ideological philosophy to dilute Christ's Gospel. We can see how these politically correct beliefs are slowly changing the minds of the American people to accept Satan's new kingdom of Anti-Christ. The American people have embraced the Liberal, Socialist and Communists ideologies for they are ignorant of the final outcome that will bring slavery to the masses. God and Christ are being taken totally out of our Society. Examples can be seen in the fact that Christ is slowly being taken out of Christmas, God out of our national pledge of allegiance, our money and prayer is illegal in public as a Christian but not to other religions such as Islam and that lying and stealing is OK as long as you don't get caught. As we know, this is just a few of the outrageous attacks on our Society to remove Christ. We, as Christians, and patriotic citizens must realize that the Socialist Liberal organizations and groups behind these attacks are Satan's Children (Matt 13:38, Act 13:10, Eph 5:6) for he is the arch deceiver of illuminist (I Cor 4:11 & 11:14). Secret Societies are his tools of advancement cloaked in secrecy where his power is given to his earthly children through channeling, wealth and supremacy of government through high corporate levels.

With that fact in mind, Satan and his earthly children are behind the onslaught to destroy our traditional moral values and ultimately the Constitution of this nation. We need to prepare ourselves with the knowledge of God's Word as his preserving salt. This is our only defense and should be alert to that fact. God needed a powerful nation to protect and wage war in the name of Justice just as Satan imitates and also need a nation to counter act Gods New Covenant of righteousness and judgment under the house of Israel of the western Christian culture. This is why the Arab nations of Ishmael (Islam) and the Communist nations of Esau are determined to destroy our western Christianized culture. The Arab Islamic countries and the Communist bloc nations are Satan's tool that is determined to destroy Gods Covenant People of the house of Israel that is the Christian nations of the world. This includes the Jewish state of Israel where God plans to set on his throne in Jerusalem.

There is a Spiritual force at work in our three-dimensional world that is diametrically opposed to Gods Covenant and Christ's Church. This force is a Spiritual war to the death and man's souls and nations are the main pawn. From the moment Satan the Devil rebelled against God, the war for man's souls began. He is aware that for him to win the war, he has to subdue the human race and be accepted as God in the eyes of man. Satan imitates God in every aspect and is able to distort man's thinking to believe evil is good and good is evil, moral relativism. Satan has the power to make man believe that he is God for this belief is rampant in the world today and is called Luciferians or the worship of Lucifer. He realizes his time is short and has devised a brilliant plan to enslave man and implement his Christ-less Lucifer worshiping New World System. To complete this task, he has to create a humanistic mechanism that could overcome and destroy Gods Church and Christian nations. This system had to be a powerful Godless, Social, ideological, political and tyrannical platform which is called Communism. It has been created by Satan or Lucifer (the Devil) and implemented by his human agents to attack man's intellectual sympathies and sinful nature. Satan communicates with his human servants by channeling. Ancient religions of Manicheism, Atheism, Freemasonry, Social Darwinism, Scientific Progressionist, Luciferians, Pantheism, Reincarnation, Spiritualism, Wicca and many more have been harbored and implemented by Secret Societies down through the ages. They have culminated into the human empire of Communism as Satan's control mechanism but, we are told by the world media, Communism no longer exist after the Soviet Union fell. In 1829 a meeting was held by the Illuminated leaders (Illuminati Secret Societies) in New York City to initiate their system where the term Communism was first coined. Within a hundred years Russia fell to Communism (1917) and presently almost one half of the world has been engulfed into their slavery. The Western nations are presently under an extreme attack veiled through their Liberal organizations.

Communism is the most powerful humanistic ideological force ever established by man and has been the most destructive. There is an aspect of evil philosophy that we as Christians and patriots must understand if we want to continue our American way of life. The Satanic orchestrated agenda of the Liberal; Socialist, Humanist, Gnostic, Nihilist and Communist groups are slowly chipping away at our Constitution and Christian way of life.

The New World Order is being constructed through the World Council of Churches dominated by the Catholic Church, the United Nations organized by

Communism and the World Trade Organization (Babylon's World Economic System). This system is being forced upon the Western Christian nations and is only a matter of time before we will be engulfed if we don't wake up to this fact. In the 1960's, the State of Alabama conducted an investigation into the United Nations finding them to be organized and dominated by Communist that still exist today.

We are kidding ourselves if we think that our system can survive this assault and must realize Satan is controlling the forces behind these groups, not man. We are physically fighting Satanic Principalities for Jeremiah 11:19 says that there are forces out to destroy our nation. This verse will come true due to our ignorance. The Christian is fighting evil Principalities of great force and power and the only way to combat this force is through the armor and truth of the Holy Scriptures. If we continue to allow these groups to influence our Republican and Democratic system, it is only a matter of time before we will be subjugated by their agenda of a New World Order dedicated to total human control. What is more important, the ideologies of Humanism, Liberalism, Racism, Civil rights, Political Correctness, or the freedoms of our American way of life. These words along with all the other "ism" words are being uses by the Liberals to destroy the freedoms of this nation. This new ideology has created the great falling away of our Churches and moral fiber of our Society mentioned in II Thessalonians 2:3. Let's wake up America to the Liberal lies before it is too late.

Warning of Destruction by the Prophets

The prophet Isaiah went to the house of Israel and Judah by mouth to warn them of their soon coming destruction due to national sins of idolatry. They had very little written Scriptures at that time and the Prophetic books had not been completed. The house of Israel was a separate nation with their own line of Kings and the warnings to Israel and Judah were later transcribed into the Scriptures to apply as a forewarning to the end time Church of today. The warning of destruction that was to occur in ancient days due to national sins is just as valid today for Jeremiah 11:19 states that there are forces trying to destroy us. It is necessary to re-quote this verse to make a point, **"Let us destroy the tree with the fruit thereof, and let us cut him off from the land of the living, that his name may be no more remembered."** Study this verse for the word fruit and tree means Christian or righteousness and is an exact alignment of nations against the western Christian culture of today determined to destroy our way of life. The term "the land of the living" means Christian for Christ is life. That is why the Muslim and Communist nations hate us so much for they deal in death and destruction, the tools of Satan fighting against the Christian nations of the world.

This brings up a question that needs to be answered. There was very little Scripture or Bible during Isaiah's day to warn Gods people of the coming destruction so God personally sent his Prophets. Therefore, what people were to receive the warnings after the Prophets wrote their prophetic books? Jonah, Obadiah, Joel, Amos, Hosea, Isaiah and Micah were sent to both houses as a warning prior to the ten northern tribes of the house of Israel being taken captive to Assyria that began in approx. 740BC. Zechariah, Haggai, Malachi, Nahum, Zephaniah, Jeremiah, Habakkuk, Daniel, Ezekiel and Obadiah were sent after the Assyrian captivity but prior to and during the Babylonian captivity from approx. 720 to 586 BC. Daniel, Haggai, Zechariah, Jeremiah, Habakkuk, Zephaniah, Ezekiel and Malachi wrote their prophetic books during and after both houses had been taken into captivity in 586BC. If the captivities had already taken place, to whom were the WARNINGS written? Because some of the Prophets wrote their Books after the event of captivities tells us that these warning can only be sent to the last day Church.

The houses of Israel and Judah is still divided making the warnings of the Old Testament Prophets valid during the last days, our present time period. The WARNING given by Isaiah to the nation of Israel and Judah in approx. 740 BC, 20 years prior to their destruction, is identical to the present modern-day situation and could be an overlay warning simply by changing the date. We know that all twelve tribes will be united with the sealing of the 144,000, 12,000 from each tribe in Revelation 7:5-8 during the Tribulation Period. Note that the tribe of Dan is the only tribe not included in the sealing and is replaced by Manasseh that is the tribe of Joseph that received the firstborn birthright blessing. Dan has been left out due to migrating out of Israel leaving his brothers to fight for themselves. The house of Joseph is the house of Israel (Ephraim GB and Manasseh US) and the house of Jacob is the other nine tribes of the northern kingdom representing the nations of modern Europe. The house of Judah is the tribes of Judah and Benjamin of the southern kingdom representing modern Israel.

II Kings 19:17 tells us that they were considered nations by God when taken captive by Assyria, **"Of a truth, Lord, the kings of Assyria have destroyed the nations and their lands."** Ephraim is not mentioned in Revelation 7:5-8 but is covered under the tribe of Joseph due to being the Birthright given to Joseph and directly to Ephraim by Jacob himself in Genesis 48:16. The warnings of destruction given in the Old Testament are directed to the end time Church and the coming of World War Three in the very near future.

Isaiah 2:11-22 gives a good warning to proud and lofty people that surely meets the standard of our day. These verses refer to Lebanon, Bashan and the ships of Tarshish. From the previous segment we have learned that

Lebanon is the house of Ephraim (representing Great Britain) and all its beauty through the birthright blessing to be great nations. Bashan is the upper ancient portion of Israel that was Manasseh (representing the United States). Verse sixteen speaks of the ships of Tarshish and represents all the great nations of the world that deals in world trade by ship. Isaiah 2:17, **"And the loftiness of man shall be bowed down, and the haughtiness of men shall be made low: and the Lord alone shall be exalted in that day"**. This verse clearly states that God is going to punish man for his lofty intellectual arrogance, "in that day", which means the day of wrath during the Tribulation Period.

Isaiah 6:11-12 goes on to say, **"And he answered, Until the cities be wasted without inhabitant, and the houses without man, and the land be utterly desolate. And the Lord have removed men far away, and there be a great forsaking in the midst of the land."** Isaiah was giving this warning to the house of Judah to warn them of their soon coming destruction that is a mirror warning of today. The term "forsaking in the midst of the land" is speaking also of the term "in the land of the living" mentioned in Jeremiah 11:19 where the word land is referring to the house of Israel that was planted by God in their own land within the wilderness (Eze 34:13, 36:17&24, 37:14&21 and Jerm 23:8). Due to sin and defiance, the great blessings given to the house of Israel (Christian nations) is now turned into judgment due to national sin. Isaiah 5:13 states that the house of Israel had already been taken captive in ancient days because of the lack of knowledge which is also a mirror prophecy of soon coming destruction in the end days. We need to keep in mind that this Warning was to their present time but the ultimate warning is to the end time Church. If you closely study these verses that speak of the cities being totally destroyed to the point that man cannot enter would indicate a nuclear or biological destruction and radiation poisoning.

Jeremiah 9:13-16 & 22 also gives an account of coming destruction, **"Behold, I will feed them even this people, with wormwood, and give them water of gall to drink"**. The Hebrew meaning of wormwood is to curse, poisonous, hemlock or bitter. The Greek meaning is to shout for help in a tumultuous way, to cry. These are just a few verses in the Scriptures that indicate a destructive war and punishment in the last days or during the time of WRATH. There is a theory that the leaders of the New World Order want to depopulate the earth by 90 percent from the current eight plus billion down to 500 million. This will be accomplished through genetic engineering, Nuclear and Bio warfare and a scenario that corresponds to Jeremiah 9:13-22, **"Even the carcases of men shall fall as dung upon the open field, and as the handful after the harvestman, and none shall gather them"**, Jeremiah 4:29, **"every city shall be forsaken, and not a man dwell therein"**.

Jerusalem will not be destroyed for God will not allow that to happen but according to the Scriptures, the cities of Israel will be destroyed. Who are and where are these cities? The Arabs, the Anti-Christ and the Jews want Jerusalem and the surrounding cities for their own control and certainly will not destroy it with any type of weapon producing mass destruction. God would not allow that to occur for he needs to establish his throne in power when he comes. I do not believe God would allow his Holy City of Jerusalem to be destroyed. The cities that are destroyed within the Scriptures are speaking of the cities of the house of Israel located within the western Christian nations of Great Britain and the United States, exactly where the weapons of North Korea, China and Russia are pointed. The American Coalition represents a threat to the Communist and Arab nations, not the small nation of modern Israel.

We truly need to seek our God for salvation and pray for individual repentance as well as for our nation. This great nation needs to bow down before God and turn back to his laws of righteousness and eradicate Liberal Relativism from our land before he brings judgment upon us. The Scriptures above clearly indicates a soon coming destruction of our cities and the end of our way of life.

We the People held accountable

This chapter is a warning to our nation of the soon coming destruction due to national sins of immoralities and forgetting our God. We must recognize that the people of a nation are held responsible for the sins of the King or the government of that nation. In the case of the United States, we vote our leaders into office, so the American people are directly accountable for the actions of the government. Throughout the Scriptures, God always held the Israelite people responsible for their evil Kings, Gods Kingdom on earth. The population of our nation is no different for God established the United States (His Kingdom) for one purpose, to spread his end time Gospel. Our Declaration of Independence, Preamble, and Constitution is based on "We the People" exalting God as our creator. We will be held accountable for our national sins in Gods Judgment. The United States has turned from a righteous nation to a Liberal Socialist nation in just the past fifty years. Read Isaiah chapter 32:5-8 on how God feels about a vile liberal. The liberal movement with their agenda in the past fifty years has destroyed the family, businesses, Governmental, Religious, moral and ethical values of this nation. In the past thirty years we have killed forty million of God's children through abortion; taken God and prayer out of our schools, public buildings, the Government and court rooms; promoted same sex marriages and perversion; pornography; turned children against their parents; rendered the Constitution of this great nation obsolete and vanquished the moral, honest ethical values of our forefathers. We will be held accountable when our sins are full.

At this very moment, the homosexual movement is infiltrating our nation's schools teaching our children the damming sin that their life style is normal. It has permeated our society to the point that normal people along with Christians have fallen for their lies to the point that they are beginning to think this life style is OK. We are labeled as racist or bigots if we fail to agree or accept their life style of death and disease that defy the natural laws of reproduction as survival of the species. Now that God and the Bible is basically taken out of the way, they can implement their evil ideology of homosexuals. God's truth by the Scriptures, are being totally ignored and done away with. This is our only defense against this degenerate sin. We are quickly approaching the sinful level of Sodom and Gomorrah and we know the end result of those two cities. If we continue to accept homosexual activity as a normal life style as a nation as fail to repent of these sins, we will see the same destruction.

How do you destroy a world class Christian Society? First you take God and his Word out of Society and then teach the young boys and girls that homosexual activity is normal through their education system. This stagnates a national population growth and implements disease and death preventing a healthy growth of Society. You teach liberalism and open the borders to all nations allowing them rights as citizens to our Social Programs. This destroys our medical and Social Systems from within and bankrupts the nation. The influence of immigrants quickly changes the moral, ethical, and religious principles of the nation eliminating hundreds of years of Christian traditions and values. This is exactly what is happening to our nation and is working very quickly. Their agenda is obvious if we only open our eyes to the truth. This is the program of the center core of the Liberal Democratic Leaders of our nation for they know the destruction of the United States has to occur before the New World Order can be implemented which are their final goal.

Every great civilization such as the Greek and Roman Empires failed due to basically one reason, immorality. Under the ideology of moral relativism, moral, immoral and a-moral values are irrelevant allowing truth of morals to be immaterial. This is the Liberals excuse to indulge in sin without judgment. Morales of a nation is the fiber of their social, economic, religious and governmental systems. When the morals of a nation fail, the system fails and we as Americans must understand this fact if we are to survive as a Republic. Moral truths are absolute and must be maintained if we are to remain a strong nation. If we repent as a nation for our national sins, God will heal our land (II Chron 7:14).

WW III Jihad (Holy war between Russia/Muslim and Christianity)

In light of what is happening within current world events, it is obvious, to the normal bystander, that a war between the Russian/Muslim extremist and the western Christian nations is inevitable. World War III or the Palestinian war is documented very well within the Scriptures and this segment will prove that fact. The battle of Jehoshaphat is recorded in Joel 3:2, Ezekiel 38:1-11 and Isaiah 34:6-7 as the bull (United States) and unicorn (Great Britain) and is the battle that takes place in the valley of Hamongog in Ezekiel 39:11. The war mentioned all through the book of Isaiah refers to World War III at the beginning of the seven year period of Judgment strictly dealing with judgment on the house of Israel and Judah (Isa 11:14, 13:4). Armageddon is the last battle at the end of the seven-year period of Wrath that judges the Anti-Christ and his followers. The war in the valley of Hamangog recorded in Ezekiel 39:11 is the same war in Micah 5:1 and 7-15 that occur at the beginning of the Tribulation.

The current Palestinian and Israeli issue in the Middle East over the west bank and Gaza strip will be the area of the flash point and the Bible calls the modern Palestinian's, Palestina, Philista and Philistine. In Hebrew, the word Palestina means, the west coast of Canaan, rolling, migratory, a region of Syria, to roll in dust and roll (wallow) self. Philista means, land of the Philistia and Philistine means, an inhabitant of Philistia. The Palestinian problem dates back thousands of years and deep rooted in extreme hatred between the two sons of Abraham, Ishmael and Isaac. The current war with Iraq and the coming war with Iran, stems from the Palestinian terrorist problem in the Middle East. The story is recorded in Genesis chapter sixteen and seventeen.

The fact that the United States is determined to destroy terrorism and turning Iraq into a democracy could very well trigger the Palestinian war mentioned above. All the verses relating to God gathering and planting his people in the wilderness within a safe peaceful land can in no way be speaking of the promised land of Canaan due to all the hatred that has been documented in the past 3500 years surrounding Palestine. This peaceful dwelling place can be found in Jeremiah 23:6, 32:37, 33:16, Ezekiel 28:26, 34:25&28, 38:8,11&14, and 39:26. The Scriptures are clear that Isaac was to receive the great blessing of receiving the promised land, not Ishmael (Gen 16:11-16, 17:19-22) and Isaac were to be the covenant people of God for their name is to be called after their seed of Isaac's sons or Saxon (Gen 21:12, Heb 11:18). Satan has emulated the Muslim religion to counteract Gods Covenant with Israel allowing this problem to occur in the last days just as the Bible has foretold. The Muslim Religion and the ideology of communism (The Red Horse) were developed in the last days to destroy Christianity and establish Lucifer's world system.

There are two distinct major wars recorded to take place during the Tribulation Period. The first battle takes place at the beginning of this seven-year period in the valley of Hamon-Gog (Ezekiel chapter 38 and 39 and Dan 11:40-45) for the purpose of bringing judgment upon the house of Israel and Judah due to national sin. This war establishes the Anti-Christ into power at the middle of the Trib. and destroys the Palestinian Arab and Russian coalition along with the fallen away western Christian culture. The first war occurs due to religious hatreds between Christianity, Islam, atheist and nihilism. This war causes so much destruction creating an extreme distain for organized religion that the world leader is able to change age old traditions of times and laws (Dan 7:25). The changing of these laws creates a great religious void and allows the Anti-Christ to step in and proclaim himself as god, the Apotheosis in the middle of the seven-year period. This battle occurs at the beginning of the Tribulation period for it takes the Israelites seven years to burn their weapons (Eze 39:9). The battle of Hamon-God could very well be the war against terrorism where President Bush invaded Iraq and in time triggers the war where God destroys the house of Israel and their cities (Mic 5:14) as a punishment for falling away from his commandments. The event of 09-11 in New York City could very well be the precursor of World War III. The second war is the Battle of Armageddon that occurs seven years later, at the end of the period of Wrath and is the war of all wars, (Rev 16:16). This war is not against the Children of Israel but to bring final judgment upon the wicked people of the world. It takes place at the end of the seven-year Tribulation just prior to the return of Christ in power claiming his throne in Jerusalem.

The Old Testament prophetic books are laced with warnings of destruction to the cities of Israel in the last days (Isa 24:12, Jerm 4:29, 15:8, Mic 5:14 and II Esdras 15:15-19 "Apocrypha"). First, we must understand the division of Israel in our present day to know the identification of the true Israel. This war could very well be the Judgment of the destruction of our cities due to present day immoralities mentioned in the previous segment. According to Genesis 48:16, the name Israel was given only to Ephraim and Manasseh, the Bull and Unicorn, as the house of Israel which is modern day England and the United States. The cities of Israel being destroyed would be the cities of the western culture, the Common Wealth of Great Britain and the United States. This war is recorded in Isaiah 34:6-10 where Britain is the unicorns and the United States the bullocks. Bozrah, Seir and Idumea are the Communist Bloc nations of Eastern Europe as outlined within the chart in chapter 7, Tracing Ancient names of the house of Israel. Verse 9-10 speaks of the nuclear war that destroys our cities.

The Scriptures are clear on an end time war that destroys Israel's cities prior to God coming in power. To better understand why this occurs, we must read and study Leviticus chapter 26 and Deuteronomy 28 for why God brings punishment to his nations for disobedience of his laws. We must also remember that modern day Israel is the house of Judah and not the whole house of Israel.

The inheritance blessing under the primogeniture law gave Ephraim (Ephratah Mic 5:2) the leadership of the house of Israel (ten northern tribes) and received the family name Israel above Judah, the Jews. It is recorded in Micah 5:1-2 placing Ephratah (Ephraim) above Judah as leader of the troops which is Gods battle ax and army as in Jeremiah 51:19-20.

Because of Gods inheritance law (Gen 48:16, I Chron 5:1-2) the cities of Israel that is destroyed during the up-coming war of Jacobs trouble would be the cities of the house of Israel in the wilderness (US and GB), not the cities of modern Israel as we all think. Why would Satan want to destroy Jerusalem for that is where he plans to establish his earthly Headquarters? When you study just where the nuclear missiles of China and Russia are pointed, it is not toward Israel but the United States and Great Britain. We as the house of Israel (Gods Battle Ax) are his main threat, not the small nation of Modern Israel. This answers a lot of Scriptural questions.

According to Chronicles 5:1-3, the firstborn or the chosen inheritance was to receive his kingdom; therefore, Ephraim and Manasseh became leader of the largest part of Gods kingdom receiving the double portion. They received the total kingdom when Jesus rebuked the Jews in Matthew 21:43, giving the complete kingdom to the house of Israel to be led by Ephraim, England. They were given the responsibility of maintaining the family name of Israel as recorded in Genesis 48:16 and the kingdom in I Kings 11:11-13 in approx. 992 BC to be completely overturned in Matthew 21:43, approx. 30AD, to Ephraim and Manasseh. King David 's throne was overturned to England (Eze 21:25-27, 17:21-24).

Now let's review Scripture that documents the soon coming Palestinian war. First, we must identify the difference between the battle of Jehoshaphat mentioned in Joel 3:2, the battle in the valley of Hamon Gog (Eze 39:11&15) and the battle of Armageddon (Rev 16:16). The battle of Jehoshaphat and Hamon Gog are the same war that brings Gods judgment upon the house of Israel and Judah. This war occurs at the beginning of Daniel's 70th week or seven-year prophecy for Ezekiel 39:9 states that it takes the people of the cities seven years to burn their weapons. This indicates that it begins at the beginning of Daniel 's prophecy. The Hebrew word Jehoshaphat means; a place of Judgment. There is no ancient Biblical record of the valley of Jehoshaphat for in the 4th century AD it was named the Kidron Valley. Jehoshaphat is believed to be a symbolic valley where all the nations of Israel is gathered by Jehovah for judgment. The Hebrew meaning of Armageddon means to pluck or to gather and this is the gathering of all heathen nations for Gods judgment. The battle of Armageddon is not nation fighting nation but all nations gather to fight God at the pouring of the 6th Vial in Rev 16:12-16. Read it closely.

The war that takes place in the valley of Hamon Gog occurs at the very beginning of Daniel's seven-year prophecy for two main reasons. The first is to punish the house of Israel (Christian nations) that has been left behind after the taking of the Church due to their falling away from Gods covenant. The second is to show the world that he is God the Almighty and for his people to accept his truth (Eze 39:22&28). The Church will be taken away (I Thes 4:14-17) prior to the nuclear war and the beginning of Wrath for I Thessalonians 1:10 and 5:9 clearly states that his Church will not see his Wrath on the wicked, **"even Jesus, which delivered us from the wrath to come."** and **"For God hath not appointed us to wrath but to obtain salvation"**. Couple these verses with Jasher 5:5 where God took all that followed him before the flood, **"And all who followed the Lord died in those days, before they saw the evil which God declared to do upon earth"**. God will not allow his people (the Church) to see the Wrath he brings upon the wicked in the last days of Tribulation. Another aspect to consider is why 12,000 from each tribe of Israel is sealed in Revelation 7:5-8 if the Church and Holy Spirit is still present on the earth. It makes no sense for all Christians in the Church already has the seal of the Holy Spirit. The 144,000 Hebrews and Jews are sealed because the Church and Holy Spirit has been taken away for the Anti-Christ cannot be revealed till the Church is gone (II Thessalonians 2:7). The Church age of the house of Israel and Daniel's 70th week or seven-year period of the house of Judah cannot overlap for it would interfere with Gods prophetic plans. The key is the removal of the Holy Spirit under the New Covenant and is why the 144,000 have to be sealed in the middle of the seven-year period. This is the fulfillment of the 70th week under the Old Covenant and to seal them as a protection or all will be killed by the Anti-Christ that don't take his MARK except the 144,000.

The Hebrew meaning of Gog and Hamon Gog is the same; a place East of the Dead Sea, the multitude of Gog, the fanciful name of an emblematic (symbolic) place in Palestine, a noise, tumult, crowd, wealth, abundance, company, rumbling, make a loud noise, to rage war, moan, clamor, consume, crush, to trouble and to vex. It is believed that the nation of Gog or Magog is the Russian and Communist (Anti-Christian) block coalition gathered against the house of Israel in the valley of Hamon Gog. The ancient name of Meschech found in Ezekiel 38:3 is believed to be modern Moscow in Russia. Do not fall for the lie that Communism is dead, for it plays a great role in this soon coming war as verified by Scripture. Hamon Gog is a place east of the Dead Sea and interesting to see that the tribe of Reuben (Modern France) and Moab of Edom is located due east of the Dead Sea as indicated on Biblical maps of ancient times. Ancient Reuben located east of the Dead Sea was a part of the lost tribes of the house of Israel that settled Europe and is now modern France. The Arab and Communist nations are called Edom in Ezekiel 25:12-16 where they have troubled Israel and Judah during the last days. The philosophy of Communism (Godless Religion) came from Reuben that is modern France and implemented by the nations of Edom, the Arab and Eastern European nations (Moab). This fulfills the Prophecy of the war mentioned in Ezekiel 38 and 39 and the firstborn inheritance feud between Ishmael (Islamic), Esau (Communism) and Jacob (Christian) culminating into the end time wars.

How does this war begin? I Thessalonians 5:3 tells us that, **"For when they shall say, Peace and safety; then sudden destruction cometh upon them,"**. This cannot be speaking of modern Israel (the house of Judah) for they are constantly vigilant against terrorism and war. This verse is speaking to the house of Israel (US and GB) for it perfectly matches the present state of the American and British people. We are at rest and ease that dwell safely (Eze 38:8&11) in un-walled cities for we believe our nation cannot be destroyed. Verse 8 speaks of the mountains or nations of Israel that was carved out of the wilderness or the continents of the world such as America, Australia, New Zealand and all the other colonization of the British Empire. In Hebrew, Abraham means High Father or colonizer indicating that we are the birthright tribes of Abraham's descent as world colonizers. The un-walled cities are the Christian nations in the world living in peace that dwell in safety on foreign continents across the vast oceans (Isa 16:8, Eze 27:4&24 and PS 80:11). We are presently at war with Iraq and the world is quickly aligning against us.

Something drastically changes in world politics with Russia and their coalition for Ezekiel 38:4 states, **"And I will turn thee back, and put hooks into thy jaws, and I will bring thee forth, and all thine army, horses and horsemen, all of them clothed with all sorts of armor, even a great company with bucklers and shields, all of them handling swords;"**. For an unspecified reason, Gog or Russia is quickly drawn into a mighty war according to the verse above. The next verse aligns Gog or Russia (Eastern bloc nations) with Persia (Arab nations), Ethiopia and Libya, which is the present coalition against Israel and the US in the Middle East of today. This verse is being fulfilled at this very moment. The above verse states that Gog, Magog and Tubal (Eastern Communist nations) will have hooks put into their jaw to cause them to go to war with the house of Israel (Christian Nations). This writer believes that the hook in their jaw is nothing more than political treaties between Russia and the Arab nations forcing them to go to war for Ezekiel 38:4 indicates a reluctance. The Hebrew word hooks mean to have a ring for the nose and is a way of guiding a domestic farm animal. Russia is drawn into this war due to politics along with their Arab coalition. The American war with Iraq and the coming war with Iran along with the Russian/Ukraine wars could very well be the hooks in the jaw of Gog and Magog, the catalyst for war. Russia supplies a vast amount of technical and military aid to Iraq and Iran with the intent of controlling their oil. They cannot allow Iraq or other Arab nations to become Democratic for they would lose political control in the region. Therefore, America's war with Iraq and Iran could very well trigger a massive confrontation with Russia and all the Arab nations as foretold in Ezekiel chapter 38 and 39. If we try to democratize Iraq or any nation in the Middle East that brings freedom of religion, this cannot be tolerated in the Muslim belief system and will cause an all-out war with the west.

The falling of Babylon mentioned in Revelation 18:2 where her great city is destroyed is the same war that destroys the cities of Israel in Ezekiel 38 and 39. The Babylon of Revelation chapter 18 is simply a symbolic name for it represents the same scale of wealth from the time of the Tower of Babel to King Nebuchadnezzar in ancient Babylon under the Baal religion. The Kings of Babylon controlled most of the wealth of the known ancient world just as the United States today through world banking and trade also fall under old Baal religion making the Western economic system the spiritual Mystery Babylon just as the book of Revelation state.

It is very important to have a full understanding of the identity of Mystery Babylon for it is a key in comprehending end time prophecy. Like many other Hebrew words, its identity lies within deep-rooted cross references found within the Strong's Concordance. This segment will change your perspective of Babylon's true identity. The Greek meaning comes from Revelation 18:2, (897) the capital of Chaldaea and literal or figurative as a type of **tyranny**. It is crossed referenced to (894) which means, **wormwood** as a type of bitterness or calamity (indicating war) and (895) Ezra 5:12, as being, lifeless, inanimate or mechanical without life. From (895) Babylon is crossed referenced to the most important in reference number (5590) indicating Babylon being spiritual for its meaning is; breath by <u>implying a spirit</u>, abstract or concretely from reference (4151) the rational and immortal soul; reference (5592 and 5594) indicate a coolness, cold or chill referring to wax cold (Matt 24:12) and (4151) a current of air, breath or a breeze, by analog or figurative <u>a spirit</u> of the human rational soul and implied as a superhuman, an angel, demon, divine God, Christ's Spirit and Holy Spirit. It is also crossed referenced to (2222) which means; life as living literal or figurative. Reference number (5590) also cross-reference to the Hebrew meaning given in (5315) "a breathing creature", ghost, mortally, soul, (7307) "breath" implying a spirit and (2416) "alive" a living thing. The words Spirit, wax cold, vex, Christ's Spirit and the Holy Spirit connects Babylon to the Church where the Spirit of the Church wax cold and lifeless as foretold in II Thessalonians 2:3. Prior to the removal of the Church in Revelation 18:23-24 verse 18 states, **"and the voice of the bride groom and of the bride shall be heard no more at all in thee"** meaning that at one time the Bride as the Church was in Mystery Babylon. The Hebrew meaning of Babylon is found in reference (894) meaning; confusion; Babel (Babylon) including the empire. It is then crossed referenced to (1101) meaning; primitive root; to overflow with oil; implies to mix, to fodder, anoint, confound, mingle and temper. It is then crossed referenced to (1098) which means feed for cattle, corn and fodder.

After a close study of all the above definitions and cross-reference, we come up with at least two main aspects of Babylon. One coming from the Hebrew meaning as being the physical city or empire representing the spirit of man under one single government and a polytheistic religion controlled by great wealth. Babylon is a symbol of great wealth from the nations of the earth and Spiritualism under Baal worship of many gods. This same religion can be seen in the World Council of Churches of today where all religions of many gods fall under one god that will culminate into Lucifer becoming god as the Apotheosis. By these definitions, Mystery Babylon as the western economic system of great wealth is a spirit of the old Baal religion of ancient Babylon.

The other aspect can be seen in the Greek definitions as being a symbolic meaning representing the modern spirit of man again indicating the ancient worship of Baal not the true God of Abraham. Baal worship has been passed from generation to generation never changing. By definition, Babylon is a spirit, breath, breeze, tyranny, immortal soul, cool-ness, wax cold, vex, angel or demon, divine Spirit of God and a living thing or soul. These definitions indicate how man's spirit will be manipulated by Satan and his demons to implement his final New World Order as Mystery Babylon, the world's economic system. All these aspects of the spirit of Babylon can be seen in our New Age Religions and Liberal Agenda promoted by the wealthy nations of the world just as in ancient days. The ideology and spirit of Babylon is slowly culminating into a one world government and religion just as the Tower of Babel almost 6000 years ago. History is repeating itself just as the Bible predicts.

There is another aspect that we need to consider. God brought judgment upon the people of Mesopotamia due to their pride by eliminating God for they wanted to build a stairway to heaven without including God. God brought judgment by confusing their language (Babel). Today this same ideology that man can become god himself is the same as ancient Babylon. It is simply a symbolic name of an age-old religion. God is going to bring judgment upon this organized religion (Liberalism) just as in ancient days but this time it is going to burn as recorded in Revelation chapter 18. Key Words within the definition such as, wormwood, calamity, vex and tyranny indicate a great war where God brings this judgment as recorded throughout the Bible. Revelation 18:23 states that the spirit of the light of a candle and the Bride of Christ which is the Church was no more in Babylon indicating that Babylon has to be the wealthy Christian nations of the west, United States and the British Empire. The Spirit of the Church is indicated within the definition of Babylon recorded above as a divine Spirit. That divine Spirit was taken over by a demonic spirit when the Church was removed in Revelation 18:23, therefore, Lucifer declares himself as god in the middle of the Tribulation Period.

Let's make a simple deduction. What single modern city controls most of the world's wealth of our modern time? What stock market manipulates every stock market in the world, therefore, controlling all the wealth of the world? It is the New York City Stock Exchange, the Bull of Wall Street controlled by the United State, Manasseh as the Bull (Duet 33:17). This can be proven by Revelation 18:23-24, **"And the light of a candle shall shine no more at all in thee (Babylon); and the voice of the bride groom and of the bride shall be no more at all in thee: for thy merchants were the great men of the earth; for by thy sorceries were all nations deceived."** According to this verse, Babylon at one time possessed the Church, the voice (Holy Spirit) candlestick and Bride of Christ, but before it was destroyed, the Church and Spirit have been taken out of her. Babylon is the house of Israel possessing great wealth that the Church is in but fell form Gods Covenant and grace, the great falling away, bringing judgment. Babylon represents the political and financial institutions of the world that is presently destroying the Church through liberalism and is not of God. The term, **"for thy merchants were the great men of the earth"**, indicate that Babylon symbolize the capitalistic system of the free world controlled by Ephraim and Manasseh as the Birthright tribes. The great wealth of the United States and Great Britain was Christian at one time but the power of Lucifer the Devil infiltrated our system by turning it into Mystery Babylon through Liberal Socialist Communism, Political Correctness and has totally corrupted our Christian nation.

The atheistic Communist nations of Eastern Europe, the oriental nations of Buda, the Eastern Mystic nations of India and the growing religion of Islam controlled by the Arab nations make up the majority of the nations of the earth. None of these nations has embraced or practiced Christ's Gospel of his true Church for his Spirit to be in them. The Babylon of Revelation 18:23 can only be the wealthy Christian nations of the west for this verse specifically states that Gods Spirit of the Church was in it before he destroyed its system.

The people of the house of Israel and other nations were deceived by sorceries of Satan's human agents where they penetrated governments through the massive wealth of huge Corporations. We must understand that God blessed the United States as a people first and then as a nation because of our righteousness. The government is not necessarily the will of the people for the nihilist has taken over our government. Note in Revelation 18:23 that when this war occurs, the candle and Bridegroom is gone from Babylon or Gods righteous people (the Church) has been taken out or raptured. Many Christians do not believe there is going to be a taking or Rapture at the beginning or in the middle of the seven-year period of John and Daniel's seven-year prophecy of Tribulation. They simply do not understand the timeline as outlined within this segment.

Two thousand years ago when Satan realized he could not stop the coming of the Messiah, he then tried to destroy the Church and Gods Battle Ax (the house of Israel Jeremiah 51:19-20), his inherited birthright tribes of Ephraim and Manasseh. Satan also knew that he could not physically destroy either but could slowly tear down by infiltrating from within using Secret Societies and organizations. The establishing of Secret Societies, philosophies, religion and evil governments within nations has all but completed his task. The term Babylon is used to indicate the same ancient sorceries used to destroy Babylon that is used to destroy and deceive nations of modern times as Revelation 18:23 states. Huge Corporations controlled by just a few families within the world have implemented Satan's agenda through the accumulation of great wealth. These families worship Lucifer as their religion with a final goal to place Lucifer (Satan) into power as the Apotheosis under a single world government, the New World Order called the Beast System. They truly believe that Lucifer, the Angel of Light, is the true god and Savior, not Satan or Christ. To them, Satan don't exist for Lucifer is their god. Their infiltration can be seen on the back of the American one-dollar bill (Babylon of the all-seeing eye) by the Latin term, "Novus Ordo Seclorum", New World Order written at the base of the Pyramid under the observance of Lucifer's all-seeing eye, lamination of the Illuminati. Their intent is to use the One Dollar bill to create a tax base financed by the American people so they can establish their one world system. When they have used Babylon (Capitalism) to establish their system, it will no longer be needed and its destruction is necessary just as Revelation chapter 18 predicts. The new world economic system will be implemented through the United Nations paid for by the American tax payer, the one dollar bill "Novus Ordo Seclorum ".

There is one more aspect that we need to consider in light of Lucifer (Satan) becoming the world leader and proclaiming himself as god. Understand that Satan has been planning this event for approx. 6000 years and has laid out a brilliant plan channeled to his human children or agents. For Satan to claim himself as world leader, he has to destroy the current world powers such as all Monarchs (Kings), American, Russian and China as world super powers. China will be factored in at a later date. To proclaim himself as god (the Apotheosis) he has to destroy fundamental religions such as Christianity, Atheism and Islam. All the other passive and progressive religions will conform to his new religious system due to massive death and destruction created by WW III. This war has multiple purposes for Lucifer to be placed into power. Ezekiel 38 and 39 says that the Russian coalition destroys the house of Israel and then in turn Gods power, to prove that he is the Almighty, destroys Russia and his coalition. For the benefit of the Anti-Christ, this destroys the American coalition of Christianity, the Arab nations of the Islamic Religion and the Russian coalition of Atheism, eliminating the world's major fundamental Religions.

The war that occurs in the valley of Jehoshaphat and Hamongon eliminates the world-class powers of America, Britain, Arab and Russian/China coalitions along with the influence of Christianity, Islam and Atheism. This allows the Anti-Christ to take power for the Spirit of the Church and the strength of Christianity will be taken away (Ruptured) just prior to this Great War.

To sum up this segment, there are a few dynamic chapters in Ezekiel that should be considered. The whole book of Ezekiel deserves to be closely studied for it is a progression of how God established the nation of Israel in the wilderness of their own land and overturned his throne from Jerusalem to the house of Israel within the wilderness. This can be seen in chapter 17 through 22. Chapters 34 through 39 is a walk-through time concerning the prophecies of Israel from the time they became a nation in ancient times till the last days of the time of Tribulation. This is the war of their judgment due to breaking Gods Covenant.

Chapter 34 explains how the house of Israel is scattered into the wilderness to establish Christ's Church for verse 23 states, **"And I will set up one shepherd over them, and he shall feed them, even my servant David; he shall fed them and he shall be their shepherd."** This verse places King David's throne in the wilderness under Gods New Covenant of the Church spoken of in Hebrew 8:8 and Jeremiah 31:31 where the throne was overturned to England in Ezekiel 21:25-27.

Chapter 35 is the warning to the mountains or nations of Seir that is a region south of the Dead Sea called Idumaea and its aboriginal occupants. It is this writer's belief through study that Idumaea is the descendants of Esau (the Red Baby) of Edom and Moab that became the Communist bloc nations of Russia (Red Communism of the Red Horse Rev 6:4). They call their elective legislative assembly of the lower house of parliament the Duma indicating their connection to Idumaea. This chapter is a warning of their godless evilness and soon coming destruction as predicted in Ezekiel chapter 38.

Chapter 36 is the warning to the mountains or nations of the house of Israel (Ephraim GB and Manasseh US) of their soon coming judgment and destruction. Verse 8 speaks of how Israel will shoot forth branches and be fruitful (Christian) to be tilled and sown and verse 17 state they shall dwell in their own land where they defile and pollute, turn against Gods Covenant. Verse 24-27 establishes the Church in the wilderness where the house of Israel is gathered into their own land from all countries of the world. They are given a new heart and Spirit where Gods Spirit is given them so they can keep his statutes and judgments. This can only be Christ's Gospel and Church. These verses are not speaking to the Jews of modern Israel but the Christian nations of the world. Verse 33 and 34 shows how the house of Israel will be given their own land and cities to dwell and how they came from the land that lay desolate and became as the Garden of Eden. This is their colonization of the desolate continents of the world given to the house of Israel to fulfill the promise of greatness to be nations and kingdoms given as a birthright to Ephraim and Manasseh. Just look at the great wealth the desolate continents have produced in the past 300 years and most of these lands are Christian, fulfilling Gods promise of greatness. Verse 38 calls these waste cities in the wilderness Jerusalem just as it has a duel meaning. Jerusalem is filed with flocks of men that know the Lord. In no way can this verse be speaking of the modern city of Jerusalem as the Jews for they still reject Christ their Savior.

At this point in time, the Church have been taken away by Christ so the Marriage Supper of the Lamb can take place in Heaven and the war of Ezekiel chapter 38 and 39 begins. This war is the judgment of the wicked house of Israel and Judah, not a part of Christ's Church that has been taken away by the Rapture. Read and study these two chapters for details of the soon coming war that is on the verge of occurring due to the Palestinian problem and possibly the war of Iraq and the US trying to democratize the Middle East.

__Bible references__

Ps 46, Eze 35, mount Seir- descendants of Edom or Esau the land of Seir or Edom Gen 14:6, Duet 2:1, 12, Josuah 15:1, Judges 11:17-18, I Kg 9:26. Connection to Palestinian and communist Edom, Isaiah 17:1 Damascus destroyed along with cities of Aroer Moabites. II Esdras 8:50&56 and 15:15-19.

Signs from Heaven	I Thes 5:3
Matt 16:1-3 signs of the times	Isa 13:6-9
Dan 12:1-3 time of Trouble	23:1-14, 24:6
Jude saving of all Israel	Cities Destroyed
Dan 12:4 signs travel, knowledge	Isa 24:1-&12
Matt 24:6-7 Wars and rumors of war	Jerm 4:29, 15:8
21:22 then great tribulation	Eze 9:4-9 destruction
Rev 6:3-4	of people in cities
Comfort from desolation Pro 3:25-26	26:18-19
WW III Ex 15:14, Isa 14:29 and 31	Isa 34:6-7
Philista - land of the Philistia	Eze 38:1-11
Ps 60:8, 87:4, 108:9	

Table One

Definitions

Understanding the Hebrew meaning of Old Testament names, places, nations and words, can help unravel the puzzle and mystery of God's prophetic Scriptures. As we have covered in chapter five, the Hebrew language is connected to almost all known languages on earth. Thousands of English words have a derivative to the Hebrew language. God uses symbols and parables to illustrate his prophetic meaning by using certain key words. When we can recognize and properly place the Hebrew meaning of these words, we can begin to disentangle his prophetic puzzle. This segment is just a few key words to put us on the road to solving Gods mysteries that he has placed before us. If we can understand Gods Biblical words by their root, prime, primitive and secondary meanings along with the figurative, non-figurative and literal aspects, his mystery can be revealed. It is astounding how the precision of the puzzle all fits together as we search out the meaning of his Word through the Hebrew Language.The reference numbers are based on Hebrew and Greek meanings of the New Strong's Exhaustive Concordance of the Bible, Copyright 1995 by James Strong, 1822-1894. A Hebrew word can have many meanings and the reference numbers in the Concordance will take you through the prime root, unused root, figurative, nonfigurative and literal circumstance and likeness of other words. The Secrets of God's Word is revealed in how the primary and secondary root meaning is laced and woven together. To understand the full meaning, we need to exhaustively seek all the aspects of the word in subject, for the secrets of Gods Scriptures are hidden deep within. The definitions and synopsis of the following words are more in definition form than in literary form. Words **highlighted in bold** has a significant meaning.

The following important key Biblical words are listed in alphabetical order by Hebrew and Greek definition followed by a brief synopsis:

Abram	Fruitful	Plant
Abraham	Gilead	Remnant
Adam	Hiram	Scattered
Anointed	Hebrew	Sharon
Ariel	Highway	Shiloh
Asshur	Inheritance	Sifted
Barbarian	Isle or Island	Sirion
Bashan	Isaac	Solomites
Bough	Israel	Stone
Bozrah	Jacob	Tyrus
Branch	Jew	Unicorn
Carmel	Last Days	Vineyard
Covenant	Lebanon	Wayfaring Man
Dispersed	Lost Sheep	Waymarks
Eagle	Man	Wilderness
East	Manasseh	Zarah or Zara
Eber	Mountain	Zion or Sion
Edom	Pharez	
Ephraim	Phoenicians	

Note: To complete the definitions of the following words, it will be necessary to requote many Scriptures and elaborate on information already given in other segments. It will help to fortify the memory. Underlined words have an expounded meaning to the subject word.

Abram: "abrum" (87) High father; Abram, the original name of Abraham: (48) "abiyram" father of height (i.e. lofty) refer to (1) "ab" a prime word; father in a literal and immediate or figurative and remote application, patrimony, principal, Comp, names in "Abi": (7311) "ruwm" a prime root; to be high, act, to rise or raise (in various applications, literal or figurative); bring up, exalt (self); extol, give, to up, haughty, heave (up), (be, lift up on, make on, set up on, too) high (-er, one), hold up, levy, lift (-er) up, (be) lofty; loud, mount up, offer (up); presumptuously, (be) promote (-ion), proud, set up, tall (-er), take (away, off, up), breed worms.

Synopsis- Abram was selected by God to be the High Father of his chosen people, the Hebrew. He was never a Jew and given the original birthright to be many fruitful Christian nations as Kings of Kingdoms (Gen 17:6, 22:17,28:14, 35:11 and 48:19). Abraham and his descendants were to exalt themselves just as the Hebrew tribes of the Gauthie and Goths were called "the people of God". This blessing was passed to Isaac for the seed of the birthright to be named after Isaac or Isaac sons as Anglo Saxon. The word Anglo is derived from the Latin word angle that means hook shape after a fishhook and the descendants of the Germanic people that migrated from Sleswick to Britain. The term Saxon by the American College Dictionary also list them as English-speaking Germanic tribes that settled England around the 5th and 6th century AD. The English people became known as the Anglo-Saxon as one who belongs to the English-speaking world. The Latin word Angle is very similar to the Hebrew word Angel which means messenger or ambassador and could very well be a part of the Hebrew tribes that migrated across the Caucus Mountains after the Assyrian and Babylonian captivities that became the Caucasian people of Europe.

The birthright blessing was passed from Isaac to Jacob where his name was changed to Israel which has a Hebrew meaning of, "he will rule as God" or "mighty as God". Jacob passed this blessing directly to Ephraim and Manasseh in a dual role through Joseph their father where the name Israel was passed only to them and no other sons or tribes. They were to be nations and kingdoms as listed in the verses above and have fulfilled Gods promise of greatness as his bow and Battle Ax. They were to rule the nations in righteousness and judgment under the New Covenant, to rule his earthly kingdom as God till his coming as the Anglo-Saxon English-speaking nations of the western Christian culture. This matches the Hebrew meaning of Angel as angle-land or England where the birthright tribe is responsible to spread Christ's end time Gospel as Gods messenger or ambassador to the world. Only Great Britain and the United States can be credited with spreading the end time Gospel of the Church to the world through the English translation of the King James Bible.

The Jews of Judah did not receive the Birthright to be "a great nation" of Manasseh the bull (USA) or "a company of nations" of Ephraim the unicorn (GB) as recorded in Genesis 35:11 and Deuteronomy 33:17. Study Genesis chapters 48 and 49 for the birthright blessings.

Abraham: (85) "abraham" unused root; to be populous; father of a multitude; Abraham, the later name of Abram. (11) "Abaddown" abstruct; a perishing; Hades-destruction. (6) "abad" primitive root; to wander away, to lose oneself; to imply to parish, break, destroy or destruction, not escape, fail, lose, be void.

*Synopsis- **Ab**- (father) **ra**- (ruling) **ham**-(multitude)* Abraham was to be the father of the ruling multitude of the world, God's chosen race of people, the Hebrew. Genesis 12:2-3 **"and in thee shall all families of the earth be blessed"**, Genesis 22:17-18 **"and thy seed shall possess the gate of his enemies"**. The word Gate in Hebrew means, city, door, gate, port, and gatekeeper. The families of Abraham which became the Hebrew Christian nations, Great Britain (Ephraim) and the United States (Manasseh), has controlled all major sea ports and trade routes in the past five hundred years and the only nation to ever fulfill these verses. The promise of greatness to Abraham, Isaac and Jacob has been fulfilled, for all nations have been blessed by the abundant wealth bestowed by God's Christian nations (Gen 26:3-4).

Abraham was to pass the family blessing of greatness down to Isaac and then to Jacob (Gen 28:1-4). God changed Jacob's name to Israel in Gen 32:28, therefore, changing the family name to Israel. The Hebrew family became Hebrew Israelites and Jacob passed the family name, birthright and inheritance to Joseph's two sons, Ephraim and Manasseh (Gen 48:16-22), **"The Angel which redeemed me from all evil, bless the lads; and let my name be named on them, and the name of my fathers Abraham and Isaac; and let them grow into a multitude in the midst of the earth" "and his seed shall become a multitude of nations" "Moreover I have given to thee one portion above thy brethren, which I took out of the hand of the Amorite with my sword and with my bow"**. The birthright name of Israel and double portion did not go to Reuben the firstborn or to Judah but to Joseph and his two sons Ephraim and Manasseh in verse 16 and 22.

I Chronicles 5:1-2 tells us, **"Now the sons of Reuben the firstborn of Israel, (for he was the firstborn; but, forasmuch as he defiled his father's bed, his birthright was given unto the sons of Joseph the son of Israel: and the genealogy is not to be reckoned after the birthright. For Judah prevailed above his brethren, and of him came the chief ruler; but the birthright was Joseph's"**. This makes it clear that the birthright blessings and the family name went to Joseph (Ephraim and Manasseh) and not to Judah or the Jews. Genesis 22:17-18, **"That is blessing I will bless thee, and in multiplying I will multiply thy seed as the stars of the heaven, and as the sand which is upon the sea shore; and thy seed shall possess the gate of his enemies: And in thy seed shall all the nations of the earth be blessed: because thou hast obeyed my voice"**. These verses can only pertain to the brothers of Great Britain and the United States (Ephraim and Manasseh), the only countries in the past two thousand years that fulfills that promise. In Hebrew, the word gate means, an opening (door or gate), city, door, gate, port. Great Britain and the United States as brothers has controlled and dominated all major seaports and trade routes through-out the world for the past five hundred years. This fulfills God promise of greatness.

Adam: First man created by God: (120) "Adam" ruddy, i.e. a human being (an individual or the species, mankind, etc.); another; hypocrite; common sort; low, man (mean, of low degree); person: (119) "Adam" to show blood (in the face), i.e. flush or turn rosy; be (dyed, made) red (ruddy): (121) Adam the name of the first man, also of a place in Palestine: (76)"ababuah" from an unused root (mean. to belch forth); an inflammatory pustule (as eruption); blains.

Synopsis - Man is made in God's image of flesh and blood that is the essence of life. His face is flush red, rosy, or ruddy and due to his sins, his salvation is represented through blood sacrifice of first animals and then Christ himself. Gods Covenant with his people Israel, Exodus 24:8, was baptized by animal blood. God's new Covenant representing his Church, baptized with water purified by Christ's blood on the cross, Heb 12:24, 13:20. Man is a symbol of blood, ruddy, rosy or red and is the color of his nature. This is why Communism chose crimson or red as their color for it is the color of Humanism, the Biblical color of man.

Anointed: (4886) "mashach" a prime root; to rub with oil, i.e. to anoint; to consecrate; also to paint: (4888) "mishchah" unction (the act), by implying a consecratory gift, (to be) anointed (-ing), ointment: (4899) "mashiyach" anointed; usually a consecrated person (as a king, priest, or saint); specifically the Messiah: (5480) "cuwk" a prime root; to smear over (with oil), i.e. anoint (self), at all: (5550) "collah" a military mound, i.e. rampart of besiegers; bank, mount: (5549) "calal" a prime root; to mound up (especially a turnpike); figurative to exalt; to oppose (as by a dam); cast up, exalt (self), extol, make plain, raise up: (1101) "balal" a prime root; to overflow (specially with oil); by implying, to mix; to fodder; anoint, confound, fade, mingle, mix (self), give provender, temper: (4473) "mimshach" in the sense of expansion; outspread **(i.e. with outstretched wings) anointed**: (1121) "ben" a son (as a builder of the family name), **grandson, nation, firstborn, very fruitful**, steward, stranger, young, youth: (3323) "yitshar" oil (as producing light); anointed oil: (2025) "harel" the alter of burnt offering. This definition is also found in the humanistic ideology of Communism, the red baby of Esau and philosophy of communism or Humanism of Man, the color of red.

Synopsis - God always anointed in a ceremony with authority by his priest, with oil, anything that was sacred or Holy to him. Anointed also means fruitful and olive which is a symbol of Gods righteousness or Christian nations, reference (8081). The olive tree is a symbol of Gods House. Reference number (1061) indicates that anointed is symbolic to the first fruits of the crop and represents the birthright by Hebrew Law, Exodus 22:29, Num 3:13. Ephraim and Manasseh were anointed as the birthright tribe and received the rights thereof, Gen 48:20. The single most precious item ever anointed by God, other than his son Jesus, was the stone of Bethel, Gen 35:14-15. Jacob anointed the stone pillar of Bethel which means house of God, Gen 31:13, and was later taken by Jacob into Egypt and kept in a sacred place within the Temple. It also has Hebrew meanings of, a house especially family, primitive root to obtain children. Israel carried the stone through the desert on the wilderness sojourn of 40 years where Moses struck and spoke to the rock (Jacobs Pillar Gen 28:18) for life saving water (Exodus 17:6 and Num 20:8). The water that came from the rock or the stone of Bethel in the wilderness represented Christ's water of Salvation. The stone of Bethel is a symbol of God's Children of Israel and of Christ, I Peter 2:4-5, **"To whom coming, as unto a living stone"**. Christians are called living stones, **"Ye also, as lively stones, are built up a spiritual house"**. This Bethel stone that was used for Jacob's pillow, Gen 28:18-22, is a stone 26 3/4 inches long, 16 3/4 inches wide and 10 3/4 inch deep and every King of Israel, Ireland, Scotland and England has been coroneted on the stone. The stone is a symbol of not only the Children of Israel but of King David's throne. Jeremiah's commission, Jerm 1:10, was to destroy the old and to plant and build the new overturned Kingdom to a fruitful land in the wilderness. When the last King of Israel fell to Babylon, King Zedekiah in 586 BC, Jeremiah took not only King Zedekiah's two daughters but also the Stone of Bethel. Bethel means God's House, Lia Fail. Jeremiah planted these items into Ireland where the Stone of Bethel is under the throne of England in West Minster Abby to this day. This subject is very controversial according to history. The promise of King David's throne has been preserved through the throne of England. This is well documented in the ancient chronicles of Ireland, Scotland and England.

The key definition words of grandson, as a son, nation, firstborn, very fruitful and steward matches the Commission of Jeremiah (Jerm 1:10) and Christ (Matt 10:6 and 15:24) to the house of Israel tasked to spread his end time Gospel as the stone of Israel (Church) the Bethel Stone of Jacob (Lia Fail stone) as the house of God.

Ariel: "areel", a city where David Dwelt. 1. An Emissary of Ezra. 2. (740) a symbolic name for Jerusalem: (739) **Lion of God**, i.e. heroic. **Lion like men**. Refer to **Israel** (410) (352) and (193) to twist, be strong, powerful: (717) to pluck, gather: (353) Strength, a chief (politically), a **ram**, **an oak tree**, mighty man.

Synopsis- According to this definition, Ariel is the original city of Jerusalem representing all twelve tribes under the government of Israel headquartered in Jerusalem with the Lion as their symbol, Gen 49:9, **Judah is a lion's whelp; from the prey, my son, thou art gone up; he stooped down, he crouched as a lion"**. There are key words in its definition that links the name Arial and Israel to Bashan that is the Birthright tribe of Manasseh through the words ram (bull), and an oak tree in which Bashan is famous. We know that Bashan is of the tribe of Manasseh, representing the United States.

Zion and Ariel are one and the same (Isa 29:1-2&7) for they both represent Jerusalem as a capital which is very important for both were overturned, plowed and moved to another location as the Church, stone of Israel or Bethel (Gods House) as Gods Kingdom taken from the Jews. It is also related to the words confederate or covenant. Ezekiel 8:6 states that God, "should go far off from my sanctuary", indicating that he departed his Temple in Jerusalem. Zion means (6726) a mountain of Jerusalem, (*mountain means nation*). (6725) a monumental or guiding pillar (*stone of Bethel or Lia Fial*), a desert or dry place. (6723) To parch, a desert-barren, drought, dry (land, place), solitary place, wilderness. The symbol of the Lion of Judah comes from Ariel that is used by several European countries such as Great Britain (Ephraim) and Germany, the standing Lion. The countries that use this symbol are the remnant of the tribe of Judah or other countries of Hebrew Israelite descent. The flag of the King of England bares the standing lion and represents the Lion of Judah. One thing that Christians need to understand is that God is all powerful and would not allow his Zion, Ariel and his Throne to disappear for 2587 years without showing his might and righteousness within his Throne. He promised King David that a man would always sit upon the throne till his coming and Jeremiah fulfilled that promise in Jerm 1:10 when he overturned the throne to Ireland, Eze 17:21-24, 20:34-47; 21:25-32 and Hosea 2:14-23. These are just a few verses explaining how God transplanted his throne into the wilderness, a place of peace and rest to wait for his Gospel to be fruitful nations of his lost sheep, Matt 10:5-8 and 21:43. These nations were of the fruitful birthright tribe of Joseph to receive the great double portion of blessings promised to Abraham, Isaac and Jacob, Genesis 35:11.

Asshur: "ashur" 1. The builder of the city of Nineveh. 2. A son of Shim. 3. Another name for Assyria: (804) 2nd son of Shim and his descendants also the country they occupy (Assyria) its religion and empire. Asshur, Assur, Assyria, Assyrians: (833) Primitive root; to be straight (in the widest since, to be level, right, happy), figurative; to go forward, be honest, prosper, blessed happy, go, guide, lead, relive: (838) in the sense of going, to step, going step.

Synopsis- Asshur or Assyria plays a large role.in the destiny of God's plan for his nation Israel. God used Assyria to punish Israel for their national sins by taking them into captivity and put in motion his end time prophetic scenario. Israel's captivity into Assyria was the beginning of their journey that started in the Black Sea area where they settled during the years of their captivity. Lebanon of Assyria is famous for their beautiful cedar trees that represent a symbol of God's creation. This is important to understand for Gods end time fruitful nations are called Lebanon after the cedar tree. The connection between

Lebanon and the 10 northern tribes of the house of Israel is due to their last known existence as a nation prior to captivity and the punishment applied by God that gives its significance. The end time house of Israel of today is named after the ancient name of Lebanon due to this fact which allows us to trace who we are today as a nation, Gods Christian nations of the end time. We can trace the ancient names of the house of Israel after captivity through names given to them by other nations. Some of these names the we have already covered are, Beth Omri, Bit Kumri, Humri, Kimri, Cimmerians, Gimmiri, Sakai, Sacae, Sakasuna, Scythians, Celts, Goths and Danaoi or Tauatha de Danaan of the tribe of Dan and Dara.

Barbarian: (Hebrew) (915) "badal" a part-piece: (914) Prime root; to divide (in various senses literal or figurative, separate, distinguish, differentiate, select, etc.), difference, divide (asunder), make, separate, sever, utterly. (Greek meaning) "barbaros" of uncertain, a foreigner (i.e. non-Greek) or barbarous.

Synopsis- In the Hebrew sense, a barbarian is someone that was not Hebrew or from that area. The Romans also had a name for barbarians that was popular during Paul's time. This name is what they called the fierce warrior people from the Island of Briton. They were fierce fighters that took place when Rome invaded Briton in 55BC and again in 423AD. The Britons fought so fiercely the Romans could not capture the Island. Paul knew the barbarians very well for he was in debt to them as stated in Romans 1:14, **"I am debtor both to the Greeks, and to the barbarians; both to the wise, and to the unwise"**. Paul knew the Christian Britons for they often visited Rome as did Claudia. Her British name was Gladys and the daughter of the British Royal family (II Tim 4:21). Aulus Rufus Pudens was a Roman senator that served the fighting forces in Briton when Rome invaded in 43AD where he meets Gladys/Claudia and later married (Rom 16:13). Paul first went to Rome in approx. 56AD where he knew the barbarian Britons well for, they served him in the Church in Rome. This is how he was debtor to them. Claudia or Gladys, along with the Royal family, was a member of the Church in England established by Joseph of Arimathea, Jesus Great Uncle in 36AD. The British Royal family was taken captive to Rome where Claudia established the Church prior to Paul's visit and that is why he was indebted to the barbarians from Briton. (Refer to dates in table #3)

Bashan: Kingdom of King Og: (1316) "Bashan" a region east of the Jordan river that was given to the tribe of Manasseh as their inheritance land taken from King Og.

Synopsis-. Zech 11:2, **"howl, O ye oaks of Bashan; for the forest of the vintage is come down"**. This verse refers to Bashan as a forest that is a wilderness of oak trees and the vintage represents a vineyard producing fruits of a vintage. Bashan is linked to the word Arial meaning Jerusalem for both have cross-reference meaning of an oak tree. God's vineyard is the house of Israel and Judah, Isaiah 5:7. Refer to wilderness and Vineyard. Bashan is an ancient region east of the Jordan river occupied by the birthright tribes of Manasseh. We know that Bashan and Carmel are a part of the house of Israel for in Isaiah 33:9 it states, **"and Bashan and Carmel shake off their fruits"**. Manasseh is the tribe associated with the bull and the old dominion of Bashan along with Gilead so they have to be the fruitful Christian nations spoken of in Isaiah 33:9 as the United States (the Bull). God's vineyard is the house of Israel and the house of Judah, again inIsa 5:7, that produce fruit or Christian so Bashan, Lebanon, Sharon, Carmel and Gilead have to be modern Christian nations. Refer to Wilderness and Vineyard and the segment on Bashan in chapter seven for details.

Bough: (1121) "ben" a son (as a builder of the family name), anointed one, nation, appointed to, <u>young bullock or calf</u>, colt, <u>daughter</u>, <u>firstborn</u>, foal, <u>very fruitful</u>, servant born: (7754) a branch: (6288) bright green foliage, branch, sprig: (534) a basis (of a building, a column), foundation, socket: (2793) a forest (as furnishing the material for fabric), bough, forest, shroud, wood: (6529) fruit literal or figurative, reward: (6057) unused root; to cover; a twig (as covering the limbs), branch: (7730) a thicket, interlaced branches, thick boughs: (7105) severed i.e. harvest (as reaped), the crop, the time, the reaper, harvest (man): (5577) unused root; to be pointed, a twig (as tapering), bough: (5688) a string, wreath or foliage, band, cord, rope, thick bough (branch), wreathen (chain).

Synopsis- The Hebrew meaning for bough is a special one for it means, nation, bullock, firstborn, very fruitful and anointed one or to be appointed. Genesis 49:22 calls Joseph a **"fruitful bough, even a fruitful bough by a well"**. Deuteronomy 33:17 goes into more detail on their blessing by calling Joseph a unicorn. The definition calls a bough, a builder of the family name, a forest, branch, foundation, harvest reaper, thick bough and a covering. The word bough according to Scripture is only applied to Joseph or Ephraim and Manasseh as the birthright tribe which is implied by definition as a son, the builder of the family name (Israel), appointed to, firstborn, lamb, servant born and steward as God's servants.

When we apply this definition to verses such as Isaiah 16:1-8, 41:1-8 and Jeremiah 23:3-6 where Israel is to be righteous and leaders of nations under King David's throne within the world, we can see how Gods prophetic picture begins to unfold before us. It is clear that during the end days Joseph was to be a bull and unicorn controlling King David's throne by bringing righteousness and judgment to the world under Christianity. We can simply trace the symbol of the Bull to the financial institutes of Wall Street in New York City and the unicorn to the governmental symbols to most of the nations within the

Common Wealth of Great Britain. The symbol of the bull and unicorn given in the definition of bough that is a nation of Joseph represents Manasseh the United States (the Bull) and Ephraim of Great Britain (the Unicorn).

These are the same definitions given to Branch, fruit, wilderness and plant which are all associated with the house of Israel being planted in the wilderness. A bough is a builder of the family name and the birthright so this verse has to be referring to Ephraim for he received the family name and birthright, Genesis 48:16&22. The house of Israel was a fruitful bough planted in the wilderness, anointed by God's new covenant and to spread Christ's end time Gospel. The meanings of these words complete the puzzle of God's prophecies.

A bough is a clearing for dwellings cut out of the forest, Judges 9:48-49. Isaiah 17:6 & 9 calls boughs **"cities be as a forsaken bough"**. The forests in the wilderness were cleared to build cities. The word bough is a symbol of the house of Israel settling into the desolate continents of the world spreading Christ's Gospel. Isaiah 27:11 compares boughs to branches to be broken off and burned for the lack of understanding which relates to the end days or present day due to the lack of knowledge of God's Word. Ezekiel refers a bough to the height of Israel, Ezekiel 17:23 **"In the mountain of the height of Israel will I plant it: and it shall bring forth boughs, and bear fruit, and be a goodly cedar"**. The bough Ezekiel is speaking of is the house of Israel, bearing fruit of Christianity by spreading God's Word through-out the world. This verse cannot be referring to Judah or the Jews for they have never been fruitful and still reject Christ. Refer to the segment on bough in chapter eight for more detail.

Bozrah: Capital city of Edom: (1224) "Botsrah" a place in Edom refer to: (1223) an enclosure, i.e. sheep fold refer to (1219) prim root; to clip off; to gather grapes; also, to be isolated (i.e. inaccessible by height or fortification); cut off, fenced, fortify, (grape) gather, mighty things, restrain, strong, wall (up), withhold refer to: (1210) clipped, i.e. the grape crop, vintage.

Synopsis- Bozrah was a city on the eastern side of Bashan within the tribe of Manasseh. Edom of Esau is Bozara, a Gentile nation that takes part in Gods end time wrath (Tribulation period) Isaiah 34:6-7; 63:1-2, and implies great death and war, Micah 2:12, Amos 1:12. The fortification as listed in its definition indicates the walled nations of Communism, descendants of Esau of Edom, the Red Baby. Isaiah 63:1-2 indicates that Bozrah could very well be China, Russia, and the other Communist nations called the Red Horse in Rev 6:4, the color of red or ruddy based on the color of Esau at birth (Bozrah, Seir and Edom). The ideology of Communism came from the descendants of Esau, Lucifer's Liberal Socialist System that dominates the world currently and during the Tribulation Period, the Red Horse of Communism. Red is also a symbol of Man that represents the Humanistic side of the human race. The domination of Anti-Christ sentiment is based on Esau losing his Birthright to Jacob representing a hatred for Christianity (Gen 25:30-34). The Hebrew definition states that Bozrah is isolated, inaccessible, fortification and walled up. This would indicate the security of the Communist Nations like the wall of China, the bamboo wall of Communism dividing the far East and the Berlin Wall of East and West Germany. Verses 2 of Isaiah 63 states, **"Wherefore art thou red in thine apparel, and thy garments like him that treadeth in the winefat"**. This indicates that their national symbol is Red and the Communist nations represents red as their color, Red China and the Reds of Russia, a symbol of the Red Horse of Communism in Revelation 6:4. Refer to Edom to mean red or ruddy. Idumea is also associated with Bozrah as in Isaiah 34:6, which is most likely Communist Russia. The Duma is a council or official assembly, an elective legislative assembly, constituting the lower house of the Russian Parliament.

Branch: "qaneh": (7070) a reed (as erect); by resemblance a rod (especially for measuring), shaft, tube, stem, the radius (of the arm), beam (of a steelyard); balance, bone, branch, calamus, cane, reed, spearman, stalk: (7069) "qanah"- a prime root; to erect, i.e. create; by extens, to procure, especially by purchase, by imply. to own; attain, buy (er), <u>teach to keep cattle</u>, get, provoke to jealousy, possess (or), purchase, recover, redeem, surely, verily: (2156) twig, pruned: (3127) <u>tender, young twig</u>. (3712) lead of a palm tree: (7105) severed (as reaped), the crop, the time, the reaper, or figurative also a limb (of a tree, or simply foliage); <u>bough,</u> branch, <u>harvest (man)</u>: (1121) a son (<u>as a builder of the family name</u>): (6788) highest branch, top: (534) a summit (of a tree or mountain); bough, branch: (6780) sprout, bud, spring.

Synopsis- The term branch is associated with the house of Israel, Gen 49:22 & 24, along with the words fruit, plant, bough, vineyard and stone. These are the symbols of the fruitfulness or righteousness of the House of Israel spreading Christ's Gospel in the last days. Gen 49:22, **"Joseph is a fruitful bough, even a fruitful bough by a well; whose branches run over the wall;"**. Remember that Joseph (his sons Ephraim and Manasseh) received the birthright blessing to carry on the name of Israel and receive the double portion of blessing, Gen 48:16&22. The **"well"** spoken of in Gen 49:22 is the **Well** of Salvation, the cleansing well water of our Lord Jesus Christ and the branches that ran over the wall represents the nations of Israel that departed the promised land and was planted into other parts of the world to be fruitful and multiply to bear fruit as the lost sheep of the house of Israel (Matt 10:6). Isaiah 16:8 speak of branches wondering through the wilderness and stretching over the sea, **"For the fields of Heshbon languish, and the vine of Sibmah: the lords of the heathen have broken down the principal plants thereof, they are come even unto Jazer, they wandered through the wilderness: her branches are stretched**

out, they are gone over the sea." Hesbon, Sibmah, Jazer and Elealeh are all cities east of the Jordan River located in the Tribe of Reuben and Gad which associates them with the lost sheep of the house of Israel and not Judea or the Jews. The house of Israel was taken captive by Assyria in approx. 721BC and the house of Judah by Babylon in 586BC. Both eventually migrated into Europe and overseas, due to their captivities, where they were planted in the wilderness into other lands on the wings of a great eagle (Eze 17). The Hebrew meaning of each of these names are as follows:

<u>Hesbon</u>, a Levitical city in Reuben and Gad, meaning: to contrivance, account, device with a prime root meaning to plant or interpenetrate, to plot or contrive; <u>Sibmah</u>, a city in Reuben, unused root, to be fragrant, the bolsam plant, spice, to smell sweet, an aroma (spice); <u>Jazer</u>, Levitical city in Gad, to surround, protect or aid, and help; <u>Elealeh</u>, a place east of the Jordan River, prime root, God is going up, strength, mighty especially Almighty, goodly, great, power, prime root to ascend, arise up and bring up. These Hebrew meanings are directly associated with the fruitful nations planted in the wilderness (the Lost Sheep of the House of Israel). They were of the Levitical cities which means the house of Israel in the wilderness were to represent Gods Laws and Righteousness. Ezekiel 17:23 explains it very well, **"In the mountain of the height of Israel will I plant it: and it shall bring forth boughs, and bear fruit, and be a goodly cedar: and under it shall dwell all fowl of every wing; in the shadow of the branches thereof shall they dwell"**.

A mountain is referred to as a nation (refer to the word mountain and bough). The Hebrew meaning of branch reflects directly to the character of the house of Israel. The house of Israel was a twig pruned, tender young twig, leaf of a palm tree, sprout, bud, a summit, psalms of singing and praise, bough, builder of the family name, and the top highest branch. They were planted in the wilderness and these definitions reflect that aspect. Keep in mind that the symbol of the Phoenician Empire of Enoch's descendants was a palm tree. Isaiah 16:8-9 proves that his branches are of Heshbon, Sibmah, Jazer and Elealeh, the lost Sheep of the house of Israel where they were broken down and her branches stretched out over the sea. Jesus sent his Disciples to these branches over the sea and abroad (Mat 10:5; 15:22-24 and James 1:1). God's Hebrew language is wonderful for within the meaning of root words is where the secrets of his mystery rest.

Carmel: "Karmel" 1. A mountain range in Canaan. 2. A town in Judah. (3760) the name of a hill and of a town in Palestine; fruitful (plentiful) field, (place): (3759) a planted field (garden, orchard, vineyard or park); garden produce; full (green) ears of corn, <u>fruitful field</u> (place), plentiful (field): (3754) from an unused root uncertain meaning; a garden or vineyard; vines, (increase of the) vineyard (-s), vintage: (1021) <u>a son (builder of the family name)</u>: (1029) a prime root; to build, begin to build (er), obtain children, make repair, set (up), surely.

Synopsis- The Hebrew definition of Carmel is directly linked to the meaning of the house of Israel. The words mountain, hill, <u>fruitful field</u>, <u>planted garden</u>, <u>orchard</u>, <u>vineyard</u>, a son or builder of the <u>family name</u> [Israel], obtain children and to build. All these definitions can be applied to the nations that were planted in the wilderness, Ezekiel 17:23. Carmel is a region in Bashan and associated with Gilead making them a region in Manasseh. We have already studied that Manasseh is the Bull of the United States under the New Covenant of the house of Israel. Refer to Carmel in chapter seven for details.

Covenant: (1285) "briyth" - (Brit as in British) (in the sense of cutting, a compact) (because made by passing between pieces of flesh) <u>confederacy</u>, <u>covenant</u>, league: (1262) "barah"- a primitive root; to select, to feed; to render clean choose, eat, manifest, (give) meat: (1288) "barak"- a primitive root; to kneel, to bless God (as an act of adoration), and (vice-versa) man (as a benefit); also (by euphem.) to curse (God or the king, as treason); x abundantly, **x** altogether, **x** at all, blaspheme, bless, congratulate, curse, **x** greatly, **x** indeed, kneel (down), praise, salute, *x* still, thank: (1242) "boqer"- dawn (as the break of day); morning; day, early, morning, morrow: (1239) "baqar", prim. root, <u>to plow, or (gen) break forth</u>, i.e. (figurative) to inspect, admire, search, seek out.

The American College Dictionary by Random House of New York states the following definition for the word **British** (briyth or **Brit** Covenant in Hebrew). 5. The language of ancient Britons, Welsh, Cornish and Breton; the English language was derived from all of these ancient languages. (Middle English) 1100-1500AD was the language called Brytysshe (Old English) before 1100 AD, Bryttise, Bryttas, Brettas, Britons form Celtic. The Strongs Concordance reference to Man is (376) "Iysh" (eesh) Hebrew for man, a male person, a man as an individual, companion, husband and steward. The reference in the Strongs Concordance for Land is (776) "erets" unused root to be firm; the earth (at large, or partitively a land); common, country, earth, field, ground, land, <u>nation</u>, way, <u>wilderness</u>, <u>world</u>.

Synopsis- Through-out the Scriptures there are seven Covenants God created between his Spirit and man. A Covenant is Gods Spiritual dealings with man (Zion) sealed by blood and his written Word. Gods original Covenant was covered by blood of sacrificed animals under the Law of Moses. Gods New Covenant fell under the blood of the Messiah and was given to the people of the world and his Gospel to be spread by his new covenant people in the wilderness. The kingdom was taken from his Hebrew Jews and given to a fruitful or righteous nation (Mat 21:43). It is pretty clear that according to the Strongs Concordance and the dictionary, the word British (Briythiysh) and

Britain (Briytherets) means Covenant Man and Covenant Land. The word British represents his lost sheep of the house of Israel and birthright tribe to receive great blessings. This certainly explains many verses in the Bible that refers to God planting the house of Israel in the wilderness to establish his new Christian Covenant and spread his end time Gospel (Zion), Hos 2:14; Eze 34:25; Jerm 31:31. Gods new Covenant is mentioned in Heb 8:8, **"For finding fault with them, he saith, Behold, the days come, saith the Lord, when I will make a new covenant with the house of Israel and with the house of Judah"**. Paul is writing this verse and makes a distinct difference between the house of Israel and the house of Judah that pertains to the last days. Where are both of these houses today? A covenant is a cutting compact between God and Noah and his descendants, all of mankind (Gen 9:9) through all generations. Heb 8:13, says, **" In that he saith, A new covenant, he hath made the first old. Now that which decayeth and waxeth old is ready to vanish away"**. This new covenant is the age of Christ's Gospel and was given the responsibility of the new planted nation of the house of Israel in the wilderness to be fruitful, his end time Gospel (Heb 8:7-13; 12:24; 13:20).

Disperse (ed): "puwts" (6327) prime root; to dash in pieces, to disperse, break into pieces, cast (abroad), disperse (selves), drive, retire, scatter (abroad), spread abroad: (2219) prime root; to toss about, to diffuse, winnow, cast away, compass, disperse, fan, scatter (away), spread, strew: (6555) Prime root; to break out, grow, increase.

Synopsis- The Hebrew meaning of Disperse is a single action, to break into pieces, cast abroad, disperse, scatter, or spread abroad and cast away. In almost every case the term disperse applies to the nation of Israel. The word disperse is synonymous with the word scatter, **"I lifted up mine hand unto them also in the wilderness that I would scatter them among the heathen, and disperse them through the countries,"** Ezekiel 20:23. Israel was dispersed into the wilderness because they did not execute Gods judgments, and despised his statutes. In this verse, it is emphasized that they were dispersed into the countries of the world. Again, God states the reason for dispersing Israel, **"And I will scatter thee among the heathen, and disperse thee in the countries, and will consume thy filthiness out of thee. And thou shalt take thine inheritance in thyself in the sight of the heathen, and thou shalt know that I am the Lord.",** Ezk 22:15-16. Again, in this verse it speaks of being scattered and dispersed among the heathen due to their national sins. The word countries are not mentioned as in the other verse. Verse 16 mentions their inheritance that indicate they had to be Ephraim and Manasseh of the house of Israel, the ten northern tribes, due to the birthright inheritance. Refer to wilderness for more details.

James knew of the scattered and dispersed lost sheep of Israel for he wrote the book of James to all twelve tribes that were scattered abroad, James 1:1. Peter also knew where they were and wrote to the scattered strangers in Peter 1:1. It is obvious the Apostles knew where the lost sheep of the house of Israel were located, for they wrote to them and were preparing to fulfill their commission by Jesus to go into the wilderness. They were to go and preach to the lost sheep of Israel and that is why they needed to speak in tongues of foreign language. There is a close parallel between the 12 Apostles and the sealing of the 144,000 or 12,000 from each tribe during the Tribulation Period. Twelve seems to be the key number representing the twelve tribes of the Kingdom of Israel and the 12 Apostles represent 12,000 sealed from each tribe that carries Gods Kingdom into the seventh millennium. Both represent the Church. Gods Spirit and salt of the earth was taken or raptured with the Church but the Holy Spirit was given to each of the two Witnesses through their candlestick and olive trees in Rev 11:11:3-4. Each of the 144,000 Hebrews were Sealed by God himself to represent his Kingdom to populate the world during the Millennial Reign just as Noah's family were to repopulated the earth after the flood. They are given special powers to fight the Anti-Christ just as the Apostles were given gifts of power to fight Satan.

Eagle: (5404) "nesher" an unused root; to lacerate; the eagle (or other large bird of prey), eagle: (7360) a kind of vulture (supposed to be tender toward its young): (7355) Primitive root: to fondle; by implying to love, especially to compassionate; have compassion (on, upon), love, (find, have, obtain, shew), mercy (-iful, on, upon), (have) pity, Ruhamah, surely: (105) a basin, charge. The Greek meaning is (5404) <u>Phoenix or palm tree</u> [symbol of the Phoenicians].

Synopsis- The Eagle is the national symbol of the United States due to the same attributes as stated in the Bible. The USA inherited this symbol from the tribe of Dan (the Eagle) where Manasseh replaced Dan as listed in Rev 7:5-8 due to their sins against their brother. The Bible refers to the eagles magnificent gracious flying ability, its swiftness, how it stirs up her nest high in the mountain, its hastiness to catch prey and its great wingspan. The average eagle has a wingspan of six feet or more, can fly and look directly into the sun to escape its enemy and fly for hours with-out flapping its wings by using air currents. The eagle is known to be a very wise and great majestic bird. Ezekiel chapter 17 uses the eagle to carry the house of Israel, Lebanon, Ephraim and Manasseh or the ten northern tribes of Israel into the wilderness by Phoenician ships (symbol of the Palm tree) to be fruitful nations. The Eagle was the standard or ensign (Num 2:2) of Dan as the leader of the northern Brigade and outlined in Numbers 2:25. Dan's standard of the Eagle was given to Manasseh due to their departing the land as indicated in Revelation 7:6 where Manasseh is given Dan's blessing of being sealed. This would indicate that Manasseh received Dan's symbol or banner of the Eagle. The great wings of the Eagle in

Ezekiel 17:3 that took the highest Branch (King David's Throne) of Lebanon into the wilderness is the account of the overturn of the throne from the Pharez to the Zarah bloodline of Judah representing the throne of Israel. This same account is given in Ezekiel 20:34-47; 21:25-16; 34:13-31; Hosea 2:14-23; Micah 5:7-11. Zechariah 2:11-13 makes the statement, **"And many nations shall be joined to the Lord in that day, and shall be my people: and I will dwell in the midst of thee, and thou shalt know that the Lord of hosts hath sent me unto thee. And the Lord shall inherit Judah his portion in the holy land, and shall choose Jerusalem again. Be silent, O all flesh, before the Lord: for he is raised up out of his holy habitation."** This verse states that many nations (Gen 35:11) shall be Christian in the end days being his people, the house of Israel of the ten northern tribes. They are the birthright tribes of Ephraim and Manasseh, the coalition of Lebanon, Bashan, Carmel, Gilead and Sharon.

They were flown into the wilderness by the great eagle to wait for Christ's Gospel (Eze 17:3). Note that at this point Judah was not included for they are not Christian till the Tribulation Period during Daniel's 70th week. The next verse states Judah shall inherit Jerusalem that occurred in 1967 to fulfill this, Scripture. The eagle taking Gods children of Israel into the wilderness is a symbol of the Holy Spirit guiding his people with tender loving care just as a mother eagle would tend to its young. All the attributes of the definition listed above for the eagle to be loving, merciful, compassionate, pity and tender, all fit the description of the greatest Christian nation ever in history of the world, the United States of America, the EAGLE. The eagle is also a symbol of the Phoenix Palm Tree and the Phoenician shipping empire that sailed the seven seas and carried the house of Israel across the seas on the wings of an eagle (Eze 17:3&7).

East: (6926) "qidmah" – is the forward part, on the east or in front: (6924) the front of a place or time (antiquity) ancient, aforetime, before, east (end, side-ward) eternal, everlasting: (6921) the fore or front part by orientation the east, east wind, eastward: (6930) eastern: (6931) anterior or of place, oriental, ancient, they that went before, east thing of old: (8121) unused root, to be brilliant the sun, the east figurative for a ray or arch, a notched battlement, sun rising, westward, window: (1053) house of the sun: (4161) the act of an egress or the place of an exit, dawn, the rising of the sun (the east), brought out, bud, going forth: (3318) to go or bring out, shout forth, <u>come abroad</u>: (4417) the idea of readiness in assent to bargain for a wife, <u>to wed</u>, <u>endow</u>.

Synopsis - The definition of East is associated with Eber as Hebrew. When studying this word, it is pretty clear why Satan has distorted this word and uses it in his own occult organizations as an orientation to the east. The East is sacred to God for it is where his people of Adam came (his Chosen People) for

Satan always emulates God. Certain key words in the Hebrew definition of east can be related to Gods Kingdom of the house of Israel and Christ's Gospel, the Church. Words such as, *ancient, everlasting, they that went before, east thing of old, battlement* (Battle Ax), *brought our going forth, come abroad, bargain for a wife, to wed and endow.* Many of these words are related to God planting his nations in the wilderness such as bough, plant, vineyard, wilderness and mountain. They also relate to Christ's end time Church as the bride of Christ.

For the most part, the term East is used through-out the Bible as a direction either referring to or from the East. As we come to the prophetic books, we see a different meaning in several Scriptures. The east gate of the Temple is significant for when Gods Glory departed the Temple prior to the destruction of Jerusalem in 586BC, his Glory departed by the east gate. Ezekiel 10:18-19 and 11:23 records this event, **"And the glory of the Lord went up from the midst of the city, and stood upon the mountain which is on the east side of the city."** This writer has found no other Scriptures where Gods Glory ever returned to the Temple prior to modern times. The departing of his Glory from the Temple began the overturn of his throne from Jerusalem as stated in Ezekiel 17:22-24 and 21:25-27. When this event occurred, King Zedekiah was the last king of the Phares line to set on the throne of Israel in Jerusalem. From 586 BC to this present date, there is no king sitting on the throne in Jerusalem because God took his Glory and has not returned it to his beloved city. This will not occur till he comes in Power and Glory and establishes his rule in Jerusalem on his earthly Kingdom fulfilling Luke 1:32-33. The Throne of David and Gods Spirit of Glory in the Temple goes hand and hand. When the Throne ceased to exist in Jerusalem (overturned in Eze 21:25-27), Gods Glory in the Temple come to an end. Gods Glory was overturned from Jerusalem to the world as recorded in Ezekiel 11:23, 43:1-2 and Ps 48:2. His Glory does not return to Jerusalem till the Church age is complete along w2ith the Tribulation Period (Zech 12:6-7).

Please do not misunderstand for Gods Spirit will always be with Jerusalem and his Chosen People, the Hebrews. Gods Glory and his Spirit is two different entities. The word Glory is the key for in Hebrew it means, splendor or copiousness, glorious, to be heavy in a good sense rich, honorable, great, nobles, prevail, and to be rich. Jerusalem laid in rubble for almost two thousand years so how can Gods Glory be in it. His Glory was shifted to his Birthright tribe to be great nations and kingdoms to fulfill the promise to Abraham, Isaac, Jacob and Joseph (Ephraim and Manasseh). His Glory will return to Jerusalem when Christ returns in Power to claim his Throne as King.

There are other meanings such as an East wind, Hosea 12:1, **"Ephraim feedeth on wind, and followed after the east wind: he daily increaseth lies and desolation; and they do make a covenant with the Assyrians,**

and oil is carried into Egypt." This verse directly speaks of Ephraim, the birthright tribe that is blown by the east wind by the Phoenician ships and great merchants with the world. Where does the east wind blow, it blows to the west where he migrated by ship and foot as a symbol on the wings of an eagle as stated in Ezekiel chapter 17. This was his branches that ran over the wall mentioned in Genesis 49:22 and Isaiah 16:8. Hosea 13:15 call the east wind an evil force, **"an east wind shall come".** This writer believes it is referring to the ideologies of eastern mysticisms and Communism that is diluting our way of life today by opening our borders to liberal religion, education, and culture changes.

East also means Eber of the Hebrew descendant and were wayfaring men that traveled the world. In other words, the Hebrew wayfaring men of Eber that came from the east traveled or migrated to the west by being blown via the east wind.

Eber: 1. Was a great-grandson of Shem son of Salah. 2. Descendants of Eber the Hebrew. 3. Son of Elpaal of the tribe of Benjamin (I Chron 8:12). 4. A priest of the Amok family: (5677) "Eber" is the name of two patriarchs and four Israeli; Eber, Heber: (5676) a region across, on the opposite side (especially of the Jordan; usually mean, the east), against, beyond, by, from, over, passage, quarter, (other, this) side, straight. (5680) "Ibrey" are an Eberite (Hebrew) or descendant of Eber, Hebrew (-ess, woman): (5674) Primitive root; to cross over; used very widely of any transition (literal or figurative;) specially to cover (in copulation), alienate, alter, at all, beyond, bring.

Synopsis- The important thing to know about Eber is that his descendants were to be Hebrew of Abraham the Hebrew Israelite Chosen People. The name Hebrew derived from Eber, Ibriy, eber, aber, abariym and finally Hebrew. It is interesting to know that the term wayfaring also means cross over, caravan, traveler, troop, Heber and Ibriy; Hebrew. A wayfaring man is a traveling Hebrew man. Eber represents the Hebrew tribes of the lost sheep of the house of Israel where their branches ran over the wall and over the seas into the wilderness to fulfill their birthright destiny to be great nations and kings of Kingdoms, to be fruitful (Christian) as Hebrew travelers. They were to be Hebrew travelers that crossed over to the other side of the world to spread Christ's end time Gospel as the Birthright tribe and family name of Israel, "He will rule as God".

Edom: 1. Another name for Esau 2. Descendants of Esau (Edomite): (123) means Red (see Gen 25:25) Edom the elder twin brother of Jacob; hence, the region (Idumaea) occupied by him; Edom, Edomites, Idumea: (122) rosy, red, ruddy: (119) to show blood (in the face), i.e. flush or turn rosy-be (dyed, made) red (ruddy).

Synopsis- Esau, Jacob's twin brother is the Edomites that have become the Communist Nations of the world. Red is the symbol of National Communism of both Russia and China that represent the Red Horse in Revelation chapter 6. It is very ironic that Jacob tricked Esau out of his birthright blessings, Gen 27:22-23, that became the most powerful and Christian nations in the world and the Edomites have become our natural enemies through Communism. The curse has become full circle to plague Jacob in the last days. Note that the region of Idumaea of the Edomites and Duma which is the legislative assembly of the lower House of Parliament of the Russian Government are almost the same (the Red Horse of Communism). Refer to Bozrah.

Ephraim: 1. Was the second son of Joseph. 2. One of the twelve tribes comprising Israel. 3. Mountains in Samaria. Second Son of Joseph and given the first Birthright blessings along with Manasseh, Gen 48:16 & 19, "Ephraim": (669) dual, double fruit: (672) Fruitfulness and another name for Bethlehem, also of an Israeli woman: (6509) Prime root; to bear fruit, bear, bring forth (fruit), fruitful, grow, increase.

Synopsis- Ephraim in Hebrew means double fruit due to the birthright blessings. He was the younger son of Joseph and received the firstborn birthright blessing before Manasseh even though both were to receive the blessing in a dual role (Gen 48:16 and I Chron 5:1-2). It is important to understand that the birthright blessing to Ephraim and Manasseh were given prior to the blessings of all twelve sons of Jacob as indicated in Genesis chapter 48 and 49. Joseph, (Ephraim and Manasseh) were actually blessed twice by Jacob, once in Gen 48:16-22 before he blessed any of the other sons and again in Genesis 49:22-26 when he blessed all the sons. The birthright son according to Hebrew Law, was to receive a double portion of the family fortune and responsible to carry on the family name by being the leader of the family. The family name Israel went to Ephraim and Manasseh (house of Israel, ten northern tribes), Genesis 48:16, **"let my name be named on them"**. This verse is clear that only Ephraim and Manasseh were to be called ISRAEL and no other son or grandson received this blessing from either Jacob or Joseph. The birthright inheritance by Law went to Joseph and his two sons but the blessing of the Throne, Scepter and Lawgiver went to Judah (Gen 49:10). After Shiloh (Christ) came as the Messiah, the whole Kingdom was given to the lost sheep of the house of Israel under the birthright of Ephraim the unicorn in I Kings 12:19-20 to be King over all Israel and Matt 21:43 as a fruitful nation.

Ephraim and Manasseh as the birthright inheritance received the responsibility and authority by Jesus himself to spread and preach Christ's end time Gospel. This can be seen within the meaning of Ephraim given double fruit or to be righteous as Christian. They were to bear fruit by representing Christ's Church.

The inheritance blessing created a great rift between the house of Israel of the north and the house of Judah in the south. This eventually divided the nation of Israel, I Kings 11:30-37 and 12:19-24. The primogeniture to carry on the name of Israel, given to Jacob their grandfather, was inherited by Ephraim first and to Manasseh second as recorded in Genesis 48:20 and I Chron 5:1-2. The law of the firstborn is given in the following verses (Exodus 22:29; 13:2; 34:19; Lev 27:26; Num 3:13-14; Duet 21:17 and Neh 10:36). It is very important for Christians to understand who received the family name firstborn birthright blessing for that is the key in understanding why God divided Israel and his overall purpose of end time prophecy in reference to each House. Genesis 35:11 gives the birthright blessing to be received, **"And God said unto him, I am God Almighty: be fruitful and multiply; a nation and a company of nations shall be of thee, and kings shall come out of thy loins;"**. According to the blessing of the birthright tribe, they were to be many nations and kingdoms and completely separate from King David's throne of Israel until the fulfillment of the coming of the Messiah. God reunited his Kingdom as a whole nation by overturning, plowing and plucking his throne and Kingdom into the wilderness due to the disbelief of the Jews. Mark 3:24-25 states that a divided Kingdom cannot stand, therefore, God had to reunite his Kingdom as a whole in which he did in the wilderness as the second gathering under his New Covenant of the Church fulfilling Gen 49:10 where Christ gathered his Church in the wilderness. The Church is Gods whole and complete Kingdom on earth to include his Throne, Zion (Jerusalem) and his people of the twelve tribes of the house of Israel under the Throne of England called Israel.

Note that this blessing was to take place in the last days, Genesis 49:1, and they were to be a Righteous Christian nation by being fruitful. You can trace the true identity of Israel through the Bible by the word fruitful for it will lead you to names such as, Bashan, Lebanon, Sharon, Carmel and Gilead (Gen 49:22; Isa 33:9 and 32:15). These names identify America and Britain in Bible Prophecy. These are all fruitful righteous Christian nations in the last days. This blessing was not to the Jews of Judah for they have never been righteous, but to Israel the ten northern tribes of the house of Israel.

Ephraim can also be traced by the term unicorn which is stated in Isaiah 34:7 and Deuteronomy 33:17. The term "firstling" indicate the birthright by Law of inheritance, Nehemiah 10:36, the bullocks and the bulls is Manasseh (United States), and the unicorn is Ephraim (United Kingdom of Great Britain). Note that the bullock and unicorn are mentioned in both of these verses due to the fact of the birthright inheritance together as brothers.
Isaiah 31:2-10 clearly demonstrates how God planted Israel, Ephraim in the wilderness and gathered them from all corners of the world and caused them

to rest. The word rest is the key for the Jews of Judah has never in history been at rest or peace for they have been persecuted in every nation in the world. Even today in the modern nation of Israel, they are always at war. Note that this gathering place in the wilderness is not the promised land of Israel for that gathering will occur just prior to the Tribulation Period, Ezekiel 37. The book of Hosea is basically written to Ephraim and Hosea 6:10-11 calls Ephraim Israel after the birthright, **"I have seen a horrible thing in the house of Israel: there is the whoredom of Ephraim, Israel is defiled. Also, O Judah, he hath set a harvest for thee, when I returned the captivity of my people"**. These two verses clearly separate the house of Israel and the house of Judah. Ephraim is called Israel and not Judah due to the birthright law. Israel and Ephraim (Samaria, Isa 7:9) are one and the same, Hosea 5:3 **"I know Ephraim, and Israel is not hid from me: for now, O Ephraim, thou committest whoredom, and Israel is defiled.", "And the pride of Israel doth testify to his face: there shall Israel and Ephraim fall in their iniquity; Judah also shall fall with them."**

These verses indicate Israel and Ephraim as a coalition in the last days with Ephraim the leader. The nation of Judah is mentioned separately from Israel and Ephraim. Again Hose 4:16-17 states, **"For Israel slideth back as a backsliding heifer: now the Lord will feed them as a lamb in a large place. Ephraim is joined to idols; let him alone"**. This is a very interesting verse for God fed Ephraim as a lamb in a large place indicating the Gospel of Jesus Christ in a large distant land (Isa 18). This sure sounds like Great Britain and the United States. Zechariah 10:3-12 and 11:1-2, also gives the account of how Ephraim will be gathered into the land of Bashan, Gilead and Lebanon which is not speaking of the promised land of Judea of Jerusalem. Verse 6 gives a distinct difference between the house of Judah and the house of Israel, **"And I will strengthen the house of Judah, and I will save the house of Joseph, and I will bring them again to place them;"**. Verse 7 says, **"their heart shall rejoice in the Lord."**, this indicates that they are a righteous Christian people. The Jews to this day do not believe in Christ so it cannot be speaking of them rejoicing in the Lord.

After a deep study of Ephraim, it is clear that they can be traced through the Bible as Israel, Samaria, Lebanon, Gilead, Bashan, Carmel, Sirion and Sharon. This is the coalition of 46 English speaking Christian nations of modern time. **Note**: the Hebrew meaning for Ephraim is referred to as a mountain and produce double fruitful. This matches his birthright in preserving the family name. The word mountain in the Old Testament means nation, Ezekiel explains it well in chapter 17 verses 22 and 23, **"Thus saith the Lord God; I will also take of the highest branch of the hight cedar, and will set it; I will crop off from the top of his young twigs a tender one and will plant it upon an high mountain and eminent. In the mountain of the height of Israel will I**

plant it; and it shall bring forth boughs, and bear fruit, and be a goodly cedar: and under it shall dwell all fowl of every wing; in the shadow of the branches thereof shall they dwell". It's important to understand that this verse was written by Ezekiel in approx. 594BC, after the ten northern tribes of the house of Israel was taken into captivity by Assyria in 721BC and just prior to Judah being taken by Babylon in 586BC.

Israel had been established as a nation for hundreds of years for they marched into the Promised Land and became a nation in approx. 1450BC. The overturn mentioned in Ezekiel 17 through 21 is speaking of a different event and time period for it was the throne of Israel that was chopped off, **"crop off from the top of his young twigs a tender one and will plant it upon an high mountain"**. This verse had to be speaking of how God planting his throne and Kingdom into another nation or mountain some-where in the world. It also matches Jeremiah's commission in Jeremiah 1:10 to root out, to pull down, to destroy, to throw down, to build and to plant. Ezekiel 21:22-24 speaks of the overturn of the thrown into another nation. Being Ephraim was the birthright son to receive the name Israel, it can only be speaking of how Ephraim was to receive the Kingdom that was rooted out, pulled down, destroyed, built and replanted in another nation to carry on the name of Israel. This included all the elements of Gods Kingdom of the Throne, Zion (Temple or Church) and the dual meaning of Jerusalem and Israel.

Fruitful: (6509) primitive root; to bear fruit, literal or figurative, bear, bring forth fruit, (cause to be, make) fruitful, grow, increase: (6529) fruitful, reward: (8081) grease, especially liquid as from the olive, often perfumed ; figurative, richness, **anointing**, fat things, fruitful, oiled, ointment, olive, pine: (3759) "karmel" a planted field (garden, orchard, vineyard, or park); garden produce, full (green) ears (of corn), fruitful field (place), plentiful (field): (2233) fruit, plant, sowing-time, posterity, carnally, child, fruitful, seed time, sowing-time: (6500) to bear fruit, be fruitful: (2593) practiced-trained: (2596) primitive root; to narrow, figurative-to initiate or discipline; dedicate, train up: (2592) <u>favor of God</u>: (2603) primitive root; to bend or stoop in kindness to an inferior, bestow, fair, be merciful, have shown mercy, have pity upon.

Synopsis- Ripe mature fruit is the most delicious of all foods grown from a vine or tree. This is why God uses the word fruit or fruitful to represent his righteousness in the Scriptures. Anoint, bough, reward, wealth, fulfilled, increase, flourish, intelligent, wisdom, teach, skillful and trained comes from the definition of fruitful. All of these words refer to his fruitful nations as being righteous with Christian values as being in favor with God. Karmel or Carmel means a planted field, garden, orchard or vineyard that was planted in the wilderness. It produces fruit. Refer to the word plant and wilderness. The end time fruitful nation of Carmel is mentioned in Isaiah 33:9, 35:2, Mic 7:14, Nah

1:4 as just a few verses. The nations of Carmel along with Lebanon, Sharon, Gilead, Sirion and Bashan is Gods fruitful Christian nations producing fruit of righteous in the last days and represents Great Britain and the United States as the birthright tribes of Ephraim and Manasseh. The US and UK can be identified by these names. Study the word fruit carefully for its full meaning and you will see how it relates to Christ's Church and his end time Gospel of fruitfulness.

Gilead: "ghil-e-ade" 1. District east of the Jordan River. 2. A mountain range in Gilead Israel. 3. Son of Marchir (Manasseh's son) (Gilead, Manasseh's grandson) 4. The father of Jephthah. 5. A chief of Gad. (1568) "Gilad" a region east of the Jordan River; name of three Israeli patriarchs: (1567) heap of testimony; Galeed: (1530) something rolled, a heap of stone or dung (plural ruins), by annual a spring of water (waves), billow, heap, spring, wave: (1556) primitive root; to roll (way, down, together), run down, seek, occasion, trust, wallow.

Synopsis- We know that Gilead was from the tribe of Manasseh that received the double blessing of the birthright along with Ephraim for Gilead was Manasseh's grandson and Genesis 48:16-22 gave the blessing to Manasseh. Gilead was the son of Machir and Machir the son of Manasseh (Gen 50:23) putting him in line to receive the birthright blessings of greatness. One half tribe of Manasseh located to the East was given the north half of Gilead, all of Bashan, and the region of Argob (Duet 3:13) which makes the people of Gilead and Bashan the same descendants as referred to in end time prophecy and national alignment. This would make Gilead and Manasseh the same Christian nation during end time Prophecy as the United States. We represent the Bull of Manasseh, the birthright tribe to be a single great Christian fruitful nation (Genesis 48:19) which relates to a single nation mentioned in Genesis 35:11 that takes place during the last days (Gen 49:1). Refer to the segment on Gilead in chapter seven for details.

Hiram: (2438) a King of Tyre and name of two Tyrians - Hiram and Huram: (2361) whiteness, noble: (2353) white linen, white: (2357) prime root, to blance (as with shame), was pale.

Synopsis- The term Hiram is important for it establishes a link or league (I Kings 5:12) between Tarshish (Spain and Greece), Tyre (the Phoenicians) and Israel during the times of David and Solomon. Tarshish was the son of Java (the Ionian Greeks) and world famous for sea going merchant shipping (II Chron 9:21). They were the descendants of the Hebrews of Calcol and Dara that settled in Argus of Greece and later Troy located in modern Turkey before and prior to the Exodus of Moses out of Egypt in approx. 1491 BC.

Hebrew: Descendant of Jacob: (5680) "Ibriy", an Eberite (Hebrew) or descendant of Eber-Hebrew: (5677) two Israelite Patriarchs, Eber and Heber: (5676) a region across, on the opposite side of the Jordan or the east, passage, side, straight: (5674) Prime root; to cross over, beyond, bring over, escape, carry over: (1444) a wall: (1443) Prime root; to wall in or around, close up, fence up, circumvallation.

Synopsis- We know that the Hebrew is God's chosen people (Duet 7:6 and 14:2) that they were descended from Eber and Jacob with a direct correlation to the term wayfaring man (traveler) as recorded in Isaiah 33:8. Abraham is the first Bible character to be called a Hebrew in Genesis 14:13 and never a Jew. The term Jew is not mentioned in the Scriptures till II Kings 16:6 just prior to the northern kingdom of Israel being taken into captivity to Assyria.

When we study the definition of Hebrew, it means a Hebrew traveler that crossed over to the east and can be related to the meanings of wayfaring, highway, Eber, Gilead, wilderness and East. By definition, a wayfaring man is a Hebrew traveler that migrated to the East on Gods Spiritual highway that called them to their new land in the wilderness. When you apply the words plant, vineyard, mountain, scattered, sifted and dispersed, we can begin to see the specifics of Gods prophetic plan for his chosen people. They were to be leaders of the world, Great Britain and United States of the house of Israel, his birthright inherited tribes.

The key words that trace the Hebrew are the definition of the phrase "to cross over to the East side of the Jordan River". The same Hebrew meaning is found in the words, Eber, East, Gilead, last, wayfaring and wilderness and associated with traveling. The term East means come abroad (Eber and Gilead) and to cross over to the East; last means to face the East; wayfaring means to travel or traveler; and wilderness means to drive or be driven. All these definitions pertain to traveling and directly associated with God's Chosen People, the Hebrew, which means traveler or to travel. Abraham was the first to be called Hebrew and was a traveler by his sojourn into Egypt. Jacob, the father of Israel also sojourned into Egypt (Ps 105:23) being a traveler. Sojourn means to, turn aside from the road for temporary lodging in a strange place. When we couple all the definitions of the above words together that directly pertain to God's Chosen People, the Hebrew, they were to be travelers migrating east of the Jordan River.

When we further relate Israel to the words, scatter, abroad, sift, desert, plant, forest, gather, mountain and fruitful, the scenario of Gods will for his people unfolds before us. With a close study, these words are directed at the house of Israel and not to Judah or the Jews, they were the root to be stationary. God's Chosen People of the house of Israel under the authority of the birthright was to be sojourners, travelers, to be planted in their own land (Jerm 23:8, Eze 34:14, 39:28). They were to fulfill the promise to Abraham, Isaac, Jacob and Joseph (Ephraim and Manasseh) to be nations and kings of kingdoms (Gen 17:6, 35:11 and 48:16&19). Their destiny was to be fruitful or Christian. The sojourn Hebrews of the house of Israel is now the English-speaking Christian (fruitful) nations of the world under the blessed leadership of the birthright tribes of Ephraim and Manasseh (BG and US) fulfilling all promises to Abraham, Isaac, Jacob and Joseph. They were to be the house of Israel, Battle Axe and caretaker of the Christian Church. The British colonizers also match the term wayfaring, traveler, wilderness and cross over just as they have settled the continents of the world. Refer to highway as a traveler.

Highway: (4546) a through fare, as a turnpike, a viaduct, a staircase, causeway, course, path, terrace: (5549) prime root; to mound up especially a turnpike, figuratively to oppose as by a dam, cast up, <u>exalt oneself</u>, extol, make plain, <u>raise up</u>: (4549) Prime root; to liquefy, to faint: (3598) a cluster of stars, the Pleiades; Pleiades a group of seven stars in constellation Taurus: (3558) unused root; to store away, a jewel (gold beads), tablet.

Synopsis - The term highway as pertaining to Gods Children of the house of Israel is very important and has several meanings. A highway is critical to a traveler for it is his mode of traveling or tool such as being a turnpike or path of travel. As we study this term in the Scriptures, two meanings appear, one physical and one spiritual. God commanded his Hebrew travelers in Jeremiah 31:21 to leave waymarks where ever they traveled so they could be identified, **"Set thee up way marks, make thee high heaps: set thine heart toward the highway, even the way which thou wentest: turn again, O virgin Israel, turn again to these thy cities".** During Israel's highway of migration into the wilderness, they were to mound up or raise up monuments where ever they traveled. "O virgin Israel" indicates they were Christ's Bribe the Church for they were a virgin just as a bride, they were betrothed in Hosea 2:19-20. This explains why there are stone circles and mounds scattered all over Europe and in the United States. During the migrations of the ten northern tribes, they named cities, mountains, rivers and valleys after themselves such as Denmark, the Danube River, Zaragoza Valley in Spain after Zara (Matt 1:3), London and many more as waymarks and monuments to their ancestors. Stone circles, earth mounds, Stonehenge and the Pyramids are attributes to Gods Hebrew travelers as commanded. The symbols of Ephraim's unicorn and Manasseh's bull can be traced through Europe to England and the United States along with the symbols of the other eleven tribes in Europe as their blessings are outlined in Genesis 49 and Deuteronomy 33. The spiritual aspect of their highway of travel can be found in Isaiah 35:6-10 as a righteous, holiness and fruitfulness as being Christian.

The most important meaning of highway is found in Isaiah 35:8, **"And an highway shall be there, and a way, and it shall be called the way of holiness; the unclean shall not pass over it; but it shall be for those; the wayfaring men, though fools, shall not err therein"**. This verse speaks of a highway of Holiness or Gods Salvation through his Gospel of Christ's Church and the wayfaring man is his chosen people of Jacob or anyone that accept Gods Salvation. Highway is also associated with the ancient names of Carmel, Sharon, Gilead, Bashan and Lebanon for they were the remnant of the house of Israel that departed from the Assyria captivity and the highway of migration into Europe in Isaiah 11:16, **"And there shall be an highway for the remnant of his people, which shall be left, from Assyria; like as it was to Israel in the day that he came up out of the land of Egypt"**. This verse refers only to the highway of the house of Israel for they went into captivity to Assyria not Judah. It also has a parallel meaning for a Spiritual calling as a bird (Eze 17:3&7) to migrate into the new Promised Land in the wilderness and again only applies to the house of Israel.

Isaiah 40:3 speaks of John the Baptist in the wilderness preparing the way for Christ and his Church, **"The voice of him that crieth in the wilderness, Prepare ye the way of the Lord, make straight in the desert a highway for our God"**. Here the term highway is a direct reference to the coming and establishing of Christ's Gospel. Wilderness, highway, wayfaring and Zion is used in the above verses to reference Gods Hebrew traveling people, the house of Israel, his lost sheep as they travel Gods highway spreading his Gospel.

The above verses refer to not only a physical highway through the wilderness but a spiritual highway of holiness where the glory of God is exalted. They can only be speaking of the nations of the house of Israel in the last days representing his fruitful Christian nations, the Church (Matt 10:6, 15:24, 21:43) as Zion, Gods Spirit with man.

Inheritance: (5159) something inherited, occupancy, an heirloom, an estate, heritage, possession: (5157) prime root; to inherit, to occupy, distribute, divide, take as an heritage: (5158) a stream especially a winter torrent a narrow valley in which a brook runs, a mine shaft, river, stream, valley: (3425) something occupied, a conquest, a patrimony: (3423) prime root; to occupy by dividing out previous tenants and possessing in their place, to siege, to rob, to inherit, to expel, to impoverish, to ruin, cast out, destroy, disinherit, dispossess.

Synopsis - It is very important to understand who received the Law of Moses, the Birthright blessing given by Jacob to the inheriting tribe of Israel to receive the great blessings to Abraham, Isaac and Jacob given directly to Ephraim and Manasseh through Joseph. This account is complete in Genesis chapter 48 and confirmed in I Chronicles 5:1-2. The Scriptures are very clear that the blessings promised to Abraham, Isaac, Jacob and Joseph were to be given only to the selected birthright son and not to all twelve tribes.

The recipient as Ephraim and Manasseh was to be **"exceedingly fruitful"** (wealthy) and **"nations of thee and kings shall come out of thee"** (Gen 17:6); **"possess the gate of his enemies"** and **"shall all the nations of the earth be blessed by him"** (Gen 22:17); **"shall spread abroad** (over-seas) **to the west, and to the east, and to the north, and to the south: and in thee and in they seed shall all the families of the earth be blessed"** (Gen 28:14); **"a nation** (United States) **and a company of nations shall be of thee** (Common Wealth of GB), **and kings shall come out thy loins"** (Monarchs of Europe Genesis 35:11); **"and his seed shall become a multitude of nations"** (Gen 48:16); **Joseph is a fruitful bough, even a fruitful bough by a well; whose branches run over the wall:"** (Gen 49:24); **"His glory is like the firstling of his bullock, and his horns are like the horns of unicorns with them he shall push the people together to the ends of the earth: and they are the ten thousands of Ephraim** (unicorn of England), **and they are the thousands of Manasseh** (bull of the United States)." (Duet 33:17).

These verses cannot be speaking of the modern state of Israel, the Jews, for they do not match in any way and are not fruitful for the Jew still reject Christ as the Messiah. The Jew's rejecting Christ is the proving factor of the division of Israel in the last days for the house of Israel were to be fruitful (Christian) and the house of Judah still reject the true Messiah of Christ. Genesis 48:16-23 clearly gives the account of who received the birthright and it went only to Joseph's two sons, the lads of Ephraim and Manasseh, the unicorn and bull. They are the fruitful Christian nations of Gods Church (Matt 21:43). God commanded that this birthright was not to be reckoned with, which means it cannot be changed as states in I Chronicles 5:1-2.

Isle or Island: (339) a habitable spot as desirable, dry land, a coast, an Island, country: (3520) weightiness, magnificence, wealth, carriage, all glorious, stately: (3519) splendor or copiousness, glorious, honorable: (3513) be chargeable: (338) the idea of a doleful sound, a howler, solitary wild creature, wild beast of the Island.

Synopsis - As we study the word Isle or Island, we can see that it means dry land consisting of the coast of a country or an Island that is desirable, wealthy and glorious. The Islands afar off is mentioned several times in the Scriptures and covered very well in Isaiah chapter 40-43. Isaiah 42:1 states that the Isles shall wait for his law (the New Covenant) and matches Jeremiah 31:10 referring to them as Israel. Isaiah 41:1-8 is speaking to the Islands and in verse three where the people, **"by the way that he had not gone with his feet"**, indicating travel by ship, were wayfaring men (Hebrew travelers). Verse five says that the people of the Island feared God and verse eight calls them Israel his servant. These verses are a direct link to Isaiah 16:8, **"they wandered through the wilderness: her branches are stretched out, they are gone over the sea,"** and fulfills Genesis 49:22 where Ephraim and Manasseh, the sons of Joseph, their fruitful bough (nation) whose branches ran over the wall.

Ephraim and Manasseh are the unicorn and bull (Duet 33:17) which is England (unicorn) and the Unites States (the bullock). Ancient Bible maps list Ireland as Hibernia that is a name for Heber, Eber or Hebrew, the early Hebrew Druid settlers of Calcol and Dara (I Chron 2:6). If we closely study the word Island, we can see this is the location God chose to plant his nation into the wilderness to wait for his Gospel to be a fruitful nation. As the Birthright tribe, Ephraim as leader of the house of Israel was responsible to receive and protect the Gospel and to evangelize the world under the name of Israel, "he will rule as God".

The Hebrew Island of Hibernia is mentioned all through the Scriptures as the Isles which is the Islands of Britannia or modern Britain. The term Barbarian was derived from the British people by the Romans due to their fierce barbaric like fighting. One meaning of the word Island is to howl like a wild beast in which the ancient British warriors (Silurian's) were famous. They went into battle half naked howling and this is where the confederate rebel hell derived its name. It came from the ancient Silurian warriors (Barbarians) rebels fighting against Rome. The British Princes Claudia (Gladys, British name) was a Christian that married the Roman Senator Pudens (II Tim 4:21) and established a Church in Rome prior to Paul's visit. Paul's reference to the barbarians in Romans 1:14 was the Christian Britons already establish in Rome.

Isaac: (3327) "Yitschaq" Son of Abraham and Sarah - Laughter (in mocking): (8711) prime root, to laugh outright (in to scorn); to apart; laugh, mock, play, make sport: (3446) he will laugh; jischak, the heir of Abraham: (7831) proudly; a place in Palestine: (7830) unused root, to strut; haughtiness (as evinced by the attitude).

Synopsis- We know that Abraham, Isaac and Jacob were great men of God and chosen for a special role in his overall prophetic plan. Abraham's seed was to multiply as the sands of the sea and to be a blessing to the families of the world as great nations and to be called Hebrew. Jacob's name was changed to Israel as God's Chosen People and was to be called Israel as their Biblical name. Isaac had a very important role to play in Gods prophetic plan for his name was to be called Isaac's sons (Saxon) which was also passed on to Jacob (Gen 21:2, Heb 11:18) for they were to be named after Isaac. In other words, they were to have three different names. Their Biblical name as a race of people were to be called after Abraham (Hebrew), their worldly name was to be called after Isaac or Isaac's sons (Saxon) and the family Biblical name was to be called after Jacob that is called Israel or Hebrew Israelites. Their earthly name was to be known by the nations after Isaac's seed, Isaac's sons and later translated to Saxon or Anglo-Sason (Angels of Isaac's sons or Angle-land "England"). A Hebrew word for tent is Succoth for the Israelite Hebrews lived in tents for years and celebrated a memorial festival every year called Feast of Succuth to commemorate their ancestor hardships. They were known as Sucths or tent-dwellers after the Saki or Saxon.

The name Saxon is derived from ancient Saka-suni and means "son of Saks" or Isaac's sons. In many Eastern languages, sons were often written as sunnia in which Isaac would be written as saac-sunnia. The Assyrians called the Israelites, Iskuza/Isguzai/Sakhi, the Babylonians called them Gimirra/Gimiri, the Romans Kimmiri and Goth and the Greeks called them Kimmerioi/Kimbroi.

Amos 7:16 refers to the house of Isaac after the seed of Isaac that is Beth-Sak. The Anglo-Saxons, Lowland Scotch, Normans, Danes, Norwegians, Swedes, Germans, Dutch, Belgians, Lombards and Franks all come from the Scythian, German or Gothic ancestors, Isaac's sons (Beth-Sak). The house of King Omri (I Kings 16:23) was called Omri-Bit, Kumri, Cimmiri, Gimmiri, and Scythian that is synonymous with Cimmeriani of the Babylonians. ("Uncovering The Mysteries of Your Hidden Inheritance" by Robert Alan Balaicius, p. 20-23 and "The Post-captivity names of Israel" by Rev. Pascoe Goard)

Israel: in (3478) "Yisrael" "he will rule (as) God"; Jisrael, a symbol name of Jacob; also of his posterity: (8280) "sarah" prime root; to prevail, have power (as a prince): (410) "el" (ale) short, strength; as adj. mighty; especially the Almighty (but used also of any deity) God (god), goodly, great, idol, might, (-y one), power strong: (352) "ayil" strength; hence, anything strong; especially a chief (politically) <u>also a ram</u> (from his strength); a pilaster (as a strong support); <u>an oak or other strong tree</u>: mighty (man), lintel, oak, post, ram, tree: (193) "uwl" ool, unused root; to twist, i.e. (by implying) be strong; the body (as being rolled together); also powerful; mighty strength.

Synopsis- Israel indicates the meaning of Covenant or Confederate. Genesis 35:9-12, 32:28 established Jacob as the father of the twelve tribes of Israel. As we study the Hebrew definition of Israel, we can see why God chose his name for this people. It means, "he will rule as God", to prevail, have power as a prince and to be all Mighty God. Israel is God's name. This means that whom-ever Jacob chose as the birthright and received his name, had to be righteous and holy to fulfill Isaiah 41:2-3, 65:10 and Ezekiel 36:38. Other names that relate to Israel by definition is Ariel, Bashan and daughter for they are represented by the terms, ram "Ephraim" (bull), young calf or bullock "Manasseh" (Duet 33:17), and oak tree "Bashan or Manasseh" (Zech 11:2). Bashan is the region belonging to Manasseh, the Birthright tribe called Israel (Gen 48:16). Therefore, Manasseh will "rule as God". The Hebrew word confederate also relates to, mighty, a chief and the All Mighty which means Covenant "briyth or brit", the British covenant of man.

Isaiah 41:2-3 states that the righteous man from the East is the Hebrew wayfaring traveler of Ephraim (Jerm 31:21, "O virgin Israel") given nations of the world to rule as kings with military power under righteousness, the Covenant of the Church (Christian). It even states how he traveled, "he had not gone with his feet". He traveled by ship or horse and wagon, automobile or airplain by not using his feet. Isaiah 65:10, refers to a valley called Achor, a place where his flocks and herds lie down and they are called Sharon where his people have sought him. Note that flocks and herds are plural which means many peoples and nations that sought him. This cannot be the Jews for they still reject Christ as the Messiah. This verse is speaking to Gods people in the last days and verse nine is bringing forth a seed out of Jacob and out of Judah "an inheritor of my mountains". This inheritor is speaking of Christ and his Church that takes place in the last days where the mountains are his Christian nations, his flocks and herds within his Church.

Ezekiel 36:38 is very interesting for it speaks of his holy flock of Jerusalem, the Church, and flocks of his waste cities of the house of Israel in the wilderness. In other words, he is calling the cities built out of the desolation in the wilderness within the continents of the world, Jerusalem. Jerusalem is his Church which is the Christian cities of the world, Zion. This verse speaks of his flock (the Church) filling the waste cities of the world, **"and they shall know that I am the Lord"**. Study this whole chapter and especially start with verse 24 for it speaks of God gathering his people into a new land and giving the house of Israel a new heart and spirit. This new heart and spirit are under the New Covenant of the Church that takes place in the last days. We need to remind ourselves that all the Old Testament Prophetic books were written as a warning to the end time Church to take place in our present time period.

After a close study of the above three verses, his Church was to have a powerful sword or military power to be Gods Battle Ax. Jeremiah 51:19-20 states that Israel is the rod of his inheritance which is Ephraim and Manasseh his birthright tribes to be a nation and a company of nations (Gen 48:19). The Lord of host is his name, Israel "he will rule as God" (Manasseh). The Unicorn of England and the Bull of the United States has been Gods Battle Axe for the past five hundred years under the new spirit and heart of his New Covenant Church.

In Isaiah 41:2, God was speaking to the Islands of England (Ephraim) and verse 8 calls them Israel his servant. "O virgin Israel also found in Jerm 31:4, 31:21, and Amos 5:2 means Israel is a virgin or bride making them the Church or Zion (Jerm 31:33, Heb 8:8-10) under the new Covenant. Jacob gave Joseph's two sons, Ephraim and Manasseh, the Birthright in Genesis 48:16 where only they received the name Israel and no other tribe to include Judah or the Jews. This is confirmed in I Chronicles 5:1-2. The other eleven sons of Jacob received their right to be called Israel through Ephraim and Manasseh who received the Birthright in a dual role.

The Hebrew meaning of Ephraim means double fruit and to be fruitful which is to be righteous or Christian. Gods Kingdom was given to Ephraim, leader of the house of Israel in I Kings 11:26-28 and later given David's overturned throne in I Kings 12:20, Eze 17:22-24 and 21:25-27. Christ himself gave Ephraim, the house of Israel the full Kingdom in Matthew 21:43 due to the disbelief of the Jews and fulfilled the breach of the Kingdom in Mark 3:24-25 and Amos 9:11. This fulfilled all the blessing of greatness to Abraham, Isaac, Jacob and Joseph to be a nation and a company of nations as kings (Gen 35:11).

Today, the house of Israel is still Gods earthly kingdom and falls under the authority of the Throne of England. His Kingdom has become the English-speaking Christian nations of the world, Christ's Church called Zion. Israel is the Church or any one that will accept Christ as their personal Savior. The Crown of England and the United States of America protects the Church, representing King David's Throne as his Battle Axe and sword that is called Israel "he will rule as God as a Prince ".

Jacob: is called (Israel) son of Isaac and Rebekah, father of the twelve tribes of Israel: (3290) "yauqob" heel-catcher (i.e. supplanter): (6117) Prime root; to swell out, or up; to seize by the heel; figurative to circumvent (as if holding by the heel); take by the heel, stay, supplant, utterly: (6119) Feminine: a heel (as protuberant); hence, a track; figurative, the rear (of an Army); heel, (horse) hoof, last, liar in wait (by mistake), (foot)-step.

Synopsis- Genesis 32:28 tells us that Jacob became Israel, **"And he said, thy name shall be called no more Jacob, but Israel; for as a prince hast thou power with God and with men, and hast prevailed"**. God gave Jacob the responsibility to preserve the family name of Israel and to pass it down in accordance to Hebrew birthright traditions. The oldest son was to receive the fathers name, be anointed, and to be given a double portion of family assets unless he sinned against the family causing him to lose his inheritance. Events where the eldest son lost his inheritance have happened through-out the Bible. It is the responsibility of the father to give the inheritance to a deserving son, therefore preserving the family name. Reuben was the oldest of Jacob's sons and would have received the Birthright inheritance but due to his sins, he lost the birthright to Joseph. In accordance to Gen 48:13-19, a very strange event occurred, Jacob passed the birthright blessing directly to Joseph's two sons, Ephraim and Manasseh. Again, Manasseh was the oldest but due to his sins, Jacob crossed his arms and placed his right hand on Ephraim giving him the double portion. This birthright blessing is very important to understand so we can properly divide the difference between the house of Israel (the ten northern tribes lead by Ephraim, the birthright child) and the house of Judah (the Jews, the tribe of Judah and Benjamin). The family name was not given to the Jews or Judah but to Ephraim and Manasseh in a dual role and according to Gen 35:9-12, Jacob's blessings for his name of Israel was to be, **"be fruitful and multiply; a nation** (Israel) **and a company of nations** (many nations) **shall be of thee, and kings** (many Kings) **shall come out of thy loins"**. This produces a big question for who are these nations and kings that were to be called Israel after Jacob's name? The nation of Israel was divided in I Kings 11:30-37 by the Prophet Ahijah. He separated the Kingdom and called the northern ten tribes the house of Israel led by Ephraim, the birthright tribe, and the two southern tribes the house of Judah. They are still divided to this day and will be till the events in Eze 37:11 is fulfilled where they become the whole house of Israel. God said that the nations of Jacob were to be fruitful meaning they were to be righteous or God fearing. Who are these nations today? They can only be the Christian nations of Ephraim and Manasseh that is, the Common Wealth of Great Britain, (a company of nations) and the United States of America, the most powerful Christian nation ever in history that has spread Christ's Gospel throughout the world. The Kingdom is still divided and will remain divided till the Tribulation Period. This can be proven for the house of Israel is fruitful by believing in Christ and the house of Judah (modern Jews), reject Christ as the Messiah.

Yes, the US is in Bible Prophecy, but under the ancient names of the house of Israel as Ephraim, Manasseh, house of Joseph, Bashan, Carmel, Gilead, house of Jacob and Samaria, which was the capital of the ten northern tribes of the house of Israel.

Jew: is "Yhuwdiy" ueh-hoo-dee, patron, a Jehudite (ie Judaite or Jew) or descendent of Jehudah (i.e. Judah-Jew): (3063) Celebrated; Jehuduh (or Judah) the name of five Israel; also of the Tribe descended from the first and of its territory-Judah: (3034) prime root; to use (hold out) the hand; to throw (a stone or arrow) at or away; especially to revere or worship (with extended hands) - cast (out) (make) confession, praise, shout, give thanks: (3027) a hand: (2453) "Chakmowniy": skillful, and Israelite - Hachmoni. Hachmonite: (2449) Prime root; to be wise (in mind), exceeding, teach, wisdom, be (made self, shew self), wise, deal, (never so), wisely, make wiser.

Synopsis- From the Hebrew definition of Jew, it is clear that a Jew is only from the tribe of Judah or Benjamin. The Bible first mentioned the term Jew in II Kings 16:6 in approx. 742BC, 238 years after Israel and Judah were divided into separate houses. The term was coined by the Assyrians when the house of Israel and the Assyrians were at war with Jerusalem, II Kings 16:5-6. The Jews of Jerusalem in Judea are always refereed too as Jews but the Israelites of the ten northern tribes of the house of Israel are never associated as being called a Jew in accordance to the Scriptures. The account of Israel being divided as a nation took place in I Kings 11:30-37 and 12:19-20 in approx. 980BC. The Israelites marched into the Promised Land in 1450 BC as a nation and the term Jew did not appear as a name of the Judeans of Jerusalem for 708 years, close to the end of the rule of the Israelite Kings that ended in 586 BC. King Zedekiah was the last King of Israel. Only the people that practiced Judaism of the tribe of Judah and Benjamin were called Jews. It is not Scriptural to call the Jews God's chosen people for it is clear in the Bible that the Hebrew Israelites are God's chosen people. The Jew was only a small portion of the chosen people but the modern Christian Church and Theologians make the mistake in believing that only the Jew is Gods elect people. The Scriptures are clear in defining the Hebrew race as God's chosen people and the Jews (Judah and Benjamin) are only two twelfth of his Covenant People.

The Birthright blessings went to Joseph, (Ephraim and Manasseh) and not to the Jews of Judah. Isaiah 45:4, **"For Jacob my servant's sake, and Israel mine elect, I have even called thee by thy name: I have surnamed thee, through thou hast not known me"**. This verse clearly indicates the division of Israel. Jacob represents all the children of Israel to include Judah but Israel his elect refers to the house of Israel that is the 10 northern tribes lead by Ephraim and Manasseh. The tribe of Judah was never divorced by God and did not lose their name or language after their captivity to Babylon. The house of Israel lost their name and language when they were taken into captivity to Assyria because they never returned to the promised land of Palestine as did the house of Judah. The ten northern tribes became the lost sheep of the house of Israel as spoken by Jesus in Matt 10:6 and 15:24 which was led by Ephraim and Manasseh, the birthright tribes. In the verse above where it speaks of "Israel mine elect" refers to the lost sheep of the house of Israel becoming Gods Christian fruitful nation as his Church in Matt 21:43. This is where most Christians go wrong for the responsibility to continue the name of Israel went to Ephraim and Manasseh (the house of Israel), the elect, through the birthright and not to the Jew or the house of Judah. Present day Jews are modern day Israel in Jerusalem that is the house of Judah, so, where is the modern-day house of Israel? They are the Christian, English speaking people of the world, the Common Wealth of Great Britain and the United States of America that has been fruitful to fulfill Gods Scriptures to evangelize the world. The term fruitful through-out the Bible means Christian, (to produce fruit) but God cursed the Jews (Jerm 7:29; 24:9; 25:18; 29:18; 44:8; and Eze 22:4). The curse of the Jews is because they always maintained Judaism and never accepted Christ as the Messiah and will remain cursed till the Tribulation Period when their eyes are opened and given their chance to repent. Christians do not see or understand the division of Israel that exist today and that is why they are so confused about Old Testament Prophecies. Until a person can rightly divide the Jew of the house of Judah and the Hebrew Israelites of the house of Israel, they will never be able to understand end time prophecies. (Refer to the term Hebrew)

Last Days: Through-out the Bible the term last days is synonymous with the period after Christ's death up to and including the great period of Wrath during the Tribulation Period. This time period is called the end times that include our present period and called by many different names as follows:

In the last days (Acts 2:17)
In that day (Isa 2:20)
Day of the Lord (Isa 10:3)
In the day of visitation (Isa 10:3)
The day of his fierce anger (Isa 13:13)
Day of grief (Isa 17:11
Day of trouble (Isa 22:5)
Day of the east wind (Isa 27:8)
Until this day (Isa 39:6)
Day of vengeance (Isa 61:2)
Great day of his wrath (Rev 6:17)
That great day of God Almighty (Rev 16:14)

To get a full understanding we need to break the definition of Last and Days into Hebrew and Greek.

Last: (_Hebrew_): (314) Hinder, generally late or last, especially as facing the east (western), afterward, to come, hindermost, uttermost: (309) prime root; to loiter (be behind), to procrastinate: (319) the last or end, the future, also posterity, length, remnant, residue, reward. (_Greek_) (314) to know again, to read: (309) restoration of sight, recovery of sight: (319) to make one self-known, be made known: (2078) sacrifice: (2077) a slaughter of the flesh of an animal, imply to sacrifice the victim or the act, offering: (2076) prime root; to slaughter and animal usually in sacrifice, kill, offer, do sacrifice, slay.

Days: (_Hebrew_): (3117) unused root, to be hot, a day as the warm hours, from sunrise to sunset or tone sunset to the next, perpetually, season, process of time: (_Greek_): (3117) long or time, far: (3372 length, very wide application, exceedingly great, high, large, mighty, sore, strong, to years.

Synopsis - The term last days, is synonymous with our present time period of the Church age where we are now in "the last of the last days". This period actually ranges from the time Christ died on the cross till the end of the Tribulation Period of Wrath or when Christ returns in power to rule for a thousand years. It ends man's 6000 allotted years of self-rule proving to Satan the Devil that man can not properly rule with justice, mercy, righteousness and peace without God at his center. It signifies the prophetic occurrences that take place during the last days as predicted in Scripture. A good example of this is given in Genesis 49:1 when Jacob gave his blessings to his 12 sons which would become nations and their blessing would be fulfilled in the last days. The last days is also directly related to the terms listed above which apply to the end of man's rule on earth.

Lebanon: Chief Mountain range in Syria: (3844) "Lebanown"; the White Mountains (from its snow); Lebanon, a mountain range in Palestine: (3825) heart: (3824) the heart (as the most interior organ); bethink themselves, breast, comfortable, courage, (faint, tender) hearted, midst, mind, unawares, understanding: (3820) the heart used figuratively very widely for the feelings, the will and even the intellect, likewise for the center of anything, care for, comfortably, consent, considered, courageous, friendly, broken, hard, merry, stiff, stout, double hearted, heed, kindly, midst, minded, regarded, themselves, unawares, understanding, well, willingly, wisdom.

Synopsis - The glory of Lebanon is spoken of in Isaiah 35:2 and 60:13 as the glory of God which means it has to be righteous and is referred to as a cedar tree representing the throne of David. Isaiah 29:17 states, **"Is it not yet a very little while, and Lebanon shall be turned into a fruitful field, and the fruitful filed shall be esteemed as a forest"**. Lebanon, Bashon, Carmel, Gilead and Sharon are all listed in the Bible as fruitful trees or forest and Lebanon is usually listed first. Fruitful is the key for fruitful represents Christian trees or nations. If we trace King David's throne to the Throne of England then ancient Lebanon must be modern England or the Common Wealth of Great Britain so the throne has been preserved to fulfill Gods promise to King David. These ancient nations listed above have to be the modern fruitful Christian nations of the English-Speaking world, Great Britain and the United States. Refer to the segment on Lebanon in chapter seven for details.

Lost Sheep: The term lost sheep is very unique and mentioned approx. five times in the Scriptures (Matt 10:6 and 15:24) but plays an important role in understanding just who the house of Israel is during the last days. Just a few verses that pertain to Gods sheep is: scattered sheep (Jerm 50:17, Zech 13:7); Israel is a scattered sheep (Jerm 50:17); seek out my sheep and gather (Eze 34:12-14); lost sheep of house of Israel (Matt 10:6); lost sheep of house of

Israel (Matt 15:24) sheep on right goats on left (Matt 25:33).

God chose the sheep as an example of his Chosen People and Church for its beauty, gentleness, its white to represent purity and a sheep will follow its guide or master without question.

Lost: (*Hebre:*): (622) prime root; to gather for any purpose hence to receive, take away, remove, destroy, leave behind, put up, restore, assemble, bring, consume, gather in or up again. (*Greek*): (622) to destroy fully, die, lose, mar, perish: (575) usually denotes separation, departure, cessation, completion, reversal: (3639) to destroy, ruin, death, punishment, destruction.

Sheep: (*Hebrew*): (4263) sympathy, delight, pitieth: (2550) prim. root; to commiserate, by implying to spare, have compassion, have pity, spare: (4261) delightful, hence a delight, object of affection or desire, be loved, desire, goodly, lovely, pleasant thing. (*Greek*): (4263) something that walks forward (a quadruped) a sheep: (4260) to walk forward, advance in years, be of a great age, go farther on, be well stricken: (4253) primary preposition; fore, in front of, prior (figuratively superior), to be above, ago, before, or ever: (939) to walk, a pace, by implying the foot.

Synopsis - The term lost sheep is very interesting and important when referring to the house of Israel as his lost sheep. The Jews of Judah were never called lost sheep for they have never been lost. It only pertains to the house of Israel where their name was taken from them and given a new name as Christian (Isa 45:4, 65:15, Duet 32:26, Isa 62:2, 56:5 and 28:11). The house of Israel was also divorced in Jeremiah 3:8 and betrothed or engaged in Hosea 2:19-20 under the New Covenant of the Church as Christ's Bride to be. The term lost means punishment and that is why they were sent into the wilderness to complete their time period of punishment. The house of Judah or the Jews was never divorced for the coming of the Messiah had to take place, otherwise, the Virgin Mary would not be eligible. They could not be betrothed for they were never divorced but cursed due to rejecting Christ and their portion of the Kingdom taken from them by Christ himself in Matthew 21:43. The complete Kingdom was given to the fruitful nation of the house of Israel planted in the wilderness (Hos 2:14-23, Eze 34:13-31, Jerm 31) and still exist today under the Throne of England.

It is clear in Matthew 10:5-8 and 15:22-26 that Christ sent his disciples only to the lost sheep of the house of Israel where his throne had been overturned by Jeremiah as recorded in Ezekiel 17 and 21 to a new land, Ireland in the Islands of Britannia. Matthew 15:24 unmistakably states, **"I** (Christ) **am not sent but unto the lost sheep of the house of Israel,"** and again in Matthews 15:24, **"I** (Christ) **am not sent but unto the lost sheep of the house of Israel"**. The

Disciples were not sent to the Jews or the Gentiles but only to the house of Israel in the wilderness as these verses clearly state. God had special plans, for his purpose was to send his Disciples into the world to establish his Church and not just to the Jews of Jerusalem or the Gentiles in Judea. That was left for Paul to complete. The Disciples were to stay in Jerusalem just long enough for the Church to be established and begin to grow before they departed to find his lost sheep. God knew that the Jews would not accept his Apostles and would kill them so he wasted no time on the Jews and left that to Saul/Paul. Jesus sent them into the wilderness to the house of Israel where they accepted his Gospel. They became the Christian nations of today.

Paul was sent to the Jews not the Apostles and due to their rejection of Christ's Gospel, Jerusalem was totally destroyed in 70AD by the Roman Army. God gave the Jew one generation to accept or be destroyed just as he did in the wilderness when they also rejected him and would not allow the non-believers to enter the Promised Land. That is why the wondered for forty years. The Welch Triads, the Chronicles of Ireland, Scotland and England confirms along with many ancient writers, that the Apostles along with Paul preached the Gospel all through Europe and the British Isles, the Isles as stated in Isaiah chapter 41-43.

Man: (120) "Adam", a human being (and individual or the species of man) person: (119) to show blood (in the face), flush or turn rosy, red (ruddy) (376) "iysh", unused root, to be extant, a man as an individual or a male person, husband: (377) "iysh" to be a man, act in a manly way.

Synopsis- The Hebrew definition of man means Adam and is a man with fair skin and a rosy red flush face (ruddy, red). Ruddy is mentioned four times in the Bible, (Sam 16:12; 17:42), referring to David as being Ruddy or red faced. Songs 5:10 is said to be speaking of the Church calling it **"white and ruddy, the chiefs among ten thousand"**. This verse identifies Ephraim that is called "ten thousands" in Duet 33:17, Lamentation 4:7 make the statement, **"Her Nazarites were purer than snow, they were whiter than milk, they were more ruddy in body than rubies, their polishing was of sapphire"**. Christ was a Nazarene (Matt 2:23) of Nazareth and this verse is a description of Christ's linage that came from King David. Christ were to come from the linage of God's chosen people and it is clear from the Scriptures that their race was to be white skinned, fair, and red faced (ruddy). The only race of people in the world that meets this requirement is the Caucasian people of Europe and the United States. Our ancestors migrated from Europe as God's Chosen People. There is another fascinating aspect that we cannot ignore. The Hebrew word for Covenant in the Strongs Concordance reference #1285 is "briyth". The Hebrew meaning for man in reference #376 is "iysh". Covenant "briyth", man "iysh", and together means British in modern terms. In other words, British means Covenant man, God's chosen people. Reference #127 is from the Hebrew word land meaning man or land; therefore, Britain would mean covenant land.

Another aspect of Man is the color red for it also represent the humanistic side that has turned into the ideology of Liberal Socialism that is Anti-Christ, the evil humanistic characteristic of the human race. This humanistic trait produces the Red Horse of Russia spoken of in Revelation 6:4, **"And there went out another horse that was red: and power was given to him that sat thereon to take peace from the earth, and that they should kill one another: and there was given unto him a great sword."** We can see today how Liberal Socialism is tied directly to Communism and dominates the world during our present time and will slowly become the platform for the New World Order through the United Nation Organization.

Manasseh: The oldest son of Joseph Gen 48:16 & 19, "Menashsheh": (4519) Causing to forget: (5382) primitive root; to forget.

Synopsis- Manasseh begins with the word "man" "ish" and in Hebrew meaning Manasseh is a forgetful man. He was the oldest son of Joseph and born in Egypt along with his brother Ephraim. Psalms 108:8 speaks of Gods Holiness and to whom most precious to him, **"Gilead is mine; Manasseh is mine; Ephraim also is the strength of mine head; Judah is my lawgiver"**. This verse is clear on who was to receive the name Israel and be the head of the family by Hebrew Law. It was given to Manasseh and Ephraim. The Throne of Israel and the duties of being the lawgiver went to Judah, Gen 49:10 (the bloodline of Jesus and the ultimate lawgiver) but not the name of Israel as the family head, it went to Joseph's two sons as indicated in this verse. Due to Manasseh's sins, Ephraim his brother received the majority of the birthright blessings and Manasseh was included in a dual blessing. The name Israel as the head of the family went to both sons, Gen 48:16, **"bless the lads and let my name be names on them,"**. This is very important to understand for God divided Israel and the ten northern tribes were the bulk or mass of all Israel's population. Ephraim is the head of the family by name and the name Israel were to go to the house of Israel and the name Jew went to the house of Judah, II Kings 16:6. This is how the Old Testament Prophets distinguished between the two separate houses of Israel.

We can trace Manasseh through the names of Gilead, I Chronicles 27:21, **"Of the half tribe of Manasseh in Gilead"**, they are called Bashan in I Chronicles 6:62, **"And to the sons of Gershom throughout their families out of the tribe of Issachar, and out of the tribe of Asher and out of the tribe of Naphtali, and out of the tribe of Manasseh, in Bashan, thirteen cities"**. The Tribes listed above is a coalition of nations called Bashan to this day. This coalition is again mentioned in Nahum 1:4, **"He rebuketh the sea, and maketh it dry, and drieth up all the rivers: Bashan languisheth, and Carmel, and the flower of Lebanon languisheth."** These are the end time fruitful God fearing Righteous Christian nations and Judah is not listed. The United States is Manasseh and Hosea 2:14-23 gives the account of how Manasseh is allured into the wilderness and betrothed into a new covenant. The name Ishi in verse 16 is the key to understand these verses, **"thou shall call me Ishi"**. There were two Ishi in ancient Israel, one was a descendant of Judah and Pharez of the bloodline of Israel's Kings. The other was a Chief of the tribe of Manasseh and a symbolic name for Israel due to the birthright Law which this verse is referring to.

Read and study this account in I Chron 5:23-24. This verse says that they will no longer call God Baali but will call him Ishi, this means they will be righteous Christian nations that recognize Christ as the Messiah. Keep in mind that all the prophet books were a warning not only to the current time but mainly for the Church to teach and spread Christ's end time Gospel in accordance with his written authorized King James Bible. King James was a King and lawgiver in the bloodline of King David which fulfills Gen 49:10, **"The sceptre shall not depart from Judah, nor a lawgiver from between his feet, until Shiloh come** [Christ the Messiah]**; and unto him shall the gathering of the people be** [the Church]**"**. This verse is clear by saying that the tribe of Judah will always have a King and a lawgiver till Christ comes to establish his Church. Where is the Scepter and lawgiver today fulfilling Gods promise? It was overturned to England where the fulfillment of this verse is presently King Charles of England where he sits on the current Throne of David and the government of England as the lawgiver. King Charles and Queen Elisabeth is a direct descendant of King James the I that translated the Bible and King David which fulfills, Jerm 33:14-17; I Kings 9:5. The English term, *"God Save the King"* is stated word for word in I Sam 10:24 in reference to King David's Throne. All the English coronation ceremonies are taken out of the Old Testament rituals of crowning a Hebrew King.

Mountain: (2022) "har" a mountain or range of hills (sometimes used figuratively), hill (country) mountain, promotion: (2042) "harar" unused root; to loom up; a mountain; hill, mount (ain): (3735) "kara" (Chaldean) in the sense of piercing (figurative) to grieve, be grieved: (3738) Primitive root: properly to dig; figuratively to plot; generally, to bore or open; dig, make (a banquet) open. Greek: (2022) "epicheo" to pour upon, pour in.

Mount: (55) is a Primitive root; probate, to coil upward, mount up: (4674) a station, military post: (5324) Primitive root; to station, appointed, deputy, erect, establish, lay, officer, pillar, present, rear up, set over or up, settle, sharpen: (5927) Primitive root; to ascend, arise (up), cause to ascend up, at once, break, spring up, take away (up), cut off, dawn, deport, exalt: (5550) a military mound, rampart of besiegers, bank: (7311) Primitive root; to be high, to raise or raise, bring up, haughty, heave up, lofty, presumptuously, promotion, proud, taller, take away, breed worms.

Synopsis- After reviewing all the Scriptures on the term mountain, we come up with two meanings. The first is a literal mountain or large landmass that looms upwards. The seconds is a symbol of a mountain or mountains referring to a nation or nations of people. Isaiah 13:4 clearly calls mountains people or nations, **"The noise of a multitude in the mountains, like as of a great people; a tumultuous noise of the kingdoms of nations gathered together"**. In many instances in the Scriptures, the word mountain is in reference to a nation or nations (Eze 34:5-6, Habakkuk 3:6, Jerm 51:24-26 etc). See the word mountain in chapter eight for details.

Pharez: The firstborn son of Judah: (6557) "Perets" the name of two Israeli patriarchs, Perez, Pharez: (6556) a break, literal or figurative; **breach**, breaking forth (in), forth, gap: (6555) Primitive root; to break out (in many applications, direct and indirect, literal or figurative; abroad, (make a) breach, break (away, down, forth, in, up), burst out, come (separate) abroad, compel, disperse, grow, increase, open, press, scatter, urge.

Synopsis- Pharez was the firstborn breached son of Judah and received the blessing of the throne as recorded in Genesis 49:8-12. All the kings of Israel came from the bloodline of Pharez to include King David and Jesus. Due to the breach of the scarlet threat as recorded in Genesis chapter 38, his twin brother Zarah, also received the dual heir to the throne. Zarah fulfills the prophecy of Ezekiel in chapter 17 and 21 with the overturn of the throne to Ireland which passed from the high branch of the cedar (Throne of David) of Pharez and given to the low branch of Zarah healing the breach of the throne (Amos 9:11 and Ps 60:2). This breach was corrected in Amos 9:8-15 when the Throne of King David were overturned to the Zarah bloodline as mentioned in Ezekiel above. Matthew 1:3 state the linage of Christ and lists both Pharez and Zarah as being in line for kingship. (Refer to the word Zarah)

Phenicia or Phoenicians: (5403) "fenisheah" a coastal region of northern Palestine (Acts 21:2). "neshar" - an eagle: (5404) "nesher" - unused root; to lacerate, the eagle or other large bird of prey.

Synopsis- The Hebrew meaning of Phoenicia and eagle are the same. The modern meaning for Phoenix is a mythical bird of great beauty, the only one of its kind, a bird of prey (the Fire Bird). When you look at a Biblical map of Canaan as divided among the 12 tribes, Phoenicia (Phenicia) is located in the northern coastal region of Palestine adjacent to the territory of the tribe of

Asher. The Phoenicians were of the house of Enoch where Abraham was in his linage as Hebrew. The Phoenicians held the symbol of the eagle and palm tree and were seagoing merchants of the known world and existed long before Israel became a nation. This could be why they were named after the eagle for they covered the world with their wings or fleet of merchant ships (Eze 17). Their wings were spread over the world as the eagle soars. The Phoenicians were the descendants of Enoch and Noah down through Abraham and Shem. They were the part of Shem's descendants that departed the land of Shinar to escape the evils of Babylon prior to the tower of Babel and settled the area of Phenicia. Possibly a portion of Abraham's sojourn also departed to the north and settled Phenicia. This would explain why the Israelites and the Phoenicians were always brothers. Solomon received his wealth from the Phoenician ships of Tarshish (II Chron 9:21) that came from Spain. The Hebrew alphabet was derived from the Phoenician language and later into Gallic then English. Phoenician were the most common language due to international trade just as English is today because of world commerce. The great Phoenician Empire controlled most of the world by colonizing through merchant shipping, not by an army. Their land was only a small strip on the northern coast of Palestine just as the island nation of England, a very small nation that has also controlled the commerce of the world by colonizing.

Plant (ed): (7880) "siyach" a shoot (as if uttered or put forth), i.e. (generally) shrubbery, bush, plant, shrub: (7878) Primitive root; to ponder, (by implying) converse (with oneself, and hence, aloud) or (tran.) utter, commune, complain, declare, meditate, muse, pray, speak, talk: (5193) "nata" primitive root; prop. to strike in, i.e. fix; spec. to plant (literal or fig.) fastened, plant (er): (5414) "nathan" primitive root; to give, used with greatest latitude of application (put, make, etc.) add, apply, appoint.

Synopsis- After reviewing the definition of plant, it represents a living, growing, branching out, shooting forth, garden, vineyard or an entity of living things that represent Gods green creation that bears fruit and grows. Plants are the essence of God's creation that produces beauty, the quintessence of life and is why it is always associated with his people and nations. The word plant or planted is a key word in understanding how Gods over-all plan for Israel has been implemented and carried out over the centuries and is a term directly associated with the house of Israel and the house of Judah. This word is synonymous with root, vineyard, branch, vines and wilderness. There is also a direct correlation between Plant and the terms; to root out, to pull down, to destroy, to throw down, and to build along with the association of, "will plant it upon a high mountain" and to "bear fruit", Ezekiel 17:22-23. This is an example of how one Hebrew word can have so many different meanings and important to research all definitions concerning the proper meaning in respect to the subject of circumstance. Note that all through the Scriptures the word plant is used by God to establish his people, Israel. Exodus 15:17, initially planted Israel in the Promised Land. We also know that due to national sins, God rooted up his people as a punishment, I Kings 14:15, and when-ever you root up a plant you have to replant soon or it will die. We need to understand the aspect of how God replanted the remnant of the house of Israel and house of Judah after their captivities and being scattered into the wilderness of the world in Jerm 1:10.

Their captivity was the completion of God dividing the two houses for they never again associated with each other after their separate captivities. Refer to the word wilderness. II Sam 7:10; I Chr 17:9 speaks of his people Israel (the house of Israel) by planting King David's throne in a safe place of their own. This cannot be speaking of the promised land of Israel in Palestine but the replanting after the captivities of Israel and Judah. From 586BC, there has been no King in Israel for 2610 years. Jerusalem was destroyed by Rome in 70AD so there had been no government of Israel till 1948 with the establishment of modern Israel and approx. 1878 years of nonexistence. Where are Gods promise of King David's throne given in I Kings 9:5? Israel did not gain control of Jerusalem till the 1967 Arab war. Israel was to be followed by Zion and transplanted by Jeremiah to Ireland in Eze 17:22 & 21:25-27. Isaiah 5:7 (to Israel and Judah), 37:30 (to Judah) and Eze 17:22 applies to Israel and Judah as a vineyard to be planted and to grow. Jeremiah 1:10, 18:9, Isaiah 41:19, Eze 17:22 speaks to the nations of the house of Israel and to the Isles to be destroyed, to be rebuilt and to be planted. This occurs after the captivities of both the house of Israel into Assyria in approx. 721BC and the house of Judah to Babylon in 586BC. Hosea 9:13 is to Ephraim (Great Britain) the leader of the house of Israel and God planted him in a pleasant place. Jerm 24:5-10 speaks only to the house of Judah where they are brought back into the promised land of Canaan in Palestine during the last days to complete prophecy during the Tribulation Period. This verse does not apply to the house of Israel.

Where is the house of Israel planted? They were planted in the wilderness of the Islands of Britannia and Europe, Isa chapter 41, Eze 17, Hosea 2:14-23 and 9:13. God blessed the nations that love and serve him and bear fruit. The great blessings given to Abraham, Isaac and Jacob in Genesis 49:1 is in the last days and II Sam 7:10-17 with the birthright double portion given to Ephraim and Manasseh were to continue the Throne of David to this day. These blessings could not go to the house of Judah or the Jews for they have rejected Christ. The promised land of Canaan or Palestine of Judea was to become the homeland or root of the nation of Israel (Isa 5:7) that produced Gods earthly throne and the Messiah, Jesus Christ. The planted nations were to fulfill the blessings given to Abraham, Isaac and Jacob, the lost sheep of the house of Israel that were filtered through the nations and planted to evangelize the world with Christ's

Gospel. The following verses is just a few key Scriptures that represents the word plant: II Sam 7:10; I Chron 17:9; Isa 5:17; 37:30; 41:19; Jerm 1:10; 118:9; Eze 17:22; Hos 9:13.

Remnant: (*Hebrew*): (7611) a remainder or residue of survival of final portion, that had escaped, be left, posterity, remainder, residue, rest: (3698) spelt: (319) same definition as last: (6413) deliverance, that is escaped: (8300) a survivor, alive, left, remaining, remnant rest: (*Greek*): (3062) something remaining, besides, finally: (2640) remainder, a few: (3062) remaining ones.

Synopsis - In light of the above definition, we need to apply the captivities of the house of Israel in 719BC (11 million Hebrews) and the house of Judah in 586BC (2 million Jews) of their present location after their departure from captivity. There is no indication in the Scriptures that the Hebrews of the house of Israel ever returned to Judea. After 70 years of the Jews being captive to Babylon, only a remnant of approx. 40,000 Jews returned to Jerusalem of Judea to rebuild the Temple as recorded in Ezra 6:14-15. At this point, we need to ask our-selves a very important question! Where did the mass of the Hebrews and Jews of the houses of Israel and Judah depart and where are they today? Only the remnant of the 40,000 Jews that returned to Jerusalem in Ezra and Zechariah's day became the Jews of Jerusalem during the reign of the Persian, Greek and Roman subjugations. The ancestors of the 40,000 Jews provided the Messiah and represent the modern state of Israel.

Amos 9:9 tell us that the house of Israel will be sifted among all nations and, **"yet shall not the least grain fall upon the earth"**. The fact that almost two million Jews migrated into the world that has not been accounted for fulfills Jerm 12:14-15, for the Jews were to be plucked out and scattered between Jacob and the house of Israel as a separate people. God knows where each and every one of his Chosen People is located and these unaccounted Jews fell under the great blessing of Ephraim and Manasseh to be a part of great wealthy nations. Most of these Jew amalgamated with the house of Israel and lost their Jewish identity and language. Only a portion maintained Orthodox Judaism in each nation they settled. They were to remain scattered among the countries of the world till the time for the reestablishment of Jerusalem in 1948 where a remnant returned to Israel. He planted the house of Israel, not the Jew, in the wilderness as Hebrew travelers, wayfaring men along his spiritual highway to produce nations of righteous Christian people to fulfill the promise to Abraham, Isaac, Jacob and Joseph (Ephraim and Manasseh), his birthright tribes under his New Covenant.

In reality, God took the mass of his kingdom, and sifted them into the world to fulfill his prophecies, to include most of the house of Judah, the Jews. Only approx. 40,000 Jews returned to Orthodox Judaism to rebuild the Temple in

Jerusalem and to fulfill the prophecy of the coming Messiah. They became modern Israel while 13 million Hebrew Israelites to include the mass of the house of Judah, the Jews, were sifted through the nations and given their own land planted in the wilderness. The two million unaccounted Jews enjoyed the fruits and security of the house of Israel in the wilderness with no country of their own where some kept their Orthodox Religion. The fulfillment of prophecy of Israel becoming a modern state in 1948 were for the Jews only, for the proving factor lies within the authority of the throne for it still remains with the Crown of England, King David's throne till the fulfillment of the gathering of the tried bones and joining of the two sticks in Ezekiel 37:11 and 16-17.

Scattered: (6327) "puwts" prime root; to disperse, break dash or shake into pieces, cast abroad, drive, retire, scatter abroad, spread abroad: (6555) Prime root, to break out; abroad, make a breach, come spread abroad, increase: (6557) **Pharez** is referring to the breach of Zarah and Pharez in Gen 38:29-30: (2219) Cast away, compass, strew: (2114) Prime root; to turn aside, **to be a foreigner**, stranger, profane.

Synopsis- The word scatter is important to understand for its definition explain Gods dispersion of his chosen people among the nations of the world due to their sin. Scattered is related to certain key words such as, disperse, cast abroad, make a breach, increase, cast away and to be a foreigner. All these words are also related to God planting his nations in the wilderness and the breach of the throne of David. The throne was to be overturned from Pharez to Zarah of the scarlet thread as mentioned in Genesis 38:29-30 and the linage of Christ and his throne in Matt 1:3. The breach was to be healed, Amos 9:11, at the overturn of the throne recorded in Ezekiel 17:22-24 and 21:25-27 which fulfills Matt 21:43 of the Jews. The scattering of Gods People was to fulfill the promise of greatness to Abraham, Isaac, Jacob and Joseph (Ephraim and Manasseh of the house of Israel) to take place in the last days. They were to be a great nation and a company of nations as kings of kingdoms (Gen 17:6, 35:11 and 48:19). How can these blessing be speaking of one small nation in Palestine called Israel that has always encompassed only the Jews in modern times?

Sharon: A plain of Ephraim, a plain or city in Gad: (8289) plain, the name of a place in Palestine: (3474) prine root; to be straight or even, figurative to be right, pleasant, prosperous, direct, fit, seem good (meet), please, be esteem, bring straight way, be upright.

Synopsis - The valley of Sharon is considered one of the most beautiful valleys in Israel and a coastal plain between Joppa and Mt. Carmel. The beautiful plant, rose of Sharon (Songs 2:1) is named after the valley due to its beauty and matches the definition above. Sharon is used as a symbolic name for Ephraim or the house of Israel in ancient days as well as prophecies of the end times and can be found in Isaiah 33:9, 35:2 and 65:9-10.

The Ancient name of Lebanon, Sharon, Bashan, Gilead and Carmel are listed as Christian (fruitful as beauty representing a garden producing fruit) nations in these verses and is referring to the falling away from righteousness (the Church, I Thess 2:3) in the last days. This is our present time period where these Christian nations become entangled and engulfed by the ideology called Liberalism, Socialism and Communism of the Red Horse (Rev 6:4). As we read and study these ancient names, we need to keep in mind that they are referring to Christian nations just prior to the Tribulation Period of Wrath. This can be proven in the following verses for Isaiah 33:9 states, **"Lebanon is ashamed and hewn down: Sharon is like a wilderness, and Bashan and Carmel shake off their fruits."**. Fruits is Christian and speaking of the nation Jesus spoke of in Matthew 21:43 as being fruitful. In this verse, they are losing their righteousness during the period of falling away as prophesied in I Thessalonians 2:3, **"Let no man deceive you by any means: for that day shall not come, except there come a falling away first;"**.

Isaiah 35:2 identifies the Church, **"the glory of Lebanon shall be given unto it, the excellency of Carmel and Sharon, they shall see the glory of the Lord,"**. This verse is referring to blossoming and rejoicing where Lebanon, Carmel and Sharon see the glory of the Lord and the Excellency of our God. This can only be speaking of the Church and these ancient names has to be his flock or herd of sheep as the Church.

Isaiah 65:9-10 identifies the Church in more detail, **"And I will bring forth a seed out of Jacob, and out of Judah an inheritor of my mountains: and mine elect shall inherit it, and my servants shall dwell there. And Sharon shall be a fold of flocks, and the valley of Achor a place for the herds to lie down in, for my people that have sought me."** The seed out of Jacob and the inheritor of Judah is Christ the Messiah and the mountains his Christian nations. There are four different elements of people mentioned in this verse. The *seed of Jacob* is Israel as a whole nation, *out of Judah* is the linage of Christ, *my elect* shall inherit is any person that accepts Christ as the Messiah and *his servants* that dwell there is the house of Israel, Gods Christian nations that he sent his Disciples to preach the Gospel (Matt 10:6 and 15:24).

The valley of Achor are the continents in the wilderness where he sent his lost sheep to spread his Gospel in peace which is England and the United States and all the other Christian nations of the British Common Wealth such as Austria, New Zealand and many other island colonies. Millions of people from all over the earth have come to the United States to seek religious freedom where they sought Christ's Gospel in peace and prosperity. Great Britain and the United

States are the only nations in history that can fulfill this verse and many more through-out the Bible. Sharon, Bashan, Carmel and Lebanon were located in the northern part of ancient Israel controlled by Samaria the capitol of the house of Israel. They were to be ruled by Ephraim and Manasseh as the birthright tribes. This is why their ancient names are mentioned as being fruitful for the house of Israel was tasked by God to spread his end time Gospel.

Shiloh: [Christ the Messiah] is "shi-loh" 1. Symbolic name for the ruler from Judah. 2. A city in Ephraim: (7887) A place in Palestine: (7886) tranquil, and <u>epithet of the Messiah</u>: (7951) Prime root; to be tranquil, secure or successful, be happy, prosper, be in safety.

Synopsis- Shiloh is an interesting word for it represents Christ in Genesis 49:10 and a symbol of the Tabernacle, Temple and the Church. Shiloh is a small city approx. 20 miles N.E. of Jerusalem just over the border in Ephraim and depicted on a Biblical map of Canaan as divided among the tribes. After coming out of the desert, the first Tabernacle was established in Shiloh by Joshua. Joshua was of the tribe of Ephraim and very significant for Ephraim was given charge over the Tabernacle as the Birthright tribe. The tribe of Ephraim was later given control of Gods earthly Kingdom (I Kings 11) and ruler as King of the ten northern tribes of the house of Israel.

Moses was given the responsibility as the lawgiver of the Levite tribe to be the Priest and control priestly functions of the Tabernacle and Temple. The overall charge of the Tabernacle, Temple and later the Church was given to Joshua the Ephrathite and passed to Jeroboam also an Ephrathite in I Kings 11:26-28 where he was given the kingdom to be Gods Battle Ax (Jerm 51:21, Isa 41:2, Matt 21:43-44 and Luke 20:18). Due to the sins of the tribe of Judah, they were driven into captivity and the throne was overturned and given to the house of Israel in the wilderness (Eze 17:22-24 and 21:25-27) as commissioned by Jeremiah (Jerm 1:10 and 31:28).

When the house of Judah (Jews) rejected Christ, the complete kingdom to include the Throne was taken from them and given to the lost sheep of the house of Israel, the fruitful nation in the wilderness (Matt 10:6, 15:24 and 21:43). This overturn and planting were complete when Christ died on the cross and the veil in the temple was rent representing the removal of Gods Spirit from Jerusalem to his planted nation in the wilderness. Ephraim as the caretaker of the Tabernacle and Church that is Shiloh (Isa 66:8&19, Jerm 26:18) has not changed to this day. The authority lies within the overturned throne of David to England (the Crown of England).

The most important Scriptures concerning Shiloh are as follows. Joshua 18:1 establishes the Tabernacle at Shiloh for the assembly of the children of Israel as their first recognized religious site. Joshua 18:8-10 and 19:51 is where Joshua divided the land in the city of Shiloh by inheritance to all twelve tribes signifying the authority of the birthright of Joshua as an Ephrahite (I Chron 7:27 and Numbers 13:8, Oshea or Joshua the son of Non, descendant of the tribe of Ephraim) which means Jehovah-saved. Joshua was a symbol of Christ the Messiah where the inheritance was established in Shiloh, the location of the house of God (Judges 18:31). Shiloh was the center of rule during the period of the Judges or Colonial days prior to being moved to Jerusalem. The city of Shiloh was called by certain names such as: Temple of the Lord in Shiloh (I Sam 1:9); house of the Lord in Shiloh (I Sam 1:24 and 2:14); the Lord revealed himself to Samuel in Shiloh (I Sam 3:21); the Israelites moved the Ark of the Covenant from the Tabernacle to the Battle field where it was captured due to their haughtiness (I Sam 4:3-4 & 11); the great Prophet Ahijah came from Shiloh (I Kings 14:2) where he gave Jeroboam the Ephrahite Gods kingdom; Shiloh is considered by God to be his Tabernacle and strength among men (Ps 78:60-61). One of the most important verses indicating how Shiloh is dear to God is found in Jeremiah 7:12, **"But to ye now unto my place which was in Shiloh, where I set my name at the first"**. This verse is calling God/Christ Shiloh, "where I set my name at the first". God loved Shiloh for this is where he first established his people as a nation and plays a key role in future events of the responsibilities of Ephraim in Shiloh, Gods House "Bethel".

These verses demonstrate the importance of the word Shiloh and how it is associated as the name of the Messiah, Christ, and a symbol of his Tabernacle and Church.

Sifted: (5130) primary root; to quiver, vibrate up and down or rock to and from, sprinkle, beckoning, rubbing, bastinadoing, sawing, waving, lift up, move, offer, perfume, make to go up and down, be gone away, be moveable, be promoted, rill, remove, scatter, set, shake, stagger, be vagabond, way, make wander up and down. *Greek:* (4617) is to riddle and sift.

Synopsis- The Hebrew definition is to scatter, East, highway, traveler, disperse, waymark and ensign which is synonymous with other key words such as plant, wilderness, mountain, bough and vineyard that is in direct correlation to the house of Israel. All these words demonstrate how God planted them as mountains (nations) within the wilderness or forest of the world. They were to be his wayfaring Chosen People.

If we closely study each word in the above sentence as laid out within this segment, you will begin to understand how God sifted both the house of Israel and Judah into the world to fulfill prophecy in two separate roles. The house of Judah fulfills prophecy pertaining to Jerusalem and the Messiah where the house of Israel fulfilled the blessing to Abraham, Isaac, Jacob and Joseph

(Ephraim and Manasseh) to establish the Church and evangelize the world with Christ's Gospel giving righteousness and judgment to the families of the earth (Isa 41:1-8, Jerm 23:3-6).

Note that the word vagabond in Hebrew has a different meaning in English. According to the Strong's Concordance, (4022) means to wonder, produce fruit, precious fruit or thing, something valuable, eminent or distinguished. This matches the blessing to Ephraim (double fruit) as leader of the house of Israel, the fruitful birthright tribe to be a nation and a company of nations (Gen 35:11, 48:19). These verses fulfill the present-day Christian nations of Manasseh being the single great nation of the United States (the Bull) and Ephraim as the company of nations, the Common Wealth of Great Britain (the Unicorn).

Sirion: like a young unicorn Ps 29:6 "Sir-e-on" a Sidonian name for Mount Hermon: (8304) "Srayah" jah has prevailed; Serajah, the name of nine Israeli patriarchs: (8280) primitive root; to free, direct: (3050) "Yahh" the same; Jah, the sacred name; Jah, the Lord, most vehement, names in "-iah": (3068) the self-existent or Eternal; Jehovah, the Lord: (3069) God: (430) "el-o-heem"; gods in the ordinary sense, of the supreme God; occasionally applied by way of deference to magistrates; and sometimes as a superlative: angels, exceeding, God, very great, judges, mighty: (136) "Adonay" the lord (used as a proper name of God only), my Lord. (1361) Primitive root; to soar *(as the Bull "soar or fly")* i.e. lofty; figurative; to be haughty; exalt, be made higher, lift up, be proud, rise up, great height, upward.

Synopsis- The word Sirion is found in Deuteronomy 3:9 where it is referred to as Mount Hermon but Psalms 29:6 is calling it **"to skip like a calf; Lebanon and Sirion like a young unicorn"**. This verse is comparing Sirion (Eternal Jehovah, the Lord) to a Bull and Unicorn that directly correlates to Ephraim and Manasseh as the bull and unicorn, Gen 49:22-24, Duet 33:17. The birthright tribes were to be fruitful and Christian in the last days as the America the bull and eagle. Interesting to note, America is Sirion by definition of "as the bull soar or fly" and we invented the airplane. There are other words that relate to the meaning of God the Almighty which is, Israel, daughter, Shiloh, Ishi and Stone. All these names are directly associated with the house of Israel and not Judah of the Jews. This fulfills Ephraim and Manasseh's destiny as the Birthright tribes to rule the nations as God till Christ comes in Power and Glory.

We have established that Ephraim and Manasseh were to be called the house of Israel or Israel, the family name meaning "he will rule as God". This connects the names of Ephraim and Manasseh (the unicorn and bull) to Sirion meaning our Eternal Jehovah, the Lord "jah" the supreme God. According to these definitions, Israel (the house of Israel, Ephraim and Manasseh) was to rule as God sitting on King David's Throne as a Prince on his earthly kingdom till Christ comes to claim his throne in power (Luke 1:32-33). This fulfills Jeremiah 51:19-20, Isaiah 41:2, Matthew 21:43-44 and Luke 20:18, making Ephraim and Manasseh (the house of Israel) Gods battle ax and stone sword (Christ's Gospel) of war that protects and perpetuates his end time Church. This nation or Battle Axe represents Sirion or Israel as Gods 5th kingdom or stone kingdom mentioned in Daniel 2:44-45 and is Gods Christian nations as the salt of the earth during the last days, "he will rule as God" bringing righteousness and judgment to the world (Isa 16:1-8 32:15-18 and 41:2-5).

Solomites: #4150("Uncovering the Mysteries of Your Hidden Inheritance" by Robert Alan Balaicius, p. 20-23 and "The Post-captivity names of Israel". #4150 an appointment, fixed time or season of an annual festival, an assembly, the congregation in a place of solemn assembly, synagogue, appointed set time: (3259) Primitive root; to fix upon by agreement or appointment, to meet at a stated time, to summon to trial, <u>to engage for marriage</u>, assemble selves, <u>betroth</u>, gather selves together, meet together, set time.

Synopsis- In Ezekiel 45:17 and 46:11 Solomites means synagogue and a place for appointment of assembly. It also means a time of seasonal or annual festivals held in a synagogue or solemn place. It was a place where burnt, meat and drink offerings representing feasts days festivals of the new moons and Sabbaths were conducted. This place can only be speaking of the physical Temple where only the High Priest conducted offerings of bullocks, rams and lambs for the sins of the people.

Isaiah 33:20-22 establishes solemnities as a nation called Zion and refers it to Jerusalem as a Tabernacle that shall not be taken down, not one of its stakes removed or cords broken. This solemnitie nation is, **"Look upon Zion, the city of our solemnities: thine eyes shall see Jerusalem a quiet habitation, a tabernacle that shall not be taken down; not one of the stakes thereof shall ever be removed", "a place of broad rivers and streams wherein shall go no galley with oars, neither shall gallant ships pass thereby."** This verse refers to Jerusalem being a quite habitation or Tabernacle representing the Church for its stakes shall never be removed indicating Christ's Church will last forever. The physical city of Jerusalem was destroyed in 70AD but the Spiritual Church (solemnities) of Jerusalem will last forever. This verse is also referring to a nation that was never taxed by the Romans. The Romans collected taxes from other nations by using Galleys with oars and gallant ships. This verse is saying that this nation called Jerusalem has never been taxed by another nation. The Ancient nations of Europe to include the main Island of England, Israel and Jerusalem was controlled and taxed by the Romans for hundreds of years so this verse cannot be speaking of Jerusalem of Judea.

Jerusalem a quiet resting habitation is referring to a safe land in the wilderness (Isa 32:18 and Jerm 30:10). This same nation is referred to in Isaiah chapter 18 and is identical to the continent of the United States of America. Compare Isaiah 33:20-22 to Isaiah chapter 18 as being the same nation of great rivers spoken of as Zion and never taxed by the Romans as this verse states. This nation is the fruitful nation Jesus gave the Kingdom to in Matthew 21:43 and represent the Solemnities Church that will be Gods New Covenant or Temple with man forever. Gods New Covenant represents the Solemnitie Temple and will never be destroyed as were the physical Temple in 70AD by the Roman Army. The nation spoken of in these verses is the fruitful nations of the house of Israel that has spread Christ's end time Gospel to the world, the birthright tribes of Ephraim the unicorn (GB) and Manasseh the bull (USA).

Stone: (68) to build, a stone, carbuncle, mason, plummet (chalk; hail, head, sling), stone (drivers, weigh): (1129) to build, <u>obtain children</u>: "same as #1121 <u>bough</u>": (6697) a cliff, a rock of boulder, a refuge, <u>Mighty God</u>, rock, sharp stone, strength, strong: (5619) primary root; to be weighty, (cast, gather, out, throw) stones: (7275) to cast together stones: (6263) <u>to pile together</u>: (1496) something cut, dressed or hewed stone: (8068) sense of pricking, a thorn, adornment (stone), brier, diamond.

Synopsis- The word stone is intriguing for it represents the strength and might of God to build his Church upon (Peter the stone) in a fruitful Christian bough (continents of the world) as the branch of the house of Israel (Gen 49:22). Stone means Mighty God just as the definition of Israel, "he shall rule as God" as a Prince of nations. The house of Israel under the leadership of Ephraim and Manasseh were to rule as God for they are called shepherds, the stone of Israel, Genesis 49:24. The stone that Jacob made his pillow upon in Genesis 28:18-22 represents the stone of Bethel or Gods House. This stone has remained with the nation of Israel down through time and was the stone that Moses took in the desert to receive water. It was placed within the Temple during the days of Israel as a nation and a symbol of their strength and judge to the world. Jeremiah took the stone of Lia Fail "the stone of Bethel" to Ireland when he overturned the throne of David to the Kings of Ireland in approx. 584-580BC. Every King of Israel has been crowned on this anointed stone that was Jacob's pillar. Ancient writers of Ireland have recorded where Jeremiah overturned the throne as mentioned in Ezekiel 17:21-24 and 21:25-27, commissioned Jermiah in Jerm 1:10 to Ireland to **"set thee over the nations and over the kingdoms, to root out, and to pull down, and to destroy, and to throw down, to build, and to plant"**. Jeremiah along with Baruch his Scribe, the judgment seat from the Temple, David's harp, Jacob's stone of Bethel and other artifacts arrived in Ireland around 580BC as recorded in the Chronicles of Ireland. Jacob's stone of Bethel (Lia Fail) is a symbol of the house of Israel as leader of the world and all Kings of Israel to include the Kings of Ireland, Scotland and England has been crowned on this stone and is located under the throne of England in Westminster Abby in London.

This stone represents Christ's Church as the house of Israel being its caretaker or Battle Ax and can be proven in Ephesians 2:20 where Christ himself is the Chief corner stone. Hebrew 8:8-10 gives Christ's New Covenant to the house of Israel, **"For this is the covenant that I will make with the house of Israel after those days"**. The term, "after those days" indicate the later days of our present time. This same verse can be verified in Jeremiah 31:28-31 with almost identical wording and includes the commission of Jeremiah to overturn the throne to another land. Both Hebrews chapter 8 and Jeremiah chapter 31 is speaking of the last days to Christ's New Covenant of the Church which refers to the house of Israel as his Church. Study these two chapters.

I Peter 2:4-6 calls Christ a living stone, **"To whom coming, as unto a living stone, disallowed indeed of men, but chosen of God, and precious"**. Christ is a stone or God and is called a living stone because he came in the flesh as a living man making him an actual living stone or God in the flesh. Because of our flesh and Spiritual born-again birth as a likeness to Christ, Christians are called living stones, **"Ye also, as lively stones, are built up a spiritual house,"**. For us to inherit Gods Heavenly Kingdom, we have to experience a fleshly birth and a Spiritual birth just as Christ did but in reverse. This verse is calling Christians living stones just as Ephraim and Manasseh as the birthright tribes of the house of Israel are called the shepherd and stone of Israel in Genesis 49:22&24 referring to them as his fruitful bough whose branches run over the wall, the Church. They were in-charge of establishing his Church. This verse is also calling Christians living stones, the house of Bethel or the house of God that is the house of Israel, Gods earthly Kingdom. This earthly kingdom is called Zion, **"Behold I lay in Sion a chief corner stone, elect, precious:"**. The chief corner stone is Christ and this verse is calling him Sion or in Hebrew Zion. If Christ is called Zion as the chief cornerstone of the Church and the Christians are the stones of the Church, then we as the building stones of the Church are also called Zion, Gods Spirit with man. The house of Israel has to also be called Zion making the planted nation in the wilderness in Isaiah chapter 18 and the ensign of the Christian flag in Isaiah 31:9 as Zion. Isaiah 28:16 makes an absolute statement, **"Therefore thus saith the Lord God, Behold, I lay in Zion for a foundations a stone, a tried stone, a precious corner stone, a sure foundation: he that believeth shall not make haste."** This verse absolutely makes it clear that Christ is the corner stone of the Church and in Zion he laid the foundation of the stone, Christ's Church. This verse makes Christ Church Zion therefore all Christians are a part of Zion, Gods Spirit.

Tyrus: (6864) A coastal city of Phoenicia: (6865) Hebrew, a rock, a stone (6696): primitive root - to cramp, confine, **<u>adversary</u>**, **<u>assault</u>**: (6876) Syrianman of Tyre.

Synopsis- Tyrus or Tyre is referred to as nations of people with Kings and a city located in the northern coast of Israel in Phoenicia. Hos 9:13 indicates that Tyrus is different than Ephraim, like Tyrus, Ephraim was planted in a pleasant place. Zec 9:3 says that Tyrus is a strong hold and wealthy but God cast her out and will smite her power in the sea and be devoured with fire or warfare. Ezekiel 38:2-6 gives a more detailed alignment of the nations with Gog, ancient Tyrus (Russia) that the alignment in Ezekiel 27:8-11.

Ezekiel chapter 27 and 28 lists the riches and judgment of Tyrus and Zidon. Eze 27:8-11 gives the alignment of the army with Tyrus and Zidon that is Arvad, Gebal, Persia, Lud, Put, and Gammadims. These nations are the present-day Communist bloc countries with their Arab alliance. Ezekiel 28:24 states that after the destruction of Tyrus, **"And there shall be no more a pricking brier unto the house of Israel, nor any grieving throng of all that are round about them, that despised them"**. In our present day, whom are the nations that give modern Israel and the United States a pricking brier, it is the Arab countries aligned with the Communist bloc nations of Russia or ancient Tyrus. Ancient Tyrus and Gog are one and the same as indicated in Ezekiel 27:3-12; 28:22-24; 38:2-6 and Zechariah 9:3 and represent the Red Horse of the humanistic ideology of Communism that subverts the world under a Godless rule.

The following nations are listed as an alignment with Tyrus or Gog that is modern day Russia. Some of these nations are listed pertispants during the Ezekiel 38 and 39 war. The ancient definitions are in accordance to the Strongs Concordance with a brief definition and meaning.

<u>Zidon</u>: ancient city of Asher- fishing village, Hunter, food, meat.
<u>Arvad</u>: is an Island near Zidon a refuse for the roving, an Island city of Palestine.
<u>Gebal</u>: an Edomite territory, a Phoenician trade city, a region in Idumaea, chain of hills, a mountain, to twist as a rope, border.
<u>Idumaea</u>: An offering: or a sacrifice for it: sin (offering): sinful: <u>Red</u>, <u>rosy</u>, <u>ruddy</u> (Red Horse of Communism Rev 6:4) (see Gen 25:25). Essau had red skin at birth, Edom, the elder twin-brother of Jacob, hence, the region (Idumaea) occupied by him, Edom, Edomites, Idumea. The Greek form of Edom is a region east and south of Palestine, Edom, Idumaea. Red, rosy and ruddy, the color of red is a symbol of Communism and the Duma was a council or official assembly, an elective legislative assembly, constituting the lower house of parliament, which was established in 1905 by Nicholas II of the Russian Government. Idumaea is also associated with Bozrah, Isa 34:6. Red, rosy, ruddy means man (refer to #120) and a symbol of the Edomite people of the Communist bloc nations. This writer believes that the term red,

rosy and ruddy symbolizes man and represents the Godless side of human nature or the humanistic Godless ideology and philosophies of the end days (Atheist Communism). These philosophies are preparing the world to accept the Luciferian world system and the Antichrist that is presently engulfing the world through Liberalism.

Persia: Present day Iran and Iraq, eastern countries.

Lud: Son of Shem, name of two nations Lud and Lydia a people of North Africa.

Phut: Son of Ham, name of his descendants and region, nations of North Africa.

Gammadims: defenders of Tyre, a warrior, grasping weapons, to grasp.

Hamon-Gog: a place where Gog is buried, multitude of Gog, a noise, tumult, crowd, wealth, abundance, company, many, multitude, noise, riches, to make a loud noise, to be in great commotion, rage, war, moan, to be in an uproar. Believed to be Russia or a portion of their allies.

Magog: Son of Japheth, a barbarous northern region. Believed to be Russia.

Gog: A Son of Shemarah, prince of Scythia: some northern nation possibly Russia.

Ethiopia: Cush, land south of Egypt, name of the son of Ham.

Libya: A land in Africa "Put" a son of Ham and their region, tribe, Phut, Put.

Gomer: The Son of Japheth, completion, also of a Hebrewess-Gomer. Prime root, to end (in the sense of completion of failure), cease, come to an end, fail, perfect, perform. Believed to be the old Soviet Republics of Azerbaijan, Armenia, Georgia.

Togarmah: Son of Gomer, an extension of the hand, avowal, adoration, a choir of worshippers, confession, praise, thanks (giving, offering). Togarmah and Tubal- believed to be parts of modern-day Turkey.

Cush: Believed to be modern day Sudan and Ethiopia.

Sheba and Dedan: Believed to be modern day Saudi Arabia.

Ashkelon: a Philistine city in the Gaza Strip (831) in the sense of weighing - place (8254) prime root; to suspend or poise (especially in trade), pay, receive, spend, thoroughly, weigh. Ashkelon is a part of the Palestinian Arab coalition in the last days and will be judged along with Tyrus, Zidon, Philistines, Caphtor and Gaza. Their judgment and destruction are stated in, Jerm 47:4-5&7, Amos 1:8, Zeph 2:4, Zech 9:5. They are the Palestinians.

Gaza: a Royal Philistine city- a city in Ephraim, (5804) strong (5794) vehement, harsh, fierce, greedy, mighty, power, roughly, (5810) prime root; to be stout, harden, impudent, prevail, strengthen (self) be strong. Gaza is also a part of the Palestinian Arab coalition which faces destruction by God along with Ashkelon, Jerm 47:1&5, Amos 1:6-7, Zech 9:5.

Ekron: a Philistine city (6138) **eradication** (6131) prime root; to pluck up (especially by the roots) to hamstring, dig down, Hough, pluck up root up. Ekron is also a part of the Palestinian Arab coalition that will be destroyed, Amos 1:8, Zeph 2:4, Zech 9:5&7.

Ashdod: a Philistine city- (795) ravager, (7703) prime root; to be burley, powerful (pass. impregnable) to ravage, dead, destroy, oppress, robber, spoiler, utterly lay waste. Ashdod is also a part of the Palestinian Arab coalition that is destroyed, Amos 1:8, Zeph 2:4, Zech 9:6.

<u>Philistines</u>: inhabitants of Philistia (6430) rolling, migratory, region of Syria (6428) prime root; to roll (in dust), roll (wallow), self. Philistines or modern-day Palestinians plays a part in the Arab coalition that God destroys, Jerm 47:1&4, Eze 25:16, Amos 1:8, Zeph 2:5, Zech 9:6.

<u>Jebusite</u>: Descendant of Canaan: (2983) inhabitant of Jebus: (2982) trodden (threshing floor in Jerusalem) aboriginal name of Jerusalem. Jebus: (947) Prime root; to trample, loath, tread, (down, under foot), be polluted. The threshing floor of Ornan the Jebusite, was a Holy Place for God, I Chron 21:15&18&28, II Sam 24:16. Modern Israel.

Note: All these nations are listed in Ezekiel chapters 27, 28 and 38 and presently an aligned coalition with modern day Russia which will play a part in World War III as indicated in the 38th chapter of Ezekiel.

Unicorn: (7214) "rem" rame; a wild bull (from its conspicuousness), unicorn. (7213) a primitive root; to rise; be lifted up.

Synopsis- The unicorn is a symbol of strength, Num 23:22 and 24:8, **"strength of the unicorn"**. Psalms 29:6, refers Lebanon and Sirion like a young unicorn representing its strength. Isaiah speaks of the soon coming war with Russia and the Arab world with Bozrah and Idumea (Russia), (ref to Bozrah and Idumea), in Isaiah 34:1-8. Verse 7 states, **"And the unicorns shall come down with them, and the bullocks with the bulls; and their land shall be soaked with blood, and their dust made fat with fatness"**. We have studied that Bozrah and Idumea is the Communist bloc nations and also know that Great Britain is the only nation in modern history to have the unicorn as one of their national symbols. It's common knowledge that the United States is the symbol of the Bull that represents world economics of Wall Street. This war that Isaiah speaks of in chapter 34 is the soon coming Holy War between the free Christian Democratic industrialized nations and the Communist bloc Arab coalition and is mentioned in Ezekiel 38:1-11, Isa 34:6-10 and Dan 11:40-45.

When Moses recorded the blessing given to Joseph in Deuteronomy 33:17, he calls Joseph a unicorn as a wild bull, **"His glory is like the firstling of his bullock, and his horns are like the horns of unicorns with them he shall push the people together to the ends of the earth: and they are the ten thousands of Ephraim, and they are the thousands of Manasseh."** In this verse, it is clear that the firstling of his bullock can only be speaking of the United States (Manasseh) and the horns of unicorns are referring to Great Britain. No doubt this greatness spoken of in this verse is the modern-day English-speaking nations, "and they are the ten thousands of Ephraim and they are the thousands of Manasseh.", Great Britain and the United States.

Vineyard: (3754) "kerem" unused root of uncertain; means a garden or vineyard- vines, (increase of the) vineyard, vintage: (3657) a plant: (3661) prime root; to set out or plant vineyard: (1021) <u>House (Beyth)</u> of the vineyard Beth-hak-Kerem, a place in Palestine: (1004) bayith, <u>a house in the greatest application, family</u>, palace, <u>temple</u>, home born: (1129) prime root; <u>to build</u> (literal and physical) begin to build, <u>obtain children</u>, make, repair, set (up): (290) brother of anger: (251) prime root; a brother of resemblance, another brother, kindred, like other: (4619) closure: (6095) prime root; to fasten (or make firm) i.e. to close (the eyes) shut.

Synopsis- The word vineyard means house and is why God calls his people a house or a symbol of a vineyard. Throughout the Bible, the term vineyard is used as a symbol of God's Chosen People of the Children of Israel and as a nation. Isaiah 5:7 states **"For the vineyard of the Lord of hosts is the house of Israel, and the men of Judah his pleasant plant"**. The nations of Israel are referred to as a vineyard and (Duet 33:13-17, Gen 35:9-12) are the branches or nations of his house that run over the wall (Gen 49:22). Israel (ten northern tribes) is the vineyard, his family house or Temple (the Church), and the men of Judah or house of Judah his pleasant plant (the root of the plant which is Jerusalem the promised land of Israel). They were to preserve the bloodline of Christ and claim his throne till Jeremiah overturned the kingdom as recorded in Ezekiel chapter 17 and 21 and Matthew 21:42-45 due to their rejection of the Messiah.

The house of Judah has maintained the root of Jerusalem so that the end time prophecies can be fulfilled while the house of Israel was planted in the wilderness of the world to become his house of the English-speaking nations of the world. They are the Church to spread his end time Gospel.

As we can see from the definition above, the terms garden, vines, increase, plant, brother and kindred all come into play. These words and many more indicate how God, through his prophetic plan, has planted his birthright nations in the wilderness as a vineyard to become fruitful righteous nations of Christianity to spread his end time Gospel. This fulfilled the promise to Abraham, Isaac, Jacob and Joseph to be Kings of Kingdoms and a great nation and a company of nations (Gen 17:6, 26:3-4, 35:11 and 48:19). See Vineyard in chapter eight for more details.

Wayfaring: "arach": (732) primitive root; to travel, go wayfaring man: (734) a well-trodden road, a caravan, manner, path, race, rank, traveler, troop: (5674) primitive root; <u>to cross over</u>: (5676) Eber: Eber, Heber two patriarchs: (5680) Ibriy; <u>Hebrew</u>, an <u>Eberite</u>.

Synopsis - A wayfaring man is a traveler in the Hebrew term or to cross over. If you go to the Strongs Concordance and look up the word Hebrew (5680) "eber" a region across on the opposite side east of the Jordan River and from reference (5674) which means to crossover. Jeremiah 9:2, **"Oh that I had in the wilderness a lodging place of wayfaring men; that I might leave my people, and go from them! For they be all adulterers, and assembly of treacherous men."** In other words, a wayfaring man is a Hebrew man from the opposite side that crossed over east of the Jordan River into Gods lodging place in the wilderness waiting for Christ's Gospel and God departed from due to the sin of idolatry for 2520 years of punishment. This punishment occurred during the Dark Ages when God departed from them providing no blessings. Note that when Israel entered the Promised Land (Israel) they entered across the Jordan River from the east going west. When they went into captivity and later departed, they entered the wilderness of the world by departing from the west going east across the Jordan River. They were blown west by the east wind (Hosea 12:1). There is a very interesting aspect in that both the house of Israel after the Assyrian captivity and Judah (Jews) after the Babylonian captivity, both migrated to the east over the Jordan River fulfilling Jeremiah 9:2 as quoted above. It also fits the description of the Hebrew Phoenician people of the providence of Phoenicia and all the migrating tribes of Israel. Other related words are, east, waymark, Hebrew, Isle, not gone with his feet (Isa 41:3) and haven of ships (Gen 49:13). The wayfaring man was a Hebrew traveler not only by foot to the East but by ship according to Scripture.

Waymarks: (6725) in the sense of conspicuousness, <u>a monumental or guiding pillar</u> *(Zion)*, sign, title, waymark: (6723) unused root; to parch, aridity, a desert, barren, drought, dry land or place, solitary place, <u>wilderness</u>.

Synopsis - The term waymarks have the same Hebrew definition as Zion in that the house of Israel was planted into the wilderness and left waymarks of mounds, circles and ensigns where ever they migrated. Jeremiah 31:21 calls Israel, **"O virgin of Israel"**, his bride that was betrothed Hosea 2:19-20, to be the Bride of Christ and gave them a commandment to leave waymarks to identify their national existence.

This is the only commandment by God for his wayfaring Hebrews (travelers) to mark their way for future identity. They were commanded to set up high heaps along their highway of travel and can be seen associated in other Hebrew words such as highway (to mound up), Gilead (a heap of stone), Hebrew (to wall in or around), mountain (to mound up), unicorn (Ephraim, to rise or be lifted up) and Zion (waymark or monument). All these words are directly associated with Ephraim, the birthright leader of the house of Israel, to be a Hebrew traveler that crossed over to the east and left monuments of earth mounds, stone circles, pyramids and named rivers, valleys, countries and mountains after their forefathers. Stone Hinge is a master of all stone circles and found in central England erected by the ancient Druid Hu Gadarn around 1800BC. Hundreds of stone circles are found all over Europe and in the far east to include the United States.

The migrating tribes of the house of Israel obeyed Gods commandment given in Jeremiah 31:21 as they traveled into the world and took Zion (Gods Spirit) and the Gospel of the New Covenant with them as they colonized. The United States, Austria, New Zealand and hundreds of other Christian colonies is an example of how Ephraim and Manasseh fulfilled Gods Commandments of Genesis 28:14, Matthew 10:5-8 and 28:19-20 as his battle ax and 5th Stone Kingdom as the Church. "O virgin Israel", means bride to be (Jerm 31:21and II Corinthians 11:2) associated with Ephraim and Manasseh as the bride of Christ, the Church or Zion. Study related words to get the full understanding of how God used his Hebrew wayfaring (travelers) Chosen People of the house of Israel to spread his end time Gospel.

Wilderness: (4057) in the sense of driving; a pasture, an open field, whither cattle are driven; a desert; also speech including its organs, <u>south</u>: (8414) unused root; to be waste; a desolation of surface, desert, a worthless thin, empty place, without form, nothing, vain, vanity, waste: (6160) sterile valley of the Jordan and its continuation to the Red Sea; evening, heaven, plain: (6723) unused root: to parch, aridity, <u>a desert</u>, barren, drought, dry (land, place), desert, solitary place: (6728) nomad or wild beast, wild beast of the desert that dwell in the (inhabiting) the wilderness.

Synopsis- As we can see from the above definition, the term wilderness is referred to as a place that is a desert, waste, desolate, empty and a solitary place. Whenever the Scriptures speak of a wilderness it simply means a place that is uninhabited by man and full of wild beast.

There is another aspect of wilderness that is absolutely fascinating in that the Strong's Concordance reference for Zion is 6726, 6725 and 6723 which is the same as wilderness and refers to waymark (leaving signs). In other words, wilderness and Zion are the same and explains many verses in reference to Zion being plowed and traveling into the wilderness. This is the overturn of Zion (Isa 66:8), David's throne (Ezee 21:27) and Gods Kingdom (Matt 21:43) to a fruitful nation in the wilderness. The word plant, sifted, scattered abroad, mountain (nations), wayfaring, waymark, East, vineyard and branch all come into play in reference to Zion and wilderness. Ezekiel 34:25 is an excellent verse and one of many that explains how God is going to disperse his nations of the house of Israel and plant them into the wilderness in a safe place under a new covenant (the Church). This is just a few verses in reference to a planting in the wilderness, Isaiah 32:15-16, 41:19, 49:8, Jeremiah 9:2, Ezekiel 20:34-43, 34:13-18, Hosea 2:14-23. Read and study each of the above verses and realize that the wilderness God is speaking of is a new uninhabited land where only beast of the field and heathen people live and cannot be referencing the return to the land of Palestine.

The planting in the wilderness is the uncharted continents of the world during our end days that have been settled by the English sea going people. They are the Commonwealth nations under Gods new Christian covenant as his Battle Axe and 5th kingdom (Jerm 51:19-20, Isa 41:2, Dan 2:44-45). This planting of Israel in the wilderness under a prophesied New Covenant is mentioned in many verses but the most important is stated in Ezekiel 20:37, Jeremiah 31:31 and Hebrew 8:8. Isaiah 41:1-8 speaks of the Islands of Britannia accepting Christ's Gospel as the righteous man from the east that did not come by foot (ship) for the Isles saw it, and feared. They were his servants of the house of Israel and of Jacob. This New Covenant is in reference to the end days of our present time under Christ's Gospel given to the house of Israel and the house of Judah indicating their end time separation.

The word wilderness is a key word in understanding how God scattered and sifted his people into the deserts of the world to establish his nations promised to Abraham, Isaac, Jacob, Joseph and his two sons. The Hebrew definition of wilderness means uncivilized or uninhabited by man (Eze 19:13, 34:22-25 and Hosea 2:14-23). The following verses are just a few that indicate how God overturn his kingdom to a planted fruitful bough that means nation (Gen 49:22 and Matt 21:43) into the wilderness (Eze 17:22-24, 20:34-47 and 21:25-27). Jeremiah 9:2 states that God has a lodging place in the wilderness for his wayfaring men (Hebrew traveler) and Isaiah 41:19 goes as far as to say that God will plant in the wilderness the cedar (David's throne). The cedar tree is a symbol of King David's throne (Eze 17:22) for Joseph (Ephraim and Manasseh) is considered to be branches (Gen 49:22) of the cedar tree making them the preserver of the throne of David.

According to the Strong's Concordance reference 2156 and 3127, a twig and a tender young twig is the throne of David in Ezekiel 17:22 being taken from the high cedar branch and given to the low branch by planting his young twig, a tender one into the wilderness. A tender twig (King Zedikiah's two daughters) has the same definition as branch and bough and is linked to Joseph or Ephraim and Manasseh (the house of Israel). This is the overturn of David's throne from Jerusalem to Ireland in the wilderness where Jeremiah was commissioned to tear down and to build (Jerm 1:10 and 31:16) which fulfills Matthew 10:6, 15:24 and 21:43. This is where Jesus personally took David's portion of his kingdom of two tribes as recorded in I Kings 11 from the Jews and gave it to a fruitful nation in the wilderness, the lost sheep of the house of Israel.

The Isles of England is the unicorn of Ephraim and the bull of Manasseh the United States where God planted his fruitful nations. Study words relating to Gods Hebrew travelers such as East, abroad, scattered, sifted, waymark and wayfaring.

Jeremiah chapter 31 is wonderful for it explains how God is going to gather his flock of the house of Israel, **"O virgin Israel"**, his Bride to be, the Church. We need to get out our Bibles and traverse each verse of Jeremiah chapter 31 to prove the true identity of the house of Israel. Verses one and two states that Gods family of Israel left by the sword (captivities), will be planted in the wilderness. Verse four calls Israel "O virgin of Israel" the Bride of Christ that is his Church. Verse five speaks of planting vines upon the mountains (fruitful Christian nations) of Samaria representing Ephraim's Capitol in ancient Israel. The word vine indicates being fruitful or Christian. Verse six speaks of the watcher of Ephraim, **"shall cry arise ye and let us go up to Zion unto the Lord our God"**. This is speaking of establishing the Church and Christ's Gospel, the vine to be fruitful. Verses 7 through 12 speaks of how God is going to gather his people from all over the world and calls Ephraim his firstborn or birthright tribe Israel (he will rule as God). God said that he would gather his flock and call it Zion and keep them as a shepherd does his flock (the Church).

Verse 13 through 17 says that the virgins (Christ Bride, O virgin of Israel) shall rejoice in the dance meaning the joy of Christ's Church. Verse 18 calls Ephraim a bullock which is his brother Manasseh (the United States) and in verse 19 repented of the sins of his youth where he was turned and instructed. Ephraim and Manasseh were turned from their sins and instructed to spread Christ's end time Gospel where verse 20 calls Ephraim his son or pleasant child which means his firstborn or birthright child and God will have mercy upon him.

Verse 21 gives Ephraim of the house of Israel the commandment to set up waymarks of identifying monuments or names when they travel as a migrating people through the spiritual highway of the world. This verse calls Ephraim **"O virgin Israel"** which means they are Christ's Church, the virgin or bride to be which matches verse 4 and 13 of the rejoicing virgins of his Gospel as his virgin or "bride to be".

Verse 22 calls Israel a backsliding daughter and that God has created a new thing in the earth. A new thing in the earth is Gods Spirit of his New Covenant of the Church. The definition of daughter is associated with Church, bough, branch and obtain children or builder of the family name. The term builder of the family name can be traced to bough, branch, Carmel, Gilead, stone and vineyard. These terms link the word daughter to Joseph, the fruitful bough and branches that ran over the wall in Genesis 49:22, to Ephraim and Manasseh as the house of Israel.

Verses 23 through 26 speak to the house of Judah, where up to this point, the Scriptures were directed at Ephraim of the house of Israel. Verse 28 is speaking to both houses and states that they will be taken into captivity to be sown into the seed of man or the nations of the world. This is in reference to both captivities of how the house of Israel and Judah will be sifted into the world.

Verse 28 and 29 says, **"And it shall come to pass"**, **"In those days"**, is a reference to the last days of how Jeremiah will pluck up, throw down, destroy, watch over, to build and to plant Gods new fruitful nation in the wilderness. This is the same commission as stated in Jerm 1:10 and referring to the overturn of King David's throne and the kingdom taken from the Jews by Christ in Matthew 21:43. These two verses indicate the time period of the last days that this whole chapter will occur. Verses 30 through 32 speak of the New Covenant of the Church to both the house of Israel and the house of Judah. Note that both houses are mentioned in this verse.

Verse 33 states that "after those days" or the last days, this covenant will be made to the house of Israel where God will put his law in their inward parts and write it in their hearts where he will be their God and they shall be his people. There is an important aspect that we must understand in that the house of Judah is not mentioned in this verse. The reason is that the New Covenant was given to both the house of Israel and Judah as two separate nations of people in verse 31 but in verse 33 the New Covenant was repeated but only given to the house of Israel. The reason is that the house of Judah or the Jews rejected Christ as their Messiah as the coming of Shiloh where they refuse to accept the New Covenant of the Church. God knew they would reject Christ so he took the kingdom from them and gave it to the house of Israel as a fruitful nation. They accepted Christ and have spread his Gospel as his servant and Stewart.

Verses 34 through 37 speak of the Gospel being taught throughout the world stating that the Lord of host is his name. Who has done more to spread the Gospel during the past five hundred years than Great Britain and the United States and can only be Ephraim and Manasseh, the bull and unicorn, as mentioned in this chapter. This is a fact that cannot be refuted. Verse 36 makes a clear statement that if we become evil and depart from Gods Ways, we will cease being a nation. This writer fears that we as a Christian nation of the house of Israel under the authority of Manasseh as a birthright tribe is losing our faith and falling away from Gods truth. We will lose the great blessings of wealth promised to Abraham, Isaac, Jacob and Joseph given directly to Ephraim (GB) and Manasseh (US) due to our unfaithfulness as a modern liberal nation by

Gods commandment to stay faithful. It is only a matter of time before we will see Gods wrath of destruction spoken of in this verse. If we fail to repent as a nation referred to in verse 19, we will be destroyed by God's judgment.

Verse 38 through 40 changes the time period from the last days to the future during the millennial reign where the Temple in Jerusalem is built and Christ sets on his throne in power to rule for a thousand years.

If we closely study this chapter, we can see how God has established his Church with the house of Israel, which is Ephraim and Manasseh the bull, that progresses through time. The chapter covers from the sifting after the two captivities prior to Christ, the gathering of his dispersed people under his New Covenant during the Church age of the last days and the establishing of his rule during his thousand-year reign.

Read and study Jeremiah chapter 31 very carefully for it is one of the most powerful chapters in the Bible. It explains very well how God dispersed, sifted and gathered his people of the house of Israel under the authority of his overturned Throne that was planted in the wilderness to establish his New Covenant. His new fruitful nation was given a new heart and spirit, the Gospel of the Church and Holy Spirit (Matt 10:6, 15:24, 21:43). This Chapter was written to Ephraim and the bull of Manasseh as the Virgin of Israel, the lost sheep of the house of Israel or the Bride of Christ (the Church).

Zarah: A son of Judah. The breached son, second born but due to his hand coming out of the womb first (the scarlet threaded finger), placed him in line for the throne, the account recorded in Gen chapter 38, and Matt 1:3: (2226) "Zerach" the name of three Israeli patriarchs also of an Idumaean and an Ethiopian prince: (2225) a rising of light, rising: (2224) primitive root; to irradiate (or shoot forth beams). To rise (as the sun), to appear (as a symptom of leprosy), arise, rise (up), as soon as it is up.

Synopsis- The story of Zarah and Phares as recorded in Genesis chapter 38 is the most mysterious story in the Bible and probably the most unknown. The account of this paradox created a controversy that exist to this very day in a direct reference to the inheritance of the throne of King David. It is a subject that calls for extreme study and a major key in understanding Bible prophecy. To understand the overturn of the Throne of King David three times as recorded in Ezekiel chapter 17 and 21, we must first understand the circumstance of the birth of Zarah and Phares to the future of the throne of Israel. The firstborn of these two sons were to receive the birthright blessing and the kingship of the throne of Israel. God works in wonderful mysterious ways and caused a breach to occur during the birth, thus making the right to the throne a dual heritage. The only other dual heritage that is recorded in the Bible is Joseph's two sons,

Ephraim and Manasseh, which received a joint birthright of double portion given by Jacob, the father of Israel. Both sons received the same right just as Judah and Tamar's twine sons Pharez and Zarah, study the whole chapter for their story.

The story of Zarah and Phares is recorded in Gen 38:27-30, **"And it came to pass, in the time of her travail, that, behold, twins were in her womb." "And when it came to pass, when she travailed, that the one put out his hand: and the midwife took and bound upon his hand a scarlet thread, saying This came out first. And it came to pass, as he drew back his hand, that behold, his brother came out; and she said, How hast thou broken forth? This breach be upon thee: therefore his name was called Pharez. And afterward came out his brother, that had the scarlet thread upon his hand: and his name was called Zarah."**

This breach has created a struggle for the throne of Israel to this day for both is eligible for the throne as the genealogy is stated in Matthew 1:3, **"And Judas begat Phares and Zara of Thamar; and Phares begat Esrom; and Esrom begat Aram"**. As you can see, Zarah is in the bloodline of King David and an heir to the throne. I Chronicles 2:6 gives the linage of Zarah, **"And the sons of Zerah; Zimri, and Ethan, and Heman, and Calcol, and Dara;"** These five sons became very renowned throughout the land for their wisdom and given credit in I Kings 4:31, speaking of King Solomon's wisdom, **"For he was wiser than all men; than Ethan the Ezrahite, and Heman, and Chalcol and Dara;".** The term scarlet threat has become a byword through time and turned into old sayings such as, red tape, one single red strand of thread in ropes of the British Navy, the British News Papers still tie a red cord around their bundled news papers and many more.

The Zerah bloodline accounts for many of the people of the tribe of Judah that never saw the promised land of Palestine. Zarah's descendants migrated into Europe by ship prior to the exodus of Moses out of Egypt and establish the Irish throne in approx. 1150BC as recorded by the Old British Chronicles. The throne of Ireland was established and waiting for Jeremiah to complete his commission as given in Jerm 1:10, to deliver the daughters of Zedekiah, the last king and bloodline of King David. When Princess Tea Tephi, King Zedekiah's daughter of the line of Judah-Pharez, married Eochaidh the Prince of the Scarlet Thread, a descendant of the Judah/Zarah bloodline fulfilled the high tree of Ezekiel's riddle united with the low branch of the cedar tree. This united the two branches of Judah, Pharez and Zarah, completing the first overturn of David's Throne in the wilderness removing it from Jerusalem. We must always bear in mind that it was the line of Judah Pharez that produced the Messiah. For a full account of these events refer to "Tracing Our Ancestors" by Frederick Haberman.

Zion or Sion: A term for Jerusalem: (6726) "Disown" <u>Disjoin</u> (as a permanent capital), a <u>mountain</u> of Jerusalem: (6725) a monumental or guiding pillar; sign, title, **waymark**: (6724) a **desert**, dry place: (6723) unused root; to parch, aridity, a desert, barren, drought, dry (land, place, solitary place, <u>wilderness</u>). <u>Sion</u>: (4622) Greek meaning a hill of Jerusalem, figurative to mean the Church (militant or triumphant).

Synopsis- The term Zion is hard to understand unless you read every Scripture in the Bible referring to Zion. Psalms 48:2 calls Zion **"the joy of the whole earth"** where I Kings calls Zion Jerusalem, the city of David. The Scriptures goes on to call Zion, mountains of Zion (Ps 133:3), daughters of Zion (Isa 3:16), Children of Zion (Ps 149:2), Zion is a wilderness (Isa 64:10), Lord dwelleth in Zion (Joel 3:21) and the sons of Zion (Zec 9:13). Zion was the guiding pillar of fire by night and the cloud by day while they were wondering in the wilderness according to the definition. After reviewing all the Scriptures of Zion, it simply means Gods Spirit with man for his Spirit is with all the names listed above. The most important Scriptures indicate that Zion is the Church (I Peter 2:4-6) calling Christ the chief corner stone and his Christians living stones. All Christians within the Church is Zion according to this verse and would also be called Jerusalem for they are one and the same. Jerusalem means to teach and a peaceful place and when Zion moved, the name Jerusalem also moved with it for Jerusalem has a duel meaning, physical and Spiritual. We must understand that God moved Zion from Jerusalem to the fruitful nation planted in the wilderness due to the Jews rejection of Christ (Matt 21:43). God plowed Zion (Jerm 26:18) or cultivated it with his Gospel and then moved (travailed, plowed and pluck) it to a fertile fruitful nation (Isa 66:8). These fertile nations are now the Christian nations of the world that is the house of Israel (Ephraim and Manasseh), the birthright tribes that received the great blessings to be nations and kingdoms as promised to Abraham, Isaac and Jacob (Gen 17:6, 35:11, 48:19) and given the name Israel (Gen 48:16). The name Israel did not go to any of the other eleven tribes but only to Ephraim and Manasseh to be his elect stewards and servants, Isaiah 65:9&15.

Daughter is a key word that we need to link to Zion and explains many verses correlating to the birthright tribe of Ephraim and Manasseh. The Hebrew definition of daughter; terms of relationship, apple of the eye, <u>branch</u>, <u>company</u>, <u>first means</u> **first born or first fruit**, old, town and village. The prime root is, to build, begin to build, <u>obtain Children</u>, made repair and to set up. The words daughter, when researching the concordance means bough, branch, Church and fruitful. We can then apply all these words to certain verses such as Genesis 49:22, **"Joseph is a fruitful bough, even a fruitful bough by a well; whose branches run over the wall"**. Ezekiel 17:23, **"In the mountain of the height of Israel will I plant it: and it shall bring forth boughs, and bear fruit,**

and be a goodly cedar;". After reviewing all the verses referring to bough, branch and fruitful we can only come to the conclusion that the Children and Daughter of Zion can only be Ephraim and Manasseh, the birthright tribes. They were destined to be fruitful and a company of nations that was planted in the wilderness to be Christian nations during the end days. The cedar is a direct reference to King David's throne that exist within the throne of England. See the segment on Zion in chapter eight.

Table Two

The Covenant, Birthright and Inheritance Blessings

The key in understanding Gods prophecies and why he divided the Kingdom of his nation into two houses can be found within studying the covenant and inheritance blessings. All of Gods prophecies are based upon the blessings to Israel, Gods earthly Kingdom that is the center of his creation. As we study the inheritance God gave his Chosen Hebrew People based upon the family birthright, we can see to whom it was given. Using this process, the Israelites can be traced through the generations of time. The blessings that started with Abraham through Joseph were to be of great wealth and power and to multiply into many nations dominated by his divided houses, the house of Israel and the house of Judah. From Abraham, the Covenant blessings were to be perpetuated from generation to generation governed by Hebrew Birthright law (Primogeniture) guided by Gods hand as recorded in the Scriptures. The blessings lie within the chosen son to receive the family name of the firstborn Birthright inheritance of the family's wealth and name.

There is a distinction between the Covenant and Inheritance blessings and important to differentiate the difference between the two. The generations of Abraham, Isaac and Jacob covers a broad spectrum of God's Chosen people that did not fall within the realm of being Israelite but also fell under the Covenant blessings. These other Hebrew's were the Phoenicians of Enoch and Colcal and Dara of Judah/Zarah. There were a large number of Hebrews that migrated prior to and during the Exodus that did not go with Moses into the wilderness and due to this event, they forfeited their right to be Israelite but still fell within the physical kingdom as a part of Gods people. Dan fell within this group for they leaped from Bashan (Duet 33:22) giving up their Israelite heritage, therefore, they were not given the blessing of being Israelite as recorded in the sealing of all twelve tribes in Revelation 7:5-8 where they are not listed as one of the twelve tribes. These people were Hebrew but not Israelite and still fell under the Covenant Blessings that were to be nations and Kings of

Kingdoms. The Birthright Inheritance Blessings were to be given great wealth and the family name as Israel under the control of Ephraim and Manasseh that has become our modern Capitalistic System and is called Mystery Babylon in Revelation chapter 18. The Christian nations were subdued and overcome by great wealth which is symbolic as Babylon and Revelation 18 tells us that this Capitalistic system will be destroyed by the Red Horse of Communism (Rev 6:4) which is the beginning of the period of Gods Wrath.

Whom ever received the Birthright of Israel were to be leader of all the family of God's Chosen People to include the non-Israelite Hebrew and were to receive a double portion of wealth as the head of the family. The tribes of Israel were to be called Israelite only through the selected birthright tribe and this writer emphasizes the importance of this fact, for the identity of our nation hinge upon this inheritance. The receiver of the birthright was to become a great international political influence with wealth and power in that all the families or nations of the world would be blessed. This is clearly outlined within the Scriptures below. The difference between the Covenant and Inheritance blessings is that the Covenant blessings of his people were to be wealthy as nations and to be Gods physical earthly kingdom. The selected Inheritance tribe of Israel were to be the leader of Gods Kingdom and wealthy over all the nations but more importantly, received the responsibility of establishing and protecting the Church as the Spiritual portion of Gods Kingdom. This would take great wealth and military power, controlling the gates of his enemy (Gen 22:17), seaports and trade routes. God's requirement to bestow his blessing were for his birthright nations to be fruitful and righteous (Christian) for one purpose, to spread his end time Gospel. His responsibility was to establish the earthly Kingdom through Israel, "he will rule as God" as a powerful Prince. They have one goal, to establish his end time Church for the Salvation of the World. This fulfills the coming of the Messiah and perpetuating his Church through the nation of Israel.

Covenant Blessings

The following Scriptures are Covenant blessings of the Birthright sons from Abraham to Ephraim and Manasseh. It is very important to understand that whomever received the Birthright to be named Israel were to rule the world as a Prince called Israel, "he will rule as God', the earthly representative or Ambassador as righteous nations of God till Christ takes his earthly throne in Power and Glory. This can be seen in the following blessings.

Abram or Abraham - (Gen 12:2-3) This Covenant was given to Abram by God in person because he was righteous in the eyes of God. **"And I will make of thee a great nation, and I will bless thee, and make thy name great; and thou shalt be a blessing: And I will bless them that bless thee, and curse**

him that curseth thee; and in thee shall all families of the earth be blessed.” Abraham was first called Hebrew in Genesis 14:13 to be a great nation and that all the nations of the world would be blessed through his descendants. Abraham was never a Jew.

(Gen 15:18-21) This was the promise to Abram giving him the Promised Land of Canaan, the birth of the nation of Israel. **“In the same day the Lord made a covenant with Abram saying, Unto thy seed have I given this land, from the river of Egypt unto the great river, the river Euphratis; The Kenites, and the Kenizzites, and the Kadmonites, And the Hittites, and the Perizzites, and the Rephaims, Canaaites, and the Girgashites, and the Jebusites”**. For the Christians and radio talk show hosts that say modern Israel does not belong to God's Hebrew/Jewish people are dead wrong. This verse and other Scripture clearly divide the land by borders still belong to the Hebrew people in ancient verses modern days for it has never changed. Modern Israel was flat-out given to his Hebrew/Jewish people!

(Gen 22:17-18) This blessing is given to Abram after God changed his name to Abraham meaning “High Father”. **“That in blessing I will bless thee, and in multiplying I will multiply thy seed as the stars of the heaven, and as the sand which is upon the sea shore; and thy seed shall possess the gate of his enemies; And in thy seed shall all the nations of the earth be blessed; because thou hast obeyed my voice.”** The word gate (8179) is the key to understanding this verse for in Hebrew it means, door or gate, city, port and as gatekeeper. In other words, the descendants of Abraham were to be the gatekeeper to the seaports, cities, and trade routes of the world. The families of the earth were to be blessed through the nations of Abraham by international trade, sea ports and great cities of merchandizing, Wall Street of New York City stock market. The great blessings given to Abraham, Isaac, Jacob, Joseph given directly to Ephraim and Manasseh has changed in no way in modern times.

Genesis 17:5-6, **“Neither shall thy name any more be called Abram, but thy name shall be Abraham; for a father of many nations have I make thee. And I will make thee exceeding fruitful, and I will make nations of thee, and kings shall come out of thee.”** Up till now, all his blessings were given in singular form but after the name change, Abraham were to be multiple nations as the High Father to the world. This verse clearly says that Abraham's descendants were to be many nations and kings and the families of the earth would be blessed through them.

.

Isaac- (Gen 17:19-22) this verse passes Gods Covenant with Abraham to his son Isaac selected to receive the firstborn blessing above Ishmael. **“And God said, Sarah thy wife shall bear thee a son indeed; and thou shalt call his**

name Isaac; and I will establish my covenant with him for an everlasting covenant, and with his seed after him. And as for Ishmael, I have heard thee; Behold, I have blessed him, and will make him fruitful, and will multiply him exceedingly; twelve princes shall he beget, and I will make him a great nation. But my covenant will I establish with Isaac, which Sarah shall bear unto thee at this set time in the next year". These blessing were to be multiple nations and kings now passed to Isaac and his sons, Isaac's sons later to be known as Saxon, (Gen 21:12 and Heb 11:18).

(Gen 21:12) The multiple Hebrew nations of Abraham were to be called after Isaac. **"And God said unto Abraham, Let it not be grievous in thy sight because of the lad, and because of thy bondwoman; in all that Sarah hath said unto thee, hearken unto her voice for in Isaac shall thy seed be called."** This verse says that the nations of Abraham and now Isaac would be called after their worldly name of Isaac. Shall thy seed be called Isaac "Isaac sons" or "Saxons". Their Biblical name was to be Hebrew Israelite. Hebrew 11:18, **"Of whom it was said, That in Isaac shall thy seed be called"**. This same verse is repeated in Gen 21:12 Rom 9:7 where the English language came from the Saxon's as slowly translated from Phoenician, Hebrew, Welch, Galic and into English.

 (Gen 25:23-27) This verse is to Rebekah, Isaac's wife, to bare twin sons for one to inherit Gods blessings given to Abraham and Isaac. **"And the children struggled together within her; and she said, If it be so, why am I thus? And she went to enquire of the Lord. And the Lord said unto her, Two nations are in thy womb, and two manner of people shall be separated form thy bowels; and the one people shall be stronger than the other people; and the elder shall serve the younger. And when her days to be delivered were fulfilled, behold, there were twins in her womb. And the first came out red, all over like an hairy garment: and they called his name Esau"**. This verse is clear that the descendants of Esau and Jacob were to be two different peoples but bonded together for prophetic purposes. They struggled together in the mother's womb just as they oppose each other today in our political world. The free Democratic Western nations are against the Eastern Communist nations just as the Scripture has foretold. Esau was a red baby and represents the Communist bloc nations of the world (Red horse of Communism). Study the word ruddy and Bozrah of how red represents the Communist and Arab coalition of nations. Jacob was to be the Christian fruitful nations during end times and brings this verse full circle in light of today's world political alignment of nations.

 (Gen 26:3-4) This was a blessing given to Isaac by God himself. **"Sojourn in this land, and I will be with thee, and will bless thee; for unto thee, and unto thy seed, I will give all these countries, and I will perform the**

oath which I sware unto Abraham they father; And I will make thy seed
to multiply as the stars of heaven and will give unto thy seed all these
countries: and in thy seed shall all the nations of the earth be blessed:"
Again, Abraham's blessing was passed to Isaac and he was to be a multitude
of nations where all the nations of the earth would be blessed through the
greatness and wealth of his descendants.

<u>Jacob</u>- (Gen 28:1-4), This verse passed the blessing of Abraham and Isaac
to Jacob. **"And God Almighty bless thee, and make thee fruitful, and
multiply thee, that thou mayest be a multitude of people; And give thee
the blessing of Abraham, to thee, and to they seed with thee; that thou
mayest inherit the land wherein thou art a stranger, which God gave unto
Abraham"**. They were to be a fruitful multitude of people or nations and
fruitful means to be righteous or Christian, the stone of Israel or "O virgin of
Israel" (the Bride of Christ to be).

(Gen 28:13-14) **"And, behold, the Lord stood above it, and said, I am the
Lord God of Abraham thy father, and the God of Isaac; the land whereon
thou liest, to thee will I give it, and to thy seed: And thy seed shall be as
the dust of the earth, and thou shalt spread abroad to the west, and to the
east, and to the north, and to the south; and in thee and in thy seed shall
all the families of the earth be blessed."** Abraham's blessings, was to be as
the dust of the earth, to be spread abroad (breach) West, East, North and South.
Note that abroad in Hebrew means; to make a breach (Pharez), break away,
burst out, come spread abroad, disperse, grow, increase, open, press, scatter
and urge. According to this verse, they were to spread out into the world and
be fruitful (righteous and Christian).

(Gen 32:28) This verse is where God changed Jacob's name to Israel and the
Covenant blessings to an Inheritance blessing. **"And he said, Thy name
shall be called no more Jacob but Israel: for as a prince hast thou power
with God and with men, and hast prevailed"**. Jacob's name was changed
to Israel which means, "he will rule as God" or as a Prince representing Gods
righteousness as great nations and kingdoms to be over the nations as families
of the earth to be their leader. He was to possess the gates of his enemies or
the world seaports and all the families of the earth were to benefit from his
wealth and power as a Prince through the authority of God. His Birthright
tribes were to rule the nations under Christianity just as Great Britain and the
United States has accomplished.

(Gen 35:9-12) Again God gave this blessing in person, not by the father, which
is very important to understand. **"And God appeared unto Jacob again, when
he came out of Padanaram, and blessed him. And God said unto him, Thy
name is Jacob; thy name shall not be called any more Jacob, but Israel**

shall be thy name; and he called his name Israel. And God said unto him, I am God Almighty: be fruitful and multiply; a nation and a company of nations shall be of thee, and kings shall come out of thy loins; And the land which I gave Abraham and Isaac, to thee I will give it, and to thy seed after thee will I give the land." The word "again", reemphasize the blessings that were passed from the inheritance of Abraham to Isaac and then to Jacob, who is now called Israel. All these blessing up till now were Covenant blessings but the next generation of blessing will be Inheritance blessings because of the creation of Gods earthly Kingdom, the nation of Israel where Israel is God's name. When we receive God's Spirit as a Christian, we inherit the Church to be his Bride. It was changed to Inheritance for the benefit of all mankind, for all man were to be eligible to inherit Gods Kingdom. They were to be fruitful and multiply into a nation and a company of nations as kings that would come out of Israel, not just one small nation in the Middle East called modern Israel. They were to be Christian nations representing "a nation and a company of nations" indicating one single nation verses a group of nations just as the United States and the Common Wealth of Great Britain. The study of history clearly shows that only the fruitful Christian nations of the United States and Great Britain can fulfill all these Covenant blessings.

Important Note: You may say, Abraham, Isaac, Jacob or Joseph never became many nations in ancient history so these verses are wrong. That is not true, for the blessings givens to these Patriarchs were to be only fulfilled by Joseph's two sons Ephraim and Manasseh in the last days as clearly recorded in Gen 49:1, **"And Jacob called unto his sons, and said, Gather yourselves together, that I may tell you that which shall befall you in the last days"**.

Covenant Birthright Inheritance Blessings

This is the Inheritance blessing given to the deserving and selected birthright sons of Jacob under the Covenant Blessing to Abraham passed through the generations of Isaac and Jacob to the present-day inheritance of Ephraim and Manasseh. Whomever Jacob chose to receive the family birthright to inherit the name Israel were to receive the great blessings to be nations and kings of kingdoms to rule over the families of the earth as promised to Gods Covenanted Patriarchs. This account is given in Genesis chapter 48 where Jacob passed the Covenant Blessings through Joseph directly to Jacob's grandsons, Ephraim and Manasseh. The only recorded case in the Bible where inheritance blessings are given to grandsons and not to the eldest son. The other eleven sons of Jacob were the tribes of Israel that did not receive the family name Israel or to be a multitude of nations and kingdoms where the families of the earth were to be blessed. The blessings of the first born to be called Israel only went directly to Joseph's two sons called lads of Ephraim and Manasseh in Gen 48:16. Only they were to receive the great blessings of Abraham, Isaac and Jacob passed directly through Joseph and not to no one else. The other eleven tribes were to be called Israel only through the Birthright of Ephraim and Manasseh. This point is clearly made within the following Scriptures and verified in I Chronicles 5:1-2.

Joseph - We need to note that the Inheritance blessing to Jacob's grandsons and the normal family inheritance to all twelve sons came from Jacob and not directly from God. All the previous Covenant blessings came straight from God so when Jacob gave the Inheritance blessing personally, it proves the authority of Jacob as the Prince of Israel, "he will rule as God" with the authority of a Prince or King given by God himself. Chapter 48 gives the account of where the firstborn right by Moses's Law was given to the two lads or sons of Joseph and no one else. The birthright inheritance blessing to Joseph is very unique for it went directly to the two lads and not to Joseph where they received the name Israel. This was performed to emphasize to whom received the Birthright Inheritance. Gen 48:16-19, **"The Angel which redeemed me from all evil, bless the lads; and let my name be named on them, and the name of my fathers Abraham and Isaac; and let them grow into a multitude in the midst of the earth. And when Joseph was that his father laid his right hand upon the head of Ephraim, it displeased him; and he held up his father's hand, to remove it from Ephraim's head unto Manasseh's head. And Joseph said unto his father, Not so, my father: for this is the firstborn; put thy right hand upon his heard. And his father refused, and said, I know it, my son, I know it: he also shall become a people, and he also shall be great: but truly his younger brother shall be greater than he, and his seed shall become a multitude of nations"**. The family name of Israel was given only to Ephraim and Manasseh, "bless the lads and let my name be named on them, and the name of my fathers Abraham and Isaac;". Not only were the two lads to receive the family name Israel but the Covenant blessing of greatness was to be many nations passed from Abraham, Isaac, Jacob and now only to his two Grandsons. These blessings did not go to the other eleven tribes of Israel as indicated by this Scripture. The lads received the birthright of the family of Israel, therefore the responsibility to carry on the family name as the lost sheep of the house of Israel. Manasseh were to be a single nation and Ephraim were to become a company of many nations throughout the world as given in Genesis 35:11. Ephraim and Manasseh represent the Spiritual portion of Israel as protector of the Church (Battle Ax) and Zion where the other eleven sons of Israel is the Physical portion of Israel fulfilling the prophecy of Jerusalem during the Tribulation of Wrath.

Joseph in Hebrew means to add or augment. Because of Reuben's sin of the firstborn, he lost his inheritance (I Chron 5:1-2). Joseph was selected to receive the birthright blessing, therefore, the first to be called into Jacob for this purpose (Gen 48:1-22). By Law, if the firstborn sinned against the family, it was the responsibility of the father to select the most suitable son and not necessarily in order of birth. This inheritance of double portion went to Joseph but it is a unique blessing for it was directed to Jacob's grandsons through their father Joseph. This is very significant if we are to understand today's world situation. No blessing to the other eleven sons went through the grandsons. Manasseh was to be one single great nation and Ephraim were to become a multitude of nations.

Ephraim- Carries the Hebrew meaning: double fruit, fruitfulness and was the second born son of Joseph. The right hand, by crossing his arms creating an X, was laid upon the son that was to receive the firstborn Birthright according to Hebrew Law and again this entitlement went to Ephraim and not Manasseh (Gen 48:14). The birthright blessing of the selected son was also to receive a double portion of wealth and given the family name. There is a strange ruling in this verse for the name Israel went to both lads and not just to the first blessed (verse 16). This is very important in following Israel down through time for whoever Ephraim and Manasseh (Lebanon, Sharon, Gilead, Carmel and Bashan) is during the end times, they are to be called Israel. This fact is seen all through the Old Testament Prophecy books by dividing the Children of Israel into the house of Israel, ten northern tribes lead by Ephraim and Manasseh, and the house of Judah (Judah and Benjamin). In Genesis 48:19, Ephraim were to be a multitude of nations but Manasseh were to be a single great nation.

The only nation in history that can fulfill this verse is the 46 nations of the Commonwealth of Great Britain or the British Colonial Empire. In Hebrew the word British means, brit "covenant", ish "man", or covenant man. The Hebrew name Ephraim means double fruit which matches his birthright and his ancient names were Lebanon and Sharon which is linked to the unicorn as mentioned in Ps 29:6 and Duet 33:17. Ephraim is a fruitful bough and is said to be fruitful or a Christian nation in the last days (Isa 33:9). He matches the symbol of the unicorn of the 46 nations of the Common Wealth of Great Britain controlled by King David's throne, (the overturn Ezk 17:22-23 and 21:25-27) the throne of England. The book of Hosea is written to the northern tribes of the house of Israel (Ephraim) as a warning of soon coming destruction and we can also heed this same warning if we do not repent of our national sins.

Manasseh- (Hebrew meaning: causing to forget) The firstborn son of Joseph and lost his birthright to Ephraim due to sin. As the firstborn, he held double land mass in the Promised Land of Israel proving the duality of the inheritance blessing. Look on a Bible map of Israel and you will see that Manasseh inherited land that bordered the Mediterranean Sea and a large landmass in the upper North Eastern corner called Bashan. His blessing is recorded in Gen 48:19,

"And his father refused, and said, I know it, my son, I know it: he also shall become a people, and he also shall be great: but truly his younger brother shall be greater than he, and his seed shall become a multitude of nations". During the last days, Manasseh is to be a single great nation. When you trace Manasseh back to their ancient name of Bashan, Gilead and Carmel, they were called fruitful which means righteous, Christian and God fearing (Isa 33:9). His symbol is the Bull as indicated in Duet 33:17 which represents the United States.

I Chronicles 5:1-2 verifies to whom received the birthright blessing and not the Covenant blessing to Abraham's descendants. **"Now the sons of Reuben the firstborn of Israel, (for he was the firstborn; but, forasmuch as he defiled his father's bed, his birthright was given unto the sons of Joseph the son of Israel: and the genealogy is not to be reckoned after the birthright. For Judah prevailed above his brethren, and of him came the chief ruler; but the birthright was Joseph's:)"**. This verse makes it clear that the firstborn birthright blessings did not go to Reuben or Judah but to Joseph and his two sons, Ephraim and Manasseh. This Scripture stress the fact that the birthright was not to be changed and that all the blessings given to Abraham through Jacob is now passed only to Ephraim and Manasseh, to be a great nation and kings of Kingdoms where the people of the earth would be blessed through them in the last days. The great blessings to Abraham hinged on who received the inherent blessings from Jacob called Israel.

<u>Family Inheritance Blessing to all twelve tribes</u>

The following blessings come from Genesis chapter 49 as the normal family inheritance and completely separate from the Birthright blessing given in chapter 48. From this point, all blessings are given by Jacob as the inheritance blessing in order of birth by Law. The blessings given in Genesis Chapter 49 is to take place in the last days which is our present time period (Gen 49:1), **"that I may tell you that which shall befall you in the last days"**. Note that during these blessing, Joseph is blessed as the eleventh born son in normal order of birth and Ephraim and Manasseh is not mentioned. This differentiates the difference between the Birthright Blessing above and the verses of the normal family blessing of inheritance. The birthright blessing to the descendants of Abraham to Joseph, were to be many nations and only applied to the birthright firstborn of Ephraim and Manasseh and not relevant to the following inheritance to all twelve tribes. Each son of Jacob, other than Joseph (Ephraim and Manasseh), were to be one single nation during the end times, (II Kings 19:17).

This segment is very important for it will display the order of inheritance blessing by Law of the twelve tribes of Israel from the beginning at Jacobs blessing till the end time or last days. These blessings are in accordance to Gods will and future destiny as prophecy is fulfilled. We as Christians cannot understand Bible Prophecy unless we carefully study the order and ranking of hierarchy within the tribes as given by inheritance. The following is the order of blessings given to the tribes as separate nations by order of birth and the leaders of Israel from Moses to our present time. The blessing given to each tribe can identify them through their given symbols placed on their flags, banners and ensigns. If we study the reason God established this order, we can better understand his Scriptures and Prophecies.

Jacob gave the following inheritance as a Prince to the family unit of Israel by order of birth as individual nations. The birthright is given in order of blessings in accordance to primogeniture Law and by following these instructions, we can see exactly who Israel is during the last days. Genesis 49:1 places all the birthright blessings to be implemented during this time period which is our present time or **"which will befall you in the last days"**. This accounts for the lack of blessings during the dark Ages. The birthright leadership of Israel can be traced through time by studying the rulers of each tribe down through history. We can see how the birthright tribes of the two lads were responsible for preserving the family name of Israel through their leadership. It is emphatically clear, according to the following blessings, that the twelve tribes were to be separate nations of kingdoms during their inherit destinies through the end times. This fulfills the birthright blessings to Abraham, to be multiple nations and kings of kingdoms as listed in Genesis 17:6, 35:11 and 48:19 to be ruled over by the end time birthright tribes. Again, the birthright blessing of greatness given to Abraham were only given to Joseph which was directly passed to Ephraim and Manasseh, so note this as you study.

There were two inheritance blessings given to the sons of Israel in relation as a tribe or nation. The first by their father Jacob in Genesis chapter 48 and 49. The second was given by Moses, the Law Giver, in Deuteronomy chapter 33 just prior to his death and their entry into the Promised Land. We know that Jacob stated the inheritance blessing would take place in the last days (Gen 49:1) so it would be fitting to say that the blessings of Moses would be of the same time frame. By compiling the two blessing, we can better understand their destinies during the last days and trace them through time. Geneses 49 by Jacob and from Deuteronomy 33 by Moses give the Birthright blessing to each Tribe.

Reuben: (France symbol of Water) (Hebrew meaning: to see) Gen 49:3-4, **"Reuben, thou art my first born, my might, and the beginning of my strength, the excellency of dignity, and the excellency of power: Unstable as water, thou shalt not excel: because thou wentest up to thy father's bed; then defiledst thou it: he went up to my couch. "Deue 33:6 "Let Reuben live, and not die; and let not his men be few."**

Summary: Reuben was unstable and would not excel but would have a large population of people believed to be modern France. They were to be "unstable as water" reflects their politics and instability with their allies just as indicated in today's political world situation. Reuben were to be powerful with "dignity" and "strength" but was not to excel for France never became a great super power due to their flamboyant, proud untrusting politics. They tried to colonize but have never been good warriors as described by their blessings and have lost almost every war they fought. He was a sexual man for it appeared that he had a sexual encounter with one of Jacobs wives. The French people have always been esteemed as romantics with sexual characteristics and an eloquent language again fulfilling this blessing.

Simeon: (part of all twelve tribes) (Hebrew meaning: to hear intelligently) Gen 49:5-7, **"Simeon and Levi are brethren: instruments of cruelty are in their habitations. O my soul, come not thou into their secret; unto their assembly, mine honour, be not thou united: for in their anger they slew a man, and in their self will they digged down a wall. Cursed be their anger, for it was fierce; and their wrath, for it was cruel; I will divide them in Jacob and scatter them in Israel."**

Summary: Simeon was not blessed in Deuteronomy chapter 33 due to his sin of cruelty. They were to be scattered within the house of Jacob (all twelve tribes) and within Israel, the birthright tribes of Ephraim and Manasseh. They were not to have a nation within the world.

Levi: (Hebrew meaning: attached, to twine, to unite) (dispersed into all twelve tribes) Gen 49:5-7 Jacob's blessing to Levi is the same as Simeon. Deuteronomy 33:8-12, **"And of Levi he said, Let thy Thummim and the Urim be with thy holy one, whom thou didst prove at Massah, and with whom thou didst strive at the waters of Meribah; Who said unto his father and to his mother, I have not seen him; neither did he acknowledge his brethren, nor knew his own children: for thy have observed thy work, and kept thy covenant. They shall teach Jacob thy judgments, and Israel thy law: they shall put incense before thee, and whole burnt sacrifice upon thin altar. Bless, Lord, his substance, and accept the work of his hands: smite through the loins of them that rise against him and of them that hate him, that they rise not again."**

Summary: Levi was chosen to be the Priestly tribe (Duet 10:8; 18:1-8) and commissioned to teach Jacob judgment, all twelve tribes, and instruct Israel on the law to the birthright tribes of Ephraim and Manasseh. They were to be scattered between all twelve tribes just as Simeon. The Levite tribe were the Priests and lawgivers and gave the authority to proclaim Kings among the tribes of Israel as recorded in each inheritance. The terms Thummin and

Urim in the verse above represent the authority of power for they were stones within the breastplate of the high priest that was worn in the presence of the Lord while in the Holy of Holies. They were to be the Judge and Teachers in matters affecting the nation (Exo 28:30; Lev 8:8). These stones represented great light and power and the authority of the Levite tribe as the Lawgiver to the King and the people. Being dispersed among each tribe gave Levi the authority and power to authorize each tribe to have there on line of Kings producing the Monarchs of Europe. Due to the Levite tribe being Priests within the Tabernacle and Temple, the other eleven tribes were required to tithe ten percent to support the Priests of the Levite tribe under the Old Covenant Law. Under the New Covenant Law, tithing was done away when Christ died on the Cross for tithing is not taught anywhere in the New Testament. Christ taught giving not tithing!

Judah: (Modern Israel symbol of the three crouched Lions) (Hebrew meaning: celebrated, to use a hand) Gen 49:8-12, **"Judah, thou art he whom they brethren shall praise: thy hand shall be in the neck of thine enemies; thy father's children shall bow down before thee. Judah is a lion's whelp: from the prey, my son, thou art gone up: he stooped down, he couched as a lion, and as an old lion; who shall rouse him up? The sceptre shall not depart from Judah, nor a lawgiver from between his feet, until Shiloh come; and unto him shall the gathering of the people be. Blinding his foal unto the vine, and his ass's colt unto the choice vine; he washed his garments in wine, and his clothes in the blood of grapes: His eyes shall be red with wine, and his teeth white with milk."**
Duet 33:7 **"And this is the blessing of Judah: and he said, Hear, Lord, the voice of Judah, and bring him unto his people: let his hands be sufficient for him and be thou an help to him from his enemies."**

<u>Summary</u>: The symbol of Judah is the lion and they were to be the leader of the kingdom by providing the Phares line of kings (Matt 1:3 scepter or throne) and the Lawgiver through the tribe of Levi that represented Gods Spirit with the nations through the Temple and Holy of Holies (Zion) ultimately to be the Church. They were tasked to produce the Messiah through the Phares line of kings to fulfill the prophecy of Christ coming to gather his people into the Church and establish his Gospel (Gen 49:10 "the gathering of the people be"). They were to maintain Jerusalem as a keeper but failed due to the sin of agnosticism. From the time Christ died on the cross, he gave the Jews 40 years, or one generation, to accept him as the true Messiah and they refused. Jerusalem was taken from them in 70AD and destroyed by the Romans. The Jews wanted to maintain the old religion of Judaism and God could not allow this to interfere with his Church. Therefore, he had no choice but to destroy Jerusalem and take his Spirit (Zion) from them and give it to a fruitful nation in the wilderness. This fruitful nation, the lost sheep of the house of Israel, would

accept and spread his Gospel to the people of the world proclaiming his glory and Salvation (Matt 21:43). God is going to give the Jews one last chance in the Tribulation Period to accept him and this time they will believe and fulfill Daniel's 70th week. Daniel's seven-year Prophecy is only to the Jews and the non-believing Gentiles and Hebrews of the house of Israel that was left behind when the Church was taken. This is the physical nation of Israel (Rev 12:1) called a woman not a Bride and is not the Church for the Holy Spirit and the Bride has been taken. There would be no need to seal 144000 if the Holy Spirit was present for, we are sealed at our Spiritual birth into the Church. The bride is not present for it will be taken at the beginning of the seven-year Tribulation.

Zebulun: (Holland or Netherlands Symbol of the Ship) (Hebrew meaning: habitation, to enclose, to dwell with) Gen 49:13, **"Zebulun shall dwell at the haven of the sea; and he shall be for an haven of ships; and his border shall be unto Zidon."** Duet 33:18, **"And of Zebulun he said, Rejoice, Zebulun, in thy going out; and Issachar, in thy tents."**

Summary: Zebulun was to be great mariners for they were to be, "at the haven of the sea" and "for a haven of ships" and were to rejoice, "in thy going out". Holland has always been known for ships and Rotterdam is one of the world's busiest seaports. Forty percent of their land mass has been taken from the sea by dams and dykes. The term, "in thy going out;" indicated that they were gone over the seas in search of commercial gains. They were brothers to the Scandinavian countries of Norway (Benjamin), Sweden (Naphtali), Finland (Issachar), Denmark (Dan), Iceland (Dan) and Faeroe Islands. They were to be of the sea (Gen 49:13) just as Holland is today, famous for world shipping.

Issachar: (Finland symbol of an Ass or Dondey) (Hebrew meaning: he will bring a reward) Gen 49:14-15, **"Issachar is a strong ass couching down between two burdens: And he saw that rest was good, and the land that it was pleasant; and bowed his shoulder to bear, and became a servant unto tribute."**
Duet 33:18, **"And of Zebulun he said, Rejoice, Zebulun, in the going out; and Issachar, in thy tents."**

Summary: Issachar and Zebulun were to be brothers in the same tent meaning they were combined as a people. The hard climate of Finland can be seen in the definition of their blessing as a shoulder to bear of their good land. Finland is on the same latitude as Alaska and the production of timber their lively hood. They are also mariners of the sea just as their brother Holland (Zebulun).

Dan: (Denmark and Ireland symbol of Eagle and Adder or Snake) (Hebrew meaning: judge, to rule, to judge, to strive at law) Gen 49:16-18, **"Dan shall judge his people, as one of the tribes of Israel. Dan shall be a serpent by**

the way, an adder in the path, that biteth the horse heels, so that his rider shall fall backward. I have waited for thy salvation, O Lord." Duet 33:22, "And of Dan he said, Dan is a lion's whelp: he shall leap from Bashan."

Summary: Dan was the most adventurous tribe and a wayfaring traveler fulfilling their Hebrew name. They were known as the seafaring Vikings that also fulfills their definition of blessings. Some of the ancient names of Dan were Danaan, Danaoi, Danai, Danites, Danes and Tuatha de Danaan as just a few. They were commanded to leave waymarks and high heaps where ever they went (Jerm 31:21) and to be **"an adder in the path"** leaving a path to follow like the adder snake. Where ever they traveled they left names of their forefathers such as the Danube, Dneiper and Don Rivers, London, Denmark, Doncaster, Dublin and hundreds more. The term **"I have waited for thy salvation, O Lord"** means they went into the wilderness to wait for Christ's Gospel, the Church where Joseph of Arimathea established the first above ground Church in Ireland in 36AD. God knew the ten lost tribes would accept his Gospel when he sent his Disciples (Matt 10:5-8) into the wilderness to find them and to preach his Gospel. They became the English-speaking Christian nations of the world.

Moses in Deuteronomy chapter 33 said that Dan would be a lion's whelp. His symbol was to be the lion that appears in nations all over Europe as the standing lion. The word whelp in Hebrew means, a young one, cub, prime root is to turn aside from the road, and to sojourn. Dan was to be a traveler and explorer for Moses said that he was to leap from Bashan, his dwelling place in the Promised Land. He turned his back on his brothers, the other eleven tribes, and totally departed his Promised Land in Canaan. Dan is not mentioned in the genealogies listed in I Chronicles chapters 4 through 8 meaning he was not in the land. Dan paid a price for leaving his brothers and his heritage, for God punish Dan by taking away his heritage of Salvation by not listing him when he seals the tribes in Revelations 7:5-8 at the sealing of the 144,000 or 12,000 from each tribe. Dan is not listed and Manasseh received his portion of blessings and the sealing 12,000 of Gods people (Rev 7:6). Dan was leader of the north Brigade consisting of Dan, Asher and naphtali (Nem 2:25-34) bearing the standard of the Eagle. Manasseh in Revelation 7:6 inherited Dan's symbol of the Eagle as the United States.

After reviewing the Scriptures on the blessing of Dan, he was to have the symbol of the Lion and Eagle found in most of the Christian nations of Europe. He was to be a strong nation as a judge under a Monarchy and a traveler by ship into the world **"that he had not gone with his feet"** (Isa 41:3) for this is how he leapt from Bashan, on the wings of an Eagle by ship. He was to control the seaports and trade routes of the world, the **"gate of his enemy"** (Gen 22:17) by being a world power as Great Britain, Germany, Denmark,

Iceland and portions of the United States.

Gad: (Switzerland symbol of a Lion) Hebrew meaning: in the since of distributing, fortune, primitive root: to crown upon) Gen 49:19, **"Gad, a troop shall overcome him: but he shall overcome at the last."** Duet 33:20-21, **"And of Gad he said, Blessed be he that enlargeth Gad: he dwelleth as a lion, and teareth the arm with the crown of the head. And he provided the first part for himself, because there, in a portion of the lawgiver, was he seated; and he came with the heads of the people, he executed the justice of the Lord, and his judgments with Israel."**

Summary: Gad or Switzerland is basically in the center of Europe and a gateway through the Alps where armies or troops have overrun him for hundreds of years. Switzerland has four national languages due to being overrun so many times, Swiss, German, French and Italian. He overcame by becoming a neutral nation in the last days fulfilling this blessing for Switzerland is an ambassador, heads of the people (State), bringing justice and judgments of the Lord and Israel to the world through their neutrality. Due to their neutrality, became a world banking center for secrecy just as their definition indicates, "in the since of distributing, fortune".

Switzerland was a Monarch with great power connected by marriage to the Kings of Germany and England for hundreds of years and can be seen in their blessing as, **"and teareth the arm with the crown of the head"**. Gad was to be a Monarch with a crowned King and have a portion of the tribe of Levi as the lawgiver bringing justice and judgment to their people and Israel just as God promised.

Asher: (Belgium and Germany) (Hebrew meaning: happy, to be straight, to go forward, be honest, prosper) Gen 49:20, **"Out of Asher his bread shall be fat, and he shall yield royal dainties."** Duet 33:24-25, **"And of Asher, he said, Let Asher be blessed with children; let him be acceptable to his brethren, and let him dip his foot in oil. Thy shoes shall be iron and brass; and as thy days, so shall thy strength be."**

Summary: The blessing in Genesis 49:20 clearly states that Asher were to yield royal dainties or Kings. Royal means to reign as a king and dainties in Hebrew means, delicacy or pleasure, delight, live voluptuously. Asher was to have kings of great wealth and pleasure. Deuteronomy chapter 33 goes on to say that Asher were to have great strength as iron and brass with many children and were to be anointed by dipping his foot in oil. He was to be great kings just as Germany has produced over hundreds of years as the key force within the politics of Europe. The rise of the Nazi Party in 1933 eliminated the Monarch of Germany just as the Communist destroyed the throne of Russia in 1917.

This was the beginning of the strength of the Red Horse that is out to destroy the power of Gods people and his Throne that finally culminates into the New World Order as the Beast System.

Naphtali: (Sweden with symbol of a deer) (Hebrew meaning: my wrestling, to twine, to struggle or be tortuous, unsavory) Gen 49:21, **"Naphtali is a hind let loose: he giveth goodly words."** Duet 33:23: **"And of Naphtali he said, O Naphtali, satisfied with favor, and full with the blessing of the Lord: possess thou the west and the south."**

Summary: The meaning of a hind is a doe or female deer, a ram stag or male deer, powerful, mighty or strength. Naphtali was to be Godly or righteous with God's Word for he found favor with God due to his righteousness. He accepted Christ's Gospel and by possessing the west and the south could very well be his migration to the United States into a new land.

It is important to note that during the late 1800's, due to famines, almost one fifth of the Swedish population migrated to the United States as if it were a calling from God. This fulfilled his end time Prophecies dealing with Manasseh for God often used famines to manipulate his people throughout the Bible. This same phenomenon also occurred with the other Israelite European nations because of tyranny and hardships during this time frame. It created the single greatest Israelite nation in history, the United States of America, Manasseh the Bull (Gen 35:11, 48:19 and Duet 33:17).

Joseph: (Symbol of the Bough or Branch of the Olive Tree, Bull and Unicorn) Has the Hebrew meaning: to add or augment and is the second blessing given to Joseph. The first was the birthright in Genesis 48. The blessing given in Genesis chapter 49 is the normal family inheritance blessing in order of birth by Hebrew Law and is proof that Joseph received the birthright. Note that the words fruitful, bough, archer, arms, branches, shepherd, stone and everlasting hills is only in reference to Joseph as the house of Israel and not to the other sons.

(Gen 49:22-26) **"Joseph is a fruitful bough, even a fruitful bough by a well; whose branches run over the wall; The archers have sorely grieved him, and shot at him and hated him: But his bow abode in strength, and the arms of his hands were made strong by the hands of the mighty God of Jacob; (from thence is the shepherd, the stone of Israel) Even by the God of thy father, who shall help thee; and by the Almighty, who shall bless thee with blessings of heaven above, blessings of the deep that lieth under, blessings of the breasts, and of the womb: The blessings of thy father have prevailed above the blessing of my progenitors unto the utmost bound of the everlasting hills: they shall be on the head of Joseph, and on the crown**

of the head of him that was separate from his brethren". The "fruitful bough whose branches run over the wall" indicate how the house of Israel departed and migrated into other lands to fulfill the blessings to become great nations and kingdoms. The term "the stone of Israel", indicates that Ephraim was to be the stone of the Church and the leader to spread the end time Gospel of Christ, "the living Stone" of Israel. The term fruitful bough by a well is very significant for fruitful means they were given a new Name as Christian. Bough means (1121) a nation, young bullock or bull, firstborn and to build. Being by a well is nothing more than drawing the water of life from the well of our Lord Jesus Christ. In other words, this verse means that Joseph was to be a Christian nation with the symbol of the bull as the Church and run over the wall by departing the land of Israel to become a strong mighty nation, "the arms of his hands were made strong". They were to be shepherds, the stone of Israel as the Church. The young bull or nation (UK and USA) was to build Christ's Church in the wilderness of the world by the well of living waters of our Lord. Joseph was to receive the wealth and precious things of the earth, **"the deep that lieth under," "utmost bound of the everlasting hills:"** and matches Genesis 22:17-18, 28:14 and 35:1 that were the covenant blessings to Abraham, Isaac and Jacob.

Duet 33:13-17, **"And of Joseph he said, Blessed of the Lord be his land, for the precious things of heaven, for the dew, and for the deep that coucheth beneath. And for the precious fruits brought forth by the sun, and for the precious things put forth by the moon. And for the chief thing of the ancient mountains, and for the precious thing of the lasting hills, And for the precious things of the earth and fullness thereof. And for the good will of him that dwelt in the bush: let the blessing come upon the head of Joseph, and upon the top of the head of him that was separated from his brethren. His glory is like the firstling of his bullock, and his horns are like the horns of unicorns with them he shall push the people together to the ends of the earth: and they are the ten thousands of Ephraim, and they are the thousands of Manasseh."** The term, "his glory is like the firstling of his bullock", indicate his birthright blessings by Law of giving the first fruit to God. This verse stresses how Joseph was to control all the mineral and mining wealth of the earth. The horns of unicorns and push the people together to the ends of the earth by colonizing is the key in identifying Ephraim (Great Britain) in modern times for England is the only modern nation to have a unicorn as a nation symbol. They have pushed the people together to the ends of the earth by colonizing the world and become the economic power house of all times through world trade and shipping through large US and UK Corporations. God's great blessings indicate the wealth and strength of the Commonwealth of Great Britain's 46 national coalition of the British Empire. Great Britain and their brother, the United States, is the only nations that can fulfill this verse by being Christian, fruitful and righteous, "the shepherd and stone of Israel" as the symbol of the unicorn to include the United States as the bull. Ephraim and Manasseh were brothers in ancient days just as Great Britain and the United States are brothers today identified by the unicorn and bull as their nations symbols united by a common language, English.

Ephraim and Manasseh: The two sons of Joseph that actually received the blessing through Joseph by Jacob personally. This is why there is no land mass given to Joseph in ancient or modern times for it went directly to his two sons. Genesis 49:22-26 and Deuteronomy 33:13-17 as quoted above and pertains to both Ephraim and Manasseh as the sons of Joseph that augment and fulfill all the blessings that were given to Abraham. His blessings were passed to Isaac and then to Jacob through Joseph to Manasseh to be a single nation (US) and Ephraim to be a company of nations and Kings of Kingdoms (GB the throne of David through the Crown of England). Their ancient Biblical names were Lebanon, Sharon, Bashan, Gilead and Carmel but their earthly names were Celts, Goths, Scythians, Danaoi, Saxon, Anglo, Jutes, Danes and many more.

Benjamin: (Norway and Iceland Symbol of the Wolf) (Hebrew meaning: son of the right hand, a son as the builder of the family name) Gen 49:27, **"Benjamin shall ravin as a wolf: in the morning he shall devour the prey, and at night he shall divide the spoil."** Duet 33:12 **"And of Benjamin, he said, The beloved of the Lord shall dwell in safety by him; and the Lord shall cover him all the day long, and he shall dwell between his shoulders."**

Summary*:* Benjamin were to have the wolf as their symbol and they were also of the sea just as their brothers that migrated and plundered the riches of the world seeking treasure by ship.

Note: All eleven brothers of Joseph fell under the leadership of Ephraim and Manasseh as the Birthright tribes of the house of Israel. As indicated in the blessings above, the tribes of Israel were to be righteous meaning, they were to receive the Gospel of Christ when planted into the wilderness to wait. Each of the twelve tribes were to be their own nation with Kings of Monarchs also indicated within their blessing as given by Jacob and Moses to be controlled by David's throne, the Crown of England. Yes. They had many quarrels and wars over the centuries but they were still brothers. If we closely study all of these modern Israelite nations, we can see how Great Britain and the United States were formed during the last days to be great nations and leaders of the world. The United States of America (Manasseh the bull) was a derivative and brother of Great Britain (Ephraim the unicorn). God created a heavenly calling of migration from all the other eleven tribes or Israelite nations of Europe to form the government of the single most powerful righteous God-fearing nation ever in history. The calling of all twelve tribes to create Manasseh on the North American Continent as a nation under a Republic and not a King were for one purpose, to establish the Church and preach Christ's end time Gospel to the world without the interference of a king. God opened the North American Continent to all peoples of the world that would hear his Word and calling of his Gospel (Isa 12:11-12, 16:1-8, 18:1-7,41:1-8 and 43:1-22). We were blessed as a righteous, Christian and fruitful nation under one God as our creator that our pledge of allegiance and national songs indicate under thirteen colonies representing the thirteen tribes of Israel. To get thirteen tribes you subtract Levi for he was divided between all tribes and replace Joseph with his two sons, Ephraim and Manasseh. This gives you thirteen as depicted on a Biblical map. Thirteen Tribes and thirteen colonies, what a coincidence!

Leaders of Israel up to King David's Throne

It is important to know the leaders of Israel by tribe so we can understand the birthright blessing of Ephraim and Manasseh as their predominate leader.

Moses - The Deliverer/Law Giver and first leader of the Children of Israel prior to becoming a nation in the Promised Land. Moses was a Levite and the first High Priest where he received the Laws from God to be given to the Children of Israel. The term Lawgiver is mentioned seven times in the Bible and Moses is referred to as the Lawgiver in Numbers 21:18 for he was the one that gave the directions to dig the well. Psalms 60:7 and 108:8 makes the statement, **"Gilead is mine; Manasseh is mine; Ephraim also is the strength of mine head; Judah is my Lawgiver"**. These verses refer to four different nations of Israel which is Gilead, Manasseh, Ephraim and Judah. "Ephraim is the strength of mine head" means he was the birthright tribe as the leader but the Lawgiver was of Judah which makes the throne and lawgiver inseparable (Gen 49:10). Gilead, Manasseh and Ephraim were of the ten northern tribes of the house of Israel and Judah the house of Judah again indicating the separation of the two houses. Isaiah 33:22 says that the Lord (Christ) is our Lawgiver King and Savior indicating that someday, he will fulfill all prophecies and rule in power from Jerusalem. James 4:12, also refers to Christ as the Lawgiver. From these verses we know that Christ will be the ultimate Lawgiver when he comes in power but until then, there is an earthly Lawgiver through the tribe of Levi started by Moses. The earthly lawgiver is the Levite tribe that was divided between the house of Jacob and Israel that became the law-making body of the governments of each tribe as given by their inheritance blessing in Duet 33:10. The Levite tribe was given the authority as the Lawgiver by God to establish a line of kings within each tribe after their division and dispersion.

Joshua - The successor as leader of Israel after Moses and was of the tribe of Ephraim, the birthright tribe to be leader that received the family firstborn birthright. The reason God did not allow Moses to enter the Promised Land is because he was not given the birthright, therefore Joshua received the leadership for he was Israel as Gen 48:16-22 states. God refused Moses into the Promised Land along with the old generation that came out of Egypt due to non belief. Joshua and the younger generation were allowed to enter Cannan where Joshua replaced Moses as their leader.

The following is the fifteen Judges and leaders of Israel up till the first king, King Saul. This time period was the colonial rule of the Judges. As you will see below, the Judges were selected from the different tribes but the majority of the leaders came from Ephraim and Manasseh, the birthright tribe to be leader of Israel. As you can see below, six of the fifteen judges were of the birthright tribes, two from Ephraim and four from Manasseh, indicating their right as the leader by birthright. The structure of Israel's leadership during the period of colonial rule is very similar to the Republic of the United States. The judges represent the President or Executive Branch by being elected of the people, the tribe leaders or elders represents the Senate and Congress of the Legislative Branch also being elected by the people, and the Priest Hood and Temple represents our Judicial Branch of the Supreme Court and Depart of Justice appointed by God or the Executive and Legislative Branches. God planted Manasseh (the Bull) in the wilderness for this sole purpose, for he needed a single great nation (Gen 48:19 & Duet 33:17) as a Republic (by the people) to spread his end time Gospel without the interference of a tyrannical King or totalitarian government. Study both of these systems of governance and you can see the close parallels for our Republic is based upon God himself and you can be assured he inspired our Preamble, Bill of Rights and Constitution.

Othniel - Joshua 15:17, the son of Kenaz and believed to be of the tribe of Judah.
Ehud - Judges 3:15, of the tribe of Benjamin.
Shamgar - Judges 3:31, possibly of the tribe of Naphtali.
Deborah - Judges 4:5, believed to be of the tribe of **Ephraim**.
Gideon - Judges 6:36, son of Joash of the tribe of **Manasseh**.
Abimelech - Judges 9:1, son of Gideon of the tribe of **Manasseh**.
Tola - Judges 10:1, of the tribe of Issachar.
Jair - Judges 10:3, a Gileadite of the tribe of **Manasseh**.
Jephthah - Judges 11:11, son of Gilead of the tribe of **Manasseh**.
Ibzan - Judges 12:8 from either the tribe of Judah or Zebulun.
Elon - Judges 12:11, of the tribe of Zebulun and judged for 10 years.
Abdon - Judges 12:13, son of Shashak from the tribe of Benjamin and ruled for eight years.
Samson - Judges 16:30, son of Monoah of the tribe of Dan.
Eli - I Sam 1:9, son of Aron of the tribe of Levi.
Samuel - I Sam 7:15, son of Elkanah and Hannah of the tribe of **Ephraim**.
King Saul - 1 Sam 9:2 son of Kish of the tribe of Benjamin. Anointed King by Samuel in 1095 BC.

King David - I Sam 16 thru I Kings 2:11, son of Jesse of the tribe of <u>Judah</u> (Phares blood line Matt 1:1) and anointed as King of Israel in 1056 BC.

Note that from the time of Moses till the Phares line of Kings began with King David, seven of the eighteen leaders came from the tribes of Ephraim and Manasseh which were the birthright tribes to be leaders of Israel by firstborn Mosaic Law.

Bible Prophets (approx. dates)

Gods Prophets and Patriarchs were simply a medium for his Spiritual communications to the King and his Children of Israel. His voice was open not only to Israel but to all nations and people that would believe his Word, just as his Spirit is today. Israel was his chosen people but his Salvation was open to the world and their Prophets were his form of communication till the fulfillment of Christ's Church and coming of the Holy Spirit. Don't confuse the duty of the High Priest and the Temple for they only atoned for the sins of the people and not for the purpose of communications. The Temple was Gods dwelling place on earth, Zion. Christ's death on the cross as our Savior fulfilled the need for the Prophets, Priest and Temple. Christ became our high Priest, our bodies became Gods Temple, and the Holy Spirit became a direct communication link from individual Spirits to Christ our mediator, and then to the Father on High. John the Baptist and Agabus were the last Prophets ordained by God directly. Paul was the last Apostle ordained by Christ himself on the road to Damascus (Acts 9:5).

The following Prophets are in order by date and time of service. To have a better understanding of Prophecy, we must pay particular attention to when the Prophets wrote the Scripture in direct correlation to whom it was written and to when and where the Prophecy is to take place. A good example of this is the Prophetic book of Ezekiel. This book was written to the Children of Israel but predominately to the house of Israel, the ten northern tribes approx. 150 years after their captivity and disappearance. Ezekiel mentions the house of Israel 78 times, the house of Judah five times, the house of Jacob once, and the house of Togarmah twice. The house of Israel is considered to be destroyed and never to return but is mentioned 78 times, many times more than any other house. All the different houses in Ezekiel are referred to as dissimilar peoples and nations. This brings up a very interesting point for Ezekiel speaks of being on the river Chibar during the Babylonian captivity. This had to be written after 586BC or approx. 135 years after the house of Israel disappeared into captivity to Assyria and never returned or herd of again as a nation or people. Why would Ezekiel write to the house of Israel with a Prophetic warning after their captivity and destruction had already occurred if they did not exist as a nation. The reason is simple, Ezekiel knew where the house of Israel was located and that they were to be many nations in the last days. This fulfilled Gods promise to Abraham, Isaac and Jacob that under the birthright blessings, they would be one great nation, a company of nations and kings of kingdoms (Gen 17:6; 35:11; 48:16-19).

These promises are clear and absolute within the Scriptures and irrefutable but the modern Church refuse to see the truth. Many of the Prophetic books of the Old Testament were written to the house of Israel and Judah after their division and subsequently had been taken into captivity. The house of Israel (Ephraim and Manasseh) is mentioned more than any of the other houses but they were first to go into captivity and never return to the Promised Land. This tells us that the warnings of the Prophetic books of the Old Testament of destruction due to wickedness and idol worship applies not only to the ancient times but to the end days or the end of the age of our present time period, the great falling away (II Thess 2:3). Why would the Prophets write after the fact? God knew that the evil ways of his rebellious house never change and would come full circle to the end of the age for history always repeats itself. In other words, all the Old Testament Prophetic books were written to Christ's Church of the last days that is Gods Children of Israel under the New Covenant Church (Zion/ Sion) (Heb 8:8, Jerm 31:31).

Old Testament Prophets

It is important to understand the dates and time period of when the prophets gave their Prophecies of coming judgment of the house of Israel and Judah. This indicates that all Prophecy is dual and can be applied to the end days or last days of the division of the modern-day house of Israel (Christian nations) and Judah (State of Israel). These warnings can be associated with the soon coming WW III as foretold by Isaiah, Ezekiel, Jeremiah, Daniel and all the minor Prophets.

Abraham (Gen 20:7) (1898BC) The first Hebrew as recorded in Gen 14:13 and was never considered a Jew for that term did not exist till II Kings 16:6 coined by the Assyrians for the people of Judah of Judea and Jerusalem. Abraham was the father of God's chosen covenant people and were to be nations and kings of kingdoms (Gen 17:6 and 11). His seed was to be called Israel and family name to be passed to the birthright tribe of Ephraim and Manasseh only (Gen 48:16-19). The name Israel was given directly to Ephraim and Manasseh and the other eleven tribes received the family name only through the leadership of Joseph's two sons of the house of Israel by firstborn Law of Moses as given by Jacob in Gen 48.

Moses (Duet 34:10) (1571BC) (birth) The Deliverer and Lawgiver, "drawing out, rescue" from the tribe of **Levi**. Moses was the leader of the Children of Israel out of Egyptian bondage into the wilderness (Exodus).

Aron (Ex 7:1) (1491BC) (born in Egypt during captivity), high priest of the tribe of **Levi** (Num 26:59 & Lev 8:1).

Eldad (Nu 11:26) (1490BC) (God has loved), elder and prophet.

Medad (Nu 11:26) (1490BC) (Affectionate), elder and prophet.

Balaam (Nu 22:5) (1452BC) (devouring or devourer) The tribe of **Ephraim**.

Samuel (I Sam 3:20) (1095BC) Anointed Saul as first King of Israel and the last Judge. He was a Prophet during the reign of King Saul and David.

David (Mt 13:35) (1063BC) The first Phares line of the Kings of Israel (Matt 1:3) that produced the Pharisees and the linage of Christ.

Gad (I Sam 22:5) (1062 BC) (to crown upon) Gad was a prophet during King David's reign.

Nathan (II Sam 7:2) (1042BC) A prophet of the royal court during the reign of David and Solomon.

The division of Gods Kingdom by Ahijah I Kings 11 (933 BC)

Ahijah (I Kg 11:29) (992BC) (Brother) A Prophet of Shiloh and divided Solomon's kingdom 1 Kings 11.

Shemaiah (II Cron 12:5) (972BC) (to hear) A Prophet during the time of King Rehoboam.

Iddo (II Chron 13:22) (958BC) (to advance) A seer/Prophet and wrote Chronicles of Solomon and Jeroboam.

Jehu (I Kg 16:7) (930BC) A Prophet during the time of King Ahab.

Joshua (I Kg 16:34) (910BC) A Prophet during the time of King Ahab.

Micaiah (I Kg 22:8) (897BC) (Who is like Jehovah) Prophet during the last days of King Ahab of Israel and King Jehoshaphat of Judah.

Jonah (II Kg 14:25) (862BC) The fifth of the minor Prophets, the son of Amittai of the tribe of Zebulun. Sent as a prophet of warning to Nineveh Assyria and example of how God will spare a nation that repents of their sins. The city of Nineveh was founded by Asshur the second son of Shem (Gen 10:11) making Assyria of Semitic descent and is why God sent Jonah for he showed compassion because they were his people. The uniqueness of this book is that Jonah did not go to the Hebrew or Jew but to the Gentiles of Assyria for this event occurred prior to captivity and represents a symbol of today's Church going into the world teaching Salvation and Repentance.

Elijah (I Kg 18:36) (906 BC) (Jehovah is God) A Prophet during the reign of King Ahab and believed to be from Gilead of the tribe of Manasseh. Elijah was one of the Prophets that God took to Heaven by a whirlwind and did not see death (II Kings 2:11). According to Malachi 4:1-6, Elijah shall return during the Tribulation period as one of the witnesses (Rev 11:3&10) to the world warning of Gods coming Judgment just prior to Gods-day of wrath. Enoch is the other witness for both were taken into Heaven by God without seeing physical death (Gen 5:24).

Joel (Joel 1:1) (800BC) (The Lord "Yahwey" is God) Joel was one of the minor Prophets believed to be as early as 800BC or as late as 350BC due to the style of writing. He warned of Gods wrath in the end of the Age of "The day of the Lord" which is our present time.

Amos (Amos 1:1) (787BC) (Burden or burden barrier) A Prophet during the reign of Jeroboam II of Israel and Uzziah of Judah. Amos was of the tribe of Judah and one of the Minor Prophets. His Prophecies were a warning to the Assyrian's and their destruction due to sin and symbolize the Church as a warning to the Gentile nations. This writer believes that the Prophecies of Amos is the destruction of Damascus and Palestinians during the last days. Amos 1:2-3 makes the alignment. Zion and Jerusalem are indicated as two separate entities for modern Zion is the house of Israel (Ephraim), the Christian nations of the world and Jerusalem is modern Israel. Zion or Sion in the Old and New Testament is not the Zionist of modern Israel but is the Spirit of the Church. Carmel and Gilead are Manasseh or the United States. Refer to table one for definitions. Isaiah 17:1-3 explains how Damascus will be destroyed due to their terrorist activity. Carmel and Gilead are the nations mentioned in the wilderness (Isa 16:1-8; 18:1-7) the people scattered and pealed and called mount Zion (the United States Isa 18:7). This verse can only be speaking in future tense for Damascus is one of the oldest cities in the world and according to history, has never been destroyed at the date of this book.

Hosea (Hos 1:1) (785BC) An end time prophet that wrote his book to the northern tribes of the house of Israel, a WARNING of the soon coming destruction which also pertains to end time prophecy of today's world situation. He ministered during the reign of Uzziah (783BC) to Hezekiah (686BC).

Isaiah II Kings 19:2 (760BC) (Salvation of Jehovah) Son of Amos and very little is known of Isaiah. He was one of the greatest Prophets that foretold and warned Judah and the house of Israel of soon coming destruction and captivity. Manasseh was the first to go into captivity in approx. 740BC. This warning is just as important and valid to the Church of today for Isaiah's warning is a duplicate Prophecy given in ancient times to culminate in the last days to the divided houses of Israel (Christian nations) and Judah (the Jews). Isaiah Prophesied during four reigns of Kings from Uzziah to Hezekiah (767 to 687BC) and witnessed the Assyrian captivity (740 to 718BC) of the house of Israel that did not head his warnings. Will the modern Christian nations of the house of Israel head this same warning?

Micah Jeremiah 26:18, (750BC) (Who is like Jehovah) A Prophet during the time of Isaiah and very little is known about him. He warns of the coming destruction and captivity of Samaria, the ten northern tribes of the house of Israel that was taken captive to Assyria ending in 718 BC. His Prophecies also applies to the present-day house of Israel and Judah.

House of Israel into captivity to Assyria in 740 - 718BC

Oded (I Cron 28:9) (741BC) He was a Prophet during the war between Samaria, the ten northern tribes of the house of Israel and Judah. He rebuked King Pekah of the house of Israel for not feeding and clothing 200,000 Jews of Judah during their Civil War. He gave the warning of Gods coming Wrath due to their sins and cruelty.

Nahum (Na 1:1) (663 to 612BC) (compassionate or comfort) A Prophet that foretold the down fall of Nineveh, the capital of Assyria, to Babylon, the Medes and Scythians in 612BC.

Daniel (Mt 24:15) (607BC) (God is my Judge) Born into unidentified nobility during Josiah's reign and one of the youthful hostages deported to Babylon by Nebuchadnezzar in 605 BC during King Jehoiakim's puppet reign. Jerusalem and King Zedekiah, the last King of Israel completely fell to Babylon in 586BC. Daniel as a young man was a great prophet and man of God given knowledge and the ability to interpret dreams. Daniel's name was changed to Beleshazzar (Protect his life) by the Babylonians where he was held captive in Babylon. All the prophetic books of the Old Testament are based upon the dreams foretold in the book of Daniel. We are quickly approaching the end of the age and fulfillment of Daniel's interpretations of all the Kings dreams. The book of Daniel is the key to all Bible Prophecies.

Ezekiel (Eze 1:3) (595BC) (God strengthens) A prophet of exile from a Priestly family and grew up in Judea during the last years of Hebrew independence prior to the Babylonian captivity. Departed to Babylon with King Jehoiachin in 586BC and younger contemporary of the Prophet Jeremiah and Daniel. The book of Ezekiel is a history of the two houses of Israel from the time they were taken captive and his warning of destruction through the Prophecies he foretold to take place in the last days. His Prophetic book tells of the planting of Gods house of Israel in the wilderness, the overturning of his throne to his nation in the wilderness, the gathering of his people in the last days and the warning to the end time Church of the soon coming wars of judgment. This judgment is the warning of destruction and captivity to the house of Israel (the modern Christian nations) due to their falling away from Gods Covenant, the Church. His warning during ancient days and the last days is coming full circle.

Obadiah (Obadiah 1) (587BC) The prophecy of Obadiah's time frame is uncertain but is a warning of the destruction of Edom. Edom of the Edomites were hostile to Israel in ancient days just as they are hostile to the house of Israel (Christian nations) and Judah (Jews of Israel) during the end times. Edom of Esau (Seir) and Moab, the people of Lot, will be judged in the end days (Eze 25:8-15 and 35:15) along with Edom, Seir, Moab, Bozarah and Idumea, the Eastern Communist bloc nations of Russia. They have created a Religion of Communism that is diametrically opposed to Christ's Church just as in ancient times. Their ideology has become the Red Horse of Communism (Atheism) as recorded in Revelation 6:4 and its destruction, to include the Arab nations, are recorded in Ezekiel 38 and 39, Isaiah 11:14, 13:4 and 34:6-10. This is the battle of Hamongog where God also brings judgment upon the house of Israel for their national sins. Obadiah mentions the houses of Jacob (Christian nations of Europe), Joseph (Ephraim GB and Manasseh US) and Esau (the Communist nations of Eastern Europe) as the nations to be judged that culminates at the end of the age of judgment, WW III (Obadiah 17-18).

House of Judah into captivity to Babylon in 586BC

Jeremiah (Jerm 1:5) (520BC) From the family of a **Levite** Priest and considered to be one of the greatest prophets during the time of King Josiah, the last sovereign king of Israel prior to being taken captive by Babylon. He was Commissioned to overturn the throne of King David from Jerusalem to the fruitful nation in the wilderness through the bloodline of King Zedekiah's daughters (Jerm 43:6; 1:10, Eze 20:34-43; 17:22-23; 21:25-27). God made Jeremiah the most powerful man ever in history (Jerm 1:10) for he was to be over all nations giving him total authority to overturn King David's throne from Jerusalem to a nation in the wilderness (Matt 21:43). Study Ezekiel chapter 17 through 22 for this event.

Habakkuk (Hab 1:1) (605-587BC) A prophet prior to the fall of Jerusalem in 586BC and believed to have been during the reign of King Jehoiakim to Zedekiah. He Prophesied of the end days for he says in Habakkuk 1:5, **"for I will work a work in your days, which ye will not believe, though it be told you."** This verse is speaking of the current falling away from the truth and how the people will not believe the truth when it is told unto them due to moral relativism and Political Correctness, the truth is a lie and a lie is the truth. He speaks of the gathering in the end days under the Gospel, **"For the earth shall be filled with the knowledge of the glory of the Lord, as the waters cover the sea"**, Hab 2:14. He speaks of Lebanon that is the Christian nations of the British Empire and the everlasting mountains representing the Christian nations of the world (Hab 2:17 and 3:6). He was an end time Prophet.

Zephaniah (Zep 1:1) (639-608BC) A Prophet prior to the fall of Jerusalem to Babylon. He Prophesied a judgment warning of the "great day of the Lord" and for all men to seek the Lord before he brings judgment. He is speaking to the Church and our present time period. This is the warning of the soon coming war of Hamongon of Ezekiel 38 and 39 and the last great war of Armageddon (Rev 16:16). He was an end time Prophet.

Haggai (Eze 5:1) (536-520 BC) The Jews of Judah returned to Jerusalem and rebuilt the Temple during the time of Haggai. He lived during the captivity to Babylon and contemporary to Zechariah. His rebuking and encouraging of the Jews enabled the completion of the unfinished Temple alone with the help of Zechariah.

Zechariah (Zec 1:1) (520BC?). Came from the line of Levite Priest and returned to Jerusalem to rebuild the Temple after captivity. A remnant of approx. 40,000 out of 2 million Jews returned to Jerusalem of Judea (Eze 6:14). He was Contemporary to the Prophet Haggai where they encouraged the procrastinating Jews to complete rebuilding of the Temple.

Malachi (Mal 1:1) (432BC?) (Messenger of Jehovah or my Messenger) Little is known about Malachi other than being a messenger of the end time Prophecies and last book of the Old Testament. This book is believed to have been written in the latter portion of the 5th century BC or as late as 432BC placing him after both captivities and the rebuilding of the Temple. His warning is for the last day Church to repent of their sins and to love God or receive his curse of destruction and judgment (Mal 2:2).

John the Baptist (Luke 7:28) (30AD death) Born approx. the same year of Jesus. His father was Zacharias that Prophesied the coming of the Messiah. He was a priest and John, chosen by God to be a Prophet, to prepare the way for the coming of Jesus. John preached the coming of the Messiah and Baptism representing the breaking away from sin and their old traditions to prepare for Christ's coming. The Pharisees and Priest did not understand for they thought the Messiah were to come as a King in power to lead the nation. Only the poor and lame believed in Christ for the haughtiness of the Priest and Pharisees compelled them to disregard his miracles and wisdom. John's ministry began in approx. 26 AD and ended with his imprisonment prior to Christ's ministry. He was Jesus' cousin and John said, **"He must increase, but I must decrease"** (John 3:30).

Agabus (Act 21:10) (40AD) A Prophet during the time of Barnabus and Saul (Act 11:27-30) foretold a drought and famine in the world. He warned Paul that the Jews of Jerusalem would imprison or kill him if he went to Jerusalem (Act 21:10-11).

Kings of the House of Israel: The Kings of the northern Kingdom after the division of Israel at the end of Solomon's reign. They began with the bloodline of Ephraim of the house of Joseph given to Jeroboam (I Kings 11:31) of the Birthright tribe and not of the linage of Christ. Gods Spirit did not lie within this line of kings for his throne was still in Jerusalem. The authority remained in Jerusalem till the vail was rent in the Temple after the death of Christ. The two daughters of Zedekiah was taken to Ireland by Jeremiah where they married into the Zarah line of Kings that settled into Ireland and Scottland hundreds of years earlier. The Royal Bloodline of King David was then official and the Throne was then official in Ireland. All the Kings of the northern Kingdom of Samaria were illegitimate and evil, creating greed and power struggles resulting in confusion, destruction and death. They completely turned from God to Baal worship so God punished them with the humiliation of captivity and dispersed them into the world to wait for his Gospel. Their punishment was to be times seven, 360 X 7 equaling 2520 years. They could not receive their blessings given to Abraham, Isaac, Jacob and Joseph to be wealthy nations and kings of Kingdoms till their punishment was complete in approx. 1780AD. They went into captivity beginning in 740 BC so add 2520 years and you get approx. AD 1780 when their punishment would be complete. This is approx. when the United States became an independent nation and the British Empire exploded colonizing the world. Very little is known of these kings for they were evil and insignificant to God and his Kingdom.

Prophets

1. Jeroboam, I Kings 11:28	Ephraim	933-912 BC	
2. Nadah, I Kings 14:20	son of	912-911	**Elijah**
3. Baasha, I Kings 15:16	Issachar	911-888	**Elijah**
4. Elah, I Kings 16:8	son of	888-887	**Elijah**
5. Zimri, I kings 16:15	Captain	885	**Elijah**
6. Omri, I kings 16:16	Captain	880-873	**Elijah**
7. Ahab, I Kings 16:29	son of	873-853	**Elijah**
8. Ahaziah, I Kings 22:40	son of	853-852	**Elijah**
9. Jehoram, II Kings 1:17	son of	852-841	**Elisha**
10. Jehu, I Kings 19:16	Captain	841-813	**Amos**
11. Johoahaz, II Kings 10:35	son of	814-798	**Amos**
12. Jehoash, II Kings 13:10	son of	798-781	**Amos**
13. Jeroboam II, II Kings 14:23	son of	781-753	**Hosea**
14. Zachariah, II Kings 14:29	son of	753-752	**Micah**
15. Shallum, II Kings 15:10	Contender	752	**Micah**
16. Menahem, II Kings 15:14	Contender	752-741	**Micah**
17. Pekahiah, II Kings 15:23	son of	741-739	**Micah**
18. Pekah, II Kings 15:25	Contender	739-731	**Oded**
19. Hoshea, II Kings 15	Contender	732-722	**Jonah, Amos**
* *Divorcement of the house of Israel Jerm 3:8*			**Hosea**

<u>Kings of the house of Judah</u> Southern Kingdom of King David after the division of Solomon's kingdom and some of the kings were Godly. These Kings are the linage of Christ and a part of his unbroken kingship as promised to David through the Pharez line of kings. The authority of King David's Throne promised to Christ in Luke 1:31-33 remained in Jerusalem till overturned by Jeremiah in Jerm 1:10, Eze 17:22 and 21:27 through the two daughters (Jerm 41:10&42:6) of King Zedekiah. The marriages into the Zarah line of Kings took place in Ireland and Scotland in approx. 580BC. This overturn fulfilled the purity of David's bloodline for Christ to receive the Throne.

Prophets

1. Rehoboam I Kings 11:43 — 931-913 BC — **Elisha, Elijah**
2. Abijuam or Abijah I Kings 14:31 — 913-910 — **Elijah**
3. Asa   I Kings 15:8 — 910-869 — **Elijah**
4. Jehoshaphat   I King 15:24 — 869-845 — **Elijah**
5. Jehoram   II Chron 21:1 — 845-841 — **Elijah**
6. Ahaziah   II Kings 8:25 — 841 — **Elijah**
7. Athaliah (Queen) II Kings 8:26 — 848-841 — **Elijah**
8. Joash or Jehoash   II Kings 11:2 — 835-796 — **Joel?**
9. Amaziah   II Kings 14:1 — 796-767 — **Hosea, Amos**
10. Uzziah or Azariah   II Kings 14:21 — 767-740 — **Hosea, Isaiah**
11. Jotham   II Kings 15:5 — 740-732 — **Isaiah**
12. Ahaz   II Kings 15:38 — 732-716 — **Oded, Isaiah**
13. Hezekiah   II Kings 16:20 — 716-687 — **Isaiah, Micah, Obadiah**
14. Manasseh   II Kings 21:1 — 687-643 — **Nahum**
15. Amon   II Kings 21:19 — 643-641 — **Nahum**
16. Josiah I Kings 13:2 (last King) — 641-609

17. Jehoahaz, name changed to Jehoiakim in II Kings 23:30&34 Daniel taken into captivity to Babylon in approx. 609BC 1st siege of Jerusalem.

Nahum, Zephaniah

18. Jehoiakim   II Kings 24:6 Ezekiel taken captive into **Habakkuk**
    Babylon approx. 598 BC 2nd siege of Jerusalem. 609-598
19 Zedekiah or Mattaniah, II Kings 24:17, 3rd siege, 586 BC **Jeremiah**
    Jerusalem fell to Babylon, last King of the Phares bloodline **Haggai**
    to set on King David's throne, 597-586 BC. **Zachariah**

These Prophets prophesied prior to and after the captivity of the house of Judah (Jerusalem) to Babylon. The house of Israel went into captivity 154 years prior to Assyria and is very important to understand the time frame for each of these Prophets. They spoke of the house of Israel as being a people and nation in the future. This is proof that the house of Israel and the house of Judah are two separate nations for they prophesied that there would be many nations of Israel to take place in the last days, Genesis 49:1. The bloodline of Judah to Christ had to be preserved for the coming of the Messiah through the Pharisees named after Phares (Royal blood line Mat 1:3) from Zedekiah (last King) to Mary, the mother of Christ. Joseph's bloodline was of Judah but not a factor being Mary were impregnated by the Holy Spirit.

Jeremiah	586BC	**Malachi**	432BC?
Daniel	607-520BC	**Haggi**	586-520BC
Ezekiel	595-520BC	**Habakkuk**	605-587BC
Zechariah	586BC	**Zephaniah**	639-608BC

Table Three

Important Bible Dates and events

Some of the dates below were taken from the "Chronology of the Old Testament" written by Floyd Nolen Jones in which this writer believes to be the most accurate dates based on the Masoretic Text, the Hebrew writings of the Old Testament. Mr. Jones did an outstanding job establishing Biblical dates and should be in every Christians Library. He states the following from his book. *"The earliest Masoretic Text which we have is dated 900AD translated by the Scribes of the Tribe of Levi known as the Masoretics that was given charge by God to keep the translations pure (Mal 2:7; Deu 31:25; 17:18). The Masoretic is the true text, not the Dead Sea Scrolls even though the Scrolls are more than a thousand years older. The Scrolls were written by a Jewish cult of ascetics whose teachings were rife with heresies. Jesus always quoted from the Masoretic Text and not the Greek Septuagint which exhibits considerable significant differences from the Hebrew Masoretic Text."*

We as Christians have no choice but to believe with blind faith that if God is powerful enough to create the Universe, then he is truly powerful enough to preserve his Word. Our Salvation is predicated upon our faith and that the Bible is true and accurate. He gave us the promise to preserve his Word and if we believe in totality, it makes us a true Biblicist (Jerm 1:12; PS 12:6-7; Isa 40:8; Mark 13:31). The accuracy and truth of the Scriptures can be proven through the fulfillment of hundreds of Prophecies with just a little study.

BC (Anno Hominis-year of man) Before Christ

4004 BC: Creation year of Adam (Anno Hominis-year of man) on Friday 26 Sept. (Chronology of the Old Testament by Floyd Nolen Jones)
3378 BC: 1st Egyptian Dynasty began with (Aryan) King Mena (Enoch's Birth) (each dynasty lasted 30 years called Renewal or Sed Festival).
3100 BC: 1st Phoenician Dynasty of King Barat symbol of the Phoenix palm

tree.

2658 - 2628 BC: Great Pyramid of Gizeh built by Sisithrus or Sesorthos when analyzed is a composition of Enoch and Noah (Refer to Coordinated Chronology of Israel and Egypt by Frederick Haberman)

2623 BC: The Great Pyramid of Cheops was built, Superior pyramids built during the Old Kingdom of Egypt, (Dynasties III to VI 2700-2200 BC) Isa 19:19-20, Exo 20:25 monuments to God Jeremiah 31:21 (not for blood sacrifice).

2348 BC: Year of the Flood or Deluge Gen 7:11 ended 2344, Gen 8:14

Unkn BC: The building of the tower of Babel in the land of Shinar. The date is basically unknown but happened shortly after the flood. Genesis 10:25 states that this happened during the days of Peleg for in his days were the earth divided. The earth being divided means the division of the nations by diversity of language. God dispersed them throughout the world or divided the world through language change by individual nations due to their haughtiness.

1921BC: Gen 12:1 Abraham's father Terah dies and Abraham departed into Egypt.

1910BC: Birth of Ishmael

1896BC: Birth of Isaac

1836BC: Birth of Jacob

1800BC: Stonehenge erected during the 18th Dynasty of Egyptian rule by Hu Gadarn in Hibernia (England) when Israel was in Egyptian Captivity. The descendants of Calcol and Dara departed Egypt prior to the Exodus and established the Druid Religion in England.

1756 BC: Birth of Levi by Leah (Gen 29:32-34)

1745 BC: Birth of Joseph

1730-1580 BC: Egyptian Hyksos Dynasties (XV and XVI) "Shepherd Kings" controlled Egypt for 150 years and were the Semite Hebrews of Abraham's sojourn and his family that departed with him into Egypt. Pharaohs of Abraham's descent ruled the western portion of the fertile crescent of Goshen. These Kings were in rule when Joseph and Jacob his father along with 66 members of his Hebrew family entered Egypt for their 240 years stay and is why they were so readily accepted.

1706 to 1491BC: Jacob goes to Egypt (Gen 47:9) Israel remained in Egypt under bondage till 1491 BC when lead by Moses into the wilderness. During this period of time, a portion of the Israelites, Calcol and Dara and a small portion of Dan and other tribes departed prior to and during the exodus by ship and settled into Greece and Spain. Pharaoh Thothmes III in power 17th Dynasty.

1689BC: Jacob's death

1635BC: Joseph's death

1571BC: Birth of Moses (Exo 7:7)

1520BC: Founding of Troy by Darda, Dardanus or Darius descendants of Calcol and Dara (1 Chronicles 2:6) called these names by various ancient writers. Dara was a direct descent of Judah and an heir to King David's throne destined to play a very important role in the overturn of the throne by Jeremiah (Jerm 1:10, Ezk 17:22-24 7 21:25-27) into Ireland, 584 BC. Troy was founded approx. 29 years before Israel's exodus from Egypt and totally destroyed in 1183 BC. Dardanus descendants departed and settled in the area of Rome producing later the Roman empire.

1491BC: Gen 15:13 Israel departed Egypt with Moses after 430 years with the last 200 years in bondage.

1451BC: Gods Covenant with Israel at Mt. Sinai.

1450BC: Israel entered Canaan the Promised Land after 41 years in the wilderness (Maccabees 12:20-22).

1095BC: Saul's Coronation as first King of Israel, he was not of the Tribe of Judah but of Benjamin (I Sam 9:21).

1056BC: King David's coronation as King of Israel and the first King of the Judah Pharez bloodline that ended at the Babylonian captivity. Zedekiah the last Pharez King (Gen 38:28-30) to sit on David's throne till the overturn of the throne in Ezekiel 21:25-27 to the Zarah blood line of the scarlet thread established in Ireland as early as 1800 BC. This fulfilled the promise of Judah to Tamar in Genesis 38:11 that she would marry his son to produce Kings and to the promise to David that a man would always sit on his Throne (I Kings 9:5, II Chron 7:18 and Jerm 33:17). The firstborn birthright of Jacob (Israel) was to be over all nations in Psalms 89:27. Study Genesis chapter 38 for details.

1015-976BC: Solomon's coronation as the first King of Israel beginning his Kingship.

1012BC: Solomon dedicated the first Temple to God.

976BC: Solomon's death and the beginning of the Division of Israel.

970BC: Separation of Judah and the house of Israel, the 10 northern tribes, I Kings 11:30. The house of Israel from this time own had their own line of Kings starting with King Jeroboam, King Solomon's servant, which was not of the Judah Pharez line. The promise of Judah to Tamar in Genesis 38 is very important for it corresponds with the overturn of the throne due to Israel being divided. The throne was taken from Solomon (Judah/Pharez Line) and given to Jeroboam of the house of Israel (Ephraim, I Kings 11:28). The Zarah line was given the assurance to be Kings (Eze 17:22-24 and Matt 1:3) and taken from the high (Pharez) to the low branch (Zarah) when overturned by Jeremiah to Ireland in 584BC.

740BC: Manasseh the first of the ten northern tribes to go into captivity by Tig-lath-Pileser III in the first Assyrian invasion of the house of Israel.

721-approx 670BC (II Kings 17:6) The captivity took place over a period of years, Ephraim and remaining 8 tribes taken into captivity with King Hoshea their last King by the Assyrians. They never again reigned as a nation in Samaria ending their line of Kings.

606BC: Assyria Nineveh fell to King Cyaaxares of the Saki (sons of Isaac) and Nabopolassar of Babylon. King Cyaaxares was a descendant of the 10 northern tribes taken captive in 740-721 BC fulfilling Jerm 51:19-20 the inheritance of Israel being Gods battle axe to destroy evil kingdoms.

586BC: (II Kings 25:1) The House of Judah, Jerusalem, went under siege by Nebuchadnezzar King of Babylon three different times and the 3rd siege taken into captivity. King Zedekiah was the last king of Israel and taken captive but his sons were killed except two daughters that escaped. They were protected by the Prophet Jeremiah to preserve the throne (Jerm 41:10 & 43:6) and later taken to Ireland where one of the daughters (Tea Tephi) married the King of Ireland and Scotta married Gallam the King of the Milesians of the Zarah bloodline of Scotland. The name Scotland is derived from Zedekiah's daughter Scotta. This completed the first overturn of King David's throne to Ireland by Jeremiah's commission (Jerm 1:10) (Eze 21:27) which was later moved to Scotland and now England fulfilling the term, **"I will overturn, overturn, overturn it"** (Eze 17:27).

538-320BC: The rule of the Median and Persian Empire.

390 BC Belinus and Brennus, sons of the famed British King Dunwall, assaulted and captured Rome with a British Army. ("Drama of the Lost Disciples" by Jowett p. 92)

333-31BC: The rule of the Greek Empire.

301BC: Persia fell to Seleucus of Greece the Parthian.

150BC: approx. - 476AD Military reign of the Roman Empire. The power of Roman military dominance ended approx. 476AD.

113-101BC: The Cimbri-Keltoi of Britain was the terror of Rome and could have brought their empire under subjection if desired. Confirmed by European writers and the reason for their hatred and the later invasion by Rome into Britain in 55 BC and 42 AD. ("The Drama of the Lost Disciples" by Jowett p. 92) This also fulfills Jeremiah 51:20 of God's chosen Hebrew people being his Battle Ax.

55BC: 5 Aug, Rome invades Britain for the first time from Calais France but fails, gains only 7 miles.

54 BC: On 10 May, regroups within a year and attempted the second invasion which also failed. Rome called a truce by only occupying a portion of England and the only nation Rome never completely conquered.

2BC: Birth of Christ in the fall of 2 BC, 29 September of the 1st Tishri Feast of Trumpets.

AD (Anno Domini, in the year of our Lord) Birth of Christ

26-36AD: Pilot ruled over Israel in Jerusalem.

27-30AD: Period of Christ's Ministry.

30AD: Spring, Christ's Crucifixion.

36AD: Joseph of Arimathaea, Christ's Uncle (John 19:38; Matt 27:57; Mark 15:43; Luke 23:51) arrived in Avalon Britain and established Christianity.

38-39AD: First above ground Church ever to be establish in the world at

Avalon in Ireland by Joseph of Arimathaea, a Disciple and Uncle of Christ.

42AD: Claudius Caesar declares war on Britannia (Briton) to destroy Christianity, Druidism and Judaism.

44AD: Peter first went to Rome.

45-68AD: Dates of Paul's Ministry approx.

52AD: Caradoc (Caractacus) and British Royal family captured and taken to Rome as POW and put on trial in front of the Roman Senate. Because of Caradoc's great battle strategies, Rome could not take Britain and he was admired throughout Rome. He was the only foreign leader to ever speak to the Roman Senate. His sentence was a supernatural event and the only leader captured and not killed for Caradoc received a slight punishment of 7 years house arrest in Rome and to never take up arms against Rome. He later went back to Britain after his seven-year probation. During this period in Rome, enter marriage between Royal families began. Caradoc's daughter Gladys (Claudia) married the Roman Senator Aulus Rufus Pudens along with other marriages within the families. This was the beginning of Rome turning Christian for the British Royal family was Christian (II Tim 4:21).

56AD: Paul arrived in Rome to spread the Gospel. The first Christian Church at Rome already existed at Paul's arrival in Palladium Britannicum where the British Royal Family lived also called Titulus or Hospitium Apastelorum then Pudentians to this day. The British Royal family of Claudia or Roman name Gladys was the first hostess to Apostle Peter and Paul during their visits to Rome. Gladys was the British wife of the Roman Senator Aulus Rufus Pudens, a Christian and Paul's half-brother (Rom 16:13).

70AD: Jerusalem and the Temple destroyed by the Romans and the end of Israel till 1948 and the taking of Jerusalem in the 1967 Arab war.

90-100 AD: Persecution of Christians by the domination of the Roman Army and the death of the Apostle John ending the Apostolic Age.

300AD: Roman persecution of early British Church.

312AD: Constantine, the great-grand son of Arviragus, leader of the British army, and son of the famous Empress Helen, a British princess, declared Rome to be Christian.

350AD: Roman Catholic Church founded.

400AD: The Vulgate Bible was the translation of the entire Bible into Latin by Jerome at Bethlehem. For a thousand years, this was the standard Bible in Latin. From 1320-1384, Wycliffe, a great English scholar, translated the Vulgate into English. He died and **William Tyndale**, a Greek scholar, completed his work with the Old and New Testament in English approx. 1530. The order of translations of the English Bibles were the **Miles Coverdale Bible** and friend of Tyndale using the translation of Tyndale's Bible from Latin and dedicated to Henry the VIII in 1535. **The Matthew Bible** of 1537 is the translation from the Coverdale and Tyndale Bibles by John Rodgers. **The Great Bible** of 1539 was translated from the Matthew, Coverdale and Tyndale Bibles. **The Geneva Bible** of 1560 was translated by scholars that fled to Geneva to escape persecution by Queen Mary and was taken from all the other Bibles. This Bible was believed to be a very scholarly version. **The Bishop's Bible** of 1568 was written by archbishop of Canterbury during the reign of Elizabeth and taken from the Geneva version that was mainly used by clergy. The **King James Bible** was finally completed in 1611.

408AD: Rome plundered by the Goths.

498AD: 2nd Overturn of the Throne of King David Circa took the Stone of Destiny to Scotland.

570AD: Mohamed created the Islam religion.

596AD: St. Augustine brought the Roman invasion of the Christian Religion to Britain from Rome where the Apostolic Church had already existed since 38 AD.

610AD: First Pope of Roman Catholic Church, Boniface III.

1611AD: The King James or Authorized Version Bible translated from the Bishop's Bible by 47 scholars under the authorization of King James I. This was the release of God's Word and Truth to all the world by his Birthright tribe as foretold in Isaiah 41:1-8 and the beginning of the great blessing to Abraham, Isaac, and Jacob. It produced the Democratic Christian nations of the British Empire and the United States spreading Gods Holy Word through using the King James authorized version that established Christ's Church into the wilderness of the world.

<u>Important Dates of Great Britain</u>

(The beginning of Christianity)

By understanding English history and how God establish the British Empire to spread his end time Gospel, we can see how his blessings to the Birthright tribe of Ephraim and Manasseh have been fulfilled through the British Commonwealth and the United States of America (Ephraim and Manasseh).

2000BC: England first settled by Kelts.

1800BC: Druidism Stonehenge erected   Hu Gadarn "Celt Druid by Elder p53".

1200BC: Dara (Judah/Zarah) of the Dannans (Tuatha de'Dannan) migrated to Ireland, Scotland and Wales from Greece after departing Egypt by ship prior to and during the Egyptian captivity of Israel.

1000BC: Milesians migrated to Ireland from Scythia by way of Spain. Simeon (Simoni) main body of Simeon most likely remained in Spain. The Dannans migrated before the Milesians after departing Greece and a war with the Assyrians. They departed for Denmark, Norway and then into Ireland. "Uncovering the Mysteries of your hidden Inheritance" by Balaicius.

700-650BC: The second migrating group of Milesian forces invaded and settled Ireland. These Milesians were from the Ionic state of Miletus

(Phoenician Greek Islands), whose people were of the tribe of Judah and descendants of Darda, the founder of Troy. They migrated to avoid Assyrian captivity. Darda, descendant of Darah son of Judah, Zarah bloodline was an heir to King David's throne (I Chron 2:5 and Matt 1:3). The Milesian's were led by Gadelius, Gadil, or Gallam (married Scotta King Zedekiah's daughter) and their celebrated standard or flag carried the sacred banner of the Milesians, on which represented the dead serpent and the rod of Moses. The new Gaelic language came from the invading Milesians and the foundation of Modern English. Stammering in Hebrew means "gael" by Young's Analytical Concordance. Taken from the Irish Chronicles and H.B. Hannay, Prof. Totten and F. Haberman, "Tracing our Ancestors" page 118-119.

55 BC: First invasion of Rome into England on 5 August from Calais France gained only seven miles. The reason for invasion was due to the Druidic influence on Roman Society.

54 BC: Second invasion of Rome into England on 10 May, after reinforcing, the invasion failed and called a truce. England was the first nation to be invaded by Rome and never taken. The next invasion was 96 years later by Rome that took place in 42AD due to Christian influence on Roman Society. Rome occupied England till 320AD. Again, they failed to take all of England.

36AD: Joseph of Arimathea, Christ's Uncle, arrived in Avalon Ireland and established Christianity.

38-39AD: First above ground Church ever to be establish in the world at Avalon in Ireland by Joseph of Arimathea, a Disciple of Christ.

42-320AD: Rome declared to destroy Britain and its Druid/Christian influence, man woman and child to include all of its institutions. The Roman Senate declared believers in the Druidic or Christian faith to be enemies of the state as a Capital offence to be cast to the lions in the Coliseum. This included any person descending from King David, a Jew or a person converted to be a Jew or claiming the Orthodox Judean faith or any person claiming to be Christian. Rome's invasion into Britain was not successful and only taking the lower two-thirds up to the Plautian Wall in northern England and never entered into Ireland or Scotland. The first 9 years were extremely fierce battles between the Romans and the Silurian armies and in 45 AD a 6-month truce was called where Ariviragus Caractacus went to Rome to arrange peace but the peace talks were short lived and war continued. Britain is the only nation in history ever attacked by the full might of the Roman Army and not be totally conquered. Their effort was to purge Christianity, Druidism and the Jews off the face of the earth. ("Drama of the Lost Disciples" by Jowett, page 93)

42AD: The first Roman Embassy set up in Britain and the only country that Rome invaded that was never completely captured. The British were the only people to ever walk free in Rome and not be under taxation or bondage to the Roman Government.

45AD: Arviragus, the Silurian King (a Christian), marries Venus Julia's daughter of Emperor Claudius Caesar, this was the beginning of Rome falling to Christianity.

52AD: The capture and trial of Caractacus along with the Royal Silurian family and taken to Rome where Caractacus was put on trial before the Roman Senate. Because of his brilliant battle tactics as the British Pendragon or Commander-in-Chief, the Romans could not take Britain and was admired through-out the land. He was the first enemy of Rome to ever be let free with only a seven-year probation to be executed freely in Rome and to swear to never raise arms against Rome again. During his seven-year probation within the streets of Rome, enter marriage between the Royal families began. Caractacus daughter Gladys married the Roman Senator Aulus Rufus Pudens along with others (II Tim 4:21). He later returned to Britain with his Christian family. The release of Caractacus was the single biggest mistake the Roman Senate ever made for the Royal families intermarried causing Rome to later fall to Christianity.

53AD: Gladys (Claudia), Caractacus daughter, marries Rufus Pudens Pudentius, a Roman Senator. St. Paul and Rufus Pudens Pudentius were 1/2 Brothers due to remarriage by the same mother (Rom 16:13). Paul wrote the book of Romans to the Christians in Rome and to the British Silurian family, Claudia, II Tim 4:21.

48AD: Death of Mary (mother of Christ) in Avalon Ireland.

156AD: King Lucius established the Christian Faith as the National Faith of Britain by Act of Parliament. On February 29, 1892 the US Supreme Court declared the United States a Christian nation, making Britain and the USA the only two nations ever in history to declare themselves by government decree to be a Christian Nation fulfilling Isa 29:18 and 41:1-8.

700-1500AD: The Dark Ages or Medieval times. This was a time in European history between classical antiquity and the Italian Renaissance from the 5th century to about 1350 AD when the Latin language and literature dominated Europe. The Arts, Literature, Religion and learning was subdued by superstition and ignorance during this period of time mainly by the Roman Church due to the lack of blessings from God because his Chosen People, the house of Israel was still under their X7 punishment.

1215AD: Signing of the Magna Charta of England on 15 Jan., beginning of the 3rd day prophecy of Hosea 6:2. The house of Israel, Ephraim, started their captivity when Manasseh was taken captive in 741 BC. Two days or 2000 years from this date would be approx. 1259AD when England began to be blessed by God and their X7 punishment would be complete by 1779AD. This is approx. when their great blessing would begin and basically matches the period of the Dark Ages or Medieval times (700-1500AD).

1455AD: The printing press was invented with the Holy Bible being the first book printed. This opened the world to be evangelized by the English people under the authority of King James 1611 Bible.

1611AD: King James, authorized the translation of the Bible by 47 scholars producing the KJV authorized version, making it accessible to common man for the first time in history.

1776AD: Deceleration of Independence of the United States of America, the tribe of Manasseh. Manasseh was the first of the ten northern tribes to be taken into captivity by the Assyrians in 741 BC. In accordance to Leviticus 26:18 punishment of X7 or 7 X 360 years = 2520 years of punishment for disobedience of Gods laws, Manasseh's punishment would be completed in 1779 AD. This fulfills Gen 48:19 with the birthright blessing to Ephraim and Manasseh. Manasseh was the 13th tribe and makes our original 13 colonies very significant.

1800 AD: The approx. beginning of the greatest Common Wealth of 46 nations in the history of the world. Great Britain of the tribe of Ephraim and Manasseh received the dual birthright blessings given in Gen 35:11; 48:16-19 became the 46 nations world over by international shipping trade. They fulfilled their heritage by becoming the greatest Empire or trading block ever in history. Ephraim went into captivity in 721 BC and after their X7 punishment as stated above, their 2520 years or 721BC + 2520 years of punishment equals to 1799 AD. This fulfills Gen 35:11; 49:22-26 and Duet 33:13-17 of Gods birthright blessings and promise to Ephraim and Manasseh. Their symbol can be traced through history as the Unicorn and Bull. England is the only nation in the world that has a Unicorn on their national seal and the Bull, the symbol of Wall Street, center of world trade in New York City controlled by the United States, fulfilling Duet 33:17.

Table Four

Reference Books

The following list of Reference books were taken from **"Tracing Our Ancestors"** by Frederick Haberman, an excellent reference book for students interested in European British American Ancestry. Many of these books can be ordered at Artisan Publications Subsidiary of Hoffman Printing in Muskogee, OK (918)682-8341.

"Aryan Origin", Prof. Waddell
"Royal Genealogy", Anderson
"Royal House of Britain", Milner
"Ancient Records of Assyria and Babylon", Prof. D.D. Luckenbill
"Origin of the English", Major de Weldon
"Gods Commonwealth", Col. McKendrick
"Joseph of Arimathea at Glastonbury", Rev. Lionel Lewis Vucar of Glastonbury
"History of England", J.R. Green

"European Race Origins", Prof. Hannay

"Bible in Modern English", Finton

"The world and the Book", Prof. S.H. Allen

"Judah's Scepter", Rev. J.H Allen

"Joseph's Birthright", Rev J.H. Allen

"Tamar Tetphi", J.D. Massey

"The Royal House of Britain", Rev. Milner

"The Great Pyramid", D. Davidson

"Prehistoric London", E.O. Gordon

"Ancient Men in Britain", D.A. Mackenzie

"Phoenician Origin of Britons, Scots and Anglo-Saxons", by L.A. Waddell. This book traces evidence from hundreds of Phoenician coins and inscriptions found in both Britain and the East that the early Britons were the sea-going Aryan-Phoenicians, who appeared in Western Europe as the Celts or Kelts, which name can also be traced to ancient Chaldea from where they came.

"Early Egypt, Babylonia and Central Asia", D. Davidson

"Coordinated Chronology of Israel and Egypt", Frederick Haberman

"Aryan Origin of the Alphabet", Prof Waddell

"The Chronicles of Eric", Translated by Rodger O'Connor Encyclopedia Brittanica Vol III pg. 859

"The Kings of God", Rev. Pascoe Goard

"Faerie Queene", Rev. Pascoe Goard

"History of Ireland", Thomas Moore

"The Enduring Empire of the Brit-ish", Rev. P.H. Pratchett

Synopsis

America in Bible Prophecy will shake the very foundation of your belief system and explains in a simple and logical manner the following misunderstood Prophetic subjects not taught in secular, ancient or Biblical History, Schools or Churches. Why?

- America's true Identity and the role we play in Bible Prophecy!
- Where is King David's throne promised to all generations?
- Who received the Birthright inheritance by Hebrew Law to be many Nations and Kings of Kingdoms?
- Who are the Jews of Judah verses the house of Israel (the lost sheep)?
- Who is Gods Battle Ax of Jeremiah 51:19-20? It cannot be the Jews!
- What is the Mystery of Daniel's untold Secret revealed in the end days?
- Will the Church see Gods Wrath or be taken away (Ruptured)?
- Soon coming WW III, who's cities, according to Scripture, is going to be

destroyed? **And many more fascinating subjects.........**

This book is riveting and a critical WARNING to the American people if we are to maintain our way of life.

Bibliography

The New Strong's Exhaustive Concordance of The Bible Comfort Print Edition Copy Wright 1995 by Thomas Nelson Publishers, Nashville, Tennessee

The Apocrypha, Cambridge University Press Syndicate, The Pitt Building, Trumpington St, Cambridge CB2 1RP 40 west 20th St. New York, N.Y. 10011-4211, USA

Robert Alan Balaicius, "Uncovering "The Mysteries of Your Hidden Inheritance", Sacred Truth Ministries, P.O. Box 18 Mountain City, Tennessee 37683 (copyright 1994)

New Encyclopedia Britannica volume nine

R. H. Charles, "The Book of Enoch or I Enoch", Oxford at the Clarendon Press 1912, 1988 edition published by Hoffman Printing Co. P.O. Box 1529 Muskogee, Oklahoma 74402 (918) 682-8341.

Destiny Publishers, "The Covenant People", Merrimac, Mass. Copyright 1966.

Isabel Hill elder, "Celt Druid and Culdee" a reprint of 1973 edition by Covenant Publishing Company, Britain. Published by Hoffman Printing Co. PO Box 1529, Muskogee, OK. 74402 (918) 682-8341.

Bonnie Gaunt, "Stonehenge…. a closer look", by Bonnie Gaunt, 510 Golf Ave, Jackson, Michigan 49203, Copyright 1979 by Bonnie Gaunt.

Rev. W.M. Pascoe Goard, "The Post-Captivity Names of Israel" Artisan Sales P.O. box 1497, Thousand Oaks CA 91360 (copyright 1989) first edition 1934 reprinted in USA 1989.

Andrew Gray, "The origin and Early History of Christianity in Britain" London Skeffington and Son, Piccadilly, W. and New York James Pott and Co., 4th Ave and 22nd St NY. NY. 1897 Artisan Publishers P.O. Box 1520 Muskogee, OK 74402 (copyright 1897)

Gospel of the Kingdom Ministry, "Tracing the Ancestors of Great Britain & America" Hoffman Printing Co. P.O. Box 1529 Muskogee, OK 74402.

Frederick Haberman, "Tracing Our Ancestors" reprinted in U.S.A.

1989, America's Promise Ministries P.O. Box 157, Sandpoint, Idaho 83864.

Nick Herbert, "Quantum Reality Beyond the New Physics", Anchor Books by Doubleday div. of Bantam Doubleday Dell Publishing Group, Inc. 1540 Broadway, NY, NY 10036.

Col. J.C. Gawler, "Dan the pioneer of Israel" Publish by Artisan Sales P.O. Box 1529 Muskogee, OK copyright 1984

Floyd Nolen Jones, "Chronology of the Old Testament" 14th Edition, Kings Word Press P.O. Box 130220, The Woodland, TX 77393-0220.

George F. Jowett, "The Drama of the Lost Disciples" Covenant Publishing Co, LTD I Blades Court, Deodar Rd, London SW15 2NU (copyright first edition 1961 this edition 1996)

R. W. Morgan, "St. Paul in Britain" Publisher Artisan Sales P.O. Box 1529 Muskogee, OK 74402 (copyright 1984)
Nation Geographic Atlas of the World, 4th edition, National Geographic Society, Washington, D. C. 1975.
Rev. F.E. Pitts, two sermons preached to the U.S. congress in 1857 "The United States of America Foretold in The Holy Scriptures and The Battle of Armageddon" Published by J.W. Bull Baltimore (proprietor of copyright 1862)

Thompson's Chain-reference Bible, fourth edition, King James version, B.B. Kirkbride Bible Co. INC. Indianapolis, Indiana.

E. Raymond Capt., "Missing Links Discovered in Assyrian Tablets". Artisan Publishers Hoffman Printing Co. P.O. Box 1529 Muskogee, OK 74402.

E. Raymond Capt. "Jacob's Pillar" A Biblical Historical Study, Artisan Publishers P.O. Box 1529 Muskogee, OK 74402 (copyright 1977)

E. Raymond Capt. "The Scottish Declaration of Independence", Hoffman Printing Co. P.O. box 1529, Muskogee, OK 74402.

James Strong LL.D. S.T.D., New Exhaustive Concordance of the Bible, Thomas nelson Publishers Nashville, TN. Copyright 1995, King James version Bible.

Merrill C. Tenney, "Zondervan's Pictorial Bible Dictionary" Copyright 1963 by Zondervan Publishing House Grand Rapids, Michigan.

Ted Weiland, "God's Covenant People" Mission to Israel Ministries P.O. box 248 Scottsbluff, Nebraska 69363.

William Whiston, A.M., "Josephus the complete Works", copyright 1998 by Thomas Nelson Publishers, Nashville, Tennessee.

"British/Scottish Royal Coat of Arms"

The cover of this book carries the Banner or Arms of England (British/Scottish Royal Arms) and identifies the secrets of the true identity of the house of Israel, Ephraim and Manasseh, the Birthright tribes and leader of Israel. We give credit to "Artisan Publishers" as a token of gratitude in allowing the use of this symbol in demonstrating our heritage.

The Lion at top center is the Lion of Judah representing Gods Throne of Israel where he has a sword and scepter in his paws. He is sitting upon the crown of England atop a Knight of armor (Honor) over the standing Lion of David. The scepter is a symbol of King David's throne (Gen 48:10) and the sword is Gods Battle Ax (Jerm 51:19-20). The Lion is a symbol of Christ and his Gospel, the Word of Gods rule of law, "In Defense" at the top of each flag pole means, in defense of the faith or the Cross of Christ. The words written below the standing Lion stating "Nemo Me Imune Lacessit" means, "No One Attacks Me With Impunity". On either side is standing unicorns representing the Birthright of Ephraim (Unicorn) and Manasseh (Bulls), Num 14:19, 23:22, 24:8-9, Duet 33:17, Ps 29:6 (Lebanon "Ephraim" and Sirion "prevail or power as a Prince" and Isa 34:7 "Bulls and Unicorns"). Throughout the Scriptures, the Unicorn and Bull is associated together as brothers and indicated in the above verses. The crown around both of the Unicorns neck represents their leadership as the Birthright tribe to be Kings repairing the breach of the throne (Gen 38:29-30 and Amos 9:11) taken from the bloodline of Pharez and given to Zarah (Mat 1:3, Eze 17:22-24 and 21:25-27). The chains around their body symbolize the captivity out of Egypt and also the Assyrian and Babylonian captivities. The unicorn and Lion support flagstaffs of the Banner of Scotland to the left and the flag of St. Andrew to the right (the flag of Scotland). The **X** within the flag of St. Andrew represents Manasseh for the Ox or Bull is the first letter of the Hebrew alphabet (#505 Strongs Concordance). Deuteronomy 33:17 speaks of Manasseh as being a thousands which also means, ref. #502 and 504 as to learn or to teach and to be a family by yoking or taming of an ox or cow (the teaching of the Gospel worldwide). The X also represent the crossing of Jacobs arms when he blessed the two lads of Ephraim and Manasseh in Genesis 48:16. When you superimpose the X of the bull, the first letter of the Hebrew alphabet and the + or the last letter of the alphabet, you get the symbol of the British flag, and in Hebrew British means, "Brit" (#1285), Covenant and "ish" (#376) man, Covenant of Man.

Israel was to rule the world under the throne of David as a Prince and to be the leader of the Birthright tribes, "he will rule as God". The Unicorn represent Great Britain of Ephraim as a multitude of nations and the Bull is Manasseh the United States of American as territories under a Republic, ruled by the people. The English Crown and the Republic of America has been the protector of the faith since the establishment of the Gospel in 30

About the Author

This Author has been a student of Biblical, Ancient and Secular history from the age of thirteen and drafted into the Army in 1970. Educated while in the Military and retired as Chief Warrant Officer Three (CW3) with 21 years of active-duty Army. Field of training in Data Communications holding a Top Secret Special Intelligence Compartmented (TSSCI) security clearance Military Intelligence in the Army Security Agency and Special Operations. Completed Army Flight School in 1978 and instructor course in 1985 as a helicopter flight instructor. Retired from the US Army in 1992 and Army Fleet Support (AFS) as a TH-67 Maintenance Test Pilot in 2014. Received the Defense Meritorious Service Medal to include many other awards and decorations. Deployed to five overseas assignments receiving the following combat citations, Joint Meritorious Unit Award, Southwest Asia Service Medal with 3 Bronze Service Stars and Kuwait Liberation Medal.

God has truly blessed me with a wonderful military and civilian flying career allowing me to amass a tremendous amount of military, historical and Biblical knowledge during my world travels. He has spiritually guided me and allowed me the ability to compile the material within this book through deep prayer, study and research. This Author is not affiliated with any Party, Denomination or Organization but simply have a great desire to tell America the truth of our national heritage as an old Soldier that loves and cherish our great nation and British brothers.